INTERNATIONAL
Antiques
PRICE GUIDE

ROSS-ON-WYE ANTIQUES CENTRE

Centre of Excellence for Antiques, Fine Art and Collectables

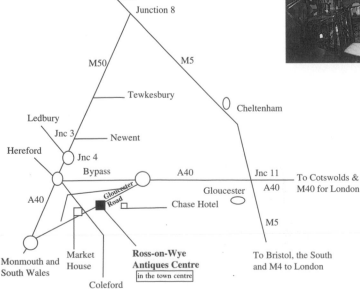

From the North and
Birmingham take M5 South,
leave at junction 8 for M50
signposted Ross-on-Wye

M5
Junction 8

M50

M5

Tewkesbury

Cheltenham

Ledbury

Jnc 3

Newent

Hereford

Jnc 4

Bypass

A40

Jnc 11

To Cotswolds &
M40 for London

Gloucester
Road

Gloucester

A40

Chase Hotel

A40

M5

Monmouth and
South Wales

Market
House

Ross-on-Wye
Antiques Centre
in the town centre

To Bristol, the South
and M4 to London

Coleford

**For all enquiries,
space and cabinets please
contact Michael Aslanian**

Opening hours:
Monday-Saturday 10.30am-5.00pm
Sunday and Bank Holidays closed

Gloucester Road
Ross-on-Wye HR9 5BU
**Tel: 01989 762290
Fax: 01989 762291**

Ross-on-Wye also has
10 other antique shops

INTERNATIONAL
Antiques
PRICE GUIDE

General Editor
Elizabeth Norfolk

2000
Volume XXI

MILLER'S INTERNATIONAL ANTIQUES PRICE GUIDE 2000

Created and designed by
Miller's
The Cellars, High Street
Tenterden, Kent, TN30 6BN
Tel: 01580 766411
Fax: 01580 766100

General Editor: Elizabeth Norfolk
Editorial and Production Co-ordinator: Sue Boyd
Editorial Assistants: Catherine Carson-Parker, Jo Wood
Production Assistants: Gillian Charles, Léonie Sidgwick
Advertising Executive: Elizabeth Smith
Advertising Assistants: Jill Jackson, Melinda Williams
Designers: Kari Reeves, Alex Warder, Shirley Reeves
Advertisement Designer: Simon Cook
Indexer: Hilary Bird
Additional Photographers: Ian Booth, Roy Farthing, David Merewether, Denis O'Reilly, wRobin Saker

First published in Great Britain in 1999
by Miller's, a division of Mitchell Beazley,
imprints of Octopus Publishing Group Ltd,
2–4 Heron Quays, London E14 4JP

Distributed in the USA by
Antique Collectors' Club Ltd
Market Street Industrial Park, Wappingers' Falls, New York 12590
Reader enquiries: 914 297 0003

© 1999 Octopus Publishing Group Ltd

A CIP catalogue record for this book is
available from the British Library

ISBN 1-84000-230-1

Illustrations and film output: CK Litho, Whitstable, Kent
Colour origination: Pica Colour Separation Overseas Pte Ltd, Singapore
Printed and bound: Lego SPA, Italy

Front cover illustrations:
top left: A Stourbridge blue cameo glass vase, overlaid with white and
carved with ferns, c1885, 6in (15cm) high.
$1,400–1,600 BELL
top right: A parcel-gilt silver sugar basket, c1873, 6in (15cm) high.
$400–500 CSK
centre: A George III-style painted satinwood and
quarter-veneered commode, c1910, 33in (84cm) high.
$2,500–3,200 S

5

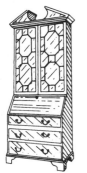

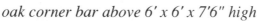

7

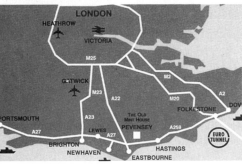

Private purchase or trade buyer you always get a warm welcome at

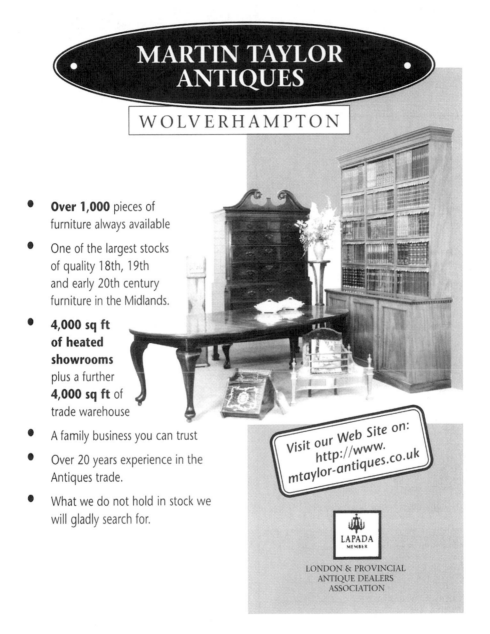

MARTIN TAYLOR ANTIQUES

WOLVERHAMPTON

- **Over 1,000** pieces of furniture always available

- One of the largest stocks of quality 18th, 19th and early 20th century furniture in the Midlands.

- **4,000 sq ft of heated showrooms** plus a further **4,000 sq ft** of trade warehouse

- A family business you can trust

- Over 20 years experience in the Antiques trade.

- What we do not hold in stock we will gladly search for.

Visit our Web Site on:
http://www.
mtaylor-antiques.co.uk

LAPADA
MEMBER

LONDON & PROVINCIAL
ANTIQUE DEALERS
ASSOCIATION

Tel: **01902 751166** Fax: 01902 746502

Web site: http://www.mtaylor-antiques.co.uk
E-mail: enquiries@mtaylor-antiques.co.uk

140B Tettenhall Road Wolverhampton West Midlands WV6 0BQ

Don't Throw Away A Fortune!
Invest In
Miller's Price Guides

Please send me the following editions

❑ **Miller's Collectables Price Guide 2000** – £17.99
❑ **Miller's Chinese & Japanese Antiques Buyer's Guide** – £19.99
❑ **Miller's Clocks & Barometers Buyer's Guide** – £18.99
❑ **Miller's Collectors Cars Price Guide 1999/2000** – £19.99
❑ **Miller's Classic Motorcycles Price Guide 1999/2000** – £14.00

I enclose my cheque/postal order for £.................post free (UK only)
Please make cheques payable to *'Octopus Publishing Group Ltd'*
or please debit my Access/Visa/Amex/Diners Club account number

Expiry Date........../...........

NAME Title   *Initial*   *Surname*

ADDRESS

Postcode

SIGNATURE

*Photocopy this page or write the above details on a separate sheet and send it to **Miller's Direct, 27 Sanders Road, Wellingborough, Northants, NN8 4NL** or telephone the Credit Card Hotline 01933 443863. Lines open from 9:00 to 5:00. Registered office: 2-4 Heron Quays, Docklands, London E14 4JP. Registered in England number 3597451*

16

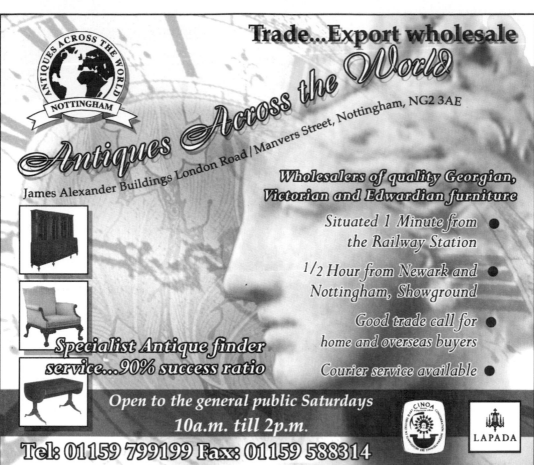

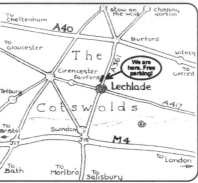
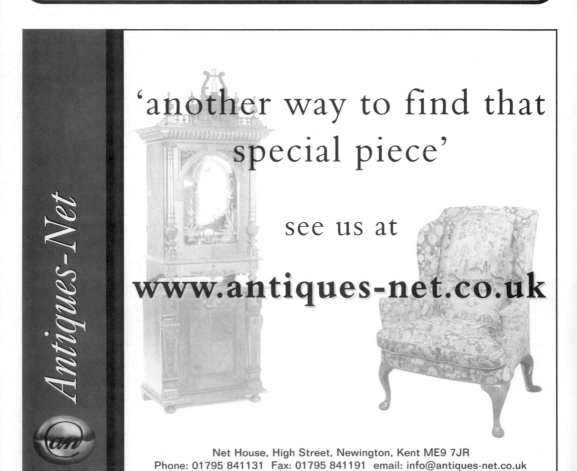

Contents

MILLER'S

2000

Acknowledgements

The publishers would like to acknowledge the great assistance given by our consultants:

FURNITURE:	Fergus Lyons, Sotheby's, 34–35 New Bond Street, London W1A 2AA
OAK & COUNTRY FURNITURE:	Victor Chinnery
PINE FURNITURE:	Ann Lingard, Rope Walk Antiques, Rye, Sussex TN31 7NA
POTTERY:	Christopher Spencer, 26 Melrose Road, Merton Park, London SW19 3HG
PORCELAIN:	John Sandon, Phillips, 101 New Bond Street, London W1Y 0AS
ASIAN CERAMICS AND ASIAN WORKS OF ART:	Peter Wain, Glynde Cottage, Longford, Market Drayton, Shropshire TF9 3PW
GLASS:	Wing Cdr R. G. Thomas, Somervale Antiques, 6 Radstock Road, Midsomer Norton, Bath BA3 2AJ
SILVER:	Eileen Goodway
CLOCKS:	Derek Roberts, 25 Shipbourne Road, Tonbridge, Kent TN10 3DN
BAROMETERS:	Michael Oxley, P.A. Oxley, The Old Rectory, Cherhill, Nr. Calne, Wilts, SN11 8UX
DECORATIVE ARTS:	Eric Knowles, Bonhams, Montpelier Street, Knightsbridge, London SW7 1HH
TWENTIETH CENTURY DESIGN:	Paul Rennie, 13 Rugby Street, London W1X 1RF
RUGS & CARPETS:	Jonathan Wadsworth, Sotheby's, 34–35 New Bond Street, London W1A 2AA
RUSSIAN WORKS OF ART:	Sheldon Shapiro, Stand 380, Grays Antique Market, 58 Davies Street, London W1Y 1LB
ISLAMIC WORKS OF ART:	Stephen Wolff, Bonhams, Montpelier Street, Knightsbridge, London SW7 1HH
METALWARE:	Danny Robinson, Key Antiques, 11 Horsefair, Chipping Norton, Oxfordshire OX7 5AL
SILHOUETTES:	Kevin McSwiggan, Sunnyside Farm, Main Street, Wath, Nr. Ripon, N. Yorks HG4 5ET
ANTIQUITIES:	Peter A Clayton FSA, Seaby Antiquities, 14 Old Bond Street, London W1X 4JL
TRIBAL ART:	Siobhan Quin, Phillips, 101 New Bond Street, London W1Y OAS
MAPS & ATLASES:	Amanda Sutcliffe, Phillips, 101 New Bond Street, London W1Y 0AS
DOLLS:	David Barrington, Yesterday Child, Angel Arcade, London N1 8EG
TRAINS:	Glenn Butler, Wallis & Wallis, West Street Auction Galleries, Lewes, East Sussex BN7 2NJ
SCIENTIFIC INSTRUMENTS AND MARINE:	Alexander Crum-Ewing, Bonhams, Montpelier Street, Knightsbridge, London SW7 1HH
CAMERAS:	Mark Jenkins, Vintage Cameras Ltd, 254 & 256 Kirkdale, Sydenham, London SE26 4NL
FISHING:	Richard Dowson, The Old Tackle Box, PO Box 55, High Street, Cranbrook, Kent TN17 3ZU

We would like to extend our thanks to all auction houses, their press offices, dealers and collectors who have assisted us in the production of this book.

How to Use this Book

It is our aim to make the Guide easy to use. In order to find a particular item, consult the contents list on page 19 to find the main heading, for example, Dolls. Having located your area of interest, you will find that larger sections have been sub-divided. If you are looking for a particular factory, designer or craftsman, consult the index which starts on page 796.

Miller's Compares

  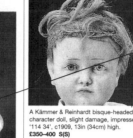

A Kämmer & Reinhardt bisque-headed character doll, slight damage, impressed '114 34', c1909, 13in (34cm) high.
£350–400 S(S)

I A Kämmer & Reinhardt bisque-headed character doll, with double-jointed toddler body, incised 'K°R 115/A', c1910, 17in (45cm) high.
£3,000–3,500 YC

II A Kämmer & Reinhardt bisque-headed character doll, with composition body, incised 'K°R 122', c1912, 15in (40cm) high.
£850–950 YC

In 1908, Kämmer & Reinhardt began producing more realistic dolls, resembling real children, in an attempt to halt falling sales figures. Item I is superbly modelled with closed, pouting mouth and double-jointed toddler body, but this design was not successful as the realistic face did not appeal to children. As it was also more expensive to produce and therefore more costly to buy, fewer examples were made and consequently they are now very rare. Doll collectors consider them artistic and desirable, which increases their value. Kämmer & Reinhardt soon began producing dolls with more idealistic faces, of which Item II is a good example.

A Kämmer & Reinhardt bisque-headed doll, c1910, 25in (63.5cm) high, with clothing and a pine bed.
£850–1,000 CAG

Further Reading
Miller's Collecting Teddy Bears & Dolls, Miller's Publications, 1996

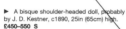
► A bisque shoulder-headed doll, probably by J. D. Kestner, c1890, 25in (65cm) high.
£450–550 S

Two Lenci dolls, with brown eyes, original clothes, trademarks to feet, 1930s, girl 17in (43cm) high.
£2,000–2,200 S

Armand Marseille
Armand Marseille was born in Russia but moved with his family to Thuringia in Germany, where he took over a porcelain factory. By 1890 he was manufacturing bisque-headed dolls with his son, also Armand. Their output was prolific and from 1900 to 1930 they also supplied dolls to other makers.

21 Years Ago ...

A Steiner doll, dressed in original clothes, 1889, 14in (37cm) high. **L**

Twenty-one years ago this Steiner doll was valued at £725–800. Although prices for many ordinary dolls have levelled, this is a good all-original example and is sought after by serious doll collectors worldwide. Today it could be expected to realize £2,300–2,600.

Miller's Compares
explains why two items which look similar have realised very different prices.

Price Guide
these are worked out by a team of trade and auction house experts, and are based on actual prices realised. Remember that Miller's is a price guide not a price list and prices are affected by many variables such as location, condition, desirability and so on. Don't forget that if you are selling it is quite likely you will be offered less than the price range. Price ranges for items sold at auction tend to include the buyer's premium and VAT if applicable.

21 years ago ...
A special box featuring selected antiques that appeared in the first edition of *Miller's Antiques Price Guide*. Our experts comment on the changing values of items over the last 21 years.

Further Reading
directs the reader towards additional sources of information.

Caption
provides a brief description of the item including the maker's name, medium, year it was made and in some cases condition.

Information Box
covers relevant collecting information on factories, makers, care and restoration, fakes and alterations.

Source Code
refers to the Key to Illustrations on page 789 that lists the details of where the item was photographed.

Introduction

As we celebrate twenty-one years of *Miller's Antiques Price Guide*, I have to admit that those years have flown by at an alarming speed. It seems odd when I think back to 1971, when I first found employment with a long-established antiques shipper in my native Lancashire. On my first day I was told by the old hands that I had arrived too late in the business. In their opinion, all the best pieces had long gone and, horror of horrors, the firm was now reduced to handling Victoriana. I am pleased to report that, by the time I was involved in the early editions of *Miller's Antiques Price Guide*, the prejudice against Victoriana and, for that matter, Art Nouveau and Art Deco, had become as distant as Queen Victoria herself.

Twenty-one years ago the word 'antique' was synonymous with only one name, Arthur Negus. The knowledgeable and affable silver-haired antiques expert found fame late in life on popular BBC television antiques programmes such as *The Antiques Roadshow*, which has now also found its way into American homes.

Miller's Antiques Price Guide can bear witness to twenty-one years that have experienced sometimes radical changes in collecting trends, attitudes and prices. During this period, the constant export of traditional antiques from the United Kingdom resulted in a depletion of quality stock which proved the impetus for the demand for Victoriana, Art Nouveau and Art Deco. It also stimulated a rapid growth in the collectables market, which attracts new buyers on the strength of both availability and affordability. For many, the established antiques collecting areas have often presented themselves as elitist and expensive. It is an odd fact to ponder that a German tinplate Mickey Mouse money bank of circa 1928 can attract a price today that could secure the purchase of at least two Chelsea polychrome goat-and-bee jugs of circa 1750. When compared with similar 'heavyweight' twentieth-century collectables, the 'antique' can often be both more readily available and affordable, but the market has always hinged upon the simple principle of supply and demand.

During my early days as a porter with Bonhams in the late 1970s, the collectors' department handled fairings, pot lids, Goss china and Stevengraphs, as well as a selection of toys and dolls, but little else. Prices rarely ventured into the realms of four figures.

The ceramics departments concentrated on the sale of 18th- and early 19th-century examples from the 'classic' factories that included Meissen, Chelsea and Worcester. Today the demand for 'classic' porcelain is still high but co-exists with a demand for such relative newcomers as Clarice Cliff, Susie Cooper, Beswick, chintzware and an endless fashion parade courtesy of Royal Doulton's bone-china figures.

The prices paid in recent times for certain examples of Clarice Cliff's ware would have been unthinkable twenty-one years ago. At the time of writing, the demand for her production continues, with specialist dealers and auctions dedicated to meeting the insatiable appetite of her devoted fans.

The reference-book market has enjoyed comparable growth over the period of time with a huge outpouring of works that encompass the whole spectrum of both antiques and collectables.

The market of today and especially during the past year has begun to undergo radical change, primarily as a result of technology at the touch of a button. The advent of the Internet and the possibility of using it to buy at auction are set to change the attitudes of the masses towards the disposal and purchase of all manner of paraphanalia.

Despite the present-day euphoria, hullaballoo and a certain amount of old-fashioned hype, I cannot help but wonder what Arthur Negus would have thought about giving up the drama of being in the saleroom on sale day in return for bidding at auction from the comfort of his home. I am also far from convinced that he would purchase from a dealer a Hepplewhite chair offered on the strength of a digital image e-mailed to a PC without being able to inspect it and offer it the gentle caress for which he became so famous.

The next twenty-one years appear set to offer as much excitement as those we now celebrate. Between now and then Miller's are determined to make sure that, whatever path the market decides to follow, the only guide you will ever need *en route* will be *Miller's Antiques Price Guide*. **Eric Knowles**

Dates	British Monarch	British Period	French Period
1558–1603	Elizabeth I	Elizabethan	Renaissance
1603–1625	James I	Jacobean	
1625–1649	Charles I	Carolean	Louis XIII (1610–1643)
1649–1660	Commonwealth	Cromwellian	Louis XIV (1643–1715)
1660–1685	Charles II	Restoration	
1685–1689	James II	Restoration	
1689–1694	William & Mary	William & Mary	
1694–1702	William III	William III	
1702–1714	Anne	Queen Anne	
1714–1727	George I	Early Georgian	Régence (1715–1723)
1727–1760	George II	Early Georgian	Louis XV (1723–1774)
1760–1811	George III	Late Georgian	Louis XVI (1774–1793) Directoire (1793–1799) Empire (1799–1815)
1812–1820	George III	Regency	Restauration Charles X (1815–1830)
1820–1830	George IV	Regency	
1830–1837	William IV	William IV	Louis Philippe (1830–1848) 2nd Empire Napoleon III (1848–1870) 3rd Republic (1871–1940)
1837–1901	Victoria	Victorian	
1901–1910	Edward VII	Edwardian	

German Period	U.S. Period	Style	Woods
Renaissance	Early Colonial	Gothic	Oak Period (to c1670)
Renaissance/ Baroque (c1650–1700)	Early Colonial	Baroque (c1620–1700)	Walnut period (c1670–1735)
	William & Mary		Walnut period (c1670–1735)
Baroque (c1700–1730)	Dutch Colonial	Rococo (c1695–1760)	Walnut period (c1670–1735)
	Queen Anne		Early mahogany period (c1735–1770)
Rococo (c1730–1760)	Chippendale (from 1750)		Early mahogany period (c1735–1770)
Neo–classicism (c1760–1800)	Early Federal (1790–1810)	Neo–classical (c1755–1805)	Late mahogany period (c1770–1810)
Empire (c1800–1815)	American Directoire (1798–1804)	Empire (c1799–1815)	Late mahogany period (c1770–1810)
	American Empire (1804–1815)		
Biedermeier (c1815–1848)	Late Federal (1810–1830)	Regency (c1812–1830)	
Revivale (c1830–1880)	Victorian	Eclectic (c1830–1880)	
Jugendstil (c1880–1920)	Victorian	Arts & Crafts (c1880–1900)	
	Art Nouveau (c1900–1920)	Art Nouveau (c1900–1920)	

Furniture

One of the most notable market trends in recent years is the interest in 19th-century furniture. As 18th-century and Regency pieces have become less accessible, attention has turned to the Victorian period. Acknowledgement of the fine cabinet-making of such firms as Holland & Sons, Gillows and Howard & Sons has been demonstrated by spiralling prices. Apart from stamped or labelled furniture, the most collectable pieces tend to be good-quality sets of dining chairs, particularly in Georgian revival styles, and 'wind-out' dining tables. Smaller items such as work tables, canterburies, davenports, whatnots and Wellington chests are also very much sought after. Preferred timbers include Brazilian rosewood, burr-walnut and bird's-eye maple. Larger pieces such as ornate inlaid walnut credenzas, Louis XV and XVI writing tables and other so-called 'Franglais' furniture have escalated in value since 1978, but bulky sideboards and wardrobes are still difficult to sell.

Edwardian inlaid and satinwood furniture has been much in demand over the past two decades, and items that were once of moderate value are now highly collectable. One of the eminent firms associated with this era is Edwards & Roberts, whose George III-style marquetry cabinets occasionally attract prices comparable to those of their 18th-century counterparts.

When *Miller's Antiques Price Guide* first went to press, the trade in 18th-century furniture was firmly established, and most collectors will have greatly benefited from their investments. The Chippendale era is still regarded as the zenith of cabinet-making in England. In 1997 a pair of English armchairs and sofas made by Thomas Chippendale to a design by Robert Adam both made record prices of over $2.4million. Only mid-18th century American furniture of an equivalent standard has the potential to match these sums. However, much 18th-century furniture has been prone to over-restoration and items in original condition should be sought wherever possible. Provenance has become an increasingly important value factor.

During the 1980s and 1990s Continental furniture fanatics continued to favour both stamped 18th-century French marquetry and Italian furniture. The Biedermeier style enjoyed a surge of popularity in the late 1980s and has maintained its niche in the market. Late 18th-century Russian brass-mounted furniture has also acquired a similar status among collectors. **Fergus Lyons**

BEDS

A Louis XV carved giltwood bed, with cream upholstered headboard and footboard, extended in width, 18thC, 81in (205.5cm) wide.
$28,000–30,000 S(NY)

A Federal cherrywood tester bedstead, with baluster-turned posts and rails with roping-pegs, American, early 19thC, 53½in (136cm) wide.
$800–1,000 SLM

A Georgian carved mahogany full-tester bed, the footposts with Gothic capitals, c1765, 63½in (161.5cm) wide.
$9,000–9,500 NOA

A Biedermeier mahogany bed, the top rail and sides with banding inlay, c1825, 36in (92cm) wide.
$550–600 S(Am)

A French painted, parcel-gilt and mahogany bed, the head and footboard surmounted by small vases above Egyptian female heads, early 19thC, 48in (122cm) wide.
$6,500–7,500 S(NY)

An Italian walnut and marquetry bedstead, with barley-twist posts, 1825–40, 52¾in (134cm) wide.
$2,000–2,200 NOA

Styles of Beds

Four-poster beds reached the peak of fashion in Britain from the mid-18th to the mid-19thC, superseded by half-testers and later by the more conventional form with headboard and footboard. The neo-classical style prevailed on the Continent from late 18th to early 19thC, and at the end of this period beds were often mahogany with gilt-brass mounts or lighter timbers with darker veneers. In France the boat-shaped bed, known as the *lit en bateau*, was very popular.

A worldwide resurgence in the revival of historical styles in the late 19thC gave rise in England to the hybrid style of Elizabethan and Jacobean, known as 'Jacobethan'. In Italy the 'Dantesque' style was a revival of 16thC renaissance influence, using ornate bone and ivory inlay. This style was also very popular in America from c1850, with an emphasis on carved ornamentation. Beds in brass and iron were fashionable in England from c1880 in the wake of the Industrial Revolution.

The late 19thC saw the revival of rococo, Louis XVI and corresponding English styles such as Chippendale and Adam, and resulted in the reintroduction of four-poster beds.

A polished teak bed, with barley-twist posts and carved headboard, c1860, 65in (165cm) wide.
$5,000–5,500 VI

A Louis Philippe Egyptian-style carved, ebonized and parcel-gilt mahogany bedstead, 1830–35, 52¾in (134cm) wide.
$2,000–2,200 NOA

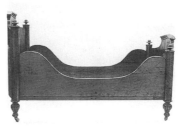

A Victorian mahogany boat-shaped single bed, mid-19thC, 46in (117cm) wide.
$1,150–1,300 E

A Victorian Gothic-style oak four-poster bed, with moulded canopy, 66in (168cm) wide.
$5,500–6,500 MEA

An American rococo revival carved mahogany bedstead, the headboard surrounded by pierced carved leaves and branches, the footboard decorated with branches, leaves and a bird, c1850, 73in (185.5cm) wide.
$5,000–5,500 B&B

This bed exemplifies the ornate cabinet-work found between the 1850s and 1870s in American furniture. An almost identical bed can be found in the White House in the Lincoln Bedroom, which is used today as a guest room for friends of the President's family. Another similar bed, made by John Belter, can be found at the Smithsonian Institution in Washington DC.

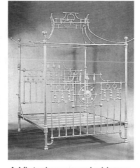

A Victorian canopied brass four-poster bedstead, the balustraded footboard centred by a wheel with ceramic balls, with corresponding headboard, 72¾in (185cm) wide.
$3,500–4,000 P(Ed)

A French Louis XVI-style painted and gilded cane bed, 19thC, 60in (152.5cm) wide.
$8,000–10,000 LaM

A French walnut four-poster bed, with carvings of Adam and Eve to head and foot, angels around the canopy, original silk drapes and tassels, c1880, 78in (198cm) wide.
$23,000–26,000 HAC

A Louis XV revival carved walnut bed, by Brandin & Gendre, Paris, c1880, 56in (142cm) wide.
$3,000–3,200 HAC

A French oak four-poster bedstead, with stucco work panel depicting a reclining lady, c1900, 60in (150cm) wide.
$14,000–16,000 SeH

This bed was reputedly made for the Paris Exhibition of 1900.

A French oak bedstead, c1890, 54in (137cm) wide.
$2,000–2,500 SeH

A pair of Continental painted and grained wrought- and cast-iron bedsteads, c1895, 36½in (92.5cm) wide.
$2,000–2,500 NOA

An oak bed, with barley-twist columns, early 20thC, 54in (137cm) wide.
$750–800 COLL

◄ A pair of Edwardian mahogany twin beds, each with ornate crossbanded and marquetry panels, 36in (91cm) wide.
$1,800–2,000 MEA

An Edwardian mahogany bedstead, the caned head and footboard with carved laurel leaf, paterae and scale decoration, 77½in (197cm) wide.
$1,200–1,400 B

BONHEURS DU JOUR

A Victorian gilt-bronze and ebony bonheur du jour, the upper section with cupboard doors all mounted with hardstone flower-filled urns, c1860, 45in (114.5cm) wide.
$9,000–10,000 S(NY)

A lady's walnut and gilt-metal-mounted bonheur du jour, with a central mirror flanked by 2 glazed doors, inlaid overall with formal scroll designs and string lines, c1870, 32¼in (82cm) wide.
$3,200–4,000 P(C)

A French-style walnut bonheur du jour, with floral marquetry and gilt mounts, 19thC, 48in (122cm) high.
$3,500–4,000 RBB

◀ A Louis XVI-style mahogany and gilt-metal-mounted bonheur du jour, with tambour cylinder and sloping fall inset with a *vernis Martin*-style panel, late 19thC, 28¼in (72cm) wide.
$2,500–3,000 P

A late Victorian satinwood classical revival bonheur du jour, crossbanded, inlaid and painted with musical instruments and floral swags, 37in (94cm) wide.
$9,000–10,000 RTo

An Edwardian grained coromandel bonheur du jour, inlaid in marquetry with etched ivory and assorted woods, the tooled-leather writing surface flanked with 2 serpentine-shaped flaps, 40in (102cm) extended.
$2,800–3,200 MEA

▶ A German gilt-bronze and ebonized bonheur du jour, the upper section with a central cupboard door and single drawer flanked by 4 pairs of drawers within free-standing floral-decorated porcelain columns, raised on a porcelain trestle-form base, late 19thC, 44in (112cm) wide.
$45,000–52,000 S(NY)

BOOKCASES

A George II walnut estate bookcase, the glazed doors enclosing a shelved interior, 54in (137cm) wide.
$5,000–6,500 B

A Dutch Empire mahogany bookcase, with protruding frieze drawer above 2 grille doors, alterations, early 19thC, 39½in (100cm) wide.
$3,500–4,000 S(Am)

A Victorian oak cabinet bookcase, by Gillows of Lancaster, the twin glazed panel doors enclosing 4 adjustable shelves, 2 linenfold panelled cupboard doors below, faults, 47½in (120.5cm) wide.
$6,000–6,500 S(S)

A George III mahogany cabinet bookcase, with 2 astragal-glazed cupboard doors enclosing adjustable shelves, the lower section with 3 chequer-banded drawers, c1790, 45¼in (115cm) wide.
$2,300–2,500 S(S)

A Regency mahogany bookcase, with astragal-glazed doors enclosing shelves, long drawer below, 52in (132cm) wide.
$4,500–5,000 WL

A Biedermeier satin birch and ebonized bookcase, the astragal-glazed doors with apron compartment below, with a simulated 3 drawer panelled door below, 19thC, 41in (104cm) wide.
$2,800–3,200 P(EA)

An Irish mahogany bookcase, on a chest of 2 short and 3 long drawers, c1800, 45in (114.5cm) wide.
$6,500–7,500 GKe

A William IV mahogany bookcase, the upper part with a pair of Gothic-style glazed doors, 62in (157cm) wide.
$2,500–3,000 L

A German walnut bookcase, in 2 sections, the 4 grille panelled doors enclosing shelves, on outswept supports, early 19thC, 77¼in (196cm) wide.
$5,500–6,500 P

A George IV figured mahogany library bookcase, with 2 glazed doors enclosing shelves, the 2 panelled doors enclosing trays, 43½in (110.5cm) wide.
$3,000–3,300 Bri

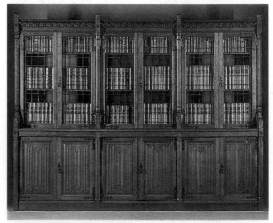

A Victorian Gothic-style oak library bookcase, the crenellated cornice carved with paterae and headed by 4 joint finials, the 3 pairs of doors with brass grille panels, the lower part enclosed by 3 pairs of linenfold panelled doors, c1850, 108½in (275.5cm) wide.
$25,000–27,000 S

The value of this bookcase lies in its superb quality and excellent condition.

Glazing Styles

- Before c1750, small rectangular panes were used, retained by fairly solid glazing bars (astragals).
- After c1750, more intricate patterns were fashionable and called for lighter glazing bars.
- From the 19thC, some bookcases had just plain glass set into a shaped panel.

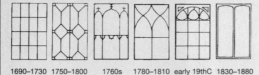

| 1690–1730 | 1750–1800 | 1760s | 1780–1810 | early 19thC | 1830–1880 |

A Victorian mahogany bookcase, 19thC, 40in (101.5cm) wide.
$2,000–2,300 JH

A pair of Victorian mahogany bookcases, each with 3 fitted adjustable shelves enclosed by a pair of arched glazed doors, one bookcase faded, 42in (106.5cm) wide.
$4,500–5,200 CAG

An Edwardian mahogany double bookcase, with 4 astragal-glazed doors, 49in (124.5cm) wide.
$4,000–4,500 DD

A George III-style mahogany breakfront bookcase, the 4 astragal-glazed doors enclosing adjustable shelves, on ogee bracket feet, c1910, 54in (137cm) wide.
$4,000–5,000 S(S)

◄ An Edwardian satin-wood bookcase, the upper section with 2 glazed doors, the base with 2 inlaid panelled doors, 28in (71cm) wide.
$1,200–1,400 MEA

A Victorian mahogany bookcase-on-chest, with 2 Gothic tracery glazed doors with interior shelves, the lower section with 2 short and 3 long graduated drawers, 38½in (98cm) wide.
$4,500–5,000 M

► An ebonized and gilt bookcase, the pair of double hinged panel doors with pierced lozenge grilles backed with silk, enclosing 4 shelves, 19thC, 46in (117cm) wide.
$1,600–2,000 P

A Victorian mahogany library bookcase, the glazed doors above an arrangement of drawers and a double dummy-fronted cellaret drawer, 70½in (179cm) wide.
$3,200–4,000 Oli

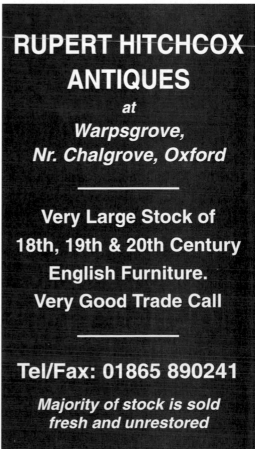

BUREAU BOOKCASES

A George III mahogany bureau bookcase, with a pair of astragal-glazed doors, the fall-front opening to a fitted interior of pigeonholes, drawers and a central cupboard, above 4 long graduated drawers, 40½in (103cm) wide.
$1,500–1,800 Bon(W)

A George III mahogany bureau bookcase, the astragal-glazed doors enclosing adjustable shelves, a fall-front below revealing a fitted interior, above 2 short and 3 long graduated drawers, parts later, 35½in (90cm) wide.
$2,500–3,000 S(S)

An American rosewood-veneered bureau bookcase, the glazed doors with applied Gothic ornament opening to 3 adjustable shelves, above 3 small drawers and a writing surface enclosing drawers and compartments, over 2 cupboard doors opening to a single shelf, 1840s, 44in (112cm) wide.
$5,000–6,000 SK(B)

▶ An Edwardian inlaid mahogany bureau bookcase, by Maple & Co, the upper part enclosed by a pair of astragal-glazed doors, the fall front above 2 short and one long drawer, 37in (94cm) wide.
$2,000–2,200 P(B)

A Victorian mahogany cylinder bureau bookcase, with 2 glazed doors above a fall-front enclosing 3 short drawers either side, pigeon-holes and a sliding writing top, 46½in (118cm) wide.
$2,800–3,200 Bon(C)

21 Years Ago ...

A Dutch mahogany bureau bookcase, inlaid overall with floral marquetry, the upper part with leaf-carved cresting, late 18th/early 19thC, 57in (145cm) wide. **S**

Twenty-one years ago this bureau bookcase was valued at $10,000–11,500. Today a similar cabinet could realize $32,000–40,000 which, taking inflation into account, does not represent a substantial increase in value. Although much prized for its decorative appeal, Dutch marquetry furniture is not known for its high standards of cabinet-making, and is not as popular today. An emerging trend is to place greater importance on high-quality construction and craftsmanship, often epitomised by 19thC furniture.

An Edwardian mahogany bureau bookcase, the astragal-glazed doors enclosing shelves, the fall-front opening to reveal stationery slides, pigeonholes, drawers and a central drawer, with 2 short and 3 long graduated drawers below, 38in (97cm) wide.
$4,000–4,500 P(HSS)

An Edwardian George III-style mahogany and satinwood crossbanded bureau bookcase, the interlaced astragal-glazed doors enclosing adjustable shelves, the fall-front enclosing drawers, pigeonholes and a cupboard door, damaged, c1910, 39½in (100cm) wide.
$6,000–6,500 S(S)

OPEN BOOKCASES

A George IV mahogany open bookcase, the top with a three-quarter solid gallery above 4 open shelves with ebony stringing, c1820, 32¼in (82cm) wide.
$6,000–6,500 S

A Regency mahogany open bookcase, inlaid with stringing, the 5 shelves united by turned and ringed supports, 50in (127cm) wide.
$2,500–3,000 P(F)

A Regency mahogany two-stage bookcase, with rosewood crossbanding, the upper part with scrolled surmount and 2 small drawers below, the projecting stand with long frieze drawer over 2 small fitted drawers, shaped undershelf, 36¼in (92cm) wide.
$3,000–3,300 AH

A George IV mahogany breakfront open bookcase, fitted with adjustable shelves, 57½in (146cm) wide.
$7,500–8,000 P

A pair of Irish mahogany graduated bookcases, with 2 drawers, c1830, 48in (122cm) wide.
$8,000–10,000 GKe

An Edwardian neo-classical style mahogany and satinwood marquetry open bookcase, with a swag, husk and urn inlaid frieze above low adjustable shelves, restored, 120in (305cm) wide.
$7,500–8,000 P

REVOLVING BOOKCASES

A mahogany and satinwood-banded revolving bookcase, the top inlaid with quarter paterae, late 19thC, 23¾in (60cm) square.
$2,000–2,500 HOK

An Edwardian mahogany revolving bookcase, with boxwood stringing and central marquetry roundel, 20in (51cm) wide.
$750–800 WBH

A William IV rosewood and mahogany dwarf revolving bookcase, the supports imitating book spines, over a leaf-carved stem on circular platform and 3 paw feet, 31½in (80cm) high.
$2,000–2,500 MEA

A Victorian mahogany revolving bookstand, the circular dished top above 3 graduated galleried triform tiers, on 3 downswept legs, damaged, restored, 37¾in (96cm) high.
$1,200–1,500 S(S)

▶ An Edwardian mahogany revolving bookcase, with parquetry banding, the top inlaid with marquetry batwing roundel, 12¾in (32.5cm) wide.
$500–600 AH

SECRETAIRE BOOKCASES

A George III mahogany breakfront secretaire library bookcase, the glazed doors with panelled astragals headed by scrolled arches and enclosing adjustable shelves, the fitted writing drawer above a pair of cupboard doors, flanked by 2 drawers over panelled doors, 89¾in (228cm) wide.
$25,000–28,000 S

A Regency brass-inlaid secretaire bookcase, the pair of glazed doors opening to 3 adjustable shelves, the lower section with *faux* marble top rising to reveal a calamander-lined fold-out secretaire, and *faux* marble stiles with gilt-metal Corinthian capitals, early 19thC, 48½in (123cm) wide.
$40,000–45,000 SLN

This is a high-quality cabinet, demonstrated by the use of *faux* marble, calamander veneers and brass inlay. Furthermore, the false book spines and fold-out, rather than fall-front, secretaire drawer are rare features.

▶ A Victorian mahogany secretaire bookcase, the glazed panelled doors enclosing adjustable shelves, the secretaire drawer over a pair of panelled cupboard doors, 47in (119.5cm) wide.
$2,000–2,300 Mit

A George III mahogany secretaire bookcase, the pierced carved swan-neck pediment above glazed doors enclosing shelves, the fitted secretaire drawer above 2 short and 2 long drawers, c1765, 46¼in (118cm) wide.
$25,000–30,000 S

A mahogany secretaire bookcase, the astragal doors enclosing adjustable shelves, the panel-front writing drawer revealing a fitted interior with satin-birch drawers, the panelled lower part enclosed by a pair of doors, c1825, 49½in (126cm) wide.
$6,500–7,200 S

A Regency mahogany crossbanded secretaire bookcase, with ebony stringing, 2 astragal-glazed doors enclosing shelving, the associated base with fitted deep secretaire drawer, 2 panelled doors below, 43in (109cm) wide.
$2,500–2,800 AH

A William IV mahogany secretaire bookcase, the Gothic glazed doors enclosing shelves, a fitted drawer below and 2 further long drawers, 48in (122cm) wide.
$2,800–3,200 L

▶ An Edwardian Adam-style mahogany lady's secretaire bookcase, with applied decoration of swags and medallions, the lower part fitted with a slide with tooled-leather surface, above a drawer and a pair of panelled doors, stamped 'E. T. Downham', 27¾in (70.5cm) wide.
$1,300–1,600 P(F)

A Regency rosewood and brass-inlaid secretaire, the astragal-glazed doors enclosing adjustable shelves, with a long drawer and a secretaire drawer below, altered, 50½in (128cm) wide.
$5,000–6,000 P(L)

A late Victorian walnut secretaire bookcase, c1880, 49in (124.5cm) wide.
$2,000–2,200 Doc

BUCKETS

A pair of George III mahogany plate buckets, the sides pierced with Gothic tracery, 12½in (31cm) high.
$8,500–9,500 L

A George III mahogany and brass-bound bucket, with brass handle, 13¾in (35cm) wide.
$2,000–2,200 Bon

A George III mahogany and brass-bound peat bucket, 15¾in (40cm) high.
$2,000–2,200 P

A pair of George III mahogany and brass-bound peat buckets, each with ribbed body, 18in (45.5cm) high.
$16,000–18,000 HCC

These buckets have an Irish provenance, and a saleroom battle involving a number of Irish bidders accounted for their high price.

A Georgian mahogany and brass-bound bucket, with lead lining and carrying handle, 14¼in (36cm) wide.
$500–600 P

A pair of George III mahogany and brass-bound peat buckets, with brass swing handles, 15in (38cm) high.
$6,000–7,000 JAd

A mahogany and brass-bound peat bucket, with a brass liner, the staved sides with brass bands, 19thC, 14¼in (36cm) high.
$800–1,000 P(Ed)

A pair of mahogany brass-bound buckets, missing brass carrying handles, late 19thC, 18¼in (46.5cm) high.
$7,000–8,000 S(NY)

BUFFETS

A mahogany three-tier buffet, with scroll corner supports, c1830, 45in (114.5cm) wide.
$2,100–2,300 HUB

An early Victorian mahogany three-tier buffet, 43¼in (110cm) wide.
$2,100–2,300 Bri

A Victorian pollard oak three-tier buffet, by Lamb of Manchester, the shaped galleried top with a central oval shield, the mirror-back above a bowed second tier with a carved frieze drawer, 60in (153cm) wide.
$2,000–2,500 S(S)

James Lamb (1816–1903) produced high-quality furniture, although no formal business documents survive. He did not take part in any of the important exhibitions until the International Exhibition of 1862 and was awarded the gold medal at the Paris Exhibition of 1878.

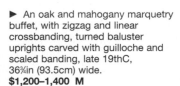

▶ An oak and mahogany marquetry buffet, with zigzag and linear crossbanding, turned baluster uprights carved with guilloche and scaled banding, late 19thC, 36¾in (93.5cm) wide.
$1,200–1,400 M

BUREAUX

A William and Mary walnut and featherbanded bureau, the fall-front revealing a fitted interior, on later stand, restored, 37in (94cm) wide.
$4,000–4,500 S(S)

A figured-ash bureau, the fitted interior with 8 small mahogany-fronted drawers and pigeonholes enclosed by a fall-front, over 4 long drawers, 18thC, 37in (94cm) wide.
$8,500–9,500 B

A Flemish oak marquetry bureau, with floral decoration and rococo scrollwork, the fall-front enclosing a recessed cupboard with concealed compartment, small drawers and slide to well, the 3 long graduated drawers forming serpentine front, 18thC, 36in (91.5cm) wide.
$7,500–9,000 WBH

LOCATE THE SOURCE
The source of each illustration in Miller's can be found by checking the code letters below each caption with the Key to Illustrations, pages 789–795.

A burr-walnut bureau, inlaid with herringbone banding, the fall-front enclosing a fitted interior of drawers and pigeonholes, restored, early 18thC, 34in (86.5cm) wide.
$8,000–9,500 S

Facts in Brief

- Evolved as a steeper version of the 17thC writing box, set on a chest of drawers.
- Early examples were often made in 2 parts, the join being concealed by moulding.
- Small examples under 36in (91.5cm) wide are particularly desirable.

A Dutch mahogany cylinder bureau, the upper part with a tambour door, above a cylinder front opening to a fitted interior and a writing surface, late 18thC, 44½in (113cm) wide.
$4,500–5,200 S(Am)

A walnut bureau, with feather-banding, the fitted interior above 2 short and 2 long drawers, on bracket feet, early 18thC, 31in (78.5cm) wide.
$2,500–3,000 RBB

A walnut bureau, decorated with feather-banding and crossbanding, the fall-front opening to reveal an assortment of pigeonholes, drawers, a central cupboard and a well, 18thC, 36in (91.5cm) wide.
$6,200–6,800 Bon(W)

An American child's walnut bureau, inlaid with maple, the fall-front opening to a fitted interior with 6 pigeonholes above 3 drawers, a sliding drawer opening to a well, New England, 18thC, 20in (51cm) wide.
$5,000–5,750 B&B

◀ A Regency mahogany cylinder-front bureau, the ebony bordered fall enclosing drawers, pigeonholes and a pull-out writing slide, 36in (91.5cm) wide.
$3,500–4,000 GOR

A mahogany tambour bureau, cross-banded in satinwood with boxwood and ebony stringing, the interior with pigeonholes, small drawers and a writing slide, 19thC, 40in (101.5cm) wide.
$9,000–10,000 DN

A Louis XV-style rosewood and floral marquetry bureau, with a three-quarter gilt-bronze cast gallery and fitted interior, 19thC, 27½in (70cm) wide.
$2,300–2,800 TMA

A mahogany bureau, the hinged fall with boxwood and ebony stringing, on reduced bracket feet, 19thC, 41⅛in (105.5cm) wide.
$1,200–1,400 P(NW)

A lady's inlaid satinwood and crossbanded rosewood bureau, the cylinder fall enclosing 2 small drawers, late 19thC, 22in (56cm) wide.
$2,500–3,000 B&L

An Edwardian mahogany, satinwood-banded, boxwood and ebony line-inlaid cylinder bureau, 36½in (92.5cm) wide.
$1,500–1,800 E

An Edwardian mahogany and marquetry cylinder bureau, the tambour front opening to reveal a sliding writing surface, reading slope and pigeonholes, 40in (101.5cm) wide.
$3,000–3,500 P(C)

An Edwardian mahogany fall-front bureau, with satinwood inlay and marquetry, on bracket feet, 30in (76cm) wide.
$1,000–1,300 BUSH

A lady's walnut bureau, the demi-lune top above a shaped fall-front opening to reveal a fitted interior of pigeonholes, drawers and central cupboard, on cabriole legs and pad feet, stamped 'Maple & Co', early 20thC, 29in (73.5cm) wide.
$750–800 Bon(W)

◀ A French rosewood cylinder bureau, with marquetry decoration, on gilt-mounted cabriole legs, early 20thC, 31½in (80cm) wide.
$2,600–2,800 SWO

CABINETS

A kingwood cabinet, with a cushion drawer to the cornice, the doors inlaid with segmented roundels, possibly Dutch, late 17thC, 47in (119.5cm) wide.
$18,500–20,000 L

A walnut cabinet, the fall enclosing a fitted interior of pigeonholes and drawers around a pair of cupboard doors, c1700, 47½in (120.5cm) wide.
$11,500–13,000 Bon

A Dutch walnut and burr-walnut cabinet, the top with shaped central carving, above 2 conforming panelled doors, 18thC, 71½in (181.5cm) wide.
$13,000–14,500 S(Am)

A George II walnut cabinet, the crossbanded cupboard doors enclosing shelves, the lower part with similar cupboards, c1750, 31in (78.5cm) wide.
$7,000–8,000 S

A George III mahogany library pedestal cabinet, the cupboards enclosing triangular shelves, flanked by banks of 4 graduated drawers, c1800, 45½in (115cm) wide.
$13,000–16,000 S

▶ A Victorian mahogany two-tier cabinet, the base with a frieze drawer, 30in (76cm) wide.
$1,800–2,000 TRL

An Italian carved walnut cabinet, the doors inlaid with Italian scenes and 6 medallions of classical profiles in the outer border, the freestanding columns at the base resting on a plinth, c1900, 48in (122cm) wide.
$8,500–9,000 DuM

A William and Mary-style oyster-veneered cabinet, with 2 pairs of short drawers above a pair of cabinet doors enclosing a fitted interior, the base with a long drawer, late 19thC, 52in (132cm) wide.
$4,500–5,000 SK

BEDSIDE CABINETS

An early George III figured mahogany bowfront bedside cabinet, with a shaped panel tambour cupboard door below a shaped gallery tray top, with carrying handles, 21in (53.5cm) wide.
$2,500–3,000 P(WM)

A mahogany tray-top bedside cabinet, fitted with a drawer, late 18thC, 14½in (36cm) wide.
$550–600 HOK

A Regency mahogany bedside cabinet, the tray-top above a panelled door, on turned tapering legs, 17in (43cm) wide.
$1,200–1,400 P(Sc)

A French mahogany bedside table, the front with ormolu mounts, the back with open compartments centred by a wooden slide, early 19thC, 17¼in (44cm) wide.
$4,500–5,200 S(NY)

A Victorian burr-walnut bedside cupboard, 16in (40.5cm) wide.
$750–900 BUSH

A maple and simulated bamboo bedside cabinet, with a drawer and fall flap, c1870, 27in (68.5cm) wide.
$1,000–1,200 S

A late Victorian walnut bedside cabinet, on casters, 35½in (90cm) high.
$450–520 AnSh

An Edwardian Sheraton-style mahogany bedside cabinet, c1900, 13½in (34.5cm) wide.
$1,200–1,400 NOA

BUREAU CABINETS

A burr-elm bureau cabinet, with walnut feather-banding, the later cornice above a pair of doors enclosing a fitted interior, the sloping fall opening to reveal a replaced velvet writing surface and a fitted interior, on a later plinth base, early 18thC, 39¾in (101cm) wide.
$11,500–13,000 P(NW)

A walnut bureau cabinet, the arched fielded panelled doors enclosing pigeonholes and folio racks with a pair of candleslides beneath, the lower part with a sloping front, 2 short and 2 long drawers, on bun feet, restored, early 18thC, 36in (91.5cm) wide.
$4,500–5,500 L

A walnut and mulberry bureau cabinet, with crossbanding and feather stringing, the upper part with a later cornice and fitted interior, enclosed by arched figured doors, the centre section with a sloping fall enclosing a fitted interior, on later bracket feet, early 18thC, 38½in (98cm) wide.
$9,000–10,500 P

A George III mahogany bureau cabinet, the panelled cupboard doors enclosing shelves, the fall-front opening to reveal a carved and inlaid interior fitted with drawers, cupboards and pigeon-holes, above 2 short and 3 long graduated drawers, 48in (122cm) wide.
$13,000–16,000 Mit

◄ A north Italian black japanned bureau cabinet, the interior fitted with pigeonholes surmounting small drawers, c1780, 38½in (98cm) wide.
$15,500–17,500 NOA

► An American brass-inlaid rosewood bureau cabinet, created from a piano, the glazed upper section fitted with 5 shelves, with later fitted writing surface, c1825, 48½in (123cm) wide.
$11,500–13,500 NOA

Brass-inlaid furniture of this form was extremely costly, and manufactured by only a few of the finest cabinet-makers in New York and Philadelphia.

A George III-style mahogany bureau cabinet, with satinwood banding and boxwood stringing, the panelled doors enclosing adjustable shelves, the inlaid fall-front enclosing drawers and pigeonholes, 19thC, 52¾in (134cm) wide.
$1,000–1,200 P(Sc)

CORNER CABINETS

A bowfront hanging corner cupboard, with 3 graduated open shelves above 2 doors painted with a nativity scene, mid-18thC, 21in (53.5cm) wide.
$3,500–4,000 DN

► A north Italian marquetry bowfront corner cabinet, inlaid in various woods and ivory with hunting scenes and stylized scrolling foliage, 18thC, 36½in (92.5cm) wide.
$5,500–6,500 Bea(E)

An Edwardian inlaid mahogany corner cabinet, the top with finials over 3 shelves and mirror back, the shaped base enclosed by a door, on turned supports, with undertier, 23in (58.5cm) wide.
$2,200–2,500 RHE

A George III mahogany standing corner cupboard, with 2 long panelled doors enclosing an arched interior, over 2 short doors, 42½in (108cm) wide.
$2,500–3,200 AH

A Biedermeier mahogany corner cupboard, the frieze drawer and door with shaped panels, chamfered corners and carved foliate decoration, late 19thC, 35½in (90cm) wide.
$800–900 S(Am)

A late George III mahogany standing corner cupboard, the astragal-glazed doors enclosing shelves, the base with a cupboard enclosed by 2 panelled doors, 40in (101.5cm) wide.
$2,000–2,500 E

A mahogany hanging corner cabinet, the cornice with 3 turned urn finials above a drop bead decorated frieze, with an astragal-glazed door enclosing shaped shelves, early 19thC, 35in (89cm) wide.
$2,200–2,500 DN(H)

► An Edwardian mahogany and satinwood-banded corner cabinet, decorated with inlaid classical urns and trailing scrolling foliage, the broken swan-neck pediment above an astragal-glazed door, c1910, 19in (48.5cm) wide.
$1,800–2,000 Bon(C)

A George III mahogany hanging corner cupboard, with interlaced astragal-glazed doors enclosing 3 shelves, 27½in (70cm) wide.
$1,600–2,000 P

A mahogany corner cabinet, with a pair of arched panelled doors enclosing a series of painted shelves, the base fitted with a pair of similar doors also enclosing shelves, 19thC, 44in (112cm) wide.
$2,300–2,600 Mit

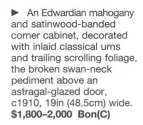

DISPLAY CABINETS

A pair of George III mahogany alcove display cabinets, inlaid with ebonized stringing, the astragal-glazed doors enclosing 4 shelves, damaged, c1800, 35in (89cm) wide.
$3,500–4,000 S(S)

A French Gothic-style carved fruitwood display cabinet, the interior fitted with 4 shelves and painted, c1825, 43½in (110.5cm) wide.
$2,800–3,200 NOA

A Dutch walnut and marquetry display cabinet, inlaid with vases of flowers, cornucopias and meandering flowers and foliage, 19thC, 57in (145cm) wide.
$6,000–7,000 Bea(E)

A walnut display cabinet, with cartouche cresting above an arched glazed door, with glazed sides, mid-19thC, 42in (106.5cm) wide.
$2,000–2,300 HOK

A mid-Victorian walnut display cabinet, decorated with boxwood outline stringing, the shaped panelled glazed door enclosing 3 shelves, flanked by gilt-metal mounts, 40in (101.5cm) wide.
$3,000–3,300 Bon(W)

An Italian ebonized display cabinet, inlaid with ivory and blonde tortoiseshell, decorated with stylized and scrolling foliage, winged mythical beasts, masks, urns and figures, inset with blue variegated hardstone and onyx panels, all bordered with ivory lines, 19thC, 48in (122.5cm) wide.
$1,500–1,800 P(E)

A Victorian mahogany bowfronted display cabinet, the upper section with a cupboard door flanked by mirror-backed shelving, the base with glazed display cabinet, 2 carved cupboard doors and an arcaded under-shelf, 31in (78.5cm) wide.
$2,300–2,600 AH

A walnut display cabinet, by Collinson & Lock, London, designed by T. E. Collcutt, c1880, 64in (162.5cm) wide.
$5,800–7,200 MoS

A late Victorian mahogany display cabinet, the twin astragal-glazed doors enclosing 3 glass shelves, on block column supports, 48in (122cm) wide.
$1,200–1,400 BWe

A Dutch Louis XV-style burr-walnut display cabinet, the top with a carved crest above 2 glazed doors, with chamfered glazed sides, the serpentine lower part with 2 short and one long drawer, on carved cabriole legs, c1900, 63¾in (160cm) wide.
$1,800–2,200 S(Am)

An Edwardian inlaid mahogany display cabinet, of part bowed outline, the shaped back decorated with foliate scrolls, the lined interior fitted with 2 glazed shelves, enclosed by a leaded-glass panel door, on cabriole legs with pad feet, 77¼in (196cm) wide.
$1,000–1,400 P(NE)

A French kingwood vitrine, with gilt-metal mounts, glazed door and sides, marquetry panels below depicting baskets of flowers, 19thC, 33in (84cm) wide.
$2,500–3,200 AH

An Edwardian Chippendale-style mahogany inverted breakfront display cabinet, the glazed panelled doors enclosing shelves, with carved gadrooning, rococo, scallop and floral decoration, 60in (152.5cm) wide.
$4,500–5,000 Gam

An Edwardian inlaid mahogany bowfront display cabinet, with arched ledge back and a pair of astragal-glazed doors, with shaped front undershelf, on square tapered legs with spade feet, 48in (122cm) wide.
$1,600–1,800 CDC

A Napoleon III gilt-bronze-mounted mahogany vitrine cabinet, attributed to Viardot, with a gilt-bronze dragon emerging from a pagoda-form cornice, flanked by a pierced gallery above a glazed door and side panels, revealing tiers of asymmetrical interior shelves and a single short drawer, c1870, 38½in (98cm) wide.
$13,000–14,500 S(NY)

Gabriel Viardot established his own workshop in 1860 in rue du Grand Chantier, Paris. The shop relocated several times and finally settled at 36 rue Amelot where the company remained until the end of the century. Viardot specialized in exotic furniture of Japanese and Chinese inspiration. He was a participant and a jury member at the Expositions Universelles of 1867 where he acquired 4 medals for his designs. In 1878 he gained a silver medal, and was awarded a gold medal in 1889.

A satinwood and painted display cabinet, the glazed door enclosing a glass shelf, with 2 drawers and a pair of doors below, c1920, 28in (71cm) wide.
$2,200–2,500 S(S)

A Sheraton design mahogany display cabinet, the broken swan-neck pediment mounted with a central urn within diaper-pierced panels, the astragal-glazed doors enclosing 2 fixed shelves above a projecting satinwood and crossbanded base, the boxwood-strung square tapering legs formerly united by stretchers, c1900, 35in (89cm) wide.
$1,600–2,000 EH

An Edwardian mahogany and marquetry display cabinet, in the manner of Edwards & Roberts, the glazed upper section with an inlaid dentilled cornice over a panel inlaid with ribbon-tied swags of bellflowers, the projecting lower section with a pair of panelled doors inlaid with classical urns and ribbon-tied swags, the square tapered legs with spade feet, 36in (91.5cm) wide.
$3,200–3,500 HYD

MUSIC CABINETS

A mid-Victorian burr-walnut music cabinet, decorated with boxwood stringing and foliate inlays, with a glazed door under, legs missing, 23in (58.5cm) wide.
$800–950 Bon(W)

A Victorian walnut and marquetry music cabinet, with a gilt-brass gallery back, the glazed door fitted with shelves and a drawer, flanked by baluster leaf-carved and turned columns, 24½in (62cm) wide.
$1,500–1,650 HYD

A Victorian walnut and inlaid music cabinet, the pierced galleried top on conforming openwork supports, the glazed panel door below enclosing a shelved interior, restored, 22¾in (58cm) wide.
$1,300–1,500 S(S)

A Victorian maple music cabinet, the leather-inset top over a mirrored door and a drawer, 24½in (62cm) wide.
$800–900 Bri

An Edwardian inlaid mahogany music cabinet, 18in (45.5cm) wide.
$350–400 TRU

A late Victorian rosewood music cabinet, with inlaid decoration and stringing, with a stained lead-glazed panelled door, 2 panelled doors and a drawer above, 23½in (59.5cm) wide.
$750–900 Gam

SECRETAIRE CABINETS

A William and Mary inlaid dark walnut escritoire, the upper part with cushion drawer, the fall-front revealing a fitted interior, the later stand fitted with 2 drawers, some veneer missing, 41¾in (106cm) wide.
$3,000–3,500 P(F)

A George III mahogany secretaire cabinet, possibly by Gillows, the panelled doors enclosing linen slides, 51¼in (130cm) wide.
$10,000–11,500 P(L)

A Louis Philippe mahogany, amaranth and satinwood *secrétaire à abattant*, the black marble top above a frieze drawer, the hinged flap enclosing a Gothic-style fitted interior with open arched compartments and drawers, inlaid with scrolling flowering foliage, above 2 doors opening to 3 drawers, mid-19thC, 41in (104cm) wide.
$4,500–5,200 S(Am)

A Queen Anne walnut and seaweed marquetry cabinet on secretaire chest, the pair of marquetry-inlaid doors enclosing a fully fitted interior, the base with a secretaire drawer fitted with drawers and pigeonholes, 2 short and 2 long drawers below, on bun feet, c1705, 42¾in (108.5cm) wide.
$9,000–10,000 S

A George III mahogany, satinwood and gilt-brass-mounted writing cabinet, in the manner of Seddon, Sons & Shackleton, the upper section fitted with brass-moulded glazed doors, the lower part centred by a roll-top bureau enclosing a fitted interior above a leather-lined slide, the inverted breakfront sides fitted with 2 drawers above banded oval panelled doors enclosing shelves, c1795, 51¼in (130cm) wide.
$50,000–55,000 S

This superb piece of furniture is in the manner of Seddon, Sons & Shackleton who were the successors of the celebrated firm of George Seddon. The partnership included George Seddon's sons, George and Thomas, and his son-in-law Thomas Shackleton, who together worked from 150 Aldersgate Street, London.

Miller's is a price GUIDE not a price LIST

21 Years Ago ...

A walnut fall-front escritoire, with crossbanding and herringbone inlay, early 18thC, 41in (104cm) wide. **B&L**

Twenty-one years ago this escritoire was valued at $2,300–2,800. A similar example in original condition, retaining good colour and patina, might fetch a price of $25,000–28,000 in today's market. The value for good-quality walnut has held up well, largely because there is so little high-calibre furniture of its kind available. The level of expertise among collectors of walnut furniture has increased, with the result that suspect or over-restored walnut pieces are far more likely to be disregarded in favour of good genuine items.

A Dutch satinwood, rosewood and lacquered *secrétaire à abattant*, the frieze drawer and fall-front with panels depicting sheep enclosing a fitted interior, above 2 doors with lacquered panels, altered, c1800, 34½in (87.5cm) wide.
$10,000–11,500 S(Am)

▶ A rococo revival bombé-shaped rosewood and marquetry-inlaid escritoire, with gilt-brass metal mounts, the marble top above a convex fall enclosing 2 drawers, with 3 serpentine drawers below, 19thC, 27in (68.5cm) wide.
$1,800–2,000 EH

An American rosewood *secrétaire à abattant*, the fall-front opening to reveal a bird's-eye maple fitted interior, with 2 panelled cupboards containing pigeonholes and compartments, early 19thC, 47in (119.5cm) wide.
$2,300–2,800 SLN

A tulipwood crossbanded mahogany semi-circular bowfront commode, the drawer with a sliding and adjustable surface, with a pair of oval inlaid panel doors below, 18thC, 47½in (120.5cm) wide.
$50,000–55,000 MCA

This piece was part of a consignment from a deceased estate that aroused enormous interest. Most of the items had been purchased about 40 years ago from leading London dealers and had not been restored in the intervening years.

A Dutch mahogany side cabinet, inlaid with chequer stringing, the top with a lift-up folding set of shelves, side drawers and dummy front drawers, late 18thC, 51in (129.5cm) wide.
$2,500–3,000 WW

A pair of mahogany side cabinets, each with a marble top, the brass trellis-panelled doors with fabric backing, early 19thC, 49in (124.5cm) wide.
$3,200–3,500 P(NW)

A George III purple heart and marquetry serpentine commode, the top inlaid with a lozenge-shaped panel, the sides similarly inlaid, the doors enclosing an interior shelf, cross-banded with tulipwood outlined with stringing, c1775, 47in (119.5cm) wide.
$14,000–16,000 S

A late George III mahogany side cabinet, with a shaped back, the panelled doors flanked by fluted pilasters, 43½in (110.5cm) wide.
$1,300–1,600 L

A late Regency mahogany chiffonier, the shelved superstructure with ebonized spindle gallery, the lower part fitted with a drawer with a baize-lined slide and enclosed by a pair of panelled doors, 34in (86.5cm) wide.
$8,000–9,500 P

The moulding is similar to designs of Robert Wright of Hull, Yorkshire.

A mahogany, tulipwood and parquetry bowfront dwarf commode cabinet, with trellis pattern and flowerhead inlay, fitted with a drawer with tambour doors below, slight damage, late 18thC, 34½in (87.5cm) wide.
$6,500–7,200 MCA

A Regency inlaid rosewood breakfront side cabinet, the central grille-inset doors flanked by shelves, formerly fitted with a superstructure, early 19thC, 61in (155cm) wide.
$10,500–12,000 S(NY)

A Regency rosewood chiffonier, with raised shelf to the back, the fitted single frieze drawer above 2 doors inset with grille panels, flanked by turned and lotus-carved pillars, 43in (109cm) wide.
$2,800–3,000 WL

A William IV mahogany breakfront side cabinet, the centre with 2 glazed doors flanked by cylindrical columns and 2 outer conforming doors, 57½in (146cm) wide.
$3,500–4,000 MEA

A Victorian rosewood breakfront side cabinet, inlaid with arabesques and stringing, the central frieze drawer above a galleried mirror-backed recess and a glazed cupboard door, flanked by bevelled astragal-glazed doors with urn and scroll decorated lower panels enclosing shelves, stamped 'Maple & Co', damaged, formerly with a superstructure, 59⅜in (152cm) wide.
$1,200–1,400 S(S)

A Victorian figured walnut breakfront credenza, with boxwood and ebony stringing and gilt-metal mounts, the central door with a palmette and flanked by glazed doors, 65¾in (167cm) wide.
$3,000–3,300 P(Ed)

A Regency figured-mahogany chiffonier, with 2 panelled doors enclosing shelves, 46in (117cm) wide.
$2,800–3,000 Bri

A William IV mahogany chiffonier, with a raised gallery back surmounted by acanthus leaf and C-scroll carved cresting, above a pair of serpentine moulded frieze drawers, 40in (101.5cm) wide.
$1,500–1,700 HYD

A Victorian marquetry-inlaid side cabinet, with carved crest and triple mirror to the back, marble top, 61in (155cm) wide.
$2,000–2,500 JM

A late Regency rosewood chiffonier, the bowfront with shallow frieze drawer above 2 long doors with pleated fabric centres flanked by reeded pilasters, 34in (86.5cm) wide.
$5,200–5,800 B

An early Victorian rosewood-veneered breakfront side cabinet, the mirror back on petal-carved pillars, the central glazed door flanked by blind fret domed panelled doors and 4 graduated drawers, stencilled stamp for Holland & Sons, London, 63in (160cm) wide.
$5,200–6,000 WW

A Victorian mahogany chiffonier, with a foliate-carved pediment above a serpentine shelf, the marble top above a serpentine drawer and a pair of mahogany panelled doors with applied foliate mouldings, 43in (109cm) wide.
$1,800–2,000 Mit

◄ A Victorian brass, ebonized and boulle breakfront side cabinet, the door inlaid with Bérainesque motifs, flanked by glazed doors, c1860, 72in (183cm) wide.
$5,500–6,500 S

An American Renaissance revival rosewood marquetry and parcel-gilt credenza, 1865–70, 71½in (181.5cm) wide. **$21,000–24,000 SK**

A Victorian inlaid rosewood side cabinet, formerly with a super-structure, 54⅛in (138.5cm) wide. **$500–600 Doc**

A mid-Victorian walnut credenza, with a central panelled cupboard door opening to reveal shelves, flanked by 2 bowfront glazed panelled doors, decorated with gilt-metal applied mounts, boxwood and ebony foliate scrolling inlays and boxwood stringing, 60in (152.5cm) wide. **$3,500–4,000 Bon(W)**

A rosewood and marquetry credenza, the carved pediment with neo-classical-style inlay of urns and swags flanking a central mirror and shelves, the base with central bowed cupboard with marquetry panelled doors, flanked by 2 drawers and an open section, on an undertier, fluted legs, late 19thC, 59¾in (152cm) wide. **$2,300–2,500 TRL**

A Victorian figured walnut, inlaid and metal-mounted credenza, with blue and white Wedgwood-style plaques, restored, 73¼in (186cm) wide. **$5,500–6,500 TEN**

A late Victorian rosewood and marquetry serpentine side cabinet, the base fitted with a pair of convex cupboard doors, 48in (122cm) wide. **$1,000–1,300 EH**

Miller's Compares

I A mid-Victorian walnut pier cabinet, the single glazed cupboard door enclosing shelves, with gilt-metal foliate mounts, decorated with floral marquetry scrolls, crossbanding and stringing, 32in (81.5cm) wide. **$1,300–1,500 Bon(W)**

II A mid-Victorian walnut pier cabinet, the single glazed door opening to reveal shelves, the exterior with gilt-metal mounts, decorated with boxwood foliate inlays and stringing, 31½in (80cm) wide. **$800–950 Bon(W)**

Although both these side cabinets are made of walnut and inlaid, item I sold well in excess of its estimate. This is likely to be because item I is veneered in particularly well-figured timber, in contrast to item II where some of the grain has the appearance of being 'combed in'. The superior quality of item I is further enhanced by the more pronounced and decorative marquetry of floral scrolls and crossbanding.

A French walnut credenza, c1900, 36in (91.5cm) wide. **$1,300–1,500 HAC**

CABINETS-ON-STANDS

A William and Mary laburnum oyster-veneered cabinet-on-stand, inlaid with central ebony and boxwood stars, the doors enclosing 11 small drawers flanking a central door with 3 internal drawers, the stand with a shallow frieze drawer, 43in (109cm) wide.
$34,000–37,000 B

A black japanned cabinet, with chinoiserie decoration, on later stand, 17thC, 29in (73.5cm) wide.
$3,000–3,300 L

A George III gilt-decorated black japanned cabinet-on-stand, with doors opening to an interior of 10 drawers, the stand with pierced frieze, mid-18thC, 27½in (70cm) wide.
$3,500–4,200 S(NY)

A satinwood and rosewood crossbanded cabinet-on-stand, with amboyna, boxwood and ebony string inlays, c1820, 40¼in (102cm) wide.
$8,000–9,000 B&L

A penwork-decorated cabinet-on-stand, with a shelved interior, early 19thC, 25in (63.5cm) wide.
$4,000–4,400 WW

An ebony and pietra dura cabinet-on-stand, by Enrico Bosi, Florence, the pierced gallery centred by a timepiece, above 8 small drawers each inset with panels of flowers and centred by a small cupboard enclosing further drawers, the stand with a frieze drawer, c1870, 30¼in (77cm) wide.
$16,500–19,500 S

Enrico Bosi was known as a worker in mosaics in Florence from 1858 until c1900. He specialized in pietra dura panels and cabinet-making. He extended his business by opening further branches in Turin, Paris and London and by participating at the main exhibitions in the 1860s. Many pieces of furniture by Bosi are now in the collection of the Palazzo Pitti in Florence.

An Edwardian mahogany cabinet-on-stand, in the manner of Thomas Chippendale, with 2 blind fret-carved frieze drawers, on square chamfered legs, 32¾in (83cm) wide.
$1,300–1,500 S(S)

An Edwardian black japanned cabinet-on-stand, the panelled doors enclosing pigeonholes and drawers, 41in (104cm) wide.
$2,000–2,500 Bon(C)

TABLE CABINETS

A south German walnut table cabinet, inlaid with flowers, animals and architectural motifs, damaged and restored, early 17thC, 23½in (59.5cm) wide.
$3,800–4,000 S(S)

A George III inlaid rosewood specimen cabinet, with brass and ebony stringing, the 6 drawers with ivory handles, 18in (45.5cm) wide.
$3,000–3,300 JAd

A rosewood table cabinet, with mother-of-pearl inlay, the lift-up top fitted with a mirror above a tray, early 19thC, 11½in (29cm) wide.
$900–1,000 HOK

A Victorian Killarney work cigar cabinet, inlaid with yew and arbutus wood, decorated with views of Glena Cottage, Ross Castle and Muckross Abbey, 13½in (34.5cm) wide.
$3,200–3,500 JAd

An early Victorian mahogany collector's chest, the top with boxwood stringing above a frieze drawer, with 4 graduated drawers flanked by turned mouldings, 19¾in (50cm) wide.
$800–900 P(NE)

A burr-walnut cigar cabinet, c1860, 10in (25.5cm) wide.
$1,200–1,400 GeM

CANTERBURIES

A Regency rosewood and mahogany canterbury, with block and ring-turned supports, damaged, 18in (45.5cm) wide.
$2,200–2,500 S(NY)

A William IV rosewood canterbury, the frieze drawer with brass lion-mask knob handles, 20in (51cm) wide.
$3,800–4,000 WW

A Victorian inlaid walnut canterbury, with gilt-metal-mounts, with turned supports, and a drawer, c1860, 21½in (54.5cm) wide.
$8,000–9,000 S(NY)

A Victorian rosewood canterbury, with turned supports and drawer below, 22in (56cm) wide.
$900–1,000 HAX

A Regency mahogany four-division canterbury, with ring-turned supports surmounted by turned finials above a drawer with ebony line, 19in (48.5cm) wide.
$1,300–1,500 P(Ed)

An early Victorian rosewood canterbury, with 3 pierced leafy and C-scroll divisions, above a base drawer, 21in (53.5cm) wide.
$1,000–1,200 HYD

A Victorian rosewood three-division canterbury, 23in (58.5cm) wide.
$2,000–2,500 JH

A Regency mahogany four-division canterbury, with turned legs and original casters, c1820, 20in (51cm) wide.
$3,000–3,300 LCA

A William IV rosewood canterbury, after a design by John C. Loudon, the 3 divisions each centred by a garland and with spindle turnings to the sides, above a drawer, c1835, 20in (51cm) wide.
$3,200–4,000 S

John Claudius Loudon was a landscape gardener and horticulturalist by trade. He wrote the *Encyclopedia of Cottage, Farm and Village Architecture and Furniture* in 1833 which by 1867 had been reprinted 11 times and was to be the most comprehensive study of English furniture to be published in the 19thC. The book featured not only fashionable period pieces but also invalid, mechanical and inexpensive utilitarian furniture, due to Loudon's interest in vernacular styles.

A Victorian walnut canterbury, with turned supports and finials above one drawer, 21in (53.5cm) wide.
$1,000–1,200 DN

◄ A Victorian oak canterbury, with lyre-shaped divisions and drawer to frieze, 19¾in (50cm) wide.
$1,000–1,200 M

OPEN ARMCHAIRS

Miller's Compares

I A George I walnut shepherd's crook armchair, with plain shaped splat, outwardly curved and moulded arms, the drop-in seat supported on cabriole legs with scrolled brackets and terminating in pointed pad toes, c1720.
$14,500–16,000 S(NY)

II A George II-style mahogany armchair, the flat shaped splat with curved uprights, outswept arms with shepherd's crook supports, on cabriole legs with scrolled brackets, carved at the knees with shells, terminating in claw-and-ball feet, 19thC.
$5,000–5,800 S(NY)

A genuine Georgian armchair is naturally more valuable than a 19thC copy but there are other factors that make item I more desirable than Item II. Firstly, it is constructed from walnut rather than mahogany, which automatically places it in a much rarer category as walnut is a much less durable timber, mainly due to its susceptibility to woodworm. When the chairs are compared on stylistic grounds, item I stands out as being more elegant, particularly as the front legs of item II are more cumbersome. Item I is of a better colour and patina and has the added bonus of being upholstered in 18thC tapestry, which is very much in vogue today with both interior decorators and private collectors.

A George III mahogany armchair, the leaf- and scroll-carved top rail above a pierced Gothic-carved splat, with shepherd's crook arms and buttoned-leather covered seat.
$5,500–6,500 S

A George III mahogany open armchair, with pierced splat, serpentine front and stuff-over seat, c1790.
$1,200–1,400 ANT

A mahogany open armchair, the arched and carved ladder-back above carved, scrolled and sweeping arm supports, with upholstered dish seat, 18thC.
$3,200–3,500 Bon(W)

A Regency ebonized and parcel-gilt armchair, the backscrolled cresting carved with a mask and foliate decoration above a reeded backsplat, the caned seat flanked by scrolled armrests on female term figures, raised on a curule support, early 19thC.
$9,500–10,500 S(NY)

◄ A pair of Regency ebonized beechwood tub-shaped chairs, with solid vase splats and scroll arm supports, repaired.
$3,500–4,000 P

A Dutch floral marquetry-inlaid mahogany armchair, with scrolled arms, early 19thC.
$1,000–1,200 GOR

A pair of Regency beechwood elbow chairs, with ormolu mounts and scroll arms, with reeded and turned cresting rails and cane seats.
$2,500–3,000 MAT

A pair of giltwood open armchairs, each scroll and foliate carved frame with shaped upholstered back and serpentine cushioned seat, c1835.
$5,000–5,700 P(R)

A rosewood elbow chair, with slightly splayed arms, raised on foliate moulded uprights, mid-19thC.
$900–1,000 GAK

A George II-style mahogany armchair, with pierced interlaced splat, outswept scroll arm supports and stuff-over seat, on cabriole legs with C-scroll and rocaille decorated knees, 19thC.
$1,600–2,000 P

A Regency fruitwood open armchair, c1815.
$650–750 AnSh

A William IV rosewood armchair, with deep buttoned spoon-shaped back, armrests and seat.
$1,500–1,700 MEA

A pair of French carved giltwood armchairs, the upholstered oval panel backs within a frame carved with swags of flowers, 19thC.
$2,500–3,000 MEA

A Regency rosewood open armchair, with sabre legs, c1820.
$800–900 LCA

A carved walnut gentleman's open armchair, the scalloped-shaped padded back with scroll and foliate carved uprights, on cabriole foliate carved legs, mid-19thC.
$800–900 P

A French Régence-style beechwood carved *fauteuil*, with scroll arms and serpentine seat, mid-19thC.
$1,200–1,400 P

Insurance Values

Always insure your valuable antiques for what it would cost to replace with a similar item, regardless of the original price paid. Both auctioneers and dealers will provide a written valuation for a fee.

A stained fruitwood grotto chair, the scallop shell carved back and seat with dolphin open arms, on carved ribbed legs, 19thC.
$1,200–1,400 P(NW)

A French Louis XIV-style carved walnut chair, with figural and floral petit point upholstery, c1880.
$2,000–2,500 NOA

A pair of George III-style mahogany armchairs, by Bertram & Son, the backs carved with pierced anthemion splats within laurel leaf surrounds, with outscrolled arms, on fluted and leaf-carved tapering legs, late 19th/early 20thC.
$5,000–5,600 S

Bertram & Son are first recorded as trading from 100 Dean Street, Soho, London, in 1839.

A pair of Edwardian satinwood elbow chairs, the rail backs with oval painted landscape panels and cane seats.
$6,500–8,000 JAd

An Edwardian Adam-style simulated satinwood floral painted armchair, with shield-shaped back and tapering legs, terminating in rosette and husk drops.
$800–900 P(Ed)

A mahogany elbow chair, of cock-pen form, with cane seat, early 20thC.
$1,500–1,700 P(F)

An American Charles II-style carved mahogany open armchair, with label 'Karpen Company, Chicago and New York', c1900–20.
$900–1,000 NOA

An Edwardian inlaid mahogany armchair, with shield-shaped back above a cushion seat, on cabriole legs with pad feet.
$700–800 MEA

An Edwardian rosewood open armchair, the inlaid top rail above similar central splat and upholstered seat, decorated with stringing.
$160–200 Bon(W)

UPHOLSTERED ARMCHAIRS

A George I walnut needlework-upholstered wing armchair, the moulded seat rail with carved fleur-de-lys motifs, above cabriole legs with double-scrolled and husk-carved knees, restored, c1720.
$26,000–28,500 S

A George II ash upholstered wing armchair, on cabriole legs with pad feet, c1740.
$16,000–18,000 S

A French-style upholstered armchair, with scrolling arms, the cabriole legs with foliate and acanthus decoration, 18thC.
$48,000–52,000 B

This chair of generous proportions is in excellent condition and the seat has a particularly attractive showframe that cants outwards. Its desirability is further enhanced by its unrestored condition.

A William IV wing armchair, on turned mahogany legs with casters.
$650–800 DN

A mid-Victorian upholstered armchair, with scrolled-carved mahogany frame and legs.
$900–1,000 Bon(W)

A Victorian button-back fully sprung upholstered armchair, stamped 'Cope & Son'.
$900–1,000 LCA

A George III-style hoop-back upholstered armchair, with mahogany frame, 19thC.
$2,200–2,500 DaH

A George III-style mahogany tub chair, with blue leather upholstery, 19thC.
$3,200–3,500 S(NY)

A mahogany wing armchair, with ribbed hide upholstery, on carved and pierced Gothic fretwork legs, 19thC.
$6,000–6,500 S

◄ A pair of Victorian armchairs, on mahogany ring-turned tapering legs.
$3,200–3,500 P(Sc)

An Irish mahogany upholstered armchair, c1850–60.
$2,500–3,000 GKe

An upholstered armchair, with original brass and brown porcelain casters, late 19thC.
$1,800–2,000 LCA

A late Victorian mahogany-framed upholstered armchair, on turned legs.
$650–750 Bon(W)

A George II-style carved mahogany wingback armchair, with velvet upholstery, c1875–90.
$1,800–2,000 NOA

A late Edwardian mahogany upholstered tub armchair, the arms with acanthus-carved fluted terminals.
$900–1,000 P(Sc)

A late Victorian wing-back armchair, with a wind-out foot section, c1890.
$1,500–1,800 Bon(C)

A pair of mahogany upholstered armchairs, on square section legs and casters, late 19thC.
$1,400–1,650 Bon(C)

BERGÈRE CHAIRS

A Louis XV walnut bergère chair, upholstered in velvet, with moulded frame and cabriole legs.
$1,600–2,000 P(Z)

A Regency leather-upholstered mahogany bergère chair, raised on tapering square legs, c1800.
$5,500–6,500 S(NY)

A Regency mahogany bergère chair, on turned tapering fluted legs.
$2,500–2,700 HYD

A George IV mahogany bergère chair, on ring-turned legs headed by paterae, c1820.
$3,700–4,000 S

▶ A pair of French Louis XVI-style carved giltwood bergère chairs, with paterae and stop-fluted turned arm supports, mid-19thC.
$1,700–2,000 P

A George IV mahogany bergère chair, the adjustable reading slope with ratchet mechanism, and scrolled arms, c1825.
$13,000–14,500 S

A George IV mahogany bergère chair, the arms with scrolled terminals.
$4,500–5,000 L

A pair of simulated rosewood bergère chairs, with caned bowed seats, upholstered in old tapestry, 19thC.
$3,200–3,500 HOK

A George IV mahogany bergère chair, the plain seat rail on turned legs, headed by roundel paterae, c1830.
$4,500–5,200 S

An Edwardian mahogany bergère chair, with boxwood stringing and later leather cushions.
$900–1,000 CF

A pair of Louis XV-style carved giltwood upholstered bergère chairs, with cabriole legs, mid-19thC.
$6,500–7,200 B&B

CHILDREN'S CHAIRS

An early Victorian mahogany child's bergère chair, with cane seat and back, raised on cabriole legs.
$550–650 JAd

A mahogany child's bergère chair, with matching stand, 19thC.
$1,000–1,200 BUSH

An American child's rocking chair, c1910.
$400–500 COLL

An early Victorian rosewood child's chair, in Carolean revival style, the needlework panel back with scrolls and a leaf cresting, on turned block front legs with a turned H-stretcher.
$350–400 WW

CORNER CHAIRS

A Georgian walnut corner chair, with pierced splats and square chamfered supports.
$650–725 WilP

An American maple corner chair, with replaced rush seat, late 18thC.
$1,000–1,200 SK(B)

◄ A pair of ebonized and parcel-gilt corner armchairs, by Kimbel & Cabus, New York, the backs with stencilled panels and spindles, c1870.
$4,500–5,200 SK

An Edwardian mahogany corner armchair, c1900.
$650–720 NOA

A French beech corner chair, with rush seat, c1900.
$450–500 CF

An Edwardian caned corner chair.
$550–650 COLL

An inlaid mahogany corner chair, c1910.
$550–650 OOLA

DINING CHAIRS

A set of 6 Continental carved walnut dining chairs, c1690.
$10,000–11,500 NOA

A set of 10 George III mahogany dining chairs, including carvers, with pierced waisted splats and stuff-over seats.
$9,500–10,500 AH

A set of 6 George III mahogany dining chairs, including 2 armchairs, one of a later date, the rosette-carved camel backs above honeysuckle-carved pierced vase-shaped splats, c1780.
$3,500–4,000 Bon(C)

A set of 8 mahogany dining chairs, including 2 carvers, with pierced vase-shaped splats, c1800.
$5,200–5,600 MAT

A set of 6 George II walnut dining chairs, with vase-shaped back splats and rush seats, damaged and restored, c1730.
$10,000–10,500 S(S)

A set of 4 George III mahogany dining chairs, with pierced undulating splats.
$1,600–2,000 P(EA)

A matched set of 8 George III mahogany dining chairs, the moulded panelled top rails above X-form splats centred by carved flowerheads, c1800.
$11,500–13,000 S

A pair of George II mahogany dining chairs, with pierced scallop shell vase-shaped splats and drop-in woolwork seats, damaged and restored, c1740.
$1,500–1,800 S(S)

A set of 6 George III mahogany dining chairs, each with 5 slender splats and stuff-over upholstered seats, with 2 later matching elbow chairs, labelled 'John Kiel Ltd, Bristol' to underside.
$5,000–5,700 P(NW)

A set of 10 George III mahogany shield-back dining chairs, the backs with Gothic arch openwork splats, restored, 3 chairs later, c1790.
$5,000–6,000 S(S)

A set of 6 Regency mahogany chairs, the turned top-rails over panelled cross bars inlaid with brass anthemia, altered, c1810, with 2 other chairs.
$7,300–8,000 S

A set of 6 Dutch fruitwood dining chairs, with interlaced oval backs and serpentine stuff-over seats, early 19thC.
$4,300–4,800 P

A set of 8 late George III Sheraton design mahogany dining chairs, including a pair of elbow chairs, each with 4 vertical reeded bars over drop-in seats, late 18th/early 19thC.
$4,200–4,800 HYD

A set of 10 Regency Irish mahogany dining chairs, with carved top and centre rails, drop-in seats with cane seats below, on sabre legs, c1810.
$14,500–16,000 GKe

A set of 8 Regency mahogany dining chairs, including 2 armchairs, the ebony-lined top rails above pierced lattice horizontal splats, centred by a brass-lined tablet engraved 'W.W.' in Gothic script.
$10,000–10,500 P(Sc)

A set of 6 Regency brass-inlaid rosewood dining chairs, the rail backs with arabesques, the seats upholstered with floral gros point.
$4,000–4,500 GSP

A set of 8 Regency mahogany dining chairs, on sabre legs.
$4,500–5,000 SWO

A set of 4 Regency mahogany dining chairs, with carved top rails and carved and pierced mid rails, including one elbow chair, c1825.
$500–600 P(F)

A set of 8 Regency mahogany dining chairs, each with rope-twist centre rail and inlaid satinwood stringing, c1815.
$13,000–14,500 ChS

Dining Chairs • FURNITURE 59

A set of 12 oak dining chairs, including a pair of armchairs, the arched crestings carved with shells and anthemion scrolls above slender centre rails, the arms terminating in carved anthemion devices on scrolled supports, c1825.
$10,500–12,000 S

A set of 8 William IV Irish dining chairs, each with carved over-hanging top rail and centre rail, on octagonal turned front legs, c1830.
$6,500–7,200 GKe

A set of 10 early Victorian mahogany dining chairs, with padded backs above conforming serpentine fronted seats.
$6,000–6,500 MEA

A set of 6 George IV mahogany dining chairs, the centre rails with tablets, the padded seats on turned tapering legs.
$2,500–2,800 DN

A set of 5 mahogany dining chairs, including one armchair, the horizontal carved pierced splat with concentric discs, 19thC.
$1,300–1,600 TRL

A set of 8 William IV rosewood dining chairs, each with a curved and leaf-capped bar back.
$4,000–4,500 P(C)

A set of 4 Victorian Gothic-style carved oak dining chairs, attributed to Pugin.
$2,100–2,500 MEA

▶ A set of 8 early Victorian mahogany rail back dining chairs, including a pair of elbow chairs.
$4,500–5,000 P(F)

A set of 6 William IV mahogany dining chairs, the backs with curved bar top rails and splats.
$1,800–2,000 P(B)

A set of 9 early Victorian mahogany dining chairs, including 3 carvers, on turned fluted front legs.
$1,600–1,800 HAX

A set of 6 Victorian mahogany dining chairs, the backs and legs with lappet carving, with padded seats.
$1,600–2,000 DN

A set of 17 Victorian oak dining chairs, with stuffed backs and seats, the backs set with cabochons.
$7,500–8,000 L

A set of 6 late Victorian mahogany spoon-back dining chairs, each with a centre pierced splat, reupholstered.
$2,000–2,500 MEA

A set of 6 Victorian mahogany balloon-back dining chairs, with pierced scrolled mid-rails, c1860.
$2,000–2,400 Bon(C)

A set of 6 mahogany dining chairs, with carved top rails above pierced and carved splats, embroidered serpentine seats, legs decorated with blind fretwork, 19thC.
$3,200–4,000 Bon(W)

A set of 12 mahogany dining chairs, with pierced slat backs and stuff-over seats, labelled 'R. Garnett & Sons, Cabinet Makers, Warrington', late 19thC.
$5,000–5,750 Bri

◀ A set of 8 mahogany dining chairs, including 2 armchairs, the shield backs with wheatsheaf motifs, late 19thC.
$5,500–6,500 Bri

▶ A set of 8 dining chairs, including 2 carvers, each with Y-pattern splats, late 19thC.
$4,000–5,000 CAG

A set of 6 Victorian walnut dining chairs, the pierced balloon-backs applied with carved foliate C-scrolls, c1860.
$2,800–3,200 Bon(C)

A set of 12 Victorian carved mahogany and leather-upholstered dining chairs, with gadrooned and scroll-carved cresting, c1890.
$3,700–4,000 S(S)

A set of 10 17thC-style walnut dining chairs, the backs with carved scrollwork and centre turned spindle frieze, upholstered in hide, late 19thC.
$2,000–2,200 WBH

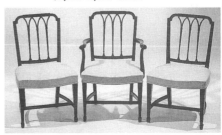

A set of 8 late Victorian dining chairs, including a pair of armchairs, with leaf-carved arms and supports, on turned tapered fluted and leaf-carved legs headed by flowerhead paterae, c1900.
$7,500–9,000 S

A set of 12 Victorian mahogany dining chairs, in the George III style, including 4 armchairs, the acanthus-carved top rails above C-scroll openwork back splats, the stuff-over seats covered in distressed red leather, on blind fret-carved legs, damaged, c1900.
$21,000–24,000 S(S)

A set of 8 mahogany dining chairs, including 2 carvers, each with a cupid's bow crest and interlaced splat, early 20thC.
$3,500–4,000 CDC

> **Miller's is a price GUIDE not a price LIST**

A set of 6 walnut ladder-back chairs, with rush seats, c1900.
$1,000–1,200 LPA

A set of 12 mahogany dining chairs, including a pair of open armchairs, with pierced and leaf-carved splats and leather stuff-over seats, late 19th/early 20thC.
$13,500–15,500 P(WM)

A set of 8 George III-style mahogany shield-back dining chairs, including a pair of armchairs, each with pierced drapery and fleur-de-lys splats, the stuff-over seats covered in machine tapestry, c1910.
$5,000–5,600 S(S)

▶ A set of 10 Edwardian mahogany dining chairs, including a pair of armchairs, the pierced vase-shaped splats carved with wheatsheaves, paterae and trailing bellflowers, the stuff-over seats covered in foliate tapestry, restored, c1910.
$7,500–8,000 S(S)

A set of 6 French Empire-style satinwood dining chairs, c1900.
$2,300–2,600 HAC

A set of 8 Georgian-style mahogany dining chairs, with pierced and foliate-carved back splats and stuff-over seats, late 19thC.
$7,500–8,000 P(O)

A set of 8 Edwardian mahogany dining chairs, with shepherd's crook arms, pierced vase-shaped splats and drop-in seats, c1910.
$2,700–3,200 S(S)

HALL CHAIRS

A pair of George II 'red walnut' hall chairs, with dished seats, on similarly shaped and dished supports joined by a shaped rail.
$1,200–1,500 DN

A pair of George III mahogany hall chairs, the balloon-shaped backs with armorial devices, the solid dished panel seats on fret-shaped dual trestle supports with armorial crests.
$2,800–3,200 P

A pair of Regency mahogany hall chairs, with carved shaped backs and reeded legs.
$800–900 JD

A pair of George IV mahogany hall chairs, attributed to Gillows, the carved backs in the form of scallop shells above scrolled mouldings, centred by painted armorial crests, c1825.
$8,000–9,000 S

A pair of William IV mahogany hall chairs, the scrolled backs with sunken oval panels.
$650–750 JH

A pair of oak hall chairs, with moulded roundel backs pierced with a cartouche, stamped 'Peter Sheridan & Son, 114–116 Capel Street, Dublin', 19thC.
$750–800 HOK

A pair of walnut and ebonized hall chairs, with canted, shaped and pierced splats, the top and front rails with satinwood key-type pattern decoration, 19thC.
$1,000–1,200 P(F)

An American Renaissance revival walnut hall seat, with a lift-up seat, c1875.
$750–900 NOA

► A Victorian oak and brass-mounted hall stool, by Shoolbred, the reeded splat back with downward sweeping arms, the sides with large roundels, stamped with a registration mark.
$1,500–1,750 P(Ed)

A pair of French walnut hall chairs, c1900.
$650–750 HAC

INVALIDS' CHAIRS

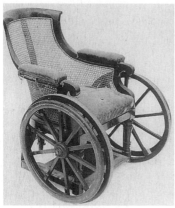

A three-wheeled bath chair, with upholstered seat, 19thC.
$1,000–1,200 E

An early Victorian mahogany invalid's chair, of caned bergère form, with buttoned-leather seat, pull-out footrest, brass shod wheels, hub caps, maker's label 'J. Ward, Leicester Square, London'.
$1,300–1,600 L

John Ward traded at 6 Leicester Square, London from c1845 to 1903, initially in partnership with Thomas Griffin until the latter's retirement c1851.

A Victorian mahogany invalid's wing armchair, with pull-out adjustable footrest and adjustable brass support fitted with a rectangular reading stand, with a tag 'J. Ward, London', late 19thC.
$4,500–5,000 B&B

◀ A late Victorian mahogany and upholstered invalid's armchair, covered in distressed patterned fabric, with an undertier incorporating an adjustable footrest, damaged, with a label 'John Ward, London', c1900.
$3,200–3,600 S(S)

LIBRARY CHAIRS

A Regency beech library chair, painted to simulate rosewood, with a curved and reeded frame, the sabre legs headed with roundels.
$5,000–5,750 DN

A George IV carved rosewood and upholstered library armchair, attributed to Gillows, covered in nailed hide, the lyre-shaped arm facings carved with acanthus scrolls, on acanthus-carved turned legs with gadrooned bun feet and casters, c1825.
$11,500–13,000 S

> **Cross Reference**
> See Reading Chairs

◀ A French walnut-framed library chair, the adjustable back and seat with carved leaf-scrolled crest centred by a mask, the arms with lion-head terminals on scrolled supports, with a sliding footrest, 19thC.
$1,150–1,400 AH

A William IV mahogany library armchair, upholstered in hide, c1835.
$6,000–6,500 S

A William IV rosewood library chair, on carved lotus-leaf turned tapering legs.
$1,500–1,650 P(Sc)

A George III satinwood, purple heart and tulipwood crossbanded bonheur du jour, the bottom section with a hinged writing surface, c1790, 25¾in (65.5cm) wide.
$14,500–16,000 Bon

A Louis XVI fruitwood marquetry bonheur du jour, in the manner of Charles Topino, the top and stretcher veneered to represent still life motifs, late 18thC, 24½in (62cm) wide.
$65,000–72,000 S(NY)

A Swedish maple bonheur du jour, the stepped super-structure incorporating a drawer, c1800, 28in (71cm) wide.
$5,500–6,500 Bon

An early Regency rosewood and tulipwood crossbanded and brass-mounted bonheur du jour, in the manner of John McLean, the lift-off upper part with high pierced gallery, the turned tapering supports with brass caps and casters, 26¾in (68cm) wide.
$40,000–48,000 MCA

A Victorian Louis XV-style kingwood and tulipwood marquetry serpentine bonheur du jour, with gilt-metal mounts, c1870, 39¼in (100cm) wide.
$6,800–7,800 P

A George III mahogany bureau, on ogee bracket feet, c1760, 35in (89cm) wide.
$3,200–4,000 BUSH

A Chippendale walnut bureau, on ogee bracket feet, Delaware River Valley, c1770, 36in (91.5cm) wide.
$24,000–26,500 SK(B)

A south German neo-classical burr walnut, walnut and larch cylinder bureau, with a writing slide and fitted interior, late 18thC, 46½in (118cm) wide.
$7,300–8,000 S(Am)

A Dutch bureau, with mahogany veneer and floral marquetry, late 18thC, 47¼in (120cm) wide.
$9,000–10,500 HVH

A walnut bureau, the fall-front opening to reveal a well and an arrangement of small drawers and pigeonholes, early 18thC, 33in (84cm) wide.
$5,000–5,750 P(HSS)

▶ A north Italian walnut and ivory marquetry bureau, heightened in pewter, enclosing an inlaid fitted interior, probably Piedmontese, 18thC, 49½in (126cm) wide.
$25,000–30,000 P

A decorated satinwood bureau, late 19thC, 40¼in (102cm) wide.
$5,000–5,500 P

A George III-style carved mahogany four-poster tester bedstead, restored, 19thC, 64in (162.5cm) wide.
$22,000–24,000 S(NY)

A Victorian iron and brass bed, each brass capital embossed with acanthus, late 19thC, 54in (137cm) wide.
$2,100–2,400 DD

A George III mahogany four-poster bed, the tester with an arched cornice decorated with leaves and flowers, c1790, 61¾in (157cm) wide.
$21,000–24,000 S

▶ A Louis XV-style carved bedstead, with upholstered panels and bow-shaped footboard, c1890, 60in (150cm) wide.
$7,300–8,000 SeH

A French carved fruitwood day bed, c1810–30, 70in (178cm) long.
$4,000–4,500 NOA

A Louis XV-style walnut bed, with solid panels, late 19thC, 54in (137cm) wide.
$1,600–1,800 SWA

A Regency ebonized chaise longue, the moulded sabre legs headed by carved panels, on brass casters, c1815, 76¾in (195cm) long.
$5,000–5,750 S

A rosewood framed scroll-end chaise longue, on turned and leaf-capped legs with brass casters, c1840, 76in (193cm) long.
$2,300–2,600 CAG

A French red japanned day bed, by Gabriel Viardot, signed and dated '1887', 71in (180cm) long.
$57,000–60,000 S

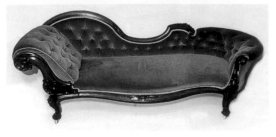

◀ A Victorian mahogany serpentine-front chaise longue, 85in (216cm) long.
$3,200–3,500 COLL

A George I inlaid bureau bookcase, the doors inlaid with starbursts and enclosing a fitted interior, early 18thC, 39½in (100.5cm) wide.
$52,000–56,000 S(NY)

A George III mahogany bureau bookcase, in 3 sections, the fall-front enclosing pigeonholes, drawers and a cupboard, 41¾in (106cm) wide.
$8,000–9,500 P

A Dutch walnut marquetry and ivory-inlaid bureau cabinet, later inlaid with scrolling leaves and flowers, 18thC, 50½in (128cm) wide.
$32,000–35,000 S(Am)

A George III inlaid satinwood secretaire bookcase, the frieze with carved paterae, on flaring bracket feet, late 18thC, 31in (78.5cm) wide.
$40,000–48,000 S(NY)

A George III mahogany secretaire bookcase, the interior fitted with satinwood-veneered drawers, c1790, 46¾in (119cm) wide.
$30,000–32,500 S

A Regency rosewood and brass-inlaid secretaire bookcase, the upper part enclosed by a pair of brass grille panelled doors, 35¾in (91cm) wide.
$11,500–13,000 P

A Venetian rococo-style green lacquer and parcel-gilt bureau bookcase, with chinoiserie decoration, fitted with later gilt-metal mounts, paint restored, late 19thC, 44¼in (112.5cm) wide.
$10,500–12,000 S(NY)

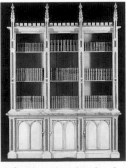

An Edwardian mahogany satinwood-lined bureau bookcase, with domed cornice, on ogee bracket feet, 39in (99cm) wide.
$3,000–3,500 BUSH

An Edwardian Sheraton-style inlaid mahogany bureau bookcase, 38in (96.5cm) wide.
$1,600–2,000 TMA

An Edwardian satinwood inlaid secretaire bookcase, with sliding fitted secretaire drawer, 36in (91.5cm) wide.
$6,800–7,800 JNic

A Gothic-style painted and parcel-gilt library bookcase, paint restored, 19thC, 92in (234cm) wide.
$10,000–11,500 S

◄ A George IV mahogany bookcase cabinet, with adjustable shelf, c1820, 27½in (70cm) wide.
$5,500–6,500 S

A George II mahogany bookcase, the projecting lower part with a pair of shaped and fielded panelled doors, c1750, 47¼in (120cm) wide.
$12,000–14,500 S

A George III Irish mahogany breakfront bookcase, with panelled doors to base, c1800, 96in (243.5cm) wide.
$12,000–14,500 GKe

A Regency mahogany breakfront bookcase, with 4 astragal-glazed doors enclosing adjustable shelves, 97¾in (248cm) wide.
$25,000–27,000 TEN

▶ A Victorian mahogany bookcase, with 2 arched glazed doors enclosing shelves, the protruding base with frieze cushion drawer, 49in (124.5cm) wide.
$2,200–2,500 AH

A George II mahogany library bookcase, the pair of astragal-glazed doors enclosing adjustable shelves, 69¼in (176cm) wide.
$12,000–13,000 CGC

A mahogany and boxwood-inlaid bookcase, the base with 3 doors with oval veneered panels, c1800, 78in (198cm) wide.
$5,500–6,500 HOK

A George III stained pine and parcel-gilt bookcase cabinet, the base with a pair of doors mounted with urns and opening to 4 drawers, adapted, 72in (183cm) wide.
$11,500–13,000 S(NY)

A pair of George III mahogany concave bookcases, in the style of Thomas Sheraton, the lower doors with grilles, c1815–20, 44¾in (114cm) wide.
$16,500–20,000 NOA

A Victorian mahogany bookcase cabinet, by Shoolbred & Co, the lower section with 3 panelled cupboard doors each centred by shell-carved angular vacant cartouches, damaged, c1880, 77¼in (196cm) wide.
$3,500–4,000 S(S)

A pair of Regency mahogany bookcases, the stepped cornices over leaf-inlaid friezes and open compartments flanked by brass grille doors, c1820, 82in (208.5cm) wide.
$16,500–20,000 S

A George IV rosewood breakfront dwarf bookcase, c1825, 49¾in (126.5cm) wide.
$7,200–8,000 Bon

A Victorian rosewood breakfront dwarf bookcase, with grey marble top, 62¼in (158cm) wide.
$4,000–4,500 TEN

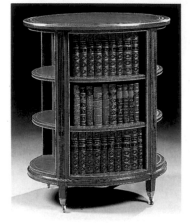

A Victorian mahogany and brass-mounted book stand, the leather-lined top with milled brass-moulded edge, c1890, 26½in (67cm) wide.
$7,500–8,000 S

A mahogany three-tier buffet, mid-19thC, 44in (112cm) wide.
$1,600–2,000 BUSH

A pair of Victorian gilt-metal-mounted mahogany three-tier buffets, each with a gilt-metal pierced three-quarter galleried top, 33½in (85cm) wide.
$23,000–26,000 S(NY)

A Continental mahogany twin-flap bedside cabinet, 1860–80, 32in (81.5cm) high.
$1,000–1,200 BUSH

A Flemish baroque-style ebonized, inlaid and *faux* tortoiseshell-mounted cabinet, with later marble top, upper cabinet lacking, restored, 19thC, 39in (99cm) high.
$3,500–4,000 B&B

A pair of Louis XVI tulipwood, marquetry and parquetry ormolu-mounted corner cupboards, of bowed outline, each with moulded white marble top, 29½in (75cm) wide.
$24,500–26,500 P

A Viennese enamel and gilt-bronze-mounted ebonized table cabinet, late 19thC, 17½in (44.5cm) wide.
$11,000–12,000 B&B

A William IV rosewood canterbury, after a design by John C. Loudon, c1835, 19¼in (49cm) wide.
$5,000–5,600 S

An early Victorian rosewood canterbury, 20½in (52cm) wide.
$3,000–3,250 Bon(C)

A south German fruitwood and marquetry cabinet, the panel drawers inlaid with mythological animals, the central compartment with panel doors, 17thC, on later stand, 48in (122cm) wide.
$7,500–9,000 P

A Charles II style scarlet lacquer cabinet and giltwood stand, decorated with chinoiseries, the interior fitted with 2 shelves and one drawer, c1900, 38in (96.5cm) wide.
$4,500–5,000 CAG

A Queen Anne burr walnut bureau cabinet, the pair of mirrored doors enclosing a fitted interior above a pair of candle slides, c1710, 41¾in (106cm) wide.
$43,000–48,000 S

A George I walnut and herringbone-banded bureau cabinet, the 2 crossbanded panelled doors enclosing adjustable shelves, small drawers and pigeonholes, above 2 candle slides, with later brass handles and escutcheons, 37in (94cm) wide.
$18,000–21,000 DN

A George II mahogany bureau cabinet, the mirrored door enclosing shelves and drawers, with candle slide below, on bracket feet, 28in (71cm) wide.
$13,000–14,500 P

An amboyna escritoire, the fall-front revealing pigeon-holes, writing surface and fitted interior, early 19thC, 41in (104cm) high.
$8,000–9,000 L&E

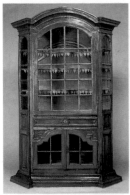

An Italian fruitwood display cabinet, the upper and lower doors glazed, fitted with carved giltwood shelves, 1730–50, 68½in (174cm) wide.
$16,500–20,000 NOA

A Dutch walnut and burr walnut display cabinet, with glazed doors, with light wood banding, on claw-and-ball feet, 18thC, 63in (160cm) wide.
$15,500–17,000 S(Am)

A William IV simulated rosewood display cabinet, the doors with circular and lozenge trellis astragals, c1835, 42½in (108cm) wide.
$5,500–6,500 S

An Edwardian painted satinwood breakfront display cabinet-on-stand, c1910, 52¾in (134cm) wide.
$5,700–6,500 Bon

A French kingwood, *vernis Martin* and gilt-bronze display cabinet, the panels painted with lovers in a landscape, c1900, 53¼in (135cm) wide.
$5,500–6,500 S(Am)

A George III painted demi-lune commode, the doors opening to a shelf, restored, late 18thC, 31in (78.5cm) wide.
$11,000–12,000 S(NY)

A satinwood, marquetry, harewood and gilt-metal-mounted commode, with hinged serpentine top above a shaped cupboard, late 18thC, 52in (132cm) wide.
$78,000–90,000 S

A pair of rosewood and brass-inlaid side cabinets, each with a panelled door enclosing a shelved interior, later alterations, early 19thC, 39¼in (100cm) wide.
$24,500–27,000 P(L)

► A late Victorian satinwood breakfront commode, in the manner of Robert Adam and Angelica Kauffmann, decorated with classical scenes, 56¾in (144cm) wide.
$22,500–26,000 P

A Charles X Gothic-style rosewood and marquetry commode, with white marble top above a frieze drawer, the panelled doors enclosing sliding trays, 1815–30, 51½in (131cm) wide.
$8,000–9,500 P

A George IV mahogany side cabinet, the brass grille doors with pleated silk panels enclosing adjustable shelves, c1825, 53in (134.5cm) wide.
$6,500–7,500 S

An Edwardian satinwood commode, painted with garlands of flowers and figures, with frieze drawer, damaged, early 20thC, 60in (152.5cm) wide.
$21,000–24,500 S(NY)

A George II 'red walnut' open armchair, with a rocaille carved crest rail, on cabriole legs with scroll feet.
$5,000–6,000 DN

A pair of George III Gothic-style yew wood and elm Windsor armchairs, restored, c1760.
$32,000–40,000 S(NY)

A pair of Louis XV carved walnut *fauteuils*, with serpentine fronts, decorated with flowers and leaves, on cabriole legs with acanthus leaf feet.
$7,000–8,000 MCA

A pair of American Transitional carved mahogany side chairs, with moulded curving crest rails, the splats with carved neo-classical elements, c1788.
$5,500–6,500 SK(B)

A pair of Regency-style parcel-gilt ebonized armchairs, on circular turned tapering legs, decoration later and restored, 19thC.
$8,000–9,500 S(NY)

▶ A pair of Louis XVI-style gilt *fauteuils*, with guilloche-moulded frames, on tapering fluted legs headed with rosettes, 19thC.
$4,000–4,500 MEA

A pair of walnut X-framed chairs, the arms ending with lion masks, c1850.
$2,500–2,800 HUB

A pair of Victorian lady's and gentleman's chairs, with relief-carved figured-walnut frames, c1870.
$7,200–8,000 BERA

A Victorian carved walnut gentleman's armchair, with foliate and shell-carved crest, the seat with Berlin tapestry.
$2,500–3,000 Mit

A pair of Louis XVI giltwood side chairs, on circular tapered stop-fluted legs headed by paterae, late 18thC.
$44,000–48,000 S(NY)

These chairs are marked on the seat rails with the crowned 'F' for the Château de Fontainebleau.

A George I walnut wing armchair, the shell-carved cabriole legs with pointed pad feet, c1725.
$5,500–6,500 S

A Louis XVI painted bergère chair, with moulded frame, on circular tapered fluted legs headed by paterae, signed 'N. S. Courtois', late 18thC.
$4,500–5,200 S(NY)

A George III mahogany library bergère chair, one arm fitted with an adjustable brass candle holder, on moulded sabre legs with brass casters, c1805.
$9,000–10,000 S

◄ A William IV rosewood library chair, with carved scrolling top rail, plain front rail, on lappeted supports, c1835.
$2,400–2,800 Bon(C)

► A George IV rosewood and brass-inlaid library armchair, the upholstered scrolled padded back, seat and arms with brass inlay, on turned tapering reeded legs and casters, c1825.
$13,000–14,500 S

A set of 6 George III painted and caned dining chairs, the curved backs with brass handholds, the tablets painted *en grisaille* with putti, c1800.
$21,000–24,000 S(NY)

A set of 12 George III mahogany dining chairs, the reeded backs with pierced trellis mid-rails above drapery-carved subsidiary rails, c1800.
$32,500–35,000 S

A set of 6 Regency simulated rosewood and brass-inlaid dining chairs, with clasp-shaped mid-rails, carved seats and sabre legs, c1815.
$6,200–6,800 S

A set of 4 Regency beechwood dining chairs, attributed to Gillows, 3 with ebony inlay, one with conforming ivory-painted decoration, c1815.
$2,800–3,200 S

A set of 12 William IV mahogany dining chairs, with simulated leather drop-in seats, probably Scottish.
$16,500–18,000 Gam

◄ A set of 8 Regency mahogany bar-back dining chairs, the top rails with scroll-carved ends, on sabre legs.
$4,000–4,500 SWO

► A set of 10 Gothic revival carved oak dining chairs, with quatrefoil pierced top rails on X-frame legs, late 19thC.
$5,500–6,500 P

A set of 12 Regency mahogany dining chairs, with reeded swag backs, the embroidered drop-in seats on shaped and reeded sabre legs, 4 chairs being later copies.
$11,500–12,500 P(S)

A set of 6 Victorian mahogany dining chairs, the balloon backs with carved splats, on panelled baluster legs.
$2,000–2,300 MSW

A set of 4 birch dining chairs, with carved paterae between the top and mid-rails, 19thC.
$1,600–1,800 TEN

A set of 6 Victorian oak dining chairs, original upholstery worn.
$1,600–2,000 COLL

The Chair Set Antiques

Specialists in sets of chairs, furniture and accessories for the dining room

We have a wide range of sets of 18th and 19th Century chairs in stock
Also dining tables, dressers and accessories for the dining room

A George I walnut and feather-banded bachelor's chest, the quartered, feather-inlaid and crossbanded fold-over top with curved corners to the back, the interior probably later veneered with mahogany to replace the baize, original brass handles, replacement escutcheons, 32in (81.5cm) wide.
$40,000–45,000 P(WM)

A Georgian mahogany chest of drawers, the top with moulded edge and blind fret canted corners, on ogee bracket feet, mid-18thC, 48in (122cm) wide.
$6,200–6,800 TMA

A Dutch walnut and marquetry serpentine commode, 18thC, 34in (86.5cm) wide.
$4,000–5,000 HYD

◀ An American mahogany reverse serpentine chest of drawers, with cabriole legs on claw-and-ball feet, 1760–80, 34¾in (88.5cm) wide.
$50,000–56,000 B&B

aA George III mahogany serpentine chest of drawers, inlaid with chevron stringing, c1765, 37in (94cm) wide.
$26,000–30,000 S

A Dutch oak bombé-shaped chest of drawers, the shaped top with rounded corners, the 3 drawers with brass handles and escutcheons, on hairy paw feet, early 19thC, 35in (89cm) wide.
$2,000–2,300 GD

A Louis XV-style gilt-metal-mounted green lacquer commode, with red and white marble top, possibly German, 19thC, 51in (129.5cm) wide.
$20,000–23,000 S(NY)

A walnut chest-on-chest, the lower drawer inlaid with concave sunburst, on bracket feet, early 18thC and later, 43in (109cm) wide.
$5,200–5,600 Gam

◀ An American carved walnut *schrank*, the panelled doors opening to a compartment with rows of hooks, late 18thC, 67¼in (171cm) wide.
$45,000–52,000 B&B

▶ A Dutch Baroque-style rosewood and ebony cupboard, the top with central carving of 2 putti, on ball feet, 19thC, 80¾in (205cm) wide.
$5,200–6,200 S(Am)

A William and Mary oyster-veneered walnut chest-on-stand, with later brass handles, stand reduced in height, c1695, 37½in (95.5cm) wide.
$21,000–24,000 HAM

A Victorian walnut davenport, with boxwood and mahogany inlay, 21in (53.5cm) wide. **$2,000–2,500 OTT**

A George III mahogany Carlton House desk, the curved superstructure with pierced and moulded brass gallery, on square tapered reeded legs headed by carved flowerhead paterae, c1790, 63in (160cm) wide. **$85,000–90,000 S**

A late Victorian figured walnut harlequin piano-top davenport, with a panelled door enclosing 4 satin birch drawers, 23¼in (59cm) wide. **$6,200–6,800 Gam**

A Sheraton revival rosewood and satinwood-banded kneehole writing desk, inlaid with penwork ovals, late 19thC, 48⅛in (123cm) wide. **$4,000–5,000 P(R)**

An Edwardian painted satinwood desk, decorated with ribbon-tied trophies, flowers and foliage, early 20thC, 53in (134.5cm) wide. **$11,500–12,500 S**

An Edwardian painted satinwood Carlton House desk, the drawers with bone handles, on tapering legs with brass casters, 56in (142cm) wide. **$8,000–9,500 P(S)**

A William and Mary walnut and marquetry mirror, the shaped fretted foliate crest with a panel of floral marquetry and bone, later plate, damaged, c1690, 33½in (85cm) wide.
$24,500–26,500 S(NY)

An Irish giltwood flat-carved mirror, with scroll cresting, mid-18thC, 28¼in (72cm) wide.
$5,000–5,600 HOK

A George II walnut and parcel-gilt mirror, the broken pediment centring a foliate-carved cartouche and garland of flowers, mid-18thC, 30½in (77.5cm) wide.
$13,000–14,500 S(NY)

A pair of Venetian rococo walnut, blue glass and parcel-gilt mirrors, each surmounted by a portrait medallion, mid-18thC, 38¼in (97cm) wide.
$65,000–80,000 S(NY)

A Regency gilt convex mirror, surmounted by an eagle flanked by acanthus scrolls, 43⅜in (111cm) high.
$2,000–2,500 P(S)

A George III mahogany fret-carved wall mirror, with gilded *ho-o* bird, c1780, 20in (51cm) wide.
$900–1,000 ANT

A Louis XVI giltwood mirror, with pierced basket and floral-carved crest above a volute and grapevine-carved frame, late 18thC, 40½in (103cm) wide.
$10,000–11,500 B&B

A Louis XVI-style painted and giltwood mirror, the cresting carved with a Grecian urn garlanded with roses and tassels, late 19thC, 38½in (98cm) wide.
$3,800–4,200 P(Z)

A George III-style carved giltwood overmantel mirror, the cresting centred by an anthemion flanked by scrolls, 19thC, 55in (139.5cm) wide.
$26,000–29,000 S

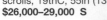

► A Venetian micro-mosaic mirror, the moulded frame decorated with multi-coloured summer flowers on a mosaic ground, c1900, 30¼in (77cm) wide.
$14,500–16,000 S

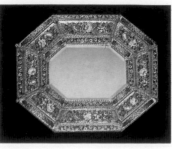

A pair of Venetian 18thC-style marginal mirrors, the foliate etched borders applied with glass flowers and green leaves, late 19thC, 21in (53cm) wide.
$2,000–2,500 P

A Louis XVI-style giltwood and composition mirror, the crest with 2 putti and central swag-carved cartouche, late 19thC, 41in (104cm) wide.
$5,200–6,000 B&B

A George III mahogany and satinwood marquetry sideboard, crossbanded in tulipwood, 66in (167.5cm) wide.
$13,000–15,500 DN

▶ A Georgian Irish mahogany sideboard, with a stepped shelf and reeded frieze, possibly Cork, 88in (223.5cm) wide.
$12,500–13,500 MEA

A George III mahogany inlaid semi-elliptical sideboard, legs later inlaid, c1790, 84in (213.5cm) wide.
$23,000–26,000 S

An American carved mahogany sideboard, with 2 Gothic-style panelled cupboard doors opening to a shelved interior, on acanthus-carved hairy paw feet, c1820–30, 59½in (151cm) wide.
$2,600–3,000 B&B

A Victorian carved oak inverted breakfront pedestal sideboard, the central oval bevelled mirror with carved game hanging each side, c1850, 139in (353cm) wide.
$11,500–13,500 Bon

A Victorian Gothic revival pale oak carved and inlaid sideboard, in the manner of Bruce Talbert, on a potboard plinth base, 84¼in (214cm) wide.
$52,000–58,000 TEN

A figured mahogany sideboard, the central drawers flanked by cupboards with applied mouldings, the raised metal trellis back with urn finials, on leaf-carved cabriole legs, late 19th/early 20thC, 72in (183cm) wide.
$420–480 HBC

A George III green-painted and parcel-gilt four-seater settee, on fluted square section tapered legs and spade feet, c1780, 82in (208.5cm) long.
$5,000–5,600 Bon

An American Federal mahogany settee, on ring-turned and reeded tapering legs, 19thC, 74in (188cm) long.
$5,000–6,000 B&B

A Dutch Empire mahogany settee, with lotus-leaf carved claw feet, early 19thC, 78in (198cm) long.
$4,500–5,000 S(Am)

A pair of Regency ebonized and parcel-gilt sofas, the out-splayed sabre legs with brass caps and casters, c1815, 80½in (204.5cm) long.
$24,000–26,000 S

A George IV simulated rosewood, rosewood and cut-brass inlaid sofa, the winged carved paw feet with brass casters, c1825, 93¾in (238cm) long.
$9,500–11,500 S

A Viennese Biedermeier mahogany, ebonized and gilt-bronze mounted canapé, the back centred by a gilt-bronze mount, restored, c1830, 87⅛in (222cm) long.
$4,400–5,200 S(Am)

A Victorian oak Chesterfield sofa, on tapering moulded legs with brass casters, c1850, 102in (260cm) long.
$3,800–4,500 S

A Dutch neo-classical marquetry and walnut settee, on scrolling sabre legs, mid-19thC, 74⅛in (189cm) long.
$2,500–3,000 B&B

A Victorian walnut cameo-back sofa, with carved cabriole legs, c1865, 61in (155cm) long.
$3,200–3,600 HUB

An Edwardian inlaid mahogany settee, 43in (109cm) long.
$1,600–2,000 COLL

An Empire-style gilt-bronze-mounted mahogany fire screen, late 19thC, 45½in (115.5cm) high.
$1,300–1,500 B&B

A walnut stool, with carved paw feet and casters, reupholstered, c1840, 19in (48.5cm) square.
$750–810 LCA

A pair of Swedish neo-classical parcel-gilt beechwood stools, 19thC, 16½in (42cm) wide.
$2,300–2,800 B&B

A Victorian walnut and marquetry-inlaid three-tier whatnot, 42in (106.5cm) high.
$900–1,100 BUSH

A George III carved mahogany reading stand, the adjustable top with book rest and 2 retractable candle holders, c1765, 21¼in (54cm) wide.
$23,000–26,000 S(NY)

A rosewood stool, with cabriole legs, c1850, 15in (38cm) diam.
$550–650 SPU

A George IV mahogany teapoy, with a fitted interior, c1825, 16in (40.5cm) wide.
$5,500–6,500 S

A George III mahogany and boxwood-strung wine cooler, 27in (68cm) wide.
$3,000–3,300 TEN

A pair of Regency *faux*-grained and gilt-metal-mounted window benches, restored, 42in (106.5cm) wide.
$23,000–25,000 S(NY)

▶ A mahogany, satinwood-lined and inlaid shaving stand, with adjustable mirror, c1820, 59in (150cm) high.
$1,200–1,400 BUSH

A pair of George IV rosewood stools, with later needlework upholstery, restored, 24½in (62cm) wide.
$24,500–26,000 S(NY)

A pair of Portuguese neo-classical painted and parcel-gilt torchères, late 18thC, 72¾in (185cm) high.
$18,000–20,000 S(NY)

A William IV cellaret, with leaf-carved finial, the front and sides with arched panels, 33in (84cm) wide.
$6,000–6,500 MEA

▶ A George III mahogany and satinwood-inlaid wine cooler, c1790, 18in (45.5cm) wide.
$5,500–6,500 S(S)

A pair of Italian Renaissance-style patinated bronze torchères, with associated drip pans, late 19thC, 65½in (166.5cm) high.
$9,000–10,000 B&B

A George II mahogany gateleg table, the drawer with later brass knob handle, 1730s, 54¼in (138cm) wide.
$5,000–5,750 HAM

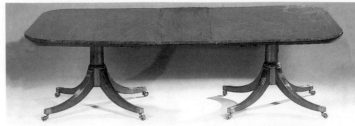

A George III mahogany dining table, c1790, 115½in (293.5cm) extended.
$16,000–19,500 S

A Louis XVI brass-mounted mahogany dining table, with 4 leaves, late 18thC, 45½in (115.5cm) long.
$14,000–16,000 S(NY)

A Regency Irish mahogany centre table, 30in (76cm) diam.
$16,000–18,000 P(Sc)

A German neo-classical mahogany and parcel-gilt tilt-top centre table, c1810, 37⅜in (96cm) diam.
$10,000–11,500 S(Am)

A William IV mahogany and marble-inlaid snap-top table, 51½in (131cm) diam.
$7,500–8,500 P(L)

► A William IV rosewood snap-top breakfast table, 47½in (121cm) diam.
$4,000–4,400 P(F)

A William IV mahogany extending dining table, after a design by Robert Jupe, made by Johnstone, Jupe & Co, c1835, 59¾in (152cm) diam.
$100,000–110,000 S

A French mahogany and marquetry-inlaid tilt-top table, mid-19thC, 38¼in (97cm) diam.
$9,200–10,200 B&B

A Victorian walnut, marquetry and gilt-brass-mounted table, c1850, 57in (145cm) diam.
$45,000–52,000 S

A Victorian concertina-action extending dining table, with 6 leaves, c1860, 178in (452cm) extended.
$11,500–13,000 S(S)

A Victorian rosewood breakfast table, 60in (152.5cm) wide.
$4,200–4,800 CAG

► A walnut tilt-top table, inlaid with flowers and foliage, 19thC, 53in (134.5cm) diam.
$5,500–6,500 E

A pair of George III Gothic revival inlaid mahogany card tables, each with a baize-lined playing surface, possibly associated, damaged, 42in (106.5cm) wide.
$17,000–20,000 S(NY)

A Regency baize-lined card table, with swivel top, 36in (91.5cm) wide.
$4,000–4,500 WW

A William IV mahogany card table, with figured-veneered top, on an acanthus carved column, c1830, 32⅛in (82.5cm) wide.
$5,500–6,000 BERA

A William IV mahogany and scagliola games table, with ebonized mouldings, the frieze with 3 real and 2 dummy drawers surmounted by a pair of slides, c1835, 25in (63.5cm) square.
$9,000–10,000 S

A George III satinwood games table, with envelope top, the underside fitted with a sliding workbag frame, c1790, 18in (45.5cm) square.
$7,500–9,000 S

A pair of Regency rosewood, simulated rosewood, maple and brass-inlaid card tables, with baize-lined swivel tops, the splayed legs with later trailing metal foliate ornament, 35¾in (91cm) wide.
$10,500–12,000 P

A Victorian walnut folding card table, with amboyna banding and string and marquetry inlay, 36in (91.5cm) wide.
$2,000–2,500 AH

A Dutch neo-classical inlaid mahogany games table, legs partially restored, early 19thC, 33⅛in (85cm) wide.
$4,500–5,000 B&B

A pair of Regency rosewood card tables, with swivelling fold-over tops, c1815, 35⅛in (90cm) wide.
$32,500–35,000 S

A pair of William IV rosewood card tables, inlaid with stringing, c1830, 35¾in (91cm) wide.
$11,500–13,000 S

A Louis XV-style ormolu-mounted rosewood and marquetry console card table, lined with green baize, late 19thC, 34in (86.5cm) wide.
$2,500–3,000 TMA

An Italian neo-classical lemon, walnut, mahogany and ebonized parquetry games table, signed 'Saltini 1848', probably Piedmontese, 30in (76cm) wide.
$14,000–15,500 S(NY)

A George III marquetry, painted and parcel-gilt pier table, in the manner of Thomas Chippendale, c1775, 48¾in (124cm) wide.
$21,000–25,000 S

A French carved, painted and parcel-gilt console table, with a marble top above 2 naturalistically carved swans, c1890, 76½in (194cm) wide.
$13,000–16,000 S

A George II walnut side table, with later marble top, repaired, mid-18thC, 59½in (151cm) wide.
$20,000–22,000 S(NY)

A Dutch mahogany and marquetry side table, with a cupboard enclosed by tambour shutter doors, late 18th/early 19thC, 30¾in (78cm) wide.
$2,500–3,200 P

A Regency rosewood brass-inlaid sofa table, in the manner of George Oakley, c1810, 59in (150cm) wide.
$40,000–45,000 S

An Irish mahogany side table, 19thC, 60¼in (153cm) wide.
$8,000–9,000 HOK

An Irish satinwood tea table, c1840, 36in (91.5cm) wide.
$3,500–4,000 CHA

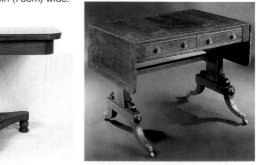

A Regency rosewood sofa table, with crossbanding, satinwood and boxwood stringing, the sabre legs with gilt-brass anthemion mounts, joined by later stretcher, brass cups and casters, 58¾in (149cm) extended.
$6,200–7,200 P(Sc)

A Regency crossbanded and brass-inlaid rosewood sofa table, with a pair of frieze drawers, 59in (150cm) wide.
$6,500–7,500 P(L)

A Victorian burr walnut veneered, rosewood and crossbanded writing table, by Holland & Sons, 40in (101.5cm) wide.
$2,800–3,200 MAT

◄ A William IV rosewood and mahogany work table, c1830, 48in (122cm) wide.
$10,000–11,000 SPU

A mahogany writing table, in the style of Gillows, 19thC, 29in (73.5cm) wide.
$5,500–6,500 SPU

READING CHAIRS

An early Georgian mahogany reading chair, with adjustable writing board, the leather upholstered chair with 2 brass mounts to take a lamp.
$4,200–5,000 B

A George III mahogany and caned reading armchair, with loose black leather cushions, adjustable reading arm, c1800.
$4,500–5,200 SK

A mahogany-framed reading wing armchair, with leather upholstery, and adjustable footrest, 19thC.
$1,600–2,000 P(Ed)

▶ A carved oak reading chair, with fold-away lectern, candle or lamp slide and pipe or tobacco compartment, c1880.
$1,000–1,200 RPh

◀ A Victorian reading chair, upholstered in hide, with a detachable brass and mahogany tray on one side and an adjustable brass and mahogany book rest on the other, stamped 'Godfrey Giles & Co, London W', late 19thC.
$5,500–6,500 S

SIDE CHAIRS

A pair of George II walnut side chairs, on acanthus leaf and scroll-carved cabriole legs, with pad feet, c1735.
$6,500–7,500 S

A William and Mary walnut chair, with pierced arched top, solid seat, the back with a cane panel.
$350–420 L

▶ A George III mahogany pierced ladder-back chair, with scroll-carved rails.
$500–550 DN

A pair of George II mahogany side chairs, the seat rail with central scallop shell, the cabriole legs with shells and leaves on claw-and-ball feet, restored, c1750.
$11,500–13,000 S(NY)

A pair of beech side chairs, painted to simulate rosewood, with ring-turned spindles, mouldings and legs, early 19thC.
$520–560 DN

A Portuguese carved mahogany and cane side chair, in the 18thC rococo style, the knees carved with lion masks, c1850–65.
$1,300–1,600 NOA

A pair of George III-style maple side chairs, with painted tablet backs and upholstered seats, c1930.
$700–800 SK

A pair of mahogany side chairs, in the manner of Gillows, the moulded arched backs filled with Gothic tracery and with leaf and scroll-carved top rails, the buttoned-leather seats on cluster-column front legs, early 19thC.
$5,000–5,500 S

A pair of Italian painted and parcel-gilt salon chairs, the cartouche-shaped backs with padded panels, the stuff-over seats on moulded inswept legs and scroll feet, early 19thC.
$1,800–2,200 P

A set of 5 late Victorian satinwood and painted side chairs, including 2 armchairs, with shield-shaped backs, the centres pierced with plume motifs, and stuff-over seats.
$2,200–2,500 HAM

A set of 4 painted beech side chairs, with simulated bamboo frames and rail backs with spheres, painted with musical trophies, diaper patterns and leaves, early 19thC.
$900–1,000 DN

A set of 6 Empire painted and parcel-gilt side chairs, with moulded upholstered backrest, painted white and highlighted with gilding, early 19thC.
$11,500–13,000 S(NY)

Each chair bears the stamp for the Palais de Fontainebleau and is stencilled with a series of inventory numbers for Fontainebleau during the Restauration period.

A pair of Edwardian carved walnut side chairs, by Jetley of London, in the George II style, the frames decorated with foliate, shell and interlaced designs, the saddle-shaped slip-in seats covered in brown hide, with a label, 'Jetley, Manufacturer, 8 South Audley Street, London W', c1910.
$3,200–3,600 S(S)

The London furniture dealer G. Jetley traded from South Audley Street in Mayfair. The company handled some of the finest furniture on the English market at that time.

◄ A rococo-style carved giltwood side chair, with stuff-over seat, on cabriole supports, early 20thC.
$130–160 Bri

CHAISES LONGUES & DAY BEDS

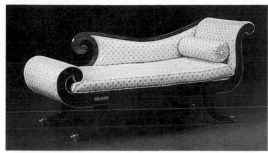

A Regency rosewood veneered and upholstered chaise longue, covered in patterned cream fabric, inlaid with brass, c1815, 67in (170cm) long.
$1,300–1,500 S(S)

An American classical mahogany chaise longue, school of Duncan Phyfe, with ormolu-mounted scroll arm and back, c1825, 80in (203cm) long.
$12,000–13,500 NOA

Duncan Phyfe (1768–1854) is one of the best-known makers of American Federal furniture. Scottish by birth, he lived in New York and specialized in light, elegant seat furniture, which he usually made from mahogany because of its rich colour.

A Victorian walnut-carved chaise longue, with a C-scroll carved apron, on cabriole legs with scroll feet, 69¾in (177cm) long.
$1,300–1,500 P

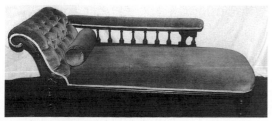

A Victorian mahogany chaise longue, with button-back upholstery, c1880, 71¾in (182.5cm) long.
$1,500–1,800 OOLA

A Regency mahogany day bed, with scrolled and reeded ends, legs reduced, c1815, 84in (213.5cm) long.
$8,500–9,000 S

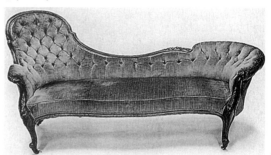

A Victorian walnut-framed chaise longue, with exposed scrolling and foliate carved show frame, upholstered in velvet, 86in (218.5cm) long.
$1,700–2,000 Mit

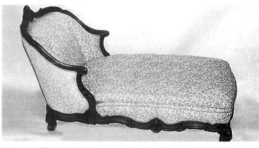

A Louis XV-style mahogany chaise longue, by Nelson Matter, with floral upholstery, c1900, 72in (183cm) long.
$2,000–2,300 DuM

The Nelson Matter Furniture Company operated in Grand Rapids, Michigan, USA, from 1854 to 1917.

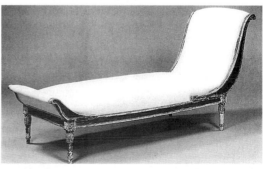

A French decorated *recamier*, in the Consulat taste, with panelled frieze on turned tapered legs, 19thC, 66in (167.5cm) long.
$5,000–5,750 P

The day bed is often referred to as a *recamier*, after Madame Recamier who was depicted in a celebrated painting of her reclining on a day bed with similar scroll ends by Jacques Louis David.

A Charles II walnut marquetry chest, the top, front and sides inlaid with floral sprays on an ebonized ground, 37in (94cm) wide.
$26,000–30,000 L

A William and Mary walnut chest, crossbanded in yew and with quartrefoil stringing to the top panel, with later turned feet, altered, 31in (78.5cm) wide.
$4,000–5,000 L

A walnut bachelor's chest, the top with 4 matched veneered panels opening to reveal plain panels, inlaid with herringbone banding and with wide crossbandings, requires restoration, early 18thC, 31in (78.5cm) wide.
$30,000–32,500 CAG

This chest was in such poor condition that it had been relegated to the vendors' cellar after they had inherited it. Eventually they decided to take it to the rubbish tip, but consulted their local auctioneers beforehand, who informed them that it was worth at least $1,600. However, in keeping with current buying trends, its unrestored condition created great excitement in the trade, and the purchaser, bidding from a train via mobile phone, had to go to many times over the estimate to secure it.

A walnut and oyster laburnum veneered chest of drawers, with 2 short and 3 graduated long drawers, early 18thC, 38½in (98cm) wide.
$23,000–26,000 E

This attractive chest sold for well in excess of its estimate because it was in its original, unrestored condition.

A George I walnut and boxwood strung chest of drawers, with moulded quarter-veneered top, 38¼in (97cm) wide.
$3,200–3,500 CGC

21 Years Ago …

A Chippendale mahogany and crossbanded serpentine-fronted chest of drawers, the top drawer fitted with lidded compartments for toiletries, 18thC. **P(WM)**

Twenty-one years ago this chest of drawers was valued at $1,700–2,000. Given the present boom in good-quality Chippendale period furniture this chest could today realize a saleroom price of $20,000–24,000. The market trend for this calibre of furniture has shown consistent growth over the past two decades. It has the desirable and rare feature of a fitted top drawer, and the serpentine sides add further appeal. The well-matched and figured veneers are another sign of quality.

A George II mahogany and walnut D-shaped chest of drawers, in need of restoration, 29¼in (74.5cm) wide.
$5,500–6,500 Bri

A mahogany chest of drawers, mid-18thC, 32in (81.5cm) wide.
$2,000–2,300 GD

A north Italian rococo walnut commode, with serpentine front, the corners with leaf and pendant floral carving, on leaf-carved scrolling feet, mid-18thC, 49in (124.5cm) wide.
$10,000–11,500 B&B

A Dutch walnut and marquetry bombé commode, inlaid with vases of flowers, scrolling foliage, floral sprays and birds, mid-18thC, 33½in (85cm) wide.
$5,200–5,700 Bea(E)

A George III mahogany bachelor's chest, the baize-lined flap top above 8 drawers, oak-lined with later brass swan-neck handles, 36½in (92.5cm) wide.
$6,500–7,200 WW

A kingwood and rosewood veneered commode, the breakfront top above 3 frieze drawers with 2 long drawers below, the whole decorated with parquetry panels, crossbanding and stringing, late 18thC, 49½in (125.5cm) wide.
$2,300–3,000 Bon(W)

A George III mahogany chest of drawers, 42in (106.5cm) wide.
$1,400–1,650 LRG

A mahogany chest of drawers, with brushing slide and 4 graduated drawers, late 18thC, 34in (86.5cm) wide.
$3,500–4,500 B&L

◄ A Louis XVI walnut and inlaid commode, with marble top, damaged, late 18thC, 50¼in (127.5cm) wide.
$7,200–8,000 Bri

► A Maltese olivewood commode, with satinwood and olivewood inlays, on square tapered legs, 18thC, 53in (134.5cm) wide.
$6,800–7,500 DaH

An American carved walnut chest of drawers, damaged and restored, late 18thC, 44in (112cm) wide.
$13,000–14,500 B&B

An American walnut chest of drawers, the 4 drawers flanked by fluted quarter column stiles, original brasses, on moulded ogee bracket feet, c1770, 40¼in (102cm) wide.
$5,000–5,700 SLN

A French Empire mahogany commode, with pierced-brass three-quarter gallery, over 3 short and 2 long drawers, flanked by gilt fluted quadrant stiles, early 19thC, 49in (124.5cm) wide.
$4,000–5,000 P(HSS)

A Biedermeier walnut chest of drawers, early 19thC, 53in (134.5cm) wide.
$3,200–4,000 B&B

A Colonial teak campaign chest, with brass corner mounts, recessed handles and iron carrying handles, 19thC, 31¼in (79cm) wide.
$3,500–4,000 Bea(E)

A Regency mahogany chest of drawers, with original knob handles, possibly Scottish, 51in (129.5cm) wide.
$1,800–2,000 DQ

A Regency mahogany chest, with brass lion-mask handles, 41¼in (105cm) wide.
$1,600–1,800 DN

A George IV mahogany bowfront chest of drawers, the drawers flanked by spiral reeded pilasters, on gadrooned bun feet, 48½in (123cm) wide.
$1,500–1,700 S(S)

A French mahogany chest of drawers, with later mounts, c1835–45, 41¼in (105cm) wide.
$2,300–3,000 NOA

A teak military chest, with brass-bound corners and steel carrying handles, 19thC, 39in (99cm) wide.
$1,300–1,500 TRL

A Victorian mahogany dressing chest, the top with chamfered border and rounded corners, 48in (122cm) wide.
$800–900 WBH

A pair of mahogany chests of drawers, with brass fittings, c1880, 36¼in (92cm) wide.
$2,800–3,500 OOLA

A Continental walnut and rosewood crossbanded serpentine commode, in the Louis XV style, applied with gilt-metal mounts, 21½in (54.5cm) wide.
$2,000–2,500 P

► An Edwardian mahogany serpentine chest of drawers, 45in (114.5cm) wide.
$2,800–3,200 L

TALLBOYS

A walnut and feather-banded tallboy, early 18thC, 37½in (95.5cm) wide.
$3,200–4,000 B&L

A George III mahogany tallboy, the upper section with moulded and dentil cornice and fluted canted corners, 42in (106.5cm) wide.
$4,000–4,500 AH

A George III mahogany tallboy, with moulded dentil cornice above an arrangement of drawers, the lower section with 3 long graduated drawers, on bracket feet, 40½in (103cm) wide.
$4,000–4,500 JAd

A walnut double-herringbone crossbanded secretaire tallboy, the upper part with canted corners inlaid with Corinthian columns above a secretaire drawer, with brass drop handles, on bracket feet, 18thC, 42in (106.5cm) wide.
$28,000–32,000 DN(H)

This tallboy realized over 4 times its top estimate because it was in unrestored condition and had a good colour and attractive inlaid canted corners.

A George III mahogany tallboy, the upper part with a dentil cornice, over drawers with satinwood banding, 46in (117cm) wide.
$2,800–3,200 L

A George III mahogany secretaire tallboy, the writing drawer with a fitted interior of pigeonholes and small drawers, c1780, 48¾in (122.5cm) wide.
$6,500–7,200 S

LOCATE THE SOURCE

The source of each illustration in Miller's can be found by checking the code letters below each caption with the Key to Illustrations, pages 789–795.

A Hepplewhite period mahogany secretaire tallboy, with original brass swan-neck handles, the secretaire drawer with a fitted interior, late 18thC, 48in (122cm) wide.
$11,500–13,000 WW

A George III mahogany tallboy, with broken architectural cornice and fluted columns, the top drawer with later pine interior, 47¼in (120cm) wide.
$5,200–5,600 P(B)

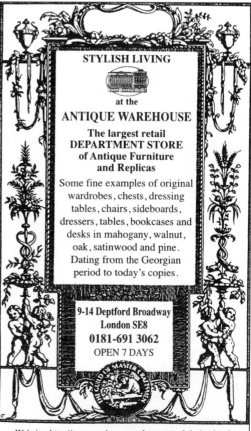

CHESTS-ON-STANDS

A William and Mary walnut and featherbanded chest-on-stand, the upper part with a quarter-veneered top, the base with a later frieze drawer and later supports, 41¼in (105cm) wide.
$9,000–10,000 P

A Queen Anne walnut chest-on-stand, with 3 short and 3 long graduated drawers, the stand with 2 long drawers, on later legs, c1710, 42½in (108cm) wide.
$7,500–9,000 S

A Queen Anne inlaid walnut veneered chest-on-stand, with 3 short and 2 long cockbeaded drawers, the lower section with a short central drawer and one deep drawer either side, 39½in (100.5cm) wide.
$5,000–5,750 HCC

A George I walnut chest-on-stand, the upper part with 2 short and 3 long drawers with crossbanded edges, the stand with 3 short drawers, restored, 38½in (98cm) wide.
$2,300–2,600 L

A George II walnut chest-on-stand, the upper part with a band of carved stiff leaves above 2 short and 3 long drawers with holly and ebony stringing, the stand with 3 similarly strung short drawers, 40in (101.5cm) wide.
$4,000–4,500 DN

A walnut chest-on-stand, the drawers with inlaid banding and later brass handles, 18thC, 38in (96.5cm) wide.
$4,000–4,500 DA

▶ A Queen Anne-style walnut and oak chest-on-stand, inlaid with stringing, the top section with canted fluted corners, some damage, early 20thC, 39½in (100cm) wide.
$3,000–3,250 S(S)

Miller's Compares

I A walnut chest-on-stand, crossbanded with herringbone stringing, early 18thC and later, 39¼in (99.5cm) wide.
$8,000–9,000 AH

II A walnut chest-on-stand, with oak crossbanding, early 18thC and later, 38½in (98cm) wide.
$4,200–4,600 AH

Both these chests are of a similar date and have been restored, but item I retains more of its original features, and is in what might be termed 'shop condition'. It has undergone sympathetic restoration and polishing, has an attractive colour and herringbone banding. In comparison, item II has plainer crossbanding and the mouldings around the top and between the top and the stand are completely new. Moreover, the proportions of item II are not so elegant as those of item I.

An American maple chest-on-stand, with replaced brasses, probably Massachusetts, c1760, 38in (96.5cm) wide.
$10,000–11,500 SK(B)

An American maple, pine and cherrywood chest-on-stand, with 5 graduated long drawers, replaced brasses, restored, New England, late 18thC, 36in (91.5cm) wide.
$1,400–1,650 SK(B)

A European lacquered chest-on-stand, decorated with Eastern views with flora and fauna, on fretwork bracket legs, 19thC, 34½in (87.5cm) wide.
$1,500–1,750 Bon(W)

LINEN & BLANKET CHESTS

A George II mahogany mule chest-on-stand, the hinged top opening to reveal a lined interior, with 2 drawers below, 51½in (131cm) wide.
$2,500–3,000 P(Ed)

A George III mahogany linen chest, the hinged top opening to reveal a camphor-lined interior, with 4 short drawers below, flanked by brass side handles, 48in (122cm) wide.
$2,500–3,000 Bon(W)

A Dutch Colonial teak and camphor chest, with ebonized mouldings, the hinged top over 2 apron drawers, c1830, 52⅛in (133.5cm) wide.
$2,500–3,000 S

An Irish mahogany blanket chest, on carved cabriole legs, c1770, 49in (124.5cm) wide.
$3,000–3,250 GKe

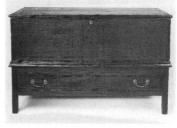

A Bermudian mahogany and inlaid chest-on-stand, with moulded lift-up top, the base with long drawer, late 19thC, 53in (134.5cm) wide.
$1,400–1,650 SK

An Edwardian inlaid and poly-chrome satinwood coffer, in the manner of Robert Adam, fitted with brass handles, c1900–10, 29in (73.5cm) wide.
$5,000–5,600 NOA

SECRETAIRE CHESTS

An Italian walnut secretaire-on-stand, the upper part with a hinged top and panelled front enclosing a fitted interior containing a drawer below, with carrying handles to the side, restored, 17thC, 65½in (166.5cm) wide.
$3,200–3,600 P

A French mahogany secretaire commode, with brass fluted terminals, the later marble top above fitted writing drawer, c1800, 42in (106.5cm) wide.
$3,200–3,600 S(S)

◀ A mahogany brass-bound secretaire campaign chest, the secretaire drawer with a satinwood interior, flanked by iron carrying handles, early 19thC, 37½in (95.5cm) wide.
$2,100–2,500 HOK

A mahogany and brass-banded secretaire campaign chest, the secretaire drawer concealing a fitted interior with burr-maple drawers and a folding folio compartment, flanked by deep drawers to either side above a long drawer, early 19thC, 38½in (98cm) wide.
$3,800–4,000 HOK

▶ A military chest, the secretaire drawer with drop-front enclosing 4 drawers and pigeonholes flanked by 2 small drawers and 3 graduated drawers below, with brass recessed handles and bound corners, 19thC, 39in (99cm) wide.
$4,000–4,400 P(G)

WELLINGTON CHESTS

A William IV rosewood Wellington chest, the 7 graduated drawers flanked by pilasters with carved corbels, damaged, c1830, 22¾in (28cm) wide.
$4,500–5,000 S(S)

A Victorian figured walnut Wellington chest, with 7 graduated drawers, a plain locking bar and carved volutes, 22in (56.5cm) wide.
$2,500–2,700 TMA

A William IV mahogany Wellington chest, with 8 drawers between locking stiles, 23¼in (59cm) wide.
$5,200–5,750 P(EA)

A Victorian walnut Wellington chest, with 8 long graduated drawers and a locking pilaster, damaged, 22in (56.5cm) wide.
$3,000–3,300 S(S)

◀ An American mahogany Wellington chest, the 6 panelled drawers flanked by hinged reeded half columns operating as locking devices, c1860, 33½in (85cm) wide.
$1,600–1,800 SLN

▶ A Victorian rosewood Wellington chest, with a stepped top and frieze, the 6 drawers with a locking pilaster, damaged, 21¼in (54cm) wide.
$2,100–2,500 DN

CLOTHES & LINEN PRESSES

A George II mahogany linen press, the upper part with a moulded dentil cornice and fitted with 3 trays enclosed by fielded cartouche panelled doors, damaged, 49½in (125.5cm) wide.
$8,000–9,000 P

A George III mahogany clothes press, the moulded panelled doors enclosing tray shelves, with 2 short and 2 long drawers, on ogee bracket feet, c1780, 49½in (125.5cm) wide.
$8,000–9,500 S

A George III mahogany clothes press, the panelled doors with carved rosettes, the base with 4 short drawers and one long drawer, with brass handles, 51¼in (130cm) wide.
$2,500–3,000 DN

A George III mahogany clothes press, the detachable moulded cornice with a veneered frieze, the hanging compartment enclosed by a pair of panelled doors, the drawers with brass swan-neck handles, 50in (127cm) wide.
$3,000–3,300 WW

A George III mahogany clothes press, 49in (124.5cm) wide.
$3,000–3,250 Doc

A mahogany clothes press, with interior sliding trays enclosed by shaped fielded panelled doors, on bracket feet, probably North Country, c1770, 49in (124.5cm) wide.
$6,000–6,800 WW

An oak and mahogany clothes press, cross-banded and with string inlay, the panelled doors enclosing shelving, on bracket feet, early 19thC, 46½in (118cm) wide.
$1,500–1,700 AH

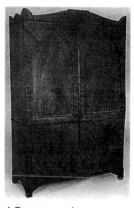

A Regency mahogany linen press, the upper part enclosed by lancet panelled doors, the lower panelled doors with roundels, with label 'John ...owat, 20 Castle Street, Aberdeen', 54in (137cm) wide.
$5,500–6,500 L

A Regency mahogany linen press, decorated with boxwood and ebony outline stringing, the panelled doors enclosing slides above a base with panelled reeded doors enclosing 2 short and 2 long graduated drawers, 50in (127cm) wide.
$2,500–3,200 Bon(W)

A mahogany linen press, the pediment with central carved shell, enclosing 2 shelves, the associated lower section with a brushing slide and cockbeaded drawers, on bun feet, 19thC, 49¼in (125cm) wide.
$1,500–1,700 P(NW)

A George IV mahogany gentleman's clothes press, with bow-shaped panelled doors enclosing 2 drawers and 3 sliding trays, with a long drawer below, on turned feet, damaged, 49¼in (125cm) wide.
$1,800–2,000 L&E

A Victorian mahogany linen press, the panelled doors enclosing sliding trays, with 2 short and 2 long drawers, on turned feet, 55in (139.5cm) wide.
$1,300–1,600 S(S)

DAVENPORTS

A Regency mahogany davenport, the swivel-top with leather-inset writing slope and a stationery drawer, above 4 drawers to the side faced by a slide and 4 false drawers, c1810, 15½in (39.5cm) wide.
$6,500–7,200 Bon

A William IV burr-walnut davenport, with gilt-brass baluster galleried hinged top enclosing a fitted interior, 4 drawers, 4 dummy drawers and a slide with hinged support, 23in (58.5cm) wide.
$2,300–3,000 Gam

A Victorian walnut serpentine-fronted davenport, with gilt leather-inset writing slope enclosing a fitted interior, with 4 side drawers below a fitted drawer and 4 dummy drawers, 21in (53.5cm) wide.
$1,600–2,000 Gam

▶ A late Victorian figured-walnut davenport, with original green morocco gilt-tooled writing surface, 21in (53.5cm) wide.
$1,000–1,200 L

A Regency rosewood davenport, with leather-inset hinged writing slope and drawers to the interior, 21in (53.5cm) wide.
$1,500–1,800 Bon(C)

A mid-Victorian walnut davenport, with boxwood foliate inlay, the hinged top above a sloping surface opening to reveal a fitted interior, with 4 drawers and 4 dummy drawers, 21½in (54.5cm) wide.
$1,200–1,400 P(NW)

A Victorian walnut davenport, the hinged top enclosing drawers, with 4 drawers and 4 dummy drawers, c1870, 21in (53.5cm) wide.
$1,200–1,600 Bon(C)

21 Years Ago ...

A walnut harlequin davenport, with a sprung superstructure operated by a lever concealed within the right-hand drawer, 1860s, 23in (58.5cm) wide. **S**

Twenty-one years ago this davenport was valued at $1,200–1,500. Today this desk might realize $6,000–7,000 at auction. Davenports of harlequin design, which incorporate a mechanical device to raise the superstructure, are among the most sought-after Victorian examples likely to come on the market, and their value grew at a rapid rate during the 1980s, peaking at the end of the decade. Values are likely to increase in the future, owing to their winning combination of ingenuity and fine cabinet-making.

A Victorian walnut and inlaid harlequin piano top davenport, the super-structure with a rising top and fitted stationery compartment, the curved hinged fall enclosing an interior with 2 drawers, sliding adjustable leather-inset writing surface, fitted pen tray and recesses, 22in (56cm) wide.
$5,200–5,700 P(E)

A burr-walnut davenport, with fitted maple interior, 4 drawers and 4 dummy drawers, 19thC, 21¼in (54cm) wide.
$1,500–1,800 Bri

A Victorian walnut davenport, the raised back with a hinged lid enclosing stationery compartments, the slope enclosing fitted drawers, 21in (53.5cm) wide.
$3,000–3,300 AH

A Victorian figured-walnut and marquetry davenport, the brass galleried top revealing a compart-mented interior above a fall-front with leather writing surface and inlaid with foliate roundels, the pedestal fitted with 4 drawers and 4 dummy drawers, damaged, 21in (53.5cm) wide.
$2,600–3,000 S(S)

DESKS

A Queen Anne walnut secretaire kneehole desk, with a crossbanded and quarter-veneered top, the frieze drawer enclosing drawers and pigeonholes, with a recessed cupboard door below, the secretaire drawer possibly later, 32¼in (82cm) wide.
$7,000–8,000 P(O)

A George III satinwood tambour writing desk, the top enclosing a fitted interior of drawers and pigeonholes above a leather-lined slide, c1790, 34¼in (87cm) wide.
$26,000–28,500 S

A George II mahogany kneehole desk, the writing drawer with a pull-down front enclosing a fitted interior with drawers and pigeonholes, with a concealed drawer over the recessed cupboard, 33¼in (84.5cm) wide.
$7,000–8,000 HYD

A George III Irish mahogany kneehole desk, the fitted top drawer with slide, c1780, 34in (86.5cm) wide.
$5,200–6,000 GKe

A pair of mahogany desks, each inset with a green leather top, early 19thC, 82¾in (210cm) wide.
$9,000–10,500 HOK

A Federal mahogany inlaid lady's desk, the 3 doors with inlaid floral vines and chequer-banding enclosing drawers above openings flanking 2 central compartments, over a fold-out writing surface, restored, Massachusetts, early 19thC, 40¾in (103.5cm) wide.
$4,500–5,000 SK(B)

▶ A mahogany kneehole desk, with one long and 2 short drawers around the fret-bordered kneehole, early 19thC, 38in (96.5cm) wide.
$800–1,000 DN

A Regency mahogany partners' pedestal desk, the top inset with a panel of tooled leather, 59½in (151cm) wide.
$4,500–5,000 P

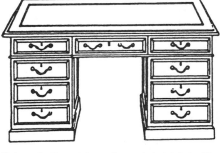

A mahogany pedestal desk, with shaped gallery back, stamped 'Gillows Lancaster', inscribed 'B. Hartley', c1840, 46in (117cm) wide.
$5,000–5,500 S

The pencilled inscription on the right-hand drawer is of a type commonly found on furniture by Gillows and gives the identity of either the cabinet-maker or the original owner.

A Victorian birch partners' desk, the top inset with brown leather, with 3 frieze drawers and opposing dummy drawers, the pedestals each with 3 drawers and a cupboard to the reverse, 66in (167.5cm) wide.
$4,000–4,500 TEN

A late Victorian Sheraton revival satinwood pedestal desk, the top with a gilt-tooled green leather writing surface, the corners of each drawer inlaid with plume-pattern spandrels and triple-strung in ebony and boxwood, the back panels in mahogany, 42in (106.5cm) wide.
$1,600–2,000 HAM

A late Victorian mahogany desk, the top divided into 7 leather-inset sections, the central hinged section opening as an adjustable bookrest, 47½in (120.5cm) wide.
$2,000–2,500 P(NW)

A Victorian burr-walnut pedestal desk, the top with leather writing surface, 48in (122cm) wide.
$2,000–2,500 AH

A pollard oak pedestal desk, on bun feet, c1870, 48in (122cm) wide.
$4,000–5,000 ANV

A mahogany partners' pedestal desk, the top inset with a panel of tooled-leather with 6 opposing frieze drawers, the pedestals with 3 drawers and opposing quatrefoil panelled doors enclosing shelves, late 19thC, 72in (183cm) wide.
$5,500–6,500 P

A late Victorian inlaid and painted satin-wood Carlton House desk, the fitted central cupboard flanked by 6 drawers and concave cupboards, decorated with painted portraits of ladies, ribbons and bellflowers, above a pull-out writing section with tooled-leather writing surface, 51in (129.5cm) wide.
$21,000–24,000 JAd

An oak pedestal desk, the frieze with a central drawer flanked by 2 further drawers, each pedestal with 2 banks of 3 drawers, late 19thC, 110in (279.5cm) wide.
$2,300–2,500 SLM

A Victorian mahogany inverted breakfront desk, with a drawer above the central cupboard, flanked by graduated drawers, 47¾in (121.5cm) wide.
$750–900 Bri

A late Victorian cylinder desk, with a three-quarter gallery above the fitted interior, the writing slide with 3 leather-covered and gilt-tooled recesses, 60in (152.5cm) wide.
$2,000–2,500 DN

A late Victorian mahogany pedestal desk, with a cloth-lined slope enclosing a fitted well, flanked by small drawers and baize-lined writing surface, stamped 'Coates', 54¾in (139cm) wide.
$2,800–3,200 TEN

Carlton House Desks

- D-shaped table with superstructure of drawers and cupboards around the back and sides.
- Designs for this type of table were first published in 1793 by both Hepplewhite and Sheraton.
- Name derives from the Prince Regent's (later George IV) London residence, for which a desk of this design was reputedly commissioned.
- Became popular again in the late 19th/early 20thC, but usually with more elaborate decoration.

A Sheraton revival mahogany and marquetry kidney-shaped desk, with borders of trailing flowers, ribbons and garrya, panels of urns and scrolling leaves, the top with a tooled-leather inset, c1900, 52¾in (134cm) wide.
$3,200–4,000 DN

An Edwardian lady's mahogany desk, the low superstructure with a broken arch pediment over a kidney-shaped mirror panel, flanked by concave hinged flaps enclosing stationery and writing accessory compartments each with a short drawer below, 36in (91.5cm) wide.
$1,500–1,650 CDC

A mahogany roll-top desk, the tambour front enclosing a fitted interior, each pedestal with a slide and 4 drawers, early 20thC, 49in (124.5cm) wide.
$1,300–1,500 DN(H)

A mahogany roll-top desk, the tambour top enclosing a fitted interior, with a single frieze slide drawer below, early 20thC, 48in (122cm) wide.
$1,100–1,300 BWe

A Georgian-style mahogany pedestal desk, with leather-inset top, the pedestals with canted leaf-carved corbels, early 20thC, 53in (134.5cm) wide.
$5,000–5,500 HOK

An Edwardian inlaid satinwood Carlton House desk, with polychrome portraits in the manner of Thomas Gainsborough, c1900, 46in (117cm) wide.
$9,000–10,000 NOA

An Edwardian mahogany kidney-shaped pedestal desk, with a leather-lined top, fitted with 9 short drawers with tulipwood crossbanding and inlaid with foliate and floral scrolls, stamped 'Edwards & Roberts', 47½in (120.5cm) wide.
$10,000–11,500 L

An Edwardian mahogany and satinwood-inlaid kneehole desk, with oak-lined central cupboard door, the drawers with brass swan-neck handles, on bracket feet, 32in (81.5cm) wide.
$1,600–2,000 BUSH

An Edwardian mahogany bowfront desk, with narrow satinwood banding, c1910, 48in (122cm) wide.
$1,600–2,000 Bon(C)

DUMB WAITERS

A George III mahogany three-tier dumb waiter, on turned column and tripod splayed legs with pad feet, 42½in (108cm) high.
$2,800–3,200 P

A George III mahogany two-tier dumb waiter, on baluster column and tripod splayed supports with casters, 40in (101.5cm) high.
$2,800–3,200 Sim

A Georgian mahogany two-tier dumb waiter, on fluted tapered column and tripod splayed foliate-carved legs, 41in (104cm) high.
$1,300–1,600 P

A mahogany three-tier dumb waiter, the tiers with drop-flaps divided by turned baluster columns, probably Irish, early 19thC, 44½in (113cm) high.
$4,000–5,000 P(Sc)

A pair of Regency mahogany dumb waiters, with 2 hinged tiers on turned ebonized and mahogany columns, with moulded outswept legs, altered, 38in (96.5cm) high.
$3,200–4,000 Bon

A mahogany three-tier dumb waiter, the dished tops on turned supports, with outswept legs, 19thC, 44½in (113cm) high.
$1,500–1,800 P

A mahogany two-tier dumb waiter, with a tambour cupboard, vase-shaped stem and cabriole legs with pad feet, 19thC, 43½in (110.5cm) high.
$1,500–1,800 AH

Facts in Brief

- Dumb waiters of multi-tiered form were first produced in England during the second half of the 18thC, but became less popular towards the end of the Regency period.
- Intended for use next to the dining table, eliminating the need to have servants constantly in the room.
- Some examples are revolving; more elaborate ones have special compartments for bottles and plates.

FRAMES

A pair of Italian giltwood picture frames, with foliate borders and surrounds, 17thC, 20½ x 15½in (52 x 39.5cm).
$4,000–4,500 P

A Flemish red tortoiseshell and ebonized mirror frame, late 17thC, with a later plate, 48¼ x 39½in (122.5 x 100.5cm).
$14,000–16,000 S

A carved and gilded Sunderland frame, with scrolling leaves running from a grotesque mask bottom to a blank cartouche crest top, mid-17thC, 40½ x 31¼in (103 x 79.5cm).
$1,400–1,600 Bon

A carved giltwood picture frame, with foliate decoration, 18thC, 33¼ x 22½in (84.5 x 57cm).
$950–1,000 WW

A giltwood frame, carved with gadroons and stylized foliage, 18thC, 74½ x 40½in (189 x 103cm).
$9,000–10,000 S(S)

A French gilded eight-sided frame, with incised scrolling leaves to the frieze and initialled quatrefoil centres, early 19thC, 23 x 17¼in (58.5 x 44cm).
$650–750 Bon

A gilded composition Watts frame, with plain sight, husked leaf, oak frieze and triple bead-and-reel below the leaf edge, late 19thC, 29½ x 19½in (75 x 49.5cm).
$1,500–1,700 Bon(C)

A Continental pierced and gilded composition frame, with stepped sight, scrolling acanthus to the sanded reverse hollow, and triple bead-and-reel back edge, late 19thC, 20 x 15½in (51 x 39.5cm).
$650–750 Bon(C)

A Continental carved, pierced and gilded frame, with clasp centres and pierced cabochon corners, late 19thC, 26½ x 21in (67.5 x 53.5cm).
$1,000–1,200 Bon

HALL STANDS

A Victorian oak hall stand, carved with Gothic tracery and linenfold panels, the mirror flanked by iron coat hooks, the base with a glove drawer on turned and spiral-carved supports flanked by quadrant umbrella rails, 43¼in (110cm) wide.
$3,000–3,200 TEN

A French Gothic revival hall stand, with 10 wooden pegs over and around an arched mirror, with linen-fold panels on either side, c1880, 43in (109cm) wide.
$2,100–2,300 HAC

An Australian hardwood hall stand, with arched surmount, mirror and glove box, carved panels of kangaroos, emus and other Australian animals, late 19thC, 42in (106.5cm) wide.
$1,800–2,000 RID

A Victorian Gothic-style carved oak mirror-back hall stand, the pierced and interlaced pediment with spire finials, the lower section with a hinged seat, restored, c1880, 45¾in (116cm) wide.
$1,600–2,000 S(S)

JARDINIERES

A Dutch neo-classical-style carved fruitwood jardinière, with brass and galvanized metal liner, c1780, 16in (40.5cm) diam.
$2,500–3,000 NOA

A French carved rosewood jardinière, with brass decoration and copper liner, c1825, 32in (81.5cm) wide.
$4,000–5,000 NOA

A Victorian Louis XV-style kingwood and walnut jardinière stand, with gilt-metal mounts, pierced galleried top, veneered cover and metal liner, c1870, 27½in (70cm) wide.
$2,000–2,250 P(NW)

Jardinière stands often had covers so that they could be used as tables in winter when there were few flowers available.

An Egyptian revival silvered and gilt-bronze jardinière-on-stand, attributed to F. Barbedienne, set with figural panels and opposing enamelled panels, the stand centred on opposing sides with an Egyptian torso with arms outstretched, fitted with onyx panels and Egyptian forms and figures, late 19thC, 43in (109cm) wide.
$25,000–30,000 S(NY)

Ferdinand Barbedienne (1812–92) was a prominent Second Empire furniture-maker and perhaps the best known 19thC Parisian bronze founder. By 1847 he had established a factory for the production of bronzes in Paris where, in addition to sculptures, he produced silver and reproduction furniture in a variety of styles.

A Victorian walnut and marquetry jardinière, with gilt-metal mounts and tulipwood crossbanding, metal-lined interior, c1870, 24in (61cm) wide.
$900–1,000 Bon(C)

A pair of French Louis XIV-style ebonized and scarlet tortoiseshell serpentine jardinières, applied with gilt-metal mounts, the tops enclosing zinc-lined interiors, c1870, 21½in (54.5cm) wide.
$1,200–1,400 P

A French boulle jardinière, with gilt-metal mounts and metal liner, c1870, 28in (71cm) wide.
$750–900 MEA

LOWBOYS

A Dutch mahogany and floral marquetry serpentine lowboy, 18thC, 31in (78.5cm) wide.
$4,500–5,000 P

A George I walnut lowboy, the top crossbanded and quarter-veneered, fitted with 3 short drawers, 31in (78.5cm) wide.
$3,300–4,000 L

An American walnut lowboy, with one long and 3 short drawers, Massachusetts, c1740, 35in (89cm) wide.
$8,000–9,000 SLN

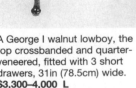

► A George III yew lowboy, with 3 frieze drawers and central scrolling niche, on cabriole legs with pad feet, 34½in (87.5cm) wide.
$1,800–2,000 P(Sc)

MINIATURE FURNITURE

A mahogany miniature bureau, the rosewood crossbanded fall-front enclosing a maple and ebony-veneered interior of drawers and pigeonholes, on turned feet, 19thC, 11½in (29cm) wide.
$1,800–2,000 P(S)

A mahogany miniature chest of drawers, with reeded sides, on later compressed cabriole legs, 19thC, 21¼in (54cm) wide.
$750–800 Bon(W)

A Victorian mahogany miniature chest of drawers, the top with a satinwood panel above 3 chequer-lined frieze drawers and 3 long drawers, 13in (33cm) wide.
$950–1,000 P(Sc)

A Continental marquetry inlaid walnut miniature chest, inlaid with scrollwork, damaged, 19thC, 18in (45.5cm) wide.
$1,800–2,000 SK(B)

A Victorian walnut and mahogany miniature Wellington chest, with boxwood stringing, the 6 drawers flanked by 2 pilasters, one locking, 14½in (37cm) wide.
$1,500–1,700 P(F)

A late Regency mahogany tilt-top miniature pedestal table, the top centred with a brass star, early 19thC, 12¾in (32.5cm) diam.
$2,500–3,000 SLN

◀ A pair of Victorian mahogany miniature breakfast tables, with tapered pedestals, 9¾in (25cm) diam.
$750–900 Bri

▶ A beech miniature armoire, with an arched and moulded cornice and 2 panelled doors, possibly French, early 20thC, 22½in (57cm) high.
$400–500 DN

A late Georgian mahogany miniature chest of drawers, one handle missing, 15in (38cm) wide.
$1,200–1,300 JH

A Victorian mahogany miniature chest of drawers, on bracket feet, 12in (30.5cm) wide.
$350–400 SK

A William IV rosewood miniature breakfast table, with a fluted tapering column and carved collar, on a tripartite base with scroll-carved feet, 5½in (14cm) wide.
$450–520 TMA

CHEVAL MIRRORS

A George III mahogany cheval mirror, crossbanded and inlaid with ebony stringing and ivory turned roundels, c1795, 30in (76cm) wide.
$5,000–5,500 S

A mahogany cheval mirror, with S-shaped supports, raised on 4 scroll legs, c1840, 32in (81.5cm) wide.
$1,200–1,400 MEA

A Napoleon III-style gilt-bronze-mounted boulle marquetry cheval mirror, the frame inlaid in brass with scrolling foliage on a red tortoiseshell ground, late 19thC, 71in (180.5cm) high.
$8,000–9,000 S(NY)

► A mahogany cheval mirror, with moulded surround, 19thC, 26in (66cm) wide.
$1,500–1,800 WBH

A French Empire mahogany and ormolu-mounted cheval mirror, the cornice centred by a female mask and anthemion scrolled decoration, the mirror-plate within a moulded frame held by turned columns with cast twin candle sconce to one side, c1810, 45¾in (116cm) wide.
$9,000–10,000 Bon

A Victorian mahogany cheval mirror, the plate within a moulded frame, on moulded and faceted tapering uprights, with carved collar and lotus-leaf carved finials, 63½in (161.5cm) high.
$2,000–2,500 AH

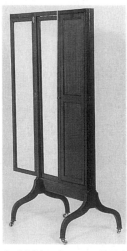

A George IV mahogany cheval mirror, the swing frame with square tapering supports, joined by a turned and reeded rail, 25in (63.5cm) wide.
$1,300–1,500 DN

An inlaid mahogany cheval mirror, the panelled front enclosing 3 mirrors, 19thC, 58in (147.5cm) extended.
$4,500–5,000 MEA

A mahogany cheval mirror, the Lewty patent telescopic brass brackets incorporating adjustable trays and candle arms, c1840, 37in (94cm) wide.
$1,500–1,800 MEA

A mahogany cheval mirror, with ring-turned frame, 19thC, 27½in (70cm) wide.
$800–1,000 HOK

An Edwardian mahogany cheval mirror, with boxwood stringing, c1910, 28in (71cm) wide.
$3,800–4,000 S

◄ An Edwardian mahogany cheval mirror, inlaid with scrolling foliage, floral festoons and pendant husks, 30in (76cm) wide.
$1,400–1,600 AH

The Tenterden Galleries

DRESSING TABLE MIRRORS

A George I walnut dressing table mirror, with later mirror-plate and 3 cavetto moulded drawers, c1725, 17¾in (45cm) wide.
$4,000–4,500 S

A George II walnut dressing table mirror, the plate with a gilt inner border, the plinth with a long concave-fronted drawer, 14½in (37cm) wide.
$650–800 L

A George III mahogany dressing table mirror, the later plate above a slope-fronted base and drawers, c1760, 19½in (49.5cm) wide.
$3,000–3,300 S

A George III mahogany dressing table mirror, attributed to Gillows, the adjustable pivoted mirror frame on a baluster-turned support, the serpentine plinth with 3 drawers, c1800, 18in (45.5cm) wide.
$2,800–3,200 S

A design for a dressing table mirror of near-identical form is recorded in Gillows' *Estimate Sketch Book*, 1797.

A George III mahogany and inlaid swing-frame dressing table mirror, the frame and serpentine base crossbanded in tulipwood, with 3 short drawers, 17¾in (45cm) wide.
$900–1,000 P

A George III mahogany dressing table mirror, the bowfront base with 3 frieze drawers, decorated with boxwood outline stringing, 18½in (47cm) wide.
$650–750 Bon(W)

A Victorian mahogany dressing table mirror, 35½in (90cm) high.
$780–820 COLL

A Regency mahogany dressing table mirror, the plate between turned uprights and surmounted by a volute-scrolled cresting, the base with a central drawer flanked by bowfront drawers, 21¼in (54cm) wide.
$1,200–1,400 TEN

A Swedish mahogany and brass-mounted dressing table mirror, c1800, 12in (30cm) wide.
$1,000–1,200 S(Z)

▶ A walnut triple mirror, 1920s, 37½in (95.5cm) wide.
$500–550 OOLA

WALL MIRRORS

A pair of Charles II walnut mirrors, the plates within frames carved with strapwork and leaves, the crestings centred by a crown cipher flanked by winged putti and leafy scrolls, restored, c1665, 27¼in (69cm) wide.
$8,000–9,500 S

A walnut wall mirror, the cushion frame with an arched fret-carved cresting, late 17thC, 15½in (39.5cm) wide.
$4,000–5,000 TEN

An early Georgian giltwood and gesso pier glass, the foliate cartouche and swan-neck pediment with ovolo decoration, the frieze with palmette spray ornament, with later trailing ornament to the sides, parts later, 26¾in (68cm) wide.
$7,000–8,000 P

A Chippendale period carved giltwood and gesso wall mirror, decorated in the rococo manner with foliate scrolls and flowerheads, late 18thC, 30in (76cm) wide.
$9,500–10,500 MCA

A George II parcel-gilt walnut mirror, the swan-neck pediment with a central phoenix, the later mirror-plate flanked by fruit and floral-carved pendants, mid-18thC, 27¼in (69cm) wide.
$7,000–8,000 B&B

Miller's Compares

I A George II carved giltwood mirror, the cresting centred by an acanthus leaf spray and with a scroll and leaf-carved apron, c1760, 29in (73.5cm) wide.
$14,500–16,000 S

II A George III carved giltwood mirror, the plate within a scroll and flower-carved frame with spray cresting, c1765, 24in (61cm) wide.
$8,000–9,500 S

Mirror glass was relatively expensive to produce in the 18thC and, as the mirror plate of item I is considerably larger, it would initially have been a far more expensive mirror to buy than item II. This inevitably accounts for the rarity of large mirrors of this period and the consequent differential in current auction prices.

A Chippendale design gilt-framed mirror, with *ho-o* bird cresting, the plate bordered by foliate scrolls, rocaille and trailing fruit, 18thC, 25in (63cm) wide.
$3,500–4,000 LRG

◄ A French Empire mirror, c1800, 17in (43cm) wide.
$650–750 CF

A lime wall mirror, in the manner of William Kent, the Greek key and reeded border with acanthus leaf and foliate surround, flanked by oak leaves and acorns, 18thC, 32¼in (82cm) wide.
$20,000–22,500 P(EA)

William Kent (1685–1748) began his career as a painter but later turned to architecture, interior decoration and furniture design. His style is characterized by heavy, carved, baroque features including masks, shells, acanthus foliage and key-pattern borders. Many of his designs were executed in giltwood for specific architectural contexts.

◄ A Federal giltwood and gesso overmantel mirror, with central frieze in relief, c1820, 56in (142cm) wide.
$4,000–5,000 SK(B)

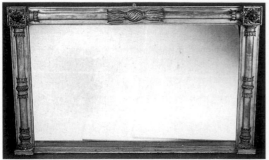

A George IV gilt overmantel, the top and sides with nulled, tasselled and leaf-carved columns terminating in carved paterae, 54in (137cm) wide.
$2,100–2,500 DN

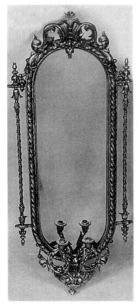

A pair of parcel-gilt convex wall mirrors, each with a cherub, a leaf surmount and open fretwork decoration of leaves and flowers, 19thC, 22½in (57cm) wide.
$1,500–1,700 P(C)

A pair of Victorian gilt girandole wall mirrors, with scroll and cartouche cresting and 2 candle branches, 20in (51cm) wide.
$5,000–5,750 MEA

A Dutch-style giltwood mirror, 19thC, 51in (129.5cm) wide.
$900–1,000 Doc

A Louis XVI-style giltwood and gesso wall mirror, surmounted by a wreath and garlands, with floral and foliate motifs, 19thC, 44in (112cm) wide.
$3,000–3,500 SLN

A giltwood and gesso mirror, c1880, 23in (58.5cm) wide.
$950–1,000 BAB

An American giltwood and gesso wall mirror, with turned pilasters and foliate carving at the corners, c1820–40, 27¼in (69cm) wide.
$1,000–1,200 NOA

A giltwood wall mirror, with a scrolling foliate frame, 19thC, 39½in (100.5cm) wide.
$1,600–2,000 Bon(C)

A Gothic revival oak mirror, with bevelled glass, c1880, 36in (91.5cm) wide.
$2,300–2,500 HAC

▶ A pair of George III-style giltwood and gesso pier mirrors, the fluted borders with paterae corners and scroll and urn surmounts, c1910, 31in (78.5cm) wide.
$4,500–5,200 S(S)

A pair of gilt gesso pier glasses, with leaf-moulded frames, the tops with pierced rococo cartouches, mid-19thC, 35in (89cm) wide.
$2,500–3,000 WW

A Continental parcel-gilt wall mirror, with central mask surmount flanked by griffins and urns, 19thC, 48in (122cm) wide.
$1,500–1,800 RBB

PEDESTALS

A mahogany dining room pedestal, the lift-up top above a fielded panelled door, the corners with carved acanthus-decorated knees, c1800, 40½in (103cm) wide.
$1,400–1,650 HOK

An American walnut pedestal, with ebonized details and masonic symbols, a plaque inscribed 'V. M. C. Lilley & Co, Columbus, Ohio', c1880, 26in (66cm) wide.
$250–300 DuM

A pair of Edwardian neo-classical-style satinwood pedestals, crossbanded with stringing and parquetry inlay, painted with flowers and ribbons, 45½in (115.5cm) high.
$3,200–4,000 AH

A pair of mahogany Adam-style urns on pedestals, the urns fitted for cutlery, the pedestals containing frieze drawers and panelled doors, early 20thC, 73½in (186.5cm) high.
$14,500–16,000 P

SCREENS

An Aubusson tapestry four-fold screen, depicting cherubs frolicking among fruit hanging from rings with parrots, 18thC, 88¼in (224cm) wide.
$8,000–9,000 B&L

A French chinoiserie block-printed paper four-fold screen, c1820, 135in (343cm) wide.
$2,400–2,600 NOA

A French Louis XV-style polychrome leather and oak six-panel screen, c1855–70, 72in (183cm) wide.
$16,000–19,000 NOA

A four-fold screen, the panels painted after Uccello with *The Battle of San Romano*, 19thC, 84in (213.5cm) high.
$4,200–4,600 RBB

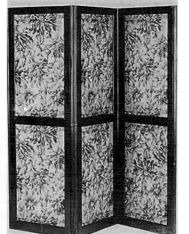

A mahogany-framed three-fold screen, with printed floral fabric panels and countersunk brass hinges, late 19thC, 66in (167.5cm) high.
$850–950 S(S)

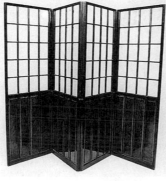

A mahogany reversible four-fold screen, each fold with 20 astragal-glazed panels above 4 moulded panels, 19thC, 96in (244cm) wide.
$2,300–2,600 P(Sc)

▶ A Victorian four-fold mahogany-framed screen, each panel painted in oils on one side with a panoramic scene, c1880, 90in (228.5cm) wide.
$550–650 Hal

A baroque ebonized firescreen, with gros and petit point needlework, early 18thC, 20in (51cm) wide.
$3,200–3,500 S(Z)

A French maple and amaranth firescreen, decorated with a neo-classical urn containing flowers, c1825, 30in (76cm) wide.
$1,600–1,800 S(Am)

A French carved giltwood firescreen, the sliding centre panel with a needlepoint panel depicting a neo-classical vase, c1780, 25½in (65cm) wide.
$1,600–2,000 NOA

A George III mahogany and satinwood lady's writing firescreen, the shield-shaped upper section with rising screen and a fall-front flap revealing a tooled-leather inset, a pair of doors and 3 small drawers, on paterae-inlaid splayed legs, c1790, 15¾in (40cm) wide.
$5,000–5,650 S

◄ A William IV brass and rosewood polescreen, the panel with red pleated fabric inside a parcel-gilt frame, on a turned and fluted stem with triform base, 56in (142cm) high.
$900–1,000 MEA

A George III mahogany firescreen, with decorative fretwork, brass candle holders and sliding silk screen, 18thC, 48in (122cm) wide.
$2,000–2,500 STK

A Victorian rosewood firescreen, 38½in (98cm) high.
$800–950 COLL

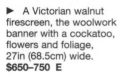

A Victorian walnut firescreen, the floral tapestry framed with rococo floral scrolls, c1870, 24in (61cm) wide.
$500–550 Bon(C)

► A Victorian walnut firescreen, the woolwork banner with a cockatoo, flowers and foliage, 27in (68.5cm) wide.
$650–750 E

21 Years Ago …

A walnut firescreen, containing a glazed woolwork panel, on trestle feet, 1860s, 33in (84cm) wide. **S**

Twenty-one years ago this firescreen was valued at $450–600. Saleroom prices for firescreens in general have been relatively static and this example is no exception with current prospects of $1,200–1,600. As fewer households have open fires, screens have become less sought after and their value has been relegated to decorative status. The practicality of an item of furniture is often an important value factor.

SETTEES & SOFAS

A settee, with 2 mahogany front legs decorated with chained bellflowers and 2 legs replaced, 18thC, 72in (183cm) long.
$3,500–4,000 MEA

A Regency rosewood sofa, the cresting and frieze with decorative box stringing, damaged, 82¾in (210cm) long.
$2,000–2,200 L&E

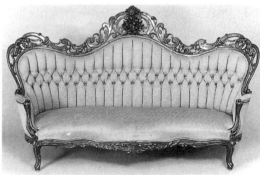

An American rococo revival laminated rosewood sofa, the back with pierced open scroll carving centred by a carved floral crest, c1850, 86½in (219.5cm) long.
$6,500–7,500 NOA

A Victorian mahogany sofa, the arms carved to the front with cherubs playing a lute and a pipe, with a panelled seat rail, 74in (188cm) long.
$750–900 P(Ed)

A mahogany sofa, the padded back with a double eagle head cresting and scroll-carved arms with similar decoration, early 19thC, 86¼in (219cm) long.
$3,800–4,500 P

A Regency mahogany and leather-covered settee, with curved and twist-turned arm supports, on turned tapering reeded legs, c1820, 78in (198cm) long.
$10,500–11,500 S

◄ A British Colonial carved and inlaid teak caned sofa, with S-scroll back and arms, c1840, 93in (236cm) long.
$10,000–11,500 SK

A Victorian four-section conversation seat, on walnut turned tapering legs, 68in (172.5cm) wide.
$4,000–4,500 Gam

A Victorian walnut sofa, 66in (167.5cm) long.
$2,500–3,000 RID

An Edwardian mahogany sofa, on cabriole supports with leaf carving, 56in (142cm) long.
$900–1,000 Bri

A mahogany settee, upholstered in leather, the arms with acanthus leaf-carved terminals, late 19th/early 20thC, 43¾in (111cm) long.
$10,000–10,500 S

An Edwardian settee, with a pierced and carved panel back, reupholstered, 60in (152.5cm) long.
$1,200–1,400 MEA

An Edwardian painted mahogany salon settee, reupholstered, 45½in (115.5cm) long.
$1,200–1,400 COLL

An Edwardian Sheraton-style inlaid mahogany settee, with bellflower decoration, quarter paterae and stringing, 42½in (108cm) long.
$2,200–2,500 JAd

◄ An Edwardian inlaid mahogany settee, c1910, 43in (109cm) long.
$750–900 BAB

SHELVES

A set of French Louis XVI style brass-mounted rosewood and marquetry hanging shelves, c1850–65, 23¼in (60.5cm) wide.
$550–600 NOA

A set of north Italian folding olivewood and marquetry hanging shelves, carved with foliate scroll fretwork decoration and with marquetry panels, 19thC, 18in (45.5cm) wide.
$950–1,000 P(G)

◀ A set of early Victorian stained beechwood hanging shelves, with turned spiral reeded frame, with spindle-filled curved sides at the base, 22¾in (58cm) wide.
$1,500–1,800 DN

SIDEBOARDS

A Federal walnut and yellow pine sideboard, with 2 dummy drawers and 2 short drawers flanking a central cupboard door, Virginia, restored, c1790–1810, 56in (142cm) wide.
$5,500–6,000 SK(B)

A Scottish mahogany breakfront sideboard, the raised back with sliding compartments, early 19thC, 79½in (202cm) wide.
$4,000–5,000 AH

A George III mahogany sideboard, the top fitted with a brass rail with baluster uprights and urn finials, the frieze fitted with a shallow drawer flanked by 2 drawers and a cellaret drawer, c1795, 72in (183cm) wide.
$6,500–7,500 S

A mahogany sideboard, with 3 drawers to the frieze, early 19thC, 94in (239cm) wide.
$3,000–3,300 WW

◀ A Dutch Empire mahogany and brass-mounted sideboard, the 2 drawers and 2 doors flanked by half-round side doors, early 19thC, 67¾in (172cm) wide.
$5,000–5,500 S(Am)

A Regency mahogany breakfront pedestal sideboard, boxwood-strung and inlaid with ebony line and trefoil decoration, one pedestal with cellaret drawer, early 19thC, 75in (190.5cm) wide.
$2,800–3,200 Bon(C)

A mahogany sideboard, possibly Irish, early 19thC, 85in (216cm) wide.
$2,800–3,200 Doc

A Regency mahogany bowfront sideboard, with a frieze drawer and arched apron flanked by 2 drawers with ebony inlay, c1820, 54in (137cm) wide.
$5,500–6,000 ANT

A William IV mahogany sideboard, the frieze drawer with carved spandrels, supported by pedestals with scrolled bases, 75¼in (191cm) wide.
$2,100–2,500 P(Sc)

A George IV mahogany bowfront sideboard, with a frieze drawer above foliate and lotus-leaf carved spandrels, flanked by a cupboard door with a further side cupboard and a compartmented bottle drawer, damaged, c1830, 76in (193cm) wide.
$5,500–6,000 S(S)

A Victorian mahogany sideboard, the raised back with carved foliate scroll border, the central section fitted with drawers and shelves enclosed by a pair of carved panelled doors, 72½in (184cm) wide.
$1,600–1,800 TRL

An Edwardian George III-style demi-lune sideboard, the later top above a central frieze drawer and tambour front cupboard flanked by 2 further cupboard doors modelled as 2 short drawers, damaged, 52½in (133.5cm) wide.
$1,000–1,200 S(S)

▶ A carved oak sideboard, c1935, 48in (122cm) wide.
$650–800 OOLA

A William IV mahogany sideboard, the raised back with 2 tambour-fronted cupboards above a frieze drawer and cellaret cupboard, 51in (129.5cm) wide.
$5,000–6,000 DN

A George III-style mahogany bowfront sideboard, the top with ebony-strung and crossbanded edge, the cupboard and drawer front with ebony and boxwood stringing and cockbeading, 19thC, 54in (137cm) wide.
$6,500–7,500 Mit

A late Victorian mahogany mirror-back sideboard, the lower section with frieze drawers above a central deep lead-lined drawer modelled as 2 drawers, flanked by cupboard doors, with label 'Sewell & Sewell, Worship Street, London', 71in (180.5cm) wide.
$1,400–1,600 S(S)

An American mahogany sideboard, the white marble top supported by a base fitted with turned columns, c1830, 80in (203cm) wide.
$3,800–4,000 NOA

An American mahogany sideboard, fitted with 3 short drawers, over 2 large half drawers and 2 cupboard doors, flanked by reeded columns, on acanthus-carved pad feet, c1840, 50½in (128.5cm) wide.
$1,200–1,400 NOA

A Victorian mahogany inverted breakfront sideboard, the panel back centred by a patera and bellflower motif and with short lotus columns to each end, above a long frieze drawer flanked by short frieze drawers with semi-secret locking mechanisms, c1880, 76in (193cm) wide.
$2,000–2,500 Hal

An Edwardian Sheraton revival satinwood bowfront sideboard, with ebony, satinwood and boxwood stringing and inlay, 47in (119.5cm) wide.
$1,500–1,750 Mit

A George III mahogany kettle stand, with waved gallery over a slide, the legs inlaid with boxwood lines, c1780, 12in (30.5cm) diam.
$1,200–1,400 GH

◄ A Regency mahogany candle stand, with reeded rim and turned legs, 10in (25.5cm) diam.
$300–350 ANV

A George III mahogany candle stand, the hexagonal top with pierced gallery above a turned and fluted standard, restored, 11in (28cm) diam.
$3,200–3,600 S(NY)

A George III satinwood urn stand, the frieze with an inset cup stand, restored, c1790, 14in (35.5cm) wide.
$13,000–15,000 S(NY)

► An Edwardian mahogany coaching stand, hinged and opening to a gilt tooled-leather writing surface, on a folding stand, c1900, 24in (61cm) wide.
$1,300–1,500 S(NY)

A Renaissance style carved *guéridon*, possibly Italian, mid-19thC, 37½in (95cm) high.
$900–1,000 P

ACCESSORY STANDS

A Regency whip rack, c1820, 22¾in (58cm) wide.
$500–550 GBr

A cast-iron umbrella stand, made by Falkirks, 19thC, 23in (58.5cm) wide.
$550–650 RUSK

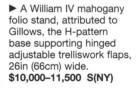

A late Georgian mahogany hat stand, with 4 tiers of graduated S-shaped hooks, on a tripod plinth base, c1830, 79½in (202cm) high.
$800–1,000 LAY

An oak umbrella or cane stand, 19thC, 24in (61cm) wide.
$350–400 CAT

◄ A William IV mahogany whip and boot stand, restored, c1835, 44in (112cm) high.
$1,400–1,600 S(S)

A mahogany boot rack, the top rail with a pierced carrying handle and turned pegs, 19thC, 26in (66cm) wide.
$400–500 P(Sc)

A walnut stick stand, early 20thC, 35½in (90cm) high.
$320–350 AnSh

FOLIO & MAGAZINE STANDS

A George IV rosewood folio stand, with turned spindles and square cross bars, c1825 41½in (104cm) wide.
$5,200–5,700 S

LOCATE THE SOURCE

The source of each illustration in Miller's can be found by checking the code letters below each caption with the Key to Illustrations, pages 789–795.

► A William IV mahogany folio stand, attributed to Gillows, the H-pattern base supporting hinged adjustable trelliswork flaps, 26in (66cm) wide.
$10,000–11,500 S(NY)

A rosewood folio stand, the trestle base raised on sabre legs, mid-19thC, 30½in (78cm) wide.
$3,200–4,000 B&B

A William IV rosewood folio stand, with double-sided ratchet adjustable wings, formed by squared cross bars and tapering vertical bars, 23in (58.5cm) wide.
$4,000–5,000 TMA

◄ A satinwood folio stand, the fall-front with floral marquetry, roundels and quarter fan designs, 19thC, 43in (109cm) wide.
$900–1,000 L

MUSIC STANDS

A George III mahogany music stand, the adjustable slide with mirror-plate hinged rest and retractable arms, c1790, 51¼in (130cm) high.
$4,000–4,500 Bon

A Regency part-gilt ebonized music stand, with brass hinged candle arms, early 19thC, 43in (109cm) high.
$6,500–7,500 S(NY)

A Victorian mahogany duet stand, the twin adjustable top with pierced lyre decoration 42½in (108cm) high.
$1,000–1,200 TRL

A rosewood double-sided adjustable music stand, with lyre decoration, on turned column and shaped platform base, on turned feet, c1840, 42in (106.5cm) high.
$2,500–2,750 E

STEPS

A set of George III bleached mahogany steps, with original ironwork hinged braces, damaged, 54in (137cm) high.
$700–800 WW

A set of late George III mahogany bed steps, the top rising, the middle sliding forward to reveal a chamber pot, on turned legs, 19in (48cm) wide.
$900–1,000 L

A set of Regency mahogany bed steps, with gilt tooled-leather inset treads and panelled fronts, the top and centre steps with hinged treads, on turned reeded legs, early 19thC, 21¼in (54cm) wide.
$4,000–4,500 S(NY)

A set of George IV mahogany library steps, with leather-lined treads and mahogany top step, the moulded handrail with turned supports, 84½in (215cm) high.
$8,000–9,000 S

A set of George IV library/bed steps, with lift-up lid, c1820 28½in (72.5cm) wide.
$1,600–1,800 HUB

A set of William IV commode/library steps, with hinged steps, 20in (51cm) wide.
$4,000–4,500 P(F)

◄ A set of William IV mahogany folding library steps, the scroll-shaped sides supporting 4 carpet-covered treads, with hinged legs joined by a turned cross stretcher, 18½in (47cm) wide.
$5,500–6,500 S(S)

STOOLS

A George II walnut stool, with a
drop-in seat, 18in (46cm) wide.
$5,000–5,600 DN

A pair of Louis XV painted and
parcel-gilt tabourets, the serpentine
upholstered seat above a volute-
carved rail, raised on cabriole legs,
mid-18thC, 19in (48cm) wide.
$4,000–4,500 B&B

A George III mahogany stool, with a
Victorian gros point floral and
cartouche design slip-in seat, the
cabriole legs with acanthus leaf and
flowerhead knees, 18in (45.5cm) long.
$8,000–9,000 P

A Victorian mahogany drawing room
stool, upholstered in silk tapestry, on
cabriole legs carved with flowerheads
and scrolls, 40in (101.5cm) wide.
$2,000–2,500 MAT

---

21 Years Ago ...

A George II carved 'red walnut'
stool, upholstered in 18thC
floral needlework. **P**

Twenty-one years ago this stool was valued at $1,800–2,000.
The demand for English furniture of this period has recently
been at its highest level since the late 1980s. The last 3 years
have seen some dramatic increases in value for Georgian
upholstered furniture and this stool could potentially realize
$13,000–20,000 in the present market. A further factor underpinning
this example's saleability is the current vogue for 18thC
needlework upholstery.

A walnut stool, the drop-in padded
seat on a veneered frame, parts
early 18thC, 21in (53.5cm) wide.
$5,000–5,500 WW

A William IV mahogany stool, in the
manner of Gillows, with upholstered
seat, 39¾in (100cm) wide.
$6,500–7,000 S

A Victorian mahogany stool,
upholstered in gros point tapestry,
22in (56cm) wide.
$600–650 P(Sc)

A Regency mahogany and
ormolu-mounted X-framed
stool, with upholstered scroll
sides, on arched supports,
32in (81cm) wide.
$8,000–9,000 P(EA)

An Edwardian Adam-style giltwood
dressing stool, with stuff-over
velvet seat with Berlin tapestry,
24in (61cm) wide.
$300–350 Mit

◄ A Victorian mahogany stool,
upholstered in gros point tapestry,
22in (56cm) wide.
$600–650 P(Sc)

MUSIC STOOLS

A Regency simulated rosewood music stool, the rosewood-veneered top rail with cut-brass trailing leaf and flower inlay, surmounted by a gadrooned cresting, the pierced lyre-shaped splat above a revolving nailed hide seat, c1820, 32in (81cm) high.
$4,000–4,500 S

A William IV rosewood music stool, with revolving shaped seat, on a baluster column, 18in (45.5cm) wide.
$1,000–1,200 L

An American rococo revival mahogany piano stool, the revolving and adjustable octagonal seat supported by a carved pedestal and quadruped base, c1850, 16¾in (42.5cm) diam.
$900–1,000 NOA

An early Victorian mahogany revolving piano stool, on carved acanthus leaf-decorated pillar, c1840, 17in (43cm) diam.
$550–650 FHF

An early Victorian walnut revolving piano stool, on carved cabriole legs, 14in (35.5cm) diam.
$1,000–1,100 BERA

► A Victorian rosewood lift-top piano stool, with fret-cut panels and spiral pilasters, with label 'T. Cleere, Wolverhampton', 22⅛in (57cm) wide.
$1,600–1,800 MEA

A Victorian walnut revolving piano stool, on turned bulbous pedestal and tripod legs, 19in (48.5cm) high.
$260–300 HAX

A Victorian brass piano stool, with velvet cushion seat, low brass back and on stretchered legs, 24in (61cm) high.
$220–260 HAX

An ebonized beech piano stool, with reupholstered tapestry seat, c1920, 24in (61cm) wide.
$100–120 BAB

LOCATE THE SOURCE

The source of each illustration in Miller's can be found by checking the code letters below each caption with the Key to Illustrations, pages 789–795.

BEDROOM SUITES

A Victorian walnut pedestal dressing table, with 8 drawers flanking a central frieze drawer with carved foliage, 59in (150cm) wide, and a matching wardrobe.
$1,800–2,200 AH

A late Victorian marquetry-inlaid oak bedroom suite, by Gillows, comprising a wardrobe, 62in (157.5cm) wide, dressing table and bedside cupboard.
$2,300–2,600 WW

An Edwardian inlaid satinwood five-piece bedroom suite, in George III-style, comprising a wardrobe, kidney-shaped dressing table, writing table, bedstead and a bedside cupboard.
$6,000–6,800 MEA

A figured walnut five-piece bedroom suite, comprising kidney-shaped dressing table, writing table, triple wardrobe with cast silver-plated allegorical panels, double bedstead and stool, early 20thC.
$3,000–3,500 DD

A French-style satinwood five-piece bedroom suite, comprising a headboard and footboard, chest of drawers, dressing table with unattached shield-form mirror and a bedside cabinet, c1930.
$1,300–1,600 DuM

◄ An Edwardian rosewood five-piece bedroom suite, inlaid with stringing and foliate scrolls, comprising a wardrobe, dressing table, washstand, pot cupboard and side chair, damaged.
$5,500–6,500 S(S)

SALON SUITES

A Napoleon III gilt-bronze and boulle salon suite, comprising a canapé and 2 side chairs, the frames decorated with arabesques and centred by a mask, c1860, settee 55¼in (140cm) wide.
$15,000–18,000 S

This suite was illustrated in Christopher Payne's *The Price Guide to 19th Century European Furniture* (Woodbridge, 1981). Payne points out that boulle seat furniture is rare and describes this design as typical of the original boulle period of c1700.

A Louis XV-style carved giltwood salon suite, comprising a canapé and 2 armchairs, c1890, canapé 67¾in (172cm) wide.
$11,500–14,000 S

▶ A Louis XVI-style carved giltwood five-piece salon suite, comprising a canapé and 4 *fauteuils*, upholstered with Aubusson tapestries, 19thC, canapé 52¾in (134cm) wide.
$3,200–3,800 P

A Victorian salon suite of 10 mahogany and upholstered chairs, comprising a lady's and gentleman's occasional chair and 8 side chairs, covered in dark green leatherette, restored.
$2,800–3,200 S(S)

HORNCASTLE

Two large trade calls, 5,000 sq. ft. plus 1 hour from Newark

Seaview Antiques
Stanhope Road, Horncastle
Tel: 01507 524524
Fax: 01507 526946

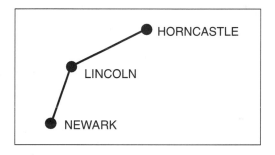

Norman Mitchell Simmons Ltd
The Wong, Horncastle
Tel: 01507 523854
Fax: 01507 523855

LINCOLNSHIRE UK

ARCHITECTS' & DRAWING TABLES

A George III mahogany architect's/library table, the top with a tooled-leather inset, raised on a hinged double-ratchet frame, above 3 frieze drawers and opposing drawers, 49¼in (125cm) wide.
$10,000–10,500 CGC

A George II gilt-metal-mounted mahogany drawing table, the frieze drawer with a sliding panel opening to divided compartments, the sides fitted with slides and retractable brass candle holders, restored, feet reduced, 36in (91.5cm) wide.
$60,000–65,000 S(NY)

The market for English furniture from the third quarter of the 18thC in the Chippendale manner is particularly strong at present. This example combines the attributes of fine quality with function. Furthermore, this table is stylistically advanced for the period. It also appears to retain a rich brown colour with good figuring to the veneers.

A George II mahogany architect's table, the ratcheted hinged top with candle stands to each side, the frieze pulling forward to reveal a fitted interior, on square and turned legs, 36in (91.5cm) wide.
$2,800–3,200 GH

► A George III mahogany architect's table, converted to a writing table, the pull-out apron drawer with fitted interior, 40¼in (102cm) wide.
$2,000–2,200 P(W)

A George III mahogany architect's table, the fitted interior with an adjustable slope and hinged panel, restored, 32¼in (82cm) wide.
$2,500–3,000 P

BREAKFAST TABLES

A George III mahogany breakfast table, with tip-up top, on ring-turned column, 48in (122cm) long.
$2,300–2,600 AH

A George III mahogany breakfast table, with crossbanded top, restored, late 18thC, 52¼in (132.5cm) long.
$16,000–18,000 S(NY)

A George III mahogany breakfast table, the top with a telescopic-action and one leaf insertion, c1800, 60in (153cm) extended.
$3,500–4,000 S(S)

◄ A Regency mahogany breakfast table, the tilt-top crossbanded with boxwood and ebony stringing, 52in (132cm) diam.
$5,500–6,500 P(HSS)

► A Regency rosewood breakfast table, with inlaid brass stringing and scrolled corner designs, 60in (152.5cm) long.
$10,000–11,500 RBB

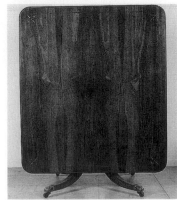

A Regency rosewood tilt-top breakfast table, the 4 outswept tapered legs with applied brass stud decoration, 53in (134.5cm) diam.
$5,000–5,500 BWe

A Regency mahogany drop-flap breakfast table, with a drawer at either end, on turned column and reeded quadruped legs, 44in (112cm) extended.
$1,000–1,200 P

A Regency mahogany breakfast table, with tilt-top, on a turned vase-shaped column with reeded collars, on 4 sabre legs, 55¾in (142cm) long.
$5,000–5,500 HAM

A pedestal breakfast table, veneered in faded rosewood, the tilt-top inlaid with a band of burr elm with a crossbanded edge and frieze, mid-19thC, 52in (132cm) diam.
$4,200–4,600 WW

Tilt-Top Tables

The pedestal on a tilt-top table is usually tenoned through a block that supports the table top. To establish whether the top has always been associated with the base, check that:

- the underside of the top retains its original bearers and not the marks of other bearers, or plugged holes, which would indicate that the top is from another table.
- the tenons, which often stand slightly proud of the block, have caused corresponding marks on the underside of the top.
- the base belongs with the block and there are no indications that it originally supported a different top.

A Victorian walnut and satinwood inlaid oval tilt-top breakfast table, on 4 slender turned columns, with carved leaf motif and quadruple scroll feet, 48in (122cm) diam.
$1,000–1,200 HAX

CARD TABLES

A George III tulipwood and harewood crossbanded mahogany and satinwood card table, the lined serpentine fold-over top with marquetry decoration, c1775, 37½in (94.5cm) wide.
$20,000–24,000 MCA

▶ An early Victorian rosewood card table, 36in (91.5cm) wide.
$1,400–1,600 MiA

A Dutch walnut fold-over card table, the parquetry top with card and counter recesses, with fitted drawer and single gate action, on cabriole legs, early 18thC, 33½in (85cm) wide.
$3,500–4,500 L&E

◀ A Victorian walnut fold-over card table, with inlaid decoration and leather top, c1870, 38in (96.5cm) wide.
$2,500–3,000 RBB

An Edwardian inlaid rosewood envelope card table, with a fitted frieze drawer, damaged, 22¾in (58cm) wide.
$1,500–1,700 P(F)

CENTRE TABLES

A William and Mary laburnum oyster-veneered and marquetry centre table, with shallow frieze drawer, 37in (94cm) wide.
$18,000–20,000 B

The top of this table is of the finest quality English marquetry.

A Restauration walnut and mahogany centre table, the marble top supported on a triform spreading pedestal applied with gilt-metal mounts, c1815, 35½in (90cm) diam.
$5,500–6,500 P(Z)

A Victorian figured-walnut centre table, after a design by W. Smee & Sons, the tilt-top with a carved gadrooned edge, the pillar with foliate scroll-carved brackets, c1850, 54¼in (138cm) diam.
$13,000–16,000 S

A mahogany centre table, the moulded top above a foliate carved frieze, mid-19thC, 48¾in (124cm) diam.
$1,400–1,600 P

A Regency rosewood and brass-inlaid centre table, the crossbanded tilt-top centred by a brass-inlaid panel with a scrolling border, the shallow frieze similarly inlaid, on a tapered octagonal support and 4 splayed legs with gilt-metal paterae mounts, c1815, 47¾in (121.5cm) diam.
$10,000–10,500 S

A George IV rosewood and marquetry centre table, the tilt-top inlaid with a band of scrolled vine and flowerhead decoration, c1830, 51in (129.5cm) diam.
$5,500–7,000 Bon(C)

A Louis XV-style rosewood and kingwood marquetry serpentine centre table, by Maison Le Marchand A Lemoine, with gilt-metal mounts, the top inlaid with a scrolling cartouche and spandrels, mid-19thC, 35½in (90cm) wide.
$2,500–3,200 P

André-Gabriel Lemoine traded at 17 rue des Tournelles, Paris, from 1852 and carried out various work for the Garde-meuble Imperial, the Ministère d'Etat and the Palais de Saint-Cloud.

A Biedermeier walnut and ebonized extending centre table, the top with radiating panels of walnut, c1815, 56in (142cm) diam.
$8,500–9,500 S(Am)

A William IV rosewood table, with later granite marble inset top above a bead-and-reel cavetto frieze, the pillar supported by a foliate-carved and scrolled tripod, c1835, 28½in (72.5cm) diam.
$3,800–4,000 S

A neo-classical gilt-bronze-mounted mahogany centre table, on tapered square legs, 19thC, 31½in (80cm) diam.
$3,500–4,000 B&B

A Victorian walnut centre table, the top inlaid with a floral spray to the centre, within a similarly inlaid border, 50¾in (129cm) diam.
$6,000–7,000 P(L)

A walnut centre table, the top with an inlaid panel of flowers and foliage and a similarly inlaid broad outer ring, 19thC, 53in (134.5cm) diam.
$5,500–6,500 E

A Gothic-style oak centre table, attributed to A. Pugin, with a central frieze drawer and opposing dummy drawer to the reverse, the supports united by a stretcher, 19thC, 58in (147.5cm) wide.
$2,500–3,000 MEA

A Victorian walnut centre table, the top with a burr-grain border and crossbanding to the leather inset, the frieze fitted with 2 drawers and carved with paterae, the lower part with carved ends joined by a baluster stretcher, 57in (145cm) wide.
$5,000–5,600 RBB

A rosewood centre table, in the style of Belter, the veneered top above a heavy foliate-carved frieze, 19thC, 48½in (123cm) wide.
$900–1,000 WW

◀ A late Victorian Sheraton revival centre table, the top with an oval inlaid panel with foliate scrolls in boxwood and harewood, the frieze inlaid with bellflower swags and repeating floral designs, c1900, 44in (112cm) wide.
$8,000–9,000 Mit

A French Empire mahogany centre table, with applied gilt-metal mounts and black marble top, on concave triform stem, lion-paw feet and casters, 19thC, 32in (81.5cm) diam.
$9,000–10,000 AH

A mid-Victorian walnut centre table, the serpentine top on fretwork supports and turned and carved stretcher, c1870, 40in (101.5cm) wide.
$3,200–3,800 BERA

CONSOLE & PIER TABLES

A French Empire cherrywood console table, surmounted by a marble top over a frieze drawer, on plain square supports, the columns with gilt-bronze cappings and bases, on cylindrical feet with ovoid toes, c1810, 35½in (90cm) wide.
$3,500–4,000 B&B

An oak console table, the green marble top above a central frieze drawer, mid-19thC, 59in (150cm) wide.
$2,300–2,600 LRG

A mahogany console table, the marble top on scrolled supports carved with flowerheads, c1835, 30½in (77.5cm) wide.
$3,500–4,000 S

◀ A Spanish console table, the marble top on carved wood and gilded supports, c1870, 44in (112cm) wide.
$1,000–1,200 BAB

DINING TABLES

A mahogany dining table, altered, 18thC, with an additional 19thC double leaf, 188½in (478.5cm) extended.
$2,800–3,200 P(L)

A George III inlaid mahogany three-section dining table, late 18thC, 88in (223.5cm) extended.
$3,500–4,000 B&B

A mahogany combination dining table, in the form of 2 Pembroke tables joined together, c1790, 84¼in (214cm) extended.
$14,500–16,000 S

A mahogany concertina-action extending dining table, including 4 extra leaves, early 19thC, 115½in (293.5cm) extended.
$7,500–9,000 Bea(E)

A mahogany dining table, with one extra leaf, early 19thC, 74¾in (190cm) extended.
$3,700–4,000 P(S)

A north European fruitwood tilt-top dining table, c1815–30, 45in (114.5cm) diam.
$1,200–1,400 NOA

A Regency mahogany telescopic extending dining table, in the manner of Gillows, including 4 extra leaves, 151½in (385cm) extended.
$13,000–14,500 P

A Regency mahogany twin-pedestal dining table, on a dividing baluster-turned column and splayed legs, including 2 extra leaves, 46in (117cm) extended.
$9,000–10,500 P

A Regency mahogany dining table, with gateleg action and 2 leaves, c1820, 93in (236cm) extended.
$5,000–6,000 LRG

A Regency mahogany concertina-action dining table, by Wilkinson, the extending fold-over top with a plain apron at one end with applied disc-turned mouldings and ebonized banding, c1820, 131in (332.5cm) extended.
$14,500–16,000 S

The firm of Wilkinson was established c1766 in Moorfields, London, by Joshua Wilkinson. By 1784 the firm had moved to 7 Broker's Row, Moorfields, and was trading as Wilkinson & Sons. Six years later the firm had expanded and was run by Joshua Wilkinson's second son, William, and his cousin Thomas. The partnership disbanded in 1808 when William established his own business at 14 Ludgate Hill, London. Thomas Wilkinson remained at 10 Broker's Row until 1828, specializing in the production of patent dining tables.

A Regency mahogany twin-pedestal dining table, with one extra leaf, 69in (175.5cm) extended.
$6,000–7,000 Bon(C)

A Regency mahogany triple-pillar dining table, with a later matching centre section and 2 extra leaves, c1820, 124½in (316cm) extended.
$25,000–30,000 Bon

A Federal cherrywood and bird's-eye maple two-section dining table, with drop-leaf ends, c1820, 82in (208.5cm) extended.
$1,800–2,000 SK(B)

A George IV mahogany dining table, in the manner of Gillows, with 3 extra leaves, c1825, 51in (129.5cm) long.
$14,500–16,000 Bon(C)

A mahogany twin-pedestal dining table, with tilting ends and one extra leaf, 19thC, 88½in (225cm) extended.
$4,500–5,200 P

A Dutch colonial padouk and teak dining table, 19thC, 57in (145cm) diam.
$6,000–7,000 S(Am)

A William IV mahogany tilt-top dining table, with cross-banded top above a beaded frieze, 48¾in (124cm) diam.
$3,000–3,500 P(S)

A William IV mahogany telescopic dining table, with 3 extra leaves, c1835, 137½in (349.5cm) extended.
$12,000–14,000 S(S)

▶ A Victorian mahogany dining table, with breakfront frieze, 4 extra leaves, restored, c1840, 123¼in (313cm) extended.
$11,500–13,000 S(S)

A William IV mahogany dining table, with 4 extra leaves, including a leaf stand with scroll brackets, 150in (381cm) extended.
$10,500–12,000 P(S)

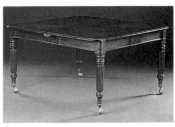

21 Years Ago ...

A William IV rosewood table, with chamfered pillar support and triform base, on carved claw feet and casters, 51¼in (130cm) diam. **S**

Twenty-one years ago this table would have been worth $500–550. A comparable example might now command a sum of $4,000–5,000. Functional items such as dining tables have remained consistently in demand. Circular dining tables are currently as popular as ever due to booming property prices and their space-efficient nature. The Brazilian rosewood veneers and pre-Victorian date of manufacture are an added bonus.

An early Victorian mahogany dining table, by John Howard, Oxford, the top extending on 8 pull-out lopers and 4 elliptical sections, c1840, 91in (231cm) diam extended.
$18,000–21,000 Hal

A Victorian mahogany dining table, with 2 extra leaves, c1860, 96¾in (246cm) extended.
$5,000–6,000 S(S)

A mid-Victorian mahogany D-end dining table, with 2 extra leaves, 95in (241.5cm) extended.
$2,500–3,000 L

A Victorian walnut dining table, the top opening to reveal 6 extra leaves, 196in (498cm) extended.
$13,000–16,000 P(Sc)

A Victorian mahogany wind-out dining table, the legs headed by scroll carving, with grape and vine carving to the knees, on hairy paw claw feet, with 3 extra leaves, c1860, 60in (152.5cm) long.
$6,500–8,000 Bon(C)

A George III-style mahogany two-pillar dining table, 19thC, 60in (152.5cm) long.
$1,500–1,700 DN(H)

A mahogany dining table, late 19thC, 95¾in (243cm) extended.
$2,300–3,000 L&E

A Victorian mahogany telescopic dining table, with one extra leaf, 94½in (240cm) extended.
$3,000–3,300 MEA

A mahogany dining table, by Maple & Co, the beaded and paterae-carved frieze on foliate, scroll and husk-decorated cabriole legs, late 19thC, 120in (305cm) extended.
$8,000–9,500 P

An American mahogany double-pedestal dining table, with 4 extra skirted leaves, 19thC, 154in (391cm) extended.
$8,000–9,500 NOA

LOCATE THE SOURCE
The source of each illustration in Miller's can be found by checking the code letters below each caption with the Key to Illustrations, pages 789–795.

An Adam-style mahogany three-section dining table, with scrolling foliate and urn-decorated friezes, on trailing husk-carved legs headed by paterae, early 20thC, 63¾in (162cm) long.
$2,000–2,500 P

DISPLAY TABLES

A Dutch marquetry display table, the glazed hinged top with trailing flowers in green, ivory and mother-of-pearl, on later base, late 18th/early 19thC, 41¼in (105cm) wide.
$1,200–1,400 P

A George IV Irish mahogany display table, with 9 glazed compartments, beaded borders and reeded scroll feet, 49in (124.5cm) diam.
$7,500–9,000 JAd

A late Victorian mahogany display table, the top with moulded scrolling glazing bars above glazed sides, 26¾in (68cm) diam.
$2,500–3,000 P(Sc)

A Louis XV-style kingwood and gilt-metal-mounted vitrine, the hinged top with a glazed insert within a cast border of entwined vines, c1880, 25½in (65cm) wide.
$3,800–4,000 Bon

An Edwardian satinwood and tulipwood crossbanded display table, with glazed sides containing a door, 17¾in (45cm) diam.
$2,300–3,000 P

An Edwardian fiddle-back mahogany and marquetry display table, with glazed top, inlaid with scrolling foliage and flowerheads, above a frieze decorated with classical urns, c1910, 24in (61cm) wide.
$1,700–2,000 Bon(C)

An Edwardian ebonized mahogany display table, the hinged cover and 4 sides with bevelled glass panels, 27in (68.5cm) wide.
$1,500–1,700 MEA

An Edwardian mahogany display table, with serpentine top, and shaped undertier, c1900, 24in (61cm) wide.
$800–1,000 BUSH

DRESSING TABLES

A George III mahogany dressing table, with a frieze drawer in the form of 3 dummy drawers enclosing a baize-lined slide, c1790, 39¼in (99.5cm) wide.
$4,000–5,000 S

A French tulipwood and purple heart dressing table, with easel mirror flanked by quarter-veneered rising panels, c1770, 30in (76cm) wide.
$5,000–6,000 B&L

▶ A George III gentleman's mahogany dressing table, the 2 hinged covers enclosing an adjustable mirror, 24in (61cm) wide closed.
$2,000–2,500 DN

A George III mahogany gentleman's dressing table/washstand, the hinged divided top enclosing a mirror surrounded by lidded compartments, the front with a dummy drawer above a true drawer, the lower concave section with a tambour cupboard door above a drawer, c1790, 26in (66cm) wide.
$2,500–3,200 Bon

A mahogany dressing table, with lift-up and fold-out top, fitted with a mirror and lidded compartments, the frieze with a slide, late 18thC, 32in (81.5cm) wide.
$3,500–4,000 HOK

A French mahogany dressing table, with a white and grey veined marble top, early 19thC, 35in (89cm) wide.
$4,000–4,500 P(Z)

A Biedermeier walnut, rosewood and parcel-gilt tilt-top toilet table, the top enclosing a mirror over a compartment with 2 hinged flaps enclosing a removable drawer, c1820, 37in (94cm) diam.
$9,000–10,000 S(Am)

A Federal mahogany carved and brass-inlaid dressing table, the cockbeaded mirror on scrolled acanthus leaf-carved supports, New York, c1825, 36¼in (92cm) wide.
$1,800–2,000 SK(B)

A William IV rosewood dressing table, after a design by T. King, the central frieze drawer fitted with a pen compartment, flanked by 2 small drawers, c1830, 42½in (108cm) wide.
$2,500–3,000 S

Thomas King was a London furniture designer who published some 15 pattern books between 1829 and 1839.

A walnut-veneered dressing chest, 19thC, 55in (139.5cm) wide.
$1,600–1,800 HOK

An American Renaissance revival walnut dresser, the marble top base with 3 drawers over a slipper drawer, c1865, 47in (119.5cm) wide.
$1,800–2,000 NOA

A Victorian walnut dressing table, the bowfront base with a frieze drawer, 47⅛in (120.5cm) wide.
$800–1,000 AH

An Edwardian mahogany pedestal dressing table, marquetry-inlaid with exotic timbers and etched ivory, 57in (145cm) wide.
$1,500–1,700 MEA

◄ A Victorian walnut dressing table, the bowfront base with a frieze drawer, 47⅛in (120.5cm) wide.
$800–1,000 AH

DROP-LEAF TABLES

A George II 'red walnut' double gateleg-action oval drop-leaf table, 78¼in (199cm) extended.
$10,000–11,500 P(E)

A George III mahogany wake table, 91in (231cm) long.
$5,200–5,800 B&B

An American mahogany drop-leaf table, Massachusetts, damaged, late 18thC, 47in (119.5cm) extended.
$8,000–9,000 B&B

A Federal cherrywood drop-leaf table, the spiral-carved tapering legs ending in ball feet, New England, damaged, 1820s, 45½in (115.5cm) long.
$500–600 SK(B)

An American French provincial-style walnut gateleg drop-leaf table, with scroll feet, early 19thC, 47¾in (121.5cm) wide.
$1,600–1,800 NOA

An early Victorian mahogany telescopic drop-leaf table, with 2 extra leaves, c1840, 48in (122cm) long.
$3,500–4,000 Bon(C)

DRUM TABLES

A George III mahogany drum table, the leather-inset top above 4 shallow drawers interspaced by 4 dummy drawers, 51in (129.5cm) diam.
$11,500–13,000 B

A Regency rosewood library drum table, with a leather-lined top over an arrangement of 4 frieze drawers alternating with simulated drawers, 50½in (127cm) diam.
$5,000–5,600 HYD

A mahogany drum table, the moulded leather-lined top above an alternating arrangement of 4 drawers and 4 dummy frieze drawers, base possibly associated, early 19thC, 44in (112cm) diam.
$5,500–6,500 S

An Italian neo-classical drum table, possibly Lucca, with 4 drawers and alternating dummy drawers, painted in dark green and highlighted with gilding, altered, early 19thC, 42½in (108cm) diam.
$16,000–18,000 S(NY)

◄ An American classical mahogany drum table, the gilt-embossed leather-inset top above 4 long drawers, c1820, 51in (129.5cm) diam.
$4,000–5,000 B&B

A Maltese walnut and fruitwood drum table, the top segmentally veneered and centred with a Maltese cross, the frieze with 4 drawers and 4 dummy drawers, early 19thC, 18¼in (46.5cm) diam.
$4,200–4,500 HAM

An Edwardian brass-mounted rosewood rent table, in the style of Thomas Sheraton, with replacement gilt tooled-leather top, c1900, 45½in (115.5cm) diam.
$3,500–4,000 NOA

GAMES TABLES

A Queen Anne walnut triple-top games and tea table, the top enclosing a baize-lined interior with candlestand corners, counter wells and a backgammon board, fitted with a drawer, c1710, 36in (91.5cm) wide.
$16,000–20,000 S

A Regency rosewood and specimen wood inlaid games table, the divided top enclosing a games board centred by a painted panel of a Jewish moneylender and forming the game 'The Jew', enclosing a leather-embossed backgammon board, 22in (56cm) wide.
$5,500–6,500 P(S)

A Victorian black lacquer and gilt games table, the top inset with a mother-of-pearl chess board, the moulded frieze with a drawer, c1850, 24½in (62cm) wide.
$800–1,000 S(S)

A late George III mahogany games table, the reversible top with a satinwood chequerboard and cribbage scorer enclosing a backgammon board above one drawer, on square tapering legs, 18in (45.5cm) square.
$2,800–3,200 DN

A Regency mahogany games table, the centre of the top sliding to reveal a leather-lined backgammon board and reversing to form a chess board within a purple morocco leather border, flanked by D-shaped compartments with hinged tops, the frieze with gilt-metal banding, 51¼in (130cm) long.
$20,000–25,000 P(O)

A French mahogany games table, the leather-centred writing top lifting to reveal a backgammon board, c1830, 30in (76cm) wide.
$5,500–6,500 NOA

An American mahogany games table, the fold-over top above a conforming crossbanded apron with figured maple panels, c1825, 36in (91.5cm) wide.
$2,000–2,500 NOA

◄ An American Empire mahogany games table, with fold-over top, mid-19thC, 34½in (87.5cm) wide.
$650–800 NOA

A mahogany chess table, the simulated glass top decorated with marbleized and gilt squares on a green and gilt background, on a turned baluster column, c1860, 18in (45.5cm) square.
$1,000–1,200 HUB

LIBRARY TABLES

A George IV rosewood library table, with 2 frieze drawers, on stop-reeded baluster supports with gadrooned collars, 56in (142cm) wide.
$4,000–5,000 Oli

A Victorian mahogany library table, the top with a panel of tooled-leather and containing 3 drawers to each side, 70½in (179cm) wide.
$5,000–5,500 P

A mahogany library table, the top veneered with figured segments centred by a marquetry panel within broad rosewood crossbanding, c1850, 50in (127cm) wide.
$5,200–6,000 S

A Victorian mahogany library table, with a leather-lined top, fitted with 6 frieze drawers, 60in (152.5cm) wide.
$2,200–2,500 TMA

A Gothic revival oak library table, with a single drawer, decorated with acanthus leaves and fleur-de-lys, c1880, 54in (137cm) wide.
$2,300–2,500 HAC

A Victorian walnut library table, with 3 frieze drawers, on barley-twist supports joined by an X-form stretcher, 59¾in (152cm) wide.
$8,000–8,500 P(NE)

NESTS OF TABLES

A nest of 3 George III mahogany tables, the beaded tops cross-banded in kingwood, c1800, largest 19¾in (50cm) wide.
$5,200–5,800 S

A set of Regency rosewood quartetto tables, the tops veneered with amboyna and crossbanded with zebrawood and satinwood, 19in (48.5cm) wide.
$14,500–16,000 TEN

◄ A nest of 3 amboyna tables, the crossbanded tops with applied ebony beading, the metal X-supports of a later date, c1840, 19½in (50cm) wide.
$4,000–4,500 B&L

► A set of George III-style satinwood quartetto tables, the tops each inlaid with an oval panel and crossbanded in rosewood, c1910, 20in (51cm) wide.
$6,500–8,000 S

A nest of 3 Regency rosewood and maple crossbanded tables, in the manner of Gillows, c1820, largest 15½in (39.5cm) wide.
$2,800–3,200 Bon

OCCASIONAL TABLES

A Continental painted table, the shaped apron centred by shells, 18thC, 33½in (85cm) wide.
$1,300–1,600 HOK

An early Victorian papier mâché decorated occasional table, the tilt-top painted with country folk harvesting apples, heightened in gilt, 22½in (57cm) diam.
$900–1,000 P

A bird's-eye maple occasional table, the shaped top with parquetry banding, the frieze with applied giltwood ribbons, raised on 4 scrolled and leaf-carved supports with giltwood flowerheads, 19thC, 42in (106.5cm) wide.
$1,800–2,000 AH

An ash and rootwood table, supported on ebonized rootwork, early 19thC, 27in (68.5cm) wide.
$5,500–6,500 S

A Sorrento fruitwood, marquetry and walnut occasional table, the snap-top inlaid with a central landscape depicting a town with a foliate surround and panels of rustic figures with a floral garland border, with a label 'Mignon Ebéniste', 19thC, 31½in (80cm) diam.
$5,500–6,500 P

A William IV rosewood pedestal table, the top with a beaded border, 18in (45.5cm) wide.
$2,800–3,200 P(G)

◄ A late Victorian mahogany and boxwood-inlaid occasional table, c1890, 24in (61cm) wide.
$1,000–1,200 STK

A Regency rosewood table, the top crossbanded and inlaid with brass stringing and stars, c1815, 21in (53.5cm) wide.
$7,500–8,500 S

A Biedermeier walnut oval occasional table, the crossbanded frieze with a drawer, the supports in the form of Doric columns with ebonized capitals, mid-19thC, 30in (76cm) wide.
$2,200–2,500 SLN

A Torquay specimen marble table top, with a black ground, the central cream-ground roundel centred with a cruciform motif, on a later stand, c1860, 36½in (92.5cm) diam.
$10,000–11,500 HAM

Known as Torquay madrepore work, this piece is thought to be by Blacklers of the Royal Marble Works of St Mary's Church, Torquay, or perhaps from another small workshop in the area. There were several local firms that, from the 1830s onwards, manufactured furniture using marble from south Devon. The county is geologically very rich, and has over 23 known varieties of marble.

PEMBROKE TABLES

A George III mahogany Pembroke table, crossbanded with string inlay, the frieze drawer with brass handle, 35½in (90cm) wide.
$1,300–1,600 AH

A George III mahogany Pembroke table, the top with shaped flaps above a frieze drawer, c1765, 39½in (100.5cm) wide.
$13,000–14,500 S

This table relates to a design by Thomas Chippendale in *The Gentleman and Cabinet-Maker's Director*, first published in 1754.

A mahogany or 'red walnut' Pembroke table, with hinged top over a frieze drawer, mid-18thC, 43¾in (111cm) extended.
$1,200–1,400 P

A George III mahogany Pembroke table, on tapering legs with spade feet, 36in (91.5cm) wide.
$400–500 E

A Georgian French-style satinwood Pembroke table, crossbanded in rosewood with boxwood line, with a drawer at either end, all 4 legs pulling out to support the top, 33in (84cm) wide.
$7,000–8,000 B

A George III mahogany Pembroke table, the well-figured veneered top with serpentine flaps, probably associated, restored, stamped 'W. Williamson & Sons, Guildford', 39½in (100.5cm) wide.
$11,500–13,000 S(NY)

William Williamson & Sons of Guildford, Surrey are recorded as cabinet-makers and sellers of second-hand furniture, 1790–1840.

Miller's Compares

I A George III mahogany Pembroke table, the top inlaid with pollard oak, boxwood-strung and crossbanded, the burr-oak frieze drawer with later brass handles, the veneered legs banded in mahogany, c1780, 38¼in (97cm) wide.
$40,000–44,000 S

II A George III mahogany Pembroke table, the double-banded top above a frieze drawer, inlaid with stringing and headed by inlaid panels, on square tapered legs ending in caps and casters, c1790, 39in (99cm) wide.
$5,200–5,600 S

Item I is particularly desirable because of its superb golden colour and original patina, which is similar in appearance to satinwood. Moreover, the chamfered square legs are associated with the Chippendale period, suggesting the piece may be earlier than the c1780 date quoted in the catalogue description. In contrast, Item II is of a dark mahogany colour and does not retain a high degree of original patina. A further basis for speculation is that Item I shares characteristics with a recorded Pembroke table by the renowned cabinet-maker Henry Kettle. These features include the prominent use of a central veneered panel, the rectangular panelled inlay to the leaves and the ovolo moulded edges to both tops. Furniture that is attributable to a particular cabinet-maker generally commands a premium price.

An Edwardian neo-classical-style satinwood Pembroke table, painted with panels of putti and female portrait medallions surrounded by ribbon-tied floral swags, 36¼in (92cm) extended.
$2,500–3,000 P

READING TABLES

A William IV rosewood bed table, with double reading slopes supported by ratchets on an adjustable column, 36¼in (92cm) wide.
$2,200–2,500 P(G)

A William IV rosewood reading table, the veneered top with a lidded compartment and a pair of flaps on easels, a detachable book rest moulding, the height adjustment on a turned stem, 35in (89cm) wide.
$1,600–2,000 WW

A mahogany reading table, the top crossbanded in rosewood, early 19thC, 23in (58.5cm) wide.
$650–800 RBB

SERVING TABLES

A George III mahogany breakfront serving table, with a fluted frieze centred by a draped swag, 90¼in (229cm) wide.
$25,000–30,000 P(Sc)

A George III mahogany serpentine-front serving table, c1780, 54½in (138.5cm) wide.
$20,000–24,000 MCA

A Louis XV provincial mahogany serving table, with hinged top, each side with a pull-out wooden slide, the platform fitted with slides at each side, with frieze drawer and apron, altered, 33in (84cm) wide.
$16,000–18,000 S(NY)

An Irish mahogany bowfront serving table, with a reeded frieze and turned legs, c1815, 60in (152.5cm) wide.
$3,500–4,500 GKe

A George IV mahogany serving table, the three-quarter galleried top above a frieze drawer, raised on cluster column legs, 40¾in (103.5cm) wide.
$8,000–9,000 S(NY)

A William IV mahogany serving table, with a leaf-moulded frieze raised on front spiral-reeded leaf-capped legs, 58in (147.5cm) wide.
$6,000–6,500 MEA

◄ An Adam-style mahogany bowfront serving table, with beaded decoration and 2 drawers, the pierced brass back surmounted by finials, early 20thC, 30¾in (78cm) wide.
$9,500–10,500 P

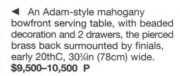

► A Victorian mahogany serpentine-fronted serving table, with carved back and frieze, raised on C-scroll cabriole legs, 106in (269cm) wide.
$6,500–7,200 MEA

SIDE TABLES

A George III mahogany side table, the frieze drawer with original brass swan-neck handle, 36in (91.5cm) wide.
$1,200–1,400 WW

An Irish satinwood side table, by W. Moore of Dublin, inlaid with panels of amboyna and tulipwood, c1770, 45in (114.5cm) wide.
$15,000–18,000 GKe

William Moore learned his craft under the London cabinet-makers John Mayhew and William Ince. He moved to Dublin in the early 1780s and advertised for commissions in the local evening paper, 'to inform those who may want inlaid work, that by his close attention to business and instructions to his men, he has brought the manufacture to such perfection, to be able to sell for almost one half his original prices . . .'. The scheme was obviously highly successful as Moore soon moved to a more desirable address in Capel Street where he remained until his death in 1815.

A George III gilt side table, the scagliola marble top in a geometric cube design, damaged, c1775 and later, 41in (104cm) wide.
$16,000–18,000 Hal

The front and back rails of this table appear to have been reduced in length.

A George III Irish mahogany side table, the ogee arched apron with a central shell flanked by flowerheads, 41in (104cm) wide.
$16,000–18,000 P

A mahogany side table, the frieze fitted with 2 drawers, mid-19thC, 42in (106.5cm) wide.
$900–1,000 HOK

A Dutch mahogany, walnut and inlaid demi-lune side table, with crossbanded top, the frieze with drawer and dentil ornament, late 18thC, 29in (73.5cm) wide.
$2,500–3,000 P

A Dutch mahogany and marquetry-inlaid side table, the tray top centred by a boxwood oval floral motif and 4 floral panels, above 2 pull-out candle slides and a cockbeaded frieze drawer, later stamped 'Edwards & Roberts', late 18th/early 19thC, 33in (84cm) wide.
$2,000–2,200 Hal

A William IV mahogany side table, with 2 dummy drawers, and one to the side, 27¼in (69cm) wide.
$2,750–3,000 P(S)

A Victorian mahogany side table, with plain gallery back and 2 frieze drawers, 42in (106.5cm) wide.
$600–700 HBC

SOFA TABLES

A Sheraton rosewood sofa table, with satinwood and boxwood banding, with 2 short and 2 dummy drawers, late 18thC, 60½in (153.5cm) extended.
$55,000–65,000 MCA

This piece sold well in excess of expectations due to its excellent, unrestored condition and the fact that it was new to the market.

A Regency rosewood, satinwood-crossbanded and inlaid sofa table, with 2 frieze drawers, 65½in (166.5cm) extended.
$6,500–8,000 P

A George IV mahogany and crossbanded sofa table, with one frieze and one dummy drawer, damaged, c1825, 62½in (159cm) extended.
$6,500–8,000 S(S)

An inlaid mahogany sofa table, with bird's-eye maple crossbanding, the 2 frieze drawers with 2 opposing dummy drawers, late 19thC, 51½in (131cm) extended.
$4,000–4,500 MEA

A coromandel sofa table, inlaid with brass lines, with a pair of frieze drawers flanked by dummy drawers, on twin ring turned end supports joined by a curved stretcher, restored, early 19thC, 58¼in (148cm) wide.
$3,000–3,500 P

A Regency rosewood and brass-inlaid sofa table, the top crossbanded in calamander and outlined with boxwood stringing, the frieze fitted with opposing brass-inlaid drawers, on shaped end supports joined by a scrolled stretcher, c1815, 72¼in (183.5cm) extended.
$16,000–20,000 S

A Biedermeier mahogany sofa table, the shaped top with 2 shaped drop-leaves and a drawer, on scrolled foliate feet joined by a stretcher with a central knob finial, mid-19thC, 26½in (67.5cm) wide.
$800–1,000 S(Am)

LOCATE THE SOURCE
The source of each illustration in Miller's can be found by checking the code letters below each caption with the Key to Illustrations, pages 789–795.

A Regency rosewood sofa table, the top crossbanded in calamander and kingwood above 2 frieze drawers, c1815, 58¾in (149cm) extended.
$20,000–25,000 S

A Regency mahogany sofa table, with satinwood crossbanding and line inlay, the frieze with 2 dummy and 2 drawers, replacement brass handles, restored, 48¾in (124cm) wide.
$11,500–13,000 P(WM)

A rosewood and satinwood sofa table, 19thC, 54¾in (139cm) wide.
$2,300–2,600 OL

A Sheraton revival mahogany sofa table, the 'plum pudding'-veneered top crossbanded in satinwood with boxwood and ebony stringing, above 2 frieze drawers, stamped 'Edwards & Roberts', late 19thC, 59in (150cm) wide.
$2,800–3,200 DN(H)

'Plum pudding' is a type of figuring in some veneers, produced by dark oval spots in the wood, found particularly in mahogany.

SUTHERLAND TABLES

A Victorian Sutherland table, with turned end supports, c1860, 34½in (87.5cm) wide.
$950–1,000 HUB

A Victorian burr walnut Sutherland table, the top with boxwood stringing and marquetry, 41¼in (105cm) diam.
$1,300–1,500 DN

A Victorian figured-walnut Sutherland table, inlaid with satinwood stringing and swagged medallions, 25½in (65cm) wide.
$1,200–1,400 M

A mid-Victorian walnut Sutherland table, the twist top above elliptical leaves, 37in (94cm) wide.
$1,000–1,200 Bon(W)

A Victorian burr walnut Sutherland table, with a quarter-veneered top, 46½in (118cm) extended.
$600–650 HYD

An Edwardian satinwood and ebony inlaid mahogany Sutherland table, 26in (66cm) wide.
$350–400 HAX

TEA TABLES

A William and Mary walnut tea table, the cross- and feather-banded fold-over top enclosing a veneered interior inlaid with line decoration, the frieze centred by a drawer, flanked by dummy drawers and candle slides, the stretcher with an inlaid star, on braganza feet, c1695, 30¾in (78cm) wide.
$18,000–20,000 S

▶ A George III mahogany tea table, the fold-over top supported by a double gateleg action above a frieze drawer, 40in (101.5cm) wide.
$1,600–2,000 S(S)

A George I walnut tea table, with double-hinged top, c1720, 34½in (87.5cm) wide.
$4,500–5,200 Bon

A George II mahogany demi-lune tea table, with fold-over top and interior well, 36in (91.5cm) wide.
$3,500–4,000 M

A George III satinwood, tulipwood-banded and ebony-strung demi-lune tea table, on square tapered legs, restored, 38¼in (97cm) wide.
$4,000–5,000 TEN

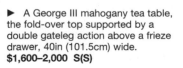

An Irish mahogany fold-over top tea table, the shaped apron centred by a shell, 18thC, 35½in (90cm) wide.
$2,500–2,750 HOK

A Federal inlaid mahogany reverse serpentine fold-over tea table, inlaid with satinwood and boxwood stringing, late 18thC, 35in (89cm) wide.
$3,000–3,500 SLN

A Regency mahogany fold-over top tea table, the turned central column raised on 4 scrolling legs terminating in carved lion-paw feet, 36in (91.5cm) wide.
$2,100–2,500 Mit

A George IV mahogany tea table, with swivel top over a volute-carved frieze, 35½in (90cm) wide.
$2,100–2,500 TEN

An early Victorian rosewood folding tea table, with leaf and scroll-carved frieze, c1840, 36½in (92.5cm) wide.
$2,500–3,000 AH

A Victorian rosewood tea table, the serpentine fold-over top above a scroll-carved frieze, 36½in (92.5cm) wide.
$1,200–1,400 P(HSS)

◄ A late Victorian rosewood tea table, the top with a central marquetry roundel, with 4 circular stands revolving on the ring-turned legs, 20in (51cm) diam.
$1,300–1,500 DN(H)

► An Edwardian gilt-brass-mounted mahogany tea table, with frieze drawer, c1900, 17¾in (45cm) wide.
$1,500–1,800 NOA

TRIPOD TABLES

A George II mahogany tripod table, the pierced carved gallery inlaid with brass stringing, the stem with acanthus leaf-carved baluster section on overscrolled tripod base carved with leaves and paterae, c1755, 23in (58.5cm) diam.
$8,000–10,000 S

A George III mahogany tripod table, with piecrust carved hinged top, on a turned stem and cabriole legs, with pad feet, 20½in (52cm) wide.
$2,300–2,600 Bon(C)

A George III mahogany tilt-top table, on a stop fluted column and 3 splayed legs with pad feet, damaged, 24½in (62cm) diam.
$1,200–1,400 DN

A George III mahogany supper table, the carved top later decorated with foliage and central stylized flowers, on baluster turned column, 24in (61cm) diam.
$950–1,000 HYD

21 Years Ago ...

A George II brass-inlaid ebonized supper table, 29in (74cm) diam. **S**

Twenty-one years ago this supper table was valued at $2,000–2,500. Today it could realize $35,000–50,000, or even more. Its considerable increase in value follows recent discoveries relating to English furniture of this type and subsequent exhibitions in Leeds and London during 1993 and 1994. Further to this research this table can be identified with a group of furniture now attributed to the German immigrant cabinet-maker, Frederick Hintz.

A Victorian mahogany tripod table, the marquetry-inlaid top with a central leaf design, 17in (43cm) diam.
$550–650 HAX

A William IV mahogany and crossbanded tripod table, 30in (76cm) wide.
$1,000–1,200 AAV

An American cherrywood dished-top candlestand, damaged, late 18thC, 18¼in (46.5cm) diam.
$2,300–2,600 SK(B)

A Victorian mahogany tripod table, 33in (84cm) diam.
$250–300 Doc

A mahogany tripod table, c1820, 22in (56cm) diam.
$1,800–2,000 OCH

A Victorian walnut tripod table, with marble inset top, on spiral fluted turned stem, c1850, 17¾in (45cm) diam.
$2,000–2,500 S

Did You Know?

Tripod tables were introduced in England during the 1730s, and were particularly popular in the Chippendale period. Most were made of solid wood, although some later examples were veneered. Tops are usually circular with a tilting action, often fixed by means of 2 bearers and held in place with a brass catch. Some have a 'birdcage' support, where the whole mechanism fits onto the top of the pedestal. A peg through the stem allows the top to rotate, tilt, or be fixed in place.

TWO-TIER TABLES

A pair of parquetry-inlaid two-tier tables, mid-19thC, 19½in (49.5cm) diam.
$8,000–9,000 S(NY)

A pair of Louis XVI-style ormolu-mounted mahogany two-tier tables, the marble tops with pierced gilt-metal galleries and a frieze drawer below, late 19thC, 27in (68.5cm) wide.
$5,000–5,000 TMA

An Edwardian mahogany two-tier tray top occasional table, the legs joined by an X-stretcher, 27in (68.5cm) diam.
$1,200–1,300 SWO

A Continental brass and painted porcelain folding tea table, the 2 porcelain plaque shelves decorated with birds and flowers, late 19thC, 25in (63.5cm) wide.
$8,000–9,000 SK

Tripod Tables • Two-Tier Tables • FURNITURE 145

WORK TABLES

A George III brass-inlaid mahogany bowfront work table, with 2 drawers, 22½in (57cm) wide.
$2,500–3,000 Bea(E)

A mahogany work table, the top with twin flaps over 2 drawers, 19thC, 21in (53.5cm) wide.
$350–420 TMA

A Victorian walnut needle-work table, the lift-up top enclosing a fitted interior, 19in (48.5cm) diam.
$600–650 HAX

A Regency rosewood work and games table, the sliding top inlaid on the reverse for chess with an inner tray and sliding well, 18in (45.5cm) wide.
$4,000–4,500 MAT

A black-lacquered work box, with hinged top, decorated with gilt foliage and floral-painted vignettes, 19thC, 17¼in (44cm) diam.
$1,400–1,600 TEN

A late Victorian Sheraton revival mahogany work table, with boxwood and ebony chequer-stringing and overpainted with a portrait of a lady, 16in (40.5cm) wide.
$750–800 DN

◀ An Edwardian mahogany sewing table, 30in (76cm) high.
$550–650 OTT

A French Empire mahogany work table, with gilt-metal mounts, the hinged lid with a mirror over 2 drawers and a dummy drawer, early 19thC, 21¼in (54cm) wide.
$3,200–3,500 HYD

A Victorian walnut work table, the burr-veneered hinged top enclosing a silk-lined interior, with a foliage scroll-carved frieze, 18in (45.5cm) wide.
$1,200–1,400 WW

▶ An Edwardian inlaid and painted satinwood work table, c1910, 12½in (32cm) diam.
$400–500 BAB

An American mahogany work table, the top with hinged ends above 2 drawers, replaced brasses, damaged, c1815, 25¼in (64cm) wide.
$2,300–2,600 SK(B)

A William IV rosewood work table, the fold-over top with a leather writing surface, frieze drawer and deep pleated well, 20¾in (52.5cm) wide.
$1,000–1,200 AH

Facts in Brief

- Introduced after 1750, particularly in France and England, as convenient tables for ladies to store needlework accessories.
- Simple examples have a hinged top revealing compartments, with a sliding pleated fabric workbag beneath for the storage of materials.
- More sophisticated tables have a sliding firescreen at the back and sometimes the additional function of a writing or games table.
- The fashion for Berlin woolwork during the 19thC helped to sustain the demand for these tables.
- During the 19thC, examples were produced in a variety of styles and mediums including Sheraton revival and boulle.

WRITING TABLES

A walnut and marquetry writing table, with crossbanded top and fitted interior, the legs pulling forward to support the fall-forward top, 17thC, 33in (84cm) wide.
$10,000–11,500 B

A George II 'red walnut' writing table, the top with mitred veneer above cross-grained shaped sides with a drawer at either end, 33in (84cm) wide.
$5,500–6,500 B

A George III satinwood and marquetry lady's writing table, after a design by Thomas Sheraton, with a green leather-lined writing surface, the stepped wings each with inward swinging hinged drawers, the arched back with a mirror panel, c1795, 36in (91.5cm) wide.
$12,000–13,000 S

This table was designed in such a way that the user could sit in comfort before the fire, the upper section serving as a protective screen. As Sheraton himself expressed it in an explanatory note, 'The convenience of this table is, that a lady, when writing at it, may both receive the benefit of the fire, and have her face screened from its scorching heat'. The construction of the table is typical of Sheraton's work, incorporating a complex system of pulleys, weights and springs. The form and decoration reflect the continuing influence of the neo-classical style pioneered by Robert Adam and his contemporaries in the mid- to late 18thC.

A George III mahogany kidney-shaped writing table, the top with reading slope, c1805, 36¾in (93.5cm) wide.
$3,000–3,300 S

A Louis XV-style lady's writing table, with inset red leather top, banded with scrolling inlaid vines, damaged, early 19thC, 40in (101.5cm) wide.
$2,500–3,000 ROS

A Regency mahogany writing table, with 2 drop-leaves, inlaid top and frieze folding outwards to form lopers, 56in (142cm) extended.
$10,000–11,500 B

A George IV parcel-gilt mahogany writing table, with 4 drawers below and 5 matching dummy drawers to reverse, 40¾in (103.5cm) wide.
$5,500–6,500 HAM

A Victorian burr walnut writing table, with line-inlaid decoration, stationery compartment, and a frieze drawer, 42in (106.5cm) wide.
$2,800–3,200 Bri

A Victorian walnut and marquetry writing table, the leather-inset top with pierced brass gallery, over a frieze containing 2 drawers and decorated with masks and scrolled line marquetry, 48in (122cm) wide.
$2,500–3,200 Bon(C)

A mahogany writing table, with central slope, the frieze with 2 sliding writing slopes flanked by a drawer to either side, 19thC, 42in (106.5cm) wide.
$3,000–3,500 AH

▶ A Louis XV-style walnut writing table, late 19thC, 24in (61cm) wide.
$1,600–2,000 ROS

TEAPOYS

A Regency rosewood and brass-inlaid teapoy, the hinged lid enclosing a fitted interior of 4 lidded caddies and recesses for mixing bowls, c1815, 15in (38cm) wide.
$2,500–3,000 Bon

A George IV mahogany teapoy, the interior fitted with 2 deep lidded compartments flanking a vacant recess, 18in (45.5cm) wide.
$650–800 L

An early Victorian rosewood teapoy, the hinged top enclosing 4 caddies and 2 circular recesses, 16in (40.5cm) wide.
$800–900 DN

A William IV burr elm teapoy, the hinged cavetto lid enclosing a fitted interior, with a label 'J. London Cabinet & Chair Maker, Upholsterer & Undertaker, 81 Stokes Croft, Bristol', 18½in (47cm) wide.
$2,800–3,200 TEN

James London is recorded as trading in Bristol from 1827 to 1839.

TORCHERES

A pair of George III mahogany torchères, each octagonal top with a fret-pierced gallery, on a slender moulded tri-form column, 49¾in (126.5cm) high.
$32,000–35,000 L

These Chippendale-style torchères are in excellent condition and were of particular interest because they were consigned by a long established local family.

A mahogany spiral pillar torchère, c1840, 60in (152.5cm) high.
$300–330 LCA

A Swiss baroque walnut torchère, with ebony veneer, c1740, 37¾in (96cm) high.
$1,600–2,000 S(Z)

A George III carved giltwood torchère, in the manner of Robert Adam, the vase carved with leaves, flutes and mouldings set with rams'-head masks supporting swags and tassels, c1775, 20in (51cm) diam.
$16,000–20,000 S

◄ An oak torchère, c1880, 45in (114.5cm) high.
$500–550 HAC

► A pair of oak torchères, with leaf-carved capitals and columns carved with leaves, each plinth base with carved winged putti masks and scrolls, 19thC, 49½in (125.5cm) high.
$1,000–1,100 DN

An ebony torchère, 19thC, 40in (101.5cm) high.
$550–650 SPa

TOWEL RAILS

A Victorian mahogany towel rail, 27¼in (69cm) wide.
$250–300 SPU

A Victorian mahogany towel rail, 26in (66cm) wide.
$100–120 CaC

An Edwardian mahogany towel rail, 33½in (85cm) wide.
$250–300 COLL

TRAYS

A George III *tôle peinte* tray-on-stand, the gallery painted with vine leaves in gilt on a black ground, the later carved giltwood stand on turned tapered and fluted legs, c1790, 28in (71cm) wide.
$5,000–6,000 S

A George III mahogany butler's tray, with hinged folding sides and pierced carrying handles, on a trestle base, early 19thC, 28in (71cm) wide.
$800–1,000 Bon(C)

A papier mâché tray-on-stand, by Henry Clay, decorated with a broad band of scrolling gilt leaves and masks on a black ground, with a modern stand, early 19thC, 27½in (70cm) wide.
$5,000–6,000 S

A mahogany butler's tray, with X-shaped stand, 19thC, 31½in (80cm) wide.
$750–900 HOK

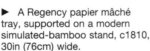

► A Regency papier mâché tray, supported on a modern simulated-bamboo stand, c1810, 30in (76cm) wide.
$3,000–3,500 CAT

An Edwardian kidney-shaped marquetry-inlaid tray, 22in (56cm) wide.
$500–600 AnSh

A pair of Victorian papier mâché trays-on-stands, each tray decorated with birds, flowers and leaves on a black ground, the simulated bamboo stands decorated in black and gilt, stamped 'Jennens & Bettridge, London', c1840, 26in (66cm) wide.
$11,500–13,000 S

Papier Mâché

- First used in France during 17thC, the term derives from the French for pulped paper.
- Developed and patented in Britain as 'paperware' by Birmingham furniture-maker Henry Clay from 1772, followed by Jennens & Bettridge in early 19thC.
- Papier mâché furniture was often japanned and decorated with painted floral designs, mother-of-pearl and gilding.
- It is easily damaged, and repair can be costly.

WARDROBES

A Flemish walnut wardrobe, the moulded panel doors with iron hinges and lockplate, enclosing a single shelf, on turned squat legs and compressed bun feet, damaged, late 17th/early 18thC, 65in (165cm) wide.
$3,500–4,500 Hal

A Continental neo-classical fruitwood and parcel-gilt armoire, the outset ends on free-standing ebonized supports headed by gilt-metal capitals, early 19thC, 66in (167.5cm) wide.
$11,500–13,000 S(NY)

21 Years Ago ...

A Dutch rosewood and ebony armoire, mid-17thC, 72in (183cm) wide. **S**

Twenty-one years ago this armoire was valued at $6,000–6,500. It is difficult to conceive it commanding a sum much higher than $8,000–11,500 in today's market, which does not represent a good investment. The possibilities for housing bulky furniture of this type today are limited and consequently so are its prospects of significantly appreciating in value.

A William IV mahogany gentleman's wardrobe, the central section with 2 doors and 2 short and 3 long drawers flanked by 2 further doors enclosing hanging space, 96in (244cm) wide.
$3,500–4,000 P(S)

A William IV mahogany double wardrobe, with central cupboard and drawers, c1830, 93in (236cm) wide.
$8,000–9,500 OOLA

An Adam revival satinwood and painted wardrobe, of serpentine breakfront form, the 2 central doors with 2 short and 3 long drawers below, flanked by mirrored doors enclosing hanging space, c1890, 83½in (212cm) wide.
$7,500–8,000 TEN

Miller's Compares

I A mahogany and walnut-veneered wardrobe, 19thC, 74¾in (190cm) wide.
$2,200–2,500 HOK

II A mahogany breakfront wardrobe, the mirror door enclosing pull-out shelves and drawers flanked by 2 panelled doors, mid-19thC, 89in (226cm) wide.
$750–900 HOK

At first glance these two wardrobes appear quite similar in style. However, features such as the partial figured walnut veneers and reed-moulded plinth of item I are indicative of its superior quality. The relative rarity of walnut coupled with its greater desirability would account for the comparatively high price. In addition, the compact proportions of item I give it a wider appeal as it is more easily accommodated.

An Edwardian breakfront satinwood-veneered wardrobe, with chequer inlay, the moulded cornice with inlaid frieze and mahogany lines, the 2 panelled doors marquetry-inlaid with flowers, above 4 graduated drawers flanked by 2 mirrored doors enclosing hanging space, 82¼in (209cm) wide.
$2,000–2,500 P(Sc)

WASHSTANDS

A George III mahogany corner washstand, the back with cut-out handles above bowl and soap reservoirs, the shelf stretcher fitted with one real and one dummy drawer, c1780, 23in (58.5cm) wide.
$6,000–7,000 S

An American inlaid mahogany washstand, the splashboard above a quarter-round shelf and pierced top below, the satinwood skirt centring a small drawer, damaged, c1800, 23in (58.5cm) wide.
$6,000–6,500 SK(B)

A George III mahogany bowfront washstand, the raised back with shaped hand-holes and shell motif inlay, with 2 short drawers decorated with satinwood stringing, 27in (68.5cm) wide.
$4,500–5,000 RBB

A Federal mahogany washstand, the shaped splashboard with 2 quarter-round shelves above a pierced top, over a shelf and cockbeaded drawer, damaged, Massachusetts, c1815, 20in (51cm) wide.
$700–800 SK(B)

◄ A late George III mahogany washstand, crossbanded and ebony strung, with a dummy drawer and a short drawer above a panelled cupboard door, 16in (40.5cm) wide.
$500–600 Bon(W)

A George III mahogany washstand, the divided top enclosing recesses, with a dummy frieze drawer above a cupboard and a drawer beneath, 17in (43cm) wide.
$400–500 L

A George III mahogany washstand, fitted for a basin, with a drawer below, c1800, 14in (35.5cm) square.
$800–900 ANT

An American tiger maple and bird's-eye maple washstand, on ring-turned legs, damaged, c1825, 21¾in (55.5cm) wide.
$1,200–1,400 SK(B)

An early Victorian mahogany kneehole washstand, with 4 drawers and a dummy drawer, 42in (106.5cm) wide.
$1,000–1,200 P(F)

► A late Victorian mahogany washstand with a ceramic washbasin, printed in blue with poppy sprays, 24in (61cm) diam.
$450–520 MSW

WHATNOTS

A late Georgian mahogany canterbury/whatnot, with reading slope top, an open tier and drawer below, and a three-division music rack under, 24½in (62cm) wide.
$2,800–3,200 P(G)

A late George III mahogany whatnot, with a drawer above 3 concave-fronted shelves, 19½in (49.5cm) wide.
$2,000–2,500 Bea(E)

A Regency mahogany whatnot, c1830, 18in (45.5cm) wide.
$4,000–5,000 SPU

A late George III mahogany whatnot, with a galleried upper tier above a cupboard enclosed by 2 doors, with a drawer at the base, 16¾in (42.5cm) wide.
$2,000–2,500 DN

A Victorian mahogany whatnot, with 3 drawers to the base, 22½in (57cm) wide.
$2,200–2,500 P(S)

An early Victorian mahogany four-tier whatnot, with bobbin-turned supports and a drawer to the base, 48in (122cm) high.
$1,200–1,400 LAY

21 Years Ago ...

A Regency mahogany whatnot, with ring-turned supports joining the 3 cane tiers, 22in (56cm) wide. **L**

Twenty-one years ago this whatnot was valued at $520–600. Regency whatnots have held their value well, showing a steady growth in prices over the past twenty years. Their easy mobility and convenient size has ensured consistent demand particularly in metropolitan markets. This example could be expected to raise keen interest due to the rare feature of cane instead of solid shelves and its practical deep drawer. Consequently, it might now possibly reach a sum of $4,000–5,500 at auction.

An early Victorian mahogany whatnot, surmounted with urn finials above 6 shelves with spiral reeded supports, c1840, 22in (56cm) wide.
$2,000–2,300 MEA

An early Victorian burr walnut whatnot, with carved gallery and side supports, a drawer to the base, 26½in (67.5cm) wide.
$4,500–5,000 BERA

▶ A Victorian figured-walnut whatnot, inlaid with boxwood scrolls and stringing, the raised back with a shelf surmounted by an arched mirror, 41in (104cm) wide.
$1,300–1,500 DD

WINDOW SEATS

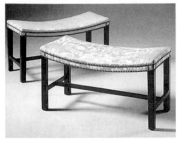

A pair of George III mahogany window seats, with over-upholstered saddle-shaped seats, late 18thC, 33in (84cm) wide.
$14,000–15,500 S(NY)

A George III simulated rosewood window seat, the upholstered seat and scrolled arms covered in nailed damask, late 18thC, 44½in (113cm) wide.
$4,500–5,200 S

A George III white-painted and parcel-gilt window seat, on tapering circular legs, with later painted and gilt decoration, late 18thC, 39in (99cm) wide.
$9,000–10,000 S(NY)

An American mahogany-veneered window seat, damaged, c1815, 39½in (100.5cm) wide.
$3,500–4,000 SK(B)

▶ A Victorian rosewood and upholstered window seat, with overstuffed seat, c1860, damaged and restored, 33in (84cm) wide.
$1,600–2,000 S(S)

A Regency *faux* rosewood and parcel-gilt seat, the loose-cushioned caned seat flanked by caned scrolled sides, damaged, c1810, 44¼in (112.5cm) wide.
$15,000–16,000 S(NY)

A William IV mahogany window seat, with overstuffed seat, requires reupholstering, 53½in (136cm) wide.
$3,500–4,000 P(S)

WINE COOLERS

A George III mahogany cellaret, the hinged cover inlaid with a central fan patera, crossbanded in satinwood and strung with ebony and boxwood, with lead-lined interior, 18½in (47cm) wide.
$3,500–4,000 P(HSS)

▶ An Edwardian mahogany drum-shaped bottle holder, inlaid with satinwood and ebony banding, with a revolving top and 4 brass dished finger grips, the rising interior fitted with 6 apertures, 22¼in (56.5cm) diam.
$1,000–1,200 M

A mahogany cellaret, the hinged lid enclosing a fitted interior, 19thC, 32in (81.5cm) wide.
$1,400–1,600 AH

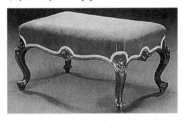

A Regency inlaid mahogany wine cooler, the top with an egg-and-dart moulded edge and bellflower swag inlay, enclosing a zinc-lined interior, with acanthus-scrolled handles, c1820, 36½in (92.5cm) wide.
$6,000–7,000 Bon

A William IV figured mahogany wine cellaret, with hinged cover enclosing a lead-lined 6 bottle interior, 26in (66cm) wide.
$1,800–2,000 TMA

METAMORPHIC FURNITURE

The adjective metamorphic defines a transformed object and aptly describes furniture that alters in form to serve more than one purpose.

Perhaps the earliest example of furniture of this description is the so-called monk's bench or chair-table. Introduced in the 17th century, these are circular or rectangular tables raised on four supports above enclosed box-type bases. They can easily be converted into a settle or an armchair by folding down a pivoted top to serve as a back. Another readily found type of metamorphic country furniture is the simple settle with a box base that extends to form a bed

During the 18th century, furniture makers developed ingenious mechanisms to alter furniture, such as a tea table with a concealed writing compartment operated by springs and weights. These were known as 'harlequin' tables. Other recorded examples of metamorphic furniture from this period include

a clothes press that converted into a bed, made by Thomas Chippendale c1775 for the actor David Garrick's villa at Hampton.

Thomas Sheraton was a leading exponent of versatile furniture, and in 1793 he published a design for a Pembroke table with a concealed ladder that converted into library steps.

During the early 19th century Morgan & Sanders published a popular design for a metamorphic armchair, with a typical 'klismos' outline and a hinged back that opened out to form a set of library steps. Another example of 19th-century metamorphic furniture is a telescopically extending table with a rectangular or circular top that rises to reveal further tiers that form a dumb waiter. These were introduced in the 1830s and remained popular until about 1850.

The tradition of metamorphic furniture has continued to the present day, and there is perhaps no better example in current use than the ubiquitous sofa bed.   **Fergus Lyons**

A Charles II oak table-settle, c1680, 72in (183cm) wide.
$11,500–13,000 PHA

An American painted maple and pine chair-table, the two-board top tilting to reveal a chair, with ring-turned legs, damaged, early 18thC, 51¼in (130cm) wide.
$20,000–25,000 SK(B)

An American walnut chair-table, the hinged top forming the back of the chair-form base, early 18thC, 44¾in (113.5cm) diam.
$1,500–1,800 SLN

A George II mahogany library step-stool, the leather-covered drop-in seat opening to reveal three-tread library steps, c1755, 30in (76cm) wide.
$16,000–18,000 S

► A Welsh oak chair-table, with a drawer in the bench seat, c1780, 27in (68.5cm) wide.
$6,000–7,000 CoA

A set of George III mahogany metamorphic library steps, the stuff-over needlework seat with a Harrow School armorial, with wrought-iron stretchers and brass locking plate, 42in (106.5cm) high.
$4,500–5,000 P

A set of George III mahogany metamorphic library chair-steps, with tooled leather-inset surfaces, the hinged fold-over top revealing 4 steps, restored, c1790, 28¼in (72cm) high.
$2,300–2,600 S(S)

An American painted maple and pine chair-table, early 19thC, 46in (117cm) diam.
$2,500–3,000 SK(B)

A set of William IV mahogany library steps/table, the hinged gilt-tooled leather inset top opening to a hand rail and hinged rest, the hinged end opening to gilt-tooled leather inset steps, the case fitted with 2 drawers, 41in (104cm) wide.
$25,000–27,000 S(NY)

◄ An early Victorian mahogany metamorphic table, the top lifting to form a three-tier étagère, c1845, 54in (137cm) wide.
$7,500–8,000 S(NY)

An American painted pine chair-table, 18thC, 31in (78.5cm) diam.
$7,000–7,500 SK(B)

A set of French bird's-eye maple and amaranth metamorphic library chair-steps, the backrest centred with a panel inlaid with an amaranth stylized flower, the scrolled arm supports raised on a carved dolphin, the chair opening to reveal 6 treads, early 19thC.
$12,000–14,000 S(Am)

A Victorian figured-walnut combined duet stand and occasional table, the top with winding action adjusting to form the stand, the cabriole scroll legs carved with bellflowers, labelled 'Swan & Milligan patent scroll and band movement', c1870, 24in (61cm) wide.
$3,000–3,500 S(S)

A George III ash and pine monk's bench, the cleated planked fold-over top revealing open arms and a box seat, with a central hinged compartment, on platform feet, early 19thC, 53in (134.5cm) wide.
$1,200–1,700 S(S)

A Regency mahogany metamorphic library armchair, after a design by Morgan & Sanders, the top rail inlaid with brass stringing above a caned panel and brass-inlaid middle rail, the caned seat flanked by scrolled open arms, c1815.
$18,000–20,000 S

This armchair follows a design published by the firm Morgan & Sanders in Rudolph Ackermann's *Repository of Arts* in July 1811. Morgan & Sanders were specialists in the manufacture of metamorphic furniture of this kind and held the patent for this particular model, which was known as the 'Patent Metamorphic Library Chair'.

An Irish pine monk's bench, c1860, 72in (183cm) wide.
$1,200–1,400 HON

An Irish pine settle-bed, c1870, 72in (183cm) wide.
$800–1,000 Byl

Oak & Country Furniture

I t cannot be over emphasized that quality and condition are the most important factors to consider when buying early furniture (mainly oak, 1550–1700), and 'country' furniture (vernacular pieces in oak, ash, elm, fruitwoods, yew and other native timbers, 1700–1850). Quality encompasses factors such as workmanship, style, decoration and rarity, while condition will include colour and patination, completeness and originality.

Although there are fewer fakes in this field than in some others, authenticity is a continuing problem for the unwary collector, ranging from out-and-out fakes to over-restored or refinished originals. It is best to be wary of Victorian and modern copies, but they will not be a problem if you take some trouble to explore the subject by reading books, attending lectures and courses, and by touring shops, museums and salerooms. Learn to identify and enjoy real patination, and avoid artificial finishes that only simulate age.

Try to find a friendly dealer whose stock appeals to you; ask advice, and who may be prepared to buy back or swap pieces should your tastes change. The main auction houses offer regular specialist oak and country furniture sales, leavened with related items such as metalwork, pottery and textiles. They offer free advice and condition reports if you don't trust your own judgement.

It is very interesting to compare the values cited in the first and current editions of *Miller's Antiques Price Guide*. Although difficult to generalize, the long-term investment values of most good-quality pieces have increased some eight- to ten-fold. Poorer quality and heavily restored items have performed much less well and often remain difficult to sell – the lesson is that poor quality is a poor investment, so buy the best you can afford. However, also bear in mind that some pieces go in and out of fashion, and it could be a mistake to buy at the top of the market. Dressers, for example, have come dramatically into fashion in recent years owing to their versatility, with the middle range currently valued from $6,500 to $20,000. Some 21 years ago, oak press cupboards were marginally higher priced than dressers, whereas today the average 17th-century piece fetches half that of a comparable 18th-century dresser. Early pieces will doubtless catch up, and this could be a good time to buy a middle-range press cupboard. **Victory Chinnery**

BEDS

An oak cradle, with 4 turned posts to the corners, with shaped canopy, 17thC, 37in (94cm) long.
$1,300–1,600 B

An oak half-tester bed, part 17thC, 56in (142cm) wide.
$5,000–5,700 REF

An early 17thC-style stained oak tester bed, 19thC, using some 17thC panels, 69in (175.5cm) wide overall.
$16,500–18,000 Doc

> **Miller's is a price GUIDE not a price LIST**

An oak four-poster bedstead, c1890, 60in (152.5cm) wide.
$8,000–9,000 SeH

◄ A Victorian oak bedstead, the pierced cornice with carved finials above a panelled back carved with grapes, the rails similarly carved with scrolling foliage and grapes, late 19thC, 46½in (118cm) wide.
$9,000–10,000 S(NY)

BENCHES

An oak and larch child's bench, c1720, 30in (76cm) long.
$1,500–1,650 DaH

A Louis XV-style provincial brass-mounted chestnut bench, with hinged seat, late 18th/early 19thC, 71in (180.5cm) long.
$1,800–2,000 SK

► An ash open-backed bench, c1820, 36in (91.5cm) long.
$300–350 SPa

An oak bench, late 19thC, 50in (127cm) long.
$500–650 BUSH

An elm hog bench, mid-19thC, 53½in (136cm) long.
$550–600 SWN

BOOKCASES

A George III oak bureau bookcase, the arched glazed cupboard doors enclosing shelves, the fall-front with an inset well, pigeonholes and drawers, bookcase and bureau associated, 38in (96.5cm) wide.
$3,000–3,500 Bon(W)

► A Regency oak glazed bookcase, c1820, 33in (84cm) wide.
$9,000–10,500 PHA

An oak bureau bookcase, c1730, 38in (96.5cm) wide.
$10,000–11,500 RED

BOXES

A Spanish walnut box, carved with paterae and scrolls, damaged, early 16thC, 10¼in (26cm) wide.
$1,500–1,650 S(NY)

A Continental walnut travelling box, with pierced metal decoration and hinged top with velvet-backed metal ornament, probably Italian, 16th/17thC, 28¼in (72cm) wide.
$1,600–1,800 P

An oak box, the hinged top enclosing 3 short drawers and a galleried shelf, on later stand, late 17thC, 27in (68.5cm) wide.
$600–700 Bon

An oak desk box, enclosing a fitted interior with drawers and secret compartments, the front carved with scrolling foliage, fruit and flowerheads, late 17th/early 18thC, 21¾in (55.5cm) wide.
$800–1,000 AH

An oak desk box, with carved front and sides, the slope inlaid, c1660, 27in (68.5cm) wide.
$3,200–4,000 CoA

> **Cross Reference**
> See Colour Review

An oak offertory box, 18thC, 7in (18cm) wide.
$300–350 SWN

BUFFETS

A French provincial oak and walnut buffet, the 3 central drawers with scroll cartouche panels between cupboards enclosed by quatrefoil panelled doors, on scroll feet, 18thC, 71¼in (181cm) wide.
$5,800–6,500 P

A Louis XVI oak buffet, with a long drawer and 2 panelled doors, late 18thC, 41in (104cm) wide.
$3,200–4,000 B&B

A French provincial Louis XV-style carved beechwood buffet, c1820, 55¼in (140.5cm) wide.
$1,700–2,000 NOA

A French provincial Louis XV-style fruitwood buffet, with wrought-iron mounts, c1825, 60¼in (152.5cm) wide.
$2,800–3,200 NOA

A French provincial elm and chestnut buffet, c1860, 49in (124.5cm) wide.
$1,300–1,600 LPA

A French provincial walnut buffet, c1860, 51in (129.5cm) wide.
$1,000–1,200 LPA

BUREAUX

An oak bureau, the interior with secret drawers and a well, c1715, 36in (91.5cm) wide.
$7,500–9,000 PHA

An oak bureau, crossbanded in walnut, c1730, 36in (91.5cm) wide.
$5,000–5,700 RED

A French provincial chestnut bureau, c1760, 35in (89cm) wide.
$3,800–4,400 B&L

A George III oak bureau, restored, c1780, 39in (99cm) wide.
$4,000–5,000 COLL

A George I oak bureau, with cabriole legs, c1720, 32in (81.5cm) wide.
$5,000–5,700 RED

An early George III provincial oak bureau, 37½in (95.5cm) wide.
$1,600–2,000 Bea(E)

A George III oak bureau, with fitted interior, 37¼in (94.5cm) wide.
$2,600–3,000 WL

An oak bureau, the interior pillared section fitted with a door and hidden slides, 18thC, 44in (112cm) wide.
$2,300–3,000 HOK

An oak bureau, the fall-front enclosing pigeonholes, small drawers and a well, with later brass handles, backplates and lock escutcheons, early 18thC, 36in (91.5cm) wide.
$2,500–3,000 P(HSS)

A Welsh oak bureau, with a deep drawer, c1760, 43in (109cm) wide.
$3,800–4,400 CoA

A George III oak bureau, the fall-front enclosing a fitted interior, 36in (91.5cm) wide.
$1,800–2,000 Bon(W)

A George III oak bureau, with mahogany crossbanding, the fall-front enclosing a fitted interior, 40in (101.5cm) wide.
$1,300–1,600 L

BUREAU CABINETS

A George II oak bureau cabinet, the fall-front enclosing a fitted interior, 39in (99cm) wide.
$5,700–6,500 P(EA)

A Welsh inlaid oak bureau cabinet, with a fitted interior, c1780, 46in (117cm) wide.
$11,500–13,000 CoA

A Welsh oak bureau cabinet, c1790, 43in (109cm) wide.
$5,200–6,200 CoA

An oak bureau cabinet, altered, 18thC, 41½in (105.5cm) wide.
$2,000–2,300 P(HSS)

CHAIRS

An oak wainscot chair, attributed to Humphrey Beckham of Salisbury, the double-scrolled crest surrounding a winged cherub above a panel of 2 stylized griffins, restored, 17thC.
$2,800–3,200 B

A joined oak panel-back armchair, c1670.
$3,500–4,000 DBA

An oak armchair, c1780.
$3,000–3,500 DBA

An oak commode chair, late 18thC.
$650–750 WELL

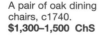

A pair of oak dining chairs, c1740.
$1,300–1,500 ChS

An oak lambing chair, the panelled back with an arched cresting carved with scrolls flanked by projecting ears, on turned legs joined by squared stretchers, basically 18thC.
$2,300–3,000 HYD

21 Years Ago ...

A carved oak armchair, mid-17thC. **RBB**

Twenty-one years ago the first edition of *Miller's Antiques Price Guide* featured a large number of 17thC panel-back armchairs, the piece pictured above falling into the middle price bracket at $1,400–1,550. The popularity of these chairs has continued unabated since 1979, and today this piece would sell for about $8,000–13,000. Examples in exceptional condition or displaying distinctive regional features can command as much as $15,000–25,000.

A set of 6 Chippendale oak chairs, c1780.
$4,000–4,500 ANV

A Welsh oak farmhouse carver, with shaped splat, c1790.
$1,200–1,400 CoA

An elm side chair, 18thC.
$250–300 SPU

A Welsh oak chair, c1795.
$130–160 OLM

Two yew and elm high-back Windsor open armchairs, early 19thC.
$3,500–4,000 Doc

An ash and elm comb-back Windsor armchair, with traces of original paint, late 18th/early 19thC.
$900–1,100 AH

A set of 6 American rod-back Windsor side chairs, each with 7 spindles and bamboo turned stiles, c1800.
$4,500–5,000 SK(B)

These chairs are branded 'W. Dalton', who was working in Boston 1799–1800.

An ash and elm comb-back Windsor armchair, with pierced splats, c1820.
$1,200–1,400 ANV

A pair of ash and elm splat-back side chairs, c1820.
$650–750 MTa

A West Country ash stick-back armchair, c1820.
$1,200–1,450 OCH

A Welsh fruitwood open armchair, c1820.
$650–750 CoA

A beech Windsor chair, c1830.
$115–130 AL

A matched set of 6 ash, elm and beech chairs, c1850.
$1,300–1,450 SWN

An ash and elm Windsor armchair, c1840.
$800–900 RED

An ash Clisset chair, with rush seat, early 19thC.
$1,150–1,300 PHA

An elm and beech spindle-back armchair, c1860.
$300–350 BOR

A matched pair of ash and elm Windsor armchairs, mid-19thC.
$1,800–2,000 ANV

An ash and elm captain's chair, c1870.
$325–400 GBr

A Victorian ash and elm rocking chair.
$450–550 CPA

A set of 4 yew and elm Windsor armchairs, with crinoline stretchers, 19thC.
$5,200–5,700 AH

An ash and elm rail-back armchair, 19thC.
$350–400 DaH

A pair of French oak armchairs, with rush seats, c1900.
$900–1,100 LPA

◀ A Spanish hall chair, painted in red and gilt, with a rush seat, c1910.
$160–200 BAB

▶ A pair of French Louis XV-style armchairs, with rush seats, c1920.
$1,000–1,250 CF

CHILDREN'S CHAIRS

A fruitwood child's captain's chair, c1830.
$550–650 BUSH

An oak child's armchair, c1840.
$325–400 AnSh

An elm child's rocking chair, with a metal strengthener to the back rail, c1840.
$500–650 STK

A mid-Victorian elm child's chair.
$200–250 AAN

A French provincial carved fruitwood and cane child's chair, c1890.
$480–560 NOA

◄ An oak child's wing-back rocking chair, 19thC.
$550–600 WL

> Miller's is a price GUIDE not a price LIST

► A French walnut highchair, converts into a low table and chair, 19thC.
$400–500 BaN

CHESTS OF DRAWERS

A Charles II oak chest of drawers, with rising top above an arcaded panel over 2 drawers, decorated with applied mouldings, 37in (94cm) wide.
$2,000–2,200 LRG

A William and Mary oak chest of drawers, the drawers with bolection-moulded fronts, veneered with panels of burr yew, later bracket feet, late 17thC, 38½in (98cm) wide.
$2,200–2,600 HYD

► A Charles II oak chest of drawers, c1680, 42in (106.5cm) wide.
$3,600–4,000 ANV

◄ An oak chest of drawers, with a moulded drawer and 3 further geometrically mitred drawers, on later bracket feet, originally in 2 parts, late 17thC, 40½in (103cm) wide.
$1,000–1,200 P(NW)

An Anglo-Dutch joined oak enclosed chest of drawers, inlaid with bone, mother-of-pearl and partridge wood, with moulded panel cupboard doors, altered, part 17thC, 46in (117cm) wide.
$3,000–3,300 EH

An oak two-part moulded chest of drawers, with later handles, late 17thC, 42in (106.5cm) wide.
$4,000–5,000 RED

An oak chest, the 4 long drawers with geometric and cushion-moulded fronts, bun feet lacking, late 17thC, 38in (96.5cm) wide.
$2,300–2,600 WW

A joined oak chest of drawers, in 2 sections, the top with later moulded edge above 4 panelled drawers, late 17thC, 37in (94cm) wide.
$3,500–4,000 Bon

An oak chest of drawers, with later bracket feet, late 17thC, 43½in (110.5cm) wide.
$1,300–1,450 Doc

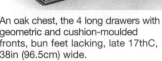

A Queen Anne oak chest of 2 short and 3 long drawers, handles replaced, c1710, 35in (89cm) wide.
$3,200–3,600 RED

An oak chest, the drawers with geometric moulded fronts, later brass handles, early 18thC, 37½in (94cm) wide.
$3,500–4,000 DN

A George II oak chest-on-chest, the base drawer with inlaid half stellar motif, 42¼in (107.5cm) wide.
$3,300–4,000 P(HSS)

An oak chest-on-chest, late 18thC, 42¼in (107.5cm) wide.
$1,400–1,600 L&E

A Louis XV provincial oak serpentine commode, with rococo keyplates and handle pulls, mid-18thC, 49¼in (125cm) wide.
$2,500–3,000 P

A French provincial oak serpentine chest, with shaped apron and panelled sides, c1800, 91¾in (233cm) wide.
$6,000–6,500 HOK

A boarded oak chest of 4 drawers, c1760, 34½in (87.5cm) wide.
$2,000–2,200 DBA

◄ An oak chest of drawers, damaged, early 19thC, 29in (73.5cm) wide.
$570–650 Hal

CHESTS & COFFERS

A walnut *cassone*, possibly from Tuscany, restored, 14thC, 18in (45.5cm) wide.
$1,600–2,000 REF

An oak chest, with foliate lunette-carved frieze, mid-17thC, 40¼in (102.5cm) wide.
$650–750 Bea(E)

An oak chest, with carving and punch-work decoration, early 17thC, 64in (162.5cm) wide.
$7,300–8,000 CoA

An oak arcaded chest, with split baluster mouldings and fitted with a drawer, c1660, 50in (127cm) wide.
$7,500–9,000 PHA

▶ An oak chest, with plain plank top over moulded double panel front, 17thC, 28⅛in (72.5cm) wide.
$3,800–4,400 GOR(B)

A Welsh oak chest, with carving and punch-work decoration, c1630, 47in (119.5cm) wide.
$3,500–4,000 CoA

An oak boarded chest, c1670, 30in (76cm) wide.
$2,100–2,400 RED

◀ An American early Colonial iron-bound elm chest, the lid with pointed strap hinges and secured by a hasp and staple, opening to a storage well, late 17thC, 24in (61cm) wide.
$1,800–2,000 SLN

▶ An oak chest, the triple panelled top and front with stiff-leaf-carved muntins and fluted frieze, 17thC, 47in (119.5cm) wide.
$800–900 L

An Italian cedar *cassone*, with carved and penwork decoration, angled steel hinges, the sides with original iron bat's-wing plate carrying handles, on later wooden casters, 17thC, 63½in (161.5cm) wide.
$4,000–5,000 WW

Construction Methods

In the past, all furniture was made by specialist craftsmen, and recognition of the method of construction is a guide to the quality of any piece. The plainest forms of case furniture are the so-called boarded chests and boxes, made by carpenters from nailed planks and decorated with simple carving. Slightly more complex were turned chairs made by turners, and finished with planked or woven rush seats.

The most satisfactory construction in the early period was joined furniture, comprising a strong rectangular frame of posts and rails held together by mortice-and-tenon joints. Tables and chairs usually had turned legs, while chests and cupboards contained panels held in grooves in the framework, often ornamented with carving and sometimes with inlay of coloured woods.

In the late 17thC, cabinet-makers introduced sophisticated Continental techniques such as dovetailed construction, veneering and marquetry.

A Charles I carved oak panelled chest, c1640, 48in (122cm) wide.
$5,700–6,500 PHA

An oak boarded chest, c1700, 32in (81.5cm) wide.
$800–900 ANV

A William and Mary joined oak chest, the top with scale-carved edge, enclosing a candle box, above a panelled front with 2 drawers below, c1700, 62in (157.5cm) wide.
$2,800–3,200 Bon

A Spanish chestnut chest, with hinged top and wrought-iron handles, on ball feet, 17th/18thC, 53¼in (135.5cm) wide.
$1,000–1,200 S(Am)

An oak boarded chest, with carved floral and fruit design, early 18thC, 45in (114.5cm) wide.
$3,000–3,300 DBA

An oak fielded panelled chest with drawers, 18thC, 60in (152.5cm) wide.
$3,600–4,400 SPU

An oak and walnut crossbanded chest with drawers, the interior with later false base, mid-18thC, 54¾in (139cm) wide.
$1,600–1,800 P

An oak boarded chest, early 18thC, 52in (132cm) wide.
$450–525 COLL

An oak and mahogany crossbanded Lancashire mule chest, c1760, 65in (165cm) wide.
$3,600–4,400 RED

An oak chest with drawers, the three-plank top above panelled front and a pair of short drawers, 18thC, 55in (139.5cm) wide.
$1,200–1,400 Mit

◀ A dark stained oak chest, with triple panelled hinged lid, the whole carved with inter-laced rosettes, 18thC, 51½in (131cm) wide.
$1,800–2,000 WL

An oak boarded chest, the hinged top with carved and moulded edges, 18thC, 35¾in (91cm) wide.
$1,000–1,100 DN

A George II Welsh oak coffer bach, with two drawers, brass handles and escutcheons, on bun feet, c1750, 25in (64cm) wide.
$5,700–6,500 PHA

A Welsh oak coffer bach, with panelled front, on a Gothic-style plinth, c1770, 44in (112cm) wide.
$3,600–4,000 CoA

A Continental oak and iron-mounted marriage chest, the top with foliate openwork iron straps, on a shaped plinth base incorporating 4 wooden wheels, damaged, dated '1771', 48in (122cm) wide.
$5,200–6,200 S(S)

A Welsh oak coffer bach, with original brasses, c1780, 18in (45.5cm) wide.
$4,400–5,200 PHA

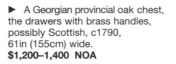

► A Georgian provincial oak chest, the drawers with brass handles, possibly Scottish, c1790, 61in (155cm) wide.
$1,200–1,400 NOA

A Welsh oak coffer bach, with drawer, inlaid in holly and bog oak, c1780, 22in (56cm) wide.
$5,500–6,000 CoA

A George III Welsh oak coffer bach, with panelled front and shaped apron, handles replaced, c1800, 20in (51cm) wide.
$3,300–4,000 PHA

A Shaker painted cherrywood panelled chest, with top lifting to reveal a cavity with lidded till, the front with 4 recessed panels, Kentucky, mid-19thC, 46in (117cm) wide.
$575–675 SK(B)

CUPBOARDS

An oak livery cupboard, with strapwork and carving, c1640, 48in (122cm) high.
$3,200–3,600 REF

An oak livery cupboard, the door inlaid with foliate scrolls and apron drawer with wrythen gadrooning, altered, 17thC, 48in (122cm) wide.
$12,000–14,500 L

A Welsh *cwpwrdd deuddarn*, the base with 2 drawers above 2 doors, early 18thC, 43in (109cm) wide.
$5,500–6,500 WBH

A joined oak press cupboard, the cornice with a lunette carved frieze, with a pair of panelled cupboard doors flanking a central panel carved with stylized flowers, mid-17thC, 58¾in (149cm) wide.
$12,000–13,500 Bon

An oak press cupboard, with moulded edge top with an egg-and-dart and guilloche moulded frieze, restored, late 17thC, 55½in (141cm) wide.
$4,500–5,500 P

This cupboard bears an old handwritten paper label stating 'This old cabinet was bought in 1878 . . . near Salisbury. It was then built in the wall of the cottage and formed part of the wall, the back being whitewashed. Cost with repairs £8.' See Victor Chinnery, *Oak Furniture* (Antique Collectors' Club, Woodbridge, 1979, reprinted 1998) pp492 and 493, for similar examples of built-in press cupboards. Chinnery refers to them as a special feature of Lakeland interiors and records examples that appear to have been made to stand freely and built-in at a later date.

A Welsh *cwpwrdd deuddarn*, the base with 2 drawers above 2 doors, early 18thC, 43in (109cm) wide.

A William and Mary carved oak press cupboard, the projecting frieze inscribed 'R.H.1689', over 2 carved panelled doors flanking a central panel, cupboard door below, 57½in (146cm) wide.
$11,500–13,000 P(HSS)

An oak hanging cupboard, the 2 central panel doors decorated with a pierced design and enclosing a shelf, restored, late 17thC, 46½in (118cm) wide.
$4,000–4,500 WW

A joined oak press cupboard, the sides of the lower part pierced, possibly from Westmorland, early 18thC, 46in (117cm) wide.
$6,500–7,500 DN(H)

◄ A Welsh *cwpwrdd deuddarn*, with 3 ogee fielded panelled doors, the lower part with 2 drawers flanking a narrow centre drawer over 2 panelled doors below, 18thC, 58¼in (148cm) wide.
$5,000–6,000 TEN

A Welsh oak food cupboard, with panelled doors, on a pine potboard base, with original paint, c1720, 39in (99cm) wide.
$4,500–5,000 CoA

A Welsh oak cupboard, with inscription 'Bydded Llawnder' (meaning 'Let There be Abundance'), c1720, 59in (150cm) wide.
$7,000–8,000 CoA

A joined oak press cupboard, the frieze carved with the initials 'RMS' and dated '1726', above 2 doors enclosing a hanging space over 2 fielded panels and 2 short drawers, damaged and restored, 62in (157.5cm) wide.
$1,600–2,000 Hal

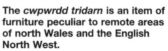

A George III oak *cwpwrdd tridarn*, the middle section with 2 arched panelled doors enclosing a void interior, north Wales, restored, mid-18thC, 56¾in (144cm) wide.
$7,500–9,000 S(S)

The *cwpwrdd tridarn* is an item of furniture peculiar to remote areas of north Wales and the English North West.

An oak press cupboard, the doors enclosing interior hanging rail and pegs above centre drawers, with 3 short graduated drawers to either side, mid-18thC, 65in (165cm) wide.
$5,500–6,000 L&E

A French oak armoire, Normandy, c1760, 60in (152.5cm) wide.
$5,500–6,500 ESA

A George III oak corner cupboard, with architectural pediment, c1770, 31in (78.5cm) wide.
$1,400–1,600 ANV

A George III oak hanging corner cupboard, 40in (101.5cm) wide.
$1,000–1,200 Doc

An oak clothes press, with moulded cornice, the upper part fitted with a hanging rail, enclosed by a pair of doors, the base fitted with 3 dummy drawers, 2 short drawers and one long drawer, 18thC, 52in (132cm) wide.
$2,800–3,200 CAG

A George III oak linen press, with a pair of twin-panelled doors enclosing hanging space, the base with 2 simulated drawers over 4 further drawers, with brass handles, 52½in (133.5cm) wide.
$3,200–3,600 HYD

A joined oak cupboard, north Wales, 18thC, 61in (155cm) wide.
$4,500–5,200 Bon

A French cherrywood armoire, with domed top, north Brittany, early 19thC, 53in (134.5cm) wide.
$3,000–3,500 MTay

A George III oak corner cupboard, with fielded panelled door and fluted sides, c1780, 26in (66cm) wide.
$1,200–1,400 ANV

A Dutch inlaid oak hanging cupboard, with shaped shelves, c1780, 31in (78.5cm) wide.
$6,000–7,000 PHA

A French elm armoire, Picardy, c1830, 50in (127cm) wide.
$2,500–3,000 ESA

An oak housekeeper's cupboard, with 4 panelled doors enclosing shelves, the lower section with double cupboard doors flanked by 3 short drawers to each side, late 18thC, 84in (213cm) wide.
$2,500–3,000 WL

A French cherrywood clothes press, early 19thC, 37in (94cm) wide.
$3,000–3,500 CF

An oak housekeeper's cupboard, with clock and brushing slides, Shropshire, c1835, 78in (198cm) wide.
$13,000–16,000 PHA

◀ A French wall-hanging bread cupboard, c1860, 41in (104cm) wide.
$2,500–3,200 LPA

DESKS

An oak desk, with geometrically panelled drawers, leather-lined writing surface, on turned front legs, c1900, 48in (122cm) wide.
$650–750 TAC

◄ An American cherrywood desk-on-stand, the lid opening to a compartmented interior set into base of thumb-moulded drawer, original brown paint, Massachusetts, c1800, 30¾in (78cm) wide.
$3,200–3,600 SK(B)

A George III oak desk-on-stand, with drawer, c1800, 22¾in (58cm) wide.
$1,300–1,500 ANV

DRESSERS

A George III oak dresser, with 3 shelves between fluted pilasters, 80¾in (205cm) wide.
$6,500–7,500 P(S)

An oak dresser, with a later rack of 3 shelves, part 18thC, 48½in (123cm) wide.
$3,500–4,000 M

A George II Welsh oak dresser, with 3 frieze drawers, damaged and restored, mid-18thC, parts possibly later, 53in (134.5cm) wide.
$7,500–9,000 S(S)

21 Years Ago …

An early Georgian oak and elm dresser, 56½in (144cm) wide. **CStJ**

Twenty-one years ago this dresser was at the top of its range with a value of $4,500–5,000. Today, as dressers are currently very popular, a similar piece would sell for $12,000–24,000 depending upon condition. However, it is wise to avoid buying at the top of a market which may falter or slow down at any time.

A George III Welsh oak breakfront dresser, Anglesey, restored, late 18thC, 64½in (164cm) wide.
$16,000–20,000 S(S)

A George III Welsh oak potboard dresser, c1770, 69in (175.5cm) wide.
$13,000–16,000 PHA

A George III oak dresser, the associated back with 3 open shelves above 4 short drawers, flanked each side by a solid panelled door, the base with a central arch flanked on each side by a drawer and twin panelled doors, 103½in (263cm) wide.
$5,500–6,500 P(Sc)

An oak dresser, with walnut and crossbanded drawers and doors, c1800, 74in (188cm) wide.
$5,000–5,500 KEY

A George III oak dresser, the rack with moulded cornice and scalloped, fluted frieze, the breakfront base with a central bank of 3 short drawers flanked on each side by a drawer with a cupboard below, 80¼in (204cm) wide.
$7,500–8,000 TEN

A George III oak dresser, the lower part with a deep frieze fitted with an arrangement of 5 short drawers, potboard below, 68in (172.5cm) wide.
$6,500–7,500 L

A Welsh oak dresser, the base fitted with 5 drawers and an open potboard below, Anglesey, early 19thC, 61½in (156cm) wide.
$3,000–3,500 L

◀ A George III oak and mahogany crossbanded dresser, c1800, 74in (188cm) wide.
$4,500–5,200 Hal

A George III cherrywood dresser, the top with 3 open shelves, the base with a central arched recess enclosing 2 shelves, flanked by later conforming fluted columns and 3 long graduated drawers, restored, late 18thC, 80in (203cm) wide.
$12,000–13,500 S(S)

A French provincial fruitwood and burr elm dresser, inlaid with chequer banding, with 2 open shelves and 3 short drawers below, over 2 frieze drawers and a pair of shaped burr-elm panelled doors, 18thC, 56in (142cm) wide.
$5,000–5,500 P

An oak and mahogany banded dresser, the breakfront base with 4 short drawers above cupboards, the central double arched doors with spindle-turned decoration, on ogee bracket feet, late 18th/early 19thC, 68in (172.5cm) wide.
$3,800–4,500 WL

LOW DRESSERS

A Jacobean oak low dresser, with a two-plank top and 5 small drawers above, with crossbanding and cockbeading, 85in (216cm) wide.
$38,000–40,000 WBH

Although the handles had been replaced, this dresser was otherwise in original condition with a very attractive colour. It was from a private source, fresh to the market, and sold for well in excess of expectations.

A Queen Anne oak low dresser, the 3 drawers with mitred surrounds, original brass escutcheons and swan-neck handles, on cabriole front legs, 72in (183cm) wide.
$5,500–6,500 B

An oak low dresser, with later middle leg and stretcher, late 17thC, 88in (223.5cm) wide.
$6,500–8,000 BIG

A George III oak and mahogany crossbanded low dresser, inlaid with stringing, the central cupboard doors flanked by 6 graduated drawers and cluster columns, Lancashire, 88in (223.5cm) wide.
$6,500–6,500 S(S)

The use of mahogany crossbanding and the drawer configuration help to attribute this item to the north west of England. Quarter columns are also a distinctive feature of this region and the use of cluster columns on this piece is particularly unusual.

LOWBOYS

An oak and crossbanded lowboy, with 2 drawers and brushing slide, c1730, 28in (71cm) wide.
$6,000–7,000 RED

Miller's Compares

I A George II oak lowboy, the shaped apron with 3 short drawers, on cabriole legs and pad feet, 30in (76cm) wide.
$2,500–3,000 L

II A George II oak lowboy, the shaped apron with 3 short drawers with burrwood fronts, on angular cabriole legs, 27¼in (69cm) wide.
$1,200–1,400 L

Item I aroused more interest among potential buyers when sold at auction because of the unusual shape of the apron, whereas item II is of a more standard design. The particularly fine colour and patination of item I also enhances its value. **L**

SETTLES

A carved oak box settle, with later incised initials and dated '1713', the boarded seat with twin hinged sections, late 17thC, 78in (198cm) wide.
$7,000–8,000 S(S)

An oak box settle, the fielded and carved panelled back within moulded stiles, over a hinged plank seat, early 18thC, 58½in (48.5cm) wide.
$2,500–3,000 WW

An elm box settle, c1725, 36in (91.5cm) wide.
$6,500–7,500 PHA

A Welsh oak settle, with panelled back, c1750, 80in (203cm) wide.
$3,800–4,200 CoA

An oak settle, with fielded panelled back, on turned front legs, c1730, 71in (180.5cm) wide.
$2,800–3,000 ANV

A George III oak bacon settle, the 3 small drawers with 2 panelled doors below enclosing an interior fitted with hooks, over a hinged seat, 63½in (161.5cm) wide.
$7,000–8,000 AH

Facts in Brief
- Box settle so named because of the box or well beneath the seat, used for storage.
- In existence in northern Europe by 15thC and one of the earliest forms of seat furniture in Europe.
- Earliest examples were usually made in oak with planked seats or linenfold panelled backs and often richly carved.
- Elm, ash yew wood and fruitwood increasingly used during 18thC, and examples continued to be made in the vernacular tradition until well into the 19thC.

A Welsh elm curved settle, c1780,
79in (200.5cm) wide.
$9,000–10,000 CoA

A walnut *cassapanca*, each fielded
panel divided and flanked by fluted
columns with Ionic capitals, with
a hinged box seat, 18thC,
75½in (192cm) wide.
$3,500–4,500 P(Z)

A French provincial turned beechwood
and rush triple chair-back seat,
c1845, 66in (167.5cm) wide.
$2,000–2,300 NOA

An oak settle, carved in Elizabethan
style possibly depicting Robin Hood
and King Richard in a castle interior,
with hinged seat above panelled
front, late 19thC, 67in (170cm) wide.
$2,200–2,600 P(S)

A Victorian oak settle, the back carved
with mermaids, 54in (137cm) wide.
$1,300–1,500 REF

An oak settle, the four-panel back
carved with agricultural scenes,
the seat with 2 hinged lids and
splayed arms, late 19th/early 20thC,
62in (157.5cm) wide.
$1,200–1,400 GAK

STOOLS

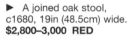

▶ A joined oak stool,
c1680, 19in (48.5cm) wide.
$2,800–3,000 RED

A small joined oak stool,
c1900, 18in (46cm) wide.
$500–600 OOLA

A joined oak stool, c1670,
18in (45.5cm) wide.
$3,000–3,300 PHA

Cross Reference
See Colour Review

A pair of Charles II
joined oak stools, with
lunette carved friezes,
damaged and restored,
17¾in (45cm) wide.
$5,500–6,500 S(S)

21 Years Ago …

A joined oak stool,
on fluted columnar
legs and square
stretchers, early 17thC,
18in (46cm) wide. **C**

Twenty-one years ago this stool was valued at
$1,600–2,000. Joined stools have long been very
popular on account of their compact size and
usefulness, and this stool is a good-quality
example. Clean and simple in design, with good
colour and rare decoration, this piece would
now fetch **$7,000–10,000.**

An elm primitive slab-top
milking stool, c1800,
11in (28cm) high.
$80–120 CPA

A pair of stools, with elm
tops and ash legs, 18thC,
14in (35.5cm) wide.
$550–650 ANV

TABLES

A Charles II oak side table, with bobbin-turned legs, brasses replaced, c1685, 31½in (80cm) wide.
$9,000–10,500 PHA

A joined oak centre table, on turned legs, c1680, 32½in (82.5cm) wide.
$3,500–4,000 DBA

A Spanish oak and walnut centre table, the carved frieze with 2 drawers, 17thC and later, 61½in (156cm) long.
$5,000–5,500 S(S)

A Queen Anne oak gateleg table, with drawer, restored, early 18thC, 60in (152.5cm) extended.
$5,000–5,500 S(S)

LOCATE THE SOURCE

The source of each illustration in Miller's can be found by checking the code letters below each caption with the Key to Illustrations, pages 789–795.

An oak side table, with chamfered fold-over top, fitted with a short frieze drawer, 17thC, 27in (68.5cm) wide.
$5,000–6,000 L

A yew gateleg table, c1700, 58in (147.5cm) extended.
$9,000–10,000 RED

An oak drop-leaf table, on baluster end supports and trestle feet, joined by a flat profile-cut double baluster stretcher, restored, early 18thC, 29½in (75cm) wide.
$1,000–1,200 TEN

An oval gateleg table, with a drawer at each end, 18thC, 57in (145cm) wide.
$2,000–2,500 P(S)

A walnut gateleg table, late 17thC, 42½in (108cm) extended.
$5,500–7,000 DBA

An oak gateleg table, with shaped frieze, late 17thC/early 18thC, 63in (160cm) extended.
$2,500–3,000 Bea(E)

Gateleg Tables

- Formed part of the luxury furnishings of grand houses in the 16thC, and became common in more modest homes by the mid-17thC, before being superseded by the swing-leg table in the early 18thC.
- 17thC examples have pegged mortice-and-tenon joints, whereas copies will have glued mortice and tenon joints.
- The flaps on early examples often consist of 2 pieces of wood joined together to complete a large oval shape. The latter part of the 17thC saw the introduction of a fixed central section, a hinged flap and a gateleg on each side swivelling out to support the flaps.
- After c1690 good-quality examples have rule joins between the flaps and central top plank in order to provide smooth contact between the 2 parts without leaving gaps. Other signs of quality are shaped friezes, turned legs and feet.
- Gateleg or drop-leaf tables were usually made to seat 4 people. Tables for 6 or more are popular today, and consequently modern copies are often found.

An ash cricket table, stretchers worn,
c1740, 18in (45.5cm) diam.
$2,500–3,000 RYA

A George III oak side table,
crossbanded with fruitwood,
Shropshire, c1780, 31in (78.5cm) wide.
$5,000–6,000 PHA

A Welsh oak occasional table, with
side flaps, Cardiganshire, c1790,
27in (68.5cm) diam.
$5,000–6,000 CoA

A Spanish walnut table, with
deep single drawer, on straight
legs and stretchers, 18thC,
39in (99cm) wide.
$350–450 E

Regional Styles of Country Furniture

Renewed awareness of specific local traditions that influenced the form
and decoration of British country furniture has resulted in an increase
in the market value of pieces with strongly defined regional features.
These variations in style were the result of local workshops producing
designs according to the requirements and preferences of the
community they served. Research in this field is ongoing and those
wishing to keep informed of developments should contact the
Membership Secretary, The Regional Furniture Society, Trouthouse,
Warren's Cross, Lechlade, Glos. Tel/Fax: 01367 252880.

A George II joined oak side table,
with a single frieze drawer, restored,
mid-18thC, 30¼in (77cm) wide.
$1,200–1,400 Bon

A George III oak tripod table,
c1780, 25in (63.5cm) diam.
$900–1,000 ANT

An oak tilt-top tripod table, c1760,
28½in (72.5cm) diam.
$800–1,000 CPA

An elm cricket table, with oak base,
c1790, 24in (61cm) diam.
$750–800 COLL

An American Federal birch table,
the overhanging top with shaped
corners and drawer below,
probably Maine, damaged, c1800,
32in (81.5cm) wide.
$1,000–1,200 SK(B)

A cherrywood tripod table, New
England, damaged, late 18th/early
19thC, 20in (51cm) wide.
$1,400–1,600 SK(B)

Tables • OAK & COUNTRY FURNITURE 177

An oak cricket table, with
stretcher base, c1800,
23¾cm (60.5cm) diam.
$1,500–1,700 ANV

A Spanish chestnut table, early
19thC, 34in (86.5cm) wide.
$700–800 GD

A French fruitwood farmhouse table, the
three-plank folding top with cleated ends,
over a plain frieze, 18th/19thC,
114in (289.5cm) extended.
$3,000–3,500 HYD

A French cherrywood farmhouse table,
mid-19thC, 77in (195.5cm) long.
$2,500–3,000 CF

A yew tripod table,
with oak base, c1820,
22in (56cm) diam.
$1,500–1,700 ANV

An oak side table, with 2 drawers,
c1840, 29in (73.5cm) wide.
$700–800 DaH

▶ A French cherrywood side table,
with 3 drawers, northern Brittany,
19thC, 71in (180.5cm) wide.
$1,600–2,000 MTay

Pine

Pine furniture started to become fashionable in the 1970s, and really took off in the 1980s. Initially, collectors had plenty to choose from, and mostly sought pieces in near perfect condition; as supply has dwindled, a certain amount of damage and imperfection has become acceptable. Fine examples of painted and decorated pine furniture can fetch high prices, but pieces that are unsuitable for modern taste are still being stripped. Recently, partly painted, distressed pieces have become very fashionable, paving the way for the latest 'shabby chic' trend in furnishing.

In spite of the diminishing supply of British pine furniture, high-quality pieces are still in demand both in the UK and abroad. Following the demise of communism, large quantities of pine furniture have been flooding in from Eastern Europe, some of which are superb quality and beautifully decorated antiques, but the vast majority was made at a later date and is, therefore, very affordable. The wood used in these later examples has none of the colour or patina of antique pine but many pieces, such as knockdown wardrobes and bedside cupboards, are eminently suitable for modern homes.

Stripped pine looks good in both period and country houses, fitting in with chintz, ginghams, stripes or the minimalist look. It is particularly suitable for children's rooms, where it is very good-tempered if the odd accident happens. Although still traditionally associated with kitchen tables, dressers, units and storage cupboards, pine furniture is so adaptable and was made in such a variety of sizes and designs that, with a little luck and perseverance, it is usually possible to find a piece for a particular space and function. Pine does not mix well with other woods, however, which means that the many people who have fully or partially furnished their homes with pine will continue to do so, enjoying the variety of colour and patina that this affordable wood provides.

If the past 21 years are anything to go by, the future of pine looks bright. Pieces purchased in the early 1980s have held their prices well, provided they have been cared for, and rarer items such as plate racks, linen presses, proving cupboards, towel rails and maids' boxes command good prices. Hopefully, the same will be true in 21 years' time for pine furniture bought today.

Ann Lingard

BEDS

A pine sleigh bed, with shaped sides and slatted base, late 19thC, 76in (193cm) long.
$450–520 OLM

A French pine single bed, c1890, 75in (190.5cm) long.
$570–650 OLM

A pair of Continental pine beds, c1920, 77in (195.5cm) long.
$730–800 DEE

BENCHES

A pine sheep bench, c1880, 48in (122cm) long.
$260–280 AL

An Irish painted pine bench, c1880, 71in (180.5cm) long.
$730–800 DFA

A Continental pine bench/stool, c1800, 24in (61cm) wide.
$320–350 MTa

◄ An American painted pine bench, Pennsylvania, with original paint, early 19thC, 96in (244cm) long.
$730–800 SK(B)

A pine bench, c1890, 48in (122cm) long.
$100–120 AL

A pine bench, c1890, 35in (89cm) long.
$200–230 AL

A pine bench, c1890, 72in (183cm) long.
$150–160 AL

A pine bench, with iron supports, c1890, 72in (183cm) long.
$100–120 AL

A pitch-pine church pew, with carved ends and
panelled back, c1905, 102in (259cm) long.
$500–550 A&H

BOOKCASES

◀ A pine bookcase,
with 9 drawers, c1840,
50in (127cm) wide.
$950–1,150 TPC

A French pitch-pine
glazed bookcase, 19thC,
45in (114.5cm) wide.
$1,500–1,800 DEE

A Regency pine bookcase,
with adjustable shelves
and panelled back, c1812,
48in (122cm) wide.
$730–800 TPC

▶ An Irish pine glazed
bookcase, c1875,
44in (112cm) wide.
$570–700 Byl

A pine open bookcase,
c1860, 50in (127cm) wide.
$650–770 TPC

◀ A Continental
glazed pine
wall cupboard,
c1864, 41in
(104cm) wide.
$320–480 Sam

A Victorian pine bookcase,
with adjustable shelves,
c1880, 57in (145cm) wide.
$1,300–1,600 ESA

An Irish painted pine glazed
bookcase, with carved
decoration, c1870,
40in (101.5cm) wide.
$1,450–1,800 HON

A Michelangelo. Only in Florence.

A Van der Tol. Only in Almere.

We carry one of the world's finest collections of antique pine furniture.

Available in unstripped, stripped and finished & painted versions. Plus

cherry/oak reproductions and decorative items. We offer quality, quantity &

profit and full packing service. Please visit our 75,000 sq.ft. warehouse

in Almere and enjoy the personal and friendly service.

Jacques van der Tol
unique antique pine furniture

Jacques van der Tol wholesale BV. (20 min. from Schiphol Airport)
Antennestraat 34, 1322 AE Almere-Stad, Holland, Industrial Estate 'Gooise Kant'
Tel.: (0)36-5362050. Fax: (0)36-5361993

BOXES

An American painted and decorated pine box, New England, some wear, 1830s, 29in (73.5cm) wide.
$800–900 SK(B)

A Victorian pine writing slope, 38¾in (98.5cm) wide.
$100–120 AnSh

A Continental pine box, c1850, 41in (104cm) wide.
$320–350 Sam

A pine domed-top box, c1860, 30in (76cm) wide.
$260–280 CPS

A Victorian pine box, with original paint, c1860, 19½in (49.5cm) wide.
$160–200 CPA

A Swedish pine sugar box, with original paint, c1860, 13in (33cm) wide.
$160–200 OLM

A Victorian pine box, c1870, 22in (56cm) wide.
$100–110 OLM

A pine domed-top box, c1870, 35in (89cm) wide.
$250–280 CPS

An Irish pine grain bin, c1875, 38½in (98cm) wide.
$300–350 Byl

A pine box, with candle box, c1880, 36in (91.5cm) wide.
$230–260 AL

A pine box, c1880, 36in (91.5cm) wide.
$160–200 WEE

A pine box, with key and candle box, c1880, 34in (86.5cm) wide.
$160–200 WEE

A pine domed-top box, c1880, 34in (86.5cm) wide.
$300–370 CPS

A pine domed-top box, c1890, 28in (71cm) wide.
$240–280 CPS

A sailor's diddy box, c1895, 12in (30.5cm) wide.
$90–100 OLM

CHAIRS

A Victorian beech Oxford carver chair.
$300–350 DEE

A child's pine chair, c1920.
$40–50 AL

A child's pine chair, 1950s.
$60–70 WaH

CHESTS & COFFERS

A American painted pine chest, inscribed 'Uniontown/J.L./1843', Pennsylvania, 54¼in (138cm) wide.
$1,800–2,100 SLN

An American painted pine chest, with original paint, Massachusetts, 18thC, 45in (114.5cm) wide.
$2,600–3,000 SK(B)

An American painted pine chest, with carved rope-twist beading, late 18thC, 43½in (110.5cm) wide.
$2,600–3,000 SK(B)

A Scandinavian painted pine dowry chest, with hinged lid, on a separate base with original wheels, wrought-iron handles, c1800, 53in (134.5cm) wide.
$1,450–1,600 DuM

21 Years Ago ...

A pine coffer, with original hinges, 19thC, 38in (96.5cm) wide. **SSP**

Twenty-one years ago this pine coffer was valued at $80–100 and was in plentiful supply. Today it is hard to find such coffers in very good condition with original ironware, and they would cost in the region of $450–550. Boxes of inferior quality are more easily found.

An American grain-painted pine chest, with one drawer, original red and yellow paint simulating tiger maple, Rhode Island, c1830, 39¾in (101cm) wide.
$2,100–2,400 SK(B)

A pine seaman's chest, with original painted woodgrain finish and Turk's-head decorative woven handles, c1850, 44in (112cm) wide.
$570–650 WaH

A pine mule chest, with 2 drawers, side carrying handles, c1870, 36in (91.5cm) wide.
$450–500 AL

An Irish pine grain bin, c1870, 47½in (120.5cm) wide.
$300–350 Byl

A pine chest-on-stand, the front opening to reveal internal drawers, c1880, 42in (106.5cm) wide.
$570–650 MLL

A Continental pine mule chest with domed top, c1880, 39in (99cm) wide.
$320–350 Sam

A carved oak armchair, dated '1655'.
$4,000–4,500 REF

A joined oak panel-back armchair, c1660.
$5,000–5,750 DBA

A Welsh oak stick chair, the single board back with pierced heart motif, c1760.
$5,000–5,600 CoA

An elm and ash Windsor chair, 1790–1820.
$580–640 OLM

An oak armchair, with rush seat, early 19thC.
$350–400 OCH

A yew and elm Windsor armchair, with crinoline stretcher, c1840.
$1,600–2,000 RED

A beech winged rocking chair, with rush seat, 19thC.
$400–500 MiA

A pair of stained beech Windsor armchairs, late 19th/early 20thC.
$7,500–8,000 S

Paul Hopwell Antiques

Early English Oak

Dressers, tables and chairs always in stock

A fine pair of George I oak side chairs.
English.   1725

A Charles II oak side table on barley
twist legs with original bun feet.
English.   c1685

A rare William & Mary walnut two seater
settee.
English.   c1695

A Charles II oak Wainscott armchair.
English.   c1690

Paul Hopwell Antiques

A fine, small Charles I oak carved joined press cupboard. Unusual carved pillars, excellent colour and patina. English. c1640

A Charles II oak side table with shaped apron and 'X' stretcher. On bobbin turned legs with original bun feet and finial. English. c1685

A fine 17thC oak panelled coffer. Gloucestershire. c1640

A Gothic Tudor boarded oak chest, with hinged plank lid, the interior fitted with a till, the front board carved with crocketed frieze and an iron lock with original wrought clasp, Northamptonshire, c1500, 57in (145cm) wide.
$20,000–24,000 EH

A joined oak chest, with linenfold panels, replacement lock and hinges, restored, c1540, 26in (66cm) wide.
$4,500–5,000 REF

A Welsh oak chest, with incised floral decoration, carved roundels and punchwork, late 16th/early 17thC, 56in (142cm) wide.
$11,500–12,500 CoA

An oak coffer, with original hinges and wrought iron safety chain, early 17thC, 49in (124.5cm) wide.
$900–1,000 HBC

An oak linen chest, with arcaded carved frieze and steel lockplate, 17thC, 39in (99cm) wide.
$2,000–2,500 WBH

An oak coffer, with carved three-panel front, 17thC, 35in (89cm) wide.
$1,600–1,800 RED

A George I oak chest of drawers, veneered with figured ash, with brass drop handles, on square chamfered legs, c1725, 38in (96.5cm) wide.
$5,000–6,000 PHA

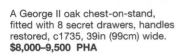

A George II oak chest-on-stand, fitted with 8 secret drawers, handles restored, c1735, 39in (99cm) wide.
$8,000–9,500 PHA

A George II 'red walnut' chest of drawers, with 4 short and 2 long drawers, on later bracket feet, 21¼in (54cm) wide.
$14,500–16,000 S(S)

A yew chest of drawers, with 3 long and 2 short drawers, c1770, 37in (94cm) wide.
$5,500–6,500 RED

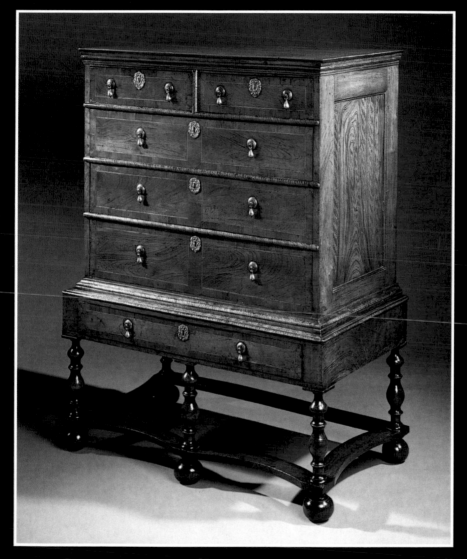

A joined oak press cupboard, Yorkshire, c1640, 71in (180.5cm) wide.
$20,000–22,500 DBA

A Charles II joined oak press cupboard, possibly West Country, dated '1684', 57½in (146cm) wide.
$16,000–19,500 PHA

A Charles II oak cabinet, inlaid with mother-of-pearl and bone, restored, dated '1684', 46⅛in (118cm) wide.
$7,200–8,200 S(NY)

A Welsh oak food cupboard, with a shelved interior, Cardiganshire, c1760, 48in (122cm) wide.
$8,000–9,000 CoA

A George III oak standing corner cupboard, fitted with shaped shelves, 44½in (113cm) wide.
$3,200–4,000 AH

► A German provincial oak cabinet, 17thC, later incised date '1774', 66¼in (168cm) wide.
$1,800–2,200 L&E

An inlaid oak corner cupboard, early 19thC, 44⅛in (113cm) wide.
$650–800 Bea(E)

An oak hanging corner cupboard, fitted with shaped shelves and drawers, 18thC, 36in (91.5cm) wide.
$2,500–3,000 CAG

◄ An oak press cupboard, 18thC, 77in (195.5cm) wide.
$7,800–8,400 Doc

An oak housekeeper's cupboard, the upper breakfront section fitted with shelves, c1800, 82in (208.5cm) wide.
$8,000–9,000 RBB

An oak press cupboard, possibly Lincolnshire, c1830, 48½in (123cm) wide.
$6,000–7,000 RED

A French chestnut armoire, 19thC, 51in (129.5cm) wide.
$2,200–3,000 MTay

A Welsh oak dresser, c1700, 53in (134.5cm) wide.
$21,000–24,000 CoA

A Welsh oak *cwpwrdd tridarn*, the upper part with open shelf, c1720, 52in (132cm) wide.
$18,000–21,000 PHA

An oak dresser, with 3 short drawers over an arcaded apron, 18thC, 52¾in (134cm) wide.
$6,500–7,500 P(E)

A Welsh oak dresser, with original brasses, c1785, 70in (178cm) wide.
$30,000–35,000 PHA

A Welsh oak 'dog kennel' dresser, c1800, 69in (175.5cm) wide.
$9,000–10,000 RED

An oak 3 drawer dresser, 18thC, 62in (157.5cm) wide.
$3,800–4,000 TMA

A George III provincial oak dresser, with 3 open shelves and shaped sides to the upper section, the base with 3 frieze drawers, and shaped arched under-frame, on baluster supports with square feet joined by an undershelf, 57½in (146cm) wide.
$7,200–8,200 Bea(E)

A French chestnut dresser, southern Brittany, dated '1881', 50in (127cm) wide.
$3,000–3,500 MTay

A French chestnut dresser, with brass hinges and mounts, central Brittany, late 19thC, 48in (122cm) wide.
$2,500–3,200 MTay

Douglas Bryan

FINE OAK & COUNTRY FURNITURE

Douglas & Catherine Bryan

The Old Bakery, St David's Bridge
Cranbrook, Kent TN17 3HN
Tel: 01580 713103 Fax: 01580 712407 Mobile: 03747 37303

Bottom of town adjacent Tanyard car park.
Resident on premises.

An oak dresser base, with later potboard, c1740, 90in (228.5cm) wide.
$14,500–16,500 RED

A George III oak dresser base, inlaid with mahogany and boxwood, c1760, 77in (195.5cm) wide.
$18,000–21,000 PHA

A North Country oak dresser base, crossbanded in oak, with panelled sides, late 18thC, 100in (254cm) wide.
$5,000–5,750 CAG

▶ A George III Welsh oak panelled box settle, c1760, 61in (155cm) wide.
$3,500–4,500 PHA

An oak refectory table, with column-turned legs, restored, mid-17thC, 120in (305cm) long.
$5,500–6,500 REF

A Charles I oak refectory table, restored, each leg stamped '1637, RD', 125in (317.5cm) long.
$25,000–29,000 S(S)

An oak refectory table, the frieze with geometric inlay, 17thC and later, 83½in (212cm) long.
$3,700–4,000 AH

A Tuscan table, with dark walnut base and light walnut top, above 2 frieze drawers, c1680, 84in (213.5cm) long.
$3,700–4,200 REF

A joined oak lowboy, with ebonized inlay to top and drawer fronts, later brasses, c1720, 33in (84cm) wide.
$5,000–5,600 DBA

An oak gateleg table, with bobbin-turned legs, c1695, 47½in (120.5cm) wide.
$6,500–7,500 PHA

A Welsh oak lowboy, with burr elm top, c1770, 27in (68.5cm) wide.
$12,000–13,500 CoA

A pine column-fronted armoire, c1870, 48in (122cm) wide.
$950–1,000 TPC

A pine two-door fielded panelled armoire, c1880, 50in (127cm) wide.
$1,200–1,500 TPC

A Victorian Irish pine chest of 8 graduated drawers, enclosed in a two-door cupboard, Dublin, c1880, 20½in (52cm) wide.
$900–1,000 DFA

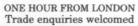

A pine cupboard, c1880, 29in (73.5cm) wide.
$360–400 AL

A pair of pine bedside cabinets, with ball feet, c1890, 17in (43cm) wide.
$650–720 TPC

A pine pot cupboard, c1900, 21in (53.5cm) wide.
$160–200 CPS

A stained and polished pine Welsh dresser, early 19thC, 64in (162.5cm) wide.
$5,000–5,600 RED

An Irish pine dresser, with 3 drawers, restored, c1840, 54in (137cm) wide.
$1,000–1,200 DFA

An Irish pine dresser, Co Tipperary, c1850, 53in (134.5cm) wide.
$1,000–1,200 DFA

A pine dresser, with 2 drawers, panelled sides and doors, c1850, 55in (139.5cm) wide.
$2,300–2,600 ESA

A pine dresser, with graduated stepped open rack, c1860, 84in (213.5cm) wide.
$2,400–3,200 TPC

A pine dresser, with open rack, 3 drawers above 3 panelled doors, c1860, 72in (183cm) wide.
$2,000–2,250 TPC

An Irish pine dresser, with moulded cornice and 3 shelves, the base with a pair of panelled doors, c1865, 48in (122cm) wide.
$800–1,000 Byl

A pine dresser, with glazed upper doors, the base with a pair of drawers and panelled doors, c1880, 48in (122cm) wide.
$1,400–1,600 TPC

A Continental pine dresser, late 19thC, 39in (99cm) wide.
$1,200–1,400 DEE

A pine box settle, c1820,
48in (122cm) wide.
$2,600–3,000 RED

A drop-leaf convent table, with
cleated top, on bobbin-turned
legs with stretchers, c1840,
108in (274.5cm) long.
$1,300–1,500 TPC

A pine box settle, c1820,
48in (122cm) wide.
$2,600–3,000 RED

A Victorian pine gallery-back
washstand, c1860,
36in (91.5cm) wide.
$400–500 TPC

A pine side table, c1870,
31½in (80cm) wide.
$750–800 AL

A pine washstand, mid-19thC,
28in (71cm) wide.
$360–400 WaH

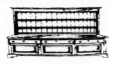

A red painted pine and maple chest, possibly Massachusetts, mid-18thC, 35½in (90cm) wide.
$52,000–60,000 SK(B)

A Victorian pine chest of drawers, with original painted finish, on turned bun feet, c1870, 36in (91.5cm) wide.
$600–700 TPC

An Austro-Hungarian pine cupboard, with glazed door and original paint, c1800, 36in (91.5cm) wide.
$600–700 OLM

A painted pine corner food cupboard, c1730, 23in (58.5cm) wide.
$3,750–4,000 INC

A Swedish baroque painted pine cabinet, 18thC, 63½in (161.5cm) wide.
$3,200–3,500 B&B

A German painted pine cupboard, dated '1802', 45½in (115.5cm) wide.
$1,600–1,800 HAM

A painted pine bowfront corner cupboard, c1840, 13½in (34.5cm) wide.
$400–500 CPA

An Irish painted pine cupboard, c1820, 59in (150cm) wide.
$3,000–4,000 HON

A painted pine armoire, c1850, 60in (152.5cm) wide.
$1,200–1,400 TPC

◄ A Continental painted pine cupboard, 19thC, 38in (96.5cm) wide.
$1,600–2,200 SPU

► A Victorian painted and grained pine dressing table, with matching wardrobe and washstand, 59in (150cm) wide.
$1,600–1,800 CDC

A painted pine marriage chest, possibly Austro-Hungarian, dated '1872', 75in (190.5cm) wide.
$1,800–2,200 B&B

A green painted pine Windsor elbow chair, 19thC.
$1,400–1,600 TEN

A French provincial painted pine chair, c1880.
$130–160 WaH

A Hungarian pine settle, with original blue paint, c1870, 76in (193cm) wide.
$800–900 OLM

◄ An Irish painted pine settle, c1820, 72in (183cm) wide.
$600–700 DFA

► A painted pine box settle, c1880, 72in (183cm) wide.
$750–900 TPC

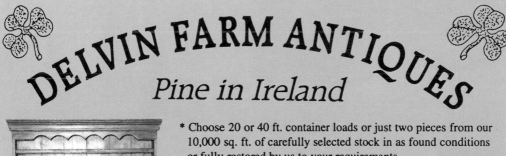

A Welsh sycamore dairy bowl,
19thC, 22in (56cm) diam.
$730–810 CoA

A copper mixing bowl, c1920,
13in (33cm) diam.
$130–160 AL

A ceramic bowl and flour shaker,
c1930, bowl 9½in (24cm) diam.
$35–50 each AL

A Welsh elm salt box,
18thC, 12in (30.5cm) wide.
$120–140 OLM

A butter churn and stand,
c1890, 46in (117cm) high.
$650–730 AL

A pine churn, c1880, 24in (61cm) wide.
$160–250 TPC

A Welsh sycamore butter scoop,
19thC, 12in (30.5cm) long.
$550–650 CoA

A Cornish ware sugar jar,
black shield mark, 1950s,
7½in (19cm) high.
$50–65 AL

A set of scales, c1910,
14in (35.5cm) wide.
$140–155 AL

A set of 5 Victorian copper ale mullers, c1860,
largest 14in (35.5cm) long.
$850–900 ANV

A Normandy apple shovel, c1880, 42in (106.5cm) long.
$130–160 MLL

A French sugar tin, c1920,
6in (15cm) high.
$10–15 AL

◄ A glass celery vase,
c1950, 6in (15cm) high.
$10–15 AL

An flight of 40 oak spice
drawers, late 18thC,
11¾in (30cm) wide.
$750–900 SPR

A George III oak spoon
rack, the 3 drawers with
original knobs, c1780,
12in (30.5cm) wide.
$1,300–1,600 PHA

CHESTS OF DRAWERS

A German painted pine serpentine-front commode, in stripped taupe-painted finish, c1775, 45½in (115.5cm) wide.
$4,500–5,000 NOA

An American red-painted pine chest of drawers, with 2 dummy drawers, New England, 18thC, 34in (86.5cm) wide.
$5,700–6,500 SK(B)

A Welsh pine chest of drawers, c1860, 41in (104cm) wide.
$570–650 OLM

A pine chest of drawers, c1860, 41¾in (106cm) wide.
$680–750 AL

An east European pine chest of drawers, c1870, 47in (119.5cm) wide.
$620–700 Sam

An east European pine chest of drawers, c1875, 40in (101.5cm) wide.
$570–650 Sam

Further Reading
Miller's Pine & Country Furniture Buyer's Guide, Miller's Publications, 1995

A pine flight of 35 drawers, c1870, 70in (178cm) wide.
$1,200–1,400 AL

A pine chest of drawers, marked 'Heal & Son, London', c1870, 44½in (113cm) wide.
$730–800 AL

A pitch-pine miniature chest of drawers, with moulded top, on bracket feet, c1870, 17in (43cm) wide.
$350–380 MB

A Lancashire chest of drawers, with marble top and tiled back, c1870, 43in (109cm) wide.
$450–500 TAN

A Victorian pine chest of drawers, with original wooden handles, 47in (119.5cm) wide.
$730–800 DEE

A pine chest of drawers, c1870, 18½in (47cm) wide.
$320–350 AL

A pine chest of drawers, c1880, 37½in (95.5cm) wide.
$700–800 AL

A Victorian pine chest of drawers, with ceramic handles, c1880, 30in (76cm) wide.
$500–550 DEE

An east European chest of drawers, c1910, 39in (101cm) wide.
$570–650 Sam

▶ A set of 6 pine graduated drawers, c1880, 16in (40.5cm) wide.
$320–370 AL

A pine miniature set of drawers, c1880, 8¾in (22cm) wide.
$100–120 AL

A flight of pine drawers, c1890,
15½in (39.5cm) wide.
$70–90 Ber

A set of 4 pine drawers, c1880, 28½in (72.5cm) wide.
$150–165 AL

A pine tray-top chest of drawers,
c1880, 40in (101.5cm) wide.
$730–800 TPC

A pine chest of drawers, c1880,
41in (104cm) wide.
$570–650 AL

A pine chest of drawers, c1880,
36in (91.5cm) wide.
$570–650 AL

CUPBOARDS

A Welsh elm and pine cupboard, c1795, 24in (61cm) wide.
$300–330 OLM

An American pine corner cupboard, New England, 18thC, 29½in (75cm) wide.
$1,600–1,800 SK(B)

◄ An American pine corner cupboard, New England, late 18thC, 37½in (95.5cm) wide.
$2,300–2,600 SK(B)

A north European painted pine wall spice cupboard, with compartmented interior, late 18thC, 16in (40.5cm) wide.
$1,450–1,650 SK(B)

An Austrian pine cupboard, in original blue paint, c1800, 43in (109cm) wide.
$1,450–1,650 ESA

A pine two-door cupboard, c1810, 32in (81.5cm) wide.
$1,100–1,300 TPC

► An American painted pine panelled cupboard, with of 2 panelled doors, New England, slight damage, early 19thC, 43½in (110.5cm) wide.
$1,000–1,200 SK(B)

An American pine panelled cupboard, the 2 sliding doors enclosing 3 shelves, New England, 18thC, 37½in (95.5cm) wide.
$9,500–10,500 SK(B)

A pine corner cupboard, with decoratively carved cornice, arched and shaped shelf interior and 2 glazed doors, c1810, 40in (101.5cm) wide.
$2,600–3,000 TPC

A Regency pine standing bowfront corner cupboard, the 4 panelled cupboard doors enclosing shelves, restored, 48in (122cm) wide.
$3,200–2,500 S(S)

An Irish pine corner cupboard, the doors with interior sunburst, c1840, 43in (109cm) wide.
$1,600–2,000 HON

An Irish pine two-part panelled cupboard, c1860, 55in (139.5cm) wide.
$1,500–1,800 HON

A Victorian pine cupboard, c1860, 72in (183cm) wide.
$900–1,000 TPC

A north European pine polychrome-decorated armoire, c1820, 63½in (161.5cm) wide.
$2,600–2,900 NOA

A pine two-piece linen press, c1880, 50in (127cm) wide.
$2,100–2,300 AL

A Scottish pine cupboard, the interior fitted with shelves and one drawer, c1860, 47in (119.5cm) wide.
$1,800–2,000 AL

A pine cupboard, with shelved interior, c1820, 48in (122cm) wide.
$730–800 HOA

Cross Reference
See Colour Review

An Irish press cupboard, c1850, 53in (134.5cm) wide.
$1,600–2,000 HRQ

An eastern European pine wall hanging corner cupboard, in original painted finish, c1860, 30in (76cm) wide.
$400–480 TPC

A Victorian pine linen press, 51in (129.5cm) wide.
$1,300–1,500 DEE

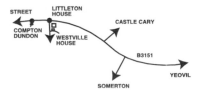

An Irish pine two-part cupboard, with interior secret drawer, c1860, 57in (145cm) wide.
$1,800–2,100 HON

A Victorian pine housekeeper's cupboard, 71in (180.5cm) wide.
$2,300–2,600 DEE

A Victorian pine pot cupboard, c1870, 14½in (37cm) wide.
$400–440 AL

A pine pot cupboard, c1870, 13½in (34.5cm) wide.
$260–280 AL

An Irish pine cupboard, c1870, 54in (137cm) wide.
$1,200–1,500 Byl

An Irish pine cupboard, c1870, 50in (127cm) wide.
$1,100–1,300 Byl

An Irish food cupboard, restored, c1870, 57in (145cm) wide.
$1,600–2,000 WEE

An Irish pine panelled cupboard, Co Galway, c1870, 51in (129.5cm) wide.
$1,200–1,500 HON

An Irish pine cupboard, c1875, 41in (104cm) wide.
$1,200–1,500 Byl

A Continental pine and fruitwood food cupboard, c1875, 38in (96.5cm) wide.
$500–600 Sam

A pine pot cupboard, c1880, 15½in (39.5cm) wide.
$330–360 AL

An east European pine display cabinet, c1880, 39in (101cm) wide.
$730–900 Sam

An Irish pine glazed cupboard, Co Clare, c1880, 32in (81.5cm) wide.
$850–1,000 HON

An Irish pine cupboard, c1880, 48in (122cm) wide.
$450–530 Byl

A pine pot cupboard, c1880, 15in (38cm) wide.
$260–300 AL

A pine pot cupboard, c1880, 15½in (39.5cm) wide.
$260–300 AL

A pine cupboard, with 2 doors, c1880, 41in (104cm) wide.
$350–400 AL

A pine pot cupboard, c1880, 14½in (37cm) wide.
$300–330 AL

▶ An Irish pine vestry cupboard, restored, c1880, 31in (78.5cm) wide.
$500–570 DFA

A French pine cabinet, with original paint, c1890, 12½in (32cm) wide.
$130–160 OLM

A Continental pot cupboard, with drawer, c1890, 15in (38cm) wide.
$140–160 MIL

A pine bedside cupboard, c1900, 16in (40.5cm) wide.
$160–200 TPC

A pine cupboard, c1900, 21½in (54.5cm) wide.
$130–160 WaH

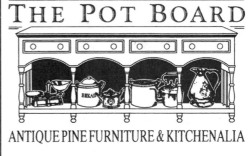

A pine and walnut bureau, with fitted interior including secret drawers, c1780, 36in (91.5cm) wide.
$1,300–1,600 TPC

A George III pine bureau, c1780, 35in (89cm) wide.
$1,800–2,100 GD

A pine desk, with secret drawer to centre, c1800, 44in (112cm) wide.
$970–1,100 WaH

An American merchant's pine kneehole desk, painted red umber to resemble wood, early 19thC, 48in (122cm) wide.
$450–575 SK(B)

This desk is inscribed 'C. Cushing: Caleb Cushing was a Newburyport, Massachusetts merchant'. Caleb Cushing (1800–79), was a congressman for 4 terms in Washington and was minister to China under President Tyler. While minister he negotiated a treaty with China enabling American ports to commence trading with China. In 1851 he was elected the first mayor of Newburyport.

A Continental pine desk, with flip-top lid and internal drawers, c1850, 53in (134.5cm) wide.
$650–800 Sam

A Victorian pine pedestal desk, in 3 pieces, with replaced leather top, 48in (122cm) wide.
$1,600–2,000 DEE

A pine pedestal desk, c1880, 60in (152.5cm) wide.
$800–1,000 TPC

A pine roll-top desk, with fitted interior, 19thC, 53in (134.5cm) wide.
$4,000–4,500 DEE

DRESSERS

A Devonshire pine glazed dresser, c1860, 72in (183cm) wide.
$3,000–3,500 **ESA**

▶ An Irish pine dresser, c1860, 85in (216cm) wide.
$1,500–1,800 **Byl**

A Hungarian pine dresser, c1860, 50in (127cm) wide.
$2,000–2,500 ESA

An Irish pine dresser, c1860, 48in (122cm) wide.
$850–1,000 Byl

An Irish pine dresser, restored, c1870, 51in (129.5cm) wide.
$900–1,000 DFA

An Irish painted pine dresser, Co Cavan, c1880, 58in (147cm) wide.
$900–1,000 DFA

An Irish pine dresser, 19thC,
55in (139.5cm) wide.
$1,900–2,500 SLN

An Irish pine dresser, restored,
later decorated, c1880,
51in (129.5cm) wide.
$650–700 DFA

◄ An Irish painted pine dresser,
c1860, 53in (134.5cm) wide.
$620–700 DFA

► An American pine two-piece
dresser, the upper section with
2 six-pane doors over an arched
open shelf, the lower section with
2 doors enclosing a shelf, 19thC,
51in (129cm) wide.
$2,200–2,500 SLN

A Hungarian pine dresser, with glazed
doors, c1900, 56in (142cm) wide.
$800–900 A&H

DRESSER BASES & SIDE CABINETS

A Georgian pine dresser base,
with original paint finish, unrestored,
c1780, 72in (183cm) wide.
$4,400–5,200 CPA

A stained-pine dresser base,
with 3 drawers and fielded panelled
doors, 18thC, 51in (129.5cm) wide.
$2,400–3,000 FHF

An Irish pine side cabinet, c1875,
44in (112cm) wide.
$300–350 Byl

An Irish pine dresser base, c1875,
39in (99cm) wide.
$260–320 Byl

An Irish pine dresser base, c1870,
48in (122cm) wide.
$350–400 Byl

A Victorian pine dresser base, with recessed cupboard, 55in (139.5cm) wide.
$800–900 DEE

A pine dresser base, with potboard, c1880, 68in (172.5cm) wide.
$730–800 AL

An Irish pine chiffonier, c1875, 42in (106.5cm) wide.
$370–450 Byl

An Irish pine chiffonier, c1880, 42in (106.5cm) wide.
$370–450 Byl

An Irish pine server, with gallery back, c1880, 42in (106.5cm) wide.
$260–320 Byl

A pine sideboard, c1880, 57½in (146cm) wide.
$970–1,100 AL

A Continental pine dwarf side cabinet, with a shelf, c1880, 31in (787.5cm) wide.
$260–300 CCP

RACKS & SHELVES

A pine rack, with original green paint, drawer missing, early 19thC, 40in (101.5cm) wide.
$570–650 CPA

A pine four-tier rack, c1920, 34in (86.5cm) wide.
$60–70 AL

Cross Reference
See Colour Review

A Continental beech hat and coat rack, c1900, 22½in (57cm) wide.
$65–75 LCA

SETTLES

A Welsh fruitwood box settle, with original paint, c1790, 57in (145cm) wide.
$1,200–1,400 OLM

A pine settle, early 19thC, 52in (132cm) wide.
$3,000–3,500 RED

A Hungarian pine box-settle, c1870, 52in (132cm) wide.
$650–750 OLM

Miller's is a price GUIDE not a price LIST

STEPS

A set of pine steps, c1900, 44in (112cm) high.
$80–100 AL

A pine step ladder, c1900, 31in (78.5cm) high.
$50–60 AL

A pine step ladder, c1930, 60in (152.5cm) high.
$80–100 AL

A painted pine step ladder, c1920, 68in (172.5cm) high.
$110–130 A&H

STOOLS

A pine stool, with 4 chamfered legs,
c1870, 23in (58.5cm) wide.
$90–100 MIL

An Irish pine milking stool, c1880,
24in (61cm) wide.
$70–90 Byl

A painted pine stool, late 19thC,
12in (30.5cm) high.
$30–40 WaH

TABLES

A painted black walnut and pine table,
with removable top, Pennsylvania,
1760–1800, 48½in (123cm) long.
$2,500–2,900 SK(B)

An American maple and pine
tavern table, New England, 18thC,
33in (84cm) wide.
$1,600–1,800 SK(B)

A pine side table, with galleried top
and 2 drawers, on turned legs, early
19thC, 36in (91.5cm) wide.
$500–650 TPC

◀ A pine
H-table, with
original painted
base joined by
an H-stretcher,
c1820, 49in
(124.5cm) wide.
$650–750 ESA

A north European turned and painted pine farmhouse
table, 1855–70, 72in (183cm) long.
$900–1,000 NOA

An Irish pine table, reduced in height, c1870,
70in (178cm) long.
$330–360 DFA

A pine sofa table, c1870,
29½in (75cm) long.
$400–450 AL

An Irish pine drop-leaf table,
with square legs, c1870,
46in (116.5cm) diam.
$300–350 Byl

A North American pine
three-legged table, c1870,
26in (66cm) high.
$280–330 WaH

A Welsh pine cricket table, c1870,
36in (91.5cm) diam.
$700–780 CoA

An Irish pine drop-leaf table, c1875,
44in (112cm) wide.
$290–350 Byl

An Irish pine table, with
2 stretchers, c1875,
53in (134.5cm) long.
$230–280 Byl

An Irish pine table, c1875,
41in (104cm) long.
$230–280 Byl

A French pine oval table, c1880,
41in (104cm) diam.
$450–570 WaH

Cross Reference
See Colour Review

A pine side table, with turned legs,
c1880, 39in (99cm) wide.
$320–350 AL

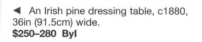

An American pine table, with hinged top, possibly
Pennsylvania, 19thC, 54in (137cm) long.
$1,400–1,600 SK(B)

◄ An Irish pine dressing table, c1880,
36in (91.5cm) wide.
$250–280 Byl

An American pitch-pine
cricket table, c1900,
25½in (65cm) high.
$280–320 WaH

WARDROBES

A pine armoire, with 2 doors, Baltic states, c1830, 50in (127cm) wide.
$1,100–1,300 ESA

An east European single-door wardrobe with original paint, c1830, 45in (114cm) wide.
$2,500–3,250 Sam

An Irish pine miniature wardrobe, with turned columns, c1840, 16in (40.5cm) wide.
$200–250 AF

A Russian pine wardrobe, c1850, 49in (124.5cm) wide.
$570–730 Sam

A Russian pine wardrobe, c1850, 52in (132cm) wide.
$570–700 Sam

A pine wardrobe, c1870, 42in (106.5cm) wide.
£1,000–1,100 TPC

An Irish pine wardrobe, c1870, 47in (119.5cm) wide.
$700–800 Byl

An east European pine single door hanging cupboard, c1860, 37in (94cm) wide.
$500–570 Sam

A Continental pine hanging cupboard, c1870, 37in (94cm) wide.
$570–650 Sam

An Irish pine wardrobe, c1875, 47in (119.5cm) wide.
$450–530 Byl

◄ An east European pine two-door wardrobe, c1875, 45in (114cm) wide.
$550–650 Sam

A pine miniature wardrobe, with original muslin curtains and secret compartment to centre, c1880, 25in (63.5cm) wide.
$290–350 WaH

An Irish pine wardrobe, c1880, 47in (119.5cm) wide.
$530–600 Byl

A Continental pine wardrobe, c1880, 46in (117cm) wide.
$970–1,100 OLM

An Irish pine wardrobe, with 2 shelves, c1880, 42in (106.5cm) wide.
$450–520 Byl

WASHSTANDS

An Irish pine washstand, c1880, 37in (94cm) wide.
$190–210 Byl

A pine washstand, late 19thC, 34in (86.5cm) wide.
$490–570 TPC

A pine washstand, with 2 drawers, c1870, 35½in (90cm) wide.
$440–490 AL

An Irish pine washstand, late 19thC, 39in (99cm) wide.
$230–280 Byl

An Irish pine single washstand, late 19thC, 23in (58.5cm) wide.
$110–140 Byl

A Continental pine washstand with lift-up lid, c1890, 36in (91.5cm) wide
$490–570 Sam

Kitchenware

An American dovetailed knife box, late 18thC, 16¼in (41.5cm) long.
$1,000–1,200 A&A

A wood and metal-bound bucket, painted with flowers, 19thC, 11½in (29cm) high.
$130–160 P

A butter churn and stand, c1880, 36in (91.5cm) wide.
$570–650 AL

A nest of pine drawers, c1840, 7¾in (19.5cm) wide.
$90–110 OLM

Two iron and brass churns, c1870, largest 20in (51cm) high.
$110–160 each AL

A sycamore butter table, c1900, 42in (106.5cm) wide.
$190–250 AL

A tin nutmeg grater, early 20thC, 3in (7.5cm) wide.
$80–100 SMI

Four storage jars, c1926, 4½in (11.5cm) high.
$15–25 each AL

A ceramic jelly mould, 19thC, 7¼in (18.5cm) wide.
$15–25 No7

A cobalt-decorated four-gallon two-handled stoneware butter churn, by W. H. Farrar & Co, Geddes, New York, damaged, 1841–71, 16¼in (41.5cm) high.
$350–400 SK(B)

A butcher's shop enamel display slab, inscribed 'Palethorpes' Royal Cambridge Sausages', c1920, 11in (28cm) wide.
$180–200 B&R

A George III silver barrel nutmeg grater, the top engraved with a crest, 1802, 2in (5cm) high.
$490–570 P

A Radiation Rhythm iron, c1930, 9in (23cm) long.
$25–35 AL

A yellow ceramic rabbit-shaped mould, c1890, 8½in (21.5cm) long.
$25–35 AL

A German fruitwood heart-shaped pastry mould, with floral decoration, 19thC, 10¼in (26cm) high.
$320–360 P(Z)

Two blue milk-glass shakers, for cinnamon and sugar, 19thC, 3½in (9cm) high.
$250–290 ASM

A Huntley & Palmers biscuit tin, in the form of a glazed cabinet, with bracket feet, c1911, 7½in (19cm) high.
$440–500 Mit

An Australian tin, c1930, 6in (15cm) high.
$10–15 AL

A copper ale muller, c1850, 11in (28cm) long.
$90–110 AL

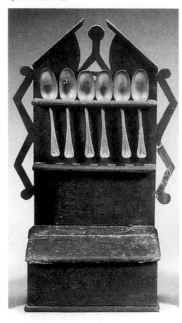

A painted pine hanging spoon rack, with 6 pewter spoons, possibly European, damaged, late 18thC, 11½in (29cm) wide.
$900–1,000 SK(B)

A Shaker iron-bound wash tub, with pierced handles, painted blue and cream, minor damage, 19thC, 20in (50.5cm) diam.
$3,600–4,000 SK(B)

A knife sharpener, c1920, 8in (20.5cm) long.
$3–6 AL

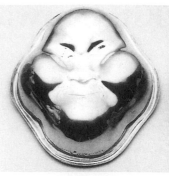

A Victorian silver jelly mould, depicting a smiling face, 1880, 4¼in (11cm) long.
$570–650 P

A set of metal pastry cutters, c1930, largest, 3in (7.5cm) high.
$15–20 AL

A ceramic ham stand, chipped, c1930, 5in (12.5cm) high.
$35–40 AL

A copper warming plate, c1890, 10½in (26.5cm) diam.
$90–110 AL

A Crawfords biscuit tin, in the form of scales, c1950, 10in (25.5cm) wide.
$190–240 PCh

226 **KITCHENWARE**

Pottery

The improvement in restoration techniques, alongside an increasing sensitivity towards the amount of restoration required, has had a considerable effect on the pottery market over the past 21 years. Delftware and majolica in particular have benefited as both are fragile and a considerable amount of restoration is acceptable, particularly on rarer pieces. The saleability of damaged items has therefore improved as dealers and collectors are aware that skilled, sensitive restoration can give the illusion of perfection.

From a purely monetary point of view, most collectors of pottery will have done well over the past 21 years, particularly those who started collections of majolica before the 1970s. Little interest had been shown in this field until an exhibition by a London dealer in 1980, and prices had been low. Since then, its popularity has risen rapidly, although today collectors are more selective, concentrating on pieces by George Jones, Minton and Wedgwood. Good French and Portuguese examples are also back in fashion.

Exhibitions and specialist auctions stimulate interest, bring in new collectors and generally lead to price increases for scarce items. Thus the sale of the Lipski delftware collection caused a jump in the market in 1982, as did the Rous Lench sale some years later. An item which bears a label from an important sale or a top dealer can often command a premium price, but beware of labels switched from inexpensive items from such sales in order to increase its market value.

There have been some periods of poor performance in various sections of the market over the past 21 years. In 1984 Dutch Delft was out of favour whilst Staffordshire figures were considered best buys. In the late 1980s, some staggering prices were paid for rare majolica, Staffordshire animals and Toby jugs, although since then the market for Toby jugs has, to some extent, stagnated. These days rare items in perfect condition are fought over, and damaged rarities do almost as well.

Fortunately most dealers, as well as collectors, are interested in pottery because of its historical associations, its beauty, and the friendship that collecting and dealing engenders. Although we complain that things will never be as good as they were 21 years ago, and our physical fitness levels fall as we trawl the internet for bargains, we can go confidently into the new millennium knowing that we will continue to derive great pleasure and profit from our enthusiasm for pottery.

Christopher Spencer

ANIMALS

A pair of tin-glazed stoneware models of a lion and lioness, restored, c1750, 6½in (16.5cm) long.
$3,000–3,300 S(NY)

Items in the Pottery section have been arranged in date order within each sub-section.

A Sicilian maiolica owl jug and cover, possibly Caltagirone, the feathers painted in blue, green, yellow, ochre and black, early 18thC, 9¾in (25cm) high.
$3,250–4,000 S

A Staffordshire tortoiseshell model of a seated cat, with mottled patches of brown, green and grey-blue, restored, c1770, 6in (15cm) high.
$1,800–2,200 S(NY)

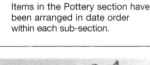

A Staffordshire model of a lion, Ralph Wood type, with a boy seated on its back, on a green and cream base, c1795, 9in (23cm) high.
$4,000–4,500 JHo

A Staffordshire model of a Suffolk Punch horse, with ochre coat and green-washed base, restored, late 18thC, 7½in (19cm) high.
$7,000–7,700 S(NY)

A Prattware model of a cow and calf, possibly Staffordshire, white with brown markings, restored, late 18thC, 2¼in (5.5cm) high.
$650–700 JHo

A Staffordshire pottery bird-shaped whistle, late 18thC, 2¾in (7cm) high.
$130–160 INC

A Staffordshire pearlware model of a white deer, with brown markings and black hooves, c1810, 3½in (9cm) wide.
$325–375 SER

A Staffordshire pottery cockerel, early 19thC, 3¾in (9.5cm) high.
$1,100–1,250 JHo

A Staffordshire leopard group spill vase, decorated in green and ochre, early 19thC, 9⅜in (25cm) high.
$1,000–1,200 PCh

A Staffordshire pearlware sheep and lamb group, on a green base, slight damage, c1825, 5½in (14cm) high.
$450–500 P

◄ Seven pearlware quail boxes and covers in a circular stand, possibly Davenport, the birds with brown and grey plumage, the stand forming a nest painted to simulate twigs and grasses in green, ochre and brown, damaged and restored, c1815, stand 11⅛in (29cm) wide.
$2,500–3,000 C

A Lloyd Shelton model of a lion, reclining beside a lamb on a pink base, inscribed 'The young Lion shall lie down with the Lamb (Isaiah XI, 6v)', with gilded tail, slight damage, c1840, 4¾in (12cm) wide.
$820–900 P

21 Years Ago …

A Staffordshire bull-baiting group, possibly by Obadiah Sherratt, the base with 2 labels 'Bull-Beating' and 'Now Captain Lad', c1830, 14in (35.5cm) wide. **L**

Twenty-one years ago this Staffordshire bull-baiting group was valued at $750–850. At this price level it was firmly in the province of wealthy collectors. Over the next 15 years, the value of this piece rose steadily while others rose spectacularly. By 1996 it represented good value in comparison with some other, more ephemeral, areas of collecting. Interest is now strong again and the value of this group has increased considerably over the past two years, to $9,000–10,000. A similar group is featured on page 274.

A Yorkshire pottery model of a swan, cream with black wings and a mottled brown base, c1850, 3¾in (9.5cm) high.
$1,000–1,100 JHo

A Staffordshire hunting group, on a green base, c1850, 8in (20.5cm) high.
$400–450 STA

A Staffordshire poodle and puppies group, on a blue base, c1855, 8in (20.5cm) high.
$575–650 JO

A pair of Staffordshire models of poodles, with black noses and gold collars, c1860, 11½in (29cm) high.
$730–830 STA

A Staffordshire model of a dog, white with black nose and glass eyes, c1860, 12½in (32cm) high.
$160–180 STA

A Rye Pottery pig, with green body and white tail, the head forming a cup, inscribed 'Wint be Druv', c1870, 8in (20.5cm) wide.
$275–325 DN(H)

A pair of Minton majolica spill vases, by John Henk, one supported by a cockerel, the other a hen, shape numbers 1982 and 1983, impressed marks and date code for 1876, slight damage, 14¼in (36cm) high.
$11,500–13,000 Bea(E)

A pair of English majolica models of seated spaniels, each wearing a collar and chain, picked out in brown, on green glazed stepped base, damaged, c1870, 10½in (26.5cm) high.
$2,000–2,500 DN

A treacle-glazed model of a lion, standing with one front paw resting on a ball, tail restored, 19thC, 10½in (26.5cm) high.
$260–320 DN

A Joseph Holdcroft majolica umbrella stand, modelled as a stork beside bulrushes, in mottled green, brown and yellow glazes, the interior of the stand in turquoise glazes, damaged, c1875, 28½in (72.5cm) high.
$5,750–6,500 Hal

Animals • POTTERY 229

A Yorkshire pottery bird, early 19thC, 4¼in(11cm) high.
$600–700 JHo

A glazed redware footwarmer, in the form of a ram, slight damage, 19thC, 13½in (34.5cm) long.
$525–575 SK(B)

A pottery figure of a man with a pony and trap, with a green base, mid-19thC, 3½in (9cm) high.
$575–650 JHo

A Ewenny pottery 'custard'-glazed cat, dated '1917', 15in (38cm) high.
$1,300–1,450 CoA

A Staffordshire pottery jug, in the form of a begging spaniel, picked out in iron-red and wearing a gilt collar, 19thC, 10¾in (27.5cm) high.
$575–650 DN

A Jackfield model of a cow and milkmaid, c1890, 6¼in (16cm) high.
$200–250 JO

A Caldas majolica monkey, seated on the back of a turtle, decorated in the style of Bernard Palissy, turtle's head missing, late 19thC, 17in (43cm) high.
$1,100–1,300 P

A Yorkshire pottery model of a horse, restored, early 19thC, 6in (15cm) high.
$4,250–5,000 JHo

A pair of Staffordshire models of spaniels, with iron-red body markings, gilt collars and black leads, grey and black tipped feet, slight damage, late 19thC, 9in (23cm) high.
$400–500 GAK

A Staffordshire model of a black elephant and baby, by W. Kent & Co, on a green and yellow base, c1900, 6½in (16.5cm) wide.
$1,000–1,150 JO

A pottery nodding cat, retailed by Thomas Goode & Co, with glass eyes, decorated with pink roses and an orange collar, c1900, 16in (40.5cm) long.
$1,300–1,450 PGA

Ewenny Pottery

- Pottery produced in Glamorgan since the early 18thC.
- In the late 19thC both the Claypits Pottery, Ewenny and The Ewenny Pottery began to produce Art Pottery.
- The Jenkins family still runs the Ewenny Pottery, which has been in the family since the early 1800s.
- Ewenny wares are easy to identify because bases are inscribed with the name of the pottery.

BOTTLES

A Portuguese blue and white bottle-shaped vase, painted with stylized flowering branches and foliage below a band of repeated spirals, the lower part with a band of lappets, slight damage, c1650, 8¾in (22cm) high.
$7,300–8,300 C

A La Cartuja faïence Persian-style bottle and stand, each brightly coloured with yellow-ground panels of stylized foliage, lappets and lattice within a turquoise-blue ground, Seville, restored, c1890, 22¼in (56.5cm) high.
$3,000–3,300 S

Miller's Compares

I A London delft wine bottle, with a grooved loop handle, inscribed in blue 'Claret 1642', 7½in (19cm) high.
$18,500–20,000 S

II An English delft sack bottle, with flat loop handle, inscribed in blue 'Sack 1659', restored, 4¾in (12cm) high.
$6,500–7,500 S(NY)

The earlier date and the unusual inscription of the word 'Claret' makes item I more desirable than Item II, as fewer claret bottles have survived. More importantly, the claret bottle is in very good condition whilst the sack bottle has several areas of restored glaze. Although item I is larger in height than item II, this did not in itself account for the higher price realized at auction. S

BOWLS

A London delft bleeding bowl, the triangular handle pierced with hearts and a circle, painted with 2 rows of evenly spaced blue and manganese marks, slight damage, c1690, 6¾in (17cm) diam.
$17,000–18,500 S

A pearlware Mocha ware bowl, with a terracotta, black and grey marbled band, 1790–1810, 6¼in (16cm) diam.
$1,150–1,300 A&A

A Dutch Delft blue and white colander bowl, the side with a rectangular pouring hole, decorated with panels of flowers, damaged, mid-18thC, 8¾in (22cm) diam.
$650–750 WW

A bargeware brown-glazed sugar bowl, inscribed 'God Bless Our Home', c1880, 7in (18cm) diam.
$400–440 DHA

◄ A Minton wash basin, decorated with Amhurst Japan pattern, c1830, 14in (35.5cm) diam.
$300–330 AnSh

A creamware punchbowl, the exterior inscribed in black beneath a blue enamelled rim, the interior with a trellis border, slight damage, dated '1790', 13¾in (35cm) diam.
$4,500–5,000 S(NY)

A Scottish bat-printed masonic bowl, c1820, 5in (12.5cm) high.
$900–1,100 BWA

A Mason's Ironstone bowl, decorated with Japan pattern and gilt rim, impressed mark, c1815–20, 10¼in (26cm) diam.
$530–580 VH

BUILDINGS

A Continental faïence inkstand, decorated in blue and yellow, the central section in the form of a country mansion, each bay with detachable roof, fitted at each corner with a metal inkwell, sander or pen holder, restored, late 18thC, 9in (23cm) wide.
$8,000–9,000 S(NY)

A pastille burner, in the 'Cottage Ornate' style, decorated with blue and pink flowers and gilt edges, c1840, 7½in (19cm) high.
$1,000–1,200 JO

This triple cottage group is unusual. Many lodge and estate cottages were built in this style during the 19thC. Their popularity is reflected in the many pottery cottage pastille burners which were produced at that time.

A Staffordshire porcellaneous castle pastille burner, decorated in pink, with green foliage, c1850, 4¾in (12cm) high.
$325–400 TVM

CENTREPIECES

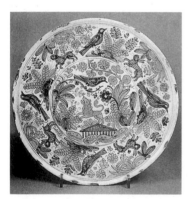

A Mason's Ironstone centrepiece, painted with Japan pattern, 1815–20, 14¼in (36cm) wide.
$800–900 EH

A Savona tazza, on a small raised foot, painted with blue songbirds and hares amongst yellow and blue flowers and foliage, surrounding a rampant lion, slight damage, c1680, 9¾in (25cm) diam.
$1,000–1,150 P

A Holics centrepiece, modelled as a naked triton, with a green, yellow and red fish's tail and red flippers, supporting a pierced quatrefoil shallow bowl decorated in shades of puce, blue, yellow and red, black HH mark, c1770, 13¾in (35cm) wide.
$5,200–6,200 C

A Mason's Ironstone fruit comport, decorated with Japan pattern, c1820, 13in (33cm) wide.
$1,000–1,150 JP

A Minton majolica nautilus-shaped centrepiece, the sides decorated with a male bust wearing a green laurel wreath, and applied with a snail and lizard, slight damage, year cipher for 1862, 7in (18cm) high.
$1,200–1,300 CGC

A George Jones majolica centrepiece, the bowl moulded with seaweed fronds and shells against a turquoise ground, the centre encircled by 3 putti and scallop shells, damaged and restored, c1875, 16in (40.5cm) high.
$10,500–11,500 S

A Victorian Minton majolica oyster stand, decorated with brown and green glazes, with 2 tiers of oyster dishes, 14in (35.5cm) high.
$2,500–3,000 HYD

DISHES

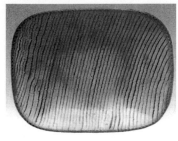

A Staffordshire pottery baking dish, the cavetto glazed with cream slip, decorated with a brown combed design, 18thC, 18½in (47cm) wide.
$1,200–1,350 Bea(E)

A pair of Continental faïence vine-leaf dishes, painted in green with raised veins picked out in pale yellow, one repaired, c1760–80, 14in (35.5cm) long.
$3,000–3,300 S(NY)

An English delft blue and white salver, c1735, 5½in (14cm) diam.
$2,000–2,200 JHo

A delftware spoon tray, Liverpool or Bristol, painted in blue with radiating panels of stylized foliage, the rim edged in brown, c1750, 6in (15cm) wide.
$3,700–4,000 S

▶ A Mason's Ironstone dessert dish, decorated with scroll pattern, c1815–20, 11in (28cm) wide.
$450–525 JP

Two Mason's Ironstone dessert dishes, one decorated in blue and white Cross Fence pattern, one in red and blue Japan pattern, c1820–30, 9in (23cm) wide.
$325–475 each JP

A George Jones-style majolica squirrel nut dish, with relief nut and leaf decoration, with registration mark dated '1868' and impressed B, 13½in (34.5cm) diam.
$1,300–1,450 Mit

◀ A Buckley slip-decorated dish, 19thC, 15in (38cm) wide.
$575–625 CoA

COVERED DISHES

A pair of Jacob Petit asparagus dishes and covers, each modelled as a bundle of asparagus, resting on an attached stand moulded with overlapping leaves and applied with onions and garlic, crossed swords with 'JP' in underglaze-blue, damaged and restored, mid-19thC, 15in (38cm) long.
$13,000–14,500 S(NY)

► A George Jones majolica cheese stand and cover, moulded in relief with dragonflies, water lilies and bulrushes, painted in tones of green, red, brown, yellow, blue and black against a pale blue ground, impressed registration mark for 18th October 1872, painted '3412' in black, 12¼in (31cm) high.
$5,600–6,400 P(F)

An English majolica sardine dish, cover and fixed stand, the cover modelled with sardines, the sides moulded with stiff leaves, on a blue ground, restored, c1860–80, 9in (23cm) wide.
$325–400 DN

An English majolica cheese stand and domed cover, with sardine handle in full relief, 1880–85, 10½in (26.5cm) diam.
$800–900 NOA

FIGURES

A pair of Milan faïence figures of Malabars, probably Clerici's factory, one figure restored, mid-18thC, 13in (33cm) high.
$9,000–10,000 S

A Milan faïence figure of a Chinese sage, Clerici's factory, restored, mid-18thC, 11in (28cm) high.
$1,600–1,800 S

► A Staffordshire figure of Mother Goose, wearing a pointed iron-red lined hat, brown-spotted lemon cape and riding a grey goose, restored, early 19thC, 7in (18cm) high.
$65–80 GAK

A Ralph Wood-type figure of an old lady, wearing a brown dress, with birds feeding from a green bowl, entitled 'The Spinner', c1790, 8in (20.5cm) high.
$5,600–6,200 JHo

A Dutch delft blue and white figure of Guanyin, the back painted with a bird perched on flowering branches, c1720, 14¾in (37.5cm) high.
$9,000–10,000 S

This figure is common in Chinese *blanc-de-Chine* but rare in Delft.

A pottery figure of Leda and the Swan, c1790, 7¼in (18.5cm) high.
$1,400–1,550 JO

Further Reading

P. D. Gordon Pugh, *Staffordshire Portrait Figures*, Antique Collectors' Club, 1987

A Staffordshire earthenware figure of John Wesley, dressed in white bands and black robes, early 19thC, 8¼in (21cm) high.
$300–330 AH

A Staffordshire figure of a showman, painted in yellow, brown and green, on a green base, damaged, 1815–25, 6in (15cm) high.
$300–330 SER

A Staffordshire figure of a girl at a pump, c1820, 6¼in (16cm) high.
$1,800–2,000 JHo

A Staffordshire pottery figure group, depicting a vicar and Moses in black cassocks, seated in a brown-glazed two-tier pulpit, 19thC, 10in (25.5cm) high.
$325–360 AH

A Staffordshire group, depicting a showman, his family and their bear, painted in red, yellow, green, brown and blue, restored, c1820, 7in (18cm) high.
$3,700–4,300 JHo

A Staffordshire figure of Christ in the Garden, painted in green, red and yellow and inscribed 'Christ's Agony', c1830, 9½in (24cm) high.
$5,600–6,200 JHo

◄ A Staffordshire figure of John Liston as Sam Swipe, painted in brown, green and yellow, early 19thC, 8¾in (22cm) high.
$1,200–1,400 JHo

A set of Staffordshire figures of the Four Evangelists, each standing in front of flowering trees and wearing yellow-lined cloaks over brownish red or purple robes, on green mound bases, with black stamped inscriptions, c1830, 8½in (21.5cm) high.
$4,000–4,500 S

Items in the Pottery section have been arranged in date order within each sub-section.

► A Staffordshire figure of Louis Napoleon, wearing a blue tunic, c1830, 16in (40.5cm) high.
$520–570 RBB

A Staffordshire figure entitled 'Samuel Anointing David', c1830, 7in (18cm) high. $2,000–2,200 JHo

A Staffordshire figure of Britannia, wearing a white and gold dress and holding green snakes, c1830, 6¼in (16cm) high. $480–560 JO

A Staffordshire whistle depicting Grimaldi, or Tom Mathews, decorated in red, c1840, 3½in (9cm) high. $160–220 SER

A Staffordshire figure of Captain James Cook, modelled wearing the full dress uniform of a captain, breeches repainted, c1845, 7¾in (20cm) high. $1,800–2,000 P

This figure was modelled after the portrait by Nathaniel Dance, dated 1776, which now hangs in the National Maritime Museum.

A pair of Staffordshire equestrian figures, portraying Queen Victoria and Prince Albert, c1845, 8in (20.5cm) high. $730–800 RWB

A Staffordshire porcellaneous group, modelled as a couple dancing beneath a green umbrella, brightly decorated in blue, pink, orange, yellow, green and gilt, on an oval gilt-lined base, slight damage, c1845, 7¼in (18.5cm) high. $300–330 WW

A Joseph Meir & Co slip-cast figure group of 2 black boys sitting on a wall, one writing and one with a book, each dressed in jackets, shirts and knee-length trousers, with impressed mark 'JM' and 'No. 9628', mid-19thC, 12in (30.5cm) high. $1,100–1,450 Mit

A Staffordshire figure of William Penn, with his hand resting on a group of mossy rocks, wearing a black tricorn hat, blue jacket and yellow waistcoat, holding the sealed charter of Pennsylvania, slight damage, mid-19thC, 8½in (21.5cm) high. $900–1,000 P

A Staffordshire figure of a Turk, painted in pink, green and gilt, c1848, 4¾in (12cm) high. $250–300 JO

A pair of Staffordshire figures of a boy and girl with their dogs, c1860, 8¾in (22cm) high. $450–550 STA

A Staffordshire figure of Abraham Lincoln, wearing an orange cloak and seated on a white spotted charger, on a titled base, c1860, 15in (38cm) high. $800–1,000 P

A Staffordshire group of children and their dog, painted in shades of green, pink, blue and brown, c1850, 8in (20.5cm) high. $200–230 JO

A pair of Minton majolica figures of a young boy and girl, picked out in coloured enamels, impressed marks for 1863, 7¾in (19.5cm) high.
$1,100–1,300 DN

A pair of Minton majolica putti matchpots, each putto with a cornucopia basket strapped to his shoulders, impressed 'Mintons', c1876, 7in (17.5cm) high.
$5,200–5,700 S

A Staffordshire figure, entitled 'Grandma's Hope', decorated in pale pink and yellow, c1880, 9¼in (23.5cm) high.
$325–400 JO

A Staffordshire group of lovers on a seat, with green bocage, 19thC, 9½in (24cm) high.
$250–300 PCh

Two Staffordshire figures, entitled '6 A.M.' and '6 P.M.', c1890, 12½in (32cm) high.
$400–500 JO

A Meissen 'Böttger' stoneware group of sleeping vagabonds, modelled by Ernst Barlach, incised crossed swords mark, c1923, 17in (43cm) wide.
$13,500–15,500 S

A Quimper hand bell, in the form of a lady, her legs forming the clapper, c1920, 4in (10cm) high.
$260–300 VH

A pair of Continental pottery figures, late 19thC, 38½in (98cm) high.
$2,600–3,300 AH

A Quimper group of dancers, painted in blue, burgundy and green, c1920, 4in (10cm) high.
$350–400 VH

FLATWARE

An Urbino maiolica shallow bowl, probably from the workshop of Guido Durantino, painted with a scene of Deucalion and Pyrrha in blue, green and yellow, damaged and restored, c1535–40, 8½in (21.5cm) diam.
$5,200–5,700 S

A Lyon maiolica dish, painted in green, blue and brown, with 2 tritons, a dolphin and a monster amid swirling waves, restored, c1570–80, 11½in (29cm) diam.
$3,700–4,900 S

An Urbino maiolica tondino, painted in blue, green and yellow, with a putto standing between 2 scantily clad figures of a man and a woman, slight damage, mid-16thC, 9in (23cm) diam.
$3,200–4,000 S

A tondino is a plate with a depressed centre.

A Venice maiolica dish, from the workshop of Maestro Lodovico, painted in blue with a landscape scene, restored, late 16thC, 11¼in (28.5cm) diam.
$2,450–2,900 S

A Dutch maiolica armorial dish, probably Graft, painted in orange, blue and green, restored, c1610–30, 13in (33cm) diam.
$1,900–2,500 S(Am)

A Dutch Delft blue and white charger, probably Haarlam, c1660, 14in (35.5cm) diam.
$4,900–5,300 JHo

> **Cross Reference**
> See Colour Review

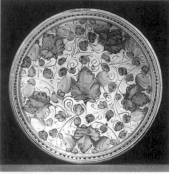

A German slipware dish, possibly by Wanfried an der Werra, decorated in cream, ochre and blue on a brown ground with Adam and Eve flanking the Tree of Knowledge, 17thC, 12in (30.5cm) diam.
$4,000–5,000 S

A Montelupo dish, painted with scattered green fig leaves and ochre figs, 17thC, 12½in (32cm) diam.
$2,000–2,500 C

An English delft plate, painted in blue with a Chinaman presenting a lady with a gift, the blue line border with a sunburst, slight damage, early 18thC, 8¾in (22cm) diam.
$350–450 WW

Italian Maiolica

- Tin-glazed earthenware. Name probably derived from Tuscan word for Majorca through which Hispano-Moresque wares were shipped to Italy from 14thC.
- Late 15thC maiolica painted in broad range of colours with stylized designs such as scrolling leaves, palmettes and geometric motifs.
- 16thC decoration included fantastic creatures, biblical or mythological scenes, trophies of arms and portrait medallions.
- Innovations to late 17th and 18thC decoration were the introduction of perspective into landscape scenes and the influence of Chinese porcelain designs.
- High-quality reproductions of 16thC designs, particularly by Ulysse Cantagalli of Florence, were popular in 19thC.

A Castelli maiolica saucer, painted in greens and browns with a wooded landscape scene, the rim edged in ochre, slight damage, mid-18thC, 6¼in (16cm) diam.
$1,000–1,300 S

A Bristol delft blue and white plate, with dolphin design, c1740, 9in (23cm) diam.
$2,450–2,600 JHo

A London delft polychrome plate, the centre painted in blue and manganese with a sailing ship, the rim with green lappets edged with blue loops, slight damage, c1750, 8¾in (22cm) diam.
$2,600–2,900 C

A Dublin delft blue and white plate, c1740, 9in (23cm) diam.
$750–900 STA

A London delft dish, polychrome painted with a parrot perched on a peony tree within a border of pine cones and trailing foliage, slight damage, c1750, 13½in (34.5cm) diam.
$320–400 Bon

An Irish delft charger, by Henry Delamain, the off-white ground decorated in blue with a basket of flowers c1750–57, 14in (35.5cm) diam.
$3,250–3,500 JAd

A Dublin delft lobed plate, by Henry Delamain, painted in manganese with 2 figures beneath a tree, slight damage, c1760, 10¼in (26cm) diam.
$6,500–7,500 C

A Marseilles faïence dish, painted in a pale grey, puce and yellow palette with 3 fish and a shell on seaweed, c1765, 12½in (32cm) diam.
$14,000–15,500 C

A Dutch Delft charger, painted in shades of blue depicting a Chinese figure strolling in a garden, 18thC, 14in (35.5cm) diam.
$800–900 S(Am)

A 'Jackfield' black-glazed plate, early 19thC, 10½in (26.5cm) diam.
$2,600–3,000 JHo

A Bristol delft plate, the border with *bianco-sopra-bianco* borders, c1760, 9in (23cm) diam.
$800–900 JHo

Bianco-sopra-bianco **is a border of raised decoration in white. It is occasionally used on English delftware, and is popular with collectors. The white decoration stands out strongly against the blue tinted background and is thought to be an attempt to imitate the underglaze carved decoration developed by Chinese potters.**

An English delft blue and white charger, decorated with a bird in a still life with various pots, and a scrolled foliate and floral border, slight damage, 18thC, 13½in (34.5cm) diam.
$530–580 SK

A Dutch Delft plate, polychrome decorated with flowers and trees on a pale green ground, 18thC, 9in (23cm) diam.
$130–160 E

A Liverpool delft plate, decorated in blue, yellow and brown with a chinoiserie of flowers in a fenced garden, c1760, 8¾in (22cm) diam.
$800–950 JHo

A Dutch Delft blue and white charger, with a figural and floral border and a central lion figure, slight damage, 18thC, 13in (33cm) diam.
$730–830 SK

An Italian maiolica charger, painted in tones of yellow, cobalt and green with a scene of Venus and Cupid, slight damage, 18thC, 17½in (44.5cm) diam.
$1,000–1,200 Bon(C)

A Staffordshire black and white child's plate, c1820, 7½in (19cm) diam.
$65–80 SER

◄ A Mason's Ironstone dish, transfer-printed in underglaze blue with bird and peony pattern, impressed mark, c1815–20, 9in (23cm) wide.
$200–230 JP

An Enoch Wood & Sons commemorative pearlware plate, printed in blue with Queen Caroline, inscribed, impressed mark with eagle, c1820, 5½in (14cm) diam.
$400–500 P

A Mason's Ironstone cheese coaster, decorated in blue, pink, orange and yellow with a long-tailed pheasant, c1825, 12in (30.5cm) diam.
$520–570 JP

A Palissy-style majolica platter, moulded with a serpent and a pike, the cobalt blue border moulded with ferns, ivy and various creatures, restored, c1880, 21¼in (54cm) wide.
$4,500–5,200 WW

A set of 6 Morley & Ashworths ironstone plates, the border decorated with orange and pink flowers, printed and impressed marks, c1860, 8½in (21.5cm) diam.
$570–600 VH

A pearlware plate, printed in black with a portrait of Queen Victoria, surmounted by a crown and ribbon inscribed 'Hail Victoria', with gadrooned rim, slight damage, c1838 8¾in (22cm) diam.
$320–400 DN

A set of 6 Salins asparagus plates, c1880–1900, 9in (23cm) diam.
$530–600 MLL

A pair of Quimper plates, from the Hubaudière faïencerie, c1883–85, 9½in (24cm) diam.
$800–900 VH

Cross Reference
See Colour Review

A Ulysse Cantagalli maiolica dish, depicting rural scenes of Urbino in greens, blues and red, 19thC, 10¾in (27.5cm) diam.
$1,300–1,500 HBC

A French faïence charger, with a band of stylized foliage and blossoms, the central scene with blue, red, yellow and decoration, late 19th/early 20thC, 21in (53.5cm) diam.
$300–350 SLM

FLASKS

A Doulton & Watts flask, depicting Mrs Caudle, early 19thC, 7½in (19cm) high.
$400–460 JHo

A Doulton & Watts cordial flask, early 19thC, 7½in (19cm) high.
$300–350 JHo

A Blois flask by Ulysse, with fleur-de-lys and crown motifs, c1905–10, 5in (12.5cm) high.
$300–320 VH

A Quimper Malicorne snuff flask, in the shape of a book with navy-blue spine, decorated with a cockerel and a pheasant with bright plumage, c1890, 3in (7.5cm) high.
$240–280 VH

FLOWER BRICKS

A London delft blue and white flower brick, restored, c1710, 5½in (14cm) wide.
£1,100–1,250 JHo

An English delft flower brick, one side painted in blue with a bird perched amongst Oriental flowers, the other with chinoiserie foliage, the top pierced with seven rows of four holes, slight damage, c1750–60, 6½in (16.5cm) wide.
$750–900 S

An English delft flower brick, probably London, slight damage, c1760, 5½in (14cm) wide.
$800–900 JHo

Delftware flower bricks were popular in 18thC England, and were also occasionally found in Holland. The design is thought to derive from late 17thC Japanese pen holders.

FOOTBATHS

A Victorian Staffordshire pottery footbath, with bead-moulded rim, printed with 'Canton groups' in green, printed mark in green, 19¾in (50cm) wide.
$650–750 P(HSS)

LOCATE THE SOURCE
The source of each illustration in Miller's can be found by checking the code letters below each caption with the Key to Illustrations, pages 789–795.

A Staffordshire footbath, transfer-printed in black with Athens design of columned buildings, black printed mark, 19thC, 21in (53.5cm) wide.
$800–900 Bon(W)

A pair of Staffordshire glazed caneware footbaths, probably designed by George Bullock, each painted in orange with stylized laurel bands, within orange line borders, the handles and rim picked out in red, c1817–20, 20in (51cm) wide.
$5,200–6,500 DN

This pair of footbaths formed part of a washstand set, reputedly intended for Napoleon's use on St Helena. It was not delivered as the decoration was thought to resemble too closely the victor's laurels.

GARDEN SEATS

A pair of glazed stoneware garden seats, with flowering convolvulus moulded in relief and picked out in white and blue, on a glazed celadon ground, c1865, 17¼in (44cm) high.
$1,100–1,300 P

A pair of John Adams & Co majolica garden seats, each with basket-weave moulded tops, the sides with ears of corn alternating with sheaves of wheat adorned by ribbons, restored, c1870, 19in (48.5cm) high.
$2,750–3,250 SK

A Minton majolica garden seat, with linen-moulded top bound with a turquoise ribbon and decorated with pink and yellow chrysanthemums above a turquoise foot band, date code for 1872, 18in (45.5cm) high.
$650–730 DN(H)

A George Jones turquoise-ground garden seat, with birds and plants in coloured relief and wicker moulded top and footrim, slight damage, c1874, 18in (45.5cm) high.
$5,200–5,700 SK

A Minton hexagonal garden seat, decorated with brown flowers on a yellow background, c1897, 20in (51cm) high.
$1,800–2,200 RUSK

A Minton majolica garden seat, modelled as bamboo canes tied by a banana leaf, the top with *jui* motifs encircling a carrying handle, glazed green, ochre, brown and plum red, impressed 'Mintons, 9111' and date cypher for 1878, damaged, 19½in (49.5cm) high.
$800–900 WW

Jui **motifs are symbols of good luck and long life.**

INKSTANDS

A Staffordshire stoneware inkwell, with incised decoration in cobalt blue, dated '1761', 1⅛in (4cm) high.
$3,250–3,800 JHo

A Mason's Ironstone inkstand, in mazarine blue, gilded, complete with pots, c1820, 6¼in (16cm) wide.
$1,300–1,500 JP

A Quimper inkstand, painted in blue, orange and green, HR Quimper mark, c1895, 12in (30.5cm) long.
$700–770 VH

JARS

A Florentine maiolica two-handled globular jar, painted in dark blue and manganese-purple with foliate motifs, slight damage, c1450, 5½in (14cm) high.
$22,000–25,000 Bon(C)

A German brown salt-glazed stoneware jar, with a hinged pewter lid, slight damage, dated '1609', 8¾in (22cm) high.
$1,450–1,600 WW

An Italian blue and white albarello, inscribed 'V. Mastiaton', 17th/18thC, 10in (25.5cm) high.
$650–730 AAV

A Cologne stoneware bellarmine, restored, mid-16thC, 7in (18cm) high.
$4,000–5,000 JHo

The faces applied to the neck of this type of jar are believed to be caricatures of the Italian Cardinal Bellarmino (1541–1621), who was hated in Protestant countries for his influence during the Counter-Reformation.

A pair of Sicilian pharmacy jars, in the manner of Palermo, painted in colours with panels of a male and female saint against a yellow ground, reserved on a ground of trophies, slight damage, dated '1648', 9¾in (25cm) high.
$3,250–3,500 P

Drug Jars

- Dry drug jars were used by pharmacists to store powders and ointments.
- Often with grooved surface below the lip so that a waxed parchment cover could be held firmly in place with string.
- Wet drug jars with spouts were used to store ingredients such as syrup.

An armorial bellarmine, stamped with a smiling bearded man's face, above an oval panel bearing a coat-of-arms below a crown, slight damage, early 17thC, 8½in (21.5cm) high.
$770–850 P

An English delft drug jar, painted with crescents within blue bands and dashes at neck and base, slight damage, late 17thC, 8in (20.5cm) high.
$650–730 P(EA)

A Sicilian Caltagirone oviform jar, boldly painted with 2 white flowers and scrolling yellow and green leaves on a blue ground, 17thC, 7¾in (19.5cm) high.
$900–1,000 P

A Dutch Delft Arita-style blue and white jar, painted with figures in a stylized landscape, restored and fitted for electricity, early 18thC, 13¼in (33.5cm) high.
$1,100–1,300 P

A north Italian wet drug jar, with short spout, inscribed in manganese on a narrow band, painted with a yellow and green flower on a ground of blue scrolling flowers, slight damage, dated '1719', 7¼in (18.5cm) high.
$970–1,150 P

A French Perigord oil jar, 18thC, 14in (35.5cm) high.
$400–570 CF

A Sicilian albarello, painted in blue and green with a naive portrait of a man, damaged and restored, 18thC, 9½in (24cm) high.
$260–320 P

A pair of Brussels faïence tobacco jars, painted in shades of blue, with brass domed covers and lion-mask handles, damaged, c1800, 16in (41cm) high.
$2,400–2,900 S(Am)

▶ A Mason's Ironstone combined flower pot and potpourri jar, decorated after a Chinese *famille rose* pattern, with orange lustre rims, c1820, 7½in (19cm) high.
$2,500–2,700 P

A French stoneware salt jar, c1830, 24in (61cm) high.
$400–480 CF

A French stoneware snuff jar, with pewter top, c1890, 6½in (16.5cm) high.
$250–290 INC

◀ An American four-gallon jar, by Lyman & Clark, Gardiner, Maine, decorated in brown, c1840, 15¼in (38.5cm) high.
$1,300–1,500 SK(B)

JUGS

A creamware ale jug, inscribed in black within a foliate C-scroll cartouche of red, green and yellow flanked by a floral spray and a church, damaged and restored, dated '1776', 8¾in (22cm) high.
$1,100–1,300 Bon(C)

A Sowter & Co blue and white salt-glazed covered sugar box and cream jug, with moulded body and applied relief decoration of an American eagle and Liberty head, c1800, jug 5in (12.5cm) high.
$650–730 A&A

A puzzle jug, printed and painted with a couple taking tea in the garden, monogram 'RB' below a pierced and funnel-style border, purple lustre rims, early 19thC, 8¼in (21cm) high.
$650–730 P(NE)

► A Mason's Ironstone miniature jug and bowl, decorated in blue, iron-red, green and gold, c1820, 3in (7.5cm) high.
$1,000–1,100 JP

A creamware masonic jug, with rust-coloured rim, painted with birds at a bird bath, within a floral garland in coloured enamels, sepia transfer and coloured masonic emblems, text to reverse, late 18thC, 6in (15cm) high.
$450–570 WBH

A white stoneware jug, the decoration heightened with black glaze, attributed to Turner & Co, c1810, 4½in (11.5cm) high.
$80–110 SER

A Liverpool jug, transfer-decorated with 'Washington in Glory, America in Tears', the reverse with 'The Macedonian & The United States', slight damage, early 19thC, 9in (23cm) high.
$2,300–2,600 SK(B)

Creamware

Cream-coloured earthenware, known as creamware, was developed by Staffordshire potters during the 1740s and further improved by Josiah Wedgwood. 18thC creamware is light in weight – much more so than modern equivalents. However, some late 19thC creamwares are close copies of 18thC wares, and were made using similar techniques. These can be deceptive.

The finely grained creamware body proved ideal as a medium for plaster of Paris moulds. It could be thinly potted and provided an ideal surface for enamelled decoration and transfer prints. Continental competitors were unsuccessful in copying the technique until after 1800, thus allowing English manufacturers to enjoy a boom period for 60 years as they produced not only creamware but associated bodies such as pearlware and queensware.

Precise identification of individual factories remains difficult and ongoing excavations on factory sites show that close attention must be paid to moulded details on and around handles, lids, spouts etc, as variations are small but significant.

A pink lustre jug, the body printed in puce and inscribed 'Women carrying away from a Town besieged what they love best', c1815–20, 6½in (16.5cm) high.
$970–1,100 P

A Mason's Ironstone jug, decorated in pink, orange and green in table flower pot pattern, c1820, 7in (18cm) high.
$730–810 JP

A Mason's Ironstone ewer and washbasin, the jug with dragon handle, decorated with Imari sprays of peonies and other Oriental flowers, slight damage, c1830, 9½in (24cm) high.
$650–730 P

A Davenport cream jug, transfer-printed in green with a country scene, c1830, 4½in (11.5cm) high.
$25–30 AnSh

A Liverpool & Manchester Railway commemorative jug, printed in puce and inscribed 'Entrance to the Liverpool and Manchester Railway', slight damage, c1830, 5½in (14cm) high.
$200–240 P

A Scottish blue and white puzzle jug, c1830, 6½in (16.5cm) high.
$570–730 BWA

A C. J. Mason relief-moulded jug, depicting Falstaff, c1840, 5in (12.5cm) high.
$240–280 VH

A Scottish black and white transfer-printed marriage jug, inscribed 'Margaret Pon 1835', 8in (20.5cm) high.
$200–240 BWA

A bargeware jug, with blue flowers on a brown glazed ground, c1880, 8in (20.5cm) high.
$230–270 DHA

A Victorian Minton majolica beer jug, in the form of an ivy-clad tower with 2 couples in medieval country dress, the pewter-mounted cover with a jester's head finial, slight damage, date code for 1867 and numbered '1231', 13in (33cm) high.
$730–810 MCA

◄ A Thun pottery jug, decorated with white flowers on a black ground, c1890, 5½in (14cm) high.
$100–120 DSG

LOVING CUPS

An earthenware two-handled mug, the inscription scratched into the body, slip-decorated with leaves, north Devon, dated '1800', 5½in (14cm) high.
$320–350 GAK

A bargeware brown-glazed loving cup, with inscription 'Let Us Enjoy Ourselves', c1880, 5in (12.5cm) high.
$440–480 DHA

A George Jones majolica two-handled trophy tankard, the central panels moulded with wildlife decorated in colours on a turquoise ground, slight damage, patch mark and registration tablet for 2nd May 1872, 7in (18cm) high.
$2,000–2,500 P(S)

MUGS & TANKARDS

◄ A London glazed stoneware half-gallon tankard, moulded with a stag hunt, c1729, 8in (20.5cm) high.
$2,700–3,200 JHo

► A creamware cylindrical mug, printed and painted with a Tythe Pig group, above a verse beneath a black line rim, damaged, c1790, 5¾in (14.5cm) high.
$400–480 DN

A creamware 'Revolutionary' mug, printed in black with figures being pushed through a grinder and inscription below, within green line borders, c1790, 4¾in (12cm) high.
$730–800 DN

A pottery mug, commemorating the wedding of Victoria and Albert, c1840, 3¼in (8.5cm) high.
$475–575 W&S

Items in the Pottery section have been arranged in date order within each sub-section.

A pottery frog mug, attributed to Anthony Scott, with pink lustre rim and foot, c1840, 5in (12.5cm) high.
$570–650 IS

A Mocha ware pottery mug, decorated with blue and brown cat's-eye pattern on a white ground, slight damage, mid-19thC, 4in (10cm) high.
$800–900 SK(B)

An Irish spongeware mug, decorated in red and green with bird motif, 19thC, 3¼in (8.5cm) high.
$130–150 Byl

PLAQUES

Castelli

Maiolica was made at Castelli, in the Kingdom of Naples, from the mid-17thC. The principal workshops were those of the Grue and Gentili families both of whom specialized in romantic landscapes as background to rustic, religious and mythological figure groups. Many Castelli painters signed their work.

A Pratt ware plaque, depicting a lady wearing a scarlet dress, with green border, c1790, 8in (20.5cm) high.
$400–500 BWA

A Castelli plaque, probably from the Gentili workshop, painted with a landscape scene in blues, browns and greens, mid-18thC, 7¾in (19.5cm) diam.
$2,000–2,500 S

A lustreware plaque, printed with a view of All Saint's Church, Newcastle, c1840, 8in (20.5cm) wide.
$730–830 IS

A pearlware plaque, printed in black with a portrait of Queen Victoria and a view of Windsor Castle beyond, within black and yellow bands, c1840, 7in (18cm) diam.
$500–575 DN

A Dutch Delft plaque, painted in shades of blue, with a chinoiserie scene, with raised border, pierced for hanging, 18thC, 12¼in (31cm) wide.
$2,000–2,500 S(Am)

▶ A Scottish pottery plaque, decorated in red and yellow with a blue border, c1860, 8in (20.5cm) diam.
$325–400 BWA

POT LIDS

21 Years Ago ...

A Prattware pot lid, entitled 'High Life', 19thC, 4¼in (10.5cm) diam. **AB**

Twenty-one years ago this pot lid, with a Pratt printed scene, 'High Life', was valued at $40–50. Interest was then stimulated by the publication of a comprehensive book about pot lids, and prices increased dramatically over the next 10 years. Today the price of this lid is down from a high of $200 in the early 1980s to $65–80 today. This could be a good investment as prices might shoot upwards should interest be rekindled when another good collection comes onto the market.

'Russian Bear's Grease, Delicately Scented', printed in black, c1850, 3in (7.5cm) diam.
$450–525 SAS

'Polar Bears', No. 18, with gold line border, c1850, 3in (7.5cm) diam.
$350–425 SAS

'The Rivals', 19thC, 4¼in (11cm) diam.
$65–80 CGC

'Funeral of the Duke of Wellington', No. 163, c1852, 5in (12.5cm) diam.
$1,300–1,600 SAS

SERVICES

A Sewell yellow glazed earthenware part tea service, comprising 7 pieces, each with red transfer Tea Party print, c1810, teapot 5in (12.5cm) high.
$1,400–1,550 SK

A Ridgway stone china part dinner service, comprising 91 pieces, with gadrooned borders, brightly decorated in polychrome with flowers and foliage, pattern No. 1226, damaged, c1820–30.
$3,250–4,000 WW

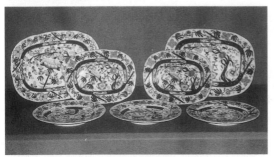

A Mason's Ironstone dinner service, comprising 71 pieces, decorated in the Japan pattern in Imari colours, c1820.
$5,750–6,500 JH

A Ridgway blue-tinted pottery fruit service, comprising 24 pieces, each piece with a shaped outline in gilt and enamelled flowering baskets, pattern No. 285, c1820–30.
$1,300–1,600 L&E

◄ A Mason's Ironstone part dinner service, comprising 53 pieces, decorated in polychrome, early 19thC.
$3,700–4,000 WW

► A Mason's Ironstone part dinner service, comprising 17 pieces, decorated with The Mandarin and His Wife pattern, c1825–30, dinner plate 9½in (24cm) diam.
$2,000–2,400 NOA

An Ironstone part dinner service, comprising 77 pieces, decorated in an Imari palette with gilt highlights, mid-19thC, large platter 22in (56cm) wide.
$2,500–3,000 SK(B)

An Ashworth Brothers Ironstone china part dinner service, comprising 58 pieces, each printed in puce with a vase and scrolling flowers and leaves, and picked out in iron-red, black and gilt, pattern No. B3194, c1880.
$2,000–2,500 DN

A Choisy-le-Roi fruit stand and 6 plates, decorated with peaches in green and red, c1880, stand 9in (23cm) diam.
$575–650 MLL

A Continental majolica dessert service, painted in blue, green and yellow, restored, c1900.
$13,000–14,500 S(NY)

TEA & COFFEE POTS

A Dutch redware teapot and cover, by Lambertus van Eenhoorn, applied with a seated figure of Budai below the spout, the cover attached to the loop handle by a chain, the foot mounted in metal, embossed unicorn mark, spout riveted, 1680–1720, 5in (12.5cm) high.
$3,000–3,500 S

The mark of Lambertus van Eenhoorn is very rarely found on redware; his brother Samuel was in partnership with Arij de Milde, and in 1679 appealed for a monopoly in making this ware. The appeal was not granted but it is nevertheless only de Milde's mark which is frequently seen.

A Staffordshire redware teapot, with applied foliate decoration and miniature hunt scene to either side, c1770, 7½in (19cm) high.
$650–800 DD

A Ridgway coffee pot, decorated with pink and purple flowers and gilt rim, c1900, 9½in (24cm) high.
$80–100 AAC

A Staffordshire solid agate teapot and cover, on 3 moulded lion mask and paw feet, marbled in shades of chocolate brown, blue and cream, spout and foot restored, c1750, 4½in (11.5cm) high.
$800–975 S

A majolica teapot and sugar bowl, moulded in the form of a cauliflower, naturalistically coloured, 1870–80, teapot 6in (15cm) high.
$575–650 A&A

A majolica teapot, formed as a monkey astride a melon, the melon blue glazed and with applied foliage, the base impressed 'J R & L', damaged, 19thC, 7¼in (18.5cm) high.
$800–900 TMA

A Minton majolica teapot, in the form of a monkey and a coconut, the monkey wearing a mazarine jacket, impressed marks and 'No. 1844', restored, 19thC, 9in (23cm) high.
$2,750–3,250 WBH

A Whieldon teapot and cover, with manganese tortoiseshell decoration, slight damage, mid-18thC, 5½in (14cm) high.
$350–400 Bon

A creamware coffee pot and cover, probably Leeds, painted in iron-red with Miss Pitt preparing a cup of tea at a tripod table, restored, c1775, 9½in (24cm) high.
$2,000–2,500 S(NY)

A brown glazed bargeware teapot, applied with white flowers, c1880, 12in (30.5cm) high.
$450–525 DHA

A Staffordshire teapot, decorated in blue and gold, c1890, 6in (15cm) high.
$115–130 CSA

TILES

An English delft blue and white tile, depicting Lot and his daughter, c1750, 5in (12.5cm) square.
$130–150 JHo

A Liverpool blue and white tile, c1760, 5in (12.5cm) square.
$100–115 JHo

◄ A set of 15 Dutch Delft blue and white tiles, each painted with a religious scene, 6 damaged, mid-18thC, 5in (12.5cm) wide.
$450–525 Bea(E)

A hand-painted tile, by W. B. Simpson, c1890, 8in (20.5cm) square.
$70–80 HIG

A set of 4 Dutch Chinese-style tiles, late 19thC, 5in (12.5cm) square.
$60–65 each No7

A set of 4 Minton tiles, 1890–1910, 8in (20.5cm) wide.
$50–60 RAW

TOBY JUGS & CHARACTER JUGS

A Ralph Wood Toby jug, c1790, 10in (25.5cm) high.
$1,200–1,400 DHA

A Neale jug, dressed in brown jacket and black hat, late crown mark, c1800, 10in (25.5cm) high.
$2,000–2,500 DHA

A Neale jug, with brown jacket, turquoise waistcoat and black hat, c1810, 10in (25.5cm) high.
$2,500–2,800 DHA

Ex-Bute Collection.

A Prattware Martha Gunn jug, her dress painted in Pratt colours with flower sprigs, c1800, 10in (25.5cm) high.
$1,600–2,000 S

A majolica Toby jug, by Edward Steel of Hanley, depicting Falstaff, with yellow jacket, blue trousers and blue and pink hat, c1888, 10in (25.5cm) high.
$780–550 DHA

A character jug, designed by Sir F. Carruthers Gould for Wilkinson Ltd, depicting President Wilson, with inscription 'Welcome! Uncle Sam', c1914–18, 10½in (27cm) high.
$800–900 HAM

A character jug, designed by Sir F. Carruthers Gould for Wilkinson Ltd, depicting Lord Kitchener, the yellow jug with inscription 'Bitter for the Kaiser', c1914–18, 10in (25.5cm) high.
$730–800 HAM

A Leonard Jarvis character jug, depicting Winston Churchill, wearing 18thC dress in tones of brown, green and yellow, signed by the artist and titled on the base, restored, c1950, 7¼in (18.5cm) high.
$400–450 P

TOILET SETS

A Mason's Ironstone transfer-printed toilet set, comprising 15 pieces, c1845–50.
$900–1,100 NOA

Miller's is a price GUIDE not a price LIST

A Mason's Ironstone bedroom set, comprising 13 pieces, printed and coloured with Japan pattern, pattern No. 1233, c1910.
$1,300–1,600 TEN

◀ A Mason's Ironstone toilet set, comprising 3 graduated jugs, 2 bowls, a chamber pot, soap dish and strainer, 2 small dishes and covers and 2 rectangular dishes and covers, each decorated in Imari colours, with hydra modelled handles, c1840.
$2,200–2,500 HAM

TUREENS

A Hicks & Meigh ironstone soup tureen, cover and stand, the body moulded with acanthus leaves, painted in polychrome with stylized flowers and leaves with gilt details, printed marks, the cover damaged, c1810–20, 13½in (34.5cm) wide.
$800–900 WW

A Staffordshire soup tureen, cover and stand, printed in grey with Indian scenes, the tureen with gilded handles, the stand with a view based on the Taj Mahal at Agra and shaped gilded handles, slight damage, c1830–40, 15in (38cm) wide.
$475–575 DN

▶ A pair of Mason's Ironstone octagonal sauce tureens, decorated with Japan pattern, c1820, 7in (18cm) wide.
$700–800 JP

An ironstone oval tureen and cover, late 19thC, 14in (35.5cm) wide.
$420–480 PCh

VASES

A pair of Dutch Delft documentary blue and white vases, late 17th/early 18thC, 10in (25.5cm) high.
$5,000–5,750 S

A pair of Dutch Delft vases with covers, each painted in blue with oval panels enclosing flora and grasses, restored, 18thC, 17¾in (45cm) high.
$2,500–3,000 S(Am)

A pair of Mason's Ironstone vases, the mauve ground with gilt overlaid butterflies and birds, applied with gilt female mask handles, on circular green bases, c1813–25, 10in (25.5cm) high.
$320–360 RTo

A Dutch Delft tulip vase, painted in shades of blue, the lower section decorated with ducks and exotic birds in flight amid flowering branches, slight damage, c1700, 4in (10cm) high.
$600–700 S(Am)

A Dutch Delft blue and white vase, painted with a scene of Chinese figures in a landscape within leaf borders, 18thC, 10¾in (27.5cm) high.
$1,000–1,150 HAM

A Mason's Ironstone cylindrical vase, decorated in mazarine blue and gilt, with bat's-head handles, c1815–20, 5in (12.5cm) high.
$325–375 VH

◄ Three Mason's Ironstone cylindrical vases, decorated with Japan pattern and gilding, c1820, largest 5½in (14cm) high.
$730–800 VH

A pair of Palmer creamware vases, applied with twin ram's-head handles, husk bands, swags and a portrait medallion, with traces of gilding, against a simulated porphyry ground, with black basalt plinths, missing covers, slight damage, c1770–78, 9¼in (23.5cm) high.
$2,000–2,500 P

A pair of Naples creamware vases, with powdered-purple ground, black monochrome views of Naples, black angular handles with white mask terminals, restored, c1800, 11½in (29cm) high.
$6,800–7,800 S

A pair of Mason's Ironstone vases, decorated in mazarine blue and gilded with Oriental flowers, slight damage, c1820, 12in (30.5cm) high.
$2,300–2,600 Bon

A Mason's Ironstone vase, decorated with red and blue flowers and gilding, c1820, 7in (18cm) high.
$450–500 JP

A pale-blue tinted earthenware potpourri vase, with pierced domed cover and inner cover, painted in gilt with 2 birds and a nest in a tree, restored, c1820, 20½in (52cm) high.
$575–650 DN

An ironstone vase, decorated with a peony and fence pattern in iron-red, blue and gilt, unmarked, slight damage, c1820, 16½in (42cm) high.
$1,400–1,550 WW

A Mason's Ironstone vase, with twin gilt scrolled handles, decorated in the Imari style with panels enclosing flowering peonies painted in iron-red, on a deep blue ground gilt with swirls, below a border of gilt floral medallions, c1830, 4¼in (11cm) high.
$525–575 P

A pair of Mason's Ironstone vases, decorated with iron-red and yellow flowers on a deep blue ground, c1835, 9in (23cm) high.
$1,300–1,450 JP

◄ A Samuel Alcock & Co Indian ironstone vase, the pierced and domed cover with blue and gilt dog of Fo finial, the vase with grotesque mask handles, printed and coloured with exotic birds amid flowers and shrubs, slight damage, marked 'No. 25' in iron-red, c1840, 20½in (52cm) high.
$575–650 TEN

An ironstone Chinese-style vase and cover, the deep-blue ground decorated in copper lustre with pheasants amid flowering prunus, the reverse and cover decorated with butterflies, slight damage, c1840, 21¼in (54cm) high.
$650–800 TEN

An earthenware vase and cover, with a gilt lion finial, decorated with flowers and leaves in iron-red, blue and gilt, unmarked, restored, c1835–45, 21½in (55cm) high.
$900–1,000 WW

An Italian maiolica 16thC-style two-handled vase, decorated with the Chariot of Apollo, and Orpheus on the reverse, c1855–90, 19in (48.5cm) high.
$1,600–2,000 NOA

An Italian maiolica-covered double serpent-handled vase, decorated in Renaissance style with a battle scene, and the Chariot of Apollo, c1880–85, 34½in (87.5cm) high.
$1,600–2,000 NOA

BLUE & WHITE TRANSFER WARE

A blue and white basket, depicting a scene from the Quadrupeds Series of Aesop's *Fables*, 'The Fox and Rooster', c1820, 12in (30.5cm) wide.
$1,000–1,150 SCO

A pair of blue and white transfer-printed tea bowls, c1820, 3in (7.5cm) diam.
$115–130 AnSh

A Davenport blue and white comport, decorated with Tudor Mansion or Bisham Abbey pattern, c1815–20, 14in (35.5cm) wide.
$520–570 GN

A blue and white transfer-printed cup, c1820, 2¼in (5.5cm) high.
$40–50 AnSh

A pair of Pountney & Allies blue and white comports, c1825, 10in (25.5cm) square.
$1,000–1,200 SCO

► A blue and white egg cup stand, decorated with sheet pattern, c1830, 7in (18cm) long.
$325–400 GN

A Rogers blue and white transfer ware plate, decorated with fallow deer, c1815, 10in (25.5cm) diam.
$180–240 Nor

► A Spode blue and white plate, printed with the Death of the Bear pattern from the Indian Sporting series, early 19thC, 9½in (24cm) diam.
$325–360 GAK

◄ A Mason's blue and white warming plate, c1820, 10in (25.5cm) diam.
$375–425 JP

► A Minton blue and white plate, decorated in the Monks Rock series, depicting a watermill, c1820, 10in (25.5cm) diam.
$160–200 GN

A blue and white warming dish, decorated with Grazing Rabbits pattern, c1825, 10in (25.5cm) wide.
$570–650 GN

A blue and white soup plate, decorated in English Scenery pattern, c1830, 9¾in (25cm) diam.
$100–115 AnSh

A blue and white tureen stand, decorated with the Village Church pattern, c1830, 16½in (42cm) wide.
$300–350 AnSh

A Hamilton blue and white plate, decorated in Hawking pattern, c1840, 12in (30.5cm) wide.
$300–330 GN

A Mason's blue and white warming plate, with pewter base, c1890, 9in (23cm) diam.
$375–425 JP

◄ A Copeland & Garrett blue and white platter, c1850, 26in (66cm) wide.
$600–660 Doc

A Swansea puzzle jug, c1810, 14in (35.5cm) high.
$650–750 GN

Puzzle jugs were a popular joke in the 18th and early 19thC. They were produced in a variety of bodies, including delft, stoneware and earthenware. By blocking all but one of the spout holes, the remaining spout could be used like a straw to suck the contents of the jug.

A pair of blue and white floral-decorated jugs, c1830, 5in (12.5cm) high.
$220–260 Nor

A blue and white commemorative jug, depicting the Duke of Wellington, c1815, 14in (35.5cm) high.
$900–1,000 SCO

▶ Two blue and white sauce ladles, one decorated with Spode Tower pattern, the other with a floral pattern, c1815–20, 8in (20.5cm) long.
$150–200 each Nor

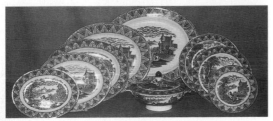

A Cauldon blue and white dinner service, comprising 49 pieces, decorated with chariot design, 19thC.
$1,600–1,800 JH

WEDGWOOD

Josiah Wedgwood was born in 1730 at Burslem, the heart of Staffordshire's pottery industry, so it was not surprising that he became an apprentice in this field. However, it was not as a potter that Josiah gained his reputation. His interest soon turned to the investigation of the materials used in pottery production, and following the establishment of his own company, his development of creamware confirmed his reputation for producing the finest and most fashionable services.

The growth of Josiah's business soon necessitated the opening in 1769 of a larger factory, which was celebrated by the production of six black basalt vases thrown by Josiah Wedgwood himself. At Etruria, as the factory was known, the range of products increased to encompass ornamental wares in newly developed or adapted bodies. As well as basalt and creamware, various colours of jasper ware were introduced in a range of styles influenced initially by Sir William Hamilton's collection of Greek and Roman antiquities, and later by other similar collections. Wedgwood's reputation was further enhanced by the creation of a one-thousand-piece creamware dinner service for the Empress Catherine of Russia.

By the time of his death in 1795, Josiah Wedgwood had firmly established himself as the leading figure in English pottery production. Unfortunately, Wedgwood's sons took less interest in the factory than their father, and the firm became a follower rather than a leader in the industry. It was not until the Great Exhibition of 1851 that the company was stimulated into appointing new designers who restored Wedgwood to its leading position in competition with Minton, as a manufacturer of exciting new products such as parian statuary ware and majolica. Wedgwood continued to be influential, and other makers once more sought to emulate its products. Among the more desirable of their early 20th-century pieces are Fairyland lustre wares (*see page 259*), which demonstrated that Wedgwood was capable of more than retrospection.

As with other areas of pottery collecting, the market is galvanized by the sale of a specialist collection, such as that of Harry Sheldon, where all areas of Wedgwood production sold well (*see following examples*). During the week of this sale similar items in general sales sold below estimate or were bought-in, indicating the continuing polarization of the market towards specialist auctions and dealers. **Christopher Spencer**

A Wedgwood basalt hedgehog crocus pot and tray, slight damage, c1810–20, hedgehog 9¼in (23.5cm) long.
$2,000–2,200 P

Ex-Harry Sheldon Collection

A Wedgwood model of Taurus the bull, modelled by Arnold Machin, impressed and painted marks, c1930, 15in (38cm) long.
$770–840 RUSK

Arnold Machin designed the portrait of Queen Elizabeth II for the definitive issue of British postage stamps and for Britain's decimal coinage first issued in 1971.

A Wedgwood model, 'Duiker Lying', designed by John Skeaping, c1930, 7in (18cm) long.
$230–260 RUSK

A Wedgwood black jasper ware biscuit barrel, with silver-plated top, c1860, 7in (18cm) high.
$900–1,000 PGA

A Wedgwood majolica Naiad centre bowl, modelled as 2 female figures supporting a net-form bowl on a wave-moulded base, base restored, c1873, 17in (43cm) wide.
$1,800–2,500 SK

◀ A Wedgwood black jasper ware biscuit barrel, with silver-plated top, c1860, 7in (18cm) high.
$900–1,000 PGA

A Wedgwood creamware bowl and cover, with 2 entwined rope-twist loop handles, pierced and moulded with interlinked leaf, scroll and oval panelled bands, on spirally fluted round foot with a laurel moulded band, restored, c1775, 8in (20.5cm) high.
$1,300–1,500 DN

A Wedgwood Queen's ware orange bowl and cover, c1879, 12in (30.5cm) diam.
$1,000–1,150 SK

A Wedgwood blue jasper ware cup and saucer, sprigged in white relief on dark blue with canaries, c1930–34, saucer 4in (10cm) diam.
$260–300 P

Ex-Harry Sheldon Collection. This cup was presented to Harry Sheldon by Hensleigh Wedgwood in 1977 in recognition of Harry's interest in breeding roller canaries.

A Wedgwood earthenware charger, decorated with a hand-painted landscape scene, titled on the reverse 'Pont Tyntur, N. Wales, H. Gummery, 1883', 16in (40.5cm) diam.
$500–550 SK

A Wedgwood armorial footbath, decorated in a brown stylized grape motif, above a crest inscribed 'Spes patientia et Perseverentia', 19thC, 17in (43cm) wide.
$800–900 B

A Wedgwood Fairyland lustre octagonal bowl, the exterior decorated with Castle on a Road pattern, the interior with fairies and peacocks centred by a flaming pearl, c1920, 7¼in (18.5cm) wide.
$2,600–3,000 AH

A Wedgwood Queen's Ware dish, with incised decoration in brown in the centre with a portrait of Garibaldi, by Matthew Elden, the border by Emile Lessore with allegorical figures above the rising sun, impressed Wedgwood and date code for 1861, 12¾in (32.5cm) diam.
$580–650 P

Ex-Harry Sheldon Collection. Matthew Elden was introduced to Wedgwood in 1860 by Emile Lessore where the 2 artists collaborated on a small number of pieces. Elden later took over as Director of Minton's Art Pottery studio before mental illness forced him into an asylum. Emile Lessore was a pupil of the French painter Ingrès and formerly worked at the Sèvres factory.

A Wedgwood Fairyland lustre plate, glazed and printed in gilding with a version of Imps on a Bridge pattern, c1920, 10½in (26.5cm) diam.
$5,800–6,400 S

A Wedgwood Fairyland lustre footed bowl, enamelled and gilt with fairies, goblins and birds, the interior with spiders and fairies, c1925, hairline crack, 8¾in (22cm) diam.
$730–830 Bri

A pair of Wedgwood plates, painted in enamel colours by Emile Lessore, each with a girl seated in a landscape within borders of turquoise and ochre, dated '1870', 8¾in (22cm) diam.
$320–360 HAM

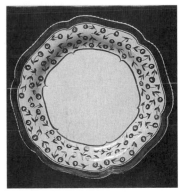

A pair of Wedgwood plates, decorated in gold lustre by Louise Powell, printed monogram and impressed marks, c1930, 9in (23cm) diam.
$200–240 RUSK

A Wedgwood caneware game pie dish, cover and liner, sprigged around the sides with fruiting vine between rope-moulded borders, the cover with a cabbage knop, c1820, 10¼in (26cm) wide.
$730–830 S(NY)

A Wedgwood black basalt jardinière, the sides applied in relief with cupids carrying a laurel garland, cover missing, c1785–90, 8in (20.5cm) wide.
$275–325 P

In the 18thC black basalt was popular with aristocratic ladies who used it to contrast with their elegant white hands.

A Wedgwood encaustic decorated black basalt bulb pot and cover, the bamboo-moulded body with enamel decorated leaves in blue and white, impressed mark, late 18thC, 8in (20.5cm) wide.
$3,000–3,500 SK

A Wedgwood dark-blue jasper dip Canopic jar, with applied white bands of hieroglyphs and zodiac signs above architectural designs, the cover with applied blue leaf designs, early 19thC, 10in (25.5cm) high.
$6,500–7,500 SK

Early jasper ware has solid colour throughout the body. Later examples were dipped in order to apply a surface of contrasting colour. Modern jasper ware, in typical green and blue, is once again solid rather than dipped.

A Wedgwood white earthenware jug, painted in colours with a group of agricultural implements, the reverse with a coloured landscape print, the initials 'JJ' below the lip, slight damage, c1810, 5in (12.5cm) high.
$300–330 P

Ex-Harry Sheldon collection.

A Wedgwood basalt Egyptian jug, decorated in iron-red, black and white with sphinxes to either side of a bird in flight, c1854, 9in (23cm) high.
$3,200–3,600 SK

A Wedgwood majolica jardinière and stand, the panelled sides with vases and scrolled flowers on a stippled ground, with brown and green glazes, impressed marks, restored, c1864, 17in (43cm) diam.
$5,000–5,700 SK

A Wedgwood white lithophane hanging light shade, the centre with a medallion of saw-edged leaves and flowers, below a border of a frieze of The Dancing Hours, with 3 brass hooks for suspension, c1920, 13¼in (33.5cm) diam.
$1,400–1,600 P

A Wedgwood blue jasper ewer, attributed to Charles Toft, in dark blue jasper dip, applied in high relief with ivy in white jasper and a band of snowdrops around the rim, incised '171', c1876–86, 7¾in (20cm) high.
$1,100–1,250 P

Ex-Harry Sheldon collection.

A Wedgwood blue and white jasper portrait plaque of Horatio, Viscount Nelson, modelled by John De Vaere in 1798, early 19thC, 5in (12.5cm) high.
$480–560 S

A Wedgwood majolica part fish service, comprising 5 pieces, decorated with naturalistically coloured fish on beds of leafage, date code for 1879, platter 25in (63.5cm) wide.
$3,000–3,300 S(NY)

A Wedgwood blue and white part dinner service, decorated in Fallow Deer pattern, comprising 18 pieces, each piece printed with deer before buildings, date codes for 1930–32.
$2,300–2,600 DN(H)

A pair of Wedgwood *rosso antico* vases, applied with black basalt acanthus and bellflower relief, 19thC, 7in (18cm) high.
$2,300–2,600 SK

A pair of Wedgwood blue and white jasper ware potpourri vases and covers, with pierced internal fitments, the bodies raised on dolphin supports and triform bases, the covers with pierced spiralling tracery, early 19thC, 5in (12.5cm) high.
$3,000–3,300 WW

A Wedgwood blue jasper dip vase, cover missing, c1820, 7¾in (19.5cm) high.
$650–750 P

Ex-Harry Sheldon Collection.

A Wedgwood black basalt vase and cover, modelled as a covered bowl with swan-head handles supported by winged sphinxes, cover restored, 19thC, 14in (35.5cm) high.
$5,600–6,400 SK

A Wedgwood Queen's ware two-handled floor vase, decorated by Emile Lessore, depicting the Defeat of Porus, handles restored, signed, c1863, 60in (152.5cm) high.
$16,000–19,500 SK

A Wedgwood vase and cover, with cream and gilt serpent handles, painted with pink flowers, leaves and butterflies on a cream ground, with gilt line rims, date letter for 1877, 20in (51cm) high.
$480–560 P(NE)

A Wedgwood Golconda ware vase, decorated with gilt and enamel raised slip floral and foliate design, c1885, 16in (40.5cm) high.
$680–820 SK

A Wedgwood black and white jasper Pegasus vase and cover, decorated with the Apotheosis of Homer, after John Flaxman, the domed cover with knop formed as Pegasus on a cloud, restored, 19thC, 26½in (67.5cm) high.
$11,000–12,000 S(NY)

The original Pegasus or Apotheosis of Homer vase is first recorded in the factory records in 1786. The companion Apotheosis of Virgil vase was probably in production by 1790.

A Wedgwood Unique Art Pottery vase, by Norman Wilson, the hand-thrown jar covered with a metallic dribbling brown glaze resembling Oriental hare's fur, c1936, 7½in (19cm) high.
$2,600–3,000 P

Norman Wilson joined Wedgwood in 1927 as a chemist and designer. His so-called 'Unique' pieces were mostly the result of weekend experiments and were not sold through Wedgwood stores.

A Wedgwood Fairyland lustre ovoid vase, decorated with Candlemas pattern, c1920, 7½in (19cm) high.
$3,000–3,500 RTo

A Wedgwood vase, designed by Keith Murray, with a straw-coloured glaze, facsimile signature, c1930, 6in (15cm) high.
$560–640 RUSK

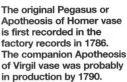

Harry Sheldon

Harry Sheldon worked in the Wedgwood factory as a young man where he became friends with many of the master potters. Although he later left the factory to run his own business, he continued to collect Wedgwood all his life and was an active participant in the International Wedgwood seminars.

A Wemyss goose sauce boat, painted in blue, green, orange and yellow, c1900, 6¼in (16cm) high.
$650–750 RdeR

A Wemyss Plichta pig, by Joseph Nekola, painted with clover leaves, c1930, 6in (15cm) long.
$650–750 RUSK

A Wemyss Low Kintore shape candlestick, decorated with cows, c1900, 4¼in (11cm) high.
$1,000–1,150 RdeR

A Wemyss heart-shaped inkstand, decorated with pink roses, c1900, 7in (18cm) wide.
$450–500 RdeR

A Wemyss black and white pig, with ears and toes picked out in pink, the base with painted mark, tail missing, c1900, 18in (45.5cm) long.
$1,600–2,000 TMA

A Wemyss Dundee bowl, the stem decorated with cherries, the base with a green geometric design, c1920, 6in (15cm) high.
$650–750 RdeR

A Wemyss egg cup, decorated with pink roses, c1900, 2½in (6.5cm) high.
$300–330 RdeR

A Wemyss mug, decorated with flowering clover, with green rim, c1925, 5½in (14cm) high.
$650–750 RdeR

A Wemyss pig, painted with thistles, Bovey Tracey, slight damage, post-1930, 11in (28cm) high.
$2,500–3,000 S(S)

A Wemyss button, probably painted by Karel Nekola, with the head of a dog against a green ground, early 20thC, 1½in (4cm) diam.
$2,000–2,400 S

A Wemyss Gypsy flower pot, decorated with the Oranges design, c1900, 6in (15cm) diam.
$325–375 RUSK

A Wemyss match striker, decorated with sailing ships in the sunset, c1900, 4¾in (12cm) diam.
$800–900 RdeR

◄ A Wemyss mug, decorated with flowering clover, with green rim, c1925, 5½in (14cm) high.
$650–750 RdeR

A Wemyss strawberry plate, c1900, 8¼in (21cm) diam.
$300–330 RdeR

A Wemyss plaque, by Karel Nekola, painted with a bird of prey, entitled 'The Hobby, Falco Subbuteo', perched on a pine branch within a green scalloped border, dated '1908', 10½in (26.5cm) diam.
$7,300–8,300 S

Karel Nekola was the chief decorator of Wemyss at the factory of Robert Heron in Fife, and continued working there until his death in 1915. This plaque appears to be the only known example of this large size painted with a bird by Nekola.

A Wemyss Gordon plate, decorated with roses, c1900, 8¼in (21cm) diam.
$450–500 RdeR

A Wemyss quaiche, decorated with blackcurrants, c1900, 10½in (26.5cm) wide.
$800–900 RdeR

A Wemyss plate, decorated with Victoria plums, c1900, 7¼in (18.5cm) diam.
$300–330 RdeR

A Wemyss bread and butter plate, decorated with oranges, c1930, 9¾in (25cm) diam.
$500–570 RdeR

▶ A Wemyss vase, painted with roses, 19thC, 11½in (29cm) high.
$600–700 HOK

A Wemyss vase, with green crimped rim, early 20thC, 5½in (14cm) high.
$360–400 GAK

Porcelain

The world of antique porcelain is shrinking. Twenty-one years ago an auction of Royal Worcester in Sydney would have attracted only Australian dealers and local collectors. I recently conducted such a sale and was astounded by the level of international interest. Instead of waiting for the catalogue to arrive in the post, potential buyers could see clear illustrations of every lot on their computer screens via the Internet. Bidding took place not only in person but by telephone, fax and e-mail from all over the world and, consequently, the sale was a great success with every lot sold.

The result of all this technology has been to level out prices worldwide. As Europe adopts a single currency, porcelain has a single value. Allowing for fluctuations in the exchange rates, a piece of Meissen will command much the same price in sales in New York, London, Munich or Melbourne, for the same buyers are active everywhere. Economic factors still matter a great deal. The English economy is thriving, and prices for porcelain that appeals to the British taste are rising. Academic pieces from the earliest English factories are particularly in demand. Germany, on the other hand, still has economic worries, and porcelain that appeals to the German market is not faring so well. Good Meissen, however, seems to weather any economic storm, remaining as strong as ever, although high prices have brought rather too much 19th-century Meissen onto the marketplace leading, I feel, to near saturation in some areas.

With more to choose from worldwide, porcelain buyers need to be much more selective. The top bidders all chase the same lots – the best of everything – and in the best condition. Pieces from the best-known factories are all performing well, but damaged and especially restored pieces are much more difficult to sell, and in many cases are falling in value. Dresden-style ornaments by minor German makers, unattributed Staffordshire, or unmarked Paris-type porcelain wares fetch high prices only if of exceptional quality. Many buyers are digging deeper into their pockets to acquire the best they can afford.

Unexciting porcelain is more difficult to sell, and the gulf between the best porcelain and the more ordinary is growing wider and wider. This is a trend that I personally support wholeheartedly; for me, fine porcelain in fine condition will always give a lot more pleasure. **John Sandon**

ANIMALS

A Belleek wall plaque, in the form of a dog's head, black printed mark, First Period, 1863–90, 8¼in (21cm) diam.
$2,000–2,300 P(NE)

A Meissen model of a sheep, on a polychrome floral-encrusted base, c1760, 4in (10cm) high.
$900–1,000 HYD

A Bow model of a brown lion, on a yellow washed base, minor damage, impressed 'B' on base, early 1750s, 4in (10cm) long.
$6,500–7,300 S(NY)

This is a particularly early example, which accounts for its high price.

> Items in the Porcelain section have been arranged in factory order, with non-specific pieces appearing at the end of each sub-section.

▶ A Meissen swan tureen and cover, modelled by J. J. Kändler, the feathers pencilled in brown and black, the bill in black and iron-red, the feet black, rim chips, crossed swords in blue, c1774, 14¾in (37.5cm) high.
$18,500–22,500 S

A Lowestoft model of a black and white tabby cat, seated on a green washed mound base, c1780, 2¼in (5.5cm) high.
$7,000–7,800 P

This Lowestoft cat was included in a specialist sale of ceramic cats, attracting added interest.

A pair of Meissen models of pug dogs, after J. J. Kändler, with fawn bodies, dark brown stripes and black muzzles, some damage, crossed swords marks, mid-19thC, 7in (17.5cm) high.
$2,500–3,500 P

Pugs of this type were made in different sizes over a long period. Size and age are important factors when assessing value.

A Jacob Petit spill-holder, in the form of a monkey wearing clothes, factory mark, c1845, 8½in (21.5cm) high.
$1,800–2,000 NOA

This type of model is particularly popular in the United States.

A Royal Worcester model of a meadow pipit, by Dorothy Doughty, decorated in coloured enamels beneath a matt glaze, No. 30 of a limited edition of 500, printed mark in black for 1975, 5½in (14cm) high.
$550–600 DN

▶ A pair of stirrup cups, in the form of foxes' heads, one ear restored, c1830, 4½in (11.5cm) long.
$1,200–1,500 DAN

A Meissen model of a parrot, with orange head and breast, yellow body, green and blue wings and tail, restored, crossed swords mark, late 19th/20thC, 12½in (32cm) high.
$1,300–1,500 P

A Royal Worcester model of a Dairy Shorthorn bull, by Doris Lindner, No. 183 of a limited edition of 500, 1966, 7½in (19cm) high.
$650–750 CAG

A Royal Worcester model of a Percheron stallion, by Doris Lindner, No. 297 of limited edition of 500, 1966, 9½in (24cm) high, on a hardwood base.
$1,000–1,100 CAG

A pair of Meissen models of Bolognese hounds, after J. J. Kändler, with brown and white decoration, underglaze mark in blue, late 19thC, 8¾in (22cm) high.
$1,600–1,800 CAG

A Rockingham model of a cat, sponge-decorated in yellow and black, seated on a cushion with a puce top, damaged, impressed marks, c1830, 1¾in (4.5cm) high.
$1,100–1,300 RTo

A Royal Dux group, in the form of 2 horses, the details picked out in gilt, applied pink triangle mark, early 20thC, 10¾in (27cm) high.
$730–800 S(S)

A Royal Worcester group, The New Born, by Doris Lindner, picked out in coloured enamels, No. 268 of limited edition of 268, printed marks in black for 1975, 8in (20.5cm) high, on a mahogany plinth.
$900–1,000 DN

BASKETS

A Belleek flat rod single-strand basket, First Period, 1863–90, 5¼in (13.5cm) diam.
$900–1,000 MLa

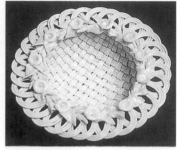

A Belleek basket, Second Period, 1891–1926, 5¼in (13.5cm) diam.
$650–750 DeA

◄ A pair of Meissen pierced baskets, with panels of coloured flowers within gilt *rocaille* cartouches, crossed swords mark in blue, c1755–60, 16½in (42cm) wide.
$10,500–12,000 S

A Minton basket, the exterior painted in coloured enamels with flowers and leaves, within turquoise and gilt scroll moulded cartouches, on a basket moulded ground picked out in puce, the interior decorated in gilt with a scroll and diaper band, impressed mark for 1861, 10¼in (26cm) wide.
$2,000–2,500 DN

A pair of Spode miniature baskets, the cobalt blue ground with gilded scales painted with floral sprays, one cracked, pattern No. 1166, c1825, 4¼in (11cm) wide.
$600–700 DD

A Royal Worcester cream and gilt porcelain basket, the interior with hand-painted motif of roses, slight damage, c1909, 7½in (19cm) high.
$200–250 RID

A Worcester card basket, Flight, Barr & Barr period, the gilded handle with a mask to the centre, painted within a reserve titled 'A View of Malvern with Peasants Sheltering from a Storm', on a claret ground within a gilded gadrooned rim, slight wear, printed Worcester and Coventry Street mark, c1825, 10¾in (27.5cm) wide.
$1,800–2,000 Bon

BOWLS

A Belleek pink bowl, applied with roses, Second Period, 1891–1926, 8¾in (22cm) diam.
$900–1,000 MLa

A Longton Hall bowl, in the manner of the Castle painter, with a landscape vignette, the reverse with a vignette of trees and bushes, and a brown-edged rim, slight damage, c1755, 6¼in (16cm) diam.
$2,800–3,200 S

A Meissen monteith, the twin acanthus leaf-moulded handles edged in blue, painted in blue with a continuous floral festoon, above small floral sprigs, crossed swords and star mark, slight damage, c1780, 11¾in (30cm) wide.
$650–730 P

◄ A Paris porcelain pedestal bowl, the exterior painted with 2 panels of garden flowers on a gold decorated deep-blue ground, c1830–40, 9¾in (25cm) diam.
$600–680 Bea(E)

▶ A Sèvres footed bowl, with blue background and gilding, maker and gilder's mark, c1884, 24in (61cm) diam.
$7,300–8,000 HAC

A Vauxhall bowl, painted in underglaze blue with a pine tree, pagoda and building on an island, slight damage, c1760, 5in (12.5cm) diam.
$650–730 JUP

A Worcester blue and white bowl, painted with The Argument pattern, late 18thC, 8¾in (23cm) diam.
$280–320 PCh

A Royal Worcester porcelain bowl, painted by Harry Stinton with Highland cattle scenes, on gilt raised foot rim, signed to interior, the base with date code for 1937, 9in (23cm) diam.
$2,000–2,500 EH

Miller's is a price GUIDE not a price LIST

A Sèvres-style gilt-bronze-mounted porcelain covered potpourri bowl, with alternating parcel-gilt *bleu de ciel* and floral stripes, c1890–95, 13¼in (33.5cm) wide.
$1,500–1,800 NOA

A Continental porcelain punchbowl, painted with figural scenes and floral sprays on gilded ground, 19thC, 10¾in (27.5cm) wide.
$1,200–1,400 AH

BOXES

A Belleek forget-me-not trinket box, Second Period, 1891–1926, 2½in (6.5cm) high.
$570–650 MLa

A Berlin snuff box, with gilt-metal mounts and hinged cover, painted in 18thC style with lovers in rural landscapes within moulded borders of flowers, the interior with a lady dancing, sceptre mark, late 19thC, 4in (10cm) wide.
$2,800–3,200 P

◄ A Meissen porcelain gilt-bronze-mounted casket, in Naples style, gilt and painted in colours, crossed swords in underglaze blue, c1865, 9¾in (25cm) wide.
$6,500–7,300 S(Am)

◄ A Mennecy silver-mounted snuff box, each side painted with sprays of roses, 1756–62, 3in (7.5cm) wide.
$1,000–1,100 S

BUSTS

A parian ware bust of John Bright, by Wyon for Adams & Co, c1870, 18in (45.5cm) high.
$800–900 JAK

John Bright was a Liberal statesman and economist who led the anti-corn league with Cobden.

A biscuit portrait bust of a woman, possibly from Comte d'Artois' factory, on a later biscuit pedestal, slight damage, c1785, 17¾in (45cm) high.
$2,000–2,500 S

Parian ware

- Name derives from its similarity to marble quarried on the Greek island of Paros.
- Consists of bone china containing a high degree of feldspar which negates the need for a separate glaze, allowing pieces to be displayed without becoming dirty.
- Both Copeland and Minton claimed to have first developed parian in the mid-1840s; both displayed extensive ranges at the Great Exhibition in London in 1851.
- Its most desirable feature was that it could be moulded without losing detail, enabling sculptors to have their works successfully reproduced for the mass market.

A Copeland parian ware bust of Princess Alexandra, by F. Miller, c1863, 12in (30.5cm) high.
$550–650 JAK

This model was issued to commemorate the engagement of Princess Alexandra to the Prince of Wales, later Edward VII.

A Copeland parian ware bust of Apollo, c1870, 13in (33cm) high.
$750–900 JAK

A Copeland parian ware bust of Queen Victoria, to commemorate her Golden Jubilee, modelled by Owen Hall, impressed marks for 1887, 13¼in (33.5cm) high.
$550–650 DN

A Kerr & Co parian ware bust of Prince Albert, by Jones, c1855, 15in (38cm) high.
$800–900 JAK

A parian ware bust of Dr Todd, physician and co-founder of King's College Hospital, London, c1860, 17in (43cm) high.
$650–730 JAK

A Robinson & Leadbeater parian ware bust of Edward VII, the reverse named and impressed with R & L mark, early 20thC, 7½in (19cm) high.
$200–220 SAS

A pair of Vienna biscuit busts of Emperor Franz Joseph I and Empress Elisabeth, on glazed socle bases, bearing their Imperial arms in gold, impressed shield marks, slight damage, dated ,'1856' and '1857', 13½in (34cm) high.
$1,450–1,600 P

A Robinson & Leadbeater parian ware bust of W. E. Gladstone MP, published by John Stark, c1866, 19in (48.5cm) high.
$650–730 Mit

▶ A bisque veiled bust, with inscription 'When as His Mother Mary was espoused to Joseph', mid-19thC, 20in (51cm) high.
$5,000–5,700 JAK

This is a very rare model.

CANDLESTICKS

A pair of Meissen five-light candelabra, depicting the four seasons, late 19thC, 15in (38cm) high.
$4,500–5,000 SK

A pair of Meissen four-branch candelabra, painted with coloured enamels and gilt, crossed swords and incised marks, damaged, late 19thC, 19in (48.5cm) high.
$1,100–1,300 WW

◀ A pair of Sitzendorf porcelain candelabra, one with Cupid and Venus below gilt bocage, the other with Diana and 2 hounds, late 19thC, 10½in (26.5cm) high.
$530–650 DN(H)

CENTREPIECES

A Copeland bowl on a Minton base, the bowl of Royal service pattern, with 4 painted medallions of fruit and flowers connected by gilt laurel swags, on a pierced ground within tooled gilt bands, supported on a pale green celadon plinth applied with 3 maidens in white with celadon hair decoration and with 3 upturned scallop shells, slight damage, mid-19thC, 15in (38cm) high.
$4,000–4,500 P

This piece realised a high price because it is very decorative.

A pair of Copeland porcelain figural comports, damaged, 19thC, 10in (25.5cm) high.
$1,300–1,500 SK

LOCATE THE SOURCE
The source of each illustration in Miller's can be found by checking the code letters below each caption with the Key to Illustrations, pages 789–795.

▶ A Swansea two-handled comport, painted with specimen flowers, c1814–26, 12¾in (32.5cm) wide.
$2,300–2,600 S

A Meissen tazza, modelled as putti supporting a pierced basket, indistinct blue crossed swords mark, c1750, 12¼in (31cm) high.
$1,300–1,600 Bon(C)

A Meissen blue and white centrepiece, surmounted with a boy holding a garland of roses, damaged and repaired, late 19thC, 16¼in (41cm) high.
$1,200–1,300 DORO

CLOCKS

A Meissen ormolu-mounted clock, modelled by J. J. Kändler and P. J. Reinicke, with figure of Columbine, wearing a yellow hat, a white bodice and yellow and purple skirt, minor restoration, crossed swords mark, mid-18thC, 12in (30.5cm) high.
$13,000–14,500 S

A Meissen mantel clock and stand, with figures of Mars, Flora and Peace, crossed swords mark, incised '452', restored, c1870, 28¼in (72cm) high.
$6,500–7,300 P

A Sèvres-style gilt-metal-mounted clock and vase garniture, the lower section painted with a pair of lovers in a landscape within a turquoise jewelled border, the pair of jewelled vases reserved with panels of lovers, some jewels missing, late 19thC, clock 14in (35.5cm) high.
$3,200–3,600 S

A Meissen mantel clock, the case surmounted by a putto, with 3 further putti on the base, decorated with applied garden flowers and highlighted in gilt, crossed swords mark, late 19thC, 24in (61cm) high.
$8,000–9,000 B&B

A Meissen and onyx gilt-metal-mounted mantel clock, painted with classical lovers, flanked by 2 figures of children, slight damage, late 19thC, 17¾in (45cm) high.
$3,200–3,600 Bon

A Sitzendorf porcelain clock garniture, the case encrusted with flowers and gilt scrollwork, applied to the base with children playing musical instruments and surmounted by a boy, with a pair of five-light candelabra, restored, c1900, 17¾in (45cm) high.
$2,000–2,500 S(Am)

Sitzendorf (c1840–present)

- Founded c1840 by the Voigt brothers in Sitzendorf, Thuringia, Germany.
- Voigt was the principal porcelain factory in Sitzendorf.
- Manufactured pieces in the Dresden/Meissen style.
- Most popular decorations were putti or encrusted flowers in a pastel palette.
- Later pieces are more boldly coloured.

COFFEE & TEAPOTS

A Belleek Tridacna teapot, with pink handle and finial, Second Period, 1891–1926, 5in (12.5cm) high.
$320–360 MLa

> Miller's is a price GUIDE not a price LIST

A Fürstenberg coffee pot and cover, painted with landscapes on a white ground, chips to spout, 'F' mark in underglaze blue, late 18thC, 7in (18cm) high.
$730–800 P

A Meissen powdered purple-ground coffee pot and cover, each side with a panel edged in gilding, knop restuck, crossed swords mark, c1740–45, 9¼in (23.5cm) high.
$2,000–2,500 S

A Sèvres teapot and cover, the body painted on each side with a wreath of flowers suspended from a pink bow within a scalloped panel reserved on a blue ground with gold spots, the cover with a yellow flower knop, slight chips, painter's mark for Antoine-Toussaint Cornailles in blue, date code for 1767, 5in (12.5cm) high.
$3,700–4,000 S(NY)

A Worcester teapot, the lid with flower finial, enamelled in colours with floral sprays, 18thC, 4¾in (12cm) high.
$700–800 CAG

A Worcester teapot and cover, each side painted with a bird perched on a branch with scattered butterflies and a ladybird, the spout with a foliage scroll in red, the cover painted with a branch and a butterfly, slight damage and restoration, c1754–55, 4¾in (12cm) high.
$5,000–5,700 C

A Worcester teapot and cover, brightly painted in coloured enamels with sprays of European flowers and leaves, within gilt line borders, c1785, 5¾in (14.5cm) high.
$650–730 DN

A Worcester teapot and cover, transfer-printed in black, by Robert Hancock, after Pillement, c1758–60, 5in (12.5cm) high.
$9,000–10,000 S(S)

The prints on this teapot are very rare.

A Worcester teapot and cover, the body painted in *famille rose*-style enamel colours with the Lady at the Loom pattern, she wears a green skirt and puce jacket, finial restored, c1765–70, 5½in (14cm) high.
$600–650 P

CUPS

A Chelsea *trembleuse* tea bowl and saucer, each painted with a landscape vignette of 2 children and scattered flower sprigs within the brown-edged rims, red anchor marks, c1755.
$5,000–5,700 S

A *trembleuse* has a saucer with a ring to support the cup.

A Chelsea acanthus-moulded cup and saucer, painted with Meissen style-flowers, slight damage, c1755, cup 2¾in (7cm) high.
$1,800–2,000 JUP

A Cozzi coffee cup and saucer, painted with chinoiserie landscape vignettes of figures, flowering plants and a fountain below gilt-edged rims, gilt anchor marks, slight damage, c1775.
$2,500–2,600 S

◀ A C. J. Mason cup and saucer, with gilt rims, c1810–13.
$290–320 VH

A Christian's Liverpool coffee cup, teabowl and saucer, painted in blue with a songbird perched within a flowering branch of peony, within a hatched diaper rim, c1768.
$500–550 P

A Höchst tea cup and a saucer, painted in colours with riverscapes, buildings and figures surrounded by flower sprigs, the inside of the cup with an insect, gilt line borders, cup wheel marked in puce, saucer with crowned wheel mark in underglaze blue, probably married, c1765.
$450–500 P

21 Years Ago ...

A Liverpool Chaffer's blue and white tea bowl and saucer, decorated with the Jumping Boy pattern, c1758. **HA**

Twenty-one years ago this teabowl and saucer were valued at $270–300. Bernard Watney's pioneering book about English blue and white created a new collector's market, and in 1978 rarities from the different Liverpool factories were starting to rise in price. Today's value of $2,000–2,500 goes hand-in-hand with rarity, and obscure Liverpool makers are worth much more than commercial Worcester, Lowestoft or Bow.

A Meissen tea bowl, with silver-gilt metal mount, each side painted with a chinoiserie scene in the manner of J. G. Höroldt within a gilt and iron-red scrollwork cartouche filled with Böttger lustre, the well with a similar circular vignette below a gilt scrollwork border, c1724. **$1,100–1,300 S**

A Spode Prince of Wales tea cup and saucer, decorated with a border of the Prince of Wales' feathers above crowns in gilding linked by foliate scrolls and flowerheads on a deep orange ground, below a buff lustre band and gilt rim, c1808. **$650–750 S**

This cup was probably designed to commemorate the Prince of Wales' visit to the Spode factory in 1806.

A pair of Sèvres double-walled cups and stands, pierced with an interlaced Gothic border outlined in gold, the handles formed as gilded bamboo, green clay marks dated 1878–82 and printed 'Doré à Sèvres', marks for 1890. **$1,600–1,800 P**

A Vienna chocolate cup, cover and saucer, painted in green with river-landscapes and scattered gilt flowersprays, below gilt borders, the cover applied with a flower finial, blue shield marks, c1780. **$1,100–1,300 C**

A Worcester moulded tea cup and saucer, painted in underglaze blue with Chrysanthemum pattern, c1765. **$550–650 JUP**

A Worcester coffee cup, painted in the *famille rose* palette with an agressive goose perched on an iron-red fence attacking an Oriental man, the reverse with a willow tree and grasses, c1756. **$4,500–5,000 C**

Examples of Chinese figure cups from the 1750s are rare.

◄ A German porcelain cabinet cup, painted in coloured enamels with figures before a building, probably the Hanover Post Office, with the cipher of George V of Hanover above the door, within gilt line borders, saucer lacking, c1855–60. **$520–570 DN**

A Chamberlain's Worcester armorial breakfast cup and saucer, with the crest of Sir James Lucas Yeo, encircled with the motto of the Order of the Bath on a pink band and within a laurel wreath, c1815–20. **$900–1,100 Bon**

Commodore Sir James Yeo, KCB, led an assault by Portuguese troops on the island of Cayenne, French Guiana, on 14th January, 1809, and was knighted as a result of the brilliant leadership he had shown. In overall command of the warships on the Great Lakes during the Anglo-American war of 1812, he was created a Knight Commander of the Order of the Bath in 1815.

A Bristol delft two-handled jar, decorated in polychrome with a bird on a branch, cover missing, c1715, 4¾in (12cm) high.
$3,200–4,000 JHo

A Lipscombe salt-glazed stoneware filter, with applied decoration, 19thC, 29in (73.5cm) high.
$1,000–1,200 SPU

A creamware commemorative jug, probably Yorkshire, handle restored, c1772, 8in (20.5cm) high.
$3,800–4,300 JHo

A Bideford slipware harvest jug, incised with coat-of-arms, dated '1788', 9¼in (23.5cm) high.
$7,300–8,300 P

A lustreware jug, attributed to Carr & Patton, North Shields Pottery, c1838, 9½in (24cm) high.
$1,000–1,200 IS

► A Hicks & Meigh ironstone jug, decorated in Water-lily pattern, c1820, 12in (30.5cm) high.
$1,000–1,150 JP

A Bovey Tracey Pottery jug, depicting the Battle of Sebastopol, c1860, 8in (20.5cm) high.
$450–500 GN

► A George Jones majolica 'Pallissy Vase', in the style of Bernard Palissy, restored, c1873, 17¼in (44cm) high.
$10,500–11,500 S

A pair of Dutch Delft polychrome models of seated cats, slight damage, c1700, 4in (10cm) high.
$3,500–4,000 S(NY)

A Staffordshire Pratt ware model of a horse, possibly after Stubbs, restored, late 18thC, 8in (20.5cm) high.
$11,000–12,500 JHo

A Staffordshire model of a cat, early 19thC, 6¼in (16cm) high.
$3,200–3,600 JHo

A Staffordshire pearlware bull baiting group, restored, c1830, 12½in (32cm) long.
$9,000–10,000 S(NY)

A pair of Staffordshire models of ponies, c1845, 5½in (14cm) high.
$2,500–2,800 JO

A Staffordshire castle on a base, in 2 parts, c1830, 8½in (21.5cm) high.
$1,400–1,550 JO

A Staffordshire figure group of the Crucifixion, restored, c1820, 10¼in (26cm) high.
$7,300–8,300 JHo

▶ A pair of Staffordshire figures of the King and Queen of Prussia, titled and decorated in coloured enamels and gilding, 19thC, 16½in (42cm) high.
$500–600 FW&C

A Staffordshire group of a gentleman and his companion on a fishing expedition, c1850, 13¼in (33.5cm) high.
$350–400 SER

A Staffordshire figure of Red Riding Hood, c1860, 8½in (21.5cm) high.
$180–220 JO

▶ A Staffordshire Sampson Smith flat-back figure entitled 'Balaam and his Ass', mid-19thC, 10¾in (27.5cm) high.
$130–160 HBC

A Faenza Casa Pirota Berettino-ground dish, decorated in blue, orange and green, chipped, c1520–30, 9¾in (25cm) high.
$6,500–7,500 C

An English delft blue-dash charger, painted with a figure of Prince Eugene of Savoy, chipped, c1714–20, 14in (35.5cm) diam.
$18,500–20,000 P

A Bristol delft plate, hand-painted and sponged with a cockerel, c1730, 8in (20.5cm) diam.
$3,200–3,600 JHo

A pair of Dutch Delft topographical Rotterdam chargers, painted in shades of blue, minor damage to rim, c1730–40, 13¾in (35cm) diam.
$27,000–30,000 S(Am)

▶ A Mason's Ironstone drainer, decorated in Water-lily pattern, c1820, 14in (35.5cm) wide.
$730–830 JP

A set of 4 Anglo-Dutch Delft polychrome dishes, 18thC, 13½in (34cm) diam.
$4,000–4,500 HOK

An Irish pottery plate, decorated by Donovan, with Lotus Leaf pattern, c1815, 8¼in (21cm) diam.
$450–550 STA

A Mason's Ironstone soup plate, decorated in Green Mandarin pattern, c1820, 10in (25.5cm) diam.
$200–250 JP

A Rogers blue and white platter, depicting Boston State House, c1820, 21in (53.5cm) wide.
$1,400–1,800 GN

A set of 6 Llanelly cockerel plates, c1900, 10in (25.5cm) diam.
$5,600–6,200 CoA

A Prattware plaque, moulded in high relief, with 2 reclining lions within a moulded frame, minor damage, c1800, 10½in (26.5cm) wide.
$2,500–3,000 S(NY)

An Italian pottery charger, c1870, 24in (61cm) diam.
$1,400–1,600 JAK

◀ A Victorian ironstone 41-piece dinner service, decorated in Indian Tree pattern with blue borders, marked 'Vesper'.
$2,000–2,500 RBB

An English delft fuddling cup, with 3 baluster-form vessels joined by their entwined handles, slight damage, c1640, 3½in (9cm) high.
$11,000–12,000 S(NY)

A Mason's Ironstone cider mug, with flared base, 1813–20, 5½in (14cm) high.
$550–650 JP

A London delft tankard, from Pickleherring Quay, Southwark Pottery, with inscription, slight damage, dated '1638', 5½in (14cm) high.
$138,000–154,000 C

This previously unrecorded mug is a significant addition to the corpus of wares attributed to Christian Wilhelm's workshop at Pickleherring Quay, Southwark in London.

▶ A Prattware Toby jug, depicting Martha Gunn, c1790, 12in (30.5cm) high.
$4,000–5,000 DHA

A Ralph Wood Toby jug, c1790, 10in (25.5cm) high.
$3,200–4,000 DHA

A Wilkinson Toby jug, designed by Sir F. Carruthers Gould, depicting King George V, slight damage, c1914–18, 12½in (32cm) high.
$1,400–1,550 HAM

A Liverpool delft tea canister, cover missing, c1740, 5in (12.5cm) high.
$3,500–4,000 JHo

An Elers Brothers gilt-metal-mounted redware teapot and cover, Bradwell Wood, Staffordshire, damaged and restored, c1695, 4¾in (12cm) high.
$9,000–10,500 S

A Staffordshire tea canister, restored, c1765, 3½in (9cm) high.
$1,100–1,300 JHo

A Thomas Fell teapot, decorated with 'The Woodman', c1820, 9in (23cm) high.
$450–500 GN

An English majolica teapot and cover, possibly Minton, c1875, 8in (20cm) high.
$2,300–2,600 DN(H)

A Mason's Ironstone teapot, decorated with Water-lily pattern, c1820, 7in (18cm) high.
$1,300–1,450 JP

A cheese dish, decorated with Arcadian Chariots pattern, c1840, 10in (25.5cm) wide.
$400–450 GN

A pair of Minton majolica jardinières on stands, modelled in the style of Albert Ernest Carrier-Belleuse, dated '1867', 26in (66cm) high.
$46,000–52,000 S(NY)

A pair of Le Nove faience wall mirrors, each mirror panel reverse-engraved with a masked female figure, restored, late 18th/early 19thC, 26¾in (68cm) high.
$4,500–5,200 S(NY)

A pair of sauce tureens and covers, by John & William Ridgway, each decorated with a view of Trinity Hall, Cambridge, c1820, 6½in (16.5cm) high.
$575–650 each SCO

A George Jones majolica garden seat, shape No. 5384, c1870, 18¾in (47.5cm) high.
$6,000–7,000 DN

A Sarreguemines majolica jardinière, c1880, 9in (23cm) high.
$575–650 MLL

A pair of Staffordshire sauce boats, in the form of dolphins, restored, c1775, 6½in (16.5cm) wide.
$1,300–1,450 JHo

A George Jones majolica strawberry set, comprising dish, cream jug and sugar bowl, damaged, c1875.
$2,000–2,200 S

A maiolica tray, painted with a Mediterranean scene, one handle missing, 18thC, 20in (51cm) wide.
$1,000–1,150 FW&C

An English delft hand warmer, in the form of a book, slight damage, clasps now missing, c1660, 6in (15cm) high.
$16,500–18,000 P

A Minton majolica jardinière and stand, slight damage, with impressed marks for 1883 and incised shape No. 923, 15in (38cm) high.
$5,500–6,000 DN

A Davenport pearlware sauce boat and stand, decorated by Donovan, c1810, 4½in (11.5cm) wide.
$550–600 STA

A Mason's Ironstone tureen, c1825, 17in (43cm) wide.
$1,000–1,150 JP

◄ A maiolica tray, painted with a Mediterranean scene, one handle missing, 18thC, 20in (51cm) wide.
$1,000–1,150 FW&C

A pair of Dutch Delft doré gilt-bronze-mounted vases, restoration to rim, 17thC, 12¼in (31cm) high.
$9,700–11,400 S(Z)

A Meissen Böttger stoneware vase and cover, minor damage, c1708, 6in (15cm) high.
$21,000–24,000 S

A Dutch Delft garniture, minor damage, finial restored, 18thC, tallest 13in (33cm) high.
$9,700–11,400 S(Am)

A Dutch Delft garniture, damaged and restored, c1770, 16in (40.5cm) high.
$4,000–5,000 C

A Mason's Ironstone urn, c1815–20, 17in (43cm) high.
$5,600–7,300 JP

A Staffordshire wall vase, restored, c1765, 9¼in (23.5cm) high.
$1,600–1,800 JHo

◄ A Mason's Ironstone gilded lily vase, moulded with flowers and butterflies, c1820, 22in (56cm) high.
$3,800–4,500 JP

► A Mason's Ironstone hall vase, with reverse panels, c1835, 37½in (95.5cm) high.
$4,000–5,000 JP

A Mason's Ironstone alcove vase, c1835, 22in (56cm) high.
$4,000–5,000 JP

A Minton majolica vase, modelled by Albert Ernest Carrier-Belleuse, damaged and restored, impressed mark and date code for 1872, 32¼in (82cm) high.
$32,500–35,500 S

A Rogers Paladian Porches vase, c1815, 7in (18cm) high.
$675–775 GN

A Wemyss vase, with flared rim and rose decoration, c1900, 8in (20.5cm) high.
$325–375 Sim

A Wedgwood tri-coloured jasper bowl, late 19thC, 4¾in (12cm) high.
$900–1,000 P

Ex-Harry Sheldon collection.

A Wedgwood Fairyland lustre bowl, decorated with the Woodland Bridge pattern, 1920s, 8¾in (22cm) diam.
$3,000–3,500 S(S)

A pair of Wedgwood coffee cans and saucers, and a slop bowl, late 18th/early 19thC, slop bowl 5in (13cm) wide.
$3,200–3,600 S

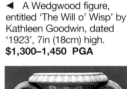

A Wedgwood drabware leaf-moulded dessert service, comprising 35 pieces, some damage, c1820.
$7,300–8,000 DN

◄ A Wedgwood figure, entitled 'The Will o' Wisp' by Kathleen Goodwin, dated '1923', 7in (18cm) high.
$1,300–1,450 PGA

A Wedgwood jasper ware inkwell, with gilt-bronze mounts, early 19thC, 7in (18cm) high.
$1,200–1,350 PGA

A Wedgwood preserve jar, with plated mounts, late 19thC, 5½in (14cm) high.
$1,000–1,500 PGA

A Wedgwood vase, applied with Procession of Deities, 19thC, 12½in (32cm) high.
$2,000–2,200 RTo

◄ A Wedgwood Fairyland lustre vase, painted with a version of the Imps on a Bridge pattern, painted 'Z5360', incised No. '2351', 1920s, 9in (23cm) high.
$4,800–5,600 S

► A Wedgwood Fairyland lustre vase, decorated with Willow pattern, shape 2034, pattern No. Z5360, 1920s, 8¾in (22cm) high.
$2,500–3,000 S(S)

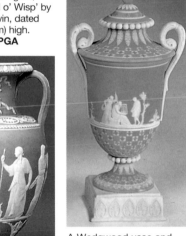

A Wedgwood vase and cover, damaged, late 19thC, 6¾in (17cm) high.
$775–900 P

Ex-Harry Sheldon Collection.

A Wedgwood gilded basalt vase and cover, pattern No. Z3242, early 20thC, 9½in (24cm) high.
$4,000–5,000 P

Ex-Harry Sheldon collection.

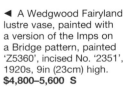

A Wedgwood Fairyland lustre jar and cover, 1920s, 13¼in (33.5cm) wide.
$22,000–24,000 POW

A Belleek basket, Third Period, 1926–46, 9¼in (23.5cm) wide.
$2,500–2,800 DeA

A pair of Irish spill vases, decorated by Herbert Cooper, marked 'HC, Dublin', c1870, 5¾in (14.5cm) high.
$600–650 STA

An Irish bowl and cover, decorated by Herbert Cooper, Dublin, marked, c1870, 5in (12.5cm) diam.
$500–575 STA

A Chamberlain's Worcester shell-shaped dish, c1840, 11¾in (30cm) wide.
$450–500 JAK

A Chelsea 'Hans Sloane' dish, painted with apple blossoms, butterflies and beetles, red anchor mark, c1755, 8in (20.5cm) diam.
$6,500–7,500 S

A pair of Chelsea dishes, each with gilt-lined rims and painted with exotic birds, gold anchor marks, c1760, 8¾in (22cm) wide.
$3,000–3,500 C

A Meissen peony dish, the edge picked out in gilding, marked, c1765, 9¾in (25cm) wide.
$3,200–3,500 S(NY)

A Mason's moulded dessert dish, c1813, 7in (18cm) wide.
$450–550 JP

A pair of Sèvres concave-sided dishes, painted in enamels with flowers and fruits, marks for 1771, decorator's mark 'K' for Dodin, 8¼in (21cm) wide.
$3,200–3,500 DN

A pair of Minton Sèvres-style pot-pourri vases, painted with figures, c1850, 3¾in (9.5cm) square.
$4,000–5,000 TMA

A Royal Worcester potpourri vase, with coloured etched flowers on a matt ivory ground, c1901, 6¾in (17cm) high.
$1,200–1,400 TH

◀ A pair of Chelsea vases, each painted with scrolling flowerheads and lotus, the scroll-moulded handles picked out in gilt, restored, c1765, 10½in (26.5cm) high.
$2,000–2,500 DN

A Sèvres-style urn, with gilt floral and swag decoration, painted with 4 portraits of ladies, marked, 19thC, 36in (91.5cm) high.
$7,300–8,300 FBG

A Continental model of a monkey, late 19thC, 22in (56cm) high.
$3,200–3,500 ARE

A Bow figure of a flower seller, with impressed ladder mark, c1756–60, 6in (15cm) high.
$3,000–3,300 BHa

A set of 4 Bow figures, emblematic of the seasons, restored, marked, c1765, 6¼in (16cm) high.
$7,300–8,300 C

A Meissen figure of a dancing shepherdess, by P. Reinicke, c1750, 6in (15cm) high.
$4,000–4,500 BHa

A Chelsea figure of a huntsman, on a flower-encrusted base, damaged and restored, marked, c1765, 11½in (29cm) high.
$1,600–1,800 S

A Frankenthal figure of a trinket seller, by Johann Friedrich Lück, on a scroll-edged base heightened in gilding, restored, marked, c1765, 7in (18cm) high.
$6,000–6,500 S

A Meissen figure of a lady of the Mopsorden, by J. J. Kändler, with 2 pug dogs, the base decorated with *faux* marble panels, damaged, marked, c1744, 11¼in (28.5cm) high.
$9,500–11,500 S(NY)

► A pair of French coloured bisque figures of a hunter and huntress, wearing Native American costume, restored, marked, mid-19thC, 27½in (70cm) high.
$1,800–2,000 B&B

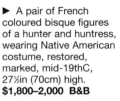

A Meissen figure of Cupid disguised as a lady taking tea, c1860, 4in (10cm) high.
$350–400 JAK

A Samson figure of Harlequin, slight damage, c1890, 5in (12.5cm) high.
$160–200 JAK

◄ A German Meissen-style group of 2 gentlemen in 18thC dress, restored, late 19th/early20thC, 9in (23cm) high.
$500–600 CAG

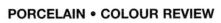

A pair of Chamberlain's chocolate cups, covers and stands, cups probably painted by John Wood, entitled 'Hope Nursing Love' and 'Hope', c1805, 4¾in (12cm) high.
$7,000–8,000 P

A Belleek Limpet teapot, Third Period, 1926–46, 6in (15cm) high.
$350–400 MLa

A Royal Worcester reticulated double-walled teapot and cover, marked, dated '1889', 4½in (11.5cm) high.
$5,000–5,500 P

A Barr, Flight & Barr trio, painted with river views on an apricot ground, gilded with foliate scrolls, incised 'B', c1810, coffee can 2¾in (7cm) high.
$3,200–3,600 Bon

A Meissen tea and coffee service, comprising 38 pieces, probably painted by Heinrich Christian Wahnes after Boucher, slight damage, marked, c1763.
$13,500–15,500 P

► A Meissen Böttger porcelain Hausmaler teapot and cover, gilded at Augsburg in the workshop of Abraham Seuter, after designs by J. G. Höroldt, c1720, 5¼in (13.5cm) high.
$42,000–45,000 P

A Royal Worcester double-walled cup and stand, painted in Middle Eastern style, restored, marked, dated '1890', cup 1½in (4cm) high.
$650–750 P

A Longton Hall Kakiemon teapot and cover, painted with *ho-o* birds, flowers and blossom, slight damage, c1750, 3¼in (8.5cm) high.
$11,500–13,500 C

A Coalport armorial part tea and coffee service, comprising 13 pieces, decorated with gilt stripes on a pink ground with central coat-of-arms, crest and motto, c1810.
$3,500–4,000 C

A Coalport tea and coffee service, comprising 42 pieces, decorated with floral sprays on a deep-blue ground within gilt borders, pattern No. 310, c1820.
$3,200–3,600 P(E)

A Rockingham part tea and coffee service, comprising 34 pieces, painted in coloured enamels with flowers and leaves, pattern No. '1473' in iron red, some damage, c1838.
$3,000–4,000 DN

A part breakfast service, comprising 46 pieces, London-decorated with pink and white roses on a pale yellow ground, minor damage and restoration, one plate with impressed Swansea and trident mark, c1820.
$4,500–5,000 S(NY)

A cream boat, possibly from Nicholas Crisp's factory at Bovey Tracey, c1767, 5¼in (13.5cm) wide. **$4,000–5,000 P**

A Meissen Kakiemon tobacco jar, painted with 2 birds perched on a branch, minor wear, marked, c1735, 5¾in (14.5cm) high. **$3,000–3,300 C**

A Liverpool jug, Richard Chaffer's factory, painted with 2 Orientals after Jean Pillement, c1762, 7in (18cm) high. **$13,500–16,000 C**

A Meissen gold-ground jug and cover, each side decorated with flowers and insects in the manner of J. G. Klinger, c1745, 6in (15cm) high. **$5,500–6,500 S**

A Meissen ewer, emblematic of Earth, after a model by J. J. Kändler, with figures of Diana, Pan and animals, chipped, marked and incised '309', c1860, 26in (66cm) high. **$4,000–4,500 WW**

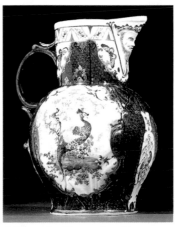

A Worcester blue-scale cabbage leaf-moulded mask jug, marked, c1770, 11¾in (30cm) high. **$6,500–7,500 C**

A Worcester, Barr, Flight & Barr jug, by Samuel Smith, painted with 3 shells and seaweed, framed in gold and reserved on a grey marbled ground, incised 'B', dated '1807', 6¾in (17cm) high. **$87,000–97,000 P**

This jug was made by the artist for his own use, and was signed and dated by him.

A Royal Copenhagen 'Flora Danica' soup tureen, cover and stand, painted with botanical specimens, marked, c1965, stand 13¼in (34cm) diam. **$4,000–5,000 S**

A Royal Worcester plaque, by Charley Baldwyn, marked, dated '1907', 9¾in (25cm) wide, in wooden frame. **$5,200–6,000 P**

A KPM Berlin plaque, painted by Dittrich, after Sichel, impressed mark, No. 336-200, c1890, 13½ x 8in (34.5 x 20.5cm). **$3,500–4,000 TEN**

◄ A porcelain plaque, by W. Porter, painted with bees, butterflies and a landscape, 1868, 14½in (37cm) wide. **$700–800 RBB**

A Belleek pierced plate, decorated with blue and yellow, First Period, 1863–90, 9¼in (23.5cm) diam.
$600–700 DeA

A Belleek dessert plate, hand-painted in pink, cream, blue and green, crest in black, Second Period, c1891–1926, 9½in (24cm) diam.
$3,000–3,300 MLa

A Chelsea Kakiemon style saucer, decorated in brown and blue, damaged, c1752, 4¾in (12cm) diam.
$320–360 P

A Coalport plate, by Stephen Lawrence, decorated with a tulip, c1845, 11in (28cm) diam.
$500–600 JAK

A French dinner service, comprising 72 pieces, decorated with blue floral sprigs on a white ground, gilt rims, early 19thC.
$5,000–6,000 JAd

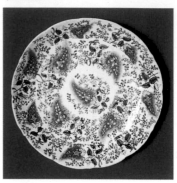

A Mason's porcelain plate, decorated with Sea-spray pattern, c1840, 9in (23cm) diam.
$70–80 JP

A Mintons cabinet plate, by A. Gregory, decorated with a basket of flowers within a gilt frame, the rim with reticulated panels, signed, impressed mark and date codes, late 19thC, 10in (25.5cm) diam.
$7,000–8,000 S

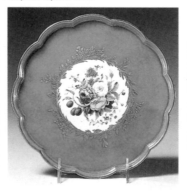

A Sèvres salver, painted with fruit and flowers within a gilt foliate border, the raised, scalloped rim with gilt edge, interlaced 'L's, painter's mark 'FB' for François-Marie Barrat, date letter 'y' for 1776, 9in (23cm) diam.
$11,500–13,000 S(NY)

A Vincennes stand, from a service made for Louis XV, painted by Pierre-Joseph Rosset, with a spray of fruit and flowers surrounded by birds in flight, painter's mark in blue, interlaced 'L's enclosing date letter 'A', c1753, 20⅛in (52cm) wide.
$110,000–120,000 S

A Minton dessert service, comprising 26 pieces, each centre enamelled with a different flower, turquoise and gilt borders, pattern No. G.781, impressed date code for 1871.
$3,000–3,300 CAG

A Berlin dinner service, comprising 103 pieces, decorated with *deutsche Blumen*, underglaze blue sceptre mark, iron-red or brown orb with 'KPM' mark, mid-20thC.
$5,000–5,750 B&B

A Derby group of lovers before bocage, restored, incised 'N.254' and patch marks, c1775, 13⅝in (34.5cm) high.
$2,200–2,500 DMA

A pair of Derby figures of a shepherd and shepherdess, c1765, largest 9in (23cm) high.
$2,700–3,000 JUP

Two Derby busts of the Laughing and Crying Philosophers, one restored, one with Isaac Farnsworth's star mark, c1780, 6in (15cm) high.
$1,600–1,800 DMA

A pair of Derby ornithological plates, each painted with a river landscape, slight damage, gilt crown, crossed batons and 'D', marks for Duesbury & Kean, c1805, 8½in (21.5cm) diam.
$3,500–4,000 C

.... A Royal Crown Derby dinner plate, from a service made for Judge Elbert Gary, painted and signed by Albert Gregory, gilded and signed by George Darlington, c1910, 10¼in (26cm) diam.
$2,400–2,700 JUP

A Derby seated figure of a girl tatting, restored, patch marks, c1770, 6¾in (17cm) high.
$1,300–1,450 P

A Derby cabaret tray, probably by George Robertson, painted with a naval battle, crossed batons, crown and 'D', c1790, 13in (33cm) wide.
$4,000–5,000 Bon

A pair of Derby two-handled sauce tureens, covers and stands, painted with nautical scenes, marked, c1797, 9in (23cm) wide.
$32,500–35,500 C

A pair of Derby tureens, covers and stands, from the Earl Ferrers service, c1825, tureens 9in (23cm) wide.
$7,300–8,000 JAK

A Derby vase and cover, painted by Zachariah Boreman and Richard Askew with classical figures, cover restored, gold painted anchor mark, c1790, 15in (38cm) high.
$5,000–5,500 Bon

▶ A Royal Crown Derby ewer, by Desiré Leroy, enamelled in white on cobalt blue ground in Limoges style, signed, dated '1894', 10⅜in (26.5cm) high.
$4,600–5,200 HAM

◀ A Derby (Robert Bloor & Co) vase, probably painted by Thomas Steele and Richard Dodson, repaired, crowned crossed batons and 'D' in red, c1815, 19in (48.5cm) high.
$9,700–10,500 S

A *sancai*-glazed pottery model of a horse, Tang Dynasty, 19¼in (49cm) high.
$14,500–17,500 S(NY)

A pair of *famille verte* models of Buddhistic lions, restored, Kangxi period, mounted on French 19thC ormolu bases, 14in (35.5cm) high.
$12,000–13,500 P

A *sancai*-glazed pottery model of a camel, with raised head, restored, Tang Dynasty, 22in (56cm) high.
$6,800–7,800 B&B

A pair of biscuit models of parrots, each on a pierced rockwork base, 18thC, 8in (20.5cm) high.
$6,500–7,500 S

A pair of moulded pottery figures of soldiers, minor damage and restoration, Northern Wei Dynasty, 17¼in (44cm) high.
$37,500–40,500 B&B

A pair of models of phoenixes, 18thC, 22in (56cm) high.
$43,500–48,500 S(Z)

These figures are of exceptional size and quality.

▶ A set of 7 glazed pottery figures of attendants, Ming Dynasty, largest 31¼in (79.5cm) high.
$24,500–27,000 S(Am)

A glazed biscuit figure, known as Louis XIV, painted in the *famille verte* palette, holding a hat in his hand, restored, Kangxi period, 9⅜in (24.5cm) high.
$13,000–14,500 S(Am)

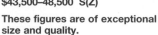
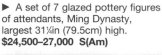

A group of 9 porcelain figures of Immortals, each painted in opaque enamels, some damage, early 19thC, largest 9¼in (23.5cm) high.
$6,500–7,500 B&B

A pair of glazed pottery figures of attendants, Ming Dynasty, 41in (104cm) high.
$9,500–11,000 S(NY)

▶ A *famille rose* figure of a lady, Guangxu period, 24¼in (61.5cm) high, on a giltwood base.
$2,500–2,800 S

Two Chinese export punchbowls, each painted with lotus petals, chipped, c1750, 15½in (39.5cm) diam.
$14,500–16,000 S(NY)

A *fahua* jar, decorated with a scene of Immortals in a landscape, c1500, Ming Dynasty, 13¾in (35cm) high.
$10,500–12,000 S(NY)

Fahua is a type of decoration consisting of enamel on biscuit, popular during the 16thC.

A pair of *famille rose* jars and covers, c1735, 27in (68.5cm) high.
$90,000–105,000 C&C

A blue and white hexagonal vase, Qianlong seal mark and of the period, 26in (66cm) high.
$97,000–130,000 Wai

A hexagonal *famille rose* lantern stand, c1800, 6¾in (17cm) high.
$3,000–3,500 GeW

◄ A *doucai*-decorated porcelain moon flask vase, with *ruyi* sceptre handles, restored, repainted, Qianlong period, 12½in (32cm) high.
$6,500–7,500 B&B

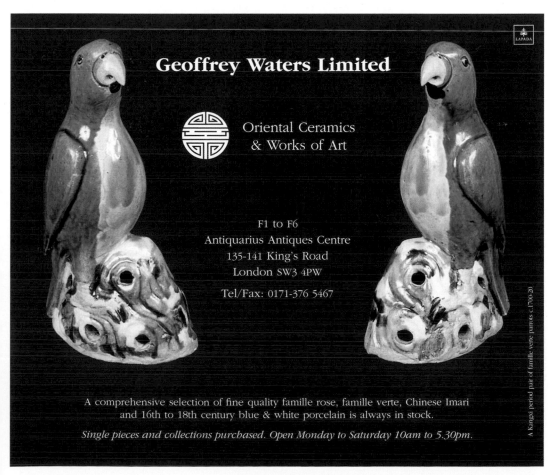

A pair of Chinese Imari chargers,
Kangxi period, c1720,
15½in (39.5cm) diam.
$3,000–3,500 GeW

A Chinese Imari plate,
early 18thC, 9in (23cm) diam.
$400–500 GeW

A pair of *famille rose* plates,
Yongzhong period, c1730,
9in (23cm) diam.
$1,200–1,500 GeW

A pair of *doucai* saucer dishes,
Yongzhong marks and of the
period, 6in (15cm) diam.
$32,500–35,500 S(HK)

A *doucai* plate, painted with deer,
slight crack, Yongzhong mark and of
the period, 8in (20.5cm) diam.
$3,200–3,500 B&B

A *famille rose* ruby-back plate,
Yongzhong period, 8¼in (21cm) diam.
$11,500–13,000 S(Am)

A *'fencai'* saucer dish, decorated
with peaches, Yongzhong mark in
underglaze blue, 8¼in (21cm) diam.
$52,000–56,500 P

A 'Nanking cargo' soup dish,
decorated with Lattice Fence
pattern, c1750, 9in (23cm) diam.
$750–800 RBA

A Chinese export plate, painted
with European flowers, c1745,
9in (23cm) diam.
$6,500–7,500 S(NY)

◄ A *famille rose* charger, Qianlong
period, 15in (38cm) diam.
$1,200–1,300 JAK

A *famille rose* dish, Qianlong period,
12⅛in (32cm) diam.
$1,400–1,600 C&C

► A blue and white meat dish,
Qianlong period, 17¾in (45cm) wide.
$700–900 GeW

A Chinese export plate, enamelled
with the arms of D. Gaspar de
Saldanha de Albuquerque, the name
picked out around the border,
Qianlong period, 9in (23cm) diam.
$19.500–22,500 C&C

A Satsuma bowl, signed, Meiji period, 5in (12.5cm) diam.
$2,600–2,900 MER

An Imari 'black ship' bowl, Meiji period, 13½in (34cm) diam.
$3,700–4,000 S(Am)

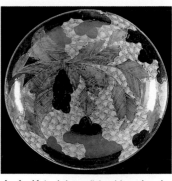

An Ao-Kutani deep dish, chipped and repaired, late 17thC, 15in (38cm) diam.
$26,000–29,000 S

An Imari dish, slight wear, late 17thC, 21½in (54.5cm) diam.
$3,500–4,000 P

A Satsuma figure of a *bijin*, Meiji period, 10in (25.5cm) high.
$1,700–2,000 MBo

A pair of Imari chargers, embellished in gilt, 18thC, 13in (33cm) diam.
$1,200–1,400 AH

A jar and cover, signed by Makuzu Kozan, and with Tokugawa crest, 1880, 28in (71cm) high.
$19,500–23,000 MCN

A Satsuma *koro* and pierced cover, signed and with blue enamel Satsuma *mon*, Edo period, 10in (25.5cm) high.
$5,500–6,000 MER

A Satsuma tea bowl and saucer, signed 'Seikozan', Meiji period, saucer 3¼in (8.5cm) diam.
$1,600–2,000 MER

A Satsuma vase, decorated with a hunting scene, signed 'Kinkozan', Meiji period, 7½in (19cm) high.
$11,500–13,000 MCN

A Satsuma vase, decorated in coloured enamels, signed beneath the *mon* of Lord Shimazu, Meiji period, 11in (28cm) high.
$3,200–3,500 Bon

◄ An Imari vase, some restoration, 17th/18thC, 22½in (57cm) high.
$4,500–5,000 B&B

A set of 3 wine bottles, with gilt-metal stoppers, in a papier mâché stand, c1830, 14in (35.5cm) high.
$1,100–1,300 BELL

An amethyst ribbed spirit bottle, with ball stopper, c1840, 11¼in (28.5cm) high.
$500–550 Som

A pair of carafes, with diamond-moulded bodies, c1820, 9in (23cm) high.
$1,200–1,400 Som

▶ A pair of Bristol decanters, with lozenge stoppers, c1820, 11¾in (30cm) high.
$1,100–1,300 JHa

A rib-moulded amethyst decanter and stopper, c1835, 13in (33cm) high.
$400–500 BELL

A green spirit bottle, with looped moulded body, c1840, 14in (35.5cm) high.
$650–720 CB

A glass decanter, with moulded body, 19thC, 7in (18cm) high.
$320–350 SHa

A Bohemian ruby-flashed decanter, engraved with fruiting vines, c1880, 15¼in (38.5cm) high.
$250–280 CB

An Italian clear glass decanter, with white and turquoise *latticinio* decoration, Venice, late 19thC, 10¾in (27cm) high.
$520–570 DORO

A 'Nailsea' hip flask, c1860, 7in (18cm) long.
$260–300 Som

A pair of glass ewers, with crenellated rims and applied clear glass handles, decorated with enamel arabesques, 19thC, 10½in (26.5cm) high.
$130–160 HBC

▶ A 'Nailsea' gimmel flask, with 2 compartments, c1860, 10¾in (27cm) long.
$260–300 Som

A Bristol blue glass finger bowl, signed on base 'I. Jacobs, Bristol', c1810, 4¼in (11cm) diam.
$2,500–2,900 Som

A blue glass finger bowl, decorated with a band of gilt anthemion within gilt panels, c1810, 3¼in (8cm) high.
$900–1,000 Som

A rib-moulded green glass finger bowl, c1840, 4¾in (12cm) diam.
$260–300 CB

A glass cream jug and sugar basin, both with gilt inscription 'A Present from Newcastle 1845', slight damage, jug 3¼in (8cm) high.
$530–600 Som

A pair of glass caviar bowls and stands, by Count Harrach's factory, Neuwelt, Bohemia, c1845, 9in (23cm) diam.
$12,000–14,500 ALiN

A pair of French opaline glass stands, c1870, 3½in (9cm) high.
$450–500 CB

A Thomas Webb & Sons gem cameo glass bowl, decorated with birds and trees, signed, c1880, 9in (23cm) diam.
$27,500–30,000 JAA

A vaseline glass jug and bowl, with applied trailed decoration and feet, c1880, jug 6in (15cm) high.
$400–500 BELL

▶ A blue glass jug and bowl, with fluted edges and applied white trailed decoration, c1880, jug 5in (13cm) high.
$320–350 BELL

A cranberry glass bowl, on a clear baluster stem and conical foot, c1890, 5in (13cm) diam.
$250–300 CB

▶ A vaseline and opaline glass bonbon dish, with frilled edge, c1890, 4in (10cm) high.
$150–180 BELL

A reverse-cut cameo and intaglio glass dragon bowl, by Joshua Hodgetts for Stevens & Williams, c1917, 9in (23cm) diam.
$2,500–2,900 ALiN

A Bohemian opaline glass casket, with enamel and gilt decoration, c1855, 5¼in (13.5cm) wide.
$4,000–5,000 ALiN

An ormolu-mounted glass casket, by Koloman Moser, with silver and gilt decoration, original key, c1875, 4½in (11.5cm) wide.
$1,300–1,600 ALiN

A French ruby glass casket, with gilt-brass mounts, and 4 scent bottles, c1880, 5½in (14cm) wide.
$730–800 CB

A French pillar-cut glass casket, with gilt-brass mounts, c1890, 4in (10cm) wide.
$1,000–1,200 CB

A Daum glass comport, on a WMF metal stand, 19thC, 14in (35.5cm) wide.
$500–600 AH

▶ A glass jar, with ormolu cover and collar, decorated with roses, c1855, 9in (23cm) high.
$5,600–6,500 ALiN

A pair of blue glass rummers, with barrel-shaped bowls, knopped stems and conical feet, c1830, 4½in (11.5cm) high.
$800–1,000 Som

A Bohemian cameo and intaglio-engraved goblet, signed 'F. Zach', c1860, 6¼in (16cm) high.
$3,500–4,000 ALiN

A Bohemian clear glass beaker, with blue overlay and gilded rim, decorated with flowers, on a star-cut base, c1875, 5¾in (14.5cm) high.
$300–360 CB

A pair of Bohemian glass goblets and covers, early 20thC, 21in (53.5cm) high.
$3,200–4,000 C

A Flemish stained-glass panel, depicting 'Sorgheloos in Poverty', 16thC, 9in (23cm) diam.
$29,000–32,500 P

A German armorial stained-glass panel, damaged and restored, dated '1582', 14in (35.5cm) wide.
$2,400–2,700 S(Z)

A German-Swiss stained leaded-glass panel, with double armorial bordered with flowers and heads, dated '1619', 21in (53.5cm) wide.
$7,300–8,000 RAG

An armorial stained-glass panel, by Wittnawer & Mueller, Basle, dated '1670', 13¼in (33.5cm) wide.
$3,700–4,000 S(Z)

A German painting on glass, depicting Frederick the Great on horseback, 18thC, 7¾in (20cm) wide.
$1,200–1,300 P

◄ An enamelled glass perfume bottle, by Koloman Moser, with jewelled and silver top, hallmarked '1885', 2½in (6.5cm) high.
$800–1,000 ALiN

► A gold-mounted opaline glass vinaigrette, c1820, 1in (2.5cm) wide.
$1,600–2,000 ALiN

A Bohemian cranberry glass tankard, with white overlay and applied handle, c1870, 4¾in (12cm) high.
$400–500 CB

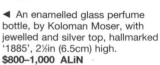

A Baccarat pansy paperweight, 1845–60, 2¼in (5.5cm) diam.
$2,500–3,000 SWB

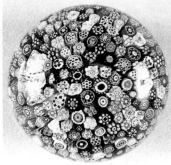

A Baccarat close-pack millefiori paperweight, signed and dated '1846', 3in (7.5cm) diam.
$5,700–6,500 STG

A Baccarat garlanded butterfly paperweight, the insect set within a garland of alternate claret and white canes, with a star-cut base, mid-19thC, 2¾in (7cm) diam.
$1,400–1,600 C

A Clichy millefiori paperweight, with central rose cane centred within 2 concentric rows of coloured canes, set in a spaced latticinio ground, mid-19thC, 2½in (6.5cm) diam.
$1,900–2,100 P

A St Louis paperweight, the red and green crown with twisted ribbons, c1850, 3in (7.5cm) diam.
$4,000–4,500 DLP

A Paul Ysart paperweight, 1930s, 3in (7.5cm) diam.
$325–375 SWB

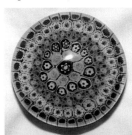

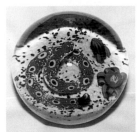

A pair of Swedish neo-classical ormolu-mounted cobalt blue glass vases, late 18thC, 10¼in (26cm) high.
$40,000–45,000 S(NY)

A pair of Baccarat enamelled double-overlay glass vases, by Jean-François Robert, slight damage, c1855, 11¾in (30cm) high.
$7,000–8,000 S

◄ A Lobmeyr Persian-style enamelled and gilt two-handled vase, with painted 'JLL' grid mark in white, c1875, 6¾in (17cm) high.
$13,500–15,500 S

A pair of Bohemian overlay glass bottle vases and covers, possibly Neuwelt or Adolfhütte bei Winterberg, slight damage, c1860, 25¼in (64cm) high.
$56,500–65,000 S

A pair of French opaline glass vases, by Jean-François Robert, painted with flowers, c1870, 14in (35.5cm) high.
$1,800–2,100 CB

A pair of Bohemian enamelled and gilt glass vases, c1875, 13in (33cm) high.
$5,000–6,500 ALiN

◄ A Chinese-style cameo glass vase, by Thomas Webb & Sons, carved with a frog and leafy branches, c1885, 7¾in (19.5cm) high.
$7,300–8,100 P

A pair of Bohemian ruby glass and 'jewelled' vases, each of baluster form, decorated with trails of foliage, on a cylindrical base, c1880, 37in (94cm) high.
$18,000–19,500 S

A Mat-Su-Noke cased and applied glass vase, designed by Northwood for Stevens & Williams, c1884, 6½in (16.5cm) high.
$2,500–3,000 ALiN

A cranberry glass vase, c1890, 6in (15cm) high.
$230–260 BELL

A Bohemian blue-flashed glass vase, 19thC, 12½in (32cm) high.
$1,600–1,800 HOK

A pair of Bohemian overlay glass and enamel-decorated vases, late 19thC, 14in (35.5cm) high.
$3,200–3,600 B&B

A double-cameo glass vase, by Thomas Webb & Sons, decorated with a spray of budding and leafy branches on a Burmese ground, late 19thC, 10in (25.5cm) high.
$8,000–9,500 P

DISHES

A Chelsea dish, the border moulded with scrolls and diaper panels, painted with scattered flowers, brown line rim, restored, red anchor mark, c1755, 13¼in (33.5cm) wide.
$1,000–1,100 WW

A Frankenthal Hausmalerei spoon tray, painted in puce with a gazebo before a church and other buildings, edged below with a scrolling foliage cartouche, signed and dated 'R. F./1762' in puce, 6in (15cm) wide.
$2,000–2,500 C

A pair of Meissen-style dishes, supported by a recumbent lady and gentleman in 18thC costume, crossed swords mark, late 19thC, 8¾in (22cm) high.
$1,000–1,100 WL

A Meissen sweetmeat dish, modelled as a reclining maiden holding a shaped bowl, applied with colourful summer flowers, cancelled crossed swords mark in underglaze blue, incised '2858', c1880, 12¾in (32.5cm) long.
$800–900 HAM

21 Years Ago …

A Worcester blue-scale dish, painted with European flowers, crescent mark, 1751–74, 9in (23cm) diam. **RD**

Twenty-one years ago this dish was valued at $550–600. Having been in great demand during the 1960s, the value of 1770s coloured Worcester porcelain has stagnated and its value today would be $650–800. Since 1978 collectors have favoured earlier Worcester from the 1750s, while blue-scale and similar coloured patterns have continually fallen from fashion.

A Sèvres dessert dish, from the service ordered by Baron de Kendall, the centre painted with a black bird perched on a leafy branch, within a green-ground border patterned with gilt-centred blue *oeils-de-perdrix*, restored, c1784, 8½in (21.5cm) wide.
$2,300–2,600 S(NY)

> Items in the Porcelain section have been arranged in factory order, with non-specific pieces appearing at the end of each sub-section.

A Worcester hors d'oeuvres tray, painted with the Willow Rock Bird pattern, c1760, 3¼in (8.5cm) wide.
$500–570 JUP

A Worcester pickle dish, painted in *famille rose* style enamels with a lotus flower within a border of flowers, with red line border and scalloped rim, c1755, 3¼in (8cm) wide.
$1,000–1,200 P

A Worcester Blind Earl pattern sweetmeat dish, moulded in relief with a spray of 2 rose buds and rose leaves, painted in blue, crescent mark, c1760, 6in (15cm) wide.
$1,800–2,000 P

This pattern is named after the Earl of Coventry, who lost his sight in a hunting accident. He owned a Worcester set of this pattern, and could feel the rose leaves that were embossed in relief.

A Worcester dish, the centre painted with a bouquet and a flowerspray, the border moulded with arched panels painted with trailing flowers reserved on a yellow honeycomb-moulded ground with brown and green vine-branch handles, slight damage, c1765, 11¾in (30cm) wide.
$13,000–14,500 C

A Worcester Blind Earl pattern sweet-meat dish, moulded with roses, painted in puce with flowersprays, and sprays within gilt cartouches, slight damage, c1770, 6in (15cm) wide.
$900–1,000 WW

A Worcester dish, Flight, Barr & Barr period, painted in coloured enamels with a bird in a nest amid flowers and leaves, on a pale green ground, within a gilt gadrooned border, printed mark in brown, c1825, 5¼in (13.5cm) wide.
$2,000–2,500 DN

EWERS & JUGS

A Belleek white and gilt jug, with harp handle, First Period, 1863–90, 8in (20.5cm) high.
$800–900 MLa

A pair of Belleek floral encrusted Aberdeen jugs, Second Period, 1891–1926, 9¾in (25cm) high.
$1,000–1,100 DeA

A moulded jug, possibly Coalport, each side painted with flowers, inscribed in gilt 'J. Boult 1846', 7¼in (18.5cm) high.
$275–325 WW

A porcelain jug, painted with exotic birds in landscapes and with gilt embellishment, 19thC, 10in (25.5cm) high.
$300–350 AH

◄ A Nove jug, painted with 4 panels of colourful flowersprays alternating with applied flower sprigs, the shell-moulded rim and acanthus-moulded foot picked out in bright yellow, cover missing, slight damage, mark in blue, late 19thC, 7¾in (20cm) high.
$160–200 P

21 Years Ago ...

A Royal Worcester reticulated ewer, painted by H. Chair, signed, pierced by G. Owen, details lightly gilded, printed mark, pattern No. 1581, Rd. No. 189077, date code for 1907, 6¼in (16cm) high. **S**

Twenty-one years ago this ewer was valued at $300–400. Today a similar ewer could be expected to realize $4,800–5,400. The fine workmanship of later English porcelain has become more important to the collector than size. Small, top-quality pieces with tooled gold and 'jewelled' borders are greatly in demand, especially from factories such as Royal Worcester.

A Vienna hot milk jug, painted with pink rose sprigs and puce borders, late 18thC, 8in (20.5cm) high.
$140–160 MCA

A Worcester cream jug, painted in puce with Oriental figures, the inner rim with a band of flowers, cracked, c1757, 3¼in (8.5cm) high.
$2,000–2,500 P(B)

FIGURES

A pair of white Bow figures, emblematic of Taste and Hearing, after the Meissen originals, damaged, c1758, 6in (15cm) high.
$800–1,000 P

A pair of Bow figures of the New Dancers, standing on a scroll base before a flowering bocage, restored, c1765, 9¼in (23.5cm) high.
$2,500–2,800 JUP

A Bow figure of a girl dancing, wearing a pink hat, after a Meissen model by Kändler, on a puce scroll base, c1765, 7½in (19cm) high.
$3,200–3,600 MCA

An Ansbach cane handle, modelled as a mermaid feeding a mythical sea creature, her hair pencilled in black, her tail heightened in gilding, with a jewelled yellow-ground flowered band around her neck, mounted in a silver-gilt scrollwork collar, gilding rubbed, c1770, 4¼in (11cm) high.
$19,500–22,500 S

This is a very rare piece by a desirable maker.

A Bow figure of a boxer, wearing gilt-striped dark blue breeches, c1770, 6¾in (17cm) high.
$2,600–3,000 MCA

Items with a boxing association are keenly sought after.

A Capodimonte white figure of a drummer, wearing a high peaked fur hat, standing against a rockwork support, damaged, c1750, 10in (25.5cm) high.
$10,500–12,000 P

The Capodimonte factory of the 1750s should not be confused with modern so-called Capodimonte porcelain.

A Chelsea figure of a woman, emblematic of Smell, from The Senses series, wearing a headdress and flowered robe and standing beside a purple marbled plinth, c1758, 9½in (24cm) high.
$2,500–2,900 S

A Copeland coloured parian figure, entitled 'Maidenhood', after E. G. Papworth Jnr, wearing a blue-flowered white dress and a gilt-edged blue cloak, late 19thC, 10in (25.5cm) high.
$650–800 P

◄ A Copeland parian figure, entitled 'Master Tom', by J. Durham, 1872, 21½in (54.5cm) high.
$1,200–1,400 Mit

Master Tom is the main character in Charles Kingsley's *The Water Babies*.

A Copeland parian figure of Lady Godiva, by Raphael Monti, c1870, 21in (53.5cm) high.
$1,800–2,000 JAK

A Frankenthal group of Venus and Cupid, by K. G. Lück, restored, marked CT monogram beneath crown, 18thC, 8¼in (21cm) high.
$2,500–2,700 S(Am)

A Heubach figure of a young girl in balletic pose, wearing a green pleated dress, the base moulded with roses and applied with a tambourine, printed sunburst mark, early 20thC, 15½in (39.5cm) high.
$520–570 S(S)

The Heubach porcelain factory was established in 1843 at Lichte in the Saxon province of Thuringia, Germany. The factory is best known for bisque and made many fine 'piano babies' and dolls' heads.

Cross Reference
See Colour Review

A Meissen group of Europa and the Bull, with applied flowers and gilt highlights, underglaze blue mark, late 19thC, 8½in (21.5cm) high.
$2,000–2,500 SLM

A Meissen group of Venus and Cupid, with pale enamel colouring, slight damage, blue crossed swords mark to rear, c1750, 12¼in (31cm) high.
$1,400–1,600 Bon

A Minton figure of a man, wearing a blue coat and green hat, sitting on a wicker seat, on a scroll-moulded green base, base cracked, c1830, 5¼in (13.5cm) high.
$550–600 Bea(E)

A Minton parian group, by John Bell, entitled 'Una and the Lion' from Spenser's *Faerie Queen*, slight damage, c1850, 15in (38cm) high.
$1,600–1,900 JAK

◄ A Minton parian figure of Dorothea, seated on a rock, diamond and John Bell mark, slight damage, 1847, 14in (35.5cm) high.
$500–575 MSW

A Meissen group, in the form of a harvester seated upon wheat sheaves and his companion with a lute, painted in coloured enamels and heightened with gilt, crossed swords mark, 19thC, 5¾in (14.5cm) high.
$650–800 P(S)

An Orléans figure of America, from a set of the Continents, depicting a Native American woman seated on a rock with an alligator curled around it, white with traces of cold enamel colours, mid-18thC, 8¼in (21cm) high.
$1,800–2,000 P

A Meissen figure of a young man in 18thC dress, wearing a mauve and gilt-trimmed coat and patterned and gilt-bordered waistcoat, restored, blue under-glaze mark, c1860, 7½in (19cm) high.
$320–350 CAG

A French group, possibly Orléans, modelled as putti with dogs by a tree growing from rockwork, c1750, 11¼in (28.5cm) high.
$2,000–2,500 C

Minton (1796–present)
- Founded in 1796 in Stoke-on-Trent by Thomas Minton, a former apprentice at Caughley.
- Early production was earthenware, followed c1798 by the introduction of bone china wares, usually painted or printed with neo-classical designs.
- Production strongly influenced by Dresden in 1830s, and by c1850 the Sèvres style had become extremely important.
- In the 1870s and '80s, Minton was influenced by the current fashion for Japanese style, and some of their reproductions in porcelain of cloisonné metalwork were designed by Dr Christopher Dresser.
- In 1872 Marc-Louis Solon arrived from Sèvres and introduced the *pâte-sur-pâte* technique, whereby white slip is built up in layers on a dark coloured ground. This continued to be used into the early 20thC but pieces lack the vitality of 19thC examples.

A Royal Copenhagen group, modelled as a naked couple embracing on a rock, naturalistically coloured, green printed and underglaze blue marks, dated '1950', 18½in (47cm) high.
$1,900–2,100 S(S)

This is a relatively modern issue of a famous model made for many years. Earlier examples are worth more.

A parian group, possibly by Robinson & Leadbeater, entitled 'The Power of Love', by Meli, c1860, 11¾in (30cm) high.
$1,100–1,300 JAK

A Sèvres biscuit group, entitled 'La Leçon de Flute', or 'Le Fluteur Boucher', slight damage, mid-18thC, 8¾in (22cm) high.
$9,000–10,500 P

A pair of Sèvres biscuit figures, entitled 'Le Batteur en Granges' and 'La Batteuse de Beurre', modelled by Suzanne and Fernex after Boucher, c1755–60, 8½in (21.5cm) high.
$5,200–5,700 DN

An Italian white figure of a sage, probably Turin, wearing long robes and holding a flower in his right hand, c1740, 7in (18cm) high.
$3,800–4,000 S

A Royal Worcester white figure of Pierrot, c1930, 7in (18cm) high.
$200–230 JAK

A Royal Worcester figure, entitled 'The Bridesmaid', by Freda Doughty, wearing a blue dress and holding an armful of rose blooms, shape No. 3224, dated '1950', 8¼in (21cm) high.
$570–600 P

A German figure of a Mandarin, with nodding head, articulated tongue and moving hands, 19thC, 6½in (16.5cm) high.
$450–530 FHF

This is a copy of a more valuable Meissen model.

A parian figure, entitled 'The Birth of Venus', c1870, 10in (25.5cm) high.
$450–500 JAK

A German bisque garniture of 3 figures, depicting The Farm Boy and The Farm Girl flanked by 2 single figures, all under glass domes, c1890, figures 12in (30.5cm) high.
$650–800 CAG

▶ A Continental group, depicting an allegorical female figure holding flowers, a putto at her feet, 19thC, 12¾in (32.5cm) high.
$600–700 AH

A Belleek side plate, decorated with gilt rim, First Period, 1863–90, 6in (15cm) diam.
$200–250 DeA

A Capodimonte saucer, painted with an Italian landscape scene of a stream and tree before a castle, slight damage, fleur-de-lys mark in blue, c1750, 5½in (14cm) diam.
$450–530 P

A Berlin cabinet plate, painted with Magdeburg Cathedral within a gilded well and border of foliate scrolls, c1825, 9½in (24cm) diam.
$2,100–2,500 Bon(C)

A Chamberlain's armorial plate, decorated with the arms of Sir John Hullock above a ribboned motto, a border of pink rose heads within gilded foliate cartouches on a cobalt blue border, red printed factory mark with royal flower swag, c1825, 10in (25.5cm) diam.
$570–700 Bon

A set of 9 Chelsea dishes, painted with scattered flowers and insects in polychrome enamels, brown line rims, one with hair crack, red anchor marks, c1755, 9in (23cm) diam.
$4,000–5,000 WW

A Chelsea soup plate, the border moulded with trellised C-scroll panels and painted with sprays of flowers, chocolate brown line rim, slight damage, red painted anchor mark, c1752–58, 9½in (24cm) diam.
$650–730 Bon

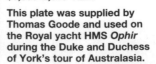

A Copeland dessert plate, the green border gilt-lined and decorated, c1901, 9½in (24cm) diam.
$1,600–2,000 ALiN

This plate was supplied by Thomas Goode and used on the Royal yacht HMS *Ophir* during the Duke and Duchess of York's tour of Australasia.

A set of 10 Copeland dessert plates, the borders pierced with a trellis design, outlined with gilt lines and bands of raised gold dots, painted with panels of fruit and flowers, probably by C. F. Hürten, the centres with monogram, dated '1875', '1878' and '1880', 8¾in (22cm) diam.
$4,800–5,200 P

A Doccia plate, the border painted with brightly coloured floral festoons between urns and putti, within deep blue borders with gilt husks, c1780, 7¾in (19.5cm) diam.
$350–400 P

▶ A pair of Dresden plates, each painted with a portrait of Mme Adelaide de France and Louise de France, within a gilt cartouche, blue border and gilt floral swags, underglaze blue printed crowned 'D' mark, late 19thC, 8¾in (22cm) diam.
$1,300–1,500 M

A set of 12 Limoges botanical dessert plates, each centred by a different painted floral specimen within a raised gilt festooned border, titled on the reverse, underglaze green printed mark 'D & C France', late 19thC, 9¼in (23.5cm) diam.
$2,300–2,600 B&B

A Limoges plate, with a photographic decoration of George Washington, c1910, 7½in (19cm) diam.
$80–100 MSB

A Longton Hall strawberry leaf plate, moulded in low relief around the rim with strawberry plants with green leaves and puce veining, the centre painted with 2 exotic birds within a wooded landscape, slight damage, c1758, 8¾in (22cm) diam.
$1,350–1,550 P

A C. J. Mason plate, depicting Provost's Lodge, King's College, c1840, 9in (23cm) diam.
$80–100 JP

A Meissen blue and white tureen stand, from the Kinder à la Raphael service, painted with 2 children playing a ball game, the rim with a border of ribbon-tied laurel swags, crossed swords and dot mark in underglaze blue, c1770, 17½in (44.5cm) long.
$3,600–4,000 S(NY)

A Meissen deep dish, slip-decorated with raised foliate and scrolled cartouches and enamelled floral sprays, early 19thC, 15¼in (38.5cm) diam.
$1,300–1,500 SK

A Meissen plate, painted with Diana, Cupid and Pan, the rim pierced with gadroons picked out in gilding, crossed swords mark, mid-19thC, 9¼in (23.5cm) diam.
$2,000–2,300 P

A Minton royal dessert plate, made for Queen Victoria for use at Balmoral, the border pierced with fine trellis and reserved with a panel at the top bearing the crowned cipher 'VRI', the centre painted with a spray of pink and white heather, impressed and printed marks, dated '1879', 9¾in (25cm) diam.
$1,100–1,300 P

A pair of Sèvres plates, painted by Nicolas Bulidon, the centre with a spray of flowers, the green-ground rims reserved with 3 flower panels and gilt scrolls strung with continuous flower swags, marked with interlaced 'L's, date letter 'S', c1771, 9½in (24cm) diam.
$5,000–5,700 S

A Worcester plate, painted in underglaze blue with Hundred Antiques pattern, c1775, 7¼in (18.5cm) diam.
$730–800 JUP

◀ A Vienna-style cabinet plate, hand-painted with a scene depicting the Rape of Europa, the border decorated in gold with garden scenes in cartouches and panels of scrolled dolphins on a cobalt ground, signed 'Wagner', marked with underglaze blue beehive, c1900, 9½in (24cm) diam.
$1,400–1,550 JAA

ICE PAILS & WINE COOLERS

A pair of Sèvres ice pails, painted with *feuille de choux* panels in blue enamel and gold containing painted flowersprays, interlaced 'L's marks with date letter 'R', both with painter's mark of 3 dots for Jean Baptiste Tandart, dated '1770', 5in (13cm) high.
$1,300–1,500 P

A pair of Spode ice pails, liners and covers, painted with sprays of flowers between bands moulded with foliate scrolls on a claret ground with gilt foliate sprigs, beneath rims moulded with 'jewels' and stiff leaves, slight damage, marked in black 'Spode', c1820, 13½in (34.5cm) high.
$1,600–2,000 Bon(C)

A Spode ice pail and cover, painted on one side with a named view of Pembroke Castle, the reverse painted with a view from a river of a wooded landscape and a castle, the deep blue ground gilt with bands of scrolled foliage and lambrequin, script mark in black, c1825, 13½in (34.5cm) high.
$4,000–5,000 P

JARDINIERES

A pair of Belleek Finner flower pots, encrusted with sprays of flowers, black printed marks, Second Period, 1891–1926, 11½in (29cm) diam.
$3,000–3,250 HOK

A jardinière, possibly Doccia, painted *en grisaille* with a panoramic scene of mermaids, mermen, putti and goddesses at play in a river, a gilt floral and stem border, between gilt and green line bands, traces of a red star mark, c1810–20, 6in (15cm) high.
$500–570 P

A pair of Royal Bonn Sèvres-style cachepots, by Franz Anton Mehlem, each painted with panels of flowers in a vase, signed 'Roder', within gilded cartouches on a cobalt blue ground, c1900, 8¾in (22.5cm) high.
$2,700–3,000 HAM

Mehlem & Co traded as Royal Bonn.

A Minton jardinière, painted with 3 panels of coastal scenes within tooled gilt borders of dotted chains, impressed 'Minton' and indistinct date cipher, mid-19thC, 7¾in (19.5cm) high.
$1,000–1,150 Bon

Sèvres-style

Some Sèvres-style porcelain was made in the 19thC using old Sèvres blanks, in factories in Paris, Limoges and sometimes even in England, to copy the famous old porcelain that was proudly displayed in museums. Sèvres-style pieces usually bear fake 18thC marks, and the date letters are often too early for the style of decoration. Vast quantities were made and sold, even then, as 'Sèvres'. This term became generic and it is now usual to find copies referred to in auction catalogues as 'Sèvres' today. Sèvres-style is a preferable description as this implies the piece is a copy and not made at the Sèvres factory.

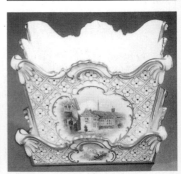

A Minton jardinière and stand, painted with village scenes and fishing boats, gilt details to the moulded floral and trellis ground, printed mark in turquoise with banners beneath, late 19thC, 8in (20.5cm) square.
$650–700 RBB

Cross Reference
See Colour Review

MIRRORS

A Dresden-style mirror, the frame encrusted with floral sprays, blue crossed swords to top outer frame, 19thC, 28in (71cm) high.
$650–800 M

A German mirror, the frame encrusted with floral sprays, enriched in gilt, underglaze blue 'R' mark, late 19thC, 18in (45.5cm) high.
$850–900 M

A pair of Meissen mirrors, each moulded with a coloured beaded border, surmounted by a pair of cherubs holding a floral garland, restored, underglaze blue crossed swords mark, late 19thC, 9½in (24cm) high.
$1,100–1,300 Oli

MUGS & TANKARDS

A Worcester mug, painted with flowersprays and an insect, slight damage, c1756–58, 3½in (9cm) high.
$5,200–5,700 C

A porcelain loving cup, painted with flowers and foliage, with gilt borders, 19thC, 4½in (11.5cm) high.
$200–250 E

A Worcester tankard, decorated with the Beckoning Chinaman pattern, wearing a puce coat, the reverse painted with a spray of Oriental flowers, workman's mark of an anchor and chain in red, c1754–56, 5½in (14cm) high.
$6,800–7,800 P

A Worcester mug, painted in underglaze blue with the Walk in the Garden pattern, slight damage, c1758, 3½in (9cm) high.
$1,450–1,650 JUP

Miller's Compares

A Copeland tyg, to commemorate the centenary of the death of Admiral Lord Nelson, printed and painted with a portrait of Nelson, and with roundels depicting Britannia, HMS *Victory* and a contemporary naval vessel, printed mark in black, pattern No. E1520, c1905, 5¾in (14.5cm) high.
$1,900–2,100 DN

A Copeland tyg, to commemorate the Transvaal War, 1899–1900, printed and painted with a portrait of Queen Victoria, flanked by flags and emblems of the Empire, with portrait roundels of Field Marshall Lord Roberts and the Marquis of Salisbury, inscribed 'Subscriber's Copy', c1900, 5¾in (14.5cm) high.
$1,200–1,300 DN

Limited edition mugs commemorating special events are not a modern phenomenon, as is demonstrated by the tygs pictured above. These were manufactured by Copeland for T. Goode & Co at the beginning of the century for an already established collectors' market. Clearly it was thought that there would be more subscribers for a piece celebrating the Transvaal War which had just ended, than for the centenary of Nelson's death, and fewer of the latter were produced. Ironically, however, today there are more collectors of Nelson memorabilia than of South Africa war commemoratives.

PLAQUES

▶ A pair of Dresden plaques, decorated by F. M. Beetz, Dresden, with portraits of Sir James and Lady Reid, he in naval uniform, she in court dress in yellow-patterned satin with grey bodice and lace trimmings, signed, late 19thC, 9¾ x 7in (25 x 17.5cm).
$2,000–2,200 P

A Berlin plaque, depicting a female warrior, impressed KPM and sceptre marks, late 19thC, 13 x 11in (33 x 28cm).
$3,500–4,000 S(NY)

A Vienna plaque, painted by Knoeller with a Tyrolean interior scene, after the original by Franz von Defregger, signed and dated '1882', 14½ x 21in (37 x 53.5cm).
$4,000–5,000 Bon

A Berlin plaque, decorated with The Immaculate Conception after the painting by Murillo, the back with impressed 'KPM' under an impressed sceptre, c1900, plaque 17in (43cm) high, in a gilt frame.
$6,000–7,000 JAA

A Meissen plaque, painted in polychrome enamels with a wicker basket containing fruit, crossed swords in underglaze blue, c1850, 17in (43cm) high.
$9,000–10,000 S

Meissen plaques are much rarer than Berlin examples, and are always skilfully painted.

SAUCE BOATS

A Bristol butter boat, moulded in bold relief with 2 sprays of fruits and leaves, painted in coloured enamels with flowers within pink line borders, blue painted 'X' mark, c1770, 4¼in (11cm) long.
$575–650 DN

A Lowestoft sauce boat, moulded with scrolls and flowers enclosing panels painted in blue with a fisherman on a boat, the interior painted with sprays of peonies, slight damage, workman's numeral '5' for Robert Allen, c1765, 8¼in (21cm) long.
$575–650 P

A pair of Bow sauce boats, each painted in underglaze blue with a version of the Desirable Residence pattern, the interior with flowers, slight damage, c1758, 4in (10cm) high.
$700–800 DN

A Worcester sauce boat, painted in underglaze blue with the Triangular Platform pattern, c1756, 7½in (19cm) long.
$1,400–1,550 JUP

A Chelsea strawberry leaf sauce boat, the handle moulded with strawberry flowers and puce tendrils, the underside moulded with further strawberry plants, the interior painted with sprays of flowers, brown line rim, handle restored, c1753, 6¼in (16cm) long.
$1,000–1,200 P

A Worcester sauce boat, each side painted with an Oriental scene, the interior with flowering plants and precious objects, c1754, 7¾in (19.5cm) long.
$1,600–2,000 C

COFFEE & TEA SERVICES

► A Belleek Neptune tea service, comprising 12 pieces, moulded as oyster shells on winkle feet, printed mark in black, Second Period, 1891–1926, tray 18in (45.5cm) wide.
$1,600–2,000 MSW

A Belleek part tea service, comprising 11 pieces, including a tray, the teapot with green rope handle, Second Period, 1891–1926, tray 17in (43cm) diam.
$1,300–1,450 MEA

A Berlin part tea and coffee service, comprising 16 pieces, some damage, sceptre marks in underglaze blue, c1775, coffee pot 8¼in (21cm) high.
$3,500–4,500 S

A Cauldon porcelain tea service, comprising 37 pieces, decorated with blue and gilded panels of urns and formal scrolls, printed marks and pattern No. 2292, early 20thC.
$160–200 GAK

► A Coalport tea and coffee service, comprising 51 pieces, with blue and gilt scroll pattern, No. 5-683, registration marks for 18th April 1850.
$950–1,100 P(E)

A Grainger reticulated tea service, attributed to Alfred Barry, comprising 9 pieces, each piece double walled, modelled in Japanese taste with gadrooned matt gold borders, the outer walls in white glazed parian pierced with scrolling foliage, shield marks in brown, pattern No. 1/1240, c1885.
$4,500–5,000 P

◄ A Haviland & Co, Limoges, tea service on a tray, comprising 18 pieces, c1900, tray 15in (38cm) square.¶
$1,300–1,450 AMH

A Hilditch & Hopwood tea service, comprising 44 pieces, decorated with a broad apricot border, with foliate and scroll gilt heightening, c1845.
$500–600 P(E)

A Lowestoft blue and white part tea service, comprising 15 pieces, each reeded body painted with a leafy branch within a cell border, c1775.
$1,300–1,450 Bea(E)

A Meissen cabaret set, comprising 12 pieces, decorated with fowl in farmyard settings, cancelled crossed swords in underglaze blue, mid-19thC.
$2,000–2,500 S(S)

A New Hall tea and coffee service, comprising 33 pieces, decorated with an underglaze blue border embellished with gilt palmettes between gilt foliate bands, one cup restored, painted '638' in purple or gilding, c1790.
$6,500–7,500 S

A Paris Empire-style coffee service, comprising 28 pieces, with bird and lion-head handles, painted in colours with vignettes of children at play, the borders gilded, some damage and repair, c1830.
$1,600–2,000 P

A Spode part tea and coffee service, comprising 40 pieces, painted in gilt with scrolling leaves on a platinum lustre band, within gilt and iron-red line borders, slight damage and repair, pattern No. 840 in gilt, c1815–20.
$4,500–5,200 DN

▶ A Royal Worcester cabaret set, comprising 10 pieces, decorated with brown and cream floral swag borders reserved against a coral pink ground, puce and brown marks, pattern No. 4551, c1898.
$750–850 RTo

DESSERT & DINNER SERVICES

A Meissen dessert service, comprising 13 pieces, decorated with the Onion pattern in underglaze blue, c1900.
$1,450–1,650 Bri

A Coalport dessert service, comprising 44 pieces, decorated with trees and buildings, the border with panels of birds and flowerheads on a gilt-decorated blue ground, slight damage, c1810.
$8,500–9,500 WW

▶ A Minton part dessert service, comprising 12 pieces, moulded with 3 foliate scroll panels enclosing printed and painted scenes of birds in branches with piercing between, on a pink ground, gilt pattern No. 1480, slight damage, c1840.
$2,500–3,000 Bon(C)

A Niderviller part dinner service, comprising 19 pieces, painted in the centres with a river or coastal landscape surrounded by flower sprigs, one plate restored, crowned interlinked 'C's mark in underglaze blue, c1775, dinner plate 9¾in (25cm) diam, and a later serving dish.
$1,300–1,450 S(NY)

A John Ridgway & Co dessert service, comprising 26 pieces, painted with fruit on a marble ledge framed within an elaborate gilt border on an apple green ground, all within pierced rims picked out in buff enamel and gilding, slight damage and repair, painted pattern No. 6/6595, c1855.
$7,300–8,300 S(NY)

A Royal Worcester dessert service, comprising 15 pieces, the centres enamelled in colours with wild flowers, ferns and grasses within pink borders and with turquoise and gilt 'jewelling', gilt borders rubbed, pattern No. 8269, date code for 1884.
$1,100–1,350 CAG

A Paris part dinner, dessert and coffee service, comprising 36 pieces, each piece painted with foliate sprays and with mustard yellow borders, restored, mid-19thC.
$1,300–1,450 SK

A Rörstrand armorial part dinner and coffee service, comprising 61 pieces, the borders moulded with a shield beneath a crown and an armorial, decorated in gilt to cobalt blue borders, c1900.
$1,500–1,650 WW

A Worcester dessert service, comprising 14 pieces, decorated with the Kangxi Lotus pattern, c1770–75, plates 7in (18cm) diam.
$9,500–11,500 BWA

TEA CANISTERS

A Lowestoft tea canister, painted in blue with the Mansfield pattern, cover lacking, crescent mark in blue, c1765, 4in (10cm) high.
$700–800 P

A Meissen tea canister and cover, painted in Kakiemon style with chrysanthemums issuing from stylised rockwork, the shoulder and cover with scattered flowers, traces of crossed swords mark in blue, c1740, 4¼in (11cm) high.
$5,000–5,500 S

A Meissen tea canister and cover, moulded on each side with a scroll-edged panel enclosing a scene of peasants after Teniers, traces of crossed swords in underglaze blue, c1750, 5in (12.5cm) high.
$5,000–5,500 S

A Worcester tea canister and flat cover, painted in coloured enamels with sprays of flowers and leaves within gilt line borders, small chip, c1775, 5in (12.5cm) high.
$525–575 DN

TRAYS

A Belleek pink and gilded tray, Third Period, 1926–46, 17½in (44.5cm) wide.
$1,000–1,150 MLa

A Sèvres tray, painted with a basket of roses suspended from an orange and red ribbon, on a ground of pale blue *oeil-de-perdrix*, gilt-edged rim, interlaced 'L's above a dot in blue, c1770, 12¼in (31cm) wide.
$5,500–6,500 S(NY)

◄ A pen tray, with a green and gilt border and painted floral spray, c1830, 9½in (24cm) wide.
$250–350 DAN

A Sèvres tray, the rim with a blue enamel ground border reserved with gilt trellis panels, slight damage, interlaced 'L's enclosing date letter R, c1770, 8½in (21.5cm) high.
$4,500–5,000 S

> **Cross Reference**
> See Colour Review

TUREENS

A Frankenthal soup tureen and cover, painted on each side with colourful birds in branches, the cover similarly decorated and with an artichoke knop, crowned 'CT' monogram mark in underglaze blue, c1770, 9¾in (25cm) diam.
$4,500–5,000 S(NY)

A Worcester tureen and stand, Flight, Barr & Barr period, painted with blue floral sprays with gilt, c1813–40, 12in (30.5cm) wide, together with a fruit dish and a plate.
$650–800 AH

A Meissen tureen and cover, the double walled sides and cover pierced with scroll panels and painted in coloured enamels, the cover with armorial cartouches, the gilt interior moulded and painted with flowers and leaves, marked in blue, c1860–80, 10¼in (26cm) wide.
$10,000–11,500 DN

A Chamberlain's Worcester soup tureen, cover and stand, painted on each side with the arms and crest of Hay, Earl of Errol, reserved in a gilt frame between panels of the Rich Queen's pattern, c1800–1807, 14¾in (37.5cm) wide.
$20,000–25,000 S(NY)

This tureen is a rare and impressive shape, of large size and with a particularly decorative coat-of-arms.

A Sèvres tureen and cover, decorated on a green ground with fruit and flowers enclosed by gilt fronds, the cover similarly decorated and with artichoke finial, restored, c1763, 10¼in (26cm) high.
$9,000–11,000 S

A melon tureen and cover, the textured sides striped in green and yellow, the leaf terminals with puce veining, damaged and restored, early 19thC, 6in (15cm) wide.
$3,000–3,500 S(NY)

Further Reading

Miller's Porcelain Antiques Checklist, Miller's Publications, 1991

VASES

A garniture of 3 Alcock vases, the reserves painted with floral sprays within gilded borders, on apple green ground, damaged, tallest 12¼in (31cm) high.
$550–650 AH

A Belleek flying fish vase, First Period, c1863–90, 4½in (11.5cm) high.
$700–800 DeA

A Belleek vase, moulded with anthemia and geometric bands, on 3 hoof feet and triform base, printed mark in black, Second Period, 1891–1926, 13½in (34.5cm) high.
$650–800 DN(H)

A pair of Belleek trumpet-shaped vases, decorated with applied flowers on basket bases, Second Period, 1891–1926, 12½in (32cm) high.
$1,800–2,000 JAd

◄ A Belleek triple flower holder, Second Period, 1891–1926, 5in (12.5cm) high.
$450–500 MLa

A Bow vase, painted in Kakiemon style with an Oriental figure, c1755, 7½in (19cm) high.
$6,500–7,500 S

A Belleek vase, encrusted with flowers, Third Period, 1926–46, 10in (25.5cm) high.
$1,450–1,600 DeA

A Belleek Nile vase, with reeded neck and lower band of golden lustre leaves, Second Period, 1891–1926, 14½in (37cm) high.
$275–325 MEA

A pair of Brownfield celadon vases and covers, each with a carp and an angel fish on a wave ground, raised on a scalework arabesque moulded base, slight damage, one with printed double globe mark and shape No. 362, c1875, 14½in (37cm) high.
$2,300–2,600 S(S)

A pair of Marx Eugene Clauss vases and covers, slight wear, blue enamel 'EC' and crossed swords, c1875, 16in (40.5cm) high.
$1,200–1,350 Bon

Bow (1744–76)

- Founded by Thomas Frye and Edward Heylyn in Stratford-le-Bow, Essex, Bow shares with Chelsea the distinction of being one of the earliest porcelain factories in England.
- Patent granted in 1744 but first successful porcelain production unlikely to have been before c1748.
- Manufactured soft-paste porcelain containing bone-ash, making it coarser than true porcelain and liable to stain.
- Typical decorations are underglaze powder-blue ground, *blanc-de-Chine* sprigged prunus blossom, Kakiemon palette and, their most popular design, the 'Quail' pattern.
- Early Bow is unmarked, but after c1765 a red enamel 'anchor and dagger' mark can be found on some colourful pieces that were possibly decorated outside the factory.
- In the 1770s the figures for which they were famous became unfashionable, resulting in the closure of the factory in 1776.

A pair of Coalport vases, decorated by Thomas Baxter, painted in sepia with a panel of a young woman in a landscape, reserved against a gilt and white chequered ground, the neck and foot with bands of summer flowers, slight damage, signed, c1802, 7¼in (18.5cm) high.
$5,500–6,500 S

A pair of Coalport urns, the deep blue ground decorated with oval reserves depicting cherubs and classical females *en grisaille*, c1840, 17¼in (44cm) high.
$2,600–3,000 JAd

A pair of Dresden vases and covers, each reserved with figures in a garden landscape alternating with panels of flowers on a pink ground, within gilt foliate and scroll borders, under-glaze blue 'AR' mark, late 19thC, 12½in (32cm) high.
$1,200–1,350 S(S)

A pair of Meissen potpourri vases and covers, painted with classical lovers in rural landscapes and *deutsche Blumen,* bordered with heavy floral and fruit encrustations, the pierced scroll covers with high floral finials, damaged and restored, blue crossed swords, c1880, 17¼in (44cm) high.
$4,500–5,200 Bon

A pair of Meissen vases, with 2 coiled serpents forming the handles, the main bodies in royal blue with a guilloche band, gilding rubbed, crossed swords in underglaze blue, 19thC, 19in (48.5cm) high.
$1,200–1,450 TEN

A pair of Minton Sèvres style two-piece potpourri vases, painted with panels of birds, fruit, instruments and flowers, crowned globe mark in gilding, impressed date code, c1869, 6¾in (17cm) high.
$5,600–6,400 S

A Paris potpourri vase and cover, attributed to Jacob Petit, the apple green ground with 2 panels of relief floral sprays, on gilded swan feet, c1835–40, 5¼in (13.5cm) wide.
$1,600–2,000 NOA

A Paris vase, with swan-form handles, reserved on the front with a man and woman in Renaissance costume, gilding restored, 19thC, 26¾in (68cm) high.
$3,500–4,000 B&B

A garniture of 3 Spode urns, each enamelled in orange, blue, green and gilt with a Japan pattern, No. 967, early 19thC, tallest 8¼in (21cm) high.
$1,450–1,600 CAG

◄ A Potschappel vase, cover and stand, the front depicting a courting couple, the reverse with a floral spray, marked in underglaze blue, c1890, 37in (94cm) high.
$5,000–5,500 S(Am)

► A Staffordshire vase and cover, decorated in red blue and green with a Japan pattern of birds, fences and stylized vegetation, restored, c1825, 26½in (67cm) high.
$2,500–3,000 P

A Swansea vase, with bee handles, painted with a band of garden flowers and foliage between gilt foliate borders, set on a black hardstone square base, c1814–26, 7in (18cm) high.
$6,500–7,500 S

A pair of Worcester vases, and covers, Kerr & Binns period, painted in coloured enamels by Luke Wells with portrait medallions of Edward IV and Anne Boleyn, the borders picked out in gilt, missing knops, c1855–60, 7½in (19cm) high.
$1,150–1,300 DN

A Royal Worcester Hadley Ware vase, painted with pheasants perched in a pine tree on a lime-green ground, with gilt handles in the form of goats' heads, raised on a plinth base with gilt goats' feet, signed 'J. C. Lewis', dated 1911, 7¼in (18.5cm) high.
$1,000–1,150 HAM

A Vienna-style vase, with a hand-painted Austrian tavern scene, the neck and foot in cobalt blue, the fired gold shoulder and base with raised enamel work, signed 'F. Schreier', marked with underglaze blue beehive, early 20thC, 22in (56cm) high.
$1,200–1,350 DuM

A Royal Worcester vase, with gilded field-mice, neck and rims, minor restoration, c1898, 6½in (16.5cm) high.
$900–1,100 ALiN

A pair of Grainger's Worcester vases, with hand-painted scenes of finches on a branch of thistle below a reticulated rim, marked in green, c1900, 9in (23cm) high.
$2,000–2,200 JAA

A pair of Worcester vases and covers, painted in blue with the Fancy Bird in a Tree pattern, the shoulders with quatrefoil panels containing Chinese river scenes, restored, c1758, 15¾in (40cm) high.
$11,500–13,500 P

A pair of Sèvres-style and gilt-metal mounted vases painted by Leber after Baudoin, interlocking 'L's mark to covers and bases, c1880, 44½in (113cm) high.
$26,000–30,000 M

These vases are of imposing size, highly decorative and in excellent condition.

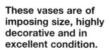

A Worcester vase and cover, Flight, Barr & Barr period, with fruit knop, painted in coloured enamels with a bird in a wooded landscape, on a gilt seaweed ground, c1820, 4½in (11.5cm) high.
$1,600–1,800 DN

A pair of French vases, painted with floral sprays on a platinum ground, late 19thC, 23¼in (59cm) high.
$5,500–6,500 S(Am)

A pair of Chamberlain's Worcester potpourri vases and pierced covers, painted in Imari palette with a Japan pattern of Oriental foliage, slight damage, c1795, 10½in (26.5cm) high.
$2,000–2,200 S

◄ A Royal Worcester vase, by George Owen, with a horizontal reticulated section between formal gilt leaf scrolls and dot patterns, puce printed mark, c1913, 3in (7.5cm) high.
$2,200–2,600 WW

DERBY

The earliest Derby porcelain is dated 1750, so the year 2000 is cause for a special celebration. The anniversary marks 250 years of mixed fortunes, ranging from the golden age of fine painting in the 1790s to bankruptcy and closure in the mid-19th century. Yet the spirit of Derby rose again. Two flourishing Victorian factories united to form Royal Crown Derby, where porcelain is still made to traditional 200-year-old designs.

Collectors usually focus on a particular period. Very early Derby figures and rare tea wares from the 1750s and 1760s appeal to connoisseurs and as a result these are always expensive. Prices for late 18th-century artist-decorated cabinet cans and saucers have returned to a more realistic level from their peak in the late 1980s, but it is not an area which a beginner can enter easily. The market for middle-range pieces from 1810 to 1840 has held steady for two decades now, but really fine pieces from this period are hard to find and tend to be expensive.

In the 18th century Derby excelled in making figures, thus compensating for its inability to make durable tea sets. Until recently the market in Derby figures had stagnated and real bargains could be found. Well-modelled examples, with only minimal damage, have been rising steadily and I feel this trend will continue.

A decline in porcelain-making in Derby after 1850 was followed by a renaissance in the 1880s. The Derby Crown Porcelain Company sold vast numbers of tea sets in popular Japanese Imari patterns. The substantial profits subsidized production of a new generation of cabinet pieces, painted and signed by artists and embellished with the finest raised and tooled gilding. One of Derby's most important services, made c1910 for Judge Elbert Gary, was sold by auction in the United States recently and subsequently offered for sale by the British antiques trade at substantial prices, with single plates, cups and saucers selling for far more than the price of 18th-century examples.

In terms of quality, fine Royal Crown Derby really does deserve the high prices it now commands, but it also highlights the fact that some older Derby is probably undervalued. Imari patterns made in the 1920s sell better than many 1820s examples, and it is these early pieces, in fine condition, that are now worth seeking. Derby collectors can afford to be selective, and consequently damaged and restored pieces should be avoided wherever possible. **John Sandon**

A Derby model of a goat, by Andrew Planché, with mottled brown markings and purple horns, supported on a mound base, damaged and restored, c1753, 5¾in (14.5cm) high.
$4,000–5,000 C

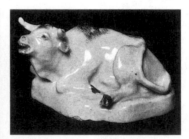

A Derby model of a recumbent cow, with a sparse grey and iron-red painted body, c1755, 3½in (9cm) high.
$900–975 HYD

A Derby basket, painted in underglaze blue with a Chinese river scene, c1765, 7in (18cm) wide.
$2,200–2,500 JUP

◀ A pair of Derby fish-head stirrup cups, each painted as a rainbow trout, with a gilt banded collar rim, inscribed 'The Angler's Delight', c1810, 5¼in (13.5cm) high.
$3,500–4,000 S(NY)

A pair of Derby models of stags, before bocage trees, each of the fawn coats speckled in white and dark brown antlers, late 18thC, c1775, 8in (20.5cm) high.
$1,300–1,600 CGC

A Derby bough pot and cover, painted with a naval battle scene, bordered by thick lines of gilding, crossed batons, crown and 'D' marks, c1790, 9¾in (25cm) high.
$15,500–18,000 Bon

A Royal Crown Derby bouillon cup and saucer, painted with floral panels, signed by Albert Gregory, gilded and signed by George Darlington, c1910, saucer 7in (18cm) diam.
$2,000–2,300 JUP

This cup and saucer is from a service made for Judge Elbert Gary.

A Derby porcelain desk set, mounted with pen tray and 3 covered pots, set on paw feet, red factory mark, early 19thC, 8½in (21.5cm) wide.
$1,000–1,200 SK

◀ A Derby figure of Water, from the Four Elements, modelled by Pierre Stephan, incised No. 3, c1770, 10in (25.5cm) high.
$1,350–1,550 DMa

Miller's is a price GUIDE not a price LIST

▶ A Derby figure of a lady with a cat, her moulded dress with a brightly coloured fringe, the detail picked out in gold and puce, patch marks, slight chips, c1775, 5½in (14cm) high.
$1,500–1,600 P

Two Derby figures, Winter and Summer from the Classical Seasons, slight damage, c1758, 11in (28cm) high.
$3,500–4,000 DMa

A pair of Derby biscuit groups, emblematic of Poetry and Music, each with a classical female figure and 2 putti, incised '216' and '217', restored, c1775, 10½in (26.5cm) high.
$2,500–3,000 DN

▶ A pair of Derby figures, The Ranelagh Dancers, on foliate scroll bases picked out in turquoise and gilt, bright enamel colouring predominantly in puce, slight damage, c1765, 10in (25.5cm) high.
$2,300–2,600 Bon

Two Derby biscuit figures of Spring and Autumn from the Grotesque Seasons, incised Derby mark and 'No. 47', c1795, 5½in (14cm) high.
$1,450–1,650 DMa

A Derby plate, the centre painted with a passion flower, with pink border and gilt rim, crowned crossed batons and 'D' in blue, wear to gilding, c1798, 9¼in (23.5cm) diam.
$900–1,000 JUP

A set of 10 Royal Crown Derby cabinet plates, by E. Ellis, printed with exotic birds amongst flowering trees, gilded rims with acorn and oak leaves, signed, dated '1930', 10in (25.5cm) diam.
$800–1,000 WBH

A Derby Imari pattern ice pail and cover, c1810–15, 9½in (24cm) diam.
$1,800–2,000 NOA

A Derby guglet, enamelled with 2 vignettes of exotic birds in parkland, patch marks, slight damage, c1760, 9½in (24cm) high.
$4,000–4,500 S

A Derby ice pail, cover and liner, in the style of William Billingsley, painted with flowersprays and scattered sprigs between gilt-line rims, slight damage, painted factory mark and impressed 'E', c1790, 9¼in (23.5cm) high.
$2,600–3,200 S

A Derby mask-spouted harvest or punch jug, painted in a soft palette with sprays and scattered sprigs of flowers on a white ground, the rim moulded with a border of leaves picked out in turquoise and puce, spout damaged and restored, c1770–75, 12¼in (31cm) high.
$730–800 P

A pair of Derby topographical Kedleston ewers, each Brunswick green body reserved with a panel depicting Launceston, Cornwall and Willersley Castle, Derbyshire, crowned crossed batons over 'D', restored, c1825, 11in (28cm) high.
$1,600–1,800 RTo

A Royal Crown Derby part dessert service, comprising 8 pieces, the centre panels painted with a spray of roses within a blue and gilt enhanced border, date ciphers for 1912 and 1915, comport, 11in (28cm) wide.
$1,000–1,200 RID

A Royal Crown Derby tureen, cover and stand, painted with floral panels, signed by Albert Gregory and signed and gilded by George Darlington, c1910, 15½in (39.5cm) long.
$2,800–3,000 JUP

This tureen is from a service made for Judge Elbert Gary.

A Derby smelling salts bottle and stopper, in the manner of Fidelle Duvivier, the 'Smith's Blue' enamel ground gilt with leaf festoons and leaf motifs, the reserved panels painted in sepia monochrome with a boy gardener, the reverse with flowers in a classical urn, damaged, c1775–80, 3½in (9cm) high.
$1,100–1,400 P

A Derby spoon, the handle moulded with gilt-edged scrolls and painted with 2 birds and a flowerspray on the reverse, the bowl painted with flower sprigs, minor wear, c1760, 8in (20.5cm) long.
$3,200–3,600 S

A Goss vase, with coloured flowers on both sides, c1870–1890, 3¾in (9.5cm) high.
$3,000–3,300 G&CC

A Goss 'jewelled' candlestick, with crest of Lord Barnard, c1890–1910, 5in (12.5cm) high.
$70–90 MGC

A Goss jar, decorated with a transfer of a Welsh lady by a rock, 1890–1920, 3in (7.5cm) high.
$200–220 MGC

A Goss figure of William of Wykeham, c1893–1930, 7¾in (20cm) high.
$3,500–4,000 G&CC

Figures such as this are seldom found. It is an early coloured parian example, and is particularly unusual as the removable crozier is still in place.

A Carlton Ware submarine, inscribed 'E. 9.', with Blackpool crest, c1915, 6in (15cm) long.
$90–110 MGC

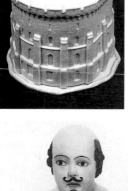

◀ A Goss Windsor round tower night light, c1900, 6in (15cm) high.
$1,100–1,300 CCC

Two W. H. Goss coloured busts of Shakespeare and Anne Hathaway, c1910–1930, 6½in (16.5cm) high.
Anne Hathaway $400–450
Shakespeare $320–350 G&CC

◀ A Savoy comical Tim the Cheshire cat, with Southsea crest, c1910–30, 4in (10cm) long.
$300–330 G&CC

A Goss Stratford Toby jug and Toby bowl, c1920, jug 3in (7.5cm) high.
$320–350 MGC

An Arcadian clip of bullets, with Kingston-upon-Thames crest, c1920, 2½in (6.5cm) high.
$50–65 MGC

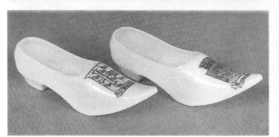

◄ Two versions of the Carlton machine gun, c1915–20, 4in (10cm) long.
$65–80 each G&CC

A Goss Perth coronation chair, with brown stone, c1910–1930, 3¼in (8.5cm) high.
$400–500 G&CC

A pair of Goss Norwegian wooden shoes, c1910–30, 4in (10cm) long.
$40–50 G&CC

A Carlton Ware model of a dog playing a banjo, with Bournemouth crest, c1920, 2¾in (7cm) high.
$65–80 MGC

A Goss model of the Longships lighthouse, c1910–30, 5in (12.5cm) high.
$50–65 G&CC

A Goss model of Portman Lodge, c1910–30, 3in (7.5cm) long.
$570–650 MGC

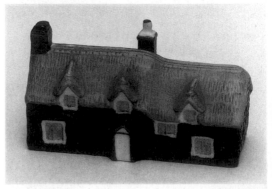

A Goss Old Maids' Cottage at Lee, Devon, c1912–1930, 3in (7.5cm) long.
$200–235 G&CC

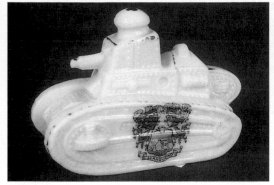

A Victoria China Renault tank, with Llandudno crest, 1915–20, 4in (10cm) long.
$145–160 MGC

A Carlton Ware motor scooter, with Southend-on-Sea crest, 1920–25, 4½in (11.5cm) high.
$80–90 MGC

A Willow Scarborough lighthouse, showing damage inflicted by German warships, 1915–20, 5¼in (13.5cm) high.
$200–230 G&CC

A Willow airman, on a plinth with the City of Rochester crest, c1916, 5½in (14cm) high.
$400–500 CCC

A Goss Hitchin posset cup, with the badge of HMS *Antrim*, c1915–20, 2in (5cm) high.
$130–160 G&CC

An Arcadian model of a point duty policeman, with Hythe crest, Hants, 1920–30, 5½in (14cm) high.
$70–80 MGC

A Shelley single decker bus, with St Anne's-on-the-Sea crest, c1920, 6in (15cm) long.
$900–1,100 CCC

A Goss Aylesbury duck, c1920, 4in (10cm) long.
$500–570 CCC

A Selection of Chinese Dynasties & Marks
Early Dynasties

Neolithic	10th – early 1st millennium BC	Tang Dynasty	AD 618–907
Shang Dynasty	16th Century–c1050 BC	Five Dynasties	AD 907–960
Zhou Dynasty	c1050–221 BC	Liao Dynasty	AD 907–1125
Warring States	480–221 BC	Song Dynasty	AD 960–1279
Qin Dynasty	221–206 BC	*Northern Song*	AD 960–1127
Han Dynasty	206 BC–AD 220	*Southern Song*	AD 1127–1279
Six Dynasties	AD 222–589	Xixia Dynasty	AD 1038–1227
Wei Dynasty	AD 386–557	Jin Dynasty	AD 1115–1234
Sui Dynasty	AD 581–618	Yuan Dynasty	AD 1279–1368

Ming Dynasty Marks

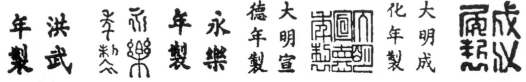

Hongwu
1368–1398

Yongle
1403–1424

Xuande
1426–1435

Chenghua
1465–1487

Hongzhi
1488–1505

Zhengde
1506–1521

Jiajing
1522–1566

Longqing
1567–1572

Wanli
1573–1619

Tianqi
1621–1627

Chongzhen
1628–1644

Qing Dynasty Marks

Shunzhi
1644–1661

Kangxi
1662–1722

Yongzheng
1723–1735

Qianlong
1736–1795

Jiaqing
1796–1820

Daoguang
1821–1850

Xianfeng
1851–1861

Tongzhi
1862–1874

Guangxu
1875–1908

Xuantong
1909–1911

Hongxian
1916

Chinese Ceramics

ANIMALS

A Sichuan pottery model of a dog, wearing a collar around the neck, Han Dynasty, 24in (61cm) high.
$4,500–5,500 S(Am)

A painted pottery model of a horse and rider playing polo, Tang Dynasty, 14¼in (36cm) long.
$13,800–15,400 S(Am)

A pair of *famille rose* models of elephants, each saddle cloth decorated with bats and emblems, restored, Jiaqing period, 12½in (32cm) high.
$11,500–13,000 S(Am)

A green-glazed buff pottery model of a horse and Persian trader, old repairs, Tang Dynasty, 14¾in (37.5cm) high.
$650–800 P

A glazed pottery model of a horse and rider, the rider in an aubergine robe, the detachable head with a red-painted hat, restored, Ming Dynasty, 20½in (52cm) high.
$2,300–2,600 S

A water pot in the form of 2 ducks, modelled together, one with a pierced beak, the plumage painted in underglaze blue, Ming Dynasty, 5¼in (13.5cm) long.
$2,800–3,200 S

A Compagnie des Indes model of a pug, the fur *en grisaille*, with green eyes and iron-red highlights to the lips and collar and traces of gilding to the bell, tail restored, Qianlong period, 7in (18cm) high.
$8,000–9,000 S

A pair of porcelain models of hawks, their bodies decorated in iron-red, sepia, *grisaille*, turquoise and yellow, the feathers outlined in gilt, slight damage, early Qianlong period, 20½in (52cm) high.
$400,000–450,000 WW

These models are exceedingly rare and beautifully modelled. Furthermore, this is almost certainly the first time they have appeared on the market since they were imported in 1740 by the Duke of Newcastle.

A Dehua model of a crane, with incised details to legs and wing feathers under a milky-white glaze, chipped, restored, 18thC, 10in (25.5cm) high.
$1,600–1,800 B&B

A pair of cockerels, glazed white with feathers incised beneath, each face, comb and wattle picked out in red, each standing on brown rockwork, slight damage and restored, Qing Dynasty, 19thC, 15in (38cm) high.
$4,500–5,200 S(S)

BOWLS

A Transitional blue and white *kraak porselein* bowl, decorated with a continuous scene of warriors in a landscape, the interior with panels of scholars and attendants alternating with panels of stylized flowers, slight damage, c1640, 13¼in (33.5cm) diam.
$5,200–5,700 S(Am)

A Canton *famille rose* bowl, decorated with Manchu/Chinese scholars and courtiers, Qing Dynasty, 20¾in (52.5cm) diam.
$5,200–5,700 Bon(C)

A *famille rose* punchbowl, painted in Mandarin palette with panels of figures and landscapes, c1770, 14in (35.5cm) diam.
$6,200–6,800 C&C

A pair of *famille rose* puce-ground medallion bowls, gilt and painted in colours with panels of antique vessels and scholar's objects, the interiors painted in underglaze blue with 4 lanterns above medallions, Daoguang seal marks in underglaze blue and of the period, 6in (15cm) diam.
$8,500–9,500 P

A blue and white bowl, with floral design and yellow rim, 17thC, 12in (30.5cm) diam.
$2,400–2,700 ORI

A Chinese Imari bowl and cover, painted with flowering plants within diaper bands, later decorated in iron-red, green and black enamels and gold, early 18thC, 9in (23cm) diam.
$800–950 Bea(E)

A Chinese Imari punchbowl, the exterior painted with sprays of chrysanthemums, the interior with a large roundel filled with a flowerspray, hairline crack, underglaze blue *zhuanshu* mark, 18thC, 13½in (34.5cm) diam.
$1,450–1,650 P

A Chinese *famille rose* medallion bowl, the exterior decorated with flowers and foliage on a sgraffito blue ground, the interior with a cartouche in underglaze blue and 4 bouquets, Daoguang seal mark and of the period, 5¾in (14.5cm) diam.
$1,150–1,300 WW

A blue and white bowl, Kangxi period, 8½in (21.5cm) diam.
$3,300–4,000 GeW

This bowl is in exceptionally good condition.

A Chinese export punchbowl, painted with masonic motifs with gilded details, c1770, 16in (40.5cm) diam.
$13,000–14,500 HAM

Chinese export porcelain for the masonic market always carries a premium price because it appeals to two different collecting fields.

A Chinese export bowl, decorated in magenta, mauve and turquoise, c1790, 10in (25.5cm) diam.
$300–350 A&A

A blue and white fish bowl, painted on the exterior with stylised lotus blooms and scrolling foliage, 19thC, 15½in (39.5cm) diam.
$525–625 P(D)

BOXES

A *famille rose* spice box and cover, with 3 compartments, painted on the exterior with scattered sprays of flowers inside brown and gilt borders, slight damage, Qianlong period, 4½in (11.5cm) wide.
$2,000–2,300 S(S)

A seal and paste box, decorated with fish and weed, by Deng Bi Suan, brother of Deng Bi Shan, 1930–35, 2in (5cm) diam.
$1,300–1,450 Wai

A seal and paste box, painted *en grisaille* with a rural lake scene, signed with the seal of Zhang Zhitang, c1930, 3in (7.5cm) diam.
$800–950 Wai

Landscapes by Zhang Zhitang (1893–1971) were reproductions based on Song and Yuan masterpieces, carefully composed and executed in fine brushwork.

CENSERS

A *sancai*-glazed tripod censer, applied with 3 polo players, 2 winged chimeras and a leaping fish in relief, below a band of cicada medallions, covered in pale ivory glaze, the figures splashed in amber and green, Tang Dynasty, 10in (25.5cm) diam.
$9,000–10,000 S(NY)

Although the polo player is a popular subject on Tang ceramic ware, it is more frequently seen as a tomb figure and is extremely rare as an applied motif on vessels. This censer appears to be the only example recorded.

The Eight Buddhist Emblems

The Eight Buddhist Emblems or happy omens are as follows:

The Chakra (Wheel) The Conch Shell The Umbrella The Canopy

The Lotus The Vase The Pair of Fish The Endless Knot

At times these emblems may be mixed up with some of the Eight Daoist Emblems.

◀ A yellow-ground censer, the surface decorated overall with the Eight Buddhist Emblems in *famille rose* enamels with gilt highlights, Qianlong mark and of the period, 14¾in (37.5cm) high.
$3,500–4,000 S(NY)

Further Reading

Miller's Chinese & Japanese Antiques Buyer's Guide, Miller's Publications, 1999

CUPS

A pair of *blanc de Chine* lotus-shaped libation cups, c1640–1700 2½in (6.5cm) high.
$900–1,000 GeW

A set of 6 black and white cups and saucers, with *café au lait* glaze, 18thC, cups 1½in (4cm) high.
$750–1,000 GeW

A 'Trumpeter' coffee cup, enamelled with 2 Moors on a turquoise and yellow field against a black ground, Qianlong period, 2½in (6.5cm) high.
$5,200–5,700 S

DISHES

A 'Swatow' blue and white deep dish, the interior decorated with a phoenix among rocks and foliage, slight damage, late 16th/early 17thC, 16in (40.5cm) diam.
$1,400–1,550 P

Swatow is a port on the northeast coast of Guangdong from which a particular type of porcelain was exported in the late Ming period. The kiln was situated on the Guangdong-Fujian border and most of the output was exported to Japan and southeast Asia.

21 Years Ago ...

A pair of late Ming blue and white *kraak porselein* dishes, slightly chipped, Wanli period, 11½in (29cm) diam. **C**

Twenty-one years ago this pair of dishes was valued at $1,150–1,300, and today could fetch $3,500–4,000 at auction. *Kraak porselein* blue and white was among the first mass-produced Chinese porcelain made specifically for the export market during the late 16th/early 17thC. The 1984 sale of the Hatcher collection of porcelain recovered from the South China Sea introduced many people to the delights of the freely painted *kraak porselein*, and this in turn led to an increase in value. Captain Hatcher subsequently went on to discover the now famous 18thC 'Nanking Cargo' which was sold in 1986, drawing even more attention to Chinese ceramics.

Two sweetmeat dishes, of chrysanthemum flowerhead form, painted with bands of waves and a brown rim, Chenghua mark, Chongzhen period, 6in (15cm) diam.
$3,700–4,200 C&C

These dishes were made for the Japanese market.

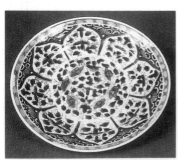

A set of 6 blue and white dishes, Kangxi period, 8in (20.5cm) diam.
$2,700–3,200 GeW

▶ A *famille rose* lotus dish, painted in the centre with a peony and dianthus, the rim painted with further peony sprays on a scroll ground, Qianlong period, 9in (23cm) diam.
$800–900 S(S)

A *famille verte* saucer dish, decorated with *Xi Wangmu* and an attendant with a chariot pulled by a deer, the reverse with borders of hundred *shou* characters, Kangxi period, 15½in (39.5cm) diam.
$10,000–11,500 S(Am)

Xi Wangmu was the Heavenly Queen of the West, a traditional Daoist figure.

A blue and white Master of the Rocks porcelain dish, Kangxi period, 10in (25.5cm) diam.
$2,400–2,600 ORI

A pair of glazed biscuit yellow-ground saucers, decorated with a green and an aubergine-coloured dragon among flames, the reverse with cranes among clouds, slight damage, Jiaqing seal mark and of the period, 5¾in (14.5cm) diam.
$1,700–2,200 S(Am)

FIGURES

A set of 6 pottery figures of court ladies, each with their hands concealed under the sleeves of their robes, restored, Tang Dynasty, 15¾in (40cm) high.
$16,500–18,000 S(Am)

A Sichuan pottery figure of a Shaman, Han Dynasty, 44in (112cm) high.
$10,000–11,500 S(Am)

Similar figures, some holding snakes, were placed at the entrances to Han tombs in Sichuan and served as guardians. Often they are of horrific aspect, with horns, bulging eyes and a protruding tongue.

A grey earthenware warrior in helmet and armour, Northern Wei Dynasty, 16½in (42cm) high.
$800–900 ORI

A green, turquoise and ochre glazed pottery ridge tile, surmounted by a bearded foreign figure riding a mythical beast, restored, Ming Dynasty, 14½in (37cm) high.
$480–530 P

These roof tiles have been made from the same moulds and same materials for 400 years. They are impossible to date without a thermoluminescence test.

A Dehua *blanc de Chine* figure of Guanyin, signed 'Chang Shan Shou', Kangxi Dynasty, 25¾in (65.5cm) high, together with an 18thC hongmu stand.
$13,000–14,500 SK

Dehua is the town in Southern China where *blanc de Chine* was made.

A *famille rose* group of an amorous couple, she wearing a diaper waistcoat over a green jacket and striped skirt, he wearing a turquoise robe and black boots, restored, Qianlong period, 8½in (21.5cm) high.
$3,200–3,600 P

These figures are unusually large and consequently realized a high price.

A Chinese export candlestick, modelled as a lady wearing an iron-red and gilt robe with a turquoise underskirt and green-patterned yellow cape, restored, c1780, 11¾in (30cm) high.
$3,500–4,000 S(NY)

A *famille rose* figure of a courtier, wearing a long green robe embroidered with flowers and butterflies, and a yellow scholar's cap, Jiaqing period, 8in (20.5cm) high.
$320–360 Bon(C)

A *famille noire* enamelled biscuit figure of an Immortal, modelled as an emaciated ascetic, on a green enamel plinth, 19thC, 15in (38cm) high.
$2,600–3,000 B&B

FLATWARE

A *kraak porselein* charger, painted with geese beside a river among water plants, within a panelled border, slight damage, Wanli period, 20in (51cm) diam.
$2,600–3,000 Bon

A pair of *famille verte* chargers, each painted with warriors battling among rocky landscapes, the rim with panels of landscapes on a floral patterned ground, damaged and restored, Kangxi period, 14½in (37cm) diam.
$2,800–3,200 P

A blue and white plate, Kangxi period, 15in (38cm) diam.
$1,800–2,000 GeW

A pair of *famille rose* plates, Yongzheng period, 11in (28cm) diam.
$1,800–2,000 GeW

A set of 20 *famille rose* plates, each decorated with birds in a garden with seats and a bench, within a band of scrolling lotus, slight damage, Qianlong period, 9in (23cm) diam.
$2,800–3,200 DN

An underglaze blue and white charger, Qianlong period, 21in (53.5cm) diam.
$1,600–1,800 P

A Meissen-style *famille rose* plate, painted with European figures loading barrels on the banks of an estuary, inside a gilt border, slight damage, Qianlong period, 13¾in (35cm) diam.
$1,300–1,450 S(S)

A set of 6 Chinese export plates, each painted with a family group outside a house, within a rim painted with panels of landscapes, flowers and geometric patterns, 2 damaged, Qianlong period, 9in (23cm) diam.
$900–1,000 Bea(E)

◀ An armorial plate, painted in *famille rose* enamels with the coat-of-arms of Ramsay within a spearhead and floral border, Qianlong period, 9in (23cm) diam.
$480–560 Bea(E)

A pair of Chinese export *famille rose* armorial plates, decorated with the crest and motto for Hussey of Scotney Castle, within a border alternately panelled with mono-chrome landscape panels and gold cell diaper on a pink ground, Qianlong period, 9¾in (25cm) diam.
$1,200–1,450 DN

Scotney Castle, near Lamberhurst, Kent, was the ancestral home of Christopher Hussey, one-time editor of *Country Life*, and latterly home to Margaret and Denis Thatcher.

A blue and white platter, painted with figures within a landscape of pavilioned islands, the rim with scrolling ribbons on a foliate ground, Qianlong period, 16¼in (41.5cm) long.
$550–650 P

A pair of *famille rose* plates, decorated with iron-red and yellow enamels, c1740, 9in (23cm) diam.
$900–1,000 GeW

A pair of Chinese export soup plates, decorated *en grisaille* and gilt with the Fortune Teller, Qianlong period, 9in (23cm) diam.
$9,000–10,500 C&C

The Chinese frequently made mistakes regarding Western customs, and here we can see the man holding the woman's hand in order to create a romantic image, whereas in reality she, as the fortune teller, should be holding the man's hand to read his palm.

A *famille rose* dish, enamelled with a cockerel, Qianlong period, 15½in (39.5cm) diam.
$4,500–5,500 C&C

A *famille rose* dish, enamelled with peonies inside an unfurled scroll, on a diaper ground strewn with floral sprays, Qianlong period, 14in (35.5cm) diam.
$2,700–3,200 C&C

A pair of Chinese export dish stands, decorated in underglaze blue with flowersprays, panelled borders and a moulded stiff-leaf border, decorated in *famille rose* enamels with a coat-of-arms, slight damage, Qianlong period, 12in (30.5cm) diam.
$650–750 DN

A pair of Chinese export soup plates, decorated in polychrome with tree shrews and pheasants among tobacco leaves, Qianlong period, 9in (23cm) diam.
$3,200–3,500 each C&C

A pair of armorial dishes, each gilt and painted in *famille rose* enamels with a floral spray beneath a crest and coat-of-arms, a gilt and coral-red border, the rim painted with scattered flowers and edged by a spearhead border, Qianlong period, 11⅛in (29cm) wide.
$3,500–4,000 P

A pair of blue and white platters, painted with clusters of flowers among scattered blossoms, the rim with a lattice-pattern border, 18thC, slight damage, 15¼in (38.5cm) wide.
$900–1,000 P

A blue and white charger, the central reserve decorated with flowers in a garden landscape with fret band and floral spray border, 18thC, 13½in (34.5cm) diam.
$650–750 JAd

A Chinese export platter and pierced insert, with blue and gilt border decoration, monogrammed, slight wear, early 19thC, 17½in (44.5cm) wide.
$1,300–1,450 SK(B)

A blue and white dish, late 18thC, 15½in (39.5cm) wide.
$600–650 JAd

Three rose medallion platters, with a family crest of a stag, 19thC, largest 17in (43cm) wide.
$2,600–3,000 SK(B)

The rose medallion pattern was popular in the USA throughout the 19thC.

GARDEN SEATS

A blue and white garden seat, decorated with chrysanthemum and bird design, 19thC, slight damage, 18¼in (46.5cm) high.
$1,100–1,250 SK(B)

A garden seat, decorated in *famille rose* enamels, with a squirrel and grapes, 19thC, 19in (48.5cm) high.
$900–1,000 SK

A *famille rose* garden seat, decorated with a vine scroll ground reserved with dragons, scrolls and bats, and panels of colourful antiques and vignettes, 19thC, 19in (48.5cm) high.
$1,000–1,200 S(NY)

JARS

A reddish-brown glazed jar, with a slender neck and ovoid body, Han Dynasty, 15¾in (40cm) high.
$3,500–4,000 S(NY)

A Cizhou sgraffitto jar, carved through the glaze with a foliate scroll, the neck with 4 lug handles, the lower body in a thick dark brown glaze, Yuan/Ming Dynasty, 20in (51cm) high.
$5,200–5,600 S(NY)

A blue and white jar, painted with Immortals, rim slightly damaged, late Ming Dynasty, 5½in (14cm) high.
$900–1,000 S(S)

A blue and white jar and cover, decorated with scholars and attendants in landscapes, cover damaged, Wanli period, 17¾in (45cm) high.
$4,000–4,500 S(Am)

It is rare for a jar of this type to have its original cover, albeit damaged.

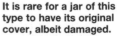

A blue and white jar, decorated with alternating pencilled double-bloom medallions and foliate lotus sprays, between infilled lappet bands, Qianlong period, 6in (15cm) high.
$6,000–6,500 S(HK)

> **Cross Reference**
> See Colour Review

A pair of blue and white jars, painted with pheasants and other birds among flowers and rocks, Kangxi period, 8¼in (21cm) high, with later wood covers and stands,
$2,000–2,200 Bon

An underglaze blue and white jar, painted in light and dark cobalt wash with 8 figures in an extensive mountainous river landscape, the reverse with an inscription composed of 15 columns, restored, late Kangxi period, 20in (51cm) high.
$2,000–2,300 P

A blue and white octagonal jar, painted with birds perched among blossoming trees, enclosed by borders of flowerheads and scrolling foliage, Kangxi period, 17in (43cm) high.
$4,000–4,500 P

A Transitional *wucai* jar and cover, decorated with ladies and attendants on a terrace in a garden, the cover with boys, cover restored, 17thC, 14½in (37cm) high.
$3,000–3,300 S(Am)

A Transitional blue and white jar, painted with bands of river landscapes, magnolias, peonies, and chrysanthemums, mid-17thC, 10½in (27cm) high.
$1,150–1,300 P(W)

A pair of Canton *famille rose* jars and covers, each with 2 panels decorated with Manchu ladies, reserved on a ground scattered with flowers, insects, fruit and scrolls, 19thC, 24¼in (62cm) high.
$7,300–8,000 Bon

JUGS

A blue and white jug, with chased silver-coloured metal mounts and shell thumbpiece, the hinged cover with a figure of a boy, the body with female figures on terraces, Kangxi period, 5¼in (13.5cm) high.
$2,000–2,300 E

An underglaze blue and white ewer, modelled after a Middle Eastern bronze shape, with later polychrome enamelling, lacking hinged cover, late 17th/early 18thC, 11in (28cm) high.
$2,700–3,000 P

The holed flange on the handle enabled a silver lid to be fitted in Europe. This distinguishes the ewer as an export piece.

A Chinese export Meissen-style soft-paste porcelain pitcher and cover, enamelled with a coat-of-arms, Qianlong period, 10¼in (26cm) high.
$11,500–12,500 C&C

A blue and white helmet-shaped jug, Qianlong period, 5in (12.5cm) high.
$575–650 GeW

▶ A *famille verte* gilt-bronze-mounted ewer, painted with cartouches of trees and exotic birds on a blue ground, 18thC, 13½in (34.5cm) high.
$5,500–6,500 S(Z)

A *famille verte* ewer, the handle modelled as a dog of Fo standing on a reticulated ball, decorated with diaper patterns in green, aubergine, yellow and black, 19thC, 9in (23cm) high.
$450–550 WW

MUGS & TANKARDS

A Chinese Imari bell-shaped tankard, c1720, 6½in (16.5cm) high.
$1,300–1,500 GeW

A set of 3 Chinese mandarin tankards, with moulded dragon handles, Qianlong period, c1780, largest 6in (15cm) high.
$4,500–5,000 C&C

▶ A Chinese export *famille rose* mug, enamelled in polychrome within under-glaze blue borders, late Qianlong period, 4½in (11.5cm) high.
$220–250 HYD

A *famille rose* armorial tankard, painted with a coat-of-arms and a mountainous river landscape, Qianlong period, 6in (15cm) high.
$4,200–4,600 P

A Chinese export *famille rose* masonic tankard, made for the American market, Qianlong period, 5½in (14cm) high.
$4,500–5,000 C&C

A Chinese blue and white mug, with ridged handle and metal rim, damaged, 18thC, 5in (12.5cm) high.
$120–140 MEG

SERVICES

A part dinner service, comprising 13 pieces, with polychrome flower and foliage decoration, slight damage, Qianlong period, tureen 14in (35.5cm) wide.
$13,000–14,500 E

A Chinese export blue and white part dinner service, comprising 29 pieces, painted with a lakeland landscape within cellular bands and foliate borders, slight damage, c1790, meat platter 16¼in (41.5cm) wide.
$4,500–5,000 TEN

A *famille rose* tea service, comprising 27 pieces, painted with sprays of roses and other flowers, slight damage, Qianlong period.
$1,750–2,000 S(S)

A part dinner service, comprising 21 pieces, painted with leafy flowers in bright *famille rose* enamels with green and gilt tendrils against a black ground, an iron-red crest at the sides, restored, Qing Dynasty.
$5,250–5,750 S

▶ An armorial part tea service, comprising 10 pieces, painted in colours with a coat-of-arms on one side and a pagoda on the reverse, 18thC, and a milk jug.
$1,400–1,600 P(Z)

A *famille verte* teapot and cover, painted in gilt and coloured enamels with vertical panels of flowers, with applied mock-bamboo handle, Kangxi period, 6¾in (17cm) high.
$4,000–4,500 P

A Chinese export blue and white teapot and cover, decorated with peony branches below a *ruyi*-head border, Kangxi period, 4½in (11.5cm) high.
$1,600–1,750 C&C

A Chinese Imari blue and red teapot, Kangxi period, 4in (10cm) high.
$730–800 C&C

A Chinese export teapot and cover, painted in *famille rose* with a European shepherdess seated by a tree and feeding a lamb, Qianlong period, 6¼in (16cm) high.
$3,250–3,750 C&C

European subjects on Chinese porcelain always fetch a high price.

A *famille verte* teapot, with Dutch decoration, c1720, 4¾in (12cm) high.
$1,100–1,400 GeW

A Chinese Imari melon-shaped teapot, Kangxi period, 4½in (11.5cm) high.
$1,000–1,200 GeW

A *famille rose* mandarin-style teapot, gilding rubbed, Qianlong period, 6½in (16.5cm) high.
$900–1,000 GeW

◄ A Chinese export mandarin coffee pot, with gilt trim, handle with entwined leaves, c1800, 10¼in (26cm) high.
$1,100–1,300 A&A

TUREENS

A *famille rose* tobacco-leaf tureen and cover, the handles formed as lotus pods, the exterior painted in underglaze blue, iron-red, gilt and opaque enamels with flowerheads, slight damage, Qianlong period, 14½in (37cm) wide.
$9,000–10,000 P

A Canton *famille rose* tureen, cover and stand, painted with ladies seated at a table playing a board game, reading or standing in a garden, beneath a border of birds, butterflies and flowers, the cover with a gilded knop, 19thC, 14¼in (36cm) wide.
$4,000–4,500 P

> **Miller's is a price GUIDE not a price LIST**

Miller's Compares

A *famille rose* tureen, cover and stand, decorated with sprays of flowers and leaves, within a narrow iron-red and gilt scroll ground, shell handles and scroll cover handle, slight damage, Qianlong period, 11½in (29cm) wide.
$9,000–10,000 Bon(C)

A *famille rose* tureen and cover, the sides decorated with sprays of flowers in an ornamental fenced garden, the cover with floral sprays and scroll knop, the tureen with animal head handles, stand missing, Qianlong period, 11¼in (28.5cm) wide.
$4,500–5,000 Bon(C)

All tureens were made with stands, but they often became separated from their stands over the years. As item I still has its original stand, it sold for far more than Item II, even though the base was cracked. The shaped oval form of Item I is also more unusual than the octagonal shape of Item II.

A rose medallion soup tureen with cover, and a platter, with woven double strap handles, the cover with gilt pineapple finial, 19thC, platter 14¾in (37.5cm) wide.
$3,250–3,500 SK(B)

A Chinese export rose medallion tureen, decorated with alternating figural and floral panels against a foliate ground, 19thC, 14in (35.5cm) wide.
$1,600–1,800 DuM

VASES

A Transitional blue and white bottle vase, made for the Dutch market, c1640, 14½in (37cm) high.
$2,000–2,500 Wai

A blue and white *yenyen* vase, Kangxi period, 17½in (44.5cm) high.
$4,500–5,000 ORI

A pair of Chinese blue and white vases, painted with peonies, slight damage, Kangxi period, 8in (20.5cm) high.
$575–650 Bea(E)

A blue and white vase and cover, Kangxi period, 17in (43cm) high.
$2,300–2,600 SOO

> **Sets/Pairs**
>
> Unless otherwise stated, any description which refers to 'a set' or 'a pair' includes a guide price for the entire set or the pair, even though the illustration may show only a single item.

Imported Blue and White

During the 17th and 18thC huge quantities of blue and white ware were imported from China to Europe. Large numbers of similar items were auctioned and bought by dealers who then made them up into pairs or garnitures. So a pair is just two of the same, and as they were hand-painted, often by different artists, there can be big differences in the patterns. The lids were packed separately from the pots so it is 'pot luck' if a lid is a good fit. Normally an allowance was made so that any lid could be put onto any pot, often resulting in quite a loose fit.

21 Years Ago ...

A blue and white vase, the elongated neck with a collar, leaf mark, Kangxi period, 7in (18cm) high. **S**

Twenty-one years ago this small but beautiful blue and white vase was valued at just $30–35. Today it is worth $1,100–1,200 in perfect condition. Damaged Kangxi blue and white is worth approximately one-tenth of its perfect value. The decoration of elegant courtesans, known as 'long Elizas', is particularly sought after. High-quality export blue and white of the late Kangxi period (c1700–20) has steadily increased in value as collectors appreciated the combination of age, beauty and affordability.

A pair of blue and white baluster vases and covers, painted with panels of birds in flowering branches below lappets and *ruyi* heads, Kangxi period, 23½in (59.5cm) high.
$29,000–32,500 **C&C**

Vases of this size are seldom found in pairs and their shape and characteristic Kangxi period decoration are particularly desirable.

An underglaze red, blue and white vase, painted with deer in a rocky landscape, restored, six-character seal mark and of the period, Qianlong, 24in (61cm) high.
$1,600–2,000 **AAV**

The price of this vase is badly affected by the damage and restoration. In perfect condition it would be valued at $19,500–24,500.

A copper-red and underglaze blue bottle vase, 18thC, 23¾in (60.5cm) high.
$5,500–6,500 **S(NY)**

A pair of enamelled porcelain bottle vases, each with a cracked ice pattern of opaque blue enamel and strewn with white and black painted prunus blossoms and bamboo sprigs, 19thC, 23½in (59.5cm) high.
$8,000–9,000 **B&B**

A yellow-ground vase, with elephant-head handles, one side painted with a diving bird and peony in *famille rose* enamels, the other side with a diving bird amongst flowers *en grisaille*, between a lappet band at the foot and a *ruyi* collar at the shoulder, gilt rims, Guangxu period, 14¾in (37.5cm) high.
$1,000–1,150 **Bon**

A Chinese export 'tobacco-leaf' garniture of 3 vases and covers, damaged and restored, c1770–80, 8½in (21.5cm) high.
$9,000–10,000 **S(NY)**

▶ A narrow-necked bottle vase, decorated with a scene of the Emperor Qianlong inspecting the troops, after a painting by Lang Shining, 1930–35, 8¾in (22cm) high.
$2,000–2,500 **Wai**

Japanese Ceramics

BOWLS

An Arita Imari barber's bowl, gilt and painted with a table supporting a vase of flowering peonies, pierced at the top with twin holes for suspension, late 17th/early 18thC, 10½in (26.5cm) diam.
$1,400–1,550 P

An Arita blue and white deep dish, painted on the interior with a crane and young feeding under a pine tree, the exterior painted with a bamboo and floral spray below the rolled rim, Meiji period, 17¼in (44cm) diam.
$2,200–2,400 B&B

An Oribe water bowl, the cream-coloured interior painted in iron oxide with splashes of green glaze, the exterior decorated with plovers and waves or swaying grasses, Meiji period, 22in (56cm) diam.
$1,000–1,150 B&B

Oribe is a type of pottery named after Furuta Oribe (1544–1615), who painted in a free style.

A Satsuma bowl, signed by Hiramatsu Gensei, Meiji period, 5in (12.5cm) diam.
$1,800–2,000 MCN

A Satsuma bowl, the interior enamelled and gilded with a thousand grains of rice pattern, the exterior with a band of enamelled flowers and insects, c1900, 9in (23cm) diam.
$4,500–5,000 HAM

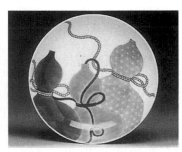

A pair of Nabeshima-style footed dishes, painted with 3 gourds in underglaze blue wash with enamels, Meiji/Taisho period, 7in (18cm) diam.
$5,700–6,500 B&B

FIGURES

A pair of Satsuma figures, restored, 19thC, 6in (15cm) high.
$570–650 JaG

◀ A Satsuma figure of Hotei, seated on his sack of treasures, restored, Meiji period, 10in (25.5cm) high.
$1,500–1,800 B&B

▶ A Satsuma figure of the Goddess of Mercy, early 20thC, 8in (20.5cm) high.
$570–650 JaG

FLATWARE

An Arita blue and white plate, painted with a boatman, the border with panels moulded with formal clouds, c1670, 8¼in (21cm) diam.
$3,250–3,500 S

An Imari charger, painted in gilt and iron-red with a vase and stylized leaves and flowers, late 17thC, 22¾in (58cm) diam.
$4,200–4,800 P

An Arita blue and white dish, decorated with *ho-o* birds, fruits and flowers encircling the central monogram 'VOC', the rim with panels of flowers, late 17th/ early 18thC, 16in (40.5cm) diam.
$16,200–18,000 S(Am)

The monogram is that of the Dutch East India Company, which operated 1602–1799 to protect Dutch trading interests in the Indian Ocean.

Cross Reference
See Colour Review

An Imari dish, decorated in underglaze blue, iron-red and gilt with a basket of flowers below a border of cockerels, c1700, 12in (30.5cm) diam.
$1,600–1,750 S(Am)

An Imari plate, decorated in blue, iron-red and gilt with flowers and quails, c1710–20, 8¾in (22cm) diam.
$450–500 MCN

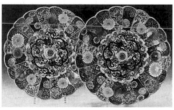

A pair of Imari dishes, by Fukagawa, the centre painted with 2 dragons chasing flaming pearls inside an elaborate panelled border, Meiji period, 11¾in (30cm) diam.
$1,500–1,750 S(S)

An Imari charger, painted with shaped panels on a butterfly and *kiku* ground, the underside with sprays of peony blooms, Meiji period, 21½in (54.5cm) diam.
$800–1,000 P(B)

An Imari charger, painted with a phoenix and 2 lotus leaves within radiating borders of *kirin* amongst flowers, 19thC, 18in (45.5cm) diam.
$1,500–1,750 S

A blue and white charger, painted with an exotic bird and an island landscape, Meiji period, 21¾in (55.5cm) diam.
$300–325 P(F)

Arita Wares

- The earliest Japanese porcelain, produced in various kilns in the area of Arita on Kyushu, the most westerly of the Japanese islands, and the closest to Korea.
- Developed by Korean potters who were brought to Japan in the late 16thC following Toyotomi Hideyoshi's invasion of Korea.
- Early Arita mainly Korean-influenced, heavily potted blue and white wares, produced principally for the domestic market.
- By c1650 decoration on pieces for the domestic market became complex, combining natural themes, such as leaf or flower forms, with geometric patterns.
- At the same time a more refined and broader range of objects was being produced for the newly established export market, with Chinese *kraak porselein* or Transitional blue and white as the main influence. Exported from the port of Imari, the name by which the wares became known in the West.
- Kakiemon-style enamelled wares were also produced from c1650, and Imari wares intended for export to Europe slightly later.
- Arita wares continued to be popular and were exported to the West until mid-18thC.

JARS

A Tokoname pottery jar, with a layer of kiln ash glaze deposited around the neck and shoulders displaying patches of opalescent blue, over a dark cinnamon brown, slight damage, Momoyama period, 19in (48.5cm) high.
$2,300–2,600 B&B

An Imari jar, the cover surmounted by an iron-red dog, c1700, 23½in (59.5cm) high.
$5,000–5,750 MCN

A Satsuma earthenware jar and cover, moulded with dragons in a landscape, 19thC, 19in (48.5cm) high.
$2,500–3,000 S(Am)

◄ An Imari jar and cover, decorated in rich iron-red and gilt, with bright underglaze cobalt, damaged and restored, signed 'Shofutei', Meiji period, 50½in (128.5cm) high.
$4,500–5,000 B&B

VASES

An Imari bottle vase, gilt and painted in typical enamels over underglaze blue with sprays of flowers, inset with 2 lobed panels with relief-worked decoration, one containing plum blossoms, the other a hen with chicks, late 17thC, 9½in (24cm) high.
$4,000–5,000 P

► A Satsuma vase, the dark blue ground decorated in gilt with birds, trailing branches and floral stems, with elephant mask handles, 19thC, 6in (15cm) high.
$450–525 TMA

A Satsuma vase, painted in blue and gilt with ornaments and vases, signed 'Bunkyu Ninen', mid-19thC, 25in (63.5cm) high.
$3,000–3,250 MER

A Satsuma vase, decorated with warriors and mythical figures on land and at sea, 19thC, 22in (56cm) high.
$1,100–1,300 MEA

A polychrome and gilt-decorated vase, the ivory-glazed ground painted with a dragon and monkeys, signed 'Shibayama', Meiji period, 21in (53.5cm) high.
$8,000–9,000 B&B

A pair of Satsuma miniature vases, decorated by Yabu Meizan with scenes of The 12 Festivals of the Year, signed, Meiji period, 1⅛in (3.5cm) high.
$9,000–10,000 MER

An Imari vase and cover, decorated in underglaze blue and iron-red with peonies and foliage within a formalized border, the cover with a *shi-shi* finial, 19thC, 20in (51cm) high.
$525–575 HYD

KOREAN CERAMICS

A Korean celadon bowl, the interior with relief floral and butterfly decoration, Koryo Dynasty, 7in (18cm) diam.
$325–375 FBG

There has been an enormous drop in prices for Korean ceramics since the collapse of the market in the Far East. Pieces of 'ordinary', ie non-exceptional, Korean ceramics, are now only worth 25 per cent of their value 3 to 4 years ago.

A Korean full-moon jar, in 2 sections joined at the waist, covered by a transparent glaze, foot unglazed, slight damage, Choson Dynasty, 17th/18thC, 17½in (44.5cm) diam.
$600,000+ Bon

Acquired by Bernard Leach in Korea in 1943. On his return to England, Leach asked Lucie Rie to look after the jar for him rather than risk a wartime train journey with it. The vase remained in Lucie Rie's studio for the next 50 years, Leach having concluded that its setting could not be improved. Rie left the jar in her will to Janet, Bernard's wife.

A Korean blue and white porcelain jar and cover, painted with 2 large peony stems beneath the cloud-patterned border, slight damage, Choson Dynasty, 19thC, 5¼in (13.5cm) high.
$1,000–1,100 B&B

A Korean bottle vase, applied with a thin white slip over a greyish body, incised and carved with a band of broad leaves, mouth rim restored, Choson Dynasty, probably 15thC, 12½in (32cm) high.
$1,000–1,200 P

A Korean white/pale celadon bowl, decorated with an even crackled glaze, Yi Dynasty, 5½in (14cm) diam.
$2,300–2,600 Bon

Provenance has added to the value of this bowl, which was formerly owned by Janet Leach.

A Korean *punch'ong* bowl, decorated with a mottled grey-cream slip and transparent glaze, damaged, Choson Dynasty, probably 15th/16thC, 7in (18cm) diam.
$2,500–3,000 Bon

A Korean *punch'ong* jar, the exterior brushed with a creamy slip and incised to form bands of flowers and leaves, all beneath the pale grey-green glaze, Choson Dynasty, 15th/16thC, 8in (20.5cm) diam.
$2,000–2,300 B&B

A Korean brown-glazed honey jar and cover, applied with a streaky glaze on a straw-coloured body, Choson Dynasty, 19thC, 8in (20.5cm) high.
$650–730 P

◀ A Korean mottled toffee-brown glazed bottle vase, some kiln grit to base, Yi Dynasty, 7½in (19cm) high.
$700–800 Bon

Dating Korean Ceramics

It is difficult to date Korean ceramics accurately because of continuing tradition. They are normally studied in 3 groups named after the Dynasties in which they were made, as follows:

Silla	57 BC–AD 936
Koryo	AD 936–1392
Yi/Choson	1392–1910

Glass

When the first edition of *Miller's Antiques Price Guide* appeared in 1979, new developments were about to take place in the field of glass collecting. Several salerooms were starting to create an interest in 19th- and early 20th-century glass, which previously had not really been a popular collecting field. Major events that brought coloured glass in particular to the public eye were the opening in 1980 of the Broadfield House Glass Museum in the West Midlands, the exhibition of Whitefriars glass in Manchester in 1994, and a smaller display in London in 1996.

The market for glass in the 1960s and 1970s was buoyant, as collectors had the opportunity to purchase fine glass from several single-owner sales during this period. In 1981–82, Sotheby's hosted the sale of the Krug collection, considered by many to be the most important collection of European glass formed in post-war years. The four parts of the sale each merited a hardback bound catalogue that made compulsive reading for most glass *aficionados*.

The past year has also seen two important sales: the Royal Brierley collection of English glass from the Stevens & Williams (later Royal Brierley) Honeybourne Museum included pieces from the 18th century to 1946. A notable feature of this sale was a cameo baluster vase by William Northwood, in turquoise glass overlaid in white, and carved with birds, flowers and foliage, which achieved $28,500. The sale that attracted the most curiosity, however, was the dispersal of an extensive glass collection, formed over many years by Thomas Standish and kept in his modest semi-detached house in Wigan. As the glass fraternity had been unaware of Standish's interest in their field, the sale was keenly attended and all lots sold, despite a number of items having minor damage. A highlight of the sale was a drawn trumpet wine glass, with a plain air-teared stem, the bowl honeycomb-moulded on its lower half, with a honeycomb-moulded foot, estimated at $400–500, which made $3,250.

The past year's results indicate that prices for good quality and rare examples have markedly increased. Moreover, the strong performance of glass in the Royal Brierley and Standish sales suggests that private collectors may now be more inclined to accept examples with minor damage.

Finally, types of glass which are likely to increase in value are engraved ratafia glasses, heavy baluster wine glasses with rare knops such as mushroom and cylinder, early 18th-century plain baluster-type candlesticks and well-engraved Stourbridge glass. **R. G. Thomas**

BEAKERS & TUMBLERS

A Continental beaker, perhaps Murano, the brown tint enamelled in white with stylized fleur-de-lys, applied footring, repaired, 14thC, 6½in (16.5cm) high.
$1,350–1,450 C

A Bohemian engraved beaker, with 3 panels engraved with religious symbols, divided by columns and panels of concave lenses, mid-18thC, 5in (12.5cm) high.
$800–1,000 P

◄ A Sunderland bridge tumbler, c1825, 4in (10cm) high.
$450–575 BELL

► A pair of Bohemian clear glass footed beakers, with transparent cobalt blue overlay and engraved decoration, minor rim chips, c1860, 5in (12.5cm) high.
$260–280 DORO

A Bohemian enamelled beaker, painted with a couple and a dog within a gilt border, Riesengebirge, regilt, minor damage, c1760, 3¾in (9.5cm) high.
$800–1,000 S

A tumbler, engraved with a Jacobite rose and a bird, c1790, 4½in (11.5cm) high.
$800–1,000 BELL

A blue glass tumbler, enamelled 'Remember Me', possibly Continental, c1840, 4in (10cm) high.
$160–200 CB

BOTTLES & DECANTERS

A shaft-and-globe decanter, inscribed in diamond-point 'Wm Skelhorn, 10th June 1747', c1720, 8in (20.5cm) high.
$1,600–1,800 S

A glass decanter, engraved with 2 bands of egg-and-tulip design, with lozenge stopper, c1790, 9½in (24cm) high.
$575–650 Som

A port decanter and stopper, engraved with a label edged with berries, vines and leaves, inscribed 'Port', chip to rim, c1760–70, 11¼in (28.5cm) high.
$500–550 P

A green glass spirit bottle, with fruiting vine metal mount, c1840, 14in (35.5cm) high.
$275–325 CB

An amethyst glass spirit bottle, with slice-cut base, c1830, 12in (30.5cm) high.
$375–430 BELL

A Bristol blue cruet set, comprising 3 gilt labelled bottles in a papier mâché stand, c1790, 6in (15cm) high.
$1,500–1,600 BELL

► A pair of spirit decanters, with triple neck rings and target stoppers, c1810, 9½in (24cm) high.
$500–650 BELL

◄ A pair of mallet-shaped decanters, with flute cut bases and lozenge stoppers, c1800, 10in (25.5cm) high.
$525–650 BELL

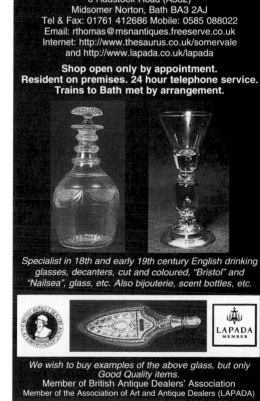

21 Years Ago ...

A Cork engraved decanter and stopper, with frilled target stopper, the base impressed Cork Glass Co, c1800, 8¾in (22cm) high. **S**

Twenty-one years ago this Irish decanter was valued at $525–600. The moulded target stopper and band of vesica engraving are particular features of Cork glass, and today this decanter is valued at $2,200–2,600. The recent sale of the Marquess of Bute's Irish glass has probably influenced its current popularity, as well as the fact that Irish glass now appears frequently at auction.

A pair of French silver-mounted cut-glass liqueur decanters, maker's mark JM, 19thC, 7in (18cm) high.
$800–900 FW&C

An amethyst glass spirit bottle, early 19thC, 14in (35.5cm) high.
$400–500 CB

A 'Nailsea' carafe and stopper, with opaque white pull-up decoration, c1860, 8¾in (22cm) high.
$300–325 Som

A cranberry glass bottle, with prism-cut neck and onion-shaped body, stopper missing, 19thC, 10in (25.5cm) high.
$180–200 PCh

◄ A pair of Stourbridge engraved decanters and stoppers, perhaps Stevens & Williams, engraved in the manner of Joseph Keller with dragon-flies and other insects among foliage, the feet with dot ornament, slight damage, c1880, 12¼in (31cm) high.
$1,000–1,200 C

Decanter Rings

Decanter rings appeared on the necks of bulbous decanters from 1800 to provide a handgrip, and varied in number from one to four. Red hot threads of glass were allowed to settle on the neck of the decanter, which was slowly rotated and then taken to the furnace mouth, where the desired shape of ring was obtained by the use of tongs. Cut rings were formed in the cutting room away from the furnace floor.

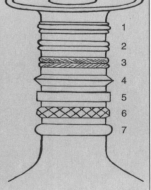

1. Triple ring
2. Double ring
3. Feathered ring
4. Triangular ring
5. Square ring
6. Cut ring
7. Plain rounded ring

A pair of Georg Jensen decanters, with ball stoppers, c1930, 10¼in (26cm) high.
$2,500–2,750 SFL

BOWLS

A cut-glass sugar basin, with fan-cut rim, decorated with small diamonds, flanked by alternate fans and star-cut under the body, c1810, 6¼in (16cm) diam.
$1,000–1,200 Som

An Irish cut-glass fruit bowl, with single knopped stem and oval rib-moulded base, c1790, 13in (33cm) diam.
$4,000–4,500 MEA

An Irish cut-glass bowl, with turn-over rim, on square lemon squeezer base, c1800, 10in (25.5cm) diam.
$2,000–2,300 CB

A Victorian cranberry and opaline glass posy bowl, c1880, 5in (12.5cm) high.
$200–260 BELL

◄ A pair of strawberry diamond- and prism-cut bonbonnières, early 19thC, 11in (28cm) high.
$1,300–1,600 BELL

A cut-glass bowl and stand, each with Brunswick star and diamond cutting, c1900, 12½in (32cm) high.
$250–300 S(S)

CENTREPIECES

A French white opaline glass tazza, with gilt wavy rim and enamelled with orange flowers, c1870, 6¾in (17cm) diam.
$400–450 CB

A graduated tier of 3 glass tazzas, each with Silesian stem and domed folded foot, 18thC, largest 12¼in (31cm) diam.
$1,200–1,400 FW&C

► A cut-glass pineapple stand, the bowl cut with tapering panels within an everted scalloped rim, c1820, 6in (15cm) diam.
$450–500 P

A Victorian epergne, the central vase flanked by a matching pair of smaller vases and a pair of spiral stem branches suspending baskets, the opalescent borders applied with turquoise glass rims, some chips and cracks, 21½in (54.5cm) high.
$600–675 P(F)

GOBLETS & WINE GLASSES

An Anglo-Venetian ale glass, the bowl with spirally-moulded decoration, on a stem with a merese and propeller knop, c1680, 6in (15cm) high.
$2,200–2,450 Som

A Dutch *façon de Venise* goblet and cover, the stem with 2 hollow quatrefoil knops set between pairs of mereses, c1690, 16in (40.5cm) high.
$3,750–4,000 C

A lead wine glass, possibly Duke of Buckingham glasshouse, of greenish tint, the bowl set on a four-sided pedestal stem and folded conical foot, late 17thC, 6½in (16.5cm) high.
$2,500–2,600 S

A set of 4 north German or Dutch roemers, of pale green tint, each stem applied with raspberry prunts beneath a milled band, 17thC, 4¾in (12cm) high.
$2,000–2,500 S(Am)

21 Years Ago ...

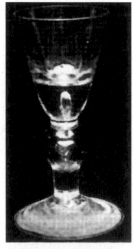

A wine glass, the heavy baluster round funnel bowl with thick base and tear, set on inverted baluster stem, folded conical foot, c1690, 5½in (14cm) high. **Som**

Twenty-one years ago this heavy baluster wine glass was valued at $730–800. It has all the desirable features typical of glasses of the early 18thC, such as a round funnel bowl, inverted baluster stemmed knop, air tears in the base of the bowl and knop, and a folded foot. For no apparent reason other than perhaps their bulk, glasses such as these have not been popular with collectors until the last couple of years, when they have justifiably caught up. Today this glass would command between $2,500 and $3,000 in the London salerooms.

A bell-bowl baluster goblet, with teared solid base of bowl, over teared inverted baluster stem with base knop and folded foot, c1710, 6¾in (17cm) high.
$1,300–1,500 JHa

A baluster wine glass, the stem with a 7 ringed annular knop and base knop, on domed folded foot, c1720, 6¼in (16cm) high.
$1,800–2,000 Som

A toastmaster's glass, with solid base, octagonal moulded stem with diamonds on the shoulder and central tear, folded conical foot, c1715, 4½in (11.5cm) high.
$1,400–1,600 S

A drawn trumpet baluster glass, of Kit-Kat type, with folded foot, c1725, 5¾in (14.5cm) high.
$650–800 GS

A toasting glass, the bowl spirally wrythen continuing on the slender stem and forming spiral ribs on the conical foot, c1740, 8in (20.5cm) high.
$1,000–1,200 P

A wine glass, with drawn trumpet-shaped bowl, on multi-spiral air-twist stem, c1750, 6¾in (17cm) high.
$275–325 DN

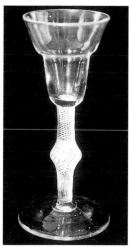

A wine glass, the pan topped bowl over a multi-spiral air-twist stem with centre swelling knop, c1750, 7in (18cm) high.
$560–730 GS

A wine glass, the bell-bowl supported on a multi-spiral air-twist stem with vermicular collar and conical foot, c1750, 6¼in (16cm) high.
$730–800 GS

A pair of cup-bowl green wine glasses, c1790, 4½in (11.5cm) high.
$200–225 FD

Miller's Compares

I A goblet, with bell bowl, the stem with an air-beaded cushion knop and an inverted baluster knop, c1730, 10in (25.5cm) high.
$1,500–1,600 Som

II A balustroid wine glass, with trumpet bowl, the ball knops each with an air tear, c1730, 6¾in (17cm) high.
$730–800 Som

The difference between these two glasses lies mainly in the amount of work that went into making them. Item I was constructed in four pieces – the bowl, followed by each knop, the stem and finally the foot. The production process was very involved and great care had to be taken. The construction of the air-beaded knop and its attractive appearance further adds to its value. Item II was made in three pieces, the entire stem with the knops incorporating air tears being constructed in one stage and was, therefore, easier and less costly to produce.

A bucket-bowl ale glass, engraved 'Welcome' over a punchbowl surrounded by hops and barley, with double series air-twist stem, c1750, 7½in (19cm) high.
$1,200–1,400 JHa

A 'Lynn' wine glass, the bowl moulded with horizontal rings, on an opaque-twist stem of a pair of intertwined solid corkscrews encircled by a multi-series spiral strand, on a conical foot, c1760–70, 5¼in (13.5cm) high.
$650–800 P

A cordial glass, with ogee bowl, on a single series opaque-twist stem, c1765, 7in (18cm) high.
$1,500–1,800 BELL

▶ A pair of green wine glasses, early 19thC, 5in (12.5cm) high.
$160–200 JAS

A pair of rummers, engraved with the Sunderland Bridge motif, the reverse with initials 'RMH' within a rectangular floral cartouche, c1820, 5½in (14cm) high.
$1,200–1,400 Som

A pair of James Powell wine glasses, designed by T. G. Jackson, c1880, 5in (12.5cm) high.
$200–235 RUSK

A pair of English ale glasses, the bowls engraved with hops and barley, on single-knopped stems and circular bases, 18thC, 5½in (14cm) high.
$325–400 E

A loving cup, engraved with a rose and thistle and the initials 'JD' within a shamrock spray on the reverse, with knopped stem and conical foot, c1825, 7¾in (20cm) high.
$900–1,000 Som

Seven clear wine glasses, with cut cranberry flashing, late 19thC, 5in (12.5cm) high.
$575–650 DQ

A rummer, engraved with masonic symbols, with capstan stem and plain foot, c1810, 6in (15cm) high.
$500–575 Som

A set of 6 green wine glasses, c1840, 5in (12.5cm) high.
$450–525 BELL

A green trumpet-bowl honeycomb-moulded wine glass, c1810–30, 5¼in (13.5cm) high.
$140–150 FD

A pair of rummers, the double ogee bowls with blazes and flute cutting, on ball knopped stem, c1835, 5in (12.5cm) high.
$300–350 GS

A Stevens & Williams green and clear hock glass, intaglio-engraved with thistles, c1895, 8in (20.5cm) high.
$1,600–2,000 ALiN

Ex-Stevens & Williams Collection, Honeybourne Museum.

JUGS

An amethyst glass cream jug, the body cold-enamelled with inscription 'Be Canny with the Cream', c1820, 4¾in (12cm) high.
$450–500 Som

A Biedermeier white alabaster and old rose pink glass jug, with gilt decoration and beading, c1835, 4in (10cm) high.
$500–550 DORO

▶ A Bohemian green-tinted glass claret jug, emerald green colouring tapering to clear glass, decorated with gilded enamel foliate scrolls and flowerheads, late 19thC, 15¾in (40cm) high.
$330–360 P(E)

LAMPS & LIGHTING

A pair of George III cut-glass two-light candelabra, each with a star finial and petal-shaped canopy, the arms hung with prismatic drops, 21¾in (55.5cm) high.
$1,600–2,000 P

A pair of glass candlesticks, the pan-top sconces on hollow sockets with circular neck rings, c1800, 6in (15cm) high.
$1,100–1,300 Som

A pair of Regency glass storm lanterns, in the manner of William Bullock, each glass shade engraved with scrolling convolvulus flowers and foliage, on a bronze base with gilt-bronze mounts, 14in (35.5cm) high.
$4,000–4,500 HYD

A pair of cut crystal glass candle lustres, c1810, 9in (23cm) high.
$2,750–3,250 CB

A pair of Bohemian clear glass table lustres, each with overlaid enamel oval plaques, alternately painted with portrait busts of ladies and flowers, surrounded by gilt overlaid foliate borders, late 19thC, 14in (35cm) high.
$650–800 RTo

A pair of Victorian cut-glass candelabra, each with 7 scrolling candle arms, each lacking one arm, late 19thC, 36½in (92.5cm) high.
$5,750–6,500 S(NY)

A Baccarat close-pack millefiori paperweight, signed 'B', dated '1847', 2¾in (7cm) diam.
$3,000–3,250 SWB

A Baccarat spaced millefiori paperweight, with 10 silhouettes, signed 'B', dated '1848', 2½in (6.5cm) diam.
$2,500–3,000 SWB

A Baccarat mushroom paperweight, set with canes in blue, red, green and white, mid-19thC, 3in (7.5cm) diam.
$2,500–3,000 Bon(C)

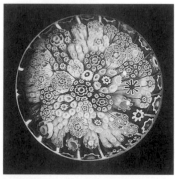

A Bacchus close-pack millefiori paperweight, c1848, 3in (7.5cm) diam.
$3,000–3,500 DLP

A Boston & Sandwich Glass Co paperweight, with a red poinsettia, c1860, 3in (7.5cm) diam.
$800–900 DLP

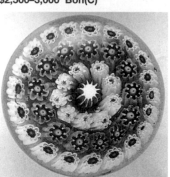

A Bacchus concentric paperweight, with a red and white central cane within 3 rows of blue and white canes, 19thC, 3¼in (8cm) diam.
$525–575 P

A Clichy paperweight, the outer canes of green, white and blue with a ring of white roses around a central pink rose, c1845–60, 3¼in (8.5cm) diam.
$1,300–1,500 SWB

A Clichy concentric millefiori paperweight, the central blue cane surrounded by 5 circles of canes in shades of pink, green, white and mauve contained in a basket of alternate blue and white purple staves, mid-19thC, 1½in (4cm) diam.
$2,500–3,000 S(S)

A Clichy paperweight, with a garland of pastry-mould canes, 7 canes including pink and green Clichy rose cane, c1850, 3in (7.5cm) diam.
$1,100–1,300 STG

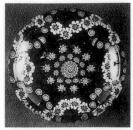

A Clichy paperweight, with 2 linked millefiori garlands around central millefiori, some broken canes, c1850, 3in (7.5cm) diam.
$700–800 STG

A Clichy paperweight, with pink rose and hidden pink rose, c1850, 2½in (6.5cm) diam.
$3,000–3,250 SWB

A Pantin paperweight, with three-dimensional flower, c1878, 3in (7.5cm) diam.
$16,000–18,000 DLP

Pantin paperweights are the most realistic three-dimensional weights from the 19thC. There are 3 or 4 known examples of this flower. Fewer than 100 Pantin paperweights are known, 2 having sold for more than $162,000.

A German paperweight, with a white edelweiss and green leaves, late 19thC, 3¼in (8.5cm) diam.
$320–400 DORO

A St Louis dahlia paperweight, the flower with overlapping rows of pink striped petals, blue and white cogwheel cane and green leaves, mid-19thC, 1¾in (4.5cm) diam.
$1,800–2,000 P

A Clichy swirl weight, with alternate turquoise and white staves radiating from a central claret cane, mid-19thC, 1¾in (4.5cm) diam.
$650–730 C

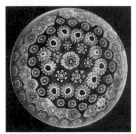

A St Louis close concentric millefiori paperweight, with 4 circles of canes in shades of pale blue, red, white and dark blue about a central lime-green, pink and white cane and within an outer circle of salmon-pink and white tubular canes, signed 'SL', mid-19thC, 2¾in (7cm) diam.
$1,000–1,200 C

A Continental close millefiori mushroom paperweight, the loosely packed canes in shades of blue, white and pink and including pink Clichy roses contained in a basket of alternate white and pairs of blue staves, probably Bohemia, mid-19thC, 5½in (14cm) diam.
$1,300–1,500 C

A St Louis garlanded flat bouquet paperweight, with blue and red canes, mid-19thC, 2½in (6.5cm) diam.
$625–700 P

SCENT BOTTLES

A Bohemian red glass scent bottle, with gold mount at base and neck, with chain attachment, mid-18thC, 3¾in (9.5cm) high.
$1,200–1,300 Som

A Bomehian red-flashed glass scent bottle, engraved with deer in landscapes, with embossed silver mount, c1860, 6¼in (16cm) long.
$900–1,000 Som

An amber glass scent bottle, with star-cut decoration, milled edge, c1790, 4¾in (12cm) long.
$730–800 Som

A gold-mounted opaline hortensia glass scent bottle, c1815–25, 2½in (6.5cm) high.
$5,000–6,500 ALiN

Hortensia is a pinky red colour, commonly called *gorge de pigeon* (throat of a pigeon), and is highly desirable.

A glass scent bottle, modelled as a lemon, with damaged silver top, 19thC, 2¾in (7cm) high.
$525–575 GH

A glass scent bottle, by Hale Thompson & Co, with cased silvered interior and cut amethyst exterior, signed, c1850, 8in (20.5cm) high.
$1,100–1,300 ALiN

Silvered-glass is made with double walls of glass that are silvered in the middle with mercury. Frederick Hale Thompson and Edward Varnish took out the British patent for the technique in 1849, and it is often called Varnish glass.

A glass scent bottle, in the form of a champagne bottle, with hallmarked silver-gilt top, c1880, 2½in (6.5cm) high.
$400–500 ALiN

A glass scent bottle, with alternate white and green swirl decoration, brass hinged cover, late 19thC, 3½in (9cm) high.
$130–150 GH

Further Reading

Miller's Perfume Bottles: A Collector's Guide, Miller's Publications, 1999

A gold-mounted ruby glass scent bottle, the hinged cover finely engraved with scrolling against a diaper ground, late 19thC, 3¼in (8.5cm) high.
$200–250 P

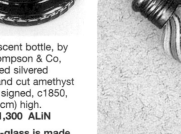

▶ A French cut-glass scent bottle, with silver screw top, c1900, 5in (12.5cm) long.
$230–260 LBr

VASES

A Bohemian *Lithyalin* sealing-wax red glass vase, possibly from Friedrich Egerman workshop, incised on the base 'Alexander Cunningham July 1842', 9½in (24cm) high.
$1,300–1,500 S

***Lithyalin* is a polished opaque glass resembling hardstones, patented by Friedrich Egermann in 1829 at his factory in Haida, northern Bohemia.**

A glass vase and cover, cut with stylized flowers and diamond panels, minor rim chips, mid-19thC, 21in (53.5cm) high.
$1,000–1,300 S

A Bohemian enamelled and cut-glass bud vase, c1870, 10¼in (26cm) high.
$280–330 CB

A pair of French lavender blue glass vases, each decorated with a partial cobalt blue overlay on the lower body and overall gilt tracery, mid-19thC, 10¼in (26cm) high.
$800–900 B&B

A cranberry glass vase, with clear foot, c1880, 12in (30.5cm) high.
$160–200 CB

A cranberry glass bud vase, with clear foot, c1890, 6½in (16.5cm) high.
$120–160 CB

A Stourbridge aquamarine cameo glass, overlaid in opaque white and carved with poppies to either side, above a banded dentil base, c1900, 9½in (24cm) high.
$650–800 Bon

A turquoise opaque glass vase, with cameo portrait, late 19thC, 10¼in (26cm) high.
$75–90 PCh

Miller's is a price GUIDE not a price LIST

Cutting

The type of cutting on glass varied according to the maker and the style in vogue at the time. Diamond cutting was generally the earliest type, and crosscut (often mistakenly called hobnail) was introduced in about 1830. These and other commonly found types of glass cutting are shown below:

DIAMOND

CROSS-CUT DIAMOND

STRAWBERRY DIAMOND

PRISM

BLAZES

PILLAR

Silver

S ilver, once conspicuously displayed as a symbol of wealth and power, has, in Britain in the 20th century, lost its lustre. Many people living outside these shores still appreciate the glamour of silver and one hopes that Britons will soon recognize that silver is the perfect foil for the vibrant hues now espoused by decorators. It looks brilliant against modern pictures and colourful furnishings, and is equally at home on a pine kitchen table.

On the whole, apart from the finest pieces with international appeal, the vast majority of British silver has appreciated little over the past 21 years. For many people, therefore, silver is far more affordable than it has ever been. For example, a pair of table candlesticks made circa 1760 might have been bought in 1979 for $2,100, admittedly 30 per cent more than a decade earlier, but it is still possible to buy a pair for $3,250 or so. Compared with the escalating price of property, British silver is undoubtedly a bargain at present!

Without doubt, taste plays an important part in determining popularity. Our 19th-century forebears, whose powerful imperial trade links brought all manner of styles to Britain, had catholic tastes. The 20th century has been much more conservative, with 17th- and 18th-century silver largely holding sway. Recent fashion has been more sympathetic towards Victorian style, and those pieces once deemed the height of bad taste are now cherished as ritzy and glitzy. Inscribed Victorian presentation pieces that record, for example, the railway inaugurations, trade ventures and great horse races are particularly interesting.

Nowadays, there are fewer collectors of silver made before 1700, but many such pieces have a simplicity of style that is very contemporary. This can be compared with, for example, the items designed in the 20th century by Georg Jensen in Denmark (*see Decorative Arts section, page 474*) and Puiforcat in France, which are much sought after. However, little has been written about their British counterparts, such as H. G. Murphy and Eric Clements, who are less well known and whose pieces are part of an emerging market. Modern silversmiths, for instance Rod Kelly and Chris Knight to name but two, are also now producing great designs – the antiques of the future – so perhaps as we enter the next 21 years of *Miller's Antiques Price Guides* it is the perfect time to look at silver with a fresh and glistening eye. **Eileen Goodway**

BASKETS

A pierced-silver sugar basket, by Henry Wilkinson & Co, inscribed, Sheffield 1867, 5in (12.5cm) high, with frosted glass liner.
$320–360 Mit

▶ A George III silver swing-handled sugar basket, by Joseph Scammell, with pierced bands of acanthus leaves, lozenges and quatrefoil motifs, further pierced with foliate medallions, blue glass liner, 1789, 5in (12.5cm) long.
$1,100–1,300 P

A silver cake basket, by William Plummer, with pierced and chased beads, scrolls, paterae and leafage, with cast leafage border and pierced swing handle, 1772, 14¼in (36cm) wide, 30oz.
$5,200–5,700 TEN

A George III silver swing-handled sugar basket, by Richard Morton, the sides pierced with beads and slats above stamped and chased acanthus leaves, the foot crested, with blue glass liner Sheffield 1778, 5in (12.5cm) diam, 4oz.
$1,100–1,300 P

LOCATE THE SOURCE
The source of each illustration in Miller's can be found by checking the code letters below each caption with the Key to Illustrations, pages 789–795.

A George III Irish silver bright-cut engraved sugar basket, by William Bond, with reeded swing handle, Dublin 1803, 4in (10cm) long, 9oz.
$1,800–2,000 JAd

A William IV silver cake basket, by H. Wilkinson and Co, with rococo scroll and floral embossed border, trailing ivy cast swing handle, the base inscribed and dated 'November 1st 1836', 10¼in (26cm) diam, 15oz.
$575–650 HAM

A silver swing-handled sugar basket, by Edward Barnard & Sons, monogrammed and dated, London 1858, 6¾in (17cm) high, with blue glass liner and a sugar sifter.
$400–500 Bea(E)

A pair of Howard & Co sterling silver baskets, after a design by Paul de Lamerie, of shell-form on dolphin feet, mid-19thC, 10½in (26.5cm) long, 68oz.
$6,500–7,500 SK

A silver cake basket, with Chippendale rim and swing handle, Sheffield 1918, 12in (30.5cm) long.
$1,150–1,300 CoHA

A silver cake basket, by Crichton Bros, the pierced and engraved edge with beaded border, London 1920, 13in (33cm) long, 25oz.
$1,300–1,450 SK

BEAKERS

A Dutch silver beaker, probably by Eelke Wyntiens, Leeuwarden, engraved with arabesques and strapwork enclosing leafy branches and flowerheads, gilt interior, the base set with a medal, c1651, 4¼in (11cm) high.
$1,800–2,000 S(Am)

► A parcel-gilt beaker, in the style of William Burges, raised on 2 falcon legs, chased with bands of medieval decoration with 2 knights jousting outside a castle, c1870, 3in (7.5cm) high, 2½oz.
$650–750 S(S)

A George III Irish silver beaker, by Michael Homer, c1778, 3¼in (8.5cm) high.
$2,600–3,000 WELD

BOWLS

A Charles II silver porringer, embossed with laurel wreaths above acanthus leaves, maker's mark 'I.S.' intertwined, London 1680, 7in (18cm) wide, 5¾oz.
$3,200–3,600 AH

A George I silver bowl, by William Duggan, with inscription, Dublin 1726, 7¼in (18.5cm) diam.
$14,500–16,000 WELD

The desirability of this bowl is due to its excellent condition and the contemporary inscription, a feature which is rarely found.

A silver rose bowl, by Edward Hutton, with a reeded band and lions' mask drop ring handles, vacant panels, reeded edging on spreading base, London 1887, 10¼in (26cm) diam, 36¼oz.
$1,150–1,400 Bea(E)

A silver rose bowl, by Charles Stuart Harris, with embossed husks, swags and ribbons, the base and foot with fluted decoration, 1907, 8in (20.5cm) diam, 12oz.
$400–500 P(EA)

A George III silver bowl, maker's mark possibly John Christie, Dublin, c1745, 6in (15cm) diam, 14oz.
$3,200–3,600 JAd

A silver quaich, c1900, 3½in (9cm) diam.
$250–325 BWA

A William IV silver-gilt sugar bowl, by Charles Fox II, decorated with trailing roses, with acanthus leaf handles and shell foot, 1833, 5in (12.5cm) diam, 14oz.
$1,000–1,150 P

An Edward VII silver fruit bowl, by George Maudsley Jackson and David Landsborough Fullerton, London 1903, 14¾in (37.5cm) long, 33½oz.
$850–950 Bea(E)

◄ An Irish silver bowl, by West & Sons, with a band of Celtic ornament around the rim, presentation inscription, Dublin 1911, 9in (23cm) diam.
$850–950 S(S)

BOXES

A Dutch silver tobacco box, with squeeze action sides, engraved with scenes from Abraham's attempted sacrifice of Isaac, maker's mark only, c1700, 3½in (9cm) long.
$6,500–7,500 P

A George III silver and parcel-gilt box and cover, the hinged cover cast with an architectural ruin after Piranesi, initialled 'RB', London 1818, 3¾in (9.5cm) long, 6¼oz.
$1,200–1,400 EH

Piranesi was a Venetian architect who visited Rome in 1740 and made a large number of etchings of classical antiquities.

▶ A silver box, set with emeralds, rubies, sapphires and pearls, c1900, 3½in (9cm) wide.
$1,000–1,150 CoHA

A German silver toilet box, the domed hinged cover with a shell and scroll cartouche and a shell thumbpiece, engraved with a coat-of-arms, on an oval lobed foot, with a key, maker's mark of Gottlieb Satzger, Augsburg, 1751–53, 8½in (21.5cm) long, 26oz.
$11,500–13,000 Bon

A silver box, by Thomas Hayes, the sides embossed with classical figures, the tortoiseshell cover inlaid in Oriental style with finches amid flowering branches, Birmingham 1899, 4¼in (11cm) wide.
$575–650 P

A George III Irish silver box, by Samuel Neville, presented by City of Dublin Corporation to James Twycross jeweller, Dublin 1808, 3¼in (8.5cm) diam.
$10,500–12,000 WELD

The inscription on this box is of great interest to silver *aficionados*.

A Continental silver repoussé box, the front with monogrammed cartouche, the lid with putti and a fairy, 7in (18cm) wide, 13oz.
$600–700 SK

A silver cigarette box, engraved with sailing ships, c1930, 6½in (16.5cm) wide.
$650–750 SFL

CADDIES

A pair of George II silver tea caddies, by John Newton, with sliding bases and domed caps, London 1739, 5in (12.5cm) high, 16½oz.
$5,200–5,700 S(NY)

A George III silver caddy set, by Emick Romer, the domed lids with cast shell finials, the bases initialled 'AS', London 1767, 5¼in (13.5cm) high, 30½oz, in a contemporary fitted mahogany box,
$9,750–11,500 S(NY)

A silver tea caddy, with domed top and fluted sides, c1909, 3in (7.5cm) high.
$650–750 GIO

CANDLESTICKS & CHAMBERSTICKS

A pair of Queen Anne silver candlesticks, by Thomas Merry, with octagonal bases, initialled 'ET', London 1708, 6½in (16.5cm) high, 20½oz.
$18,500–21,000 S

A pair of George III silver candlesticks, by Robert Makepeace & Richard Carter, base monogrammed, London 1777, 9½in (24cm) high, 46oz.
$4,800–5,600 SK

A pair of 18thC-style silver candlesticks, by William Hutton & Sons, London 1905, 8¾in (22cm) high.
$1,300–1,550 S(S)

A pair of 18thC-style silver candelabra, maker's mark 'RC', London 1936, 13in (33cm) high, 27oz.
$1,800–2,200 S(S)

A George II cast-silver taper stick, by John Cafe, on shaped square base with knopped stem, London 1743, 4in (10cm) high.
$1,000–1,150 GAK

A George III chamberstick, by Robert Makepeace & Richard Carter, with gadrooned and hairbell motif, London 1777, 4in (10cm) diam, 8oz, the snuffer also marked.
$1,000–1,100 P(Ed)

A pair of William IV silver candlesticks, by Waterhouse, Hatfield & Co, each with leaf decoration, the bases with alternating C-scroll moulded decoration, Sheffield 1836, 11in (28cm) high.
$1,200–1,400 TRL

▶ A pair of George V silver three-light candelabra, by Martin, Hall & Co, the fluted oval bases, tapering stems, drip pans and detachable nozzles with reeded edging, Sheffield 1913, 16¼in (41.5cm) high.
$3,000–3,500 Bea(E)

A pair of silver candlesticks, by Ebenezer Coker, the knopped stems with cotton reel nozzles and spiral fluted drip pans, London 1762, 10¼in (26cm) high, 47oz.
$4,250–5,000 HAM

A pair of George III silver chambersticks, by John Edwards III, the circular pan with gadrooned border, snuffers and nozzles lacking, London 1800, 3¼in (8cm) high.
$1,000–1,150 RTo

A pair of silver Adam-style candlesticks, Sheffield 1899, 10in (25.5cm) high.
$1,200–1,400 TMA

CARD CASES

A silver card case, embossed with a monument, possibly the Albert Memorial, London, within a scroll and leaf border, the hinged lid embossed with scroll decoration, Birmingham 1851, 4in (10cm) high.
$900–1,000 RTo

A silver 'castle-top' card case, by Nathaniel Mills, heavily embossed with a view of Windsor castle, the reverse with foliate scrolls and vacant panel, Birmingham 1846, 4in (10cm) long.
$1,150–1,300 S(S)

A silver 'castle-top' card case, embossed and engraved with the 1851 Great Exhibition Hall in Hyde Park, within arabesque scrolls, maker's mark DP, Birmingham 1853, 4in (10cm) long, 2oz.
$3,000–3,500 BR

A silver 'castle-top' card case, with a view of Bath Abbey within foliate scroll decoration, the reverse with a plain scroll cartouche, maker's mark of Alfred Taylor, Birmingham 1856, 4in (10cm) long.
$2,400–2,700 Bon

CENTREPIECES

A silver centrepiece, bowl damaged, maker's mark of John Mortimer and John S. Hunt, London 1843, 8¾in (47.5cm) high, 136oz.
$10,000–11,500 Bon

A German silver centrepiece, the stem formed as a grapevine surrounded by 3 putti, the bowl with scrolled tendril handles topped by seated putti, mid-19thC, 28in (71cm) high, 224oz.
$14,500–16,500 S(NY)

A silver-gilt centrepiece, inscribed and marked with a registration mark, maker's mark of George Richard Elkington, London 1857, 19in (48.5cm) high.
$6,500–7,500 Bon

A silver centrepiece, by Elkington & Co, applied with figures of a Chinaman and Sarawak tribesmen, Birmingham 1873, 19in (48.5cm) high, 115oz.
$10,500–11,500 S

Registration Marks

Registration marks are often found on items designed between 1842 and 1883, and indicate that these pieces were registered at the Patent Office Design Registry.
The marks appear thus:–

1842–67

Years

1842 – X		1855 – E	
1843 – H		1856 – L	
1844 – C		1857 – K	
1845 – A		1858 – B	
1846 – I		1859 – M	
1847 – F		1860 – Z	
1848 – U		1861 – R	
1849 – S		1862 – O	
1850 – V		1863 – G	
1851 – P		1864 – N	
1852 – D		1865 – W	
1853 – Y		1866 – Q	
1854 – J		1867 – T	

1868–83

Years

1868 – X		1880 – J	
1869 – H		1881 – E	
1870 – C		1882 – L	
1871 – A		1883 – K	
1872 – I			
1873 – F			
1874 – U			
1875 – S			
1876 – V			
1877 – P			
1878 – D			
1879 – Y			

Months

January	C	May	E	September	D
February	G	June	M	October	B
March	W	July	I	November	K
April	H	August	R	December	A

(R may be found as the month mark for 1st–19th September 1857, and K for December 1860).

(For 1st–6th March 1878, G was used for the month and W for the year).

Class
Year
IV
H
Month C RD I Day of Month
2
Parcel No.

Class
Day of Month
IV
I
Parcel No. 2 RD H Year
C
Month

1842 – 1867	
IV	Class
H	Year
C	Month
2	Parcel No
I	Day of month

1868 – 1883	
IV	Class
I	Day of month
2	Parcel No
C	Month
H	Year

CIGAR & CIGARETTE CASES

A silver 'castle-top' cigar case, with a view of Windsor Castle within foliate scroll decoration, maker's mark of Nathaniel Mills, Birmingham 1839, 5in (12.5cm) long, 2¼oz.
$1,000–1,150 Bon

A silver cheroot case, by Yapp & Woodward, engraved with a hunting scene, Birmingham 1845, 4¾in (12cm) long.
$1,000–1,100 TC

▶ A silver cigarette case, with an enamelled scene of a scantily-draped lady inside the lid, London 1896, 3in (7.5cm) wide.
$3,200–3,600 SHa

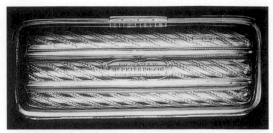

A silver three-cigar case, by Hilliard & Taylor, Birmingham 1863, 5in (12.5cm) long.
$525–600 DIC

COFFEE POTS & TEAPOTS

A George I silver teapot, by Francis Nelme, engraved with a contemporary armorial, with a wooden scroll handle, London 1724, 4½in (11.5cm) high, 12oz.
$17,000–19,000 S(S)

A George II silver teapot, by Richard Gurney & Co, with chased rocaille scroll and foliage scalework to the top and wooden scroll handle, incised initials, London 1748, 6½in (16.5cm) high, 18oz.
$2,800–3,200 WW

A George III engraved-silver teapot, by William Plummer, London 1785, 5½in (14cm) high, 15¼oz.
$3,000–3,500 TC

A George III silver teapot, by William Vincent, with reeded bands, wavy edge and hinged cover, fruitwood handle and finial, maker's mark 'W.V.', London 1788, 5½in (14cm) high, 15½oz.
$520–570 MCA

▶ A French silver coffee pot, with pineapple finial, scrolled spout with lion-mask moulded terminal, on 3 paw feet, early 19thC, 12¼in (31cm) high, 36oz.
$1,300–1,500 B&L

A silver coffee pot, by John & George Angell, with reeded decoration, engraved with shells and foliage, London 1847, 11½in (29cm) high, 29oz.
$800–900 E

COFFEE & TEA SERVICES

A silver three-piece tea service, by John Burger, New York, decorated with wheelwork bands, roundels and scrollwork, enriched with bright-cut details, with engraved monogram 'A.C.S.', c1790, sugar urn 10in (25.5cm) high, 43oz.
$4,000–5,000 B&B

A George IV silver three-piece melon pattern tea service, by William Bateman, with shell, rose and foliate scroll borders and gilt interiors, 1827 and 1828, 42oz.
$1,450–1,600 P(W)

A Dutch silver four-piece tea service, by Jacob D. Arnoldi, on vine leaf supports, with double-scroll handles, Amsterdam 1865, teapot 6¾in (17cm) high, 52oz.
$1,400–1,550 S(Am)

A Victorian silver three-piece tea service, engraved with stylized swags and strapwork, with beaded acanthus handles, Sheffield 1883, 34oz.
$750–900 P(NE)

Bright-cut engraving

Bright-cut engraving is used mainly on neo-classical silver of the late 18thC. The metal is cut with a graver at an angle to create facets that reflect the light. It should be noted that the facets are easily worn by polishing and the decoration must be crisp to enhance value.

A Dutch silver two-piece tea service, by Pierre Hyacinthe la Ruelle, the teapot with wood handle and knop finial, Amsterdam 1806, cream jug 5½in (14cm) high, 17½oz.
$2,000–2,500 S(Am)

An Irish silver four-piece tea and coffee service, by R. Sherwin, with chased alternating cartouches and leafage, Dublin 1839–41, 91oz.
$4,000–4,500 TEN

A Victorian silver four-piece tea service, with engraved foliate decoration throughout, maker's stamp 'T.W.', London 1879, 62oz.
$1,300–1,450 Mit

A George IV silver three-piece tea service, by Charles Fox, engraved with flowers and scrolls, crested, London 1826, 34oz.
$1,800–2,000 FW&C

A silver six-piece tea service, by William Gale & Son, heavily embossed with grapes and leaves, monogrammed, New York 1850–60, teapot 12¼in (31cm) high, 78oz.
$7,500–8,500 SK

A Victorian silver four-piece tea and coffee service, by James Dixon & Son, engraved with a crest within bright-cut medallions, the tea kettle and jug with inscription, stiff-leaf chased borders and handles embellished with rams' masks, Sheffield 1880, 205oz.
$7,500–8,500 S

A sterling silver Near Eastern-style five-piece tea and coffee service, by Whiting Mfg Co, Rhode Island, the surfaces fully chased in bands of various widths, inscribed, c1880, coffee pot 7¾in (19.5cm) high, 84oz.
$3,200–3,600 B&B

A sterling silver five-piece tea and coffee service, by Whiting Mfg Co, in the Baltimore style, decorated with chased and repoussé roses and foliage, c1885–1895, 74oz.
$4,000–5,000 NOA

A silver three-piece tea service, with vertical fluting and reeded body bands, Chester 1900, 33oz.
$575–650 GAK

A silver three-piece tea service, with gadrooned edges, the teapot with ebonized handles and knop, the sides with half gadrooning, early 20thC, 35oz.
$500–550 TRL

A George III style silver three-piece tea service, by Walker & Hall, each piece with shell-capped curved legs, Sheffield, c1908, 40oz.
$850–1,000 MEA

A silver early 18thC-style four-piece tea and coffee service, by Walker & Hall, Sheffield 1932, coffee pot 9¾in (25cm) high.
$1,600–2,000 CGC

A Victorian silver four-piece tea and coffee service, by C. S. Harris, with gadroon, shell and acanthus edging, engraved with flowers and scrolling foliage, London 1900, 80oz.
$1,550–1,800 Bea(E)

An Edwardian silver four-piece tea service, the teapot and hot water jug each with foliate cast finial and ebony loop handle, embossed with scrolling foliage, London 1903–4, 68oz.
$1,800–2,000 AH

An Edwardian silver five-piece tea service, by the Goldsmiths & Silversmiths Co Ltd, engraved with stylized flowers and foliage, London 1907, kettle Sheffield 1908, 99oz.
$1,300–1,600 P(F)

A silver four-piece tea service, the teapot and hot water jug each with composition handle and finial, London 1934.
$575–650 Bon(M)

CONDIMENT POTS

A pair of Dutch silver mustard pots, by Harmanus Heuvel, with blue liners and scroll handles applied with twines, hinged covers engraved with the monogram 'G' beneath a crown, one with rose finial, the other with aster finial, Amsterdam 1773, 4in (10cm) high.
$14,500–16,500 S(Am)

A set of 4 George IV silver table salts, with lobed lower bodies, gadrooned borders, and a matching mustard pot, maker's mark 'CE', London 1824, 3½in (9cm) high.
$1,800–2,000 HYD

A silver Britannia standard mustard pot, with blue glass liner, London 1903, 5in (12.5cm) wide.
$450–550 CoHA

◄ A silver three-piece condiment set, by Charles Boyton, with blue glass liner, London 1933, pepper 2¾in (7cm) high.
$650–750 BKK

CRUET STANDS

A George III silver four-bottle cruet stand, with central fluted carrying handle, the 4 silver-mounted cut-glass cruet bottles with shell finials, maker's mark of Paul Storr, London 1806, 11in (28cm) high, 24oz.
$5,000–6,000 Bon

A George III luncheon cruet stand, the base with floral and leaf repoussé border, on 4 leaf-cast and shell feet, with 5 matched bottles, marks rubbed, London, 7½in (19cm) high.
$300–350 HYD

A George III silver cruet stand, by Charles Chesterman, 6 stoppers with silver mounts, the stand with bands of bright-cut engraving and a monogrammed cartouche, with wooden base, maker's mark 'CC', London 1797, 10¼in (26cm) high.
$1,000–1,200 SK

CUPS

A William III silver two-handled cup and cover, by Matthew West, the lower body gadrooned and fluted, with decorative stamped leaves and stylized flowerheads, fully marked, London 1699, 5¾in (14.5cm) high, 18⅜oz.
$7,500–8,500 S(NY)

An early George III silver cup, by Francis Crump, the cover with a fluted ovoid finial and gadrooned edge, the body engraved with an armorial shield within floral sprays, London 1770, 12¼in (31cm) high, 44¼oz.
$1,800–2,000 P(F)

A Queen Anne silver cup, by John Rand, with cast scroll handle, marked with initials, London 1708, 3¼in (8cm) high, 8½oz.
$6,500–7,500 HAM

A Channel Islands silver two-handled cup, by Pierre Maingy, Guernsey, engraved on one side with initials 'SRB' and on the other with slightly later monogram 'EMR', maker's mark, c1770, 2½in (6.5cm) high, 3oz.
$1,650–2,000 S(NY)

A silver presentation three-handled loving cup, by Edward Barnard & Sons, with chased strapwork and raised on 3 ball feet, maker's mark, London 1873, 8in (20.5cm) high, 41oz.
$1,000–1,150 AH

A George III silver cup, by John Payne, with reeded girdle and scroll handles with heart-shaped terminals, London 1762, 5¼in (13.5cm) high, 11¼oz.
$450–550 Bea(E)

CUTLERY

A James II silver trefid spoon, by Edward Hulse, prick-dot engraved on front of stem, maker's mark EH, London 1685.
$800–900 P

A provincial silver trefid spoon, by George Trowbridge, the stem pricked with initials 'ES/TS' and dated '1724', Exeter 1711.
$500–600 Bea(E)

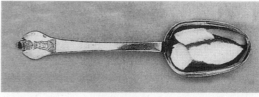

A Queen Anne trefid spoon, scratch initialled to reverse of bowl, 'A*H' over 'H*C 1705', crested to front, 7in (18cm) long, 1oz.
$350–400 Bon

A pair of George II silver Old English pattern serving spoons, each engraved with a crest, maker's mark possibly that of Thomas & William Chawner, London 1750, 5¼oz.
$800–900 JAd

A Georgian silver Old English and Hanoverian pattern table service, comprising 12 place settings, later engraved 'C', various dates and makers, 1783–1832, 78oz.
$1,300–1,450 P(EA)

▶ Six Dublin silver tablespoons, by J. Shields, c1786, 9in (23cm) long.
$1,300–1,450 WELD

A Limerick silver tablespoon, by Thomas Burke, c1785, 9½in (24cm) long.
$1,000–1,200 WELD

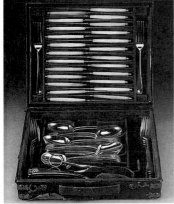

A George III Old English pattern silver-gilt dessert service, by George Smith & William Fearn, comprising 73 pieces, the terminals armorial engraved, the knife blades Edward Hunt II of London, c1790, the grape scissors Eley & Fearn, London 1814, 58oz, in contemporary brass-bound leather case.
$14,500–16,500 S

Six George III Irish silver Fiddle pattern dessert spoons, by Richard Sawyer, each engraved with crest above initials, Dublin 1813–15, 6½oz.
$400–500 JAd

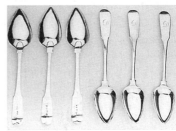

Six Scottish provincial silver Fiddle pattern tablespoons, by John Pringle, engraved initial 'D' in script, Perth, c1830, 12oz.
$800–900 P(NE)

A set of 6 Victorian silver King's pattern tablespoons, engraved with a crest, London 1872.
$325–400 JAd

A silver Queen's pattern canteen, by Chawner & Co and Elkington & Co, comprising 153 pieces, London 1888, 317½oz, in brass-mounted oak case.
$11,500–13,000 S

A pair of Queen Victoria Diamond Jubilee silver repoussé spoons, the handles set with coins of Victoria, the stems twisted, the bowls engraved '1837–97', above repoussé work of roses, thistles and clovers, monogrammed to back, 7in (18cm) long, 3oz, with fitted case.
$325–400 SK

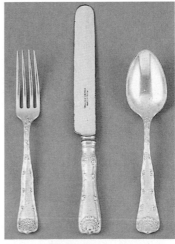

An American silver assembled Wave Edge pattern flatware set, by Tiffany & Co, comprising 111 pieces, monogrammed, New York 1884–1891, 135oz.
$7,500–8,500 S(NY)

▶ A set of 6 silver and ivory knives and forks, by Omar Ramsden, London 1929.
$2,400–2,700 BEX

DISHES

A George III Scottish silver pap boat, by Cunningham & Simpson, Edinburgh 1809, 4in (10cm) long.
$320–360 GAK

A sterling silver dish, by Tiffany & Co, Edward Moore director's mark, New York, c1880, 9in (23cm) wide.
$1,400–1,600 SHa

A pair of Regency silver meat dishes, by Paul Storr, 1818, with mazarines and later domes, by John Bridge 1823, London, for Rundell, Bridge & Rundell, 23½in (59.5cm) wide, 620oz.
$57,000–65,000 S

A silver sweetmeat dish, pierced overall with geometric and floral designs, applied floral and scrolled edge, Chester 1895, 4½in (11.5cm) wide, 4½oz.
$320–360 GAK

An Austrian silver and gilt-embossed dish, decorated with a sacrificial scene within a border depicting the signs of the zodiac, Vienna 1857, 13in (33cm) wide.
$1,450–1,650 RTo

EWERS & JUGS

An Irish silver covered jug, by J. Nowlan, Dublin 1833, 10¾in (27.5cm) high.
$5,200–5,700 SIL

A George III silver cream jug, on a square pedestal foot with applied beaded rim, London 1796, 4½in (11.5cm) high.
$300–400 PSA

A silver water pitcher, by Forbes & Son, New York, the lower body chased with acanthus leaves in a stylized band, the upper body with chased scrolling foliage framing the blank monogram reserve, the multi-scroll handle chased with flowers and leaves, c1850, 14¾in (37.5cm) high, 43½oz.
$3,000–3,500 B&B

A silver ewer, by E. & J. Barnard, the body with engraved scrolling decoration, the handle in the form of a vine with applied fruit and leaf detail, ivory insulators and leaf thumbpiece to the lid, London 1858, 14¼in (36cm) high, 24½oz.
$1,200–1,400 P(Ed)

◄ A silver wine flagon, by Stephen Smith and William Nicholson, with fawn finial, the body engraved with swags and palmette frieze, London 1864, 14¼in (36cm) high, 58oz.
$2,000–2,300 P(NW)

◄ A silver wine jug, the body with a band of reeding above scrolling foliage and 2 cartouches, London 1865, 12in (30.5cm) high, 17½oz.
$1,000–1,200 E

A Gorham coin silver water jug, the collar applied with classical portrait medallions, the handle with the figure of a draped nude maiden, marked and stamped '530', c1865, 10½in (26.5cm) high.
$2,200–2,500 NOA

The term coin silver means that the jug was made of silver of the standard used for coinage, ie .925 or sterling.

A silver hot water jug, by Martin, Hall & Co, engraved in Greek revival taste with figure frieze, masks and festoons, with Greek helmet finial and gilt interior, engraved with crest and motto, London 1877, 13in (33cm) high, with fitted case.
$2,750–3,000 S

Chasing

A relief design is created by using a chasing hammer and tracing tools to push the metal into a pattern. During the 19thC, the fashion for elaborate decoration often resulted in all-over chasing of earlier plain silver, thus 'modernising' old pieces, rather than melting them down for re-use. Assess whether the chasing is contemporary, as later-chased items are of lesser value. Chasing from the 19thC usually has broader lines than 18thC chasing and patterns are often superimposed over the hallmarks. However, take care, as 18thC pieces were also sent for chasing after they had been hallmarked!

A French parcel-gilt ewer and basin, by Hénin & Cie, cast and chased with rocaille ornament, flowers and aquatic plants, Paris, c1880, basin 18in (46cm) diam, 16½oz.
$7,800–8,500 S

An Irish silver cream jug and sugar bowl, by Weir & Sons, supported on 3 lion-mask and claw feet, both decorated with foliate scrollwork, fruit and a blank cartouche, Dublin 1902, 4½in (11cm) high, 13oz.
$700–800 P(E)

A silver-mounted glass claret jug, with etched floral sprays bordered by pierced scrolling silver overlay, the silver neck with lobed spout and dragon handle, maker's mark 'SS', London 1885, 14½in (37cm) high.
$2,300–2,700 P(NE)

A silver jug, with reeded handle, on a stepped waisted socle and square foot, Sheffield 1910, 8in (20.5cm) high, 9oz
$200–250 P(HSS)

A Mexican sterling silver water jug, by William Spratling, Taxco, with triple curve arched strap handle, c1940, 10in (25.5cm) high, 28¼oz.
$3,700–4,000 B&B

▶ A Renaissance-style French first standard silver ewer, in the form of a nautilus shell with wave chased spout, the lid mounted with a conch shell finial, the handle cast and chased in the form of a horn-blowing triton, marked 'Puiforcat, France', c1915, 12½in (32cm) high, 38oz.
$4,500–5,500 NOA

Cross Reference
See Colour Review

A Tiffany & Co sterling silver water jug, with erasure and later engraved monogram, slight damage, New York, c1865, 11in (28cm) high, 52oz.
$5,700–6,500 B&B

INKSTANDS & INKWELLS

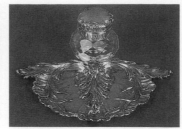

A silver inkstand, by William Elliot, with pierced panels of urns flanked by lions and bacchic heads, the top with 2 pen trays, engraved with arms and motto, on paw feet, marked, London 1819, 12¼in (31cm) wide, 103oz.
$21,000–24,000 S(NY)

▶ A silver inkstand, by Gibson & Langman, with pierced fret gallery, a pair of cut-glass inkwells, on a satinwood base with chased panel feet, London 1896, 12in (30.5cm) wide.
$1,000–1,100 WW

A silver inkwell, by Edward Ker Reid, the lozenge-faceted glass bottle with floral-embossed domed cover, London 1856, 7in (18cm) wide.
$600–700 WeH

A silver-mounted glass inkwell, by J. C. Vickery, the cover with inset watch, the front with aperture for calendar cards, London 1906, 4½in (11.5cm) square.
$800–900 S(S)

JARDINIERES

A French silver three-piece jardinière set, with sterling silver liners, by Bointaburet, c1860, largest 15½in (39.5cm) wide.
$22,000–24,500 SFL

Bointaburet pieces are usually of very fine quality and very heavy. The fact that this is a suite also enhances the price.

A Continental silver .930 standard rococo-style jardinière, with silver-plated liner, import marks for Mappin & Webb, London 1898, 22in (56cm) wide.
$5,500–6,500 B&B

KETTLES

An American silver kettle-on-stand, by Jones, Ball & Poor, chased and embossed with floral decoration, the handle with ivory insulating rings, Boston, mid-19thC, 9¼in (23.5cm) high, 24oz.
$900–1,000 SK

A silver kettle-on-stand, with gadrooned border, part ebonised handle, the stand with 4 tapered legs and claw feet, maker GH, Sheffield 1904, 12½in (32cm) high, 43oz.
$575–650 P(E)

An American silver kettle-on-stand, with swing handle and burner, monogrammed, stamped 'Sterling, Howard & Co, New York, 1893', 12¼in (31cm) high, 34½oz.
$375–400 Bea(E)

MIRRORS

A silver mirror, by W. Comyns, the frame decorated with scrolls, flowers and foliage, London 1900, 22in (55.5cm) high.
$650–800 Bea(E)

A German silver dressing mirror, probably by H. Gladenbeck & Söhne, Berlin, decorated with rocaille ornament, engraved with monogram 'MR', c1860, 26¼in (66.5cm) high.
$2,700–3,000 S(Am)

An American sterling silver chased and repoussé dressing mirror, decorated with birds and flowers, marked 'JR/925', c1900, 19½in (49.5cm) high.
$2,000–2,500 NOA

▶ A Viennese silver mirror, with star beaded edge, c1900, 18½in (48cm) high.
$800–900 DORO

MODELS & FIGURES

A silver stirrup cup, by Tudor & Leader, in the form of a fox's head, gilt interior, Sheffield 1777, 5in (12.5cm) long.
$5,200–5,700 S(S)

A pair of silver models of tricycles, with slatted seats, London 1893/4, 5in (12.5cm) high, 9oz.
$1,000–1,100 P(NE)

A silver model of a parasol, with turned handle, Sheffield 1899, 4in (10cm) long.
$200–250 AH

▶ A silver model of fairies seated at a table, marked, Chester 1900, 2in (5cm) wide, 1¼oz.
$450–500 HCC

A Portuguese toothpick holder, in the form of a soldier, the base with pierced and embossed foliate decoration, on 3 paw feet, monogrammed, maker's mark worn, c1850, 8¾in (22cm) high, 12oz.
$1,600–2,000 Bon

A pair of Norwegian peppers, by David Anderson, Oslo, in the form of a penguin and a polar bear, c1940, largest 2½in (6.5cm) high, 1¼oz.
$325–400 S(S)

> **Miller's is a price GUIDE not a price LIST**

MUGS & TANKARDS

A Norwegian silver peg tankard, with engraved foliate decoration, the lid set with a coin, inscribed, maker's mark of Suder Meyer, c1697, 8in (20.5cm) high, 30oz.
$5,500–6,000 Bon

A silver pint mug, by Thomas Farren, with moulded rim, leaf-capped scroll handle, on a moulded spreading foot, the base inscribed with initials, London 1741, 7in (18cm) high, 11½oz.
$900–1,000 WW

An American silver tankard, by Thomas Edwards, Boston, now altered to a jug, marked, c1750, 8½in (21.5cm) high, 26¼oz.
$2,300–2,800 B&B

A silver quart mug, with reeded upper and lower bands and fluted scroll handle, maker's mark 'RG', London 1770, 6¼in (16cm) high, 23oz.
$1,400–1,550 HAM

A silver pint mug, with acanthus leaf scrolled handle, maker's mark 'IK' for John Kentenber, London 1771, 5in (12.5cm) high, 14oz.
$1,000–1,100 MCA

A silver tankard, by John Langlands I, with openwork chair-back thumbpiece, the handle with heart-form terminal, Newcastle 1774, 7½in (19cm) high, 26¾oz.
$4,000–4,500 B&B

Further Reading

Miller's Silver & Sheffield Plate Marks, Miller's Publications, 1993

A silver tankard, possibly by Jan Lotter, The Cape, the cover inscribed, marked, c1800, 6½in (16.5cm) high, 24oz.
$3,200–3,600 TEN

A silver-gilt christening mug, by Charles Fox, decorated with foliate bands, beaded edging and with an angular handle, 1870, 4½in (11.5cm) high.
$400–500 Bea(E)

LOCATE THE SOURCE

The source of each illustration in Miller's can be found by checking the code letters below each caption with the Key to Illustrations, pages 789–795.

◄ A silver christening mug, by Josiah Williams & Co, engraved with ferns, Exeter 1878, 6½in (16.5cm) high, 4oz.
$260–280 P(NE)

RATTLES

A silver rattle and whistle, by Thomas Tearle, engraved with acanthus leaves and initials 'SH', coral teething stick, c1740, 6¼in (16cm) long.
$900–1,000 P

► A silver-gilt rattle, by Charles Rawlings, in the form of a pagoda, hung with bells, coral teething piece, one bell missing, London 1824, 6in (15cm) long.
$3,700–4,000 HAM

The unusual design of this rattle accounts for the high value.

A silver rattle and whistle, probably Dutch, in the form of 4 bells suspended from a lion and a chain, 18thC, 2¾in (7cm) long, 2oz.
$2,400–2,700 S(Am)

PLATES

A set of 14 silver soup plates, by Robert Makepeace and Richard Carter, engraved with armorials, applied buffed gadrooned borders, London 1778, 9¾in (25cm) diam, 255¾oz.
$5,600–6,800 B&B

A set of 12 silver dinner plates, with gadrooned borders and engraved with a coat-of-arms, maker's mark of Paul Storr, London 1814, 10½in (26.5cm) diam, 262oz.
$13,000–14,500 Bon

A set of 6 Scottish silver plates, by J. & W. Marshall, with gadrooned borders, engraved with a crest, maker's mark, Edinburgh 1867, 9in (23cm) diam.
$2,000–2,300 MCA

SALVERS & TRAYS

◄ An Irish chased silver card tray, by J. Fray, Dublin 1840, 6in (15cm) diam.
$1,150–1,300 SIL

A silver salver, with chased decoration, initialled 'CWB', maker's mark 'DL', London 1735, 6in (15.5cm) diam.
$1,800–2,000 Bon(G)

A silver salver, flat-chased with scrollwork enclosing a monogram, on 3 panelled feet, maker HW, London 1862, 7in (18cm) diam.
$200–250 HYD

A silver pin tray, by William Comyns, London 1891, 8in (20.5cm) long.
$160–200 GAK

A silver tea tray, by Harrison Brothers & Howson, initialled 'H', Sheffield 1898, 20in (51cm) wide, 106oz.
$1,200–1,450 Bea(E)

SAUCE BOATS

An Irish silver sauce boat, by Matthew West, engraved with initials, on 3 shell and hoof feet, Dublin 1787, 8in (20.5cm) wide, 9oz.
$2,250–2,750 JAd

A pair of 18thC-style silver sauce boats, by William Comyns, engraved with a crest, on shell feet, London 1913, 9in (23cm) wide, 30oz.
$1,200–1,350 WW

A silver sauce boat, marked 'Dysons of Windsor', Chester 1937, 6in (15cm) wide.
$500–575 CoHa

This piece was produced for the Coronation of 1937.

SERVING IMPLEMENTS

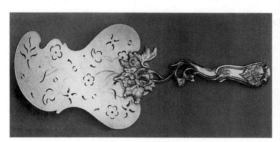

A German silver cake slice, by Gottfried Johan Boden, the blade pierced and engraved, the scroll handle with rocaille decorated terminal, c1740, 11in (28cm) long, 6½oz.
$5,000–5,500 S(G)

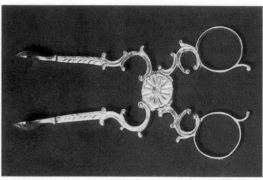

A pair of Irish silver sugar nips, Dublin 1750, 5½in (14cm) long.
$650–750 WELD

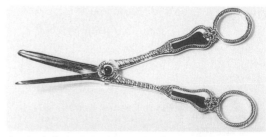

A silver serving trowel, maker's mark probably of William Plummer, London 1772, 11in (28cm) long.
$2,000–2,300 Bon

A pair of silver grape scissors, by George Adams, London 1864, 7in (18cm) long.
$675–775 BEX

George Adams worked for Chawner & Co, one of the major 19thC manufacturers of table silver.

A pair of silver grape scissors, by George Unite, Birmingham 1882, 7in (18cm) long.
$775–850 BEX

SNUFF BOXES

A German silver-gilt snuff box, in the manner of Alexander Fromery, Berlin, with rocaille decoration, inlaid with an enamel cartouche, marked 'AF', 18thC, 3in (8cm) wide.
$1,800–2,000 S(Z)

A silver-gilt snuff box, engine-turned with raised floral borders, reeded sides, maker's mark probably of Ledsam & Vale, Birmingham 1831, 3in (8cm) long.
$525–575 Bon

A silver snuff box, engraved with floral sprays between arched borders, probably German, maker's mark 'DF', c1765, 3½in (9cm) wide, 3¾oz.
$900–1,000 S(S)

A Scottish silver table snuff box, by W. J. McDonald, the cover decorated with an agate chequered panel within silver framing, Edinburgh 1861, 3½in (9cm) wide.
$450–500 TMA

A silver snuff box, by Thomas Shaw, engraved with latticework around a monogrammed cartouche, the base with latticework and foliate scroll borders, Birmingham 1831, 2¼in (5.5cm) long.
$400–450 P

A granite curling trophy snuff mull, with silver cover set with a citrine, c1880, 11in (28cm) diam.
$4,000–5,000 BWA

SUGAR CASTERS

A silver sugar caster, by Solomon Joel Phillips, engraved with rococo leaf and shell scrolls enclosing diaper and fish scale panels, London 1905, 8in (20.5cm) high, 19oz.
$950–1,100 P(NE)

▶ A silver sugar caster, with turned finial and pedestal foot, London 1908, 8¾in (22cm) high, 7½oz.
$320–360 Bea(E)

A silver sugar caster, on a stepped foot, Birmingham 1908, 9in (23cm) high, 11oz.
$450–500 GAK

TUREENS

A silver tureen and cover, by Tiffany & Co, the handles with beaded cube to centre and flat leaf terminals, and domed lid, monogrammed, 1875–91, 15in (38cm) long, 56oz.
$5,000–6,000 SK

A silver 18thC-style sauce tureen, by Crichton Bros, with bright-cut borders, London 1913, 8¾in (22cm) wide, 14½oz.
$800–900 S(S)

Crichton Brothers (c1890–1940) were noted for their fine reproductions of silverware from the 17th and 18th centuries.

A German silver tureen and cover, by Bruckmann & Söhne, Heilbronn, of ribbed form with a broad band of scrolling foliage, the cover with bud finial, cover stamped No. 12–9438, c1890, 19in (48.5cm) high.
$4,000–4,500 S(G)

VESTA CASES

A silver vesta case, modelled as a water bottle in a basket, with a hinged cover, maker's mark of A & L, Birmingham 1888, 2in (5cm) high.
$650–750 Bon

A silver vesta case, modelled as an owl, the hinged head set with glass eyes, maker's mark of S. Mordan & Co, London 1895, 2¼in (5.5cm) high.
$2,000–2,300 Bon

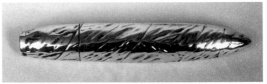

Cross Reference
See Colour Review

An American silver cigar-shaped vesta box and striker, c1890, 4in (10cm) long.
$400–500 SFL

A silver vesta case, with gold circle, Birmingham 1898, 1½in (4cm) high.
$75–90 PSA

A silver vesta case, depicting a billiard game, maker's mark 'JF', Birmingham 1907, 1½in (4cm) diam.
$750–850 S(S)

VINAIGRETTES

A silver vinaigrette, with embossed foliate decoration, the base with engine-turned decoration, the interior with a pierced silver-gilt foliate grille, maker's mark of John Shaw, Birmingham 1818, 2in (5cm) long.
$575–650 Bon

Miller's is a price GUIDE not a price LIST

A silver vinaigrette, by Edward Smith, the cover chased in low relief with Abbotsford House, the engine-turned base with vacant cartouches, Birmingham 1840, 2in (5cm) long.
$1,800–2,000 P

A silver 'lantern' *nécessaire* and vinaigrette, by S. Mordan & Co, marked 'Thornhill', date mark for 9th January 1878, 2½in (6.5cm) high.
$3,000–3,300 S(S)

Silver Plate

A pair of Sheffield plate candelabra, with flame finials on reeded turned stems, double star mark, 19thC, 21in (53.5cm) high.
$850–950 AH

A pair of silver-plated candlesticks, the shaped triangular bases applied with 3 swans with shell supports, the sconces decorated with acanthus leaves, c1870, 6¼in (16cm) high.
$1,800–2,000 P

A Sheffield plate four-branch epergne, fitted with cut-glass centre bowl surrounded by smaller bowls, c1835–50, 14½in (37cm) high.
$2,400–2,700 NOA

A Victorian silver-plated table centrepiece, 17¼in (44cm) high.
$700–800 CGC

A late Victorian silver-plated centrepiece, 20in (51cm) high.
$575–650 Doc

A Sheffield plate coffee pot, with scrolled beech handle and acanthus leaf cast spout, stamped mark of 4 stylized 'B's on neck, c1760, 10½in (26.5cm) high.
$800–900 EH

An Edwardian silver-plated five-piece tea service, by Elkington & Co, with embossed and engraved floral scroll cartouches and heraldic beast finials, kettle-on-stand 16in (40.5cm) high.
$1,300–1,450 RBB

A pair of Sheffield plate entrée dishes and covers, with detachable handles, 19thC, 13in (33cm) wide.
$500–600 PCh

▶ A silver-plated bird inkwell, c1870, 6in (15cm) high.
$400–500 BWA

◀ A pair of silver-plated fish servers, with Japanese *shibayama* handles, c1880, 12½in (32cm) long.
$900–1,000 SFL

Wine Antiques

A silver and glass spirit flask, with silver-gilt cap, Chester 1887, 6½in (16.5cm) high.
$400–450 JAS

A Victorian silver and wicker hip flask, 6in (15cm) high.
$220–250 BCA

A silver and cut-glass claret jug, by Tiffany & Co, late 19th/early 20thC, 10¾in (27.5cm) high.
$500–575 SK

A pair of French silver-mounted glass claret jugs, by Bointaburet, Paris, c1910, 9in (23cm) high, in fitted box.
$4,000–4,500 P

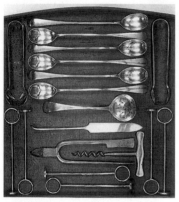

A fitted tray of cocktail accessories, with corkscrew, sugar tongs and sifter spoons, Sheffield and London 1931, 10in (25.5cm) wide, 21oz.
$450–550 WL

A Continental 18thC-style brass-mounted repoussé copper wine cooler, c1790–1810, 27¼in (69cm) wide.
$3,500–4,000 NOA

A Dutch walnut and marquetry-inlaid decanter box, late 19thC, 8½in (21.5cm) wide.
$975–1,100 PF

A Bakelite cocktail shaker, commemorating the cornonation of George VI, 1937, 11½in (29cm) high.
$975–1,100 SFL

An oak tantalus, containing 3 crystal bottles, with cigar and playing card drawer, late 19thC, 14¼in (36cm) wide.
$420–480 L&E

A set of 4 silver bottle labels, by Thomas Phipps & Edward Robinson II, engraved 'Frontiniac', 'Sherry', 'Port' and 'Madeira', London 1792, 1½in (4cm) wide.
$950–1,100 GAK

◄ A silver ladle, with turned marine ivory stem, crested, maker's mark 'WT', London 1831, 17in (43cm) long.
$430–480 S(S)

A silver wine funnel, by William Burwash, the detachable strainer with gadrooned edging, London 1814, 6in (15cm) long.
$975–1,150 Bea(E)

A brass and steel Royal Club corkscrew, with lever mechanism and brass plaque, inscribed with royal arms, 19thC, 9½in (24cm) high.
$2,000–2,200 VOS

A double-action corkscrew, with turned bone handle, the bronze barrel embossed with Autumnal Fruits pattern, c1810, 7½in (19cm) closed.
$1,450–1,650 CS

▶ A steel pocket corkscrew, 18thC, 3½in (9cm) long.
$100–120 AnS

A corkscrew, with turned rosewood handle, fitted with dusting brush and hanging ring, the steel shaft with large steel Henshall button, c1850, 6in (15cm) long.
$55–75 CS

An American corkscrew, with carved boar's tusk handle, Edwin Walker bell cap set in the centre of the shaft, bladed worm, c1900, 6in (15cm) long.
$115–140 CS

A Victorian pull ring corkscrew, 5in (12.5cm) long.
$65–80 TAC

A Tangent Lever two-part corkscrew, patented by Wolverson, 1873, 8in (20.5cm) long.
$100–120 Har

A brass and bronze corkscrew, in the form of a hand holding a Hardy fishing rod, c1940, 7½in (19cm) long.
$260–300 RTh

A brass and steel T-shaped corkscrew, with retractable ratchet-action and turned bone handle, 19thC, 5in (12.5cm) long.
$950–1,150 AH

An American Yankee No. 2 patent bar corkscrew, after Gilchrist's patent of 1907, 6in (15.5cm) long.
$400–500 JSC

Clocks

Some 21 years ago the market in antique clocks was still largely dominated by collectors, and clocks made after 1830 were of little interest. Victorian clocks and painted dial longcase clocks rarely appeared in the major London specialist sales at that time. Principal exceptions were examples by eminent makers such as Frodsham, Dent and Jump, and fine carriage clocks made between 1830 and 1900.

Today the whole market has changed. Although there are still serious clock collectors, particularly for fine, rare and unusual examples, the majority of clocks, even in the higher price range, are bought as beautiful and fascinating objects to adorn the home and complement antiques. Thus French lyre clocks with superb enamelled dials by Coteau or Dubuisson, of which maybe 35 were made between 1786 and 1815, are highly sought after and the best would now fetch around £100,000. The same can be said of those with superb cases created by such masters as Thomire and Gouthière.

At a more humble level, the mahogany longcase with painted dial, particularly with moonphase, has probably increased eight-fold in value in the last 21 years owing to its wide appeal and has now almost caught up with the value of earlier brass-dialled clocks.

The same kind of change has taken place with Georgian bracket clocks. In 1978 an ebonized breakarch bracket clock of 1720–40 was probably worth more than a similar mahogany clock made some 40 or 50 years later. Today the situation is reversed because a mahogany case fits so much more happily into the modern home.

Recently, the carriage clock market has been strong, particularly for the more decorative examples such as those with porcelain or, much rarer, Limoges enamel panels, the quality of which are quite superb. This market has been somewhat disturbed and prices have been erratic over the last year or so due to the appearance on the market of a very large number of clocks, maybe 600, from three major collections.

At the top end of the market, prices are somewhat unpredictable due to the fact that there have been very few fine English clocks for sale – far fewer than two years ago. Thus, a walnut longcase by George Graham was recently bid to over £140,000, which could well affect future prices for other rare English clocks by fine makers.

Derek Roberts

BRITISH BRACKET & MANTEL CLOCKS

A mahogany and gilt-metal bracket clock, by J. P. Acklam, London, with brass dial, twin fusee movement striking on a gong, 18thC, 16in (40.5cm) high.
$4,500–5,200 EH

An ebonized table clock, by William Adcock, London, with brass dial and silvered chapter ring, double fusee verge movement striking the hours on a bell, c1760, 18in (45.5cm) high.
$10,500–11,500 PAO

◀ An ebonized table clock, by John Aitken, Edinburgh, with enamel dial, the 3-train movement striking and repeating the hours on a bell, the going train with half deadbeat escapement, jewelled pallets, maintaining power, c1770, 15½in (39.5cm) high.
$10,500–11,500 PAO

A rosewood table clock, by Arnold & Dent, London, the twin fusee movement striking and repeating on a bell, c1830, 15¼in (38.5cm) high.
$3,500–4,000 Bon

A mahogany bracket clock, by Robert Atchison, London, with silvered-brass dial, verge movement striking and repeating the hours on a bell, c1795, 20in (51cm) high.
$9,000–10,500 PAO

◀ An ebonized mantel clock, by Barraud & Lund, London, with silvered-brass dial, single fusee movement with anchor escapement and heavy pendulum, c1850, 9¼in (23.5cm) high.
$3,750–4,250 PAO

An ebonized fruitwood table timepiece with alarm, by Paul Beauvais, London, with brass and silvered dial, single train fusee movement with 5 ringed pillars, c1714, 13in (33cm) high.
$4,000–5,000 DN

A Regency mahogany and brass-inlaid bracket clock, by J. Benjamin, London, with painted dial, single fusee movement, restored, 18in (46cm) high.
$950–1,150 Bri

A Victorian Gothic-style oak bracket clock, by John Bennett, London, with engraved silvered dial, triple fusee movement chiming and striking on 8 bells and a coiled gong, 29¾in (75.5cm) high.
$2,300–2,800 P(NW)

An ebonized bracket clock, by Bushman, London, with brass dial and silvered chapter ring, twin fusee movement converted to anchor escapement with pull quarter-repeating on 6 bells, 18thC, 17¾in (45cm) high.
$3,250–4,000 P(E)

A mahogany table clock, by Josh Cheetham, Leeds, with painted dial, 2-train fusee movement with anchor escapement and repeating the hours on a bell, c1800, 17¾in (45cm) high.
$12,000–13,000 S(S)

A mahogany bracket clock, by Harvey Denton & Co, London, the fusee movement with anchor escapement, striking and repeating the hours on a bell, c1860, 14in (35.5cm) high.
$5,500–6,000 PAO

◄ A mahogany electric mantel timepiece, by Eureka Clock Co Ltd, London, with enamel chapter ring, the brass movement with a large balance, c1900, 10in (25.5cm) high.
$1,400–1,500 Bon

An ebonized and brass-inlaid mantel timepiece, by Dwerrihouse Carter & Son, with enamel dial, single fusee movement, dial damaged, c1810, 10in (25.5cm) high.
$1,400–1,500 Bon

A rosewood and brass-inlaid table clock, by French, London, with engraved silvered dial, 2-train fusee and chain movement striking on a gong, c1830, 17¾in (45cm) high.
$3,250–4,000 S

A late George III mahogany and marquetry-inlaid table clock, by Frodsham, with painted arch dial, the 5-pillar 2-train fusee movement with anchor escapement, rack striking the hours on a bell, 21in (53.5cm) high.
$3,000–3,250 DN

▶ An ebonized table clock, by Charles Goodall, London, with enamel dials, repeat mechanism, triple fusee movement striking the quarters on 8 bells and the hour on a further bell, c1800, 18in (45.5cm) high.
$13,000–14,000 PAO

An ebonized and gilt mantel clock, by Edward Funnel, Brighton, with silvered chapter ring, the 3-train movement chiming on a series of gongs, late 19thC, 21¾in (55cm) high.
$1,600–1,800 HAM

21 Years Ago …

A Regency bracket clock, by William Patrick Greenwick, with double fusee movement and anchor escapement, 20in (51cm) high. **S**

Twenty-one years ago this clock was valued at $1,400–1,550. Today, that figure would probably need to be multiplied three to four times, to $4,000–5,500. The main reason for this change is that, whereas 21 years ago few people collected any clocks made after 1800, today the beauty of a mahogany or rosewood case is a far more important factor than mechanical details.

An ebonized bracket clock, by Henry Harper, London, the 6-pillar movement now with anchor escapement, repeat mechanism missing, c1700, 14¼in (36cm) high.
$2,500–2,750 TEN

A mahogany table clock, by Hardeman & Son, Bridge, with painted dial, twin fusee movement striking and repeating on a bell, c1820, 19½in (49.5cm) high.
$2,500–3,000 Bon

When sold at auction, clocks have sometimes had alterations to their movements or are in unrestored condition, which may be reflected in the prices realized.

◀ An ebonized bracket clock, by Robert Hodgkin, London, the brass dial with mock pendulum and date apertures, twin train fusee movement with later anchor escapement striking on a bell, the backplate with foliate scroll ornament, 18thC, 17¾in (45cm) high.
$3,250–3,500 P(EA)

A Victorian Gothic-style figured-walnut bracket clock, by Lewis, Brighton, with silvered engraved dial, triple fusee movement chiming and striking on 8 bells, with pendulum, 27½in (70cm) high.
$3,250–4,000 P(NW)

An ebonized bracket clock, by Lund & Blockley, with silvered chapter ring, triple fusee and chain movement chiming on 8 bells at the quarters and hours on a gong, c1880, 24in (61cm) high.
$3,250–4,000 Bon

A mahogany four-glass mantel timepiece, by Manning, Worcester, with silvered dial, the fusee movement with anchor escapement, c1860, 10¾in (27.5cm) high.
$3,000–3,250 S(S)

A mahogany bracket clock, by James McCabe, London, with silvered dial, 5-pillar movement, anchor escapement striking on a bell, case altered, mid-19thC, 14in (35.5cm) high.
$2,500–3,000 P

◄ A George IV mahogany table clock, by Moorhouse, Liverpool, with silvered dial, the 2-train fusee movement with anchor escapement striking the hours on a bell, the domed top case carved with borders of acanthus, a rosette and 'C' scrolls, on turned and nulled feet, 17¾in (45cm) high.
$325–400 DN

◄ A satinwood table clock, by Payne, London, with striking fusee movement, c1820, 14in (35.5cm) high.
$3,000–3,250 SO

Further Reading

Miller's Clocks and Barometers Buyer's Guide, Miller's Publications, 1995

A brass-inlaid rosewood table clock, by Thomas Rowell, Brighton, with fusee movement and anchor escapement, striking and repeating the hours on a bell, c1820, 16in (40.5cm) high.
$7,000–8,000 PAO

A Victorian ebony and gilt-metal-mounted bracket clock, by A. & H. Rowley, London, with pineapple and urn finials, brass dial and silvered chapter ring, the 3-train movement striking on 8 bells and a gong, on gilt-metal scrolled feet, 24½in (62cm) high.
$2,750–3,250 P(F)

◄ An ebony bracket clock, by Henry Russell, London, the door and corners with gilt-brass edging strips, the domed top with brass handle, the sides with fabric-backed brass grilles, with painted dial, twin fusee movement with bell strike, late 18thC, 17in (43cm) high.
$1,800–2,000 WW

An ebony and gilt bracket clock, by John Shaw, London, the silvered chapter ring and matted centre now with blocked pendulum aperture, the 5-pillar twin fusee movement with converted anchor escapement and restored trains, c1680, 16¼in (41.5cm) high.
$3,250–4,000 Bon

A mahogany and brass-inlaid table clock, by Thomas Simson, Hertford, the double fusee 5-pillar repeating movement with anchor escapement, c1800, 16in (40.5cm) high.
$11,500–12,500 PAO

An ebonized bracket clock, by William Scafe, London, with silvered-brass dial, 3-train chiming movement with anchor escapement striking the hours on a bell and chiming the quarters on 8 bells, 19thC, 22in (56cm) high.
$1,600–2,000 DN

► A Victorian Gothic-style oak bracket clock, by Adam Thomson, London, with silvered dial, twin fusee movement striking on a bell, 18½in (47cm) high.
$1,000–1,200 Bri

An ebony veneered table clock, by Francis Stamper, London, the 6-pillar 2-train fusee movement with verge escapement, late 17thC, 12¾in (32.5cm) high.
$13,000–14,500 DN

A rosewood and brass-inlaid table clock, by Thwaites & Reed, London, with double fusee movement striking and repeating the hours on a bell, 1826, 20in (51cm) high.
$7,500–8,500 PAO

An ebonized bracket clock, by William Tomlinson, London, the brass dial with silvered chapter ring, twin fusee movement with 5 ringed pillars and verge escapement, pull quarter repeat on 6 bells, dial replaced, case later, 18thC, 19½in (49.5cm) high.
$3,250–4,000 P

A Regency mahogany bracket clock, by Underwood, London, with painted dial, twin train fusee movement repeating and striking on 9 bells, deadbeat escapement, 17¼in (44cm) high.
$6,500–7,500 P(Sc)

An ebonized bracket clock, by Robert Ward, with silvered chapter ring, 5-pillar twin fusee movement with verge escapement and bob pendulum, striking on a bell, corner finials lacking, c1760, 20¼in (51.5cm) high.
$3,000–3,500 Bon

A mahogany table clock, by James Warren, Canterbury, with painted dial, 5-pillar 2-train bell striking fusee movement with anchor escapement, hands replaced, c1805, 16in (40.5cm) high.
$3,800–4,000 S

A mahogany and brass-inlaid mantel timepiece, by Richard Webster, London, the silvered brass dial with scroll engraving, chain fusee movement with anchor escapement and heavy bob pendulum, c1890, 12in (30.5cm) high.
$3,500–4,000 PAO

◀ An ebony veneered table timepiece, by John Wise, London, with silvered-brass dial, single train fusee movement with 4 baluster turned pillars, verge escapement, pull quarter repeat on 3 bells, late 17thC, 13in (33cm) high.
$7,200–8,000 DN

A George III mahogany and brass-mounted bracket clock, the movement with bob pendulum and bell, Cockspur Street, London, dial and name rubbed, 14½in (37cm) high.
$4,000–4,300 GOR

A late George III mahogany bracket clock, with white enamelled dial signed Saffron Waldon, twin fusee movement, bob pendulum, verge escapement, striking on a bell, dial later, 18½in (47cm) high.
$2,000–2,300 P(NW)

A mahogany and brass-inlaid table clock, with painted dial, 5-pillar 2-train bell striking and trip repeating fusee movement with anchor escapement, c1810, 16¾in (42.5cm) high.
$2,300–2,600 S

A mahogany and brass-inlaid mantel clock, with shallow arched top, applied foliate carving, silvered dial, 2-train fusee movement with repeat striking on a bell, anchor escapement, c1830, 17¼in (44cm) high.
$1,400–1,600 S(S)

A Victorian ebonized mantel clock, with porcelain panels decorated with flowers and acanthus leaves, the face and 6 further panels similarly decorated, the dial with arabic numerals and Gothic-style surround, 21¼in (54cm) high.
$575–650 TRL

An ebonized and gilt-brass-mounted mantel clock, with silvered chapter ring, 3-train fusee movement with anchor escapement, chiming on 10 bells and striking on a gong, c1890, 37½in (95cm) high.
$3,250–3,500 S(S)

◄ A mahogany and brass-inlaid mantel clock, with white enamelled dial, the movement striking on a gong, possibly German, late 19thC, 19½in (49.5cm) high.
$750–900 P(F)

An inlaid mahogany bracket clock, the brass dial with silvered chapter ring and matted centre, the fusee movement with anchor escapement chiming on 8 bells or 4 gongs, late 19thC, 21in (53.5cm) high, with original wall bracket.
$5,000–5,500 P

A mahogany bracket clock, the lancet-top case inlaid with brass stringing, with French striking movement, on ogee bracket feet, late 19thC, 12in (30.5cm) high.
$800–900 DD

An Edwardian mahogany bracket clock, with shell inlay, enamelled dial, striking movement, 15in (38cm) high.
$350–400 LF

A mahogany and boxwood-strung arched top mantel clock, with white enamel dial, 2-train movement striking the hours and the quarters on 2 coiled gongs, on brass feet, 1900s, 14¼in (36cm) high.
$350–400 DN

CONTINENTAL BRACKET & MANTEL CLOCKS

A French gilt-brass mantel clock, signed A. & N. Paris, with enamel dial and mercurial pendulum, striking the hours and half-hours on a gong, c1900, 11in (28cm) high.
$4,000–4,500 PAO

A French ormolu mantel clock, by Clauset, Chalons, with white enamel chapter ring, blue enamel and gold star outer border, later glass dome and ebonised stand, c1815, 20½in (52cm) high.
$2,600–2,900 HAM

A French gilt-bronze and porcelain figural mantel clock, by E. Delabrou, Paris, late 19thC, 23⅜in (59.5cm) high.
$3,250–4,000 SLN

A French black marble and bronzed mantel clock, by Dent, Paris, with perpetual calendar and subsidiary dials, visible Brocot escapement, bell striking movement with Brocot suspension, c1870, 16¼in (41.5cm) high.
$6,000–7,000 S(S)

◀ A Swiss Louis XVI-style white marble and gilt-bronze mantel clock, by A. l'Emeraude, Lausanne, the enamelled dial with Roman numerals, 19thC, 19¼in (49cm) high.
$1,200–1,400 S(Z)

A French bronze-mounted boulle bracket clock, by Le Faucheur, Paris, the enamel dial with Arabic numerals, striking the hours and half-hours on a bell, c1745, 21in (53cm) high, on original wall bracket.
$9,000–10,500 S(Z)

A French gilt and patinated bronze mantel clock, by Jacques Auguste d'Etour, Paris, surmounted by a figure of Diana the Huntress, with white enamel dial, the drum-cased movement countwheel striking, with silk suspension and flat bottom plates, c1776, 22in (56cm) high.
$10,000–11,500 JIL

French Bracket & Mantel Clocks

The extensive use of gilt-bronze and ormolu is highly characteristic of 19thC French clocks. Elaborate cases, particularly with figures in classical dress in miniature interior settings, were often far more significant than any mechanical refinements. Cases often represented classical or allegorical themes such as Love or Wisdom. After c1860 clocks were often made of spelter.

A French ormolu and porcelain-mounted mantel clock, by Jean le Gallais, with white enamel dial, the movement striking on a bell, c1860, 11½in (29cm) high.
$1,500–2,000 B&L

A French bronze mantel clock, by A. D. Mougin, with porcelain panel painted with an Indian scene, movement striking on a gong, late 19thC, 12¾in (32.5cm) high.
$700–800 Bri

A French Régence-style gilt-bronze-mounted rosewood and tortoiseshell bracket clock, by Planchon, Paris, the white enamelled dial above a reverse-engraved Venetian glass panel, the movement striking the hours and half-hours, c1880, 33½in (85cm) high.
$6,500–8,000 B&B

A French gilt mantel clock, by Richard, Paris, the movement striking the hours and half-hours on a bell, c1850, 17½in (44.5cm) high.
$1,400–1,550 K&D

An oak bracket clock, by Winterhalder & Hofmeier, quarter chiming on 8 bells, c1870, 20in (51cm) high.
$2,000–2,500 OT

A French Louis XV gilt-bronze-mounted boulle bracket clock, with enamel dial, the movement striking the quarters on a bell, c1745, 40½in (103cm) high, on original bracket.
$6,500–8,000 S(Z)

A French gilt and patinated-bronze mantel clock, with enamelled dial, c1815, 16½in (42cm) high.
$3,250–3,500 NOA

A French gilt-bronze mantel clock, with enamel dial, the bell-striking movement with outside countwheel and silk suspension, damage, c1820, 16½in (42cm) high.
$2,000–2,500 S(S)

A French alabaster and gilt mantel clock, with white enamel dial, striking movement, mid-19thC, 14in (35.5cm) high.
$500–600 L

A French Louis XVI-style gilt and patinated-bronze mantel clock, late 19thC, 14¾in (37.5cm) high.
$2,300–2,600 SK

A French slate and rouge marble mantel clock, with porcelain dial, movement striking the hours and half-hours, c1885, 13in (33cm) high.
$375–425 K&D

A French inlaid and ebonized mantel clock, supported by 4 Doric columns, 19thC, 19¼in (49cm) high.
$260–280 PCh

A French gilt-metal and Sèvres-style porcelain mantel clock, by L. Marti, stamped 'GR' and No. 42161, 19thC, 20in (51cm) high.
$4,200–4,500 P(NE)

A French boulle mantel clock, with embossed brass dial, 19thC, 9in (23cm) wide.
$800–1,000 Bon(W)

A French tortoiseshell and boulle marquetry bracket clock, the movement striking on a gong, c1880, 20in (51cm) high.
$6,000–7,000 JIL

A French gilt and marble Gothic-style mantel timepiece, with enamel dial, the movement with platform escapement, 19thC, 12in (30.5cm) high.
$325–350 Bon

A French gilt-metal mantel clock, with white enamel chapter ring, the movement striking on a bell, slight damage, 19thC, 18½in (47cm) high.
$775–850 MJB

◄ A French gilt-metal and silvered mantel clock, surmounted with a Roman soldier, a shield at his side, with floral-decorated porcelain dial and 2 conforming porcelain panels, a similar panel below, flanked with swags and scrolls, 19thC, 21in (53.5cm) high.
$900–1,000 MEA

A French gilt-metal and champlevé enamel mantel clock, with striking movement and enamelled pendulum, late 19thC, 14in (35.5cm) high.
$1,400–1,550 DN(H)

A French Louis XV-style boulle and ormolu bracket clock, late 19thC, 15in (38cm) high.
$1,100–1,300 S

◀ A Black Forest cuckoo clock, with ivory and bone hands and numerals, c1880, 16½in (42cm) high.
$450–480 K&D

▶ An Italian neo-classical painted and parcel-gilt mantel clock, with white enamel dial, 19thC, 26¼in (66.5cm) high.
$4,000–4,500 S(NY)

A French four-glass mantel clock, the dial decorated with champlevé enamel borders, the 2-train movement with anchor escapement and mercury compensated pendulum, striking the hours on a coiled gong, late 19thC, 9¾in (25cm) high.
$800–900 DN

A French brass and champlevé enamel mantel clock, the movement striking on a gong, No. 261548, late 19thC, 12in (30.5cm) high.
$650–730 Bea(E)

A French Louis XVI-style gilt-bronze and 'jewelled' porcelain mantel clock, with vase surmount, the dial painted with a bird, the bell striking movement with Brocot suspension, c1880, 20in (51cm) high.
$5,000–5,750 S(S)

Cross Reference
See Colour Review

A French mantel clock, inset with porcelain panels, 8-day movement, c1880, 14in (35.5cm) high.
$1,000–1,200 K&D

A French mantel clock, inset with porcelain panels, with 8-day movement, c1885, 20½in (52cm) high.
$1,000–1,200 K&D

CARRIAGE CLOCKS

A French tortoiseshell carriage clock, with cylinder movement, signed William Comyns, London 1908, 4in (10cm) high.
$1,400–1,600 AH

A French gilt-brass carriage clock, by Drocourt, with enamel dial signed J. W. Benson, London, the bell striking movement with lever escapement, c1875, 5in (12.5cm) high.
$900–1,200 S

> **Miller's is a price GUIDE not a price LIST**

◄ A French gorge-cased striking and repeating carriage clock, 19thC, 6in (15cm) high.
$1,000–1,200 PCh

A French gilt-brass carriage clock, by Margaine, with enamel dial, the gong striking movement with ratchet tooth lever escapement, c1880, 4¼in (11cm) high.
$1,000–1,200 S

► An ormolu carriage clock, with gilt painted cream-coloured dial, presentation inscription to top, dated '1906', 4in (10cm) high.
$325–400 GAK

A French brass carriage clock, with platform lever escapement striking the hours and half-hours on a gong, c1880, 6½in (16.5cm) high.
$2,500–2,750 PAO

CARTEL CLOCKS

A French ormolu cartel clock, the white enamel dial signed Cronier à Paris, 18thC, 27½in (70cm) high.
$3,250–4,000 HOK

◄ A gilt cartel clock, by Thomas Church, Norwich, the re-silvered brass dial with Roman and Arabic numerals, verge escapement, case re-gilt, c1760, 31in (78.5cm) high.
$15,500–17,000 JIL

A gilt-metal cartel clock, the dial with white enamel numerals, the floral and scroll case surmounted by 2 angels, c1860, 29in (73.5cm) high.
$2,300–2,600 GSP

GARNITURES

A French ormolu and marble clock garniture, with enamel dial, striking the hours and half-hours on a bell, late 18thC, clock 21¾in (55.5cm) high.
$6,500–7,500 B&L

A French gilt-bronze and porcelain-mounted clock garniture, with twin train movement striking the half-hours on a steel bell, 19thC, clock 15¾in (40cm) high.
$4,800–5,600 P(Sc)

A French marble, ormolu and spelter clock garniture, with bell striking movement, on marble and ormolu-mounted plinths, late 19thC, clock 24in (61cm) high.
$1,300–1,600 Mit

A black polished marble clock garniture, by Vinchon, with black marble dial, twin barrel movement with outside countwheel and pendulum striking on a bell, late 19thC, clock 21¾in (55.5cm) high.
$750–900 P(NW)

A white marble and ormolu clock garniture, with enamel dial, the circular movement striking on a bell, late 19thC, clock 18in (45.5cm) high.
$1,800–2,200 Bon

A French gilt-bronze and porcelain-mounted clock garniture, with painted ceramic dial, the twin barrel movement with pendulum, striking on a bell, 19thC, clock 26¾in (68cm) high.
$3,000–3,500 P(NW)

A French marble and ormolu clock garniture, late 19thC, clock 15½in (39.5cm) high.
$650–750 PCh

A French gilt-metal and porcelain-mounted clock garniture, striking on a bell, each piece on a shaped giltwood plinth, c1880, clock 14½in (37cm) high.
$1,300–1,600 P

LANTERN CLOCKS

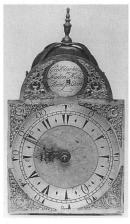

A Victorian brass lantern clock, by John Calver, Woodbridge, the twin fusee movement striking on a bell, 15¼in (39cm) high.
$1,600–2,000 P(G)

A lantern-type clock, by George Clark, London, made for the Turkish market, the brass dial with silvered chapter ring, the twin train movement with strike and verge bob pendulum, 18thC, 14in (35.5cm) high.
$1,300–1,600 P(NW)

A brass lantern clock, by Dickerson, Framlingham, with silvered chapter ring, 18th/19thC, 14in (35.5cm) high.
$2,500–3,000 GAK

A French gilt-brass lantern clock, with white enamel dial, the square brass twin train movement stamped 'C.L. à Paris', with outside countwheel, 19thC, 15in (38cm) high.
$1,000–1,150 Bon(G)

Facts in Brief

- Lantern clocks were first produced in Britain from c1600, but had already appeared c1500 in Europe, particularly in northern Italy and southern Germany.
- The name possibly derives from old English 'latten', meaning brass, of which these clocks were made, although they also resemble a domestic lantern.
- Early examples were regulated by a balance wheel escapement, but after the invention of the pendulum c1660 most pieces were made with the more precise pendulum-controlled verge or somewhat later anchor escapements.
- In the 19thC, older examples were often converted to spring-driven movements, so that they could be placed on tables.

21 Years Ago ...

A brass lantern clock, inscribed 'Tho. Wheeler, near Ye French Church', movement with anchor escapement, 17thC, 16in (40.5cm) high. **P**

Twenty-one years ago, this lantern clock by Thomas Wheeler, converted to anchor escapement and minus alarm disc and mechanism, was estimated at $3,500–4,000. A probable price today would be $10,500–11,500. For many years the price of these clocks stayed in the doldrums, partly because of the existence of many fakes and heavily restored examples. However, thanks in part to Sir George White's excellent book, *English Lantern Clocks*, they are now much better understood and good early examples, such as this one, are much sought after.

LONGCASE CLOCKS

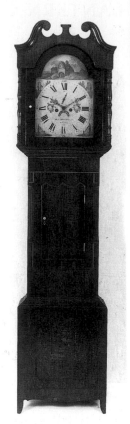

An oak longcase clock, by William Alder, Grays, the 5-pillar movement striking the hours on a bell, c1770, 79in (200.5cm) high.
$7,000–8,000 PAO

An oak longcase clock, by Joseph Allingham, Sanderstead, with brass dial, c1745, 82in (208.5cm) high.
$6,800–7,800 ALS

A mahogany longcase clock, by Bentley, Darlington, the silvered and brass arched dial with rococo spandrels and matted centre, c1776, 91in (231cm) high.
$4,800–5,600 TEN

An oak and mahogany longcase clock, by Richard Blakeborough, Otley, with painted dial, c1820, 93in (236cm) high.
$1,450–1,750 BWe

A Welsh mahogany and red walnut longcase clock, by David Bowen, Swansea, with brass dial, striking the hours on a bell, c1780, 82in (208.5cm) high.
$10,000–11,000 PAO

An oak longcase clock, by Brown, Chester, with brass dial, c1770, 86in (218.5cm) high.
$6,000–7,000 ALS

Facts in Brief

- The name longcase was adopted after the invention of the short pendulum c1650, which needed to be boxed to protect and conceal the pulleys and weights.
- At this time the pendulum was about 9in (23cm) long – cases were therefore narrow and comparatively short, around 75in (190cm) high.
- With the invention of the anchor escapement in 1670, a longer seconds-beating pendulum was required and the size of cases increased.
- Dials have also become larger, growing from 10in (25.5cm) on early clocks, to 11in (28cm) and finally to 12in (35.5cm), which is still the most popular size today.

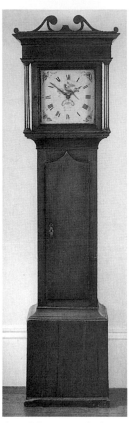

An oak longcase clock, by Boyfield, Melton, with painted dial and 30-hour bell-striking plated movement with outside countwheel, c1790, 78¾in (200cm) high.
$2,800–3,200 S

A faux tortoiseshell chinoiserie-decorated longcase clock, by Budgen, Croydon, with brass dial, mid-18thC, 89½in (227.5cm) high.
$9,000–10,500 ALS

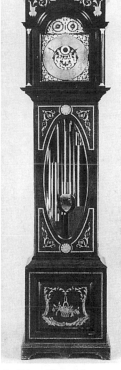

A tortoiseshell lacquer chinoiserie-decorated longcase clock, by William Carter, Southwark, with brass dial and 5-pillar movement striking the hours on a bell, c1770, 86in (218.5cm) high.
$12,500–14,000 PAO

A black lacquer chinoiserie-decorated longcase clock, by Francis Coulton, London, the 30-hour striking movement with ringed pillars, restored, c1700, 77¼in (196cm) high.
$6,500–7,500 TEN

An Edwardian mahogany and marquetry-inlaid longcase clock, by R. Collingwood, Edinburgh, the gilt-brass dial with silvered chapter ring, 3-train movement striking and bell chiming, 96in (244cm) high.
$6,500–7,500 EH

◄ An Irish mahogany longcase clock, by James Colhoun, Londonderry, with painted dial and moonphase, quarter columns to the trunk and base, c1815, 90in (228.5cm) high.
$5,000–6,000 BEE

An oak longcase clock, by John Culliford, Bristol, with brass dial and 30-hour movement, later oak case, early 18thC, 82in (208.5cm) high.
$1,000–1,150 L

A mahogany longcase clock, by John Dalrymple, Dublin, the brass dial with silvered brass chapter ring with brass corner spandrels, striking the hours on a bell, c1770, 92in (233.5cm) high.
$10,000–11,000 PAO

An oak and mahogany longcase clock, by Crawley, Wellington, with painted dial, striking the hours on a bell, c1830, 80in (203cm) high.
$2,700–3,000 K&D

An oak longcase clock, by Owen Davies, Llanidloes, with painted dial, c1820, 91in (231cm) high.
$6,500–7,500 CoA

A George III oak longcase clock, by John Draper, Maldon, with brass dial, 83⅜in (212.5cm) high.
$2,500–3,000 Oli

An oak longcase clock, by John Ebsworth, London, veneered with walnut and burr elm, the dial with brass chapter ring, the movement with 6 latched pillars, bolt-and-shutter maintaining power and countwheel striking on a bell, c1680, 76in (193cm).
$40,000–50,000 PAO

The small size, early date and 10in (25.5cm) square dial make this clock particularly desirable.

◀ A burr-walnut longcase clock, by Edward East, London, with brass dial, c1725, 94in (239cm) high.
$35,000–40,000 SOS

This clock is an excellent example from this prestigious maker, and the case is in exceptionally good condition.

An oak longcase clock, by Flight, Kinross, the painted dial with raised gilt to the corners and arch, striking the hours on a bell, c1778, 82in (208.5cm) high.
$3,200–3,700 K&D

An oak and mahogany longcase clock, by Graham, Cockermouth, with painted dial and 30-hour movement, early 19thC, 86in (218.5cm) high.
$1,450–1,700 Mit

An inlaid mahogany longcase clock, by Stephen Gwuther, Bristol, with painted dial and moonphase, 19thC, 87in (221cm) high.
$3,250–4,000 MJB

A George III oak and mahogany longcase clock, by John Latham, Manchester, with 14in (35.5cm) painted dial, 85in (216cm) high.
$1,600–2,000 Doc

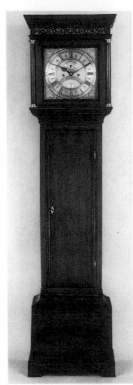

A mahogany longcase clock, by James Leigh, the arch with moonphase, dial with a matted and foliate-engraved centre, with 4-ringed pillar rack and bell striking movement, late 18thC, 93in (236cm) high.
$4,000–5,000 Bon

An oak longcase clock, by David Lockwood, Swaffham, the brass dial with applied cast-brass corner spandrels, striking the hours on a bell, c1745, 82in (208.5cm) high.
$7,500–8,500 PAO

A flame mahogany longcase clock, by Lowe, Arbroath, crossbanded and inlaid with mahogany and rosewood, with painted dial, c1830, 82¼in (209cm) high.
$6,500–7,500 ALS

A walnut longcase clock, by D. Hawthorne, Darlington, quarter repeating on 6 bells, case later, early 18thC, 84in (213.5cm) high.
$3,800–4,400 JNic

► A black and gilt japanned longcase clock, by Nathaniel Hodges, London, the dial with a brass chapter ring, the 5-ringed pillar movement with a small outside countwheel striking on a bell, early 18thC, 85in (216cm) high.
$2,000–2,300 Bon

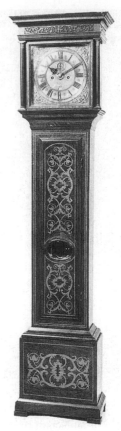

A walnut and marquetry longcase clock, by Jacob Hasius, London, the brass dial with silvered chapter ring and alarm, the 2-train movement striking on a bell, alarm missing, c1710, 82in (208.5cm) high.
$7,500–8,500 HYD

A George II silver basket, with swing handle, maker's mark of Samuel Herbert & Co, London 1754, 14½in (37cm) wide, 53oz.
$11,500–13,000 Bon

A George III silver basket, by John Lawford and William Vincent, London 1762, 13¼in (33.5cm) wide, 24½oz.
$4,500–5,500 S

A silver bread basket, with maker's mark of Harrison Brothers & Howson, Sheffield 1910, 11in (28cm) wide.
$1,000–1,200 SHa

A Commonwealth silver porringer and cover, by John Thomason, York, 1659, 5¼in (13.5cm) high, 17½oz.
$40,000–50,000 S

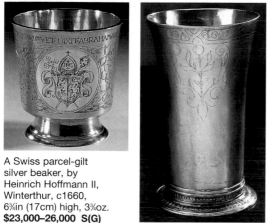

◀ A silver beaker, maker's mark 'WI', London 1599, 5½in (14cm) high, 7oz.
$18,500–21,000 S

A Swiss parcel-gilt silver beaker, by Heinrich Hoffmann II, Winterthur, c1660, 6¾in (17cm) high, 3¾oz.
$23,000–26,000 S(G)

A Charles II silver wine taster, maker's mark 'RM', London 1662, 3¾in (9.5cm) wide, 3oz.
$3,500–4,000 HAM

A silver rose bowl, by James Garrard, with detachable rim and gilt interior, 1887, 9½in (24cm) diam, 103oz.
$4,800–5,200 TEN

An American silver-gilt punchbowl, by Gorham Mfg Co, with ruby glass liner, 1893, 16½in (42cm) diam.
$32,500–35,500 S(NY)

A pair of William III silver candlesticks, repaired, maker's mark of John Laughton, London 1699, 6in (15cm) high.
$13,500–15,500 Bon

A German parcel-gilt silver toilet box, by Albrecht Biller, with applied scrolling acanthus, 9 embossed enamelled ovals, wood inserts and velvet lining, c1690, 14in (35.5cm) wide, 83oz.
$55,000–60,000 S

A pair of Dutch silver candlesticks, by Albert Gaillard, 1745, 13in (33cm) high.
$14,500–16,000 S(G)

◀ A pair of silver five-light candelabra, by Tiffany & Co, New York, c1885, 16½in (42cm) high, 115½oz.
$16,500–19,000 S(NY)

A pair of silver candelabra, by Georg Jensen, 1918, 13⅛in (34.5cm) high.
$35,000–40,000 SFL

A George I silver coffee pot, by Isaac Cookson, Newcastle 1722, 12in (30.5cm) high, 30oz.
$3,500–4,000 P(NE)

An Austrian silver three-piece tea set, teapot by Mayerhofer & Klinkosch, Vienna 1840, teapot 8½in (21.5cm) high, 77oz.
$3,500–4,000 S(G)

A George III silver epergne, by Thomas Pitts, London 1771, 16in (40.5cm) high, 131½oz.
$32,500–35,500 S

A Victorian silver five-piece tea and coffee service, maker WS, Birmingham 1875, coffee pot 12½in (32cm) high, 101oz, in an oak travelling case.
$2,600–3,200 P(E)

A silver-gilt cup and cover, raised on a plinth, by S & Co, London 1913, 24½in (62cm) high, 200oz.
$9,000–10,000 B

A silver-gilt-mounted glass claret jug, by Reily & Storer, London 1842, 12in (30.5cm) high.
$10,000–11,500 S(G)

A pair of silver embossed salts, by William Eley, London 1829, 3½in (9cm) diam.
$1,100–1,300 DIC

A Dutch parcel-gilt trophy, in the form of a drinking horn, 1867, 19¾in (50cm) high, 164oz.
$9,500–11,500 Bon

A George I silver kettle-on-stand, maker's mark of Gabriel Sleath, London 1726, 13½in (34.5cm) high.
$8,000–9,500 Bon

A pair of George IV silver wine coolers, by Thomas Blagdin, Thomas Hodgson, Samuel Kirkby, Joseph Elliott and Jonathon Woollin, Sheffield 1829, 10½in (26.5cm) high.
$21,000–24,000 S(S)

A Regency silver soup tureen and cover, by Mackay, Edinburgh 1810, 15in (38cm) wide, 123oz.
$4,500–5,500 WW

A George II silver tankard, by Thomas Whipham, London 1746, 6in (15cm) high, 31oz.
$2,500–3,000 HAM

A George III silver wine cooler, by Robert Garrard, liner missing, London 1818, 10in (25.5cm) high.
$14,600–16,200 S

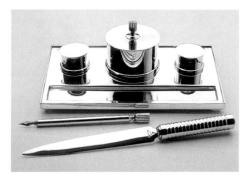

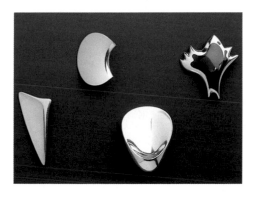

A George III brass-bound mahogany table clock, by John Ellicott, London, with fusee movement, verge escapement, parts missing, c1770, 26½in (67.5cm) high.
$6,000–6,500 S

A walnut bracket clock, by Frodsham & Baker, London, with single train fusee anchor movement, c1860, on a carved bracket, 53½in (136cm) high overall.
$2,500–3,000 TEN

A mahogany table clock, with 2-train fusee movement, anchor escapement, c1800, handle later, 15¾in (40cm) high.
$4,500–5,000 S(S)

A rosewood bracket clock, inlaid with boxwood, marked Depree & Young, Exeter, with triple fusee movement, late 19thC, 22in (56cm) high.
$2,800–3,200 TMA

A rosewood and burr-walnut mantel clock, by Wassell & Halford, London, c1875, 11½in (29cm) high.
$6,800–7,400 PAO

A Victorian ebonized bracket clock, 8-bell quarter-chiming with hour strike on a gong, 22in (56cm) high.
$2,500–3,000 P(S)

◀ A late Victorian gilt-metal-mounted ebonized bracket clock, 18in (45.5cm) high.
$2,600–3,200 GSP

A mahogany bracket clock, by Farr & Son, Bristol, with fusee movement, c1820, 19in (48.5cm) high.
$4,000–4,500 DQ

◀ A William IV walnut bracket clock, by Larard, 23½in (59.5cm) high.
$2,600–3,200 B&B

An ebonized fruitwood bracket clock, by William Robson, London, with 3-train movement, anchor escapement, c1810, 25in (63.5cm) high.
$10,000–11,000 PAO

A brass-cased bell-striking and repeating carriage clock, by Paul Garnier, with lever escapement, mid-19thC, 6¼in (16cm) high.
$1,100–1,400 Bon

A gilt-brass carriage clock, set with paste stones, with 8-day movement, platform lever escapement, c1890, 5¾in (14.5cm) high.
$1,400–1,600 JIL

A French and English gilt-brass carriage clock, with cameo glass panels, repeating gong-striking movement, platform lever escapement, c1880, 5¼in (13.5cm) high.
$3,700–4,400 S

A bronze and ormolu clock garniture, signed Le Sieur à Paris, c1820, clock 15¾in (40cm) high.
$14,500–16,000 B&L

A gilt-bronze clock garniture, by A. Carrier-Belleuse, movement signed Lemerle & Charpentier, c1870, clock 34in (86.5cm) high.
$22,500–26,000 S

A French *tôle peinte* and porcelain clock garniture, movement signed Samuel Martin, now with platform lever escapement, 19thC, 27¼in (69cm) high.
$2,400–2,700 P

◄ A German chamber clock, with iron movement, verge and balance escapement, striking on bells, 16thC, 20½in (52cm) high, with later wall bracket.
$14,500–16,000 S

A Sèvres porcelain and ormolu clock garniture, 19thC, 20in (51cm) high.
$5,600–6,200 GOR(B)

A gilt-bronze-mounted porcelain clock garniture, movement stamped Japy Frères, late 19thC, clock 19in (48.5cm) high.
$11,500–13,000 B&B

◄ A George II lantern timepiece, by Jasper Taylor, London, the 30-hour weight-driven movement with verge escapement, 8½in (21.5cm) high.
$4,200–4,800 DN

► A brass lantern clock, signed Jno Rawlings, Mortimore, 18thC, 15¼in (39cm) high.
$3,500–4,500 S(S)

A walnut 8-day longcase clock, by Thos Baker, Portsmouth, 5-pillar internal rack striking movement, c1725, 87in (221cm) high.
$14,500–18,000 ALS

A Welsh mahogany 8-day longcase clock, by John Bank, c1860, 90½in (230cm) high.
$4,800–5,200 S(S)

An oak 8-day longcase clock, by Thos Beeching, Rye, c1735, 83¾in (212.5cm) high.
$9,000–10,000 ALS

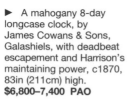

A Victorian oak and mahogany 8-day longcase clock, by Beavington, Stourbridge, 92in (233.5cm) high.
$3,200–3,600 RBB

An oak 8-day longcase clock, by Coates, Cirencester, c1785, 81½in (207cm) high.
$6,000–7,000 ALS

A mahogany 8-day longcase clock, by Meshach Britton, Devizes, c1765, 91in (231cm) high.
$14,000–16,000 PAO

A burr-walnut 8-day longcase clock, by Camerer Kuss & Co, London, striking the hours and quarters on 5 gongs, c1880, 94in (239cm) high.
$13,000–14,500 PAO

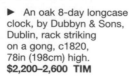

▶ A mahogany 8-day longcase clock, by James Cowans & Sons, Galashiels, with deadbeat escapement and Harrison's maintaining power, c1870, 83in (211cm) high.
$6,800–7,400 PAO

A mahogany 8-day longcase clock, by James Cowans & Sons, Galashiels, with deadbeat escapement and Harrison's maintaining power, c1870, 83in (211cm) high.

A George III inlaid mahogany quarter-chiming longcase clock, by David Collier, Gatley, damaged and repaired, 92in (233.5cm) high.
$8,000–9,500 S(NY)

▶ An oak 8-day longcase clock, by Dubbyn & Sons, Dublin, rack striking on a gong, c1820, 78in (198cm) high.
$2,200–2,600 TIM

A walnut marquetry longcase clock, by Christopher Gould, London, with anchor escapement, late 17th/early 18thC, 85in (216cm) high.
$23,000–26,000 P

A walnut marquetry month-going longcase clock, by Charles Gretton, London, the movement with 6 ring-turned pillars, bolt-and-shutter maintaining power, c1695, 78½in (199.5cm) high.
$26,000–32,000 S

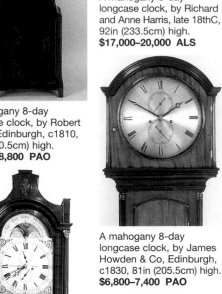

A mahogany 8-day longcase clock, by Robert Green, Edinburgh, c1810, 79in (200.5cm) high.
$7,800–8,800 PAO

A mahogany 8-day longcase clock, by Richard and Anne Harris, late 18thC, 92in (233.5cm) high.
$17,000–20,000 ALS

A mahogany 8-day longcase clock, by James Howden & Co, Edinburgh, c1830, 81in (205.5cm) high.
$6,800–7,400 PAO

A pine 8-day longcase clock, by Jacob Higman, Cornwall, c1820, 79in (200.5cm) high.
$1,800–2,200 ESA

▶ A flame mahogany 8-day longcase clock, by Joseph Hill, c1840, 86in (218.5cm) high.
$9,000–10,500 ALS

A mahogany 8-day longcase clock, by Thomas Husband, Hull, c1785, 95in (241.5cm) high.
$12,000–16,000 SoS

▶ An oak 8-day longcase clock, by Anthony Hutchinson, Leeds, movement not working, c1770, carving later, 88in (223.5cm) high.
$2,500–3,000 WBH

An oak 8-day longcase clock, by Stephen King, Chippenham, the door flanked by mahogany reeded canted corners, c1795, 81in (205.5cm) high.
$5,600–6,200 PAO

► An oak 8-day longcase clock, by James Powell, Worcester, with mahogany and shell inlay, c1820, 81in (205.5cm) high.
$5,200–6,200 PHA

A mahogany 8-day longcase clock, by James Melluish, Batheaston, early 19thC, 86in (218.5cm) high.
$5,500–6,500 ALS

A mahogany 8-day longcase clock, by Peter & Semple, Dublin, with barometer and thermometer, c1810, 78in (198cm) high.
$5,200–5,700 TIM

► A George III mahogany 8-day longcase clock, by James Stewart, London, slight restoration, 79½in (202cm) high.
$10,000–11,500 TEN

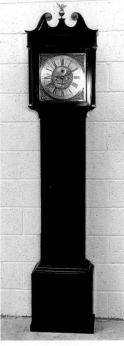

A mahogany 8-day longcase clock, by Thomas Sanderson, Dublin, c1735, 93in (236cm) high.
$10,000–11,500 BEE

◄ A flame-mahogany and brass-inlaid 8-day longcase clock, by George Lloyd, London, c1760, 85in (216cm) high.
$20,000–23,500 SoS

A George II red and gilt japanned longcase clock, by Richard Peckover, London, decoration restored, c1750, 89in (226cm) high.
$9,000–10,000 S

A Georgian mahogany 8-day longcase clock, by James Sandiford, Manchester, 87in (221cm) high.
$7,500–9,000 RBB

◄ A George III figured-mahogany 8-day longcase clock, by Adam Travers, London, c1783, 104in (264cm) high.
$11,500–13,500 HBC

John Myers, Southwark. Classic London Mahogany with rocking ship automaton "The Torbay", late 18th century, 92.5in (235cm).

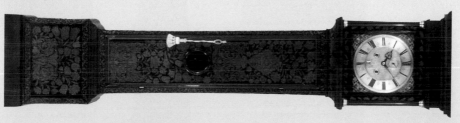

Markwick, London. Classic month going Walnut & Marquetry with original detachable caddy top, circa 1700, 89in (235cm) - 84in (213cm).

A mahogany 8-day longcase clock, by William Wasbrough, Bristol, late 18thC, 88in (223.5cm) high.
$11,500–13,000 ALS

A George III oak 30-hour longcase clock, by John Verow, Hinckley, c1800, 86in (218.5cm) high.
$5,000–6,000 PHA

An oak 8-day longcase clock, by Rob Trippet, London, early 18thC, 82in (208.5cm) high.
$2,500–3,000 HBC

A Charles II olivewood parquetry and marquetry longcase clock, with latched movement, bolt-and-shutter maintaining power and outside countwheel, c1685, 75½in (192cm) high.
$23,000–26,000 S

A Federal inlaid mahogany longcase clock, by Simon Willard, Massachusetts, slight damage, c1790, 89in (226cm) high.
$40,000–50,000 SK(B)

A George III mahogany longcase clock, with associated brass dial and movement, 91in (231cm) high.
$4,000–5,000 SWO

A walnut 30-hour longcase clock, with birdcage movement and single hand, c1740, 83in (211cm) high.
$3,500–4,000 K&D

◀ A Swedish painted longcase clock, signed Prinsz, Stockholm, late 18thC, 91¼in (232cm) high.
$10,000–11,500 S(Z)

A Louis XVI carved oak 8-day *comtoise* clock, c1800, 97in (246.5cm) high.
$3,500–4,000 B&B

◀ A French 8-day *comtoise* longcase clock, with painted pendulum, c1850, 105in (266.5cm) high.
$1,100–1,300 LPA

A 'Monarch' oak shelf clock, by Ansonia, with 8-day striking movement, c1895, 24in (61cm) high.
$850–950 OT

A Régence boulle bracket clock, signed Baltazar Baltazar à Paris, c1715, 53in (134.5cm) high.
$7,500–9,000 S(Z)

A French red boulle mantel clock, by J-B Delettrez, the bell striking movement with Brocot escapement, c1865, 17in (43cm) high.
$3,000–3,500 S

A French gilt-bronze four-glass mantel clock, by A. D. Mougin, with 8-day countwheel movement, re-gilt, c1870, 17½in (44.5cm) high.
$7,300–8,000 JIL

A Louis Philippe gilt-bronze mantel clock, signed Guymont, Paris, with 8-day half-hour striking movement, mid-19thC, 20in (51cm) high.
$5,400–6,200 B&B

A French gilt-bronze mantel clock, by Japy Frères, Paris, c1880, 21in (53.5cm) high.
$4,000–5,000 SO

An Empire gilt-bronze portico mantel clock, the dial inscribed Marcais Her. A Lafleche, early 19thC, 18in (46cm) high.
$3,500–4,500 B&B

A French porcelain and ormolu-mounted mantel clock, the movement by Japy Frères, 19thC, 19in (48.5cm) high.
$5,000–5,500 TEN

A Louis XV painted bracket clock, with single train movement, signed Musson à Paris, 18thC, 21¾in (55cm) high.
$4,500–5,500 S(Z)

An Austrian Empire carved giltwood and black painted 'moving eye' automaton mantel clock, the movement with anchor escapement rack striking on 2 top gongs, c1800, 26¾in (68cm) high.
$14,000–15,500 S(Am)

A French gilt mantel clock, with tower bell strike, c1840, 18in (45.5cm) high.
$1,300–1,600 SO

A brass-cased mantel clock, with 8-day movement, c1885, 19½in (49.5cm) high.
$850–1,000 K&D

A French gilt-spelter mantel clock, inset with porcelain panels, c1870, 17in (43cm) high.
$2,000–2,200 CHe

A French mantel clock, inset with porcelain panels, 8-day movement, c1880, 14in (35.5cm) high.
$1,000–1,200 K&D

A French simulated tortoiseshell and gilt-brass mantel clock, 19thC, 13in (33cm) high.
$2,000–2,200 Bon(W)

A French ormolu mantel clock, inset with porcelain panels, the dial with retailer's name Howell James & Co, maker to the Queen, late 19thC, 10½in (26.5cm) high.
$650–800 TMA

A Victorian skeleton clock, on velvet plinth, with glass dome, c1860, 16in (42cm) high.
$2,000–2,500 S

A brass quarter-chiming skeleton clock, 19thC, 21in (53.5cm) high.
$4,200–5,200 P

A brass-inlaid mahogany case wall clock, by G. Esplin, Wigan, c1850, dial 12in (30.5cm) diam.
$3,000–3,500 PAO

◄ A mahogany wall timepiece, signed Leroux, London, late 18th/early 19thC, 26in (66cm) high.
$4,500–5,000 P

A seconds-beating wall regulator, by Lenzkirch, with gridiron pendulum, c1880, 79½in (202cm) high.
$10,000–11,000 DRA

◄ A mahogany veneered calendar clock, by Seth Thomas Clock Co, Connecticut, with 8-day spring movement, c1863, 28in (71cm) high.
$1,100–1,300 OT

A clock, barometer and thermometer in cast-iron case, by J. J. Wainwright & Co, Birmingham, c1875, 25in (63.5cm) high.
$350–400 RTw

◄ A German 8-day weight-driven striking wall clock, c1890, 51in (129.5cm) high.
$1,200–1,300 DQ

A Regency mahogany longcase regulator, signed W. G. Connell, London, c1820, 78in (198cm) high. **$20,000–25,000 DRA**

▶ A satin-birch Vienna regulator, by Joseph Petrovits, 19thC, 39in (99cm) high. **$1,200–1,300 Bea(E)**

A mahogany Vienna regulator, by Kralik, c1840, 39in (99cm) high. **$4,000–5,000 S**

▶ An ebonized Viennese regulator, c1810, 76in (193cm) high. **$25,000–30,000 GeC**

A mahogany regulator, by Gillett Johnston, Croydon, c1900, 87in (221cm) high. **$5,000–6,500 SO**

An 18ct gold and diamond-set quarter-repeating hunter cased pocket watch, by Henry Capt, Geneva, c1900, 39mm diam.
$3,200–3,600 S(SI)

A Hebdomas 8-day pocket watch, with dial for Turkish market, c1880, 45mm diam.
$650–750 BLH

A French *oignon* watch, signed Pasquier, in a chased and engraved gilt-metal case, c1695, 58mm diam.
$4,000–5,000 PT

A gold and enamel pair-cased verge watch, by James Tregent, London, 1767, 45mm diam.
$2,500–3,000 S

An 18ct gold half hunter pocket watch, by John Walker, London, 1871, 50mm diam.
$420–480 WilP

A silver repoussé pair-cased verge watch, the full plate fire-gilt movement with square baluster pillars, signed T. Simont, 1785, 51mm diam.
$1,300–1,500 PT

A Corum 18ct gold diamond and sapphire astronomical bracelet watch, c1975, 32mm diam.
$3,500–4,000 S(SI)

An Omega 9ct gold slimline quartz watch, c1975, 28mm diam.
$1,450–1,600 BWC

A Cartier 'Tortue' 18ct gold, diamond and pearl bracelet watch, c1985, 23mm long.
$10,500–11,500 S(NY)

◀ A Patek Philippe 18ct pink gold wristwatch, 1950s, 31mm diam.
$4,500–5,000 P(Gen)

A Patek Philippe 18ct rose gold wristwatch, c1940, 6¼in (16cm) long.
$2,700–3,000 S(LA)

◀ A Rolex 18ct gold Oyster automatic wristwatch, with black dial, late 1970s, 35mm diam.
$5,000–5,700 RBB

A harbour master's wheel barometer, by Bryson, Edinburgh, in oak case, c1860, 40in (101.5cm) high.
$3,200–3,700 PAO

This barometer is unusual and possibly unique.

An inlaid mahogany wheel barometer, by Chas Aiano, London, with wooden bezel, c1785, 36in (91.5cm) high.
$5,000–6,000 AW

► An oak mercury-driven barograph, by Negretti & Zambra, London, with fusee clock, c1880, 46in (117cm) high.
$6,200–6,800 AW

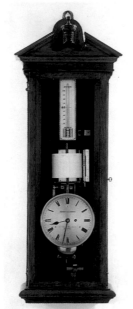

A mahogany stick barometer, by Fasana, Bath, c1810, 38in (96.5cm) high.
$4,000–4,500 PAO

A George II mahogany stick barometer, by George Hallifax, Doncaster, the mechanism with replaced siphon tube, c1750, 47in (119.5cm) high.
$23,000–26,000 S

A satinwood wheel barometer, by Porri, Nottingham, c1815, 38in (96.5cm) high.
$4,000–5,000 PAO

A mahogany stick barometer, by Lincoln, London, with silvered brass plates and fan-inlaid trunk, c1790, 37½in (95.5cm) high.
$6,000–7,000 AW

◄ An early Victorian papier mâché wheel barometer and thermometer, inlaid with mother-of-pearl and gilt, 39¼in (100cm) high.
$1,400–1,550 Bea(E)

A mahogany clock, barometer and thermometer, by Sweet, London, unrestored, 19thC, 42in (106.5cm) high.
$2,000–2,200 CAG

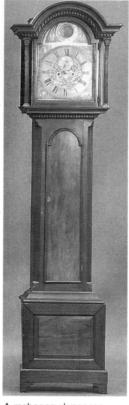

A flame-mahogany longcase clock, by Humphrey of Calne, the painted dial with moonphase, c1815, 91in (231cm) high.
$10,500–12,000 SoS

A mahogany longcase clock, by A. James, Neath, with flame veneers and inlaid with chequered stringing, white dial, striking the hours on a bell, c1850, 88in (223.5cm) high.
$8,500–9,500 PAO

A mahogany longcase clock, with brass dial, minor restorations to dial plate, late 18thC, 93¼in (237cm) high.
$3,000–3,500 P(WM)

An oak and mahogany banded longcase clock, by Jno Jaques, Wakefield, the brass dial with silvered chapter ring, late 18thC, 86in (218.5cm) high.
$2,000–2,500 M

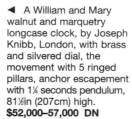

◄ A William and Mary walnut and marquetry longcase clock, by Joseph Knibb, London, with brass and silvered dial, the movement with 5 ringed pillars, anchor escapement with 1¼ seconds pendulum, 81½in (207cm) high.
$52,000–57,000 DN

Joseph Knibb is one of the most eminent of English clockmakers. Born in 1640, he moved to Oxford in 1667 where he worked as a gardener to Trinity College. This may have been a device to allow him to practise as a clockmaker in the city even though he was not a freeman. He was admitted in 1668, moved to London around 1677, and supplied clocks to Charles II. He is particularly noted for the excellence of his work and the elegance of his clocks. A sale was held of his clocks in 1697 and shortly after this he retired to Hanslope, Bucks. Examples of his clocks can be found in many major collections.

A mahogany longcase clock, by Thos Mills, Newport, with ebony and boxwood stringing and painted dial, early 19thC, 82in (208.5cm) high.
$9,000–10,000 ALS

An oak, mahogany and fruitwood-inlaid longcase clock, by D. Moore, Coventry, with painted dial, 4-pillar rack and bell striking movement, early 19thC, 89in (226cm) high.
$2,000–2,500 Bon

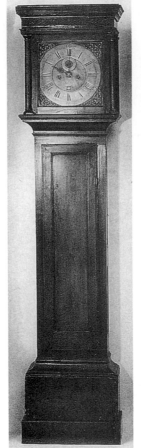

An oak and mahogany crossbanded longcase clock, by Moore, Perth, the brass dial with silvered chapter ring, late 18thC, 88in (223.5cm) high.
$2,500–3,000 MSW

An oak and mahogany crossbanded longcase clock, by Jeremy Murch, Honiton, with brass dial, silvered chapter ring and engraved centre, striking the hours on a bell, c1770, 80in (203cm) high.
$8,000–9,000 PAO

A George II oak longcase clock, by William Parry, Newport, with brass dial and 5-pillar movement rack striking on a bell, 77½in (197cm) high.
$3,200–3,500 DN

An oak and mahogany crossbanded longcase clock, by Pannell, Northallerton, with rocking ship and brass dial, late 18thC, 90in (228.5cm) high.
$3,250–4,000 DD

▶ A George III oak longcase clock, by Joseph Quarman, Temple Cloud, with brass dial and 30-hour movement, 82in (208cm) high.
$1,400–1,600 L

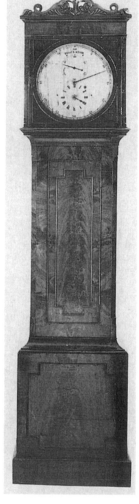
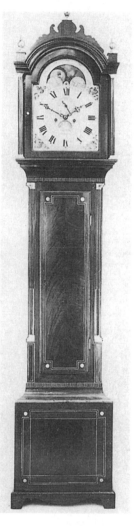

An oak longcase clock, by Richard Roe, Haslemere, the 30-hour plated movement with external locking plate, striking on a bell, c1770, 77¼in (196cm) high.
$1,600–1,900 S(S)

An oak longcase clock, by James Rule, Portsmouth, with brass dial, now with gong strike, lacks finials, 18thC, 82in (208cm) high.
$3,000–3,500 Bri

21 Years Ago …

A mahogany longcase clock, by J. Ship, Long Melford, late 18thC, 85in (216cm) high. **OL**

Twenty-one years ago this late 18th-century painted-dial longcase clock was estimated at $850–950. Today, early fine-quality longcase clocks, particularly those with moonphases, are hard to find and this clock has probably increased in value to $7,250–8,000. Interestingly, only a few examples such as this were illustrated in the first issue of *Miller's Antiques Price Guide,* and in those days auction houses rarely included them in their sales.

A Cuban mahogany longcase clock, by Richard Roughsedge, Twickenham, the case inlaid with later shells, the brass dial with silvered brass chapter ring, the 5-pillar movement with anchor escapement and striking the hours on a bell, c1770, 94in (239cm) high.
$16,000–18,000 PAO

▶ A mahogany longcase clock, by Russell, Belfast, with painted dial, early 19thC, 90in (228.5cm) high.
$7,750–8,500 ALS

An Irish mahogany
longcase clock, by
J. Russell, Kingstown,
the enamel dial decorated
with gold leaf, with
rack striking movement
striking on a gong, c1870,
82in (208.5cm) high.
$5,000–5,500 TIM

A George III oak and
mahogany crossbanded
longcase clock, by
George Searle, Chudleigh,
with moonphase to arch,
87in (221cm) high.
$3,500–4,250 MJB

A mahogany longcase
clock, by Geo Slater,
Burslem, with 4-pillar
movement striking on a bell,
19thC, 89in (226cm) high.
$2,000–2,200 Bon(C)

An oak and mahogany
crossbanded longcase
clock, by Smith and
Walton, with painted dial,
19thC, 89in (226cm) high.
$2,000–2,500 WL

A Victorian mahogany longcase clock, by William Spence Hamilton, with white painted dial, the twin train movement with anchor escapement, 82¼in (209cm) high.
$2,750–3,250 P(Sc)

A mahogany longcase clock, by Richard Stimson, Ely, with flame veneers and brass dial, striking the hours on a bell, c1780, 99in (251.5cm) high.
$14,500–16,500 PAO

A *faux* tortoiseshell chinoiserie-decorated lacquer longcase clock, by Smorthwait, Colchester, with brass dial, the 5-pillar movement with internal countwheel, early 18thC, 86in (218.5cm) high.
$9,000–10,500 ALS

A Cuban mahogany longcase clock, by Edward Townley, Dundalk, with painted dial, standing on front feet only, c1794, 93in (236cm) high.
$7,500–8,500 BEE

A mahogany longcase clock, by James Upjohn, London, with brass dial, striking the hours on a bell, c1770, 87in (221cm) high.
$19,500–22,500 PAO

◄ A mahogany longcase clock, by Tucker, Coleford, with flame veneers and white dial, striking the hours on a bell, c1845, 87in (221cm) high.
$7,000–8,000 PAO

A mahogany and line-inlaid longcase clock, by W. Vaughan, Newport, late 19thC, 82¾in (210cm) high.
$3,500–4,200 Bri

A walnut longcase clock, by Thomas Wagstaffe, London, with well-figured veneers and chequered line inlay, brass dial with separate chapter ring and spandrels, the 5-pillar movement striking the hours on a bell, c1760, 88in (223.5cm) high.
$22,000–24,500 PAO

An oak longcase clock, by Will Wilks, Wolverton, with brass dial, striking on a bell, repaired, early 19thC, 80½in (204.5cm) high.
$1,300–1,600 WW

◄ An inlaid mahogany longcase clock, by T. Wilson, Guisborough, with arched painted dial, c1800, 92½in (235cm) high.
$1,800–2,000 Bea(E)

A mahogany 8-day longcase clock, by William Wasbrough, Bristol, late 18thC, 88in (223.5cm) high.
$11,000–13,000 ALS

A mahogany 8-day longcase clock, inscribed Edm'd Whittingham, London, late 18thC, later inlaid, 86in (218.5cm) high.
$4,500–5,200 WW

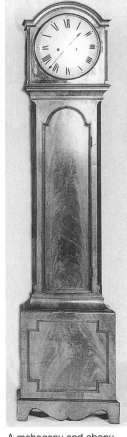

A George III oak longcase clock, by Wilmshurst, Brighton, with brass dial and 30-hour movement, 82½in (209.5cm) high.
$900–1,100 Doc

An inlaid mahogany longcase clock, by David Wyllie, Saltcoats, with brass dial, silvered chapter ring and twin train movement with anchor escapement, 19thC, 91in (231cm) high.
$1,600–1,800 P

A walnut longcase clock, with herringbone inlay, silvered and brass dial, early 18thC, 90¼in (229cm) high.
$5,750–6,500 TEN

A mahogany and ebony-inlaid longcase clock, with white enamel dial, early 19thC, 86½in (220cm) high.
$3,200–3,500 P(NW)

A mahogany longcase clock, the painted dial with moonphase, mid-19thC, 90in (228.5cm) high.
$2,000–2,300 BWe

A Regency mahogany and ebony-inlaid longcase clock, with white enamel dial and striking movement, 80in (203cm) high.
$2,300–2,600 FHF

An oak and mahogany crossbanded longcase clock, with painted dial and 30-hour movement, 19thC, 79in (201cm) high.
$1,400–1,600 WL

A northern French oak *comtoise* clock, with Flemish-influenced carving, c1850, 104in (264cm) high.
$2,000–2,500 LPA

A French provincial painted fruitwood *comtoise* clock, with embossed gilt-brass pendulum, c1820, 91in (231cm) high.
$1,600–2,000 NOA

A French provincial grain-painted and ebonized *comtoise* clock, by Felix Depay, Lamure, with enamel dial, the pendulum bob inset with an image of Napoleon, c1835, 92in (233.5cm) high.
$2,500–3,000 NOA

A Continental neo-classical style oak and fruitwood longcase clock, with embossed brass and copper dial, c1825, 94½in (240cm) high.
$1,800–2,000 NOA

A mahogany, satinwood and ebony line-inlaid longcase clock, with painted dial, inscribed Cork, c1800, 91¾in (233cm) high.
$3,000–3,500 HOK

A Scandinavian carved and painted longcase clock, with painted metal face, 18thC, 91in (231cm) high.
$3,200–3,600 SLM

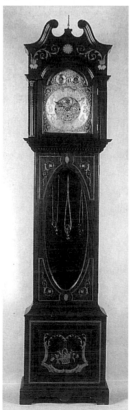

An inlaid mahogany longcase clock, c1910, 98½in (250cm) high.
$6,000–7,000 S(S)

A French musical picture clock, the gong striking movement signed Hoffman Frères, Paris, with anchor escapement, c1860, 34 x 40in (86 x 102cm).
$3,200–3,600 S

An Austro-Hungarian *grande sonnerie* musical picture clock, with 3-train silk suspension trip-repeating movement striking on 2 gongs, in a giltwood and gesso frame, c1840, 39 x 36½in (99 x 93cm).
$5,000–6,000 S

Further Reading

Miller's Clocks & Barometers Buyer's Guide, Miller's Publications, 1997

◀ A French ship's quarterdeck automaton clock, with striking movement, c1870, 11in (28cm) high.
$3,250–3,750 CHe

A Victorian oak clock, in the form of St Peter's Church, Brighton, with triple fusee movement chiming the quarters on 8 bells, striking the hours on a gong, backplate inscribed Boxell, Brighton, on an oak table, 86in (218.5cm) high overall.
$3,500–4,500 RTo

Did You Know?

The craze for novelty clocks in the 19thC produced a variety of inventive designs, such as the picture clock. The movement was concealed behind a painted canvas, the dial appearing through a hole which was usually incorporated in a church tower so that it formed part of the picture. Many also had a musical movement concealed behind the canvas, operated by pulling a trip to one side.

A French alabaster vase-shaped clock, with revolving white enamel dials, the base with applied ormolu decoration, 19thC, 11in (28cm) high.
$3,500–4,000 B&L

A Louis XVI-style urn-shaped clock, the revolving bands with enamel numerals, 19thC, 19½in (49.5cm) high.
$2,500–3,000 Bea(E)

SKELETON CLOCKS

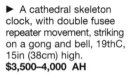

A brass skeleton clock, the fretted silvered dial with nameplate inscribed E. Bragg, Windsor, the chain and fusee movement with passing strike, on a white marble base, late 19thC, 15¾in (40cm) high, with glass dome.
$1,000–1,200 CAG

A brass skeleton timepiece, by Joseph and John Brookhouse, Derby, the month-going movement with twin fusees and barrels driving the intermediate wheel, the detached lever with jewelled pallets, 19thC, 12in (30.5cm) high.
$4,000–5,000 P

A French ormolu clock and calendar, inscribed Lepine, Paris, early 19thC, 18in (45.5cm) high.
$8,000–9,000 S(NY)

A brass skeleton clock, by Henry Marc, Paris, with enamel dial, striking movement, and a glass dome, late 19thC, 22in (56cm) high.
$700–900 E

► A cathedral skeleton clock, with double fusee repeater movement, striking on a gong and bell, 19thC, 15in (38cm) high.
$3,500–4,000 AH

◄ A brass skeleton clock, the silvered chapter ring signed Sowter, Oxford, the twin fusee movement with anchor escapement striking on a gong, 19thC, 12½in (32cm) high, with glass dome.
$2,600–3,000 P(E)

A French gilt-brass and white marble musical skeleton timepiece, with chain fusee movement, pinwheel escapement, later enamel chapter ring, musical movement in replaced ebonized and brass-mounted base, centre seconds replaced, c1800, 17½in (44.5cm) high.
$4,000–5,000 P

► A brass skeleton clock, with silvered chapter ring, the single train movement with passing strike, on a mahogany base, with glass dome, c1870, 18in (45.5cm) high.
$2,000–2,300 GH

A brass skeleton timepiece, with pierced chapter ring and fusee movement with anchor escapement, on an ebonized base, 19thC, 14¼in (36cm) high.
$725–800 P(E)

A black lacquer brass-faced wall clock, by William Andrews, London, with arched dial and 30-hour movement, 1730, 40in (101.5cm) high.
$8,000–9,500 PHA

A black japanned Act of Parliament clock, by Thomas and John Fardon, with white painted dial and gilt chinoiserie decoration, 18thC, 60in (152.5cm) high.
$8,000–9,000 S(NY)

A stained wood wall clock, by J. Hill & Son, Teignmouth, 19thC, 16in (40.5cm) diam.
$570–650 Bea(E)

A German wall clock, by Gustav Becker, with striking movement, c1890, 46in (117cm) high.
$1,100–1,300 DQ

A mahogany wall clock, by Gillett & Johnston, Croydon, marked ER for Edward Regis, with single train fusee movement, c1908, 23⅛in (59.5cm) high.
$2,000–2,300 PAO

A wall clock movement, by Seymour, Wantage, in a bird-cage frame, with brass dial and single steel hand, 30-hour movement striking on a bell, outside countwheel, early 18thC, 10in (25.5cm) high.
$650–730 WW

A Continental ormolu and mother-of-pearl wall timepiece, with associated gilt watch dial signed Breguet et Fils, verge watch movement, 19thC, 13in (33cm) high, with later mahogany case.
$425–500 P

A mahogany drop-dial station wall clock, by Thwaites & Reed, retailed by Donne & Son, London, with fusee movement, c1889, 22in (56cm) high.
$1,000–1,100 K&D

A mahogany and brass-inlaid wall clock, by S. Haslehurst, Devizes, the fusee movement with anchor escapement, c1840, 23in (58.5cm) high.
$4,000–4,500 PAO

A Regency mahogany and brass-inlaid drop-dial wall clock, with cream painted dial indistinctly inscribed Stowbridge, twin fusee movement striking on a bell, 28¼in (72cm) high.
$1,300–1,500 Bea(E)

◄ A brass bedroom alarm clock, by Pickett, Marlborough, with 30-hour weight-driven movement, c1780, 8¼in (21cm) high.
$2,300–2,500 PAO

A mahogany and brass-inlaid drop-dial timepiece, by Winterhalder & Co, London, the 4-pillar single train fusee movement with anchor escapement, 19thC, 20½in (52cm) high.
$1,800–2,000 DN

A German walnut wall clock, with two-piece enamel dial, the square gong striking movement with deadbeat escapement and ebonized pendulum rod, late 19thC, 46in (117cm) high.
$900–1,000 Bon

A mahogany and ebony-inlaid wall clock, by John Walker, London, with A-frame weight-driven movement, c1840, 44in (112cm) high.
$2,000–2,500 K&D

A German wall clock, surmounted by a horse, with turned columns and finials, enamel dial, striking mechanism, c1890, 58in (147.5cm) high.
$1,000–1,100 DQ

◄ A Dutch baroque-style walnut Friesland clock, the brass spandrels depicting the 4 seasons, striking on 2 bells, restored, 19thC, 42in (106.5cm) high.
$1,300–1,600 SK

A French gilt-bronze wall clock, the white enamel dial signed for Tiffany & Co, c1900, 14in (35.5cm) high.
$5,200–6,000 S

A French repoussé brass *comtoise* clock, with 2 weights, c1830, 55in (140cm) high.
$1,200–1,500 DuM

◄ A French wall clock, with enamel Roman numerals, striking mechanism, 19thC, 29in (73.5cm) high.
$275–325 Doc

AMERICAN CLOCKS

A Federal walnut longcase clock, with painted metal dial, Pennsylvania, c1800, 94in (239cm) high.
$9,500–11,500 SLN

A walnut shelf clock, by Ingraham Clock Co, Bristol, Connecticut, with striking movement, c1880, 23in (58.5cm) high.
$400–500 OT

A painted pine longcase clock, by S. Hoadley, Plymouth, Connecticut, with polychrome wooden dial, 30-hour wooden movement, damaged, c1820, 84in (213.5cm) high.
$2,200–2,500 SK(B)

A mahogany and stencilled shelf clock, by Norris North, Torrington, Connecticut, with polychrome and gilt white-painted dial, 30-hour wooden weight-driven movement, c1825, 23¾in (60.5cm) high.
$5,000–5,750 SK(B)

◀ A rosewood octagonal calendar clock, by Ansonia Clock Co, c1870, 24in (61cm) high.
$200–250 DuM

A walnut shelf clock, by Ansonia Clock Co, the spring-wound alarm mechanism striking on the hours, c1880, 21in (53.5cm) high.
$250–300 OT

A Federal mahogany pillar and scroll mantel clock, by Seth Thomas, Plymouth, Connecticut, with polychrome and gilt dial, 30-hour wooden weight-driven movement, c1825, 31½in (80cm) high.
$2,500–2,800 SK(B)

A *faux* marble 'Curfew' clock, by Gilbert Clock Co, Winsted, Connecticut, with solid brass bell striking the hours and half-hours, spring-wound movement, c1895, 17in (43cm) high.
$325–400 OT

A red adamantine clock, by Seth Thomas, the spring-wound movement striking on the hours, c1910, 9in (23cm) high.
$250–325 OT

A Federal mahogany shelf timepiece, by Aaron Willard, Boston, the glazed door with eglomisé tablet of lyre spandrels and foliate designs, with white painted iron dial, weight driven brass movement, slight damage, c1825, 31in (78.5cm) high.
$7,250–8,000 SK(B)

◀ A Federal inlaid mahogany banjo timepiece, with gilt finial, brass bezel, white painted iron dial, brass weight-driven movement with T-bridge escapement, Boston, slight damage, c1815, 34in (86.5cm) high.
$9,000–10,000 SK(B)

BRITISH REGULATORS

A walnut regulator, by Darling & Wood, with silver dial, steel and mercury compensating pendulum, c1866, 71in (180.5cm) high.
$19,500–23,500 SoS

A flame-mahogany longcase regulator, by David Smith, Leven, with deadbeat escapement and maintaining power, c1835, 81in (205.5cm) high.
$9,000–10,000 PAO

A mahogany regulator, by Vulliamy, with silvered dial, striking movement and deadbeat escapement, mid-19thC, 77in (195.5cm) high.
$21,000–24,500 B

A Victorian Scottish mahogany regulator, with striking movement, 85in (216cm) high.
$2,500–2,750 BR

CONTINENTAL REGULATORS

A German rosewood and walnut regulator, with striking movement, 19thC, 45in (114.5cm) high.
$1,100–1,300 WBH

◄ A mahogany year-going Viennese regulator, c1840, 52in (132cm) high.
$26,000–32,500 GeC

Watches

POCKET WATCHES

A Swiss 18ct gold full hunter watch, signed Aubert & Capt, with engine-turned silver dial, c1840, 42mm diam.
$1,600–2,200 PT

A gilt-metal pair-cased verge watch, by Barnard, London, with enamel dial, c1800, 45mm diam.
$325–400 Bon(C)

A 14ct gold keyless hunter watch, jewelled movement signed to backplate Crescent St, Waltham, Mass, 19thC, 44mm diam.
$600–675 S(S)

A gold quarter-repeating skeletonized automaton watch, by Du Bois & Fils, with enamel chapter ring, gilt full plate verge movement, c1820, 57mm diam.
$2,900–3,250 S(G)

An American gilt 21-jewel lever watch, by Elgin Natl. Watch Co, with white enamel dial, c1921, 50mm diam.
$450–525 PT

A Swedish 18ct gold watch, by Jacob Kock, Stockholm, full plate gilt fusee movement, engraved bridge cock forming initials 'GR' surmounted by a crown, c1760, 57mm diam.
$3,500–4,000 PT

The crown above the initials suggests that this watch may have been made for King Gustav III.

An 18ct gold open-faced quarter-repeating watch, by George Moore, with enamel dial, key-wound movement striking on 2 gongs, 1859, 50mm diam.
$1,000–1,200 Bon

A French silver open-faced watch, by Robert & Courvoisier, with enamel dial, gilt fusee movement and verge escapement, c1840, 57mm diam.
$900–1,000 S(S)

A gilt and painted shell pair-cased verge watch, by Sampson Morrice, London, c1800, 52mm diam.
$400–450 Bon(C)

A silver pair-cased watch, with enamel dial decorated with a hunting scene, the black letters reading Richard Wakelin to record the hours, backplate signed Jn Roe, Coventry, Birmingham 1816, 42mm diam.
$650–750 S(S)

A Dutch silver pair-cased verge watch, the pierced balance cock signed J. Strong, London, late 18thC, 50mm diam.
$450–550 Bon(C)

A tortoiseshell pair-cased watch, with enamel dial, gilt fusee movement with verge escapement, backplate signed Jo Taylor, London, late 19thC, 37mm diam.
$575–650 S(S)

An 18ct gold hunter watch, with gilt face, gilt fusee movement and verge escapement, backplate signed Chas Taylor, Bristol, London 1818, 45mm diam.
$575–650 S(S)

A gold pair-cased watch, by Jon Rowe, with gold champlevé dial, converted to lever escapement, 49mm diam, and a gilt-metal chatelaine with crank key and double seal, 18thC.
$2,750–3,250 P

A Swiss silver and enamel hunter watch, signed J. Ulmann & Co, Hong Kong, with enamel dial, c1880, 50mm diam.
$400–500 Bon(C)

An American up/down dial lever watch, signed Vanguard, Waltham, Mass, with white enamel dial, c1920, 50mm diam.
$1,000–1,200 PT

A Swiss silver masonic watch, with mother-of-pearl dial, 15 jewel movement adjusted to 3 positions, 1930s, 48mm wide, in fitted box.
$1,600–2,000 Bon

A Swiss gold, enamel and diamond-set keyless cylinder watch, with white enamel dial, c1880, 26mm diam.
$1,750–2,000 S

A Bulova Accuquartz 9ct gold watch, with Accutron movement, 1974, 38mm diam, in original box.
$725–800 BWC

A Cartier 18ct white gold and diamond bracelet watch, with silvered matt dial, signed, c1970, 20mm wide.
$3,200–3,600 S(G)

A stainless steel centre seconds military watch, by International Watch Co, the black dial with luminous quarter marks, 1948, 35mm diam.
$1,400–1,600 Bon

A Jaeger LeCoultre 9ct gold automatic centre seconds calendar watch, with silvered dial, 1962, 34mm diam.
$725–800 Bon

A Jaeger LeCoultre 18ct gold bracelet watch, with gilt dial, the damascened nickel movement in a case with a textured edge, and a similar bracelet, 1960s, 26mm wide.
$1,200–1,400 Bon

A Longines silver cushion-cased watch, with integral lugs, enamel dial, red No. XII and subsidiary seconds, c1920, 8¾in (22cm) long.
$300–350 MANS

A 14ct gold single-button chronograph watch, with register, made for the Russian market, signed H. Moser, c1915, 44mm diam.
$3,200–3,600 S(G)

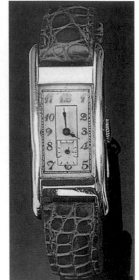

A Movado Curvex 14ct gold watch, with silvered dial, the unadjusted movement with 17 jewels, c1940, 33mm long.
$1,500–1,800 S

An Orfina chrome-plated chronograph watch, the pink gilt dial with subsidiaries for running seconds and 30 minute recording, outer timing scale, 1960s, 34mm diam.
$300–350 Bon

A Patek Philippe 18ct gold bracelet watch, with champagne dial, nickel lever movement with 20 jewels, c1970, 20mm wide.
$2,600–3,000 S

A Rolex curved back watch, the silvered water-silk dial signed for Sermon, Torquay, the 15-jewel movement signed Extra Prima, 1924, 25mm wide.
$1,200–1,400 Bon

A Patek Philippe 18ct gold watch, retailed by Max Schnabel, Madrid, with matt-gilt lever movement, jewelled to the 4th wheel, c1925, 33mm diam.
$4,500–5,000 S

An 18ct gold chronograph watch with register, by Favre-Leuba & Co, with nickel lever movement, c1925, 34mm diam.
$3,000–3,500 S(G)

A Rolex 9ct gold duo-dial watch, with flared sides, silvered dial with gilt spandrels, 15 jewels, 1930, 36mm long.
$6,500–7,250 S

A Rolex Prince stainless steel duo-dial watch, with flared sides, and silvered dial, c1935, 36mm long.
$5,000–5,750 S

A LeCoultre gold-filled moonphase watch, with tonneau nickel lever movement, c1945, 40mm long.
$1,750–2,000 S(NY)

A Rolex 9ct gold bracelet watch, the silvered dial with baton numerals, with jewelled lever movement, 1952, 19mm diam.
$320–350 Bon(C)

A Rolex 9ct gold centre seconds watch, with silvered dial, 1955, 32mm diam, with fitted box.
$1,000–1,200 Bon

A Rolex 9ct gold bracelet watch, with silvered dial, 17 jewel movement, 1956, 15mm diam.
$500–575 Bon(C)

A Rolex 18ct pink gold bracelet watch, with circular nickel lever movement, c1960, 17 jewels, 26mm wide.
$2,300–2,800 S

A Rolex Precision 18ct gold watch, the silvered dial with baton numerals, 1960, 20mm wide.
$500–575 Bon

A Rolex Oyster Perpetual 'Explorer II' stainless steel self-winding watch, with black matt dial, nickel lever movement, 26 jewels, c1972, 38mm diam.
$4,000–5,000 S(NY)

◄ A German WWII airman's watch, by Wempe, Hamburg, with gilt finished movement, 50mm diam, with leather strap.
$575–650 DD

A Rolex Oyster Perpetual Datejust watch, 1979, 37mm diam.
$1,600–1,800 BWC

A Rolex Oysterdate stainless steel watch and bracelet, with blue dial, sweep seconds hand with date, c1981, 38mm diam.
$900–1,000 P(Ed)

Barometers

STICK BAROMETERS

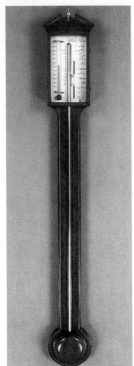

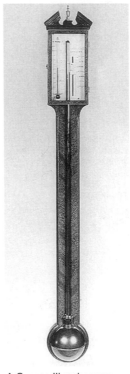

A mahogany bowfront stick barometer, by F. Amadio & Son, London, c1805, 38in (96.5cm) high.
$9,500–11,500 PAO

A mahogany stick barometer, by Balati & Bianchi, Norwich, c1800, 38in (96.5cm) high.
$3,500–4,000 PAO

A George III mahogany stick barometer, by L. Casartilli, Liverpool, 39in (99cm) high.
$2,600–3,000 P(NW)

A Victorian mahogany stick barometer, by W. Cook, Keighley, with ivorine dial, 43in (109cm) high.
$900–975 Mit

A late George III mahogany stick barometer, by Dollond, London, 41in (104cm) high.
$9,000–10,000 HYD

A mahogany stick barometer, by W. Harris, London, 18thC, 38¼in (97cm) high.
$2,000–2,500 P(C)

A Victorian walnut stick barometer, by J. Hicks, London, 40in (101.5cm) high.
$1,300–1,500 CAG

A flame-mahogany stick barometer, by Mason, Dublin, with silvered-brass register plate behind brass-framed door, concealed tube and turned cistern cover, c1790, 37in (94cm) high.
$4,500–5,500 AW

21 Years Ago ...

A mahogany stick barometer, with vernier scale, signed Henry Andrews, Royston, c1810, 38¾in (98.5cm) high. **LC**

Twenty-one years ago, this mahogany stick barometer was valued at $650–725. Although of a common style, this elegant type of barometer is much sought after and has increased substantially in value. A similar example in fully restored condition would be worth $4,000–4,500 today.

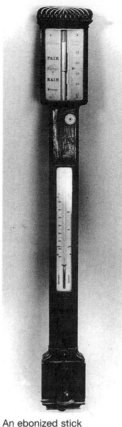

An ebonized stick barometer, by J. D. Potter, London, unrestored, c1830, 39¼in (100cm) high. **$1,100–1,300 HOK**

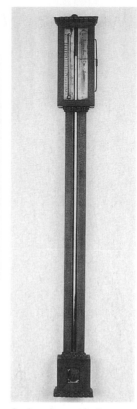

An American walnut barometer, by A. S. & J. A., New York, with silvered dial, slight damage, c1840, 35¼in (89.5cm) high. **$650–800 SK(B)**

A mahogany stick barometer, by Wisker, York, with silvered brass register plate and hemispherical cistern cover, c1810, 36in (91.5cm) high. **$3,000–3,500 AW**

An oak Admiral Fitzroy Royal Polytechnic barometer and thermometer, with silvered dial and scale, 19thC, 42in (107cm) high. **$650–725 Bon(W)**

WHEEL BAROMETERS

A William IV rosewood veneered banjo barometer, by J. Abraham, Bath, 44in (112cm) high.
$1,800–2,000 Mit

An inlaid mahogany banjo barometer, inscribed Barnaschin, Newcastle-upon-Tyne, early 19thC, 38¼in (97cm) high.
$650–800 P(C)

A Victorian rosewood and seaweed marquetry banjo barometer, inscribed S. Castelazie, Edinburgh, 38¼in (97cm) high.
$650–800 P(Sc)

A mahogany wheel barometer, by W. Cawdle, Torquay, c1830, 38in (95.5cm) high.
$1,400–1,600 PAO

A mahogany wheel barometer, by Cetti & Co, London, early 19thC, 39in (99cm) high.
$1,100–1,300 CAG

A Victorian papier mâché wheel barometer, by Ciceri & Pini, Edinburgh, the case decorated with gilt panels and inlaid with mother-of-pearl, 39½in (100.5cm) high.
$900–1,100 Bea(E)

A flame-mahogany wheel barometer, by Dollond, London, with engraved plates, c1830, 40½in (103cm) high.
$2,000–2,300 AW

A mahogany and boxwood-strung wheel barometer, by L. Gobbi, Liverpool, with hygrometer, c1845, 37in (94cm) high.
$1,600–2,000 PAO

A George III boxwood and ebony-strung wheel barometer, by T. Harris & Son, British Museum, London, the silvered dial engraved with leaves and a globe, 42in (106.5cm) high.
$2,000–2,300 DN

A mahogany wheel barometer, by Maspoli, Hull, with silvered-brass dial, c1825, 36in (91.5cm) high.
$2,300–3,000 AW

A mahogany banjo barometer, by Negretti & Zambra, London, c1875, 39in (99cm) high.
$900–1,000 RTw

A mahogany and boxwood-strung wheel barometer, by B. Porri, Skipton, with silvered-brass dial, c1835, 42in (106.5cm) high.
$1,400–1,600 PAO

A mahogany wheel clock barometer, by L. Guanna, Salop, the timepiece signed W. G. Shaw, London, No. 820, early 19thC, 37in (94cm) high.
$2,600–3,000 GH

A mahogany wheel barometer, by Somalvico, Lione & Co, London, c1805, 19¼in (100cm) high.
$1,600–2,000 S(S)

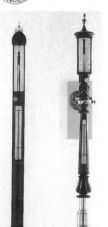

An inlaid figured-mahogany banjo barometer, by Torre & Co, London, with 2 subsidiary dials, early 19thC, 41in (104cm) high.
$1,800–2,000 MEA

A mahogany and line-inlaid wheel barometer, by Tyler, London, c1830, 37½in (95.5cm) high.
$1,300–1,500 AW

A mahogany and boxwood-strung wheel barometer, by Vanetti & Benzzoni, Brighton, with central hygrometer, c1810, 39in (99cm) high.
$3,000–3,500 PAO

A mahogany wheel barometer, by J. Verga, Chester, with silvered-brass scale, c1810, 40in (101.5cm) high.
$2,500–2,750 PAO

ANEROID BAROMETERS

A brass-cased Bourdon-style aneroid barometer, with paper scale and exposed movement, c1870, 5in (12.5cm) diam.
$600–650 AW

A forecasting set, by Negretti & Zambra, London, c1920, box 6½in (16.5cm) wide.
$1,300–1,600 AW

An oak rope-twist aneroid barometer, by J. G. Wall, Ross, with porcelain dial, c1890, 7in (18cm) diam.
$210–250 RTw

▶ An aneroid barometer, in a gilt-decorated easel strut case, on an ebonized base, under a glass dome, 19thC, 7in (18cm) high.
$160–200 Bon

◀ A brass-cased aneroid barometer, by E. J. Dent, Paris, with suspension loop, mid-19thC, 5in (12.5cm) diam.
$500–600 Bon

A German figured-walnut aneroid barometer, dated '1928', 7in (18cm) diam.
$100–140 RTw

BAROGRAPHS

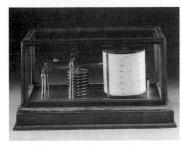

A mahogany barograph, the 8-day French movement with cylinder escapement, brass base signed Bailey, Birmingham, mounted on a moulded mahogany base with chart drawer, c1900, 13¼in (33.5cm) wide.
$900–1,000 S

An inlaid mahogany barograph, by Finnegan's Ltd, Manchester, with ancillary dial, c1910, 15in (38cm) wide.
$2,500–3,250 AW

An oak-cased barograph, by Joseph Hicks, London, with chart drawer, c1900, 14in (35.5cm) wide.
$2,000–2,300 AW

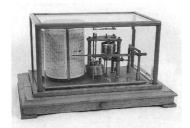

An oak-cased precision recording barograph, by Negretti & Zambra, with 4 sets of bellows and a chart drawer, dated '1952', 19in (48.5cm) wide.
$3,000–3,500 RTw

An oak-cased barograph, by John Trotter, Glasgow, early 20thC, 14in (35.5cm) wide.
$800–900 Bea(E)

▶ An oak-cased barograph, by Winter & Son, Newcastle-upon-Tyne, with barometer face, c1925, 14in (35.5cm) wide.
$1,500–1,800 RTw

A German miniature barograph, by Wegner, in chrome and ebonized case, c1950, 8in (20.5cm) wide.
$725–800 RTw

A Victorian gilt-brass barograph, the ebonized case with bevelled glass panels to top and side, the moulded base containing drawer, 14in (35.5cm) wide.
$575–650 WBH

An oak-cased barograph, with bevelled glass and chart drawer in the plinth base, 1920s, 14½in (37cm) wide.
$1,300–1,500 Bon

Decorative Arts

The past 21 years have witnessed both consolidation and expansion in the misty parameters that enclose what some choose to describe as the decorative arts and others the applied arts. Sotheby's Belgravia auction rooms had already established themselves 21 years ago as the mecca for the faithful eager to pursue the treasures of the Victorian age and early 20th century. In those days much of the business of buying and selling Art Nouveau and Art Deco appeared to be centred around London and Brighton. The adventurous, however, began to search further afield, opting to buy in Paris, Brussels or Amsterdam and, when the exchange rate allowed, in New York and at the Miami winter fairs. The established antiques trade looked on with both bemusement and incredulity when the glass of Gallé and Tiffany or the furniture of Moser and Mackintosh achieved stratospheric prices.

Japanese interest in European decorative arts during the mid-1980s helped to create a rapid movement in prices, especially for the works of Gallé, Daum and Lalique. The market for Lalique glass in particular resulted in a series of annual specialist auctions at Bonhams in London.

The emergence of a mass interest in the pottery creations of Clarice Cliff led to similar specialist auctions, with Christie's hosting sales since the mid-1980s devoted entirely to her work. These were so successful that that which was considered good for Clarice Cliff was also considered good for Susie Cooper, William Moorcroft and Poole Pottery, with Christie's South Kensington eager to provide the venue for each specialist auction.

The pottery of William de Morgan has also attracted a keen following, especially during the last ten years. Much the same is true of silver and pewter designed by Archibald Knox for Liberty & Co, and the metalwork designs of Dr Christopher Dresser, which have also found themselves in the fast track. In recent years the Japanese interest has waned in the light of a wobbly economy; prices during the early 1990s in particular began to dive, but stabilized towards the end of the decade.

The collector of today is without doubt better served than 21 years ago. Now one can find a huge number of specialist books, from Ruhlmann to Rookwood or Mucha to Majorelle, all of which are there to arm both the collector and dealer with the ultimate weapon – knowledge. Personally, I would be more than happy to settle for a small amount of hindsight.

Eric Knowles

ARTS & CRAFTS CERAMICS

An Ault 'Twist' and 'Propeller' vase, decorated in yellow and green, designed by Dr Christopher Dresser, c1893, 5in (12.5cm) high.
$300–350 NCA

◄ An Elton ware vase, the deep red body incised with flowers and berries, with 3 loop handles, painted black mark, c1900, 12in (30.5cm) high.
$900–1,000 RUSK

A pair of Brannam beaker vases, decorated in blue, green and brown, incised marks for 1904, 8in (20.5cm) high.
$600–700 RUSK

A Burmantofts vase, decorated in lime-green with dimples and sunbursts, c1885, 9in (23cm) high.
$250–300 NCA

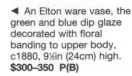

A Burmantofts jardinière-on-stand, decorated in turquoise, c1900, 41in (104cm) high.
$900–1,000 PAC

◄ An Elton ware vase, the green and blue dip glaze decorated with floral banding to upper body, c1880, 9½in (24cm) high.
$300–350 P(B)

A charger, attributed to William de Morgan, decorated in red and green with a galleon, c1890, 14in (35.5cm) diam.
$650–800 DSG

A Linthorpe moon flask, designed by Dr Christopher Dresser, decorated in green, brown and yellow glaze, c1879–1882, 5¾in (14.5cm) high.
$725–800 NCA

A Bernard Moore bowl, painted by R. R. Tomlinson, c1910, 7½in (19cm) diam.
$800–1,000 DSG

A French brown and green iridescent glazed jug, by D. Zumbo, Fréjus, in the style of Clément Massier, c1900, 7in (18cm) high.
$300–330 DSG

A William de Morgan vase and cover, painted in Persian style in shades of green, purple and turquoise with birds among foliage, painted mark, late 19thC, 13¾in (35cm) high.
$13,000–14,500 CGC

This vase is a particularly fine example of William de Morgan's work. The colours are crisp and it is in excellent condition and of a large size, commanding a high price when sold at auction.

A Maw & Co tile, possibly designed by Pugin, c1880, 6in (15cm) square.
$40–50 GIN

A Pewabic pottery bronze iridescent vase, with bubble textured surface, impressed mark, c1930, 14½in (37cm) high.
$1,600–2,000 DuM

A Losol ware comport, by Keeling & Co, painted in blues, green, and orange on a mottled beige ground with an aesthetic bird, c1920, 10½in (27cm) diam.
$130–160 P(B)

A pair of Minton tiles, depicting Shakespearean scenes, c1860, 6in (15cm) square.
$150–180 DSG

A Ruskin high-fired stoneware vase, glazed overall with greenish-cream ground mottled blue and purple with green spots, c1910, 13in (33cm) high.
$7,000–8,000 S

A Watcombe cobalt-glazed terracotta teapot, c1900, 4¼in (11cm) high.
$80–100 DSG

ARTS & CRAFTS FURNITURE

An Arts and Crafts oak bookcase, the frieze with motto, over 3 leaded doors enclosing adjustable shelves, with cupboard and 2 shaped niches below, c1890, 54in (138cm) wide.
$4,000–4,500 TEN

A pair of Arts and Crafts satin-walnut carver chairs, the top rails pierced with geometric patterns, drop-in seats over plain friezes with central circular cut, on shaped front supports, early 20thC.
$650–750 GAK

A mahogany 'Salisbury Combination Secretaire', the fall with applied prunts and leaf-carved star-shaped motifs, enclosing a fitted interior, the design repeated on the cupboard doors below, late 19thC, 38in (96.5cm) wide.
$360–420 WW

This piece bears a brass trade label of Arthur Foley, Fisherton Machine Cabinet Works, Salisbury.

An Arts and Crafts Liberty-style oak armchair, c1910.
$1,500–2,000 OOLA

An Arts and Crafts mahogany and marquetry inlaid writing cabinet, the fall front inlaid with a Continental village landscape at sunrise, enclosing pigeonholes and 2 small drawers, some damage, early 20thC, 38in (96.5cm) wide.
$2,000–2,500 S(S)

An oak rocking armchair, by L. & J. G. Stickley, with brown leather drop-in seat, with trade label, c1912.
$900–1,000 B&B

A Gustav Stickley oak desk, the panelled fall-front opening to a fitted interior, fall front replaced and 2 drawers lacking, c1904, 26in (66cm) wide.
$3,000–3,500 B&B

A pair of Arts and Crafts inlaid oak elbow chairs, c1900.
$600–700 COLL

An Aesthetic Movement mahogany and inlaid secretaire chest, the door enclosing sliding shelves to one side and a secretaire on the other over 4 drawers, inlaid overall with stylized flowers, late 19thC, 42½in (108cm) wide.
$6,500–7,500 SK

A Gothic-style oak dresser, possibly by a follower of Gilbert Scott, the lower part with panelled doors above a carved hinged fall and a panelled door flanked by 6 open shelves and panel doors to the sides, late 19thC, (139.5cm) wide.
$1,600–2,000 P

Arts & Crafts Movement

- Aimed to revive quality craftsmanship in the face of industrial mass production which had been so fêted at the Great Exhibition, London, in 1851.
- Movement dates from the early 1860s to the beginning of the 20thC.
- Its influence was established with the setting up of the Art Workers' Guild in 1884, the Guild of Handicraft in 1888 and the Arts & Crafts Exhibition Society in 1906.
- Enthusiasts favoured artistic, individually crafted wares, in contrast to the extravagant revival styles so popular in Victorian times.
- Pioneer of the movement was William Morris, whose London design company promoted a style based on medieval sources using local and natural materials and traditional handicraft techniques.
- Other leading exponents in Britain included William de Morgan, Charles Robert Ashbee and Charles Rennie Mackintosh.

An Arts and Crafts stained oak dresser, the boarded rack with 2 pegged shelves, the base with shaped frieze drawer, c1910, 42in (107cm) wide.
$320–360 P(NW)

An Aesthetic Movement oak sideboard, c1875, late 19thC, 77in (196cm) wide.
$2,000–2,200 L&E

An Arts and Crafts oak sideboard, with bevel-edged mirror plate, with Ruskin-style roundels and beaten copper mounts, early 20thC, 60in (152cm) wide.
$3,000–3,500 BWe

◄ A Ridenour oak two-tier lamp table, bearing paper label, early 20thC, 24½in (62cm) diam.
$900–1,000 B&B

An Arts and Crafts oak plant stand, c1900, 37in (94cm) high.
$650–800 MoS

An Arts and Crafts oak hall stand, with patinated copper panel and original fittings, c1905, 30in (76cm) wide.
$1,200–1,400 MoS

An Arts and Crafts oak writing table, c1900, 33in (84cm) wide.
$700–800 OOLA

◄ An Aesthetic Movement ebonized and parcel-gilt occasional table, with decorated top, late 19thC, 30½in (77.5cm) high.
$750–850 MEA

ARTS & CRAFTS METALWARE

An Arts and Crafts silver punchbowl, by West & Sons, the body chased and engraved with bands of Celtic motifs and roundels, applied with 4 plaques, Dublin 1901,
15in (38cm) high.
$4,000–5,000 JAd

A silver box, by Omar Ramsden and Alwyn Carr, the top enamelled with a Venetian scene in naturalistic colours, London 1909, 6½in (16.5cm) wide.
$8,000–9,000 SHa

A pair of Arts and Crafts candlesticks, early 20thC, 14¼in (36cm) high.
$720–800 FBG

An Arts and Crafts pedestal bowl, with embossed palmette border inset with matrix turquoise cabochon stones, Chester 1920, 12in (30.5cm) diam.
$800–1,000 P(NW)

A pair of Liberty & Co brass chambersticks, designed by Dr Christopher Dresser, c1880, 5¾in (14.5cm) high.
$1,500–1,700 P

These candlesticks are unusual in having metal handles instead of the usual combination of wood and metal.

An Arts and Crafts copper coal scuttle and cover, with small enamel insets and brass mounts, supported on brass pad feet, c1880,
23½in (60cm) high.
$230–280 P(B)

◄ A silver-mounted green glass decanter, designed by C. R. Ashbee, Guild of Handicrafts, glass by James Powell, London 1904, 8½in (21.5cm) high.
$2,000–2,300 RUSK

A Guild of Handicraft silver box, enamelled with a mallard duck, some restoration, marked, London 1903, 5¼in (13.5cm) wide.
$1,000–1,200 P

A green enamelled metal chamberstick, after a design by Dr Christopher Dresser, c1880, 5in (12.5cm) high.
$250–300 SHa

An Elkington & Co plated-metal egg stand, designed by Dr Christopher Dresser, with ebonized carrying handle, c1880, 6¼in (16cm) high.
$1,200–1,400 P

An Arts and Crafts silver boat-shaped dish, by A. E. Jones, of hammered design, pierced at either end with a panel of lily pads, the sides and pedestal foot with stud decoration, Birmingham 1913, 11¾in (30cm) long.
$1,500–1,700 P

An Arts and Crafts gong, possibly Guild of Handicrafts, c1890, 16in (40.5cm) wide.
$650–800 ANO

An Aesthetic Movement plated-metal kettle-on-stand, with burner, c1880, 12½in (31.5cm) high.
$750–850 P

An Arts and Crafts silver tyg, by Wakely & Wheeler, with hammered finish and 3 scroll handles, London 1905, 7½in (19cm) high.
$550–650 CGC

A copper jug, by W. A. S. Benson, c1880, 10in (25.5cm) high.
$900–1,000 SHa

A Hukin & Heath silver-plated travelling tea kettle and folding stand, with spirit burner, designed by Dr Christopher Dresser, fully marked, c1890, 9in (23cm) high.
$350–400 CAG

A silver milk jug and sugar basin, decorated with Celtic motifs, Dublin 1922, in original box, 4½in (11.5cm) high.
$1,800–2,000 SIL

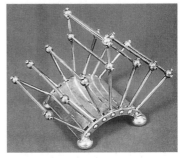

A Hukin & Heath silver articulated toast rack, designed by Dr Christopher Dresser, c1884, 6in (15cm) wide.
$800–1,000 MoS

An Arts and Crafts Aesthetic Movement copper tray, designed by Dr Christopher Dresser, with brass and pewter inlay, c1885, 9½in (24cm) diam.
$400–500 RUSK

21 Years Ago ...

A Hukin & Heath silver-plated soup tureen and ladle, designed by Dr Christopher Dresser, maker's mark, c1885. **S**

Twenty-one years ago this soup tureen was valued at $400–500 and today would sell at auction for $4,000–5,000. Dr Christopher Dresser is recognized today as being one of the most creative designers of the Victorian age, his futuristic metalware shapes pre-empting the modernist era by some 50 years. This soup tureen with cover and ladle can also be found with ivory fittings. The simplicity of design embodies Dresser's desire to integrate form with function. Recent publications and several exhibitions have contributed to the increase in both interest and prices.

DOULTON

A Doulton Lambeth jar and cover, decorated in blue, green and brown, dated '1879', 2½in (6.5cm) high.
$200–250 DSG

A pair of Doulton Lambeth stoneware vases, decorated by Frank Butler, each incised with foliate scrollwork picked out in green/grey and blue on a brown ground, incised artist's monogram, impressed factory mark and '1884', 10¼in (26cm) high.
$1,200–1,500 S

A Doulton Lambeth lemonade set, by Eliza Barker, each piece incised with a band of stylized foliage in green and white between blue borders on a buff ground, some damage, impressed circle mark and dated '1885', 8in (20.5cm) high.
$400–500 Bon(M)

A Royal Doulton tyg, by Mark V. Marshall and Rosina Brown, moulded with Art Nouveau-style flowers, decorated in treacle, blue and cream on a beige ground within blue chevron borders, impressed marks, c1890, 5½in (14cm) high.
$650–750 GAK

▶ A Doulton Lambeth jug, with honey-coloured glaze, restored crack, c1890, 7in (18cm) high.
$120–140 PAC

A pair of Doulton stoneware vases, with pierced covers, the sides tube-lined with sunflowers and leaves in shades of blue and green on a mottled ground, impressed rosette mark and incised initials 'AEP' and 'AR', c1880–91, 14in (35cm) high.
$600–700 CGC

A Doulton Lambeth faïence vase, possibly by Florence Lewis, decorated with holly on a brown ground, late 19thC, 9in (23cm) high.
$250–300 PCh

A Doulton Lambeth vase, decorated in blue, late 19thC, 10½in (26.5cm) high.
$550–650 PCh

A Royal Doulton Lambeth vase, decorated with blue and green flowers on a dark blue ground, c1902–5, 8¼in (21cm) high.
$250–350 POW

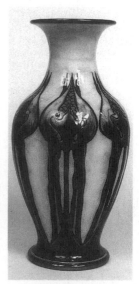

A Royal Doulton stoneware baluster vase, decorated in brown on a grey ground, by Eliza Simmance, c1907, 11½in (29cm) high.
$2,000–2,200 POW

A Royal Doulton candlestick, decorated in green and brown, c1910, 8¼in (21cm) high.
$140–160 DSG

A Royal Doulton Chang stoneware vase, by Charles Noke and Harry Nixon, the neck applied with a dragon in high relief, on a blue ground, with white running crackle glaze under green, yellow and flambé glazes, printed and painted marks, c1910–15, 7¾in (20cm) high.
$4,200–5,000 AH

A Royal Doulton figure, Geisha, HN634, by Harry Tittensor, 1924–38, 11in (28cm) high.
$5,500–6,500 Bon(M)

This model is properly known as Geisha but is commonly called 'A Japanese Lady'.

A Royal Doulton Sung vase, by C. J. Noke, c1930, 14in (35.5cm) high.
$7,000–8,000 POW

This exhibition piece is in perfect condition.

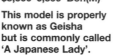

◄ A Royal Doulton bone china coffee set, by C. Hart and R. Brown, comprising 25 pieces, each painted with a signed painted scene of a castle in an extensive landscape, with gilded handles and rims, water jug with non-matching cover, c1920s.
$700–800 BWe

A Royal Doulton penguin group, HN133, c1940, 6in (15cm) high.
$350–400 PCh

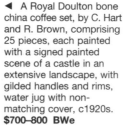

MARTIN BROTHERS

A Martin Brothers vase, incised with overlapping fans below straw-like decoration, the shoulders with pierced holes, signature mark 'Martin, London', c1880, 6in (15cm) high.
$225–275 P(B)

A Martin Brothers stoneware clock case, the white enamel dial supported by columns and an heraldic shield inscribed 'Treu Und Fest', flanked on either side by a pair of griffins, some damage, incised marks, dated '1875', 12in (30.5cm) high.
$5,000–6,000 S

The Martin Brothers made a number of clock cases during the 1870s.

A Martin Brothers vase, moulded with dentil border and decorated with geometric foliage, decorated below with incised portraits of a crusader, painted in shades of brown, with deep blue detail, signed and dated '1875', 17in (43cm) high.
$2,200–2,500 GAK

A Martin Brothers stoneware pier and capital, high-lighted with a blue glaze, some damage, 1879 and 1876, 32¾in (83cm) high.
$700–800 S(S)

A Martin Brothers stoneware vase, incised 'R. W. Martin, Southall, London', dated '30.8.80', 17in (43cm) high.
$800–900 RUSK

A Martin Brothers stoneware jug, incised and painted with lilies and Chavenhage House, 'CP' monogram on a brown salt-glazed ground, c1882, 9in (23cm) high.
$1,100–1,300 WDG

◄ A Martin Brothers bird jar and matched cover, the plumage picked out in blue and brown, incised marks, c1890, 13¼in (33.5cm) high.
$7,500–8,500 S

The variations in the incised feathers and the ground-out date codes suggest that the head and body of this bird have been matched. This may, however, have occurred at an early date as the match and fit are extremely good.

A Martin Brothers double-face spouted jug, with buff glaze, the eyes and teeth picked out in black and white, the hair in black, spout chipped, incised marks, dated '1886', 11in (28cm) high.
$5,000–5,500 S

A Martin Brothers stoneware double-faced jug, with rich biscuit brown tones, signed, c1903, 6¾in (17cm) high.
$4,200–4,800 P(O)

A Martin Brothers two-handled vase, decorated in black and beige, c1890, 8½in (21.5cm) high.
$1,600–2,000 DSG

A Martin Brothers stone-ware vase, highlighted in brown and green washes against an oatmeal ground, incised mark, c1903, 9½in (24cm) high.
£1,500–1,650 S(S)

MOORCROFT

A Moorcroft MacIntyre Florian ware vase, designed by William Moorcroft, the tube-lined decoration in 3 sections, with stylized foliage, flowers and butterflies in shades of blue, slight damage, printed marks, incised 'W.M.', c1900, 10¾in (27.5cm) high.
$2,100–2,500

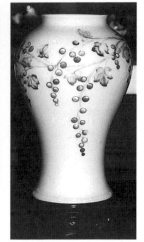

A Moorcroft yellow over-glaze Vine pattern vase, made for Liberty, c1906, 9in (23cm) high.
$4,000–4,400 RUM

A Moorcroft bowl, decorated with Pomegranate pattern on a green ground, with painted green signature and dated '1913' to base, 7¾in (20cm) diam.
$1,800–2,200 RTo

◄ A Moorcroft plate, decorated with Wisteria pattern, c1930, 9in (23cm) diam.
$325–350 PAC

A Moorcraft Flambé vase, decorated with Pomegranate pattern, c1925, 15in (38cm) high.
$2,200–2,600 DSG

A Moorcraft vase, decorated with spring flowers on a green ground, impressed facsimile signature, c1928, 10in (25.5cm) high.
$1,300–1,500 Mit

A Moorcroft bowl, decorated with Orchid pattern, c1935, 2½in (6.5cm) diam.
$320–350 NP

A Moorcroft ashtray, decorated with Columbine pattern, c1950, 4½in (11.5cm) diam.
$110–130 DAC

◄ A Walter Moorcroft vase, decorated with Grapes and Leaves pattern, impressed mark and signed, c1945, 8¾in (22cm) high.
$725–800 P

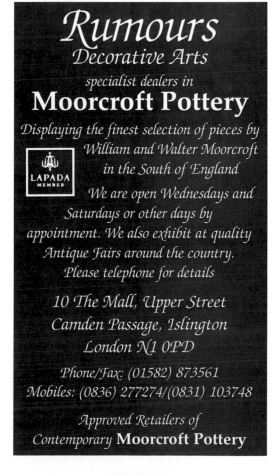

ART NOUVEAU CERAMICS

An Amphora dish, by Ernst Wahliss, Vienna, in the form of a girl on a floating lily pad, with applied enamels and encrusted flowers, c1900, 10in (25.5cm) diam.
$2,400–2,600 PGA

An Elton ware jug, decorated with orange flowers on a green ground, c1910, 7½in (19cm) high.
$350–400 DSG

A Grueby vase, with sculpted and applied overlapping leaves under tooled vertical stems supporting open flower blossoms, covered with green matt glaze, signed 'W. Post', c1900, 13in (33cm) high.
$8,000–9,000 TREA

Miller's is a price GUIDE not a price LIST

A Bretby cloisonné-style vase, decorated with yellow and pink flowers and a bird on a black ground, 14½in (37cm) high.
$200–250 DSG

A Gouda two-handled dark green vase, made for Liberty, decorated with yellow and blue pattern, c1901, 15in (38cm) high.
$725–800 OO

An Owens Pottery standard glaze lamp base, painted naturalistically with orange pansies, American, c1900, 8in (20.5cm) high.
$200–250 YAN

A Burmantofts jardinière, decorated in shades of blue and yellow, c1890, 8½in (21.5cm) high.
$725–800 ASA

A De Porceleyne Fles earthenware wall plate, designed by Leon Senf, decorated in neo-Persian style with 2 birds in shades of blue and green on a cream ground, painted factory mark and initials 'B BA', c1910, 16½in (42cm) diam.
$725–800 S(Am)

A pair of Moore Brothers vases, with 2 loop handles, each applied in relief with lilies and leaves, picked out in yellow, green and gilt on a cream ground, slight damage, c1880, 8¾in (22cm) high.
$600–700 DN

A Della Robbia vase, decorated with irises and water lilies in shades of green and ochre on a blue ground, with twin griffin handles, moulded with green glazed decoration, signed and dated '1900', 16½in (42cm) high.
$1,000–1,200 TRL

A Minton Secessionist jardinière, tube-lined with stylized flowers in turquoise and purple, slight damage, printed mark and impressed number, c1890, 12½in (32cm) high.
$520–600 Bon(W)

A Bernard Moore flambé vase, 1920s, largest 6in (15cm) high.
$320–400 PGA

◄ A Purmerend vase, decorated in pink, yellow and green, 1896–1904, 7in (18cm) high.
$1,000–1,200 OO

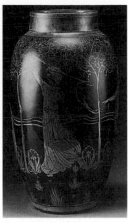

A Pilkington's Royal Lancastrian lustre vase, by Gordon Forsyth, painted with classical maidens and trees in a stylized landscape against a blue ground, impressed marks, artist's monogram and year mark for 1909, 16½in (42cm) high.
$2,000–2,500 S

A Pilkington's Royal Lancastrian green lustre bottle vase, c1910, 8¼in (21cm) high.
$800–1,000 ASA

A Foley Intarsio ware biscuit barrel, designed by Frederick Rhead, decorated with Hares pattern, with silver mounts, c1890, 7¾in (19.5cm) high.
$1,600–2,000 PGA

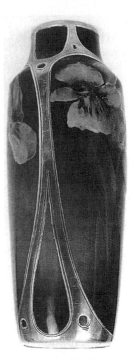

A Rookwood, Cincinnati, standard glaze vase, painted with viola flowers in dark ivory and buff tones on a light and dark green ground, encased in a silver metal mount, impressed mark for 1900, 6½in (16.5cm) high.
$1,000–1,200 P(EA)

A Rozenburg earthenware pot and cover, decorated with birds and butterflies among berried branches in shades of brown, green and purple, slight damage, painted factory mark, date code for 1897, 20in (51cm) high.
$5,200–5,600 S(Am)

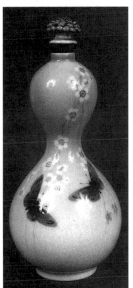

A Royal Copenhagen pink bottle, with 'flower' stopper, decorated with grey butterflies, c1900, 8in (20.5cm) high.
$1,000–1,200 FrG

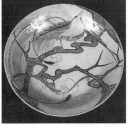

A Rozenburg ceramic plate, by Rudolf Sterken, c1900, 8¼in (21cm) diam.
$800–1,000 OO

A Tiffany Favrile crystalline glazed pottery vase, in mottled yellow-ochre, amber brown and cream, incised LCT monogram, early 20thC, 11½in (29cm) wide.
$1,000–1,200 B&B

▶ A Weller iridescent decorated art pottery vase, signed on base, American, c1900, 11in (18cm) high.
$1,300–1,600 DSG

A Brantjes & Co Purmerend earthenware clock, derived from the Rozenburg Chronosy clock, decorated with a peacock and flowers in shades of yellow, green, blue, purple and brown on a yellow-green ground, painted factory mark and number, 1895–1904, 13¼in (33.5cm) high.
$27,000–30,000 S(Am)

This clock was previously unknown and is believed unique, which accounts for the exceptional price.

A Théodore Goujon parcel-gilt-bronze figural clock, the chapter ring cast with swirling clouds reserved against a starry ground, impressed 'Louchet/Paris/Ciseleur', c1900, 19in (48.5cm) high.
$7,500–8,500 S(NY)

A Maurice Dufrêne mahogany and gilt-bronze mantel clock, by La Maison Moderne, c1902, 15¼in (38.5cm) high.
$4,000–4,400 S(NY)

A Goldscheider bronzed-pottery-cased clock, modelled as a draped couple studying a book entitled 'Historia', the case inscribed 'Cave Ne Indigmum' restored, early 20thC, 19¼in (49cm) high.
$1,000–1,200 S(S)

A Liberty Tudric pewter mantel clock, with blue enamel dial, the case decorated in relief with fern leaves, stamped 'Tudric Pewter', c1905, 11in (28cm) wide.
$2,000–2,300 RUSK

An Albin Müller marble, granite and porphyry clock, monogrammed 'AM', c1900, 15½in (39.5cm) high.
$8,000–9,000 S(NY)

A Rozenburg earthenware clock garniture, painted by J. van der Vet, decorated with dandelions and chrysanthemums in shades of blue, green, yellow, brown and purple, restored, marked, date code for 1903, clock 12in (30.5cm) high.
$4,000–4,500 S(Am)

A Liberty Tudric pewter travelling clock, decorated with stylized entwined leaves, picked out in blue enamel, c1900, 4in (10cm) high.
$800–900 DN

A Rozenburg Juliana earthenware clock garniture, painted by Sam Schellink, decorated with stylized floral ornament in shades of blue, purple, yellow and brown on a cream ground, marked, date code for 1909, clock 14¾in (37.5cm) high.
$5,200–5,600 S(Am)

A Liberty Tudric pewter timepiece, cast in relief with a tree motif, the copper dial centred with blue and green enamel, stamped 'Tudric', c1910, 7in (18cm) high.
$1,200–1,400 P

Cross Reference
See Colour Review

A silver-cased clock, by Fattorini & Sons, Birmingham, c1910, 9½in (24cm) high.
$800–900 S(S)

▶ A Gouda clock, decorated with orange flowers and leaves, c1921, 6½in (16.5cm) high.
$650–750 OO

ART NOUVEAU FIGURES & BUSTS

A Goldscheider figure of a Nubian slave, resting her elbow and knee on a tree trunk at her side, repaired, impressed mark, late 19thC, 29½in (75cm) high.
$1,800–2,000 TEN

A Rosenthal porcelain figure of a dancer, designed by Berthold Boehs, painted in polychrome colours, inscribed and impressed model No. K201, c1913, 9¼in (23.5cm) high.
$1,600–1,800 DORO

► A terracotta figure, entitled Lady with the Billing Doves, by Ernst Wahliss, c1900, 30in (76cm) high.
$4,000–5,000 ASA

A French patinated-bronze bust, entitled 'Le Matin', cast after a model by Nicolas Mayer, c1900, 22½in (57cm) high.
$1,200–1,400 B&B

A pair of Royal Dux figures, one with a tambourine, the other a violin, decorated in green and pink enamels, pink triangle mark, c1910, 18in (45.5cm) high.
$900–1,000 HYD

A pewter inkwell, signed 'Peyze', c1899, 8in (20.5cm) high.
$550–700 ANO

A Royal Dux porcelain figural centrepiece, in the form of a maiden standing on the crest of a wave holding a fishing net, flanked by 2 scallop shell-form receptacles, marked, c1900, 16¾in (42.5cm) high.
$2,000–2,200 B&B

An Art Nouveau green patinated bronze figure, by C. Wollek, depicting a naked man holding a giant conch shell, on a circular base signed and dated '1902', 9¾in (25cm) high.
$550–650 EH

► An Art Nouveau gilded-spelter table lamp, modelled as a female figure, c1900, 17½in (44.5cm) high.
$525–575 PCh

A Purmerend earthenware figure, entitled 'Venus Frigida', painted by R. Sterken, cream with shades of yellow, brown and green, restored, c1904, 24in (61cm) high.
$2,500–3,000 S(Am)

A Bohemian porcelain figure, by Ernst Wahliss, Alexandra Porcelain Works, slight damage, early 20thC, 16¾in (42.5cm) high.
$1,200–1,350 SK(B)

A Diot mahogany bookcase, carved with whiplash devices above an arrangement of shelves and partitions, with a central lower door, c1900, 36½in (92.5cm) high.
$3,000–3,300 S(NY)

An Art Nouveau mahogany double-bowfront display cabinet, with central floral inlay and 2 doors with mask panels, on square legs with undertier, c1910, 47in (119.5cm) high.
$2,000–2,200 GSP

An Art Nouveau mahogany and mother-of-pearl inlaid display cabinet, the upper part applied with a gilt-metal moulding pierced with a foliate design, 1890s, 54in (137cm) high.
$5,500–6,500 P(C)

An Art Nouveau inlaid mahogany and glazed display cabinet, with open section over double doors, raised on tapering supports, c1890, 72in (183cm) high.
$3,200–3,500 AAV

An Art Nouveau mahogany display cabinet, with 2 glazed doors enclosing shelves, late 19thC, 35½in (90cm) wide.
$1,200–1,400 P(C)

An Austro-German mahogany-veneered mirror-back display cabinet, carved with flowers, the glazed doors enclosing 3 compartments and shelves, c1900, 35½in (90cm) wide.
$3,200–4,000 DORO

An Art Nouveau fruitwood dining chair, the back intarsia-inlaid in a chestnut leaf pattern, upholstered in cotton, German, c1890, 39¾in (101cm) high.
$600–700 S(Am)

Intarsia is a type of decorative geometric wood inlay.

A mahogany dentist's cabinet, by The American Cabinet Co, with up-and-over glazed doors with metal glazing bars, enclosing drawers and shelves, on 5 carved claw feet, early 20thC, 30in (76cm) wide.
$1,600–1,800 DD

An Art Nouveau mahogany armchair, c1900.
$800–1,000 ANO

An Art Nouveau mahogany corner chair, the legs joined by X-shaped stretcher, c1895.
$350–400 STK

A pair of Art Nouveau beech elbow chairs, by William Birch, with upholstered seats, c1900.
$750–900 P

▶ A set of 4 Art Nouveau mahogany chairs, the back splats inlaid in coloured woods with stylized foliage, upholstered seats, c1900.
$750–900 P

An Art Nouveau mahogany armchair, c1900, 45in (114.5cm) high.
$1,000–1,200 ASA

A brown stained wood armchair, by J. & J. Kohn, No. 714, brand stamp and label to underside, c1905.
$1,000–1,200 DORO

An Art Nouveau cast-iron bedroom fireplace, c1901, 37in (94cm) wide.
$400–500 A&H

◄ An Art Nouveau gilt-metal-framed firescreen, the glass panel inset with stylized foliate design in colours, c1890, 32in (81.5cm) high.
$500–550 GAK

A painted wood armchair, by Wilhelm Schmidt, upholstered in white leather, c1902.
$2,000–2,200 S(NY)

A pair of upholstered armchairs, by Eugène Gaillard, the mahogany frames carved with scrolling foliate tendrils, c1905.
$10,000–10,500 S

An Art Nouveau mahogany cake stand, slight damage, c1905, 31in (78.5cm) high.
$150–180 STK

21 Years Ago …

A Gallé oak and marquetry etagère, inlaid in various fruitwoods, inlaid signature, late 19thC, 31in (79cm) wide. **C**

Twenty-one years ago, this occasional table was valued at $500–600 and today would realize $1,600–2,000. This etagère displays simple yet elegant lines with interesting marquetry inlay. The marketplace for Gallé furniture, especially larger items, appears to be centred primarily in Paris and New York. A substantial amount of furniture was produced in the style of Gallé during and after his lifetime (Gallé died in 1904), so inlaid signatures are important.

A Majorelle mahogany four-piece salon suite, each piece carved with pine cones and leaves upholstered in tan leather, c1900.
$10,500–11,500 S(NY)

An Art Nouveau bentwood salon suite, c1900, settee 42½in (108cm) long.
$1,000–1,200 WDG

► An Art Nouveau oak mirror-back sideboard, the mirror plate and shaped shelf flanked by tapered columns headed by openwork heart motifs, the lower section with 2 cupboard doors inlaid with stylized plant forms, c1900, 56¼in (143cm) wide.
$900–1,200 S(S)

A Daum etched and enamelled glass winter landscape vase, with enamelled signature, c1900, 4¾in (12cm) high.
$3,000–3,500 PSG

A Gallé enamelled decanter, with gold inclusions, c1900, 9½in (24cm) high.
$6,500–7,200 ART

A Daum rose-tinted glass vase, acid-etched with poppies and foliage, heightened with gilding and applied with a flower and foliage embellished foot, maker's mark 'LP', c1900, 5in (12.5cm) high.
$400–500 P

A Gallé green glass dish, with enamelled figures in the centre, on 3 ball-shaped feet, c1900, 6in (15cm) wide.
$1,800–2,000 ART

◄ A Gallé yellow and white glass vase, decorated with red flowers, c1907, 7in (18cm) high.
$2,000–2,500 ASA

A Daum etched and enamelled white mottled glass sweet pea vase, with orange foot, etched mark, c1910, 9in (23cm) high.
$2,300–2,500 S(Am)

A Gallé cameo glass landscape vase, with blue mountains and lake, c1900, 13in (33cm) high.
$12,000–13,500 ART

A Daum mottled yellow glass vase, graduating to aubergine at the bottom, etched and enamelled with cornflowers, c1910, 3in (7.5cm) high.
$2,000–2,200 ART

A Gallé mould-blown glass vase, decorated with clematis design in yellow, red, blue and green, c1900, 6¾in (17cm) high.
$5,000–5,600 PSG

A Légras 'End of Day' orange and yellow glass vase, over-painted with poppies, signed, c1910, 18in (45.5cm) high.
$300–330 AAV

◄ A Harrach'sche Glasfabrik vase, the violet tinted glass with a spray of flowers enamelled in gold, the lower rim decorated with a gold band, gold slightly rubbed, c1900, 9½in (24cm) high.
$1,400–1,600 DORO

Gallé Cameo Glass

Within the last 5 years a significant number of fake Gallé cameo glass vases have appeared on the market. Most have come from eastern Europe; they are signed in cameo 'Gallé Tip' (for Tip read 'Type'). It does not take too much imagination on the part of the unscrupulous to arrange the removal of the word 'Tip' by means of grinding and polishing, and many examples have had this treatment.

Careful examination of the surface often reveals a depression near the signature which should raise suspicion. The bases of most of these recent imports are moulded and lack evidence of the polished and ground pontil mark found on many of the originals.

A Loetz ruby-red glass vase, decorated with iridescent turquoise and gold streaks, with openwork silvered-metal mount, c1899, 10¼in (26cm) high.
$5,500–6,500 S

A Steuben Jack-in-the-pulpit glass vase, the iridescent amber glass decorated with silvery-blue feathering, inscribed 'aurene', c1910, 8½in (21.5cm) high.
$4,500–5,000 S(NY)

An American leaded glass window, depicting flying birds above reeds and water lilies, the sky in shades of amber with pink clouds, early 20thC, 47in (119.5cm) high.
$4,000–4,500 S(NY)

A Loetz iridescent green glass bowl, c1900, 4½in (11.5cm) high.
$450–500 RUSK

A Stevens & Williams silver-mounted rock-crystal glass rose bowl, engraved and dated '1904', 8in (20.5cm) diam.
$4,000–5,000 ALiN

A Tiffany Favrile paperweight glass vase, the pale amber glass decorated with foliage and trailings in brick-red and ochre, the interior with amber iridescence, inscribed mark, c1909, 4¾in (12cm) high.
$6,500–7,500 S(NY)

A green glass and silver-mounted claret jug, with engraved thistle decoration, silver collar and lid with thumb rest, marked for 1894, maker N & W, late 19thC, 8¾in (22cm) high.
$800–1,000 P(B)

A Moser blue glass and enamel vase, decorated with leaves and branches, painted in colours with applied metal acorns, signed, c1900, 3½in (9cm) high.
$550–650 P(B)

A Tiffany Favrile glass floriform vase, the golden-yellow iridescent glass decorated with fine lined feathering in white and orange, 1894–1918, 5½in (14cm) high.
$3,500–4,000 S(NY)

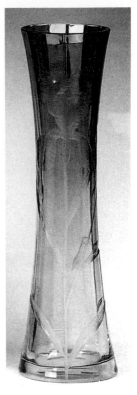

A Ludwig Moser & Söhne glass clear vase, graduating to purple and decorated with a carved iris twig, c1914, 15¾in (40cm) high.
$1,000–1,200 DORO

ART NOUVEAU JEWELLERY

◄ A French 18ct gold, pearl and diamond pendant, designed as an elegant flower, the bud and pendant pavé set with rose diamonds and baroque pearls, c1900.
$800–1,000 S(Am)

A diamond brooch, designed as a female head embellished with a diamond-set hair ornament and dog collar, original pearl drop missing, c1900.
$800–1,000 S(Am)

A silver-gilt, enamel and pearl brooch, the stem and bud with pale green *plique-à-jour* enamel leaves suspending 2 flowerhead drops, the petals of fresh water pearls, c1900.
$1,600–1,800 P(Gen)

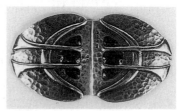

A silver buckle, the lower part in the form of a reclining lady, Birmingham, c1900, 3 1/4in (8.5cm) wide.
$500–550 SHa

A silver buckle, in a silver-plated surround, Chester, c1904, 3in (7.5cm) wide.
$350–400 SHa

A silver buckle, set with blue stones, by Deakin & Frances, Birmingham 1905, 3¾in (9.5cm) wide.
$650–750 SHa

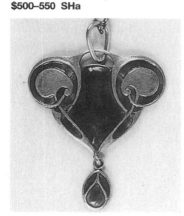

A set of 6 Art Nouveau sterling-silver buttons, c1895.
$400–500 SHa

A silver and enamel pendant, set with blue stones, by Murrle, Bennett & Co, c1900, 1½in (4cm) wide.
$650–750 SHa

A copper and lapis lazuli brooch, designed by F. Zwollo Jr, decorated with hammered stylized floral ornament, the centre set with a lapis lazuli, marked, c1915, 3¼in (8.5cm) diam.
$800–900 S(Am)

A gold and enamel pendant, modelled as 2 stylized bell-shaped flowers enamelled in shades of grey to mauve, the borders set with amethysts, diamonds and pearl berries, slight damage, c1900.
$2,000–2,500 P(Gen)

A gold, enamel and gem-set pendant, modelled as a peacock, *plique-à-jour* enamelled in white and pale green with diamond border detail, a pale ruby to the surmount and a pearl and ruby pendant drop below, c1900.
$4,000–4,500 P(Gen)

A Daum bronzed standard lamp, with pierced and stylized scrolled finials, palmette decoration with beaded bands, the shade etched and cut, marked, c1900, 63in (160cm) high.
$11,500–13,000 FHF

A Gallé cameo glass ceiling light, the shade with a design of apple blossoms cut in deep amber over a frosted ground, original brass hanger, signed, c1920, 14in (35.5cm) diam.
$4,500–5,000 JAA

An American Art Nouveau spelter and slag glass table lamp, the base with moulded poppies, early 20thC, 23in (58.5cm) high.
$2,000–2,500 DuM

A Gallé cameo glass lamp, decorated with Trees at Sunset, the domed top with butterflies hovering over blossoms, signed, c1895, 14in (35.5cm) high.
$12,000–13,500 NOA

A Handel copper-patinated-bronze and stained-glass Apple Blossom table lamp, c1910, 23¾in (60.5cm) high.
$2,800–3,200 NOA

A Tiffany Favrile glass and Rookwood standard glaze pottery lamp, decorated by Matthew Daly, inscribed, c1900, 20½in (52cm) high.
$13,000–15,500 B&B

A Rozenburg lamp, globe replaced, c1910, 17¾in (45cm) high.
$650–800 OO

An Art Nouveau gilt-metal four-light fitting, c1900, 22in (56cm) high.
$1,200–1,400 PF

A Tiffany bronze counter-balance bridge lamp base, with a brown/green patina, stamped mark, c1899–1920, 56½in (143.5cm) high.
$2,800–3,200 WW

Miller's Compares

I A Tiffany Favrile glass and bronze Poppy Filigree lamp, shade and base with impressed marks, 1899–1920, 24⅛in (51cm) high.
$90,000–105,000 S(NY)

II A Tiffany Favrile glass and bronze Dragonfly lamp, shade unsigned, base with impressed mark, 1899–1920, 21in (54.5cm) high.
$44,000–48,000 S(NY)

The market for Tiffany lamps is well and truly centred in their country of origin, with the **New York** auction houses attracting the most important examples. The Poppy Filigree lamp is considered desirable especially when combined with an interesting Tiffany Studios bronze base, as seen in item I. The overall effect is a harmonious balance between colour and form. The Dragonfly lamp in item II also employs the filigree effect in the insects' wings and the shade is only 4in (10cm) smaller than that of the Poppy lamp. The Dragonfly shade of item II, however, is unsigned, lacks its original pierced bronze cover and also appears to sit a little uncomfortably on its Tiffany Studios bronze base.

ART NOUVEAU METALWARE

A pewter biscuit barrel and cover, by Archibald Knox for Liberty & Co, embellished with 4 stylized plant-form motifs, marked 'English Pewter', c1903, 5½in (14cm) high.
$720–800 P

A silver box, designed by Kate Hams, retailed by Liberty & Co, c1910, 4½in (11.5cm) wide.
$600–650 ASA

A pair of Continental Art Nouveau bronze candlesticks, each cast as a poppy on a foliate base, the open petals forming drip pans, heightened with pale-green patination, c1900, 10¼in (26cm) high.
$900–1,000 P

A Liberty Tudric pewter two-handled loving cup, the border decorated with Art Nouveau-style flowering tree design, inscribed 'For Old Times Sake', impressed mark, 1920s, 8in (20.5cm) high.
$500–550 GAK

A Tiffany & Co sterling silver bottle holder, marked 'John C. Moore', c1910, 6in (15cm) diam.
$1,500–1,650 SHa

A pair of French gilded-pewter candelabra, by C. Bonnefond, c1900, 13½in (34.5cm) high.
$3,200–3,500 ANO

A WMF pewter four-light pierced candelabrum, c1910, 14½in (37cm) high.
$500–550 JD

A silver casket, by Nathan & Hayes, the hinged cover repoussé-decorated with a portrait of a maiden, the interior cedar-lined for cigarettes, Chester 1906, 6¼in (16cm) wide.
$500–550 WW

A pewter candlestick, by Imperial Zinn, in the form of an abstract reclining body, c1900, 11in (28cm) high.
$200–250 P(B)

A pair of Georg Jensen silver candelabra, c1919, 11in (28cm) diam.
$40,000–50,000 SFL

These candelabra are of complicated construction and of superb quality.

WMF Pewter

The popularity of WMF and Continental Art Nouveau pewter has resulted in a large influx of modern-day reproductions. Most of the copies are stamped on the reverse with an oval panel enclosing an angel and the initials 'AB'. Despite the attention to detail and simulated wear and tear, those examples that incorporate, in particular, scantily draped maidens lack the finesse of detail and modelling of the original.

An Art Nouveau hammered silver three-handled cup, maker's mark overstruck, 1910, 14½in (37cm) high.
$1,300–1,600 Gam

A Liberty Tudric pewter dish, designed by Archibald Knox, with glass liner by James Powell of Whitefriars, c1905, 5in (12.5cm) diam.
$350–400 RUSK

A WMF pewter dish, in the form of a kneeling boy watching a frog on a pond, factory mark, c1910, 7¾in (20cm) wide.
$250–300 P(B)

A silver two-handled porringer, by Wakely & Wheeler, Dublin 1901, 9½in (24cm) wide.
$1,000–1,200 SIL

A WMF figural pewter dish, decorated in relief with a maiden in long robes, maker's mark, c1900, 12¼in (31cm) wide.
$380–420 P

A pierced silver mirror, London 1901, 16½in (42cm) high.
$380–420 Doc

A silvered-bronze panel, by D. Puech, modelled in relief with a naked figure of a maiden among water and reeds, with a view of Paris in the distance, c1900, 24in (61cm) wide.
$8,500–9,500 ART

An Art Nouveau silver photograph frame, c1902, 5in (12.5cm) square.
$650–720 ASA

◄ A WMF silver-plated easel mirror, with classical female piper flanking bevelled plate, c1900, 16½in (42cm) high.
$1,600–2,000 RBB

A pair of W. A. S. Benson silver spoons, each handle with intertwined heart and flowerhead motifs, London 1911, 6¼in (16cm) long.
$1,000–1,200 WDG

A WMF pewter tea and coffee service, c1900, coffee pot 9in (23cm) high.
$720–800 DQ

▶ A gilt and patinated-bronze figural vase, by Emmanuele Villanis, the neck flanked by 2 naked female figures cast with morning glories, inscribed 'E. Villanis', late 19thC, 35in (89cm) high.
$7,500–8,000 S(NY)

ART DECO CERAMICS

An Augarten vase, designed by Franz von Zülow, polychrome-decorated and highlighted in black, marked, c1925, 6in (15cm) high.
$1,600–2,000 DORO

A Carlton Ware hand-painted cottage biscuit barrel and cover, original handle, 1932, 8in (20.5cm) high.
$130–160 BKK

A Lallemant glazed earthenware vase, painted in black and rust on a cream ground with a dockside scene, marked, c1925, 13in (33cm) high.
$1,100–1,250 B&B

▶ A Keramis earthenware vase, decorated with floral bands in blue and yellow on a cream crackled ground, stamped mark, 1920s, 10½in (26.5cm) high.
$480–560 S(Am)

A Carlton Ware box and cover, decorated with a stylized landscape on a dark red ground, over-painted in gilt, with lustre-green interior, stamped, c1920, 5½in (14cm) long.
$115–130 P(B)

A Gouda vase, decorated with Bloemen pattern, c1929, 11in (28cm) high.
$575–650 OO

A Limoges tête-à-tête, decorated with black cats on a yellow band, c1920.
$480–560 HAC

A Carlton Ware charger, enamelled and gilt with 2 Egyptianesque fan-like flowers and smaller flowers, marked, c1930, 12½in (32cm) diam.
$4,800–5,600 P

A Gouda tray, decorated in orange, turquoise and blue on a white ground, c1932, 13in (33cm) wide.
$200–250 OO

A Mougin stoneware vase, moulded in relief with figures before a temple, glazed in cream with brown outlines, slight damage, marked, c1930, 15in (38cm) high.
$2,200–2,400 B&B

A Poole Pottery biscuit barrel, Carter Stabler & Adams, impressed marks and initials, c1932, 5in (12.5cm) high.
$525–575 RUSK

A Poole Pottery vase, Carter Stabler & Adams, painted in buff, grey, black and blue with stylised flower and leaf motifs, artist's initial 'H', pattern code 'LJ', c1925, 11¾in (30cm) high.
$2,200–2,450 RTo

A Radford vase, with brown and green decoration on a cream ground, c1935, 5in (12.5cm) high.
$55–75 DSG

A Shelley Harmony dripware butter dish, c1930, 8in (20.5cm) long.
$65–75 HEW

◄ A Pilkington's Royal Lancastrian model of a scarab, c1925, 2½in (6.5cm) long.
$160–200 DSG

A Wiener Werkstätte ceramic box and cover, designed by Josef Hoffmann, decorated with green and black lines on a white ground, c1925, marked 'WW', 4½in (11.5cm) wide.
$1,400–1,550 DORO

A Pilkington's Royal Lancastrian plate, decorated in pale green on a cream ground, 1930s, 8in (20.5cm) diam.
$160–200 ASA

A Radford vase, decorated in buff on a mottled blue ground, 1936, 11in (28cm) high.
$200–230 HEW

A Shorter & Son Wave vase, shape No. 183, with mottled decoration on a red ground, c1932, 8½in (21.5cm) high.
$115–130 BKK

CLARICE CLIFF

A Clarice Cliff bowl, decorated with Red Trees and House design, 1931, 9in (23cm) diam.
$650–750 HEW

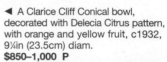

A Clarice Cliff Celtic Harvest bowl, decorated with yellow wheat-sheaves, 1930s, 9in (23cm) wide.
$270–300 DQ

◄ A Clarice Cliff Conical bowl, decorated with Delecia Citrus pattern, with orange and yellow fruit, c1932, 9¼in (23.5cm) diam.
$850–1,000 P

A Clarice Cliff figural candlestick, in the form of a woman streaked in orange and brown, holding a floral encrusted sconce, Bizarre mark, c1930, 7¼in (18.5cm) high.
$600–650 P

A Clarice Cliff Pastel Autumn candle holder, c1930, 3½in (9cm) high.
$1,400–1,600 DSG

A Clarice Cliff Bizarre coffee pot, decorated with Capri pattern in orange, marked, finial restored, c1935, 7in (18cm) high.
$275–300 GAK

A Clarice Cliff Oasis jug, c1930, 2½in (6.5cm) high.
$525–600 DSG

A Clarice Cliff jug, decorated with Capri pattern, 1935, 11in (28cm) high.
$1,000–1,150 HEW

A Clarice Cliff plate, decorated with Tropic pattern, cracked, 1933, 9in (23cm) diam.
$2,000–2,300 BKK

This rare pattern was previously called Pink Tree. The correct name is Tropic, as it was hand-painted on the back of a plate.

A Clarice Cliff Celtic Harvest pot and cover, 1939, 4in (10cm) high.
$115–130 HEW

A Clarice Cliff sugar shaker, decorated with Sungleam pattern, c1932, 5½in (14cm) high.
$1,100–1,300 DSG

◄ A Clarice Cliff sugar shaker, shape No. 489, decorated in Honolulu pattern, 1932, 5½in (14cm) high.
$3,000–3,500 BKK

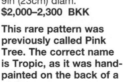

A Clarice Cliff part coffee service, comprising 15 pieces, brightly painted with Garland pattern, printed marks, 1929.
$730–830 Bea(E)

A Clarice Cliff Fantasque Bizarre vase, shape No. 342, decorated in Orange Autumn pattern, c1930, 7¾in (19.5cm) high.
$1,000–1,150 DD

A Clarice Cliff Bizarre part dinner service, comprising 22 pieces, decorated with Full Circle pattern, black rubber stamp mark, c1933.
$200–250 GAK

A Clarice Cliff toast rack, decorated with Crocus pattern, c1936, 6½in (16.5cm) long.
$600–700 BKK

A Clarice Cliff Bizarre vase, decorated with Inspiration pattern, the turquoise ground with geometric patterns in blues, black and pinks, slight damage, marked, 1930s, 8in (20.5cm) high.
$850–1,000 P(B)

A Clarice Cliff Conical vase, decorated with Forest Glen pattern, 1935, 18¾in (47.5cm) high.
$1,150–1,300 MJB

A Clarice Cliff Lotus vase, with single handle, decorated with Forest Glen pattern, 1935, 7¾in (19.5cm) high.
$900–1,000 MJB

Further Reading

Miller's Art Deco Antiques Checklist, Miller's Publications, 1991

21 Years Ago …

A Clarice Cliff wall mask, Marlene, c1933, 7in (18cm) high. **AP**

Twenty-one years ago this wall mask, entitled Marlene, was priced at $70–80. Today its value would be $250–350. The fortunes of Clarice Cliff have been somewhat mixed during the past two decades, with interest waxing and waning and then waxing again. Today interest continues at fever pitch, stimulated by the publication of several books and an active collectors' club. Masks such as Marlene have not attracted as much interest as other Clarice Cliff items, although they are still considered desirable. Watch out for fakes, poorly decorated in odd colours and a strange base glaze.

A Clarice Cliff Celtic Harvest bowl, decorated in yellow, orange and green, with corn and wheatsheaves on a cream ground, c1935, 13in (33cm) wide.
$730–830 BEV

A Clarice Cliff Fantasque Bizarre jug, decorated with Summerhouse pattern, with red hut, green tree and yellow foliage, black printed mark, c1931, 6½in (16.5cm) high.
$650–800 GAK

A Clarice Cliff jug, decorated with Canterbury Bells pattern, c1932, 7in (18cm) high.
$800–1,000 BEV

SUSIE COOPER

A Susie Cooper coffee service, decorated with brown and green on a white ground, c1960, coffee pot 8in (20.5cm) high.
$480–550 HEW

A Susie Cooper tea-for-two, decorated with a sage-green band on a cream ground, c1938, teapot 5½in (14cm) high.
$325–400 DSG

CHARLOTTE RHEAD

A Charlotte Rhead bowl, decorated with blue, pink, green and yellow, c1933, 10in (25.5cm) diam.
$400–450 HEW

A Charlotte Rhead plate, decorated in brown and green with Autumn Leaves pattern, c1935, 11in (28cm) diam.
$160–200 HEW

A Charlotte Rhead Bursleyware charger, decorated in blue and orange with pattern No. 1293, 1930s, 16in (40.5cm) diam.
$260–280 PCh

A Charlotte Rhead tapered bowl, decorated with grey and blue mottled glaze, trellis design and a band of trailed leaves and fruit, c1930s, 9¾in (24.5cm) diam.
$140–160 L&E

A Charlotte Rhead vase, decorated with Autumn Leaves pattern, c1935, 12in (30.5cm) high.
$400–450 HEW

A Charlotte Rhead commemorative mug, decorated in blue and white, 1937, 7in (18cm) high.
$300–330 HEW

Miller's is a price GUIDE not a price LIST

A Charlotte Rhead Byzantine vase, by Crown Ducal, decorated with flowers and leaves in blue, green, yellow and orange on a mottled orange ground, marked, 1930s, 12¼in (31cm) high.
$480–560 S(S)

ART DECO CLOCKS

A brass timepiece, by
Breguet, with silvered dial,
1930s, 4in (10cm) high.
$1,800–2,000 Bea(E)

A chrome-plated mantel
clock, by J. L. Reutter,
Atmos, with silvered dial,
in a glass case, 1930s,
9¼in (23.5cm) high.
$1,400–1,550 Bon

A walnut longcase clock,
the silvered-dial marked
The Enfield, Camerer Cuss
& Co, London, c1938,
75in (190.5cm) high.
$750–850 CGC

21 Years Ago ...

A Lalique opalescent glass
clock, 'Inseparables', moulded
mark 'R. Lalique', 1920s,
4¼in (11cm) high. **S**

Twenty-one years ago this Lalique clock was
priced at $525–600. Today it would be valued at
$2,500–3,000. The Lalique market has proved to
be something of a roller-coaster ride, but
Japanese interest towards the end of the 1980s
pushed prices sky high before they fell back to
earth with a bump in the early 1990s. 'Inseparables'
has always been a favourite design among
collectors and is considered even more desirable
when the clock-face centre is painted with blue
budgerigars. The original leather case can increase
the value by at least $500.

A Menneville gilt-metal and onyx figural mantel clock,
mounted with a lady in a long dress and cap, repaired,
base inscribed, c1925, 22¼in (56.5cm) wide.
$2,200–2,500 S(NY)

A silver and enamel
boudoir timepiece, the fan-
shaped case enamelled in
pink over feathered
decoration, maker's mark
possibly HH, Birmingham
1928, 4in (10cm) high.
$750–850 S(S)

A Continental Art Deco
chrome clock, c1934,
6in (15cm) high.
$100–130 BKK

Cross Reference
See Colour Review

ART DECO WATCHES

A Cartier gold, rock
crystal, enamel and
diamond open-face dress
watch, the nickel lever
movement with 19 jewels,
c1920, 47mm diam.
$6,500–7,500 S(NY)

A Cyma Watch Co gold,
silver, metal and enamel
shutter clip watch, the
nickel lever movement
with 15 jewels, case
signed Verger Frères,
c1920, 41mm long.
$2,000–2,300 S(NY)

A Dunhill silver watch,
in the form of a cigarette
lighter, with nickel lever
movement, signed,
c1925, 55mm high.
$2,200–2,500 S(NY)

A diamond bracelet watch,
with arched oblong
baguette diamond case,
on a mesh strap, c1935.
$3,000–3,300 P

ART DECO FIGURES

An ivory figure, by Joe Descomps, entitled 'Beauty of Paris', on an onyx base, c1920, 10in (25.5cm) high.
$5,500–6,500 ASA

An Art Deco spelter figure of a dancer, signed to base 'Fayral', c1920, 17in (43cm) high.
$680–740 P(B)

An Austrian Art Deco figure, holding a pink floral dress, c1930, 14in (35.5cm) high.
$1,300–1,600 ASA

A bronze figure holding a marble ball, by Guiraud Rivière, entitled 'Stella', c1925, 11½in (29cm) high.
$3,200–3,600 ART

A bronze figure, cast from a model by Y. Guerbe, engraved marks, c1925, 25in (63.5cm) wide.
$1,100–1,350 Bon(C)

An Art Deco bronze female figure, holding a lamp, c1930, 19in (48.5cm) high.
$480–560 PCh

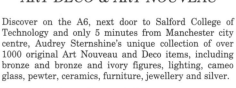

ART DECO FURNITURE

A pair of mahogany open armchairs, with curved solid backs and seats, on ebonized bracket feet, 1930s.
$525–575 P(Sc)

A French Art Deco figured-wood chest of drawers, 1930s, 31in (79cm) wide.
$3,200–3,500 S

A pair of Art Deco walnut and leather-upholstered cloud chairs, each lobed back continuing to the arms, on short curved feet, 1930s.
$1,400–1,550 S(NY)

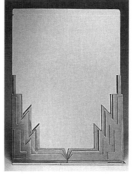

An Art Deco walnut cantilevered desk, probably French, slight damage, 1930s, 81in (205.5cm) wide.
$3,700–4,000 S(NY)

A Hagenauer chromed-metal mirror, the frame decorated with zigzags, impressed marks, c1925, 17in (43cm) high.
$4,000–5,000 S(NY)

A stained elm three-legged stool, designed by Josef Frank, Vienna, c1925, 14½in (37cm) high.
$4,200–4,800 DORO

An Art Deco walnut-veneered dining room suite, comprising dining table and 8 chairs, including 2 carvers, c1930s, table 96½in (245.5cm) long.
$2,600–3,000 P(Sc)

◄ An Art Deco burr-maple bedroom suite, by Mercier Frères, comprising a dressing table, stool, double wardrobe and double bed, c1935, wardrobe 58in (148cm) wide.
$4,800–5,600 P

ART DECO GLASS

A Daum acid-etched glass vase, enamelled in green, with silver mounts on rim and base, c1920, 8in (20.5cm) high.
$3,800–4,400 ART

A Daum acid-etched yellow glass vase, signed, c1930, 4in (10cm) high.
$1,800–2,000 ART

A Daum acid-etched granite-coloured glass vase, c1930, 6in (15cm) high.
$1,800–2,000 ART

A Lalique red glass vase, entitled 'Ronces', c1925, 9in (23cm) high.
$7,000–8,000 ART

A Lalique frosted-glass 'Skyscraper' perfume bottle, in enamelled chrome case, for Lucien Lelong, with 4 tiers of black enamel swags, with complementary stopper, c1929, 4½in (11.5cm) high.
$6,800–7,800 B&B

A Lalique opalescent bowl, decorated in the Lys pattern, c1930, 9in (23cm) diam.
$1,100–1,200 RUSK

A Powell amethyst glass bowl, by Whitefriars, with wavy decoration, c1930, 6in (15cm) high.
$120–140 RUSK

A Powell green glass square vase, c1930, 9in (23cm) high.
$120–150 TCG

Miller's Compares

I A Lalique grey frosted-glass vase, entitled 'Grande Boule Lierre', moulded in low relief with trailing ivy vines and foliage, inscribed 'R. Lalique', acid-etched, introduced 1919, 13¾in (35cm) high.
$14,500–16,000 S(NY)

II A Lalique grey frosted-glass vase, entitled 'Charmilles', with everted rim, moulded with overlapping serrated foliage, black patina, acid-stamped 'R. Lalique, France', introduced 1926, 13¾in (35cm) high.
$6,500–7,500 S(NY)

'Grande Boule Lierre', the Lalique vase in Item I, is intaglio-moulded with a Japanese-inspired ivy-leaf design, heightened with a pale grey surface stain. The glass itself is of quite thick gauge and weight and its desirability is enhanced by being a relatively rare and early production.

The design of item II, however, is less subtle, and the moulding lacks crisp definition. The thinner gauge used has resulted in a relatively lightweight vase. Because it proved less popular as a design, Lalique adapted it to a lampshade. A pair of 'Chamille' lampshades adorn the gateway to the Lalique glass church of St Mathews Millbrook on the Channel Island of Jersey.

A Lalique opalescent glass 'Chamonix' vase, signed, c1930, 6in (15cm) high.
$1,150–1,300 PSG

A Monart pink and blue glass vase, with combing, c1930, 7½in (19cm) high.
$300–330 TCG

A Czechoslovakian malachite and green glass box, the cover decorated with a nude classical maiden in relief, 1930s, 6in (15cm) wide.
$200–250 P(B)

ART DECO JEWELLERY

An Art Deco openwork diamond plaque brooch, c1930.
$1,300–1,450 WW

► A pair of Art Deco chalcedony cuff links, with diamond-set sleeves, c1925.
$1,400–1,600 P

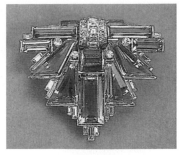

An Art Deco white gold clip, with tapering and baguette-shaped aquamarines and brilliant-cut diamonds, 1930s.
$2,800–3,200 TEN

A pair of Georg Jensen silver cuff links, 1930s.
$200–250 DID

A Lalique moulded glass necklace, the clear glass pendant fuchsia blossoms alternating with ovals and round beads, c1929, 17in (43cm) long.
$3,000–3,300 B&B

A French Art Deco platinum-set ring, c1935, ¾in (2cm) wide.
$800–900 WIM

ART DECO LIGHTING

An Ikora chromed-metal table lamp, designed by Paul Haustein for WMF, with 3 yellow glass cylindrical shades, marked, c1928, 23¼in (59cm) high.
$900–1,000 DORO

A Daum Nancy lamp, the shade and base in grey glass acid-etched with furrows, the iron mount painted silver, signed, c1925, 16¼in (41.5cm) high.
$8,000–9,000 S(NY)

► An Art Deco chrome four-branch ceiling light, with frosted glass shades, 1920–30, 19¾in (50cm) wide.
$200–250 OOLA

A Lalique glass lampshade, signed, 1920–30, 12in (30.5cm) wide.
$575–700 MARK

A *pâte de verre* ceiling light by Müller Frères, 1900–33, 12in (31cm) wide.
$480–560 P(B)

A pair of Sabino desk lamps, with bronze bases, signed, c1925, 23in (58.5cm) high.
$8,000–9,000 ART

ART DECO METALWARE

A Georg Jensen silver bowl, the rim with scrolling plant form decoration to 2 sides and underside, impressed mark and London import marks, dated '1931', 12½in (31.5cm) diam, 43oz.
$7,500–8,500 Mit

A French red and white enamel vase, with overlapping and geometric design, c1920, 4in (10cm) high.
$700–800 AAV

A Josef Hoffmann hammered silver-metal chalice, by the Wiener Werkstätte, embossed with a continuous frieze of fruiting vine motifs, the body embossed with small flowerheads within each central flute, raised on a spreading foot, marked, c1920–25, 6½in (16.5cm) high.
$6,500–7,500 WDG

An Art Deco cocktail unit, with chrome mixer, hour-glass-shaped measure, swizzle stick and corkscrew, on a mahogany base, 1930s, 13½in (34cm) long.
$150–165 P(B)

A Georg Jensen silver cocktail shaker, dated 'October 15th 1955', 13½in (34.5cm) high.
$4,000–5,000 SFL

▶ An Art Deco 9ct gold compact, with fish-scale pattern engraving, the clasp set with square rubies and brilliant-cut diamonds, hallmarked London 1948, by D. S. & S., 3in (7.5cm) wide, 5¼oz.
$730–830 WL

ART DECO CARPETS

A Chinese Art Deco rug, decorated with bamboo on a green ground, c1930, 93in (236cm) diam.
$680–730 TREA

A da Silva Bruhns floral wool carpet, woven in shades of blues, red, pink and brown on a cream ground, signed in the weave and monogrammed, c1930, 254¼ x 74½in (468 x 189cm).
$8,000–9,500 S

A Chinese Art Deco design terracotta carpet, with a rosette of flowerheads and circles in one corner, c1935–37, 124 x 132in (315 x 335cm).
$730–800 WW

This carpet is in the style of the British designer Betty Joel, whose carpets were woven in China, c1935–37.

◀ A Chinese Art Deco rug, with yellow floral sprigs on a soft green field, c1930, 36 x 24in (91.5 x 61cm).
$325–355 TREA

Twentieth-Century Design

CERAMICS

An earthenware teapot, by Bernard Leach, light brown with yellow slip-trailed design of a bird in flight to both sides, impressed seals 'BL' and 'St Ives', c1923, 10¼in (26cm) wide.
$4,500–5,000 Bon

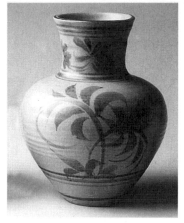

A stoneware vase, by Charles Vyse, grey-green with reddish brown foliage decoration, incised 'CV 1931' on base, 9½in (24cm) high.
$900–1,000 Bon

An Isle of Wight Pottery vase, designed by Ernest Saunders, with green decoration and orange rim, c1935, 7¼in (18.5cm) high.
$120–150 DSG

An earthenware five-piece salad set, by Piero Fornasetti, the painted fruit and vegetables incorporating face masks, factory mark, 1955, large bowl 9½in (24cm) diam.
$430–480 WBH

A Bing & Grøndahl flambé vase, with mottled brown decoration, c1950, 5¼in (13.5cm) high.
$200–250 DSG

A black and white raku bowl, by Martin Smith, the interior white with black design at the rim, c1976, 10¼in (26cm) high.
$2,000–2,300 Bon

A stoneware vase, by David Leach, decorated with ash glaze, c1950, 9½in (24cm) high.
$400–500 RUSK

▶ A spiral-shaped vase, by Chris Carter, with yellow and brown mottled decoration, c1995, 22½in (57cm) high.
$1,000–1,300 DSG

Chris Carter was a friend of Lucie Rie.

Modernism & Crafts

The minimalist style of modernism is usually justified by appeal to a set of spiritual values associated with integrity, fitness for purpose and utility. It is surprising, therefore, that modernists frequently seek to incorporate handmade objects and artisan traditions into their vision. This is how hand-tufted rugs, ceramics by Bernard Leach and Lucie Rie, and wooden furniture can all be included in modernist interiors that are otherwise austere functionalist environments. Craft objects are reinvented as pieces of sculpture and appreciated for their texture and idiosyncratic form. They work as a contrast to their surroundings.

An oak side table, by Gordon Russell, 1920s, 36in (91.5cm) wide.
$900–1,000 SWO

A light oak chest of drawers, by the School of Cotswold Furniture Designers, 1920s, 35½in (90cm) wide.
$1,000–1,100 OOLA

A nest of 4 oak tables, on block feet, 1930s, 21in (53.5cm) square.
$400–500 P

A beech, brass and leather folding chair, designed by Mogens Koch in 1932, made by Interna, Rud Rasmussens Snedkerier Aps, 1960.
$350–400 WDG

The concept for this chair was influenced by the Safari chairs designed by Kaare Klint. Considered too avant-garde to be produced in 1932, this design was not manufactured until 1960, since when it has become an icon in the history of Danish chair design.

An adzed oak dresser, by Robert 'Mouseman' Thompson of Kilburn, the 5 drawers with turned wood handles, flanked on each side by a six-panelled cupboard door with wrought-iron mounts, 1930s, 60in (152.5cm) wide.
$3,250–4,000 AH

A laminated chaise longue, by Marcel Breuer for Isokon, damaged, c1935.
$1,600–2,000 P

A laminated-birch dining chair, designed by Alvar Aalto, made by Finmar, maker's label, 1933.
$250–300 DORO

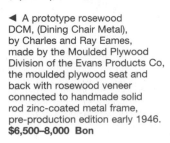

A laminated-beech and white enamelled-steel school desk and chair, by Jean Prouvé, the desk lid in solid beech, 1930s, 24½in (62cm) wide.
$1,600–1,800 DORO

A green painted sofa, designed by Børge Mogensen, made by Fritz Hansen, Denmark, with spindle back and sides, one side adjustable, c1945, 63in (160cm) long.
$2,300–2,600 WDG

◀ A prototype rosewood DCM, (Dining Chair Metal), by Charles and Ray Eames, made by the Moulded Plywood Division of the Evans Products Co, the moulded plywood seat and back with rosewood veneer connected to handmade solid rod zinc-coated metal frame, pre-production edition early 1946.
$6,500–8,000 Bon

An ash and teak Peacock chair, designed by Hans J. Wegner, made by Johannes Hansen, Denmark, c1947.
$7,250–8,000 WDG

'La Chaise', by Charles and Ray Eames, the white fibreglass free-form moulded shell supported on iron rods issuing from a wooden X-shaped base, c1990.
$5,000–5,750 Bon

This chair was originally designed in 1948 as a proposal for the Museum of Modern Art International Competition for Furniture Design. Although 'La Chaise' was not one of the prize-winning designs, its elegant form made it one of the most notable competition entries, appearing in both the catalogue and exhibition of 1950.

A 'Zigzag' white patinated elm chair, designed by G. Th. Rietveld, made by Gerard van de Groenekan, 1940s.
$3,500–4,000 S(Am)

A set of 6 'Ant' chairs, designed by Arne Jacobsen, made by Fritz Hansen, 1952.
$1,400–1,600 MARK

A birch and chromed-steel rocking stool, designed by Isamu Noguchi, c1953, made by Knoll Associates Inc, c1955, top 14in (35.5cm) diam.
$5,700–6,500 B&B

A pair of tubular armchairs, after Carlo Mollino, 1950s.
$725–800 WBH

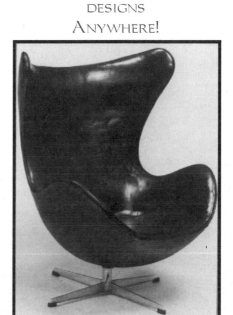
Sets/Pairs

Unless otherwise stated, any description which refers to 'a set' or 'a pair' includes a guide price for the entire set or the pair, even though the illustration may show only a single item.

A 'Champagne' chair, designed by Erwin and Estelle Leverne, with perspex seat on metal pedestal base, 1957.
$650–725 MARK

An 'Aluminium Group' armchair, designed by Charles Eames, made by Herman Miller, with ribbed red fabric on a five-support swivel base with casters, c1958.
$850–950 Bri

A 'Pastilli' chair, designed by Eero Aarnio, for Askooy, red reinforced polyester in 2 parts, 1967.
$650–800 WBH

A Brattrud & Richardson dining room suite, comprising a rosewood extending table on a pedestal base, and a set of 8 laminated palisander and chromium-plated chairs with wooden splats on metal supports, c1958, table 96in (244cm) long.
$600–725 P(B)

▶ A set of 4 Continental leather and aluminium armchairs, 1970s.
$2,000–2,500 ZOOM

A black stacking chair, designed by Vernon Panton, c1959, made by Herman Miller, 1968–79.
$500–575 MARK

A red plastic anthropomorphic chair, 'Floris', designed by Günter Beltzig in 1967, for Beltzig Bros, from an edition issued by Wolfgang F. Maurer, Munich, 1990, signed and marked '38/100'.
$1,800–2,200 DORO

▶ A 'D'Antibes' cabinet, designed by George J. Sowden for Memphis, lacquered wood with blue top and yellow sides, 1981, 23in (58.5cm) wide.
$3,500–4,000 Bon

A 'Palm Springs' dining table, designed by Ettore Sottsass, and a set of 6 'First' dining chairs, designed by Michele de Lucchi, Memphis, Milano, 1983 and 1984, table 84in (213.5cm) long.
$7,250–8,000 B&B

The Memphis Group

The Memphis Group was a studio group of architects and designers formed around Ettore Sottsass in 1980. Sottsass had worked in Milan since 1946 and was famous for his design work with Olivetti and the radical group Alchimia. The Memphis Group made a brave and successful attempt to end the rhetoric of anxiety in European design values. It allowed Sottsass to reconcile his appreciation of North American consumer culture and Asian decorative traditions to create a range of furniture, ceramics, glass and lighting that was decorative and whose defining logic was more frivolous than the functional logic of most European modernism. The Memphis Group was thus able to redefine modernism around more pleasurable and hedonistic values.

GLASS

A Leerdam Unica free-blown glass vase, designed by A. D. Copier, internally decorated with an enclosed opal layer and red coloured powders, 1946, 11½in (29cm) high.
$1,300–1,500 S(Am)

A glass vase, designed by Vicke Lindstrand for Kosta, internally decorated, with a dark purple band to base, incised 'Kosta LH 1242', c1955, 5½in (14cm) high.
$160–190 P(B)

Miller's is a price GUIDE not a price LIST

A flaring glass vase, designed by Vicke Lindstrand for Kosta, on a tall stem with 'graal' technique, vertical lines in brown, acid stamp, c1955, 7¾in (19.5cm) high.
$600–675 FF

An Iittala frosted 'Pot Hole' glass vase, designed by Tapio Wirkkala, engraved on base, 1956, 7in (18cm) high.
$950–1,050 FF

A Murano orange glass vase, with pinched lip, 9¼in (23.5cm) high.
$200–250 MARK

An Orrefors 'Ariel' technique green glass vase, by Ingeborg Lundin, signed, 1962, 5¾in (14.5cm) high.
$1,400–1,600 FF

Scandinavian Modernism

Scandinavian modernism is unusual in seeking to grow from the craft traditions of the Nordic countries. It is characterized by the use of traditional materials and in the high quality finish of its products. Alvar Aalto is the best known of its architects and designers. Other major names include Arne Jacobsen and Hans Wegner in furniture design, Wirkkala and Franck in glass and applied arts. The Scandinavian approach to modernism allowed progressive ideas of form to be reconciled with a traditional appreciation of skill. In Britain Jacobsen designed St Catherine's College, Oxford, as a coherent and integrated environment of building, lighting and furniture.

A glass ice bucket, by Strömberg, Sweden, with sterling silver mounts by Aage Dragsted, Denmark, 1960s, 8in (20.5cm) high.
$650–800 DID

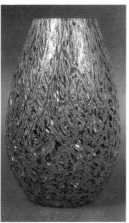

A Strathearn green speckled glass and cloisonné vase, c1963, 7½in (19cm) high.
$100–115 TCG

A Maltese Mdina 'axe' vase, 1970s, 10½in (26.5cm) high.
$200–250 MARK

◀ A Whitefriars 'Knobbly' blue glass vase, designed by William Wilson and Harry Dyer, 1960s, 7in (18cm) high.
$100–130 MARK

JEWELLERY

A diamond bangle, by G. Guillemin, set with cabochon moonstones, sapphires, rubies, citrines and diamonds, c1950, 2½in (6.5cm) diam.
$4,200–4,750 S

A 9ct gold bangle, set with an amethyst, by Elis Kauppi for Kupittaam Kulta, Turku, Finland, c1953.
$900–1,000 DID

A German gold wire brooch, by Grosse, in the form of a flower, c1961.
$500–600 S(Am)

A sterling silver torque, by Bent Gabrielsen Pedersen, for Hans Hansen, Denmark, the pendant set with black enamel, c1970.
$325–400 DID

An enamel and silver pendant, by Norman Grant, Edinburgh, c1960.
$250–325 DID

Cross Reference
See Colour Review

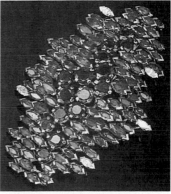

▶ An 18ct gold, sapphire and diamond brooch, by Grima, c1967.
$4,000–5,000 S

LIGHTING

A Modernist aluminium and patinated-metal triple-cone lustre, c1930, 39½in (100cm) long.
$2,400–2,600 S

A black-painted three-light floor lamp, by Arteluce, with brown, white and black shades, 1950s, 69in (175.5cm) high.
$2,700–3,000 WDG

A Rosenthal green-glazed porcelain table lamp, with plastic shade of Chinese lantern form, c1960, 22½in (57cm) high.
$200–250 DORO

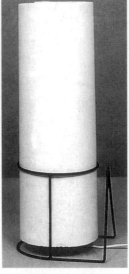

A black-lacquered metal table lamp, with hand-made paper shade, designed by Carl Auböck, c1950, 19¾in (50cm) high.
$260–280 DORO

An orange glass hanging lamp, 1950s, 18in (45.5cm) diam.
$130–160 ZOOM

A 'San Remo' lacquered metal and Perspex floor lamp, by Archizoom for Poltronova, 1968, 87in (221cm) high.
$2,500–3,000 S

Modern Lighting

Modern designers have sought to transform rooms by using lighting effects based on diffusion, reflection and deflection. In the 1950s, the Scandinavian solution was to reposition the hanging lamp to create asymmetrical lighting. The shades created for these lamps emphasize the sculptural quality that lighting can add to a room. The open planning of many modern living spaces often requires different kinds of lighting for specific tasks, reflected in the many small and adjustable lights produced since the 1960s. The 1970s' fad for spotlights was an attempt to bring dramatic cinema lighting effects into the home.

A white-painted metal and brass hanging lamp, 'Handgranate A 111', by Alvar Aalto for Valaistustyö, c1951, 17½in (44.5cm) high.
$2,500–2,700 S

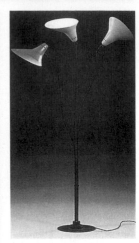

A painted-metal three-light floor lamp, by Boris Lacroix, the adjustable shades painted in yellow, grey and lilac, on an iron base, before 1954, 67¾in (172cm) high.
$9,000–10,000 S

A chromed plastic 'Pastillo' wall light, by Studio Tetrach for Valenti, stamped, 1969, 23½in (60.5cm) wide.
$320–350 DORO

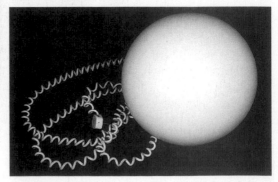

An Italian 'ball and chain' light, 1970s, 18in (45.5cm) diam.
$500–575 ZOOM

A parchment and inlaid wood armchair, by Carlo Bugatti, signed in watercolour, c1880.
$13,000–14,500 S(NY)

An Arts and Crafts oak desk and bookcase, the upper part with inscription, over leaded glass doors enclosing adjustable shelves, the desk with a leather-inset top, c1890, 42in (107cm) wide.
$5,200–5,800 TEN

A set of 14 oak dining chairs, by William Birch, High Wycombe, including 2 armchairs, with rush seats, c1900.
$6,500–7,500 MoS

A set of 6 Arts and Crafts oak chairs, including one carver, with rush seats.
$4,000–5,000 ASA

An Arts and Crafts oak settle, attributed to Jung, early 20thC, 91in (231cm) long.
$3,700–4,200 B&B

A stained-birch child's chair, by Frank Lloyd Wright, c1912.
$9,000–10,000 S(NY)

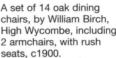

◄ An American Arts and Crafts Colonial longcase clock, dated '1911', 80in (203cm) high.
$4,300–5,000 TREA

An Arts and Crafts oak sideboard, the top cabinet with 2 doors concealing leaded glass windows, restored, c1870–1910, 90in (228.5cm) wide.
$12,000–13,500 TREA

A mahogany press cupboard, in the manner of Ambrose Heal, with decorative pewter and ebony inlay, early 20thC, 48in (122cm) wide.
$2,500–3,000 L&E

An Aesthetic Movement carved mahogany sideboard, by the Cincinnati Women's Wood Carving Movement, c1870, 97in (246.5cm) wide.
$11,000–13,000 SK

A teak and rosewood-inlaid stool, in the manner of Leonard Wyburd, with concave rattan seat, late 19thC, 25½in (65cm) square.
$800–900 TEN

A Royal Worcester 'Aesthetic' teapot and cover, by James Hadley, probably designed by R. W. Binns, marked, c1882, 6in (15cm) high.
$6,500–7,500 S(NY)

An Arts & Crafts pottery bowl, by Bernard Moore, c1890, 8in (20.5cm) diam.
$575–650 SHa

A Clutha green glass jug, by James Couper & Sons, Glasgow, designed by Dr Christopher Dresser, c1890, 8¾in (22cm) high.
$2,700–3,200 P(Sc)

A Clutha glass bowl, design attributed to Dr Christopher Dresser, retailed by Liberty & Co, c1890, 5in (12.5cm) diam.
$900–1,000 NCA

A pair of jade, hardstone and gold drop earrings, by Marie Zimmermann, c1925, 3in (7.5cm) long.
$5,000–5,750 S(NY)

A Guild of Handicrafts copper vase, attributed to J. Pearson, c1890, 11in (28cm) high.
$750–900 ANO

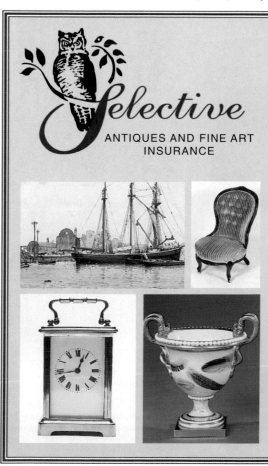

A mahogany and ivory-inlaid bookcase, designed by H. P. Berlage, 2 shelves replaced, c1900, 67½in (171.5cm) wide.
$3,200–3,600 S(Am)

A fruitwood marquetry buffet, signed 'L. Majorelle, Nancy', c1900, 58in (147.5cm) wide.
$32,000–33,500 S(NY)

An Austrian mahogany display cabinet, with replaced brass fittings and parts renewed on the back, c1900, 36¼in (92cm) wide.
$5,700–6,500 DORO

An Art Nouveau oak armchair, with 3 turned tapering front legs, c1900.
$1,600–2,000 ASA

A bamboo and cane child's rocking chair, c1900.
$200–250 P

An Art Nouveau tooled- and stained-leather and wood three-panel folding screen, in the manner of René Lalique, c1900, 73½in (186.5cm) high.
$26,000–28,500 S(NY)

A Belgian Art Nouveau fruitwood side-board, c1910, 46½in (118cm) wide.
$2,500–3,000 S(Am)

An Art Nouveau inlaid mahogany desk, attributed to J. S. Henry, c1905, 39in (99cm) wide.
$3,500–4,000 ANO

A French Art Nouveau marquetry table, Nancy School, c1900, 38in (96.5cm) wide.
$4,000–5,000 ASA

◄ A Josef Hoffman bent beech-wood salon suite, by J. & J. Kohn, comprising a settee, 2 armchairs and a table, suite model No. 728, c1906, settee 47in (119.5cm) long.
$5,000–6,000 S(NY)

An Amphora vase, restored, c1900, 19in (48.5cm) high. **$525–600 ANO**

An Amphora vase, c1900, 16in (40.5cm) high. **$200–250 ASA**

◀ An Amphora vase, c1910, 13¾in (35cm) high. **$75–90 P(B)**

An Amphora vase, by Riessner Stellmacher & Kessel, painted in the manner of Alphonse Mucha, damage to neck, c1900, 10¾in (27.5cm) high. **$900–1,000 P**

A Compton Pottery plaque, with inscription, c1900, 7 x 4¾in (18 x 12cm). **$160–200 DSG**

A Burmantofts jardinière and pedestal stand, c1900, 33in (84cm) high. **$1,600–2,000 ASA**

◀ A Gouda vase, by W. P. Hartgring, c1912, 17in (43cm) high. **$3,200–3,800 OO**

A Utrecht earthenware tulip vase, designed by J. W. Mijnlief, marked, c1896, 9¾in (25cm) high.
$3,200–3,600 S(Am)

A Pilkington's Royal Lancastrian lustre vase, by Richard Joyce, dated '1920', 5½in (14cm) high.
$800–900 DSG

A Minton 'Secessionist' ware vase, stamped No. 72, c1900, 8in (20.5cm) diam.
$575–650 ASA

A Minton 'Secessionist' ware jug and basin, marked, c1904, basin 20in (51cm) diam.
$850–950 P(B)

A Pilkington's Royal Lancastrian blue vase, c1915, 8in (20.5cm) high.
$250–350 ASA

A Primavera vase, French, c1910, 8¾in (22cm) diam.
$140–160 DSG

A Purmerend vase, c1896, 11in (28cm) high.
$1,300–1,450 OO

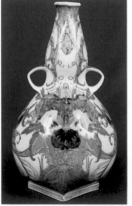

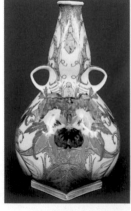

◄ A Rozenburg eggshell porcelain two-handled vase, by Sam Schellink, c1911, 7¼in (18.5cm) high.
$2,800–3,200 OO

► A Rozenburg eggshell porcelain vase and cover, c1905, 7¾in (19.5cm) high.
$2,800–3,200 OO

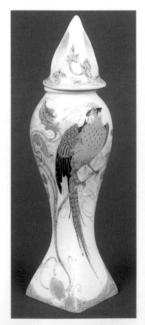

A Royal Worcester Sabrina ware jardinière, c1900, 11in (28cm) diam.
$750–850 DSG

A Royal Bonn bottle vase, c1910, 4¼in (11cm) high.
$200–250 DSG

A hand-painted figure of a maiden seated in a leaf-shaped dish, by Ernst Wahliss, c1900, 8½in (21.5cm) high.
$2,500–2,800 BKK

A Doulton Lambeth inkwell, c1877, 6in (15cm) high.
$650–750 PGA

A pair of Doulton Lambeth stoneware garden seats, by George H. Tabor, slight damage, impressed marks, c1880, 18in (45.5cm) high.
$2,000–2,200 RID

A Doulton Lambeth vase, by Elizabeth Atkins, c1882, 7¼in (18.5cm) high.
$500–575 DSG

A pair of Doulton Lambeth faïence vases, c1895, 21½in (54.5cm) high, converted to lamp bases.
$3,200–4,000 INC

A Royal Doulton Burslem Chang vase, c1930, 5½in (14cm) high.
$1,600–2,000 DSG

A Doulton Lambeth Diamond Jubilee mug, with silver rim, c1897, 8in (20.5cm) high.
$200–250 TMA

A Doulton Lambeth Slaters patent twin-handled vase, c1900, 9½in (24cm) high.
$320–360 P(B)

A Doulton Lambeth night-light, c1900, 7½in (19cm) high.
$60–75 DSG

A pair of Doulton Lambeth vases, by Hannah Barlow, incised marks, late 19thC, 10in (25.5cm) high.
$2,700–3,000 P(G)

A Royal Doulton vase, c1910, 7in (18cm) high.
$200–250 P(B)

► A Moorcroft vase, decorated with Cornflower pattern, signed and dated '1928', 16½in (42cm) high.
$4,500–5,000 S

A Moorcroft Flambé jar and cover, c1930, 7in (18cm) diam.
$800–900 PGA

A Moorcroft bowl, decorated with Fish pattern, signed, c1930, 4¾in (12cm) diam.
$800–900 CEX

A Moorcroft jardinière, decorated with Anemone pattern, signed, c1950, 9½in (24cm) diam.
$1,300–1,450 RUSK

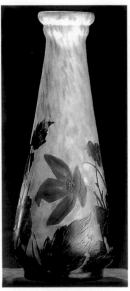

A Daum internally-decorated glass vase, signed and marked, c1900, 11¾in (29.5cm) high.
$7,500–9,000 DORO

A Daum applied wheel-carved cameo glass vase, marked, slight damage and restoration, c1909, 10¾in (27.5cm) high.
$65,000–80,000 S(NY)

A Loetz iridescent glass vase, c1900, 8in (20.5cm) high.
$2,000–2,500 ASA

A Daum internally-decorated acid-cut and enamelled glass vase, c1920, 18in (45.5cm) high.
$10,500–12,000 ART

◄ A Daum acid-cut and enamelled glass vase, c1910, 19thC, 9⅞in (25cm) high.
$1,100–1,300 AH

► A Daum acid-cut and enamelled glass vase, c1920, 4in (10cm) diam.
$3,400–3,800 ART

A Loetz iridescent glass vase, etched mark, c1900, 6in (15cm) high.
$1,000–1,150 P(B)

► An opalescent glass vase, inscribed 'L. C. Tiffany', c1890, 4¾in (12cm) high.
$2,500–3,000 JAA

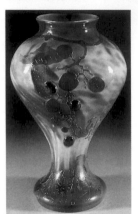

A Gallé wheel-carved, applied and fire-polished glass vase, with grape and vine decoration, signature in relief, c1900, 12in (30.5cm) high.
$3,600–4,000 FBG

A Loetz 'Papillon' iridescent glass vase, with silver deposit overlay, c1905, 4in (10cm) high.
$900–1,000 MoS

A Gallé cameo glass vase, overlaid in blue and green with flowering plants, c1900, 7in (18cm) high.
$4,000–4,500 ART

A glass vase, decorated with stag beetles, by Eugène Michel, engraved mark, c1900, 8in (20.5cm) high.
$20,000–22,000 S

A Tiffany Favrile bronze-mounted glass vase, c1900, 21¼in (54cm) high.
$26,000–32,000 S(NY)

ARTEMIS
DECORATIVE ARTS LTD

ガレ, ドーム, ルネ・ラリック

Leading dealer in 19th & 20th Century Decorative Arts. Established in 1974. Dedicated to fine quality. With 25 years experience and knowledge our Gallery offers clients professional advice and support. We carry varied stock of Galle, Daum, Lalique, Bronzes, Marbles, Lighting, Art Nouveau and Art Deco accessories.

36 Kensington Church Street, London W8 4BX
Tel 0171 937 9900 Tel/Fax: 0171 376 0377
Email: Artemis.w8@btinternet.com

LAPADA
MEMBER

A silver and copper punchbowl, set with opals, designed by Paulding Farnham, Tiffany & Co, marked on base, 1902, 21in (53.5cm) wide.
$21,000–24,000 S(NY)

A silver-coloured metal and ivory casket, by Edmond-Henri Becker for the Société Parisienne d'Orfèvrerie, stamped mark 'SPO', c1900, 6in (15cm) wide.
$7,500–9,000 S

An Art Nouveau pewter ice bucket, by Kayserzinn, retailed by Liberty & Co, stamped mark, c1902, 8in (20.5cm) high.
$900–1,000 RUSK

◀ A pewter and glass decanter, by Kayserzinn, c1900, 12in (30.5cm) high.
$1,400–1,550 SHa

▶ A pewter hot water jug, by Archibald Knox for Liberty & Co, marked, c1903, 7¾in (19.5cm) high.
$1,000–1,500 P

An Art Nouveau WMF inkwell, with glass body and plated cover, marked, c1905, 4in (10cm) high.
$320–360 P(B)

A Norwegian *plique à jour* enamel spoon, by Marius Hammer, c1900, 4¾in (12cm) long.
$300–350 AliN

An Art Nouveau green glass and silvered metal claret jug, c1900, 12in (30.5cm) high.
$900–1,000 ART

A green glass vase, by Alvin & Co, with silver overlay, c1905, 12in (30.5cm) high.
$3,500–4,000 SFL

A Liberty Tudric pewter desk clock, with copper and blue enamel dial, c1906, 4½in (11.5cm) high.
$1,300–1,450 RUSK

A pair of Art Nouveau silver frames, c1903, 13 x 10in (33 x 25.5cm).
$2,000–2,500 ASA

A silver and polychrome enamel vase, mark of Liberty & Co and Cymric, Birmingham 1902, 8¾in (22cm) high, 20oz.
$26,000–28,500 Bon

A Rozenburg earthenware clock garniture, by Sam Schellink, 1897, 14½in (37cm) high.
$5,000–5,500 OO

A Japanese-style silver and mixed metal mantel clock, by Tiffany & Co, marked, c1880, 8¾in (22cm) wide.
$52,000–57,000 S(NY)

An Art Nouveau diamond, enamel and seed pearl brooch, mounted in 18ct gold and platinum, c1900.
$3,700–4,200 S(LA)

A silver, enamel and hardstone necklace, by L. Gaillard, stamped, c1900, 27½in (70cm) long.
$16,500–18,000 P(Gen)

An opal, pearl, diamond and enamel pendant, by L. Gautrait, signed, c1900.
$28,000–32,000 S

An aquamarine and enamel pendant, by René Lalique, signed, c1903.
$40,000–45,000 S

A freshwater pearl, emerald and diamond pendant, by Philippe Wolfers, in the form of a stylized egret, marked, c1900.
$45,000–52,000 S

An amethyst, pearl and enamel pendant, c1900, 21½in (55cm) long.
$2,000–2,500 P(Gen)

▶ A silver, enamel and pearl pendant, c1900, 19½in (49.5cm) long.
$1,400–1,600 P(Gen)

A bronze figure, entitled 'Winged Victory', by L. Ernest Barrias, c1880, 16in (40.5cm) high.
$3,200–3,800 ART

A bronze figure, entitled 'Nature Revealing Herself to Science', by L. Ernest Barrias, c1890, 10in (25.5cm) high.
$8,000–9,000 ART

A French boxwood and ivory figure of a maiden, c1900, 8¾in (22cm) high.
$2,500–2,700 S(S)

An Austrian cold-painted and gilt-bronze figure of an Arabian dancer, by Franz Bergman, marked, late 19thC, 10¾in (27.5cm) high.
$2,200–2,400 CAG

A French parcel-gilt and patinated bronze figure, entitled 'Vers la Lumière', cast after a model by Louis Chalon, on a marble base, c1900, 29¾in (75.5cm) high.
$20,000–22,000 B&B

A bronze figure, entitled 'Darling', by C. J. R. Colinet, c1920, 10in (25.5cm) high.
$2,500–3,000 ASA

A gilt-bronze and ivory figure, entitled 'Crimean Dancer', by C. J. R. Colinet, c1900, 12in (30.5cm) high.
$7,000–8,000 ART

A Goldscheider terracotta bust, entitled 'La Fierté', c1900, 18in (45.5cm) high.
$2,000–2,500 ANO

A Goldscheider terracotta bust, c1900, 27in (68.5cm) high.
$4,000–5,000 ASA

A gilt-bronze figural lamp, 'Loïe Fuller', by Raoul François Larche, c1900, 13¼in (33.5cm) high.
$13,000–14,500 S(NY)

A gilt-bronze figure, 'l'Aurore', by August Moreau, signed, on an onyx stand, c1900, 9½in (24cm) high.
$900–1,000 P

◄ A gilt-bronze figure, 'La Cothurne', after a model by Agathon Leonard, signed, c1900, 20¾in (52.5cm) high.
$9,500–11,500 WDG

A French gilt-bronze and alabaster three-light lily lamp, after a model by Albert Cheuret, inscribed, early 20thC, 15in (38cm) high.
$6,500–7,500 B&B

A leaded glass and patinated-metal table lamp, possibly by Handel, slight damage, early 20thC, 27½in (70cm) high.
$4,500–5,500 B&B

A Tiffany Favrile glass and bronze filigree ball lamp, c1899, 21¾in (55.5cm) high.
$30,000–35,000 S(NY)

A Duffner & Kimberly leaded glass and gilt-bronze lamp, shade with impressed mark, c1910, 29in (73.5cm) high.
$22,000–24,000 S(NY)

A Handel reverse-painted glass and patinated-metal lamp, model No. 6688, signed, c1915, 23in (58.5cm) high.
$16,000–20,000 S(NY)

A Tiffany Favrile glass and gilt-bronze Venetian lamp, impressed marks, c1899, 19¾in (50cm) diam.
$33,000–40,000 S(NY)

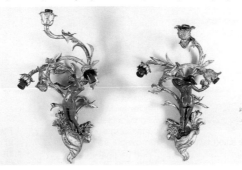

A Gallé cameo glass table lamp, signed, c1910, 22in (56cm) high.
$18,000–20,000 ART

A Müller Frères cameo glass and wrought-iron lamp, signed, c1900, 19in (48.5cm) high.
$26,000–32,000 S(NY)

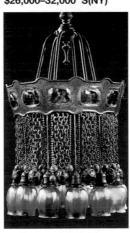

A Tiffany Favrile glass and bronze turtle-back tile Moorish chandelier, slight damage, inscribed 'L.C.T.', c1899, 38in (96.5cm) diam.
$73,000–83,000 S(NY)

A Gustav Gurschner bronze and Loetz iridescent glass lamp, impressed marks, c1900, 25in (63.5cm) high.
$13,000–15,000 S(NY)

A Pairpoint reverse-painted glass and silvered-metal butterfly and roses lamp, c1915, 20½in (52cm) high.
$9,000–10,000 S(NY)

A Jugendstil metal table lamp, on marble base, c1900, 14¼in (36cm) high.
$360–420 P

◄ A pair of gilt and patinated bronze figural three-light sconces, regilded, c1900, 25in (63.5cm) high.
$9,000–10,000 B&B

A Majorelle carved walnut
armoire, labelled, c1920,
78in (198cm) wide.
$4,000–4,500 B&B

A pair of maple-veneered tub armchairs, designed by Ray Hille, c1930.
$1,100–1,300 MoS

A limed oak armchair, c1930.
$250–300 AnSh

A pair of Le Corbusier-Jeanneret-Perriand chromed-
metal and leather chairs, 'Le Grand Comfort',
designed 1928, made by Heidi Webber, c1960.
$14,500–16,000 S(NY)

A set of 4 French Art
Deco walnut-veneered
dining chairs, 1930s.
$1,400–1,550 P(B)

A galuchat and ivory-inlaid
commode, attributed to Jean-Michel
Franck and Adolphe Chanaux,
with green marble top, c1927,
46¾in (119cm) wide.
$35,000–40,000 P(Z)

A Thonet bent beechwood six-piece salon suite,
attributed to Josef Hoffman, early 20thC, settee
46⅛in (118cm) long, and 2 similar armchairs.
$6,500–7,500 S(NY)

An oak and Macassar ebony 'Spirales' divan, by Emile-Jacques
Ruhlmann, upholstered in velvet, c1920, 72in (183cm) long.
$450,000–500,000 S

**This low divan was made in very small numbers with
variant details.**

A Dominique Macassar ebony dining table
and 8 dining chairs, stamped, c1930,
table 92½in (235cm) long.
$11,500–13,500 S(NY)

An Art Deco beechwood six-piece salon suite,
c1930, settee 50in (127cm) long.
$5,000–5,750 B&B

An Art Deco walnut and
satinwood sewing table,
the removable top
with ebonised pull
concealing another
removable tray, c1930,
22¾in (57.5cm) diam.
$600–700 P

A French Art Deco silvered-bronze
and marble console table, c1925,
40in (101.5cm) wide.
$48,000–56,000 S(NY)

A Boch Frères La Louvière
earthenware vase,
stamped factory mark,
1920s, 11¾in (30cm) high.
$800–900 S(Am)

A Susie Cooper twin-
handled vase, signed
'Bourne, Denby', c1930,
14½in (37cm) high.
$320–360 P(B)

A Burleigh Ware Golden Days
pattern dinner service, 1930s.
$1,000–1,200 BUR

► A Gouda deep dish, c1924,
18in (45.5cm) diam.
$2,500–3,500 OO

A Clews Chameleon Ware vase,
c1930, 3¾in (9.5cm) diam.
$65–80 PrB

► A Gouda Berka design toilet set,
c1925, bowl 14in (35.5cm) diam.
$1,000–1,200 OO

A Carlton Ware conical bowl,
stamped, c1935, 10½in (27cm) diam.
$1,300–1,600 P(B)

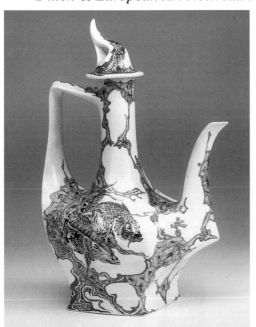

A Gouda Laric design jardinière,
c1930, 13in (33cm) diam.
$650–750 OO

A Gouda
Zenith factory,
with seagull
design, c1925,
18in (45.5cm) high.
$1,600–2,000 OO

► A Pilkington's
Royal Lancastrian
Lapis ware
vase, c1935,
8in (20.5cm) high.
$240–280 DSG

A Gray's Pottery plate, c1935,
13in (33cm) diam.
$300–350 HEW

A Myott hand-painted shallow fruit bowl,
c1932, 11in (28cm) diam.
$145–160 BKK

A Poole pottery vase,
Carter, Stabler & Adams,
impressed stamp, 1930s,
11in (28cm) high.
$550–650 P(B)

A Radford ware vase, c1935,
5¼in (13cm) high.
$100–120 DSG

A Roseville vase,
decorated with Fuchsia
pattern, American, 1940s,
8in (20.5cm) high.
$160–200 DSG

A pair of Schoonhoven earthenware tassas,
designed by Harm Ellens, one with minor
restoration, c1922, 8¾in (22cm) diam.
$5,500–6,500 S(Am)

A Shelley Sunrise and Tall Trees pattern morning
tea set, unused, c1928, with original box.
$2,400–2,800 BKK

A Ruskin pottery vase,
impressed mark, 1930,
12in (30.5cm) high.
$480–540 RBB

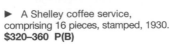

A Santa Domingo pottery vase,
c1920, 9½in (24cm) high.
$400–500 HUR

► A Shelley coffee service,
comprising 16 pieces, stamped, 1930.
$320–360 P(B)

A Shelley Harmony dripware octagonal bowl, c1930, 9in (23.5cm) diam.
$200–220 HEW

A Shelley Harmony dripware cake stand, c1930, 7in (18cm) diam.
$200–230 HEW

A Shelley Harmony dripware vase, c1930, 7in (18cm) high.
$200–220 HEW

A Shelley Acacia pattern hot water jug, c1933, 7½in (19cm) high.
$200-250 BKK

A Shelley conical dripware vase, c1930, 5in (12.5cm) high.
$160–220 HEW

A Charlotte Rhead Bursley Ware charger, c1930, 14½in (37cm) diam.
$575–650 DSG

◄ A Charlotte Rhead Burleigh Ware Sunshine teapot, c1930, 4½in (11.5cm) high.
$130–160 BDA

A Charlotte Rhead vase, c1935, 7½in (19cm) high.
$200–220 HEW

A Charlotte Rhead Bursley Ware Trellis pattern vase, with snake handle, c1942, 10in (25.5cm) high.
$480–540 BKK

A Charlotte Rhead two-handled vase, c1935, 6in (15cm) high.
$300–330 HEW

► A Charlotte Rhead three-handled vase, decorated with coloured flowers on a cream glaze, with blue rim, c1935, 8in (20.5cm) high.
$350–400 HEW

A Clarice Cliff Dover shape pot, decorated with Broth pattern, c1929, 9in (23cm) high.
$1,300–1,450 HEW

A Clarice Cliff Dover shape pot, decorated with Original Bizarre pattern, c1928, 6in (15cm) high.
$730–800 HEW

A Clarice Cliff Shape 132 ginger jar and cover, decorated with Comets pattern, c1930, 8¾in (22cm) high.
$6,000–7,000 BKK

A Clarice Cliff Shape 370 vase, decorated with Latona Knight Errant pattern, c1930, 6in (15cm) high.
$5,200–5,700 BKK

A Clarice Cliff Shape 358 vase, decorated with Gibraltar pattern, painted Fantasque Bizarre mark, minor restoration, c1930, 8¼in (21cm) high.
$1,400–1,600 M

A Clarice Cliff Fantasque wall plaque, decorated with Orange Chintz pattern, c1931, 13¼in (33.5cm) diam.
$1,800–2,200 DN

A Clarice Cliff Shape 55 bowl, decorated with Blue Heaven pattern, c1932, 10in (25.5cm) diam.
$1,600–2,000 BKK

A Clarice Cliff bowl, decorated with Secrets pattern, c1933, 7in (18cm) diam.
$730–800 HEW

A Clarice Cliff jug, decorated with Blue Chintz pattern, 1932, 7in (18cm) high.
$900–1,000 HEW

A Clarice Cliff jug, decorated with My Garden pattern, c1930, 9in (23cm) high.
$160–200 P(B)

▶ A Clarice Cliff plate, decorated with Secrets pattern, c1933, 9in (23cm) diam.
$800–900 HEW

A Clarice Cliff Greek shape jug, decorated with May Avenue pattern, mid-1930s, 9in (23cm) high.
$5,000–5,500 ROS

A Clarice Cliff Bizarre plate, c1935, 9in (23cm) diam.
$450–500 HBC

A Clarice Cliff eight-piece coffee service, c1935.
$160–200 P(B)

A Clarice Cliff planter, in the form of a flower, on a naturalistic base, 1930s, 9in (23cm) wide.
$160–200 P(B)

A pair of Clarice Cliff vases, 1930s, 8in (20.5cm) high.
$350–400 DQ

A Clarice Cliff bowl, decorated with Bamboo pattern, c1938, 7in (18cm) diam.
$500–550 HEW

A Clarice Cliff Bizarre spill vase, decorated with Farmhouse pattern, 1930s, 8in (20.5cm) high.
$1,000–1,150 P(B)

A Clarice Cliff Bizarre vase, shape 358, decorated with Secrets pattern, 1930s, 7¾in (19.5cm) high.
$900–1,000 DD

A Clarice Cliff wall pocket, in the form of 2 parrots on a branch, c1936, 9in (23cm) high.
$650–750 HEW

A Clarice Cliff Celtic Harvest jug, c1939, 11in (28cm) high.
$260–300 HEW

A Clarice Cliff Bizarre

▶ A Clarice Cliff Meiping Shape 14 vase, decorated with Farmhouse pattern, 14in (35.5cm) high.
$4,500–5,000 MJB

◀ A Clarice Cliff teapot, decorated with Blue Crocus pattern, c1930, 5¼in (13.5cm) high.
$2,000–2,500 DSG

A Clarice Cliff early morning tea service, decorated with Flora pattern, c1930.
$1,800–2,200 RBB

A Clarice Cliff vase, with applied floral decoration, c1940, 7in (18cm) high.
$80–100 P(B)

A bronze and ivory figure, by Demêtre Chiparus, entitled 'Ayouta', 1920s, 11in (28cm) high.
$13,000–16,000 ASA

A silver-patinated, cold-painted and enamelled bronze and ivory figure, by Demêtre Chiparus, entitled 'Starlight', marked on base, 1920s, 23¼in (59cm) high.
$27,500–30,000 S

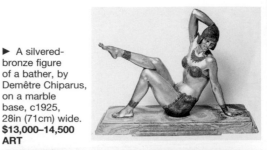

▶ A silvered-bronze figure of a bather, by Demêtre Chiparus, on a marble base, c1925, 28in (71cm) wide.
$13,000–14,500 ART

A carved ivory, cold-painted and gilt-bronze figure, by Demêtre Chiparus, entitled 'Tender Promises', on an onyx base, c1925, 29¼in (74.5cm) wide.
$21,000–24,000 S(NY)

A Goldscheider glazed ceramic fgiure, impressed signature 'Herexey', c1930, 17in (43cm) high.
$2,700–3,200 WL

A bronze figure, by Lorenzl, entitled 'Pyjama Girl', c1920, 9in (23cm) high.
$2,300–3,000 ASA

A cold-painted bronze and ivory figure, by Otto Poertzel, entitled 'Butterfly Dancers', on an onyx base, marked, 1930s, 16¾in (42.5cm) high.
$20,000–23,000 S

A gilt-bronze figure of a naked lady riding a fish, by A. Pohe, on an onyx base, c1925, 12½in (31.5cm) high.
$1,000–1,150 P

A bronze and ivory figure, by Roland Paris, c1920, 11in (28cm) high.
$12,000–14,500 ASA

A cold-painted bronze and ivory figure, after a model by Ferdinand Preiss, entitled 'Breasting the Tape', on an onyx base, signed, 10½in (26.5cm) high.
$13,000–14,500 WDG

A gilt-spelter figure of a girl, holding an alabaster ball, 1920s, 7in (18cm) high.
$400–500 CARS

A Gübelin enamelled and turquoise hardstone desk timepiece, signed, 1920s, 3¾in (9.5cm) high.
$2,400–2,700 S(Am)

A glass clock, by René Lalique, c1928, 8in (20.5cm) wide.
$4,000–5,000 ANO

An 18ct gold and enamel watch, by Uti Watch Co, signed, c1925, 1¾in (4.5cm) wide.
$9,000–10,000 S(NY)

A diamond wristwatch, by Boucheron, signed, c1940, 8in (20.5cm) long.
$4,500–5,200 S

A platinum double clip/brooch, by Drayson, London, 1930s, 1½in (4cm) wide.
$7,500–8,500 WIM

A sapphire and diamond plaque brooch, c1935.
$9,500–10,500 Bon

◄ An amethyst and diamond double clip brooch, signed 'Le Roy et Fils Ltd', c1940.
$8,000–9,000 S

A jade, sapphire and diamond brooch, the jade drop in the form of a bat and a peach, c1925.
$4,500–5,000 P

An aquamarine and diamond double clip brooch, c1930.
$7,500–8,500 P

A pair of metal bookends, by H. Moreau, in the form of birds, mounted on marble bases, c1925, 5in (13cm) high.
$250–300 P

A sapphire and diamond necklace, set with cube-shaped sections, c1935.
$4,500–5,500 P

A silver dish, by Omar Ramsden, with central boss pierced as a seeded rose on wine-coloured enamel, 1923, 3in (7.5cm) diam.
$500–600 TEN

A lacquer-on-copper vase, by Jean Dunand, signed, c1925, 8in (20.5cm) high.
$20,000–22,000 S(NY)

A Studio pottery bowl, by William Staite-Murray, decorated with *jun* glaze, impressed potter's seal, c1930, 12in (30.5cm) diam.
$1,000–1,150 RUSK

***Jun* is named after the town in ancient China where opalescent blue glaze was used from the 11thC.**

An Italian earthenware six-person coffee set, marked 'N.190/195/199', 1950s, coffee pot 7in (18cm) high.
$200–250 WBH

A Gustavsberg vase, designed by Wilhelm Kåge, Swedish, 1940s, 4¼in (11cm) high.
$200–250 MARK

An Italian table lamp, 1950s, 23in (58.5cm) high.
$525–575 ZOOM

◄ A silver and agate necklace, by MP, London, 1960, with Swedish import marks for 1969, pendant 8in (20.5cm) long.
$575–650 DID

A porcelain vase, by Dame Lucie Rie, impressed 'LR', c1965, 9in (23cm) high.
$3,250–4,000 Bon

A Strathearn glass vase, c1963, 8½in (21.5cm) high.
$115–130 TCG

A painted wood table, by Gerard van de Groenekan, designed by Gerrit Th. Rietveld, 1980s, 20¼in (51.5cm) wide.
$1,000–1,150 S(Am)

A pair of moulded plywood side chairs, by Makers of Simple Furniture, designed by Gerald Summers, c1938.
$6,500–7,500 Bon

A red lacquer sideboard, with 2 doors, brass trim and Lucite handle, 1940s, 60in (152.5cm) wide.
$2,000–2,500 TREA

A mahogany table and 4 stools, designed by Frank Lloyd Wright, the stools with inset yellow vinyl cushions, c1954, table 95½in (242.5cm) long.
$10,500–12,000 S(NY)

An Arflex suite, designed by Marco Zanuso in 1951, foam rubber upholstery renewed c1980s, marked, sofa 78¾in (200cm) long.
$3,200–3,600 WBH

A collapsible sofa, by Herman Miller, designed by Charles & Ray Eames in 1954, the black enamelled steel supports raised on chrome-plated steel legs, upholstery designed by Alexander Girard.
$3,600–4,200 Bon

Two 'Top Hat' chairs, by Evans Furniture, 1960s.
$350–400 each WBH

A set of 4 Italian chrome, plastic and green upholstered airport chairs, c1967.
$65–80 P(B)

A leather chair, in the form of a boxing glove, 1960s.
$730–830 MARK

A 'Le Témoin' seat, designed by Man Ray for Gavena, made for the Ultramobile Exhibition, 1971.
$2,000–2,500 MARK

A bronze wire chair and stool, by Knoll, designed by Warren Platner, with wool fabric upholstery, 1966.
$2,500–3,000 TREA

Six moulded plastic chairs, by Bruno Bodo Rasch, 1960s.
$3,500–4,000 ZOOM

A 'Samsone' polyester cast and moulded table, by Gaetano Pesce, for Cassina, 1980, 63in (160cm) wide.
$11,500–13,000 Bon

Lamps & Lighting

CEILING & WALL LIGHTS

A Dutch brass lantern, the base with a brass pricket, 18thC, 27in (68.5cm) high.
$2,800–3,200 S(S)

A Restauration eighteen-light patinated-bronze chandelier, the candle arm façades modelled as bearded male masks, French, 1820–30, 32in (81.5cm) high.
$8,500–9,500 NOA

A brass wall light bracket, with flower-etched cranberry glass shade, on pierced scrolling foliate support with matching backplate, 19thC, 16in (40.5cm) wide.
$1,300–1,450 AH

A brass lantern, with glass panels, c1800, 29in (73.5cm) high, with brass electric fitment.
$10,500–12,000 S

A pair of giltwood twin-light wall lights, each surmounted by a displaying eagle, 19thC, 35in (89cm) high.
$2,300–2,600 Bon(C)

A pair of Victorian brass wall gas lamps, 16in (40.5cm) high.
$250–325 RUL

A cut-glass and gilt-brass chandelier, attributed to Perry & Co, the 12 lights with S-scroll arms hung with faceted drops, the vase stem with gilt-brass mounts and corona, early 19thC, 46in (117cm) high.
$24,500–26,500 S

This chandelier has stylistic affinities with the work of Perry & Co. Founded in the mid-18thC, Perry & Co established themselves as London's most eminent glass manufacturers, providing fittings for royal residences such as Carlton House and the Royal Pavilion, Brighton. Perry & Co remained at their 72 Old Bond Street showrooms until the firm's closure in 1935.

Electric Lighting

Always check that electric lighting conforms to the current safety regulations.

◄ A pair of Victorian brass candle sconces, 13in (33cm) wide.
$400–500 RUL

A Regency brass ceiling light, of waterfall type with festoons of buttons issuing from a wire corona to a brass ball-moulded ring, 27in (68.5cm) high.
$3,000–3,300 MEA

A Victorian brass outdoor wall lamp, converted from gas to electricity, 30in (76cm) high.
$575–650 RUL

A pair of neo-classical style gilt-bronze wall sconces, converted to electricity, 19thC, 19½in (49.5cm) high.
$750–850 WW

A brass ceiling light, converted from gas to electricity, c1880, 19in (48.5cm) wide.
$350–400 RUL

A Louis XV-style ormolu and porcelain eight-light chandelier, 19thC, 37in (94cm) diam.
$4,000–4,500 RTo

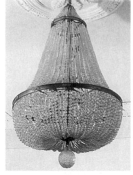

A Continental gilt-metal-banded centre light, the central stem entwined with metal flowerheads, hung with graduated facets of cut-glass drops and with central cut ball finial, late 19thC, 26¾in (68cm) diam.
$3,250–3,600 HOK

A brass rise-and-fall gasolier, late 19thC, 47in (119.5cm) high.
$2,200–2,400 Doc

An American bronze railroad table lamp, by Adams Westlake Co, with cast decoration on the font, arm and base and acid-etched amber shade, late 19thC, 22in (56cm) high.
$900–1,000 JAA

A turquoise blue holophane ceiling light, 1920s, 9in (23cm) high.
$240–280 RUL

An Austrian hall lantern, by L. G. Zimmermann, with cast-metal scrollwork frame, the 4 sides set with lithophane opaque glass panels depicting girls with doves and soldiers after a battle, set with blue glass panes, 19thC, 12½in (32cm) high.
$1,200–1,350 DD

An Edwardian cut- and moulded-crystal chandelier, the central baluster column with fluted decoration and scalloped canopy suspending pendants and swags linking 8 curved branches, 34¼in (87cm) high.
$700–800 P(S)

An Italian baroque-style walnut lantern, surmounted with putti and shells among foliage over arched glazed panels, late 19thC, 59in (150cm) high.
$4,500–5,000 B&B

A brass hanging ceiling lamp, c1910, 18in (45.5cm) high.
$730–830 RUL

A vaseline glass ceiling light, 1910–20, 12in (30.5cm) high.
$575–650 RUL

▶ A pair of rock-crystal and glass two-branch wall light fitments, with gilt-metal mounts and central bird of paradise, late 1940s, 14in (35.5cm) high.
$2,000–2,300 BWe

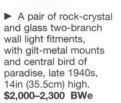

A white opaque glass office ceiling light, with brass fitting, 1930s, 11in (28cm) diam.
$230–260 RUL

TABLE & STANDARD LAMPS

A pair of Portuguese oil lamps, early 19thC, 23½in (60cm) high.
$2,600–3,200 P

A pair of brass candlesticks, each with 3 griffins on a triform support, converted to electricity, 19thC, 13in (33cm) high.
$1,000–1,150 MEA

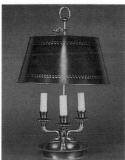

A gilt-bronze lamp, the 3 branches in the form of inverted swans' heads, with green and gold painted shade, late 19thC, 22½in (57cm) high.
$650–750 P

A gilt-bronze colza oil lamp, converted to electricity, c1815, 7in (18cm) high.
$2,000–2,300 S

A brass gas banister lamp, c1890, 43in (109cm) high.
$900–1,000 RUL

A pair of gilt-bronze candelabra, fitted for electricity, c1820, 28½in (72.5cm) high.
$6,500–7,500 S

◄ A Victorian gilt-bronze-mounted and cut-glass table oil lamp, the collar stamped Osler, converted to electricity, 24½in (62cm) high.
$2,000–2,500 WW

A Doulton stoneware oil lamp, by Mark V. Marshall, decorated with panels of mythical creatures or flowerheads in olive, green, pale blue and brown, within a brass frame, impressed and factory marks and '1885 M. V. M.', 15¾in (40cm) high.
$250–300 P(S)

A pair of painted and gilt toleware table lamps, decorated with garlands and palmette motifs, 19thC, 22¾in (58cm) high.
$3,200–3,600 S

A Royal Worcester Italian Renaissance-style table lamp, with applied masks on scroll brackets in turquoise and gilt, impressed 'Hadley', stamped and dated '1893', 37in (94cm) high.
$2,300–2,700 WBH

This piece was made for the Chicago Exhibition in 1893.

A pair of French white marble and gilt-bronze mounted lamps, each body applied with a band of foliate cast scrolls, flanked by goats'-head masks hung with vine garlands, late 19thC, 14in (35.5cm) high.
$1,600–2,000 P

A brass lacemaker's lamp, by Prince & Symmons Lion Lamp Works, London, the ruby glass reservoir supported on an adjustable column, late 19thC, 21in (53.5cm) high.
$450–500 DD

A pair of French painted-porcelain oil lamps, each depicting figures in a landscape with manor houses, late 19thC, 19in (48.5cm) high.
$1,400–1,600 SK(B)

An American astral lamp, the standard of opalescent and blue glass with gilt highlights, the shade wheel-cut with shield, lyres and foliate devices, on a brass and marble base, late 19thC, 30in (76cm) high.
$3,500–4,000 SK(B)

A pair of adjustable brass standard lamps, late 19th/early 20thC, 50in (127cm) high.
$4,500–5,000 S

A porcelain oil lamp, in the form of an owl, with relief feathers and yellow eyes, converted to electricity, c1900, 13½in (34.5cm) high.
$650–750 Bon(W)

A pair of baroque-style gilt-bronze and glass girandoles, converted to electricity, early 20thC, 36in (91.5cm) high.
$4,500–5,000 B&B

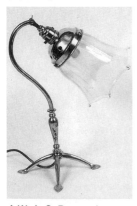

A W. A. S. Benson brass table lamp, with opaline glass shade, c1905, 15in (38cm) high.
$1,000–1,300 MoS

A brass desk lamp, c1910, 18in (45.5cm) high.
$400–450 RUL

A French oil lamp, with onyx column and base and green enamelled glass bowl, c1900, 27½in (70cm) high.
$375–425 TWa

A brass and enamel desk lamp, with steel base, c1920, 16in (40.5cm) high.
$270–300 RUL

Rugs & Carpets

An English needlepoint carpet, the walnut lattice field supporting 3 columns of pastel polychrome flower-filled medallions, damaged and restored, late 19thC, 115 x 89in (292 x 226cm).
$11,500–13,500 S(NY)

A Napoleon III Aubusson carpet, the burgundy field with an ivory floral bouquet medallion and ivory complementary border, France, 262 x 211in (665 x 535cm).
$18,500–21,000 S

A Portuguese needlework carpet, the ivory field with overall pastel polychrome palmettes and angular vines ending in flowerheads, with a blue cruciform medallion border, early 20thC, 268 x 140in (681 x 356cm).
$9,500–10,500 S(NY)

An Aubusson carpet, with scrolling foliate borders, with stylized rosettes, and a central medallion on a green ground, France, early 19thC, 168 x 118in (420 x 300cm).
$24,500–26,500 S(Z)

An Aubusson carpet, the cream open field surrounded by tassel-form inner borders, coloured in beige, terracotta and taupe, France, 19thC, 188 x 152in (470 x 380cm).
$10,000–11,500 NOA

A French or German hooked pile rug, with overall lattice of flowerheads and palmettes in blues, reds and browns on a tan field with navy blue border, late 19th/early 20thC, 115 x 76in (292 x 193cm).
$1,800–2,000 SK(B)

The rugs in this section have been arranged in geographical sequence from west to east, in the following order: Europe, Turkey, Anatolia, Caucasus, Persia, Turkestan, India and China.

Aubusson Carpets

- Workshops first set up in the French town of Aubusson in mid-17thC under the patronage of Louis XIV, although the art of weaving was thought to have been introduced there in the 8thC by the Saracens.
- Both flat-woven and piled carpets were produced in the 17th and 18thC, but Aubusson is best known for its 'tapestry' carpets produced in the 19thC.
- The foundation of these carpets is almost always cotton, with the surface weaving of wool.
- Elaborate garlands of naturalistic flowers and neo-classical and rococo themes were popular with Aubusson designers.
- Aubusson carpets in good condition are firm to handle, while a worn example will feel limp. Check carefully for any restoration. Always check that a carpet has a strong cotton or linen backing.

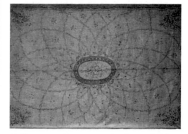

A Savonnerie carpet, the ivory field with an oval floral medallion, radiating curvilinear leaf vines and floral branches, France, late 19thC, 239 x 171in (607 x 435cm).
$18,500–22,500 S

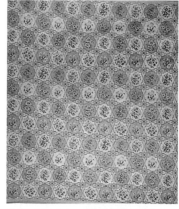

A Continental needlepoint carpet, the field with overall alternating pale blue and ivory flower-filled medallions, c1920, 154 x 137in (391 x 348cm).
$6,500–7,500 S(NY)

A Ghiordes carpet, the ivory hooked leaf field with a yellow stepped reserve enclosing a salmon stepped medallion and hooked vine border, restored, Turkey, late 19thC, 191 x 131in (485 x 333cm).
$13,000–14,500 S(NY)

A Ushak carpet, the ice-blue field with an all-over design of geometric medallions and angular vines, enclosed by multiple foliate borders, Turkey, c1910, 145 x 112in (367 x 285cm).
$3,700–4,000 P

A central Anatolian prayer rug, the ivory *mihrab* with a red hooked vine arch within a similar green arch, a walnut star flowerhead border, early 19thC, 56 x 45in (142 x 114cm).
$13,000–14,500 S(NY)

An Arabesque or Lotto rug, old cobbling and repiling, Ushak, Turkey, 17thC, 64 x 45in (162 x 115cm).
$13,000–14,500 S

Lotto Ushaks are so-called because of their celebrated depiction in the paintings of the Venetian artist Lorenzo Lotto (1480–1556).

A west Anatolian rug, the red stepped field with a yellow lozenge medallion, green spandrels and a red *gul* border, c1800, 64 x 50in (162 x 125cm).
$13,000–14,500 S

A central Anatolian kilim, the ivory field with 4 columns of polychrome stepped rectangular medallions, linked by hooked vines, some damage, mid-19thC, 152 x 63in (386 x 160cm).
$4,300–4,800 S(NY)

▶ A Melas rug, the terracotta field with a column of polychrome floral lozenge medallions, and a terracotta flowerhead border, southwest Anatolia, c1880, 79 x 50in (201 x 127cm).
$9,000–10,000 S(NY)

Turkish Rugs & Carpets

Carpets have been produced in Turkey for hundreds of years. They are usually geometric in design and are strongly influenced by Caucasian, Persian and Central Asian weavings. Generally the Turkish knot is used, exceptions being Isparta, Sivas and some Herekes, and wool is more common than cotton. Turkish weavings are on the whole produced in villages rather than by nomadic tribes, and some co-operatives and workshops have existed for centuries.

A Karapinar multi-niche rug fragment, the ivory field with alternating red and blue arched pointed reserves, an ivory polychrome rosette border, restored, possibly missing main borders, central Anatolia, 17thC, 45 x 33in (115 x 83cm).
$13,000–14,500 S

There are approximately 15 published examples of Karapinar ascending multiple-arch rugs. The origin and interpretation of this distinctive geometric design has been the subject of much speculation, with the cusped arches alternatively described as bulls' horns, fertility symbols or plants.

A Moghan rug, the blue field with a column of 8 polychrome hooked and stepped medallions, south Caucasus, c1880, 101 x 45in (256 x 114cm).
$9,000–10,000 S(NY)

A Karabagh rug, the dark indigo field with a centre row of medallions filled with floral motifs, old repairs, Caucasus, dated '1890', 99 x 47in (251 x 120cm).
$2,300–2,600 WW

A Perepedil rug, the red field with ram's horn motifs, star flowerheads and small motifs in navy and sky blue, ivory, gold, tan and pale blue-green, with midnight blue Kufic border, northeast Caucasus, late 19thC, 64 x 50in (162.5 x 127cm).
$2,400–2,700 SK(B)

A Seichur *wagireh*, the polychrome field with an overall abstract design of floral bouquets, east Caucasus, c1880, 59 x 46in (150 x 117cm).
$6,500–7,500 S(NY)

A *wagireh* is a knotted sampler used by weavers to show the field design of a section of the borders or guard stripe.

A Kazak rug, the indigo field with a pale blue medallion with 3 mid-blue and brick inner medallions, Caucasus, dated '1932', 118 x 64in (30 x 163cm).
$1,450–1,650 WW

A Konakend rug, the tomato red field with a blue pole medallion, pale blue spandrels and overall foliate motifs, ivory flowerhead and bracket border, east Caucasus, c1920, 86 x 52in (218 x 134cm).
$650–800 S(S)

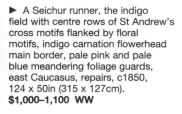

▶ A Seichur runner, the indigo field with centre rows of St Andrew's cross motifs flanked by floral motifs, indigo carnation flowerhead main border, pale pink and pale blue meandering foliage guards, east Caucasus, repairs, c1850, 124 x 50in (315 x 127cm).
$1,000–1,100 WW

A Shirvan rug, the brick field with ivory centre medallion and brick end medallions on an indigo field within a pale gold border, ivory leaf and wine glass main border and striped guards, east Caucasus, late 19thC, 87 x 45in (221 x 114cm).
$4,500–5,500 WW

A Shirvan Karagashli rug, the deep blue field with overall geometric medallion and figural design, geometric borders in reds, blues, brown, mustard and off-white, east Caucasus, dated '1905', 52 x 36in (132 x 91.5cm).
$1,600–1,800 FBG

A Soumac carpet, the terracotta field with 3 polychrome star medallions, *guls* and flowerheads, with a star-filled *gul* border, east Caucasus, c1880, 109 x 81in (277 x 206cm).
$6,500–7,500 S(NY)

A Soumac carpet, the brick field with all-over dragon, animal and medallion design in pale gold, sea-green, indigo, brick and pale blue, with pale blue main border of geometric motifs and medallions, ivory guards, brick and dark brown outer border, east Caucasus, late 19th/early 20thC, 110 x 89in (280 x 226cm).
$2,500–3,000 WW

A Kurdish rug, the field with a column of stepped medallions radiating diagonal serrated leaves, a stepped leaf and stylized tulip border, northwest Persia, c1900, 77 x 47in (195.5 x 119.5cm).
$1,300–1,450 SLN

A Kurdish rug, with 2 serrated star medallions, matching spandrels in red, slate-blue, ivory, gold, aubergine and blue-green on the black field, 2 red and ivory borders, northwest Persia, early 20thC, 98 x 62in (249 x 157.5cm).
$1,400–1,550 SK(B)

A Tabriz rug, the ivory field filled with rows of pink and blue flowering plants, pale brick main border of angular flowers and foliage, ivory scrolling floral guards, slight damage, c1880, 73 x 55in (186 x 140cm).
$800–900 WW

A Heriz carpet, the madder field of flowering vines and serrated leaves framed by an indigo samovar border, northwest Persia, c1900, 120 x 84in (303 x 213cm).
$1,000–1,100 P

A Joshagan carpet, the terracotta field of angular plants centred by an indigo diamond-shaped medallion, framed by sky blue spandrels and a flowerhead lattice border, west Persia, c1870, 125 x 91in (317 x 230cm).
$6,500–7,500 P

A Lori Pambak rug, the madder field centred by a stepped medallion and 2 octagons enclosed by leaf and calyx borders flanked by arrow-head guard stripes, west Persia, 19thC, 85 x 55in (215 x 140cm).
$2,500–3,000 Bon

512 **RUGS & CARPETS**

A Mahal carpet, the brick field with flowerheads and palmettes in gold, blue, brick, green and indigo amid floral sprays, indigo main border of flowers and foliage, pale gold and beige trailing floral guards, damage and repair, west Persia, late 19thC, 179 x 145in (455 x 368cm).
$5,700–6,500 WW

A Feraghan Sarouk rug, with a navy blue medallion within an ivory background surrounded by a navy blue border, north Persia, c1880, 81 x 48in (205.5 x 122cm).
$4,000–5,000 NOA

A Sultanabad carpet, the madder field with vines and flowerheads enclosed by deep indigo leaf and flowerhead borders, central Persia, early 20thC, 171 x 125in (435 x 317cm).
$1,100–1,300 Bon

A Sarouk rug, the blue field with a lobed medallion issuing scrolling flowering vines, palmette and scrolling arabesque border, west Persia, c1940, 58 x 40in (147.5 x 101.5cm).
$1,000–1,100 SLN

A Faraghan carpet, the terracotta *herati* field within a pale blue palmette inner border, an ivory flowering vine outer border and multiple guard stripes, north Persia, c1900, 142 x 102in (360 x 258cm).
$3,500–4,000 S(S)

A Kashgai rug, the blue field with overall *boteh*, flowerheads and animals, ivory *boteh* and gilt border, southwest Persia, c1900, 64½ x 42½in (164 x 108cm).
$575–650 RTo

A Kashan silk rug, the burgundy field of cloudbands and flowering plants centred by an ivory, pale blue and indigo medallion, framed by similar spandrels and an indigo palmette border, central Persia, c1920, 85 x 50in (215 x 126cm).
$2,500–3,000 P

21 Years Ago ...

A pair of Ispahan rugs,
84 x 55in (213 x 139.5cm). **S**

Twenty-one years ago this pair of Ispahan rugs was valued at $500–600. The market for Persian town rugs such as these has been extremely volatile, their peak being in the mid- to late 1980s, when Middle Eastern buyers were active competitors. The 1990s heralded a decline in this market and in the west such intense floral designs became less fashionable. A slow revival seems under way and such pieces should today realize $2,500–3,500.

A Kirman Ravar carpet, the compartmented field with flowering plants and cypress trees, framed by an ivory palmette border and floral guard stripes, southeast Persia, c1890, 194 x 100in (491 x 252cm).
$11,500–13,000 P

A Kirman Ravar carpet, the red field with an ivory and blue floral medallion and spandrels, inscribed '1941 remember Pearl Harbor Dec 7.', a vase and floral bouquet border, southeast Persia, c1920, 180 x 126in (450 x 320cm).
$3,000–3,500 SLN

This carpet was given anonymously to the US Government in 1942.

A Kirman pictorial rug, depicting the figure of Nadir Shah surrounded by attendants, framed by an indigo flowering shrub border, southeast Persia, c1910, 84 x 54in (213 x 138cm).
$2,000–2,500 P

The scene depicted on this rug is probably the coronation of Nadir Shah in 1736, a subject often encountered in pictorial rugs. Nadir Shah was a great commander who extended the territories of Persia after successful campaigns in Turkey, Afghanistan and India.

A Kirman rug, the cream field with flowering trees, birds and an urn with flowers below a *mihrab* enclosed by indigo palmette and flowerhead borders with double mirrored guard stripes, southeast Persia, c1920, 78 x 55in (198 x 140cm).
$1,300–1,600 Bon

A Saryk *ensi*, the deep madder compartmented field with 2 *mihrab* arches and geometric motifs, framed by multiple narrow borders, west Turkestan, c1900, 68 x 48in (172 x 120cm).
$2,500–3,000 P

An *ensi* is a rug used as a door by the Turkoman tribe on their tents.

A Yomud Turkoman *chuval*, the terracotta field with overall stepped *guls* within a serrated leaf lattice, a cruciform *gul* border, central Asia, c1900, 20 x 26in (50 x 66cm).
$1,400–1,550 SAM

21 Years Ago …

A Yomud *hatchli* rug, in tones of red, ivory, blue and brown, 64 x 48in (162 x 122cm). **S**

Twenty-one years ago this rug was valued at $200–230. The Yomud tribe is a part of a wider group of tribes called the Turkoman. Turkoman rugs as a whole are particularly favoured by collectors. An increase in understanding and awareness in this particular field has attracted more interest and this is reflected in their slow but steady rise in price. Its current value would be $1,300–2,000, but they have yet to achieve their full potential.

A Samarkand rug, the red field with overall floral design, floral borders in reds, green, brown and off-white, south Turkestan, late 19th/early 20thC, 60 x 103in (152.5 x 261.5cm).
$1,450–1,800 FBG

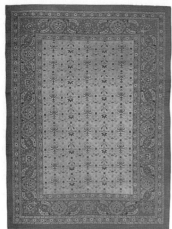

An Amritsar carpet, the ivory field with overall stylized plants, within a leaf lattice, a pale caramel floral cartouche and feather-leaf border with plain caramel surround, slight damage, north India, c1900, 150 x 109in (381 x 277cm).
$18,500–21,000 S(NY)

An Agra rug, the burgundy field linked by a hooked vine lattice, a blue flowerhead and continuous vine border, northwest India, early 20thC, 78 x 58in (198 x 147cm).
$9,000–10,000 S(NY)

A Chinese silk and gilded metallic thread carpet, the central field in blue and orange on a gold metallic ground, 19thC, 101½ x 67in (258 x 170cm).
$9,000–10,000 S(NY)

A Lahore carpet, the terracotta field with overall polychrome palmettes, animals and cloud bands issuing curvilinear scrolling vines, an ivory palmette and arabesque border, north India, c1900, 237 x 150in (601 x 380cm).
$22,500–26,000 S

A Ningshia rug, the ivory field with a blue dragon roundel, blue fret spandrels and border with plain ivory surround, west China, late 17thC, 55 x 29in (140 x 74cm).
$27,500–30,000 S(NY)

A Chinese carpet, the ivory field with a blue scrolling flowering vine medallion, a blue leaf and vine border, with plain ivory surround, c1890, 331 x 165in (587 x 419cm).
$16,000–18,000 S

An Agra carpet, the mushroom field with overall floral cartouches within a stepped vine lattice, a brown palmette and vine border, northwest India, early 20thC, 105 x 101in (267 x 256cm).
$11,500–13,500 S(NY)

A Ningshia carpet, the camel field decorated with flowering plants centred by a medallion framed by spandrels and deep sea-blue flowering vine borders, China, c1900, 122 x 113in (310 x 286cm).
$1,300–1,600 Bon

A Ningshia rug, the ivory field decorated with shrubs and butterflies, centred by a medallion and enclosed by scrolling tendril spandrels and an indigo meandering vine border, west China, c1910, 116 x 80in (294 x 204cm).
$575–650 P

Textiles

COVERS & QUILTS

A Spanish natural linen filet coverlet, the 3 vertical panels worked with motifs of unicorns, angels, stylized lions, dragons and sheep around a central vase motif, early 17thC, 90 x 68in (228.5 x 172.5cm).
$1,150–1,300 WW

An American cotton quilt, with red and pink rose appliqué pattern on ivory ground squares and serpentine vine and rose bud border, c1840, 101 x 81in (256.5 x 205.5cm).
$4,800–5,600 SLN

A patchwork coverlet, worked in mainly blue, red, black and yellow plain and printed cottons, padded and quilted, late 19thC, 84¼ x 72½in (214 x 184cm).
$375–400 P

A quilted-linen coverlet, possibly Scottish, decorated with coloured linen thread embroidery, stained and worn, marked 'AC 1749', 82¾ x 71¾in (210 x 182cm).
$2,300–2,600 P

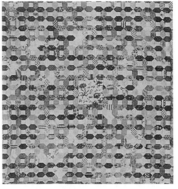

A patchwork coverlet, with a central panel of late 18thC chintz with a rose and a carnation, later lined, mid-19thC, 80 x 77in (204 x 196cm).
$380–440 P

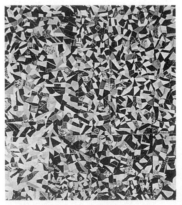

A patchwork coverlet worked in plain and brocaded silks and dark velvets, lined, late 19thC, 84¼ x 74in (214 x 188cm), with matching nightdress case and slipper bag.
$600–660 P

This quilt was made by members of the Free family of Marlborough, Wiltshire in 1880.

▶ A French gold and pink quilted bed cover, c1905, 78 x 66in (198 x 167.5cm).
$160–200 OLM

A *susani*, Uzbekistan, early 19thC, 105 x 80in (267 x 203cm).
$13,000–14,500 S(NY)

An Ura-Tube *susani*, the undyed linen ground embroidered with mainly crimson, blue, black, cream and terracotta silks, later lined with printed cotton, Uzbekistan, mid-19thC, 93 x 77¼in (236 x 196cm).
$1,000–1,200 P

EMBROIDERY & NEEDLEWORK

A silk embroidered valance, possibly English, in green coloured silk on a linen ground, with rope twist border above and below, 16thC, 33 x 300in (84 x 762cm).
$6,500–7,500 S(NY)

An embroidered picture of a lion, worked in silk long and short stitch on ivory ribbed silk, mid-17thC, 5 x 5½in (12.5 x 14cm), later framed and glazed.
$3,700–4,200 P

A petit-point picture fragment, worked in wool with silk highlights, depicting a lady kneeling with her hand being offered forward by another lady, 2 men behind, slight damage, late 17thC, 10¼ x 14½in (26 x 37cm).
$500–550 WW

Needlework Pictures

Needlework pictures first became popular in the early 18thC, when the arrival of printed dress fabrics forced embroiderers to turn their skills elsewhere. The pictures were usually worked in wools on a linen canvas and often depicted pastoral scenes. Memorial or mourning pictures became popular at the beginning of the 19thC – a fashion that probably arrived from America following the death of George III.

An English stumpwork panel, the cream-coloured silk applied with flowering plants, a blue unicorn and a lion, further enriched by brass discs, 17thC, 16 x 21in (40.5 x 53.5cm), framed and glazed.
$700–800 S(NY)

An Italian claret velvet and embroidered appliqué church hanging, depicting Christ as the young shepherd, surrounded by a scrolling cartouche borne by putti, late 17th/ early 18thC, 70 x 52in (178 x 132cm).
$1,500–1,800 Bon(C)

◀ A George III needlework picture, worked with coloured silks on a dark ground, 23½in (60cm) high, in contemporary giltwood frame.
$1,800–2,000 Bea(E)

A silkwork picture, depicting a gentleman surrounded by the 4 elements personified by 4 ladies, framed and glazed, mid-17thC, 12½ x 11in (32 x 28cm).
$4,500–5,200 Bon(C)

An embroidered picture of Queen Esther and King Ahasuerus, worked in tent stitch in coloured wools with silk thread features, the crowns and the date '1693' embroidered in seed pearls, 13½ x 17¼in (33.5 x 44cm).
$3,700–4,200 S(S)

An embroidered picture of a rural scene, worked in wool tent stitch on canvas, the sky damaged, c1720, 26¾ x 19in (68 x 48cm).
$3,200–3,500 P

LOCATE THE SOURCE

The source of each illustration in Miller's can be found by checking the code letters below each caption with the Key to Illustrations, pages 789–795.

A George III silk on sarcenet panel, worked in long stitch with a lady seated on a donkey, 9½ x 7in (24 x 18cm).
$450–550 HYD

Sarcenet is a thin tissue of fine silk.

A Kaitag silk embroidery, worked in browns and yellows, mounted, small stains, east Caucasus, c1800, 36 x 20in (91.5 x 51cm).
$6,500–7,500 S(NY)

A silk embroidered picture of a red squirrel stealing hazelnuts from a basket, worked in long and short stitch on oyster satin, early 19thC, 6 x 12¼in (15 x 31cm), framed and glazed.
$650–750 P

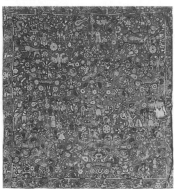

A silk pincushion, embroidered with sequins and silver tassels to commemorate a baby's birth, dated '1772', 7in (18cm) long.
$570–630 JPr

A Greek island embroidery, the linen ground worked with figures, animals and flowering branches, backed, slight damage, c1800, 55 x 50in (139.5 x 127cm).
$13,000–14,500 S(NY)

An embroidered silk picture, depicting a biblical scene, early 19thC, 17¾ x 14½in (45 x 37cm), in gilt frame.
$450–500 AH

◄ An appliquéd, pieced and embroidered wool table rug, minor losses, New England, early 19thC, 50¾ x 30¾in (129 x 78cm).
$2,600–3,000 SK(B)

► A French needlework panel, depicting 3 figures in Italian costume, in a gilt frame, early 19thC, 48½ x 35¾in (123 x 91cm).
$2,600–3,000 S(Z)

A silk picture, worked in the memory of William Applegath, aged 14, who died in 1794, 27in (68.5cm) square.
$800–950 Bon(C)

An embroidered picture of Jacob with the daughters of Laban, embroidered in long and short stitch, laid stitch and French knots on a cream satin ground, early 19thC, 19 x 29in (48.5 x 74cm).
$1,450–1,650 DN(H)

A silk appliqué and embroidered picture of a pheasant perched in an oak tree, early 19thC, 16½ x 14in (42 x 35.5cm).
$320–360 RTo

A Victorian silk embroidered picture of a flower-filled basket, on a silk ground, in a gilt frame, mid-19thC, 25 x 26¾in (63.5 x 68cm).
$2,200–2,500 S(NY)

A French needlework cushion face, the black silk ground embroidered with slightly-padded rose petals, black silk frilled edge, lined with gold damask silk, mid-19thC, 25 x 21in (63.5 x 53.5cm).
$250–300 WW

A silk and embroidered tea cosy, c1860, 15in (38cm) wide.
$300–330 HUM

A Victorian beaded pincushion, with orange and cream beads on black velvet, 5in (12.5cm) square.
$115–130 L&L

A silk and woolwork picture, entitled 'The Woman of Samaria', within a black and gilt glass mount and later composition frame, 19thC, 16¼ x 21¼in (41.5 x 54cm).
$160–200 RTo

A Continental silk embroidered satin panel, worked in 18thC style depicting an elephant and mahout kneeling before an eastern potentate within elaborate foliate scrollwork borders, 19thC, 84 x 70in (213 x 178cm).
$6,500–7,500 B&B

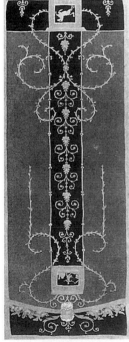

An Italian needlework panel, worked in Pompeiian fresco style, c1875–90, 65¼ x 24¾in (165.5 x 63cm).
$780–900 NOA

▶ An Irish linen tablecloth, embroidered with pink flowers and with handmade lace edging, 1930s, 48in (122cm) square.
$50–65 AIL

An Egyptian wall hanging, of undyed cotton with red, blue and brown cotton appliqué designed with a pharaoh, the border of a brick pattern, c1910, 71 x 32in (180 x 81cm).
$400–450 P

LACE

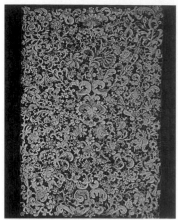

A panel of gros point Venetian needlelace, with a wide variety of fillings and raised work, joined, c1650, 31 x 19¾in (79 x 50cm).
$1,150–1,300 P

A French part flounce of Point d'Alençon needlelace, designed with a repeated curved bough of roses over a border of scrolls and foliage displaying a variety of picot detail, mid-19thC, 19¾ x 87¾in (50 x 223cm).
$4,000–4,500 P

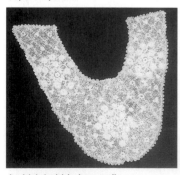

An Irish bobbin lace collar, worked with rosettes and leaves, c1900, 17¾in (45cm) long.
$100–120 EON

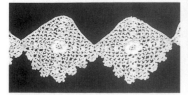

An Irish length of lace, featuring a rose, c1920, 36in (91.5cm) wide.
$35–40 JVa

A table cover, adapted from an alb flounce of Milanese bobbin lace, late 17thC, 66¼ x 76in (168 x 193cm), edged with peasant bobbin lace and lined with later light tan taffeta silk.
$1,100–1,300 P

A panel of Victorian Irish Clones lace, 5½ x 14½in (14 x 37cm).
$40–50 JVa

Clones lace always features a shamrock and a rose.

An Irish crochet lace tablecloth, c1900, 34in (86.5cm) diam.
$70–80 AIL

> **Miller's is a price GUIDE not a price LIST**

An Irish crochet lace tea cosy, 1920s, 14in (35.5cm) wide.
$40–50 AIL

A gros point Venetian needlelace bib-front, with a variety of fillings and raised picot detail, c1670.
$3,500–4,000 P

A flounce of Brussels needlelace, designed with pendant ribbon-tied flowersprays and swags of blossom, late 19thC, 14½ x 147¾in (37 x 375cm).
$300–330 P

A handmade bobbin lace collar, minor repairs, c1900, 17in (43cm) long.
$30–50 CHU

An Irish Clones lace collar, 1940–50, 2in (5cm) wide.
$75–80 JVa

SAMPLERS

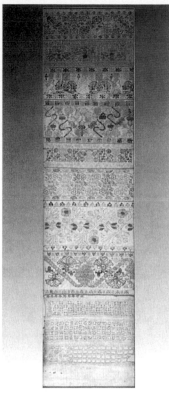

A Charles II border band sampler, worked in green, blue and cream silks with boxer figures, acorns, fruit, flowers and foliage, the lower part with pierced cutwork, possibly unfinished, 27½ x 6¼in (70 x 16cm).
$2,300–2,600 Bea

A George III cross stitch sampler, by Jane Bonny, aged 10, embroidered with the alphabet and a verse, 1790, 20 x 18in (51 x 46cm).
$1,150–1,300 DN(H)

A silk on unbleached linen sampler, worked in tent and eye stitches with raised knot detail, with part-worked dark green tent stitch ground, 1630s, 8 x 20in (20 x 51cm), framed and glazed.
$5,500–6,500 P

A needlework family register, probably Massachusetts, worked in vibrant colours, early 19thC, 25 x 17in (63.5 x 43cm).
$375–400 SK(B)

A needlework sampler, worked in coloured silks on wool with Psalm XXIII, slight damage, early 19thC, 16 x 12in (40.5 x 30.5cm), framed and glazed.
$600–700 WW

◄ A sampler, by Gwen Thomas, the floral meandering border surrounding flower arrangements and Adam and Eve beneath the Tree of Knowledge, 1807, 19 x 16in (48.5 x 40.5cm).
$650–800 Bon(C)

A sampler, by Sarah Fisher, of Exodus chapter 20, 'The Ten Commandments', 1769, late 18thC, 15 x 12¼in (38 x 31cm).
$550–650 Bon(C)

A needlework sampler, by Lucy Allen, worked in silk with the alphabet and numbers over a central vase, the base with boats, dated '1787', 13½ x 9¼in (34.5 x 23.5cm).
$375–400 WW

A needlework sampler, by Mary Wreford, aged 11, with rows of alphabets and religious verse, slight colour run, 1807, 17 x 13in (43 x 33cm).
$650–750 Bon(C)

A sampler, worked with a poem, 'On honest labour', 1808, 13in (33cm) square.
$700–800 DHA

A sampler, by Amelia Hanington, worked in coloured threads with the alphabet, a village scene, a poem and animals, within a blue foliate chain-link border, 1809, 13in (33cm) square.
$550–600 DHA

A sampler, by Sarah Barker, aged 13, worked in silk cross stitch on linen, with a verse and various motifs with an alphabet above, 1813, 17¼ x 10¼in (44 x 26cm).
$500–600 P

An acrostic sampler, by Elizabeth Norman, aged 11, 1813, 24 x 25in (61 x 64cm), framed and glazed.
$1,000–1,100 Bon(C)

A sampler, by Susanna Frost, worked in cross and satin stitch, 1816, 12¾ x 13¼in (32.5 x 33.5cm), in a mahogany frame.
$2,200–2,500 RTo

A sampler, by Salley Crowthers, aged 16, worked in gold, green and brown silk with a verse surrounded by spot motifs, 1820, 16¼ x 17in (41.5 x 43cm).
$440–480 WW

A George III sampler, by Eleanor Stone, worked in coloured threads with various animals, 1821, 16¼ x 11¾in (41 x 30cm), in a gilt frame.
$5,200–5,700 CGC

A sampler, by Sophie Bailly, silk on linen, worked in reds, blues, brown, black and greens, 1828, 13 x 11in (33 x 28cm).
$7,300–8,000 FBG

An American needlework sampler, by Sophie Bailly, silk on linen, worked in reds, blues, brown, black and greens, 1828, 13 x 11in (33 x 28cm).
$7,300–8,000 FBG

◄ A pair of woolwork samplers, by Ann Walton, each embroidered with the figure of a girl and small animals, flanked by birds and heart-shaped trees, 1836, 7½ x 8½in (19 x 21.5cm), framed and glazed.
$3,000–3,300 S(S)

A sampler, by Charlotte Shank Box, with flowers, butterflies, birds and deer within a rosebud border, slight discoloration, 1828, 20¼ x 14½in (51.5 x 37cm).
$1,200–1,450 Bon(C)

A needlework sampler, by Margaret Craigs, aged 10, with a basket of flowers surrounded by various motifs, 1837, 22 x 20in (60 x 51cm), framed.
$1,100–1,200 SK(B)

A sampler, by Caroline Mackenzie, aged 7, worked in green, brown and gold coloured silks, some holing, 1841, 18 x 13¼in (45.5 x 33.5cm), framed and glazed.
$975–1,100 WW

A Victorian pictorial sampler, by Eliza Goymer, worked in green, cream and brown silk cross stitch on a wool ground, slight damage, 1846, 17 x 13in (43 x 33cm), framed and glazed.
$1,000–1,200 WW

► A sampler, by Alex and Janet Callaway, worked in wool with silk highlights on a linen ground, 1859, 15½ x 11½in (39.5 x 29cm), framed and glazed.
$400–500 WW

A sampler, by Mary Ann Johnson, worked in silk cross stitch on tammy cloth, 1830s, 11¾in (30cm) square.
$900–1,000 P

A needlework sampler, by Marianne Gawood, with alphabet numerals and motifs, 1843, 16 x 17in (40.5 x 43cm).
$260–280 GOR(B)

A sampler, by Laura Jones, worked in coloured wools with motifs including a steamship and an exotic temple, 1848, 17½ x 18½in (44.5 x 47cm), framed and glazed.
$600–700 Bon(C)

A sampler, by Alex and Janet Callaway, worked in wool with silk highlights on a linen ground, 1859, 15½ x 11½in (39.5 x 29cm), framed and glazed.

A sampler by Maria Hawkins, aged 8, with a verse, birds, flowers and buildings, c1830, 16½ x 12¼in (42 x 31cm).
$1,500–1,650 L

Collecting Samplers

Early fine-quality examples in good condition are the most desirable. Condition is critical – check for moth or mould damage, faded colours and run-stained grounds. Professional cleaning and restoration are advisable, and original frames and backboards add to the value.

A woolwork sampler, by Ann Wade, 1849, 24 x 23½in (61 x 59.5cm), mounted on a modern firescreen.
$600–700 AH

A sampler, by Sarah Barker, decorated with a religious text, flora and fauna, 1862, 12½ x 12in (32 x 30cm), framed and glazed.
$650–800 Bon(W)

TAPESTRIES

A tapestry fragment, probably Tournai, depicting a late Gothic court scene, with Latin inscription, c1500, 93 x 68in (236 x 172.5cm).
$13,000–15,000 S

A Flemish hunting tapestry panel, late 16thC, 66 x 43in (167.5 x 109cm).
$6,000–6,500 S(NY)

A Flemish classical tapestry, perhaps from the workshop of Jeremias Coekx and Cornelis de Wael, after Pieter Spierincx and Pieter Ijkens, depicting Circe showing Ulysses the statue of Picus, damaged and repaired, Antwerp, c1680, 91 x 79in (231 x 200.5cm).
$10,000–11,500 S

A tapestry panel, of a supplicant king said to be Louis IX of France, originally part of a larger tapestry, c1675–80, 69½ x 44½in (176.5 x 113cm).
$3,700–4,200 NOA

An Aubusson tapestry panel, 17thC, 83 x 120in (211 x 305cm).
$9,500–10,500 S(NY)

A French Beauvais tapestry, 17thC, 96 x 63in (244 x 160cm).
$4,000–5,000 SLN

A panel of tapestry, designed with a strapwork pattern and pairs of shells, masks, birds and monkeys woven in red, green, yellow and blue wools, early 18thC, 69¼ x 19in (176 x 48cm).
$1,400–1,550 P

A Flemish mythological tapestry, depicting a girl wounded by an arrow, a huntsman and a dog standing in a wooded landscape, c1700, 151½ x 141¾in (385 x 360cm).
$11,500–13,500 S(Am)

▶ An Aubusson tapestry, depicting a horseman in a wooded landscape, enclosed by borders of leafy vines, early 18thC, 102 x 67in (259 x 170cm).
$4,000–5,000 Bon

An Aubusson verdure tapestry panel, depicting a peacock perched on an oak tree, 18thC, 92 x 64in (233.5 x 162.5cm).
$7,500–8,500 P

A Flemish tapestry, depicting a young man with his dog, with floral borders, 18thC, 114 x 58in (289.5 x 147.5cm).
$5,500–6,500 NOA

An allegorical tapestry border fragment, depicting part of the Triumph of Cupid, some splits and repairs, 18thC, 18½ x 101in (47 x 256.5cm).
$1,300–1,450 WW

► An Aubusson floral tapestry, with peonies, roses and dahlias in tones of blues, browns and taupe, 1830, 126 x 52in (320 x 132cm).
$6,000–6,500 SK

An Aubusson verdure tapestry, of foliage, trees and 2 perched birds, in tones of rust, green, olive, brown, gold and ivory, surrounded by foliate border, restored, 18thC, 108 x 96in (274.5 x 244cm).
$6,800–7,400 B&B

A tapestry panel, depicting Christ as the Man of Sorrows, probably Rome, early 18thC, 12 x 9¼in (30.5 x 23.5cm), in a contemporary gilt walnut frame, carved with acanthus leaves.
$1,450–1,600 S(NY)

A Flemish tapestry, in the manner of Teniers, probably from the workshop of Willem Werniers, depicting Flemish peasants playing cards and skittles and a tavern, with a floral border, minor repairs, Lille, c1730, 93 x 144in (236 x 366cm).
$18,000–19,500 S

A French tapestry panel, depicting a rural settlement by a river, with villagers fishing, boating and herding sheep, 18thC, 82 x 100in (208.5 x 254cm).
$6,000–6,500 P

An Aubusson tapestry wall hanging, the centre designed with a quiver of arrows and a garland of flowers within a border of scrolling leaves and flowers, woven in mainly pink, green and cream wool, mid-19thC, 105½ x 43¼in (268 x 110cm).
$3,200–3,600 P

An Aubusson tapestry, with Chinese figures in a garden, some repairs, 19thC, 100 x 102in (254 x 259cm).
$13,000–14,500 S

An Aubusson verdure tapestry panel, depicting 2 birds in a rural landscape, 19thC, 79½ x 41in (202 x 104cm).
$775–850 P(Z)

An Aubusson tapestry, depicting a hunting scene in the mountains, 19thC, 152 x 84in (386 x 213.5cm).
$14,500–18,000 NOA

A Flemish tapestry, in the manner of Teniers, depicting a Continental river landscape, with narrow dark brown border, 19thC, 108 x 79in (274.5 x 200cm).
$4,250–5,000 WW

An Aubusson tapestry, originally woven at Beauvais, after François Boucher, representing 'La Musique' from the *Les Fêtes Italiennes* series, c1880, 68 x 83in (173 x 211cm).
$10,000–11,500 S(Am)

An Aubusson *portière*, woven in colours depicting a flower-filled basket over a flower arrangement, within a floral border, reserved on a camel ground, c1880, 149½ x 59in (380 x 150cm).
$2,300–2,600 S(Am)

An Aubusson tapestry fragment, depicting 4 country figures and a goat, in tones of brown, green, rose, rust and ivory, late 19thC, 57 x 37½in (145 x 95.5cm).
$2,600–3,000 B&B

Four *entre fenêtres* tapestries, in wool with silk highlights, each depicting hunting, arms and armour and musical trophies, the blue borders with ribbon entwined fruiting branches, 19thC, each 132 x 27in (335.5 x 68.5cm), one panel 39in (99cm) wide.
$6,500–8,000 WW

A French tapestry, depicting a falconry party, late 19thC, 79 x 91in (200.5 x 231cm).
$5,750–6,500 SLN

Costume

A French button, with a gouache painting on paper under glass, set in silver, late 18thC, 1½in (4cm) diam.
$400–450 TB

This button is one of a set of 12, each depicting a rider in a different dressage position.

An embroidered cream silk waistcoat, c1790.
$325–400 JPr

▶ A brown and white cotton print full-length dress, c1830.
$275–325 L&L

An American copper button, engraved with 'GW' and initials of each State, c1789, 1¼in (3cm) diam.
$1,600–2,000 TB

This button was made for the inauguration of George Washington, and the engraved border represents the 13 original colonies.

A Tekke midnight blue silk *chrype,* embroidered in crimson, white and ochre silk, central Asia, mid-19thC.
$350–420 P

A Tekke Turkoman hat, central Asia, late 19thC.
$550–600 SAM

A hand-embroidered cashmere shawl, in red, gold, blue and white, c1850, 70in (178cm) square.
$900–1,200 JPr

A brown silk dress, with lace trim and tiered sleeves, 1850s.
$280–320 L&L

A Victorian cream lawn bodice, hand-embroidered with openwork Irish lace collar and hem.
$1,600–1,800 JVa

A Victorian child's hand-embroidered dress.
$70–80 CHU

A Norwich shawl, by Clabburn, Son & Crisp, of crimson, black, cream and blue woven silk, c1860, 68½ x 65¼in (174 x 166cm).
$350–400 P

A Victorian watered-silk parasol, with ivory handle, 24in (61cm) long.
$160–200 JPr

A gentleman's silk top hat, by Sam Mortlock & Son, with leather case lined in red, with brass lock, late 19thC.
$160–200 S(S)

A cotton lined young girl's brown checked day dress, c1880.
$160–200 Har

A velvet jacket, the deep burgundy ground woven with velvet flowers in greens and golds, edged with black lace and hung with tiers of faceted beads and brown silk knots to the back, lined with pale gold silk and labelled 'Worth, 7 Rue de la Paix, Paris', c1880.
$1,600–2,000 WW

A court evening dress, in royal blue shantung silk, with pink lining, late 19thC.
$160–200 RBB

A child's unbleached linen pinafore dress, the yoke, shoulder straps and side seam insertions worked in golden-yellow silk Ruskin needlelace, c1897.
$900–1,000 P

This dress was ordered by Princess Beatrice for her daughter, granddaughter of Queen Victoria.

An Egyptian black cotton net dress, with wrapped gold metal strip decoration, lined in red cotton, c1900.
$700–800 P

A lady's walking costume, of charcoal flecked tweed, the jacket faced and decorated with crimson velvet, c1890.
$320–360 P

A Victorian child's burgundy velvet dress, lined in glazed cotton.
$130–150 CCO

A silk velvet evening coat, with lamé lining, 1920s.
$200–250 TT

Fans

A French fan, the paper leaf painted with Juno attended by female companions, the carved ivory sticks and guards with *piqué* and *clouté* work, c1720, 10½in (26.5cm) wide.
$2,200–2,500 P

A Chinese export brisé cockade fan, designed with a medallion painted with a family group, the sticks of pierced and carved ivory, the surround, tips and handles designed with birds, flowers and blossom, early 19thC, 14¾in (37.5cm) long, and a cream and gilt paper and card box.
$8,000–9,000 P

A mother-of-pearl fan, with hand-painted and lithograph leaf depicting Roman soldiers and Grecians within a landscape, the pierced sticks with silver highlights, the guardsticks with gold foil set to piercing, 19thC, 10½in (26.5cm) wide, in a carved and giltwood display case.
$260–300 WW

A French fan, the vellum leaf painted with a girl by a well, with tortoiseshell sticks, signed 'L. Gatzert', c1880, 11¾in (30cm) wide.
$720–800 P

A lacquered brisé fan, painted with a vignette of a gentleman and a lady on a bridge, the top edge trimmed with a ribbon, slight damage, c1740, 6¼in (16cm) wide, in a carved and giltwood display case.
$250–300 WW

A brisé fan, of *piqué* decorated horn, the tips with painted figure and animal scenes in white and grey on a sienna ground, the whole with gilt flowers and ferns, c1810, 6¼in (16cm) wide, with green card box.
$200–250 P

A silk leaf fan, with a painted scene of lovers, designed with ribbon swags and sequins, with gilded and pierced tortoiseshell sticks and guard stick, late 19thC, 10in (25.5cm) wide.
$180–210 DN(H)

A French fan, the black net leaf with white bobbin lace, sequin and spangle appliqué, designed with leaves, blossom and tendrils, the tortoiseshell sticks with *piqué* work, c1890, 10¾in (27.5cm) long.
$520–580 P

▶ A Brussels lace fan, with gilded carved wooden sticks, c1910, 15in (38cm) high.
$450–550 JPr

A north European fan, the paper leaf painted with Paris, Mercury and Venus with attendants, the reverse with lovers, the ivory sticks inlaid with tortoiseshell and mother-of-pearl, c1750, 11½in (29cm) wide.
$750–900 P

A French lace and silk fan, by J. Duvelleroy, hand-painted with dragonflies and flora with applied multi-coloured sequins, with ivory sticks, 19thC, 12in (30.5cm) wide, in original case.
$160–200 DA

A Chinese lacquer fan, the leaf printed in red, blue and jade green with figures and pavilions in gilt on black to the sticks, in original decorated lacquer fitted box with label for Madrid retailer, c1880, 10in (25.5cm) wide.
$160–200 WW

A fan, probably Spanish, the leaf of pleated sheet cork painted with a bird and blossom, with wood sticks, the guards with cork appliqué, c1880, 11½in (29cm) wide.
$230–260 P

Jewellery

BRACELETS

A garnet bracelet, each panel with a rope-link border and applied with a half pearl, damaged, mid-19thC, in a fitted case.
$1,150–1,300 DN

A Scottish silver and agate bracelet, c1870, 6in (15cm) long.
$600–700 BWA

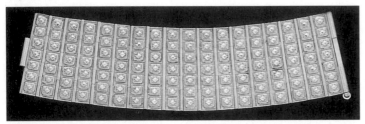

A gold bracelet, by Phillips, London, in the form of a flared cuff, each panel with raised faceted hobnail decoration and bead detailing, within rope-twist borders, c1873, in a velvet barrel-shaped case.
$9,500–10,500 S

A Victorian gold bracelet, with linked floral and diamond-shaped panels, each set with a turquoise, joined by a heart-shaped padlock.
$380–420 WL

A mid-Victorian gold bracelet, set with a garnet cluster flanked by 2 garnets, with a flexible strap, in a fitted case.
$1,800–2,000 WW

A Victorian silver-gilt bracelet.
$350–400 AnS

A 9ct gold, pearl and turquoise bracelet, of curb-link form, with padlock clasp, c1890, in original fitted case.
$1,000–1,200 HofB

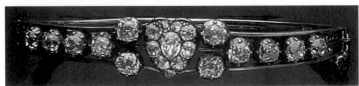

A gold and diamond-mounted hinged bangle, 19thC.
$3,750–4,000 Bea(E)

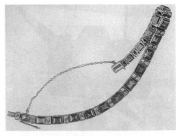

An Edwardian bracelet, the hinged panels set with square-cut sapphires and 8 cut diamonds.
$1,500–1,700 WL

A gold triple wirework bangle, mounted with an Oriental pearl within a diamond cluster, c1895.
$2,500–3,000 P

A gold bangle, set with graduated sapphires and brilliant-cut diamonds, c1900.
$5,200–5,700 Bon

A double-hinged bracelet, set with 8 graduated diamonds and 7 sapphires, rose-coloured shank, early 20thC.
$4,000–4,500 DD

BROOCHES

A flower pin brooch, set with amethysts, pearls and chrysolite, c1790, 1½in (4cm) long.
$800–1,000 WIM

A diamond spray brooch, the principal flowerhead mounted *en tremblant*, some later modifications, c1830.
$10,000–11,500 P

A diamond floral spray brooch, mounted in silver and gold, with detachable brooch fitting, c1850.
$4,500–5,500 Bon

A copy of the Glen Lyon brooch, mid-19thC, 5½in (14cm) diam.
$2,000–2,500 BWA

A diamond brooch, the centre set with a chrysoberyl, c1860.
$6,200–6,800 S

► An Irish Tara brooch, c1860, 3¼in (8.5cm) diam.
$1,000–1,200 SIL

A Celtic revival silver-gilt pin brooch, c1860, 2½in (6.5cm) diam.
$550–700 WELD

A Victorian 18ct gold and pearl-set star pendant/brooch, with central diamond and rope-twist chain.
$1,200–1,300 EH

A Victorian gold bee brooch, with central diamond, diamond-set wings, pearl body and ruby eyes.
$2,500–3,000 HYD

Insect Brooches

Jewellery representing dragonflies, bees, butterflies and even flies was popular from the mid-19thC, owing to the increase in general interest in natural history. Quality varies, and many pieces are relatively inexpensive.

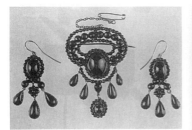

A Victorian Bohemian garnet brooch, with matching pendant earrings.
$900–1,000 WL

A Victorian diamond floral spray brooch, set with red gemstones, the main flowerhead set *en tremblant* in white gold mount.
$550–600 HYD

A Victorian gold pendant/brooch, set with turquoises, and with triple pendant drops.
$250–300 WL

A diamond brooch, in the form of a series of tied bows and diamond collet buds, c1915.
$5,000–6,000 P

A seed pearl and diamond pendant/brooch, by Hunt & Roskell, with hair slide fitment, 19thC, in original fitted case.
$900–1,000 Bea(E)

Flower Brooches

These were popular throughout the 19thC. The central flower was sometimes mounted on a spring (*en tremblant*) and could be removed to mount on a hair comb. Flower brooches were often taken apart later, and it is not unusual to see the central flower or spray sold separately. Brooches of the best craftsmanship appear as fine from the back as from the front.

A 15ct gold and half-pearl pendant/brooch, c1910, 1in (2.5cm) diam.
$1,150–1,300 WIM

Further Reading

*Miller's Jewellery
Antique Checklist,*
Miller's Publications, 1997

A Victorian gold brooch, the engraved rim supporting black enamel wirework, interspaced with diamonds, the central quartz stone with a butterfly inlaid with diamonds, 1½in (4cm) diam.
$650–750 BWe

A 15ct gold brooch with central garnet, c1870, 1¼in (3cm) wide.
$600–700 WIM

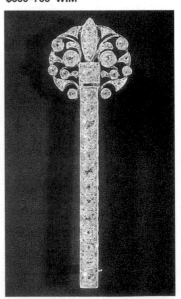

An Edwardian diamond brooch, the bar with 13 stones, with a circular openwork foliate terminal.
$4,000–5,000 DN

A diamond bar brooch, with central cushion-shaped stone, the openwork foliate husk frame set with millegrain diamonds, c1920, in a fitted case.
$7,500–8,500 S(Am)

◄ An Edwardian platinum bar brooch, with a collet-set diamond within strapwork.
$750–800 TEN

CAMEOS

A Victorian hardstone cameo brooch, depicting a classical scene, within a pierced scrollwork frame.
$400–500 P(HSS)

A pair of gold and shell cameo earrings, carved with female personifications of Night and Day, the surmounts with male masks, and a matching brooch, c1830.
$3,000–3,300 P

A Victorian hardstone cameo pendant, carved with a classical maiden within a border of diamonds and pearls, in a fitted case.
$1,000–1,200 HYD

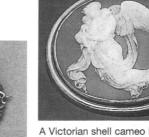

A Victorian cameo brooch, with yellow metal frame.
$420–480 WilP

A Victorian shell cameo brooch, carved with a classical female bust with elaborate flowerhead garland.
$250–300 P(G)

A shell cameo brooch, in a scroll mount, damaged, pin later, 19thC.
$300–350 DN

► A Victorian shell cameo brooch, carved with a biblical scene, in gold mount, with safety chain.
$400–500 HYD

A Victorian shell cameo brooch, carved as the angel of the night, in a plain gold border.
$750–850 P

CUFF LINKS

A pair of Victorian pietra dura cuff links, and 2 studs, each with a stylized flowerspray on a black ground, set in gold rope-twist frames.
$1,300–1,500 DN

A pair of 9ct gold cuff links, by Murrle, Bennet & Co, each with a blue and white enamelled facsimile Orange Free State 6d stamp, late 19thC.
$500–550 TEN

A pair of 18ct gold and enamel 'four vices' cuff links, Birmingham, c1897.
$3,800–4,000 S

EARRINGS

A pair of Iberian gold chandelier earrings, set with emeralds in triple-drop clusters suspended from a scrollwork and roundel support, c1750.
$5,500–6,000 P

A pair of diamond earrings, designed as paisley shapes, mounted in silver and gold, c1850.
$1,800–2,000 S(LA)

A pair of 15ct gold earrings, in the form of buckles, c1870.
$1,000–1,200 WIM

A pair of early Roman carnelian intaglios, mounted as earrings in 1810.
$1,600–2,000 WIM

A pair of Victorian drop earrings, each tear-drop cluster with a sapphire and diamonds suspended from a similar stud.
$8,000–9,000 AH

A pair of coral love-knot earrings, each set with a diamond, c1870.
$900–1,000 WIM

◄ A pair of sapphire and diamond ear clips, mounted in silver and gold, c1900.
$4,000–4,400 S(LA)

► A pair of diamond earrings, of ribbon-scroll design with bobbin-shaped drops, c1935.
$5,500–6,500 P

A pair of diamond drop earrings, each pear-shaped drop suspended from a brilliant-cut diamond terminal, c1850.
$30,000–32,500 Bon

A pair of Victorian pendant earrings, with diamond-set enamel drops, beaded borders and rose-cut diamond-set bee motifs.
$1,500–1,800 P(Ed)

A pair of natural pearl and diamond earrings, c1895.
$2,500–3,000 WIM

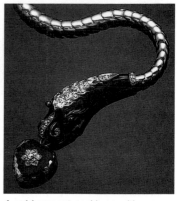

A gold serpent necklace, with blue enamel head and set with a cluster of diamonds, supporting a matching heart-shaped locket drop, c1845.
$10,500–12,000 P

A flat-cut garnet necklace, c1790.
$4,800–5,200 WIM

A topaz and diamond parure, comprising a necklace, pair of brooches and a single earring converted to a pendant, the other earring now at the end of the necklace, mid-18thC.
$9,000–10,000 P

A 15ct gold necklace, c1870, 17in (43cm) long.
$3,200–3,500 WIM

A gold collar, in the form of plain flattened oval sections with arched connections, c1880.
$3,000–3,500 P

A pearl and diamond tiara/necklace, c1890, 14½in (37cm) long.
$8,000–9,000 S

A 15ct gold, peridot and seed pearl necklet, of openwork foliate design with 3 pear-shaped drops, late 19thC.
$720–800 Bea(E)

A Victorian pearl and gold necklace, in the form of 5 graduated flowerheads, c1895.
$3,000–3,300 P

◄ A pearl necklace, with silver clasp, 1920s, 18in (45.5cm) long.
$450–500 AnS

► A 15ct gold and pearl necklace, c1910, 16in (40.5cm) long.
$2,800–3,200 WIM

PENDANTS

A Charles I silver heart-shaped locket, inscribed, enclosing a plaque decorated in relief with a portrait of the king, 1¼in (3cm) high, in a black shagreen case.
$2,000–2,300 FW&C

A diamond Latin cross pendant, with a silver chain, c1820.
$8,000–9,000 S

A mosaic and gold cruciform pendant, the reverse with a locket compartment, c1850.
$2,000–2,500 P

A Victorian pearl and diamond pendant, the reverse with a locket, set in yellow gold.
$2,500–3,000 HYD

A diamond and pearl pendant, set in platinum, c1910, 1¼in (3cm) long.
$2,500–3,000 WIM

A Victorian Roman-style pendant, the central boss in turquoise enamel, set with pearls and a diamond, the reverse with a locket for hair.
$1,200–1,400 LAY

A brown zircon, pearl and diamond pendant, mounted in silver and gold, c1880.
$2,000–2,500 Bon

◄ An Edwardian 15ct gold pendant, with an aquamarine in a half pearl and tied ribbon frame, suspending a matching drop below.
$1,200–1,500 P

RINGS

An 18ct gold cluster ring, set with emeralds, pearls and a diamond, c1820.
$1,200–1,500 WIM

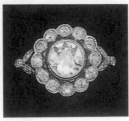

A Victorian five-stone diamond half-hoop ring, with rose diamond points.
$2,750–3,250 DN

An 18ct gold ring, set with 3 garnets and 4 diamonds, Chester 1901.
$275–325 GAK

A gold claddagh ring, by Fallen, Galway, c1885.
$500–575 WELD

Claddagh rings are often in the form of 2 hands clasping a heart, and were given as a token of eternal love.

An Edwardian diamond and platinum ring.
$1,200–1,500 HYD

A ruby and diamond cluster ring, c1910.
$6,000–7,000 S

A sapphire and diamond cluster ring, c1915.
$3,000–3,500 Bon

A yellow sapphire and diamond ring, c1925.
$2,000–2,500 P

Enamel

A Birmingham enamel bodkin case, c1780, 4in (10cm) long.
$900–1,000 BHa

An enamel patch box, the cover decorated with trees and inscribed 'A Trifle from Farnham', with mirror inside, late 18thC, 1½in (4cm) wide.
$275–325 HAM

A Cartier enamel perpetual desk calendar for 1908–18, with gold highlights, moonstone button and ivory backplate, 4in (10cm) diam.
$2,000–2,300 P

A Staffordshire enamel scent bottle, decorated with flowers within a pink and blue cartouche, gilt-metal mount, late 18thC, 3½in (9cm) high.
$800–1,000 Bon

A gold and red and blue enamel snuff box, mark of Jean-Jacques Prévost, Geneva, c1790, 3½in (9cm) wide.
$5,500–6,500 S

An Austrian enamel cup and saucer, c1890, saucer 5in (12.5cm) diam.
$1,200–1,400 SHa

A pair of French champlevé enamel frames, decorated with flowers, birds and foliage, 19thC, 12½in (32cm) high.
$800–1,000 E

A pair of Continental enamel and gilt opera glasses, decorated with musicians, late 19thC, 4in (10cm) wide, in a fitted case.
$350–400 PCh

A Bilston enamel patch box, c1780, 1½in (4cm) wide.
$550–650 BHa

An enamel and silver-gilt-mounted cameo glass powder box, enamel probably Limoges, glass possibly Webb, c1900, 3¾in (9.5cm) wide.
$1,300–1,600 RTo

A Bilston enamel nutmeg grater, c1780, 1½in (4cm) long.
$1,200–1,500 BHa

A Limoges enamel and gold scent bottle, c1870, 3in (7.5cm) high.
$2,500–2,800 SHa

Gold

A French gold snuff box, the floral engraved border enclosing a cubed geometric panel, Paris marks for 1798–1809, 3¼in (8.5cm) wide.
$2,200–2,500 B&L

A gold presentation cigar box, with inscription, the base engraved with a Scottish stag hunt, repaired, c1850, 5½in (14cm) wide.
$3,500–4,000 S(S)

A Victorian gold card case, engraved with a lakeside scene, c1850, 3½in (9cm) long.
$4,500–5,000 P

A French 18ct gold-topped glass scent bottle, c1840, 3in (7.5cm) high, in original fitted case.
$1,400–1,600 SFL

A French gold-mounted and ivory box, decorated with cupid firing arrows at 3 ladies on a pink ground, worn, late 18thC, 2¼in (6cm) diam.
$450–520 TEN

A 14ct gold pill box, by Tiffany & Co, the cover inset with a miniature of a girl, c1880, 1in (2.5cm) diam.
$6,000–7,000 SHa

A Mexican gold cheroot case, chased with birds and foliage, with diamond thumbpiece, c1800, 3in (7.5cm) high.
$3,800–4,200 S(NY)

A French 18ct gold and ivory needle and thimble case, c1760, 3in (7.5cm) long.
$1,400–1,600 BEX

► A gold vinaigrette, set with turquoises, garnets and other gems, c1815, 1¼in (3cm) wide.
$1,600–2,000 TEN

An 18ct gold snuff box, with engine-turned decoration, maker's mark of Alexander J. Strahan, London 1807, 3in (7.5cm) wide.
$2,500–2,800 Bon

A gold snuff box, by Louis Willmott, mounted with a miniature of King George V surrounded by diamonds, London 1910, 3½in (9cm) wide.
$5,200–5,600 S(NY)

A Cartier 14ct gold flask, with screw cap, New York, early 20thC, 7¼in (18.5cm) high.
$2,400–2,600 S(NY)

Russian Works of Art

In 1613, the Russian Church convened an assembly of representatives to vote for a new ruler, which resulted in Michael Feodorovich becoming the reluctant founder of the Romanov Dynasty. This was hailed as a sign that the 'troubled times' – the period of Tartar rule and the years of chaos in Russia – were over.

This period of Imperial Russia, as we know it, remained unchanged until the Revolution in 1917, and was the beginning of a new era of Russian aristocracy and a style of living that was to be unparalleled in Europe. The costumes, jewellery, palaces, churches, furniture and *objets d'art* produced for the nobility were more magnificent, more elaborate and more intricately crafted than those of the French or British monarchy, and this opulence and quality of work was reflected down throughout Russian society.

Russia had become a land of artists and artisans stretching an incredible distance from Europe in the west to the Orient in the east. Thousands of craftsmen produced wonderful pieces in glass, porcelain, papier mâché and silver while developing their own style of niello and cloisonné enamel work influenced by the Ottoman Empire and China. Thousands more devoted themselves to the making of icons or holy paintings called for by the Church, and these 'Windows on Eternity' served as symbols of the threshold between the secular world and the divine. The Russian theology was one of pictures rather than words and, within decades, every Russian home from the palace of the Tsar to the hovel of the poorest peasant displayed a vividly coloured and precisely painted holy icon.

The vast abundance of rich mineral deposits in Russia led to the use for ornamentation of many semi-precious stones found in the Ural region of central Russia, such as malachite, nephrite jade and agate. In later years the famous court jeweller, Carl Fabergé, created a wonderful array of fantasy objects from these stones.

Woodworking and carving were widespread traditional Russian art forms. By the 18th century the production of carved and decorated furniture had reached standards comparable to the west, and the craftsmen used karelian birchwood from the tundra wastes of the north to make furniture with a honey-coloured burr texture that was unique to Russia.

Sheldon Shapiro

FURNITURE

A pair of Russian mahogany and parcel-gilt tub chairs, the gold and black painted feathered front legs on claw-and-ball feet, early 19thC.
$9,000–10,000 S(NY)

A Russian mahogany campaign chest, on turned feet, early 19thC, 47in (119.5cm) wide.
$3,200–3,600 B&B

A Russian oak armchair, each arm in the form of an axe, the back carved with a Cyrillic inscription, the seat carved with a pair of woodman's gloves, label for Jacob and Joseph Kon, St Petersburg, 19thC.
$3,000–3,300 S(NY)

▶ A Russian neo-classical-style poplar daybed, the arched headboard and footboard flanked by square supports with orb finials, 1920s, 87in (221cm) wide.
$6,800–7,600 S(NY)

A Russian Tula polished and blued-steel and parcel-gilt footstool, upholstered in 18thC silk, c1790, 14¼in (36cm) wide.
$105,000–120,000 S

The Tula ironworks were founded in central Russia by Peter the Great to make small arms, but by 1725 had been partly converted into a factory making steel furniture and small ornaments. By 1736, the factory was producing large quantities of decorative objects and later in the 18thC was greatly patronized by Catherine the Great. At the time, Tula pieces were very expensive, and because of their rarity and desirability they still command a premium today.

CERAMICS

A porcelain charger, painted with a scene after the painting of Savinska, with simulated cloisonné enamel border, signed 'I. Dubin', Kuznetsov factory mark and overglaze gold factory mark, c1890, 18in (45.5cm) diam.
$14,000–15,500 S

An Imperial Russian hand-painted porcelain egg, c1880, 4½in (11.5cm) high.
$1,400–1,550 SHa

A Russian bisque porcelain figure of a street vendor, painted in polychrome colours, by Francis Gardner, Verbilki, Moscow, minor chips, impressed mark, 19thC, 7¼in (18.5cm) high.
$1,200–1,350 DORO

A Russian porcelain figure of a woodman, in a brown jacket and black trousers, green printed Nicholas II mark and incised marks, 1908, 8in (20.5cm) high.
$850–1,000 Bon

A Russian porcelain ten-piece tea set, by Kuznetsov, moulded with Art Nouveau-style leaves, painted with lavender borders, gilded with foliate motifs, c1900, teapot 5¼in (13.5cm) high.
$1,300–1,450 S(NY)

▶ A pair of porcelain vases, by the Imperial Porcelain Manufactory, the shoulders with cherubic fauns, the base moulded with acanthus tips and a wheatsheaf, underglaze green factory mark, 1855–81, 18in (45.5cm) high.
$21,000–24,500 S

A porcelain inkstand, by the Imperial Porcelain Manufactory, with gilt scroll decoration on a green ground, restored, underglaze blue factory mark, 1825–55, 9¾in (25cm) wide.
$1,800–2,200 S

BRONZE

A Russian bronze group of a peasant driving a cow, c1890, 12in (30.5cm) high.
$1,000–1,200 GOR(B)

A Russian bronze model of a peasant with an ox-cart, signed 'Khodarovich', foundry stamp, 19thC, 23in (58.5cm) wide.
$1,000–1,200 SK

▶ A Russian bronze-mounted malachite inkstand, with original cut-glass inkwell, c1810, 6in (15cm) diam.
$575–650 NOA

A Russian bronze group of a troika, by Grachev, signed, Woerffel foundry mark, late 19thC, 19½in (49.5cm) wide.
$7,500–8,500 S(NY)

SILVER

A Russian silver-gilt and niello beaker, the stippled sides with foliage and flowers within arched frames, maker's mark AK in script, Moscow 1838, 3¼in (8.5cm) high, 3¼oz.
$450–550 P

A Russian silver-filigree box, set with turquoises, the cover with melon-shaped finial, 1863, 5in (13cm) high, 9½oz.
$750–850 S(Am)

A Russian silver snuff box, decorated in niello with a courtyard scene, stamped 'J. M. Etamat Xoyaa', late 19thC, 5in (13cm) wide.
$250–300 FHF

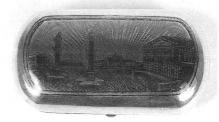

A Russian silver and niello cigarette case, marked, Moscow 1874, 4in (10cm) wide.
$900–1,000 ELI

A pair of Russian silver candlesticks, the base with scrolling stylized dolphins, the stem with flat leaf motifs, restored, late 19thC, 13¾in (35cm) high, 26oz.
$800–900 SK

A Russian silver-mounted cut-glass claret jug, by Ivan Khlebnikov, the spout in the shape of an oil lamp, the finial modelled as a swan, Moscow, c1900, 14in (35.5cm) high.
$7,000–8,000 S

An Imperial Russian silver cigarette case, with a scene of warriors, c1890, 4¾in (12cm) wide.
$800–900 SHa

A Russian silver cup, with niello decoration within scrolling foliate and floral decoration on stippled ground, gilt interior, 19thC, maker's mark 'AB', 6½in (16.5cm) high, 9oz.
$800–900 SLN

A Russian silver samovar, engraved and with vacant cartouches, gilt-washed interior, ivory fittings, maker's mark 'MP', Moscow 1887, 15¾in (40cm) high, 114oz.
$7,500–8,500 SLM

A Russian silver-gilt seven-piece tea set, in Japanese style, by Pavel Ovchinnikov, each piece applied with flowers, foliage and insects, with Imperial warrant, Moscow, 1894, teapot 4½in (11.5cm) high, in original wooden case.
$23,500–26,500 S

◄ A Russian silver tray, by Adolf Sperr, assaymaster D. Tverskoi, engraved with the Imperial eagle, St Petersburg 1849, 27½in (69.5cm) wide.
$4,000–5,000 S(G)

A Russian silver caviar jar and vodka measure, with *trompe l'oeil* decoration, c1860, measure 5¼in (13.5cm) high.
$4,500–5,000 SFL

ENAMEL

An Imperial Russian gilded-silver and champlevé enamel punchbowl, with harp-shaped handles, rim with Cyrillic inscription, maker's mark 'AK', Moscow, dated '1896', 10in (25.5cm) wide.
$7,500–8,500 JAA

A Russian cloisonné enamel cigarette box, decorated with foliage, birds and butterflies on a gold-washed stippled ground, inscribed in Russian, dated '1899', 4in (10cm) wide, 5oz.
$1,300–1,450 SK

A Russian gilded-silver and shaded enamel cigarette case, by Ivan Saltykov, decorated with flowers on a pale blue ground, Moscow, c1900, 3¾in (9.5cm) wide.
$3,000–3,300 S(NY)

A silver-gilt and shaded cloisonné enamel *kovsh*, by Alexander Benediktovich Lyubavin, decorated with flowers and scrolls, the handle with a raised St Petersburg crest surmounted by a coronet, c1896, 7½in (19cm) long.
$1,450–1,650 S(S)

A silver and cloisonné enamel tazza, by Gustav Klingert, decorated with floral scrolls in blue and red on a turquoise ground, with white pellet bands, Moscow, 1895, 5½in (13.5cm) high.
$800–950 S(S)

A Russian silver and enamel salver, the border polychrome-decorated with stylized foliage, the centre applied with the Imperial Order of St Andrew, c1900, 8¾in (22cm) diam.
$9,000–10,500 S(NY)

◄ A Russian set of 6 silver and enamel spoons, the bowls decorated with circles and silver beads on a stippled silver ground, marked, Moscow, c1908, 5¾in (14.5cm) long.
$2,000–2,300 JAA

JEWELLERY

A Russian gold bangle, with a miniature portrait of the Hon Robert Kennedy in an engraved enamel and pearl mounted band, c1850.
$2,400–2,700 Bon(G)

A Russian demantoid garnet and diamond hinged gold bangle, with removable centrepiece for conversion to a brooch, marked, Moscow, c1880.
$7,500–8,500 P

◄ A pair of Russian demantoid garnet earrings, set within clusters of diamonds, maker's mark 'MK', c1905.
$44,000–48,500 P

Demantoid is the precious transparent green variety of andradite garnet and owes its colour to traces of chromic oxide. It was first discovered in the Russian Urals in 1868, and the finest examples are sourced from the gold washings of Nizhne-Tagilsk in the Sissertsk district.

A Russian gold four-leaf clover brooch, maker's mark indistinct, c1896.
$2,400–2,600 P

A Russian demantoid garnet, half-pearl and diamond brooch/pendant, maker's mark 'MT', c1900.
$1,100–1,200 S(Am)

A Fabergé bonbonnière, with two-colour gold mounts, enamelled in opalescent rose over centred texturing on the cover flowing from an old-cut diamond, chased laurel border, workmaster M. Perchin, St Petersburg, 1896–1903, 1¾in (4.5cm) long.
$22,000–24,500 S(G)

A Fabergé diamond brooch, with rose Pompadour enamel Easter egg pendant, set with 3 diamond bands, unmarked, late 19thC, in associated Fabergé case.
$7,500–8,500 S

A Fabergé gold, silver and enamel brooch, converted from a buckle, the translucent lilac enamel on a sunburst field, signed 'KØ', Moscow, c1900.
$3,700–4,200 P

A Fabergé gold-mounted diamond brooch, with detachable fittings, workmaster A. Holmström, St Petersburg, c1900, 1¾in (4.5cm) wide, in original fitted case.
$18,000–21,000 S(G)

By family tradition, the diamonds used in this brooch were taken from the frames of portrait miniatures given by Emperor Alexander II to his Imperial Chancellor, Prince Alexander Gorchacov. His son, Prince Konstantin, commissioned Fabergé to make this jewel as an Easter present for his favourite daughter, Princess Maria. This history would account for the lack of inventory number on the piece as, being a special order, the brooch would not have entered Fabergé's stock.

A Fabergé pearl, silver and enamel timepiece, with translucent oyster ground over moiré engine-turning, on a scrolled easel support, workmaster H. Wigström, St Petersburg, 1896–1908, 4in (10cm) high.
$22,500–26,000 S(G)

A Fabergé carved nephrite, gold and enamel dish, the rim set with faceted red stones, the handles set with pearls, workmaster Michael Perchin, St Petersburg, c1900, 7in (18cm) wide.
$21,000–24,500 S(NY)

◄ A Fabergé gilt and cloisonné enamel *kovsh*, workmaster Fedor Ruckert, marked, 1908–17, 1in (2.5cm) diam, in original box.
$3,000–3,300 P

A Fabergé gold and enamel pendant, in the form of an egg, workmaster August Hollming, c1900, ½in (12mm) long.
$4,500–5,500 SHa

A Fabergé Imperial Russian matt enamel and lapis lazuli seal, workmaster E. Cundell, St Petersburg, 1893–1907, 1½in (4cm) high.
$8,500–9,500 SHa

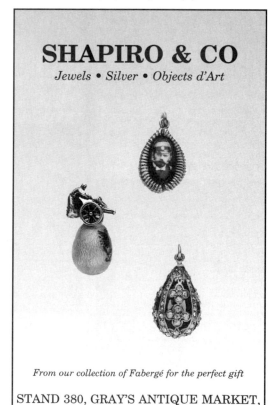

ICONS

A Russian icon of the Kazan Mother of God, the veil and Christ's garments overlaid with seed pearls and paste stones, silver-gilt and repoussé halo, the borders with a silver repoussé and chased riza, 17thC, 12½ x 10½in (32 x 26.5cm).
$4,500–5,200 JAA

A Russian icon of the Descent into Hell (Anastasis) and Principal Feasts, with Saints John, Matthew, Luke and Mark in the corners, early 19thC, 14 x 12in (35.5 x 30.5cm).
$4,000–5,000 RKa

A Russian icon of the Mother of God of Tenderness, with 4 saints on the borders, encased in a silver-gilt *oklad*, the garments composed of seed pearls, coral beads and semi-precious stones, maker's mark 'MT', 1844, 7 x 6in (18 x 15cm).
$3,700–4,400 S

A Russian icon of the Mother of God, flanked by archangels, 18thC, 20½ x 15½in (52 x 39.5cm).
$4,000–4,500 S(NY)

▶ A Russian icon of Saint Nicolas, on board, slight paint loss, 19thC, 12¼ x 10¼in (31 x 26cm).
$400–500 Bea

A Russian icon of a Bishop Saint, in a landscape with monastery beyond, gilt floral borders, early 19thC, 12 x 10½in (30.5 x 26.5cm).
$575–650 SK

A north Russian icon of the Deisis, painted with Christ enthroned as high priest, with God the Father, the Mother of God, Saint John the Baptist, an angel and Saint Phokas, late 19thC, 14 x 12¼in (35.5 x 31cm).
$2,600–3,000 DORO

▶ A Russian icon of a saint, painted on mother-of-pearl, in a silver and enamel frame, stamped 'AK 84', c1900, 2½ x 2¼in (6.5 x 5.5cm).
$250–300 Bea(E)

A Russian brass icon of Saint Nicolas, flanked by Christ Pantocrator and the Mother of God in nimbus, embellished with blue and white enamel, c1800, 10½ x 9½in (27 x 24cm).
$400–500 P

A Russian icon of the Presentation of the Virgin in the Temple, c1890, 8¾ x 7in (22 x 18cm), in a later carved giltwood shadowbox with velvet lining.
$675–850 NOA

MISCELLANEOUS

A Russian lacquered box, the cover with a troika being chased by wolves, 19thC, 5in (12.5cm) wide.
$800–900 SHa

An Imperial Russian birch cigarette box, with old gold mounts and set with a turquoise, c1900, 3in (7.5cm) long.
$1,450–1,600 SHa

A Russian powder horn, engraved with hunters, soldiers and game, initialled 'AELR' and '1867', with wooden stopper and brass cap, 9½in (24cm) long.
$600–650 JAA

A Russian papier mâché plate, from the studio of Vishniakov, 6 medals of merit mark, early 19thC, 7in (18cm) diam.
$480–560 RdeR

An Imperial Russian Karelian birch cigar box, with applied monogram on the cover, c1900, 8in (20.5cm) wide.
$3,200–3,600 SHa

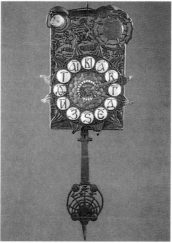

A Russian Arts and Crafts bronze, copper, brass and glass clock, the face with Slavonic letters in enamel in place of numerals, German gong-striking plated movement with deadbeat escapement, 13¾in (35cm) wide.
$5,600–6,400 S

This clock was exhibited at the Glasgow International Exhibition in 1901, probably as part of the Russian Arts and Crafts section.

A Russian portrait miniature, by B. Becher, depicting Count Kirill Grigorievich Razumovsky, wearing the sash of the Order of St Andrew, in a gilt-metal frame, 18thC, 3¾in (9.5cm) high.
$1,600–2,000 S

▶ A pair of Russian gilt-bronze-mounted *faux* porphyry and cut-glass garniture vases, c1900, 13in (33cm) high.
$1,150–1,300 NOA

A Russian lacquered box, by Vichnaichov, c1880, 6¼in (16cm) wide.
$800–900 SHa

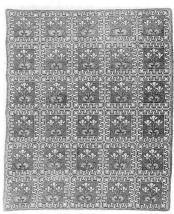

A Russian coverlet, the printed cotton ground embroidered in red, green and cream cross stitch, late 19thC, 75½ x 61½in (192 x 156cm).
$400–500 P

A set of 4 Russian walrus ivory and bone plaques, each decorated with a portrait bust of a member of the Imperial Russian family, inset on mica panels with rocaille and green stained panelled borders, late 18thC, largest 7 x 5¾in (18 x 14.5cm).
$4,000–5,000 P

Asian Works of Art

CLOISONNE

A Chinese cloisonné one-piece enamel clasp, decorated in blue, green, yellow and red on a dark blue ground, c1900, 3in (7.5cm) wide.
$100–115 JBB

A Japanese enamel vase, by Namikawa Yasuyuki, worked in silver wire with a dragon on a purple ground, the neck and foot with bands of floral decoration, signed, c1900, 3½in (9cm) high.
$10,500–12,000 S

A pair of Japanese cloisonné vases, decorated with orange flowers on a black ground, 1880–1900, 6in (15cm) high.
$2,600–3,000 MCN

A Japanese cloisonné enamel dish, the central medallion with a pale blue ground, decorated in silver wire with butterflies and flowers surrounded by a band of stylized motifs, Meiji period, 24in (61cm) diam.
$3,000–3,300 S

A Japanese cloisonné enamel vase, by Ota Kichisaburo, decorated with a pair of eagles in a maple tree watching a flight of sparrows, on a midnight-blue ground, impressed mark, Meiji period, 11¾in (30cm) high.
$4,600–5,200 S(S)

A Japanese cloisonné and gilded-bronze jar and cover, Meiji period, 4in (10cm) high.
$1,100–1,300 MCN

A pair of Chinese cloisonné covered jars, the yellow ground decorated with fruiting peach branches, late 19th/early 20thC, 14in (35.5cm) high.
$850–1,000 SK

A pair of Japanese cloisonné enamel vases, decorated on each side with birds and flowers on a patterned ground of stylized foliage and interlocking panels, Meiji period, 18in (45.5cm) high.
$1,450–1,600 P

A Chinese Canton enamel tea kettle and stand, decorated with continuous figural scenes, slight damage, early 19thC, 12¼in (31cm) high.
$1,000–1,100 SK(B)

GLASS

A Chinese cobalt Peking glass bowl, rim polished down, Qianlong mark and of the period, 6½in (16.5cm) diam.
$1,300–1,450 B&B

◄ A Chinese reverse glass painting, depicting a maiden seated at a European-style table reading a book and holding a tobacco pipe, in original frame, 19thC, 19½ x 13½in (49.5 x 34.5cm).
$650–800 Bon

A pair of Chinese yellow glass jars and covers, 19thC, 9¾in (25cm) high.
$10,000–11,500 S(NY)

JADE

A Chinese jade model of a goat, Song Dynasty, 2in (5cm) long.
$2,000–2,300 Wai

A Chinese Imperial jade headdress status badge, carved with the Imperial five-clawed dragon, early Ming Dynasty, 2¼in (6cm) wide.
$4,800–5,600 Wai

Chinese Jade

In China jade was a symbol of purity that was often used as a tomb adornment to comfort the soul and and confer immortality. Jade carving of ritual objects dates back to Neolithic times, and the popularity of the stone has continued unabated through the ages. From the Ming period, fine ornaments, small sculptures and items for the scholar's desk became the main output, and jade workshops opened up in almost every major city in China. Over the last 200 years the value of the finished object has become more dependent on the quality of the stone used than the quality of the carving.

A spinach-green jade censer and cover, carved in low relief with an archaic frieze of *taotie* masks, the cover pierced with lotus blooms and scrolls and with a coiled dragon finial, early 19thC, 5½in (14cm) high.
$2,000–2,300 Bon

A *taotie* is a mythical animal that devours wrongdoers.

A Chinese mottled green and brown jade boulder carving of a mountain, worked with the figure of Tamo in a grotto with a waterfall and gnarled trees, 18thC, 6¾in (17cm) high, the fitted wood stand carved and pierced with bamboo, grasses, flowers and *lingzhi*.
$3,500–4,000 P

◄ An Indian Mughal carved mid-green jade bowl, in the form of an oval twelve-petalled flower, with a pair of acanthus scroll handles, 18thC, 8in (20.5cm) diam.
$9,000–11,500 S

A Chinese nephrite jade boulder, of mottled olive grey-green stone with brown inclusions, carved with a scholar and 2 boys on a mountain path, restored, Qing Dynasty, 13in (33cm) high.
$2,800–3,200 Bon

An Indian Mughal jade oil-lamp, the stone of pale green tones with minor russet inclusions, the acanthus scroll handles worked in relief with foliate form designs around the foot and the rim, 18thC, 3¼in (8.5cm) high.
$22,000–25,000 S

A Chinese carved celadon jade brushwasher, in the form of a double gourd with both bulbs hollowed out, enclosed by bats and meandering vines continuing around the reverse, Qing Dynasty, 12¾in (32.5cm) long.
$3,000–3,300 S(NY)

LACQUER

A Chinese red lacquer rice barrel, mid-19thC, 14in (35.5cm) high.
$300–330 GHC

A large wooden rice barrel would be found in most houses in the south of China to store the household's supply of rice corns. They were always lacquered to add strength.

A Chinese export black lacquer and gilt-decorated games box, with a chess board on the exterior, each of the black squares with seated gilt figures, the interior with a backgammon board, with some mother-of-pearl games pieces, mid-19thC, 19½in (49.5cm) wide.
$700–800 S(NY)

A Chinese export lacquer games box, with numerous interior compartments with red and gilt chinoiserie decoration, c1860, 15in (38cm) wide.
$400–500 RBB

A Chinese export black lacquer and gilt-decorated needlework box, the interior fitted with lidded compartments and containing various ivory accoutrements, with base drawer, 19thC, 14in (35.5cm) wide.
$1,200–1,350 TMA

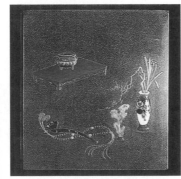

A Japanese inlaid lacquer *suzuribako*, decorated in coloured *takamakie* and inlaid wood, silver, pottery, tortoise-shell, stained ivory and stones, fitted with inkstone and a silver container in the form of 2 chrysanthemum flowers, 19thC, 9½in (24cm) long.
$5,750–6,500 S

A *nashiji* ground lacquer game box and stand, with gilt-metal mounts, slight damage, Meiji period, 18½in (47cm) high.
$1,150–1,400 B&B

▶ A Japanese gold lacquer box, in the form of a boy seated on a drum, his face and hands of ivory, Meiji period, 5½in (14cm) high.
$8,000–9,000 S

A Japanese lacquer and mother-of-pearl encrusted box and cover, the exterior applied with flower blooms, the interior and base of *nashiji*, Meiji period, 6½in (16.5cm) wide.
$3,200–3,600 P

A Japanese lacquer box, decorated with gold lacquer *chidori* on an abalone shell and brown lacquer ground, with powdered gold interior, 19thC, 6in (15cm) wide.
$900–1,000 FW&C

A Japanese gold lacquer box and cover, the inside of the cover depicting lovers in a boat in a moonlit setting, 19thC, 5in (12.5cm) wide.
$9,500–10,500 KJ

A Japanese lacquer box, decorated with branches of leaves and a butterfly, c1900, 3¼in (8.5cm) diam.
$1,450–1,650 MCN

A lacquer miniature chest, decorated with peony blossoms in red, green and gold *takamakie* against a *nashiji* ground, the silver-mounted doors opening to reveal 3 interior drawers decorated with gold butterflies against a red ground, slight damage, signed 'Senpo', 19thC, 6in (15cm) wide.
$9,000–10,500 B&B

21 Years Ago ...

A lacquer *suzuribako*, decorated in red and green *hiramakie* and gold *takamakie*, 19thC, 10 x 9¼in (25.5 x 23.5cm). **S**

Twenty-one years ago this *suzuribako* (writing instrument box) was valued at $650–750. Lacquerware has a complicated and time-consuming manufacturing process. The intrinsic value combined with the fine artwork of the Japanese master artists have resulted in a far greater appreciation of lacquerware as an art form. Most of the best lacquer work originated in the late 19th or early 20th century and, like much art of relatively modern manufacture, it has taken time to be fully appreciated. The last ten years has seen a steady increase in value and the market is still rising. Today this *suzuribako* would fetch $5,500–6,500.

A Japanese lacquer smoking box, decorated with landscape views, 19thC, 7¼in (18.5cm) wide.
$2,500–3,500 B&B

A Japanese gilt lacquer cabinet, the central doors inlaid with 2 figures before a distant Mount Fuji, above a single drawer and flanked by wings containing 4 graduated drawers, with detachable top, slight damage, Meiji period, 5½in (14cm) high.
$1,800–2,000 RTo

A Japanese lacquer tray, decorated in ivory, mother-of-pearl, coral, green hardstone and lacquer high relief with the 7 gods of good fortune in a sailing vessel, Meiji period, 16¼ x 23¾in (41.5 x 60.5cm), in a glazed case.
$11,500–13,000 HYD

◄ A Chinese lacquer figure of Buddha, of joined block construction, his curls painted in black and the remaining surfaces covered in gold lacquer, 18thC, 15in (38cm) high.
$1,150–1,350 B&B

METALWARE

A Japanese bronze elephant incense burner, Meiji period, 8in (20.5cm) high.
$2,300–2,600 BOW

A Japanese bronze model of an elephant, c1890, 10in (25.5cm) long.
$3,300–3,700 SHa

A Japanese bronze model of a fantail pigeon, Meiji period, 5in (12.5cm) wide.
$1,800–2,000 MBo

A Japanese export sterling silver punchbowl, worked in high repoussé with flowering *kiri* branches, with a conforming liner, maker's mark, stamped 'Joko', early 20thC, 15¼in (38.5cm) diam.
$4,000–4,500 B&B

A Tibetan gilt-bronze-mounted iron ewer, the handle cast as a dragon, the spout issuing from the jaws of an elephant, the cover with lotus-bud knop, decorated with a dragon surrounding by scrolling lotus, slight damage, 18thC, 15¼in (39cm) high.
$800–900 Bon(C)

A Japanese bronze figure of a girl kneeling, holding drumsticks, sealed 'Seiya' on base, Meiji period, 8in (20.5cm) high.
$480–560 FW&C

A Chinese silvered-bronze mirror, decorated with bird design, Tang Dynasty, 5in (12.5cm) diam.
$200–250 BAC

---

21 Years Ago ...

A pair of inlaid bronze vases, each decorated in gilt, silver and copper *takazogan*, late 19thC, 7¾in (20cm) high. **L**

Twenty-one years ago this pair of bronze vases was valued at $500–600. Over the past 21 years the market for Asian antiques has polarized as collectors have distinguished between quality, rarity and intrinsic value and the 'run-of-the-mill' items. Good-quality bronzes in particular have gradually risen in price as collectors have appreciated the art, skilful techniques and time taken in their manufacture. This pair of signed inlaid bronze vases might now achieve a price of $4,000–5,000 at auction.

A Japanese bronze vase, in the form of rope-tied leaves on lily pad and tendril base supports, c1900, 23½in (60cm) high.
$1,450–1,600 Bri

STONE

An Indian Ghandaran grey Schist sculpture of Skanda, the warrior-deity standing on a base incised with a lattice design, minor damage, 2nd–3rd century AD, 11in (28cm) high.
$500–600 P

A central Indian buff sandstone Jain *stele*, with a figure meditating beneath a canopy surrounded by an arch of attendant figures and riders on elephants to either side, slight damage, 8th–9th century AD, 23½in (60cm) high.
$3,500–4,000 B&B

A central Indian red sandstone carving of Dikpala, God of Wealth, flanked by an attendant and jewels, the deity's 4 hands holding a citron, lotus, mace and staff, circa 10th century AD, 18in (45.5cm) high.
$2,000–2,300 P

A Chinese carved stone head of a Bodhisattva, the back of the head unfinished, Song Dynasty, 14in (35.5cm) high.
$3,300–3,600 B&B

WOOD

A Chinese fruitwood model of a merchant's store, with hinged rear roof, 19thC, 11¼in (28.5cm) high.
$3,700–4,200 S(NY)

A Japanese model of an owl, perched on an ivy-clad tree stump, the eyes inlaid in ivory with black painted pupils, early 19thC, 1¾in (4.5cm) high.
$5,800–6,500 S

A Japanese wood and *shibayama* model of an elephant, with an ivory finial on its back, decorated with tortoiseshell, ivory and coloured glass, signed, slight damage, Meiji period, 6¾in (17cm) high.
$800–900 Bea(E)

An Indian group of carved wood polychrome figures, comprising 20 pieces, including a dignitary in a carriage drawn by 2 Brahmin bulls, with high- and low-cast male and female attendants and artisans, most titled in Hindi and English, distressed, early 19thC, figures 5in (12.5cm) high.
$480–560 FW&C

A Japanese boxwood figure of Ono no Komachi, 19thC, 3in (7.5cm) high.
$1,100–1,300 B&B

Ono no Komachi was a famous 9th century poetess who ended her life in penury.

A Chinese wooden devotional figure, Qing Dynasty, 9in (23cm) high.
$200–230 BAC

ARMS & ARMOUR

A Japanese suit of armour in Gomaido Gusoku style, with yellow brocaded silk waistcoat, gilt-metal and gold lacquer decorations, Edo period, 52in (132cm) high.
$3,800–4,200 FW&C

This suit was collected in Japan in the 19thC.

A Japanese suit of armour in the Domaru style, with leather shoes, arm guards and leg backs, in japanned lacquer box, 19thC, 62in (157.5cm) high.
$9,000–10,000 JAd

A Japanese Namban-style helmet, composed of 12 plates, decorated with gold and silver inlay of crests, dragons and various insects, 18thC, 6¾in (17cm) high.
$1,800–2,200 SK

A Japanese bronze and lacquer *tanto*, the hilt decorated with gilt cloud-like scrolls, the lacquer scabbard decorated with *nashiji* leaves and *aogai* butterflies on a mottled gilt ground and encased in silver mounts, slight damage, Meiji period, 8in (20.5cm) long.
$575–675 P

A Japanese *tanegashima*, the barrel engraved with a dragon grasping a flaming jewel, details in gilt and silver, the flat lock and fittings in brass, the stock of reddish-brown wood, pins missing, 18th/19thC, 36in (91.5cm) long.
$4,000–4,500 S(NY)

A *tanegashima* is a matchlock musket.

An Indian Mughal dagger and silver-mounted scabbard, the jade hilt inlaid on either side with a ruby-set foiled crystal, 18thC, 16¾in (42.5cm) long.
$5,200–5,700 S

A Japanese *daisho,* mounted in red and black lacquered *sayas*, signed 'Ni Ote To To Kato Ho Ju Tskuru Kore' and dated '1804', longest 25½in (65cm) long.
$7,000–8,000 GV

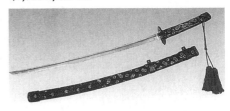

A Japanese cloisonné mounted *tachi*, the hilt, *tsuba* and scabbard decorated with flowers, foliage, dragons and birds on a midnight blue ground, signed 'Munenaga', 17thC, 41¼in (105cm) long.
$4,800–5,600 Bea(E)

TSUBA

A Japanese *tsuba*, the pitted ground pierced with a *kemari* and stylized blossoms, probably Momoyama period, 3½in (9cm) diam.
$1,450–1,600 S(NY)

A Japanese Soten School *tsuba*, worked with a Gempei battle scene, gold highlights, signed, 17th/18thC, 3in (7.5cm) diam.
$3,000–3,300 B&B

A Japanese iron *tsuba*, with 5 cloisonné enamel roundels inlaid on the front, and 3 on the reverse, signed 'Egawa Muneyoshi', 19thC, 3¼in (8.5cm) high.
$1,300–1,450 S(NY)

A Japanese gold lacquer *tsuba*, decorated with Emma, king of the underworld, and *oni* preparing hell tortures, inlaid in ivory and coloured shell lacquer, signed 'Nemoto', slight damage, Meiji period, 4½in (11.5cm) high.
$3,200–3,500 B&B

CLOCKS

A Japanese rosewood bracket clock, with verge movement, brass casing and mechanism, a revolving face and adjustable hour plates of silvered-metal engraved with Japanese numerals and windows for day and date, 19thC, 6½in (16.5cm) high.
$3,700–4,200 S(NY)

► A Japanese rosewood stick clock, with engraved brass movement, the dial with numbers and gold lacquer zodiac characters, 19thC, 18¼in (46.5cm) high.
$1,800–2,200 SK

A Japanese brass-mounted clock, the case carved with leafy peony blossoms, the face engraved with zodiac signs, the movement probably English, c1900, 8in (20.5cm) high.
$2,600–3,200 S(NY)

◄ A Japanese rosewood stick clock, with verge movement, the front plate pierced and engraved with flowers and a bird, 19thC, 18in (45.5cm) high.
$4,000–4,500 S(NY)

FURNITURE

A Japanese brass-mounted lacquer cabinet, on a European rococo-style carved wood stand, 17th/18thC, 36in (91.5cm) wide.
$5,500–6,000 HOK

An Indo-Portuguese cabinet, veneered in hardwood and with engraved ivory inlay of flowers, the fall-front enclosing small drawers, slight damage, 18thC, 25¾in (65.5cm) wide, on a later ebonized stand.
$32,500–35,500 MCA

There is currently a strong market in Portugal for items associated with the country, and this item is also a rare piece.

► A Chinese fruitwood tapered cabinet, 19thC, 42in (106.5cm) wide.
$2,000–2,500 K

An Indo-Portuguese hardwood marquetry and bone-inlaid cabinet-on-chest, the top section with 12 drawers, the base with a pair of drawers over a deep drawer, probably Goanese, 19thC, 44in (112cm) wide.
$20,000–22,000 SK

A Chinese red elm scholar's chair, 19thC.
$750–850 SOO

A Chinese five-leaf screen, made from door panels, 19thC, 35½in (90cm) high.
$900–1,000 GHC

A Japanese display cabinet, the door fronts faced in gilt lacquer applied in high relief with ivory flowers, on a separate scrolled base pierced and carved with birds, some damage, Meiji period, 42½in (108cm) wide.
$2,200–2,500 P

An Anglo-Indian brass-mounted mahogany and wrought-iron coffer, c1820, 50½in (128.5cm) wide.
$1,100–1,300 NOA

A north Indian carved-teak chest, c1840, 30in (76cm) wide.
$480–560 BAB

A Chinese export calamander chair-back settee, the crests and splats outlined with scroll carving, 18thC, 54in (137cm) long.
$2,200–2,600 DN

A Chinese black lacquer table cabinet, decorated in gilt with figures, buildings, flowers and foliage, the 2 doors each with a raised oval panel, 19thC, 13½in (34.5cm) wide.
$325–375 TRL

A Chinese export black lacquer and gilt chest-on-stand, decorated with trailing ginkgo leaves and berries, 18thC, 34in (86.5cm) wide.
$10,500–12,000 TMA

A Chinese table screen, the black and gilt lacquer panel depicting a nobleman's household at a summer palace, 19thC, 25in (63.5cm) wide.
$480–560 WW

A Burmese hardwood console table, carved with birds, scrolling foliage, fruit and masks, on scrolling supports carved with animal masks and foliage, 19thC, 66½in (169cm) wide.
$1,150–1,300 HYD

INRO

A Japanese four-case *inro*, applied in silver and gold with wisteria, inlaid with mother-of-pearl, some damage, late 17th/early18thC, 2½in (6.5cm) high.
$900–1,000 P

A Japanese boxwood four-case *inro*, carved in the form of a terrapin, with inlaid horn eyes, 18th/19thC, 4in (10cm) high.
$1,100–1,200 FW&C

A Japanese black lacquer two-case *inro*, in the style of Ogata Korin, Rimpa school, decorated with pine trees, inlaid with pewter, 17thC, 4¼in (11cm) high.
$3,700–4,200 S

▶ A Japanese black lacquer four-case *inro*, inlaid with green-tinted bone, the underside inscribed in gilt with 'Koma Kyuhaku saku', slight wear, 19thC, 3in (7.5cm) high.
$9,000–11,500 B&B

A Japanese silver-mounted lacquer three-case *inro*, slight damage, 19thC, 3in (7.5cm) diam.
$1,700–2,000 JaG

NETSUKE

A Japanese carved wood *netsuke*, in the form of a man struggling with an octopus, slight wear, 18thC, 2¼in (5.5cm) high.
$800–900 P

◀ A Japanese ivory *netsuke*, in the form of a monkey, signed 'Masatami', 19thC, 1½in (4cm) high.
$3,200–3,800 MBo

A Japanese *netsuke*, in the form of an *oni* sheltering under his straw hat, 19thC, 3½in (9cm) high.
$2,000–2,500 BOW

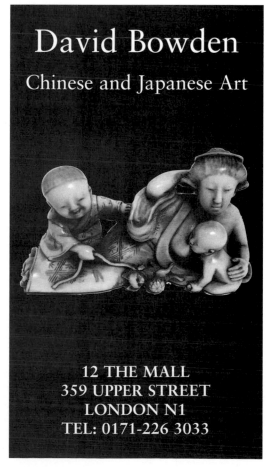

PRINTS & POSTERS

A Japanese concertina album, comprising 26 pictures, depicting girls and children at leisure, damaged, Meiji period, 8 x 14in (20.5 x 35.5cm).
$700–800 Bon

A Japanese print of a Tai bream, in shades of brown on a blue ground, by Hiroshige, published by Eijudo, c1830, 10 x 14½in (25.5 x 37cm).
$2,000–2,300 JaG

Cross Reference
See Colour Review

A Japanese print of Tanzaku, monkey and bee, by Koson, early 20thC, 13½ x 7½in (34.5 x 19cm).
$350–400 JaG

▶ A Chinese poster, entitled 'Off to the Countryside', 1976, 30¼ x 20¾in (77 x 52.5cm).
$300–330 Wai

A Chinese poster, entitled 'Defending Zhen Bao Island', 1971, 21 x 14½in (53.5 x 36cm).
$200–230 Wai

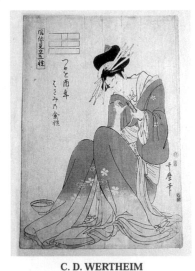
ROBES & COSTUME

A Japanese dark blue brocade and cream silk *kosode*, with small flower pattern motif, lined with terracotta silk, late Edo period, mid-19thC.
$230–260 P

A Japanese governor's dress uniform, the coatee of black wool doeskin cloth, with raised gold thread embroidery, the trousers with gold braid outer seam stripe, early 20thC.
$900–1,000 P

◀ A Chinese silk theatrical costume, with yellow upper section and pink-ground silk skirt embroidered in shades of blue, late 19thC.
$3,200–3,500 B&B

SNUFF BOTTLES

A Chinese overlay glass snuff bottle, carved as a peach, the branch picked out from the top layer of light green glass carved to the semi-translucent body of yellowish-beige with tan striations, early 19thC, 1¾in (4.5cm) high.
$3,200–3,500 S(HK)

A Chinese chalcedony snuff bottle, of warm brown tone with inclusion of ochre tones, carved to depict a dragon and phoenix, 19thC, 2¼in (5.5cm) high.
$3,500–4,000 JWA

◀ A Chinese double overlay glass snuff bottle, white on black against a snowflake ground, with the One Hundred Antiques between mock lions' mask ring handles, 19thC, 2¾in (7cm) high.
$900–1,000 B&B

21 Years Ago ...

An interior painted glass snuff bottle, by Ye Zhongsan the Younger, with an apple-green jade stopper, *yin* seal, signed and dated '1908', 3in (7.5cm) high. **S**

Twenty-one years ago this snuff bottle was valued at $160–200. Chinese snuff bottles have always been popular with collectors on account of their size and the mix of medium used in their manufacture. The past five years have seen a dramatic rise in the value of the best examples of snuff bottles as demand increases, but supply is getting very limited. Each specialist sale achieves higher prices, confirming a rising market. This snuff bottle, by Ye Zhongsan (Yey Chung-San) the Younger, would today realize $3,250–4,000. But beware of the many fakes now reaching the market.

TEXTILES

A Japanese *fukusa*, embroidered and applied with coloured silks and gold thread on a dark blue satin ground, designed with a woodcutter resting by a stream, lined with ivory silk, late Edo period, 23 x 22in (58 x 56cm).
$360–420 P

A *fukusa* is a gift-wrapping cloth.

A Chinese skirt panel, embroidered in blues and greens on a yellow ground, with Buddhistic symbols, late 19thC, 13 x 7½in (33 x 19cm).
$160–200 PBr

A Chinese red silk hanging, embroidered with 24 characters from the Peking Opera, the blue silk borders with gold thread, late 19thC, 71½ x 61in (181.5 x 155cm).
$1,400–1,550 SK

An embroidered and applied coiled thread and silk wall hanging, designed with a cockerel on a barrel, and a hen nesting, with a velvet border, late 19thC, 82 x 45½in (208 x 116cm).
$1,800–2,200 P

◀ An Indian Rescht hanging, worked in silk floss and metal thread on a blue felt ground, the central flower motif in metal thread surrounded by pink and lilac flowerheads, c1900, 69 x 67in (175.5 x 170cm).
$525–600 WW

Islamic Works of Art

A Nishapur slip-decorated pottery bowl, decorated in black, red and buff, eastern Persia, 10thC, 9½in (24cm) diam.
$3,500–4,000 S

A Seljuk cock's-head pottery ewer, painted in cobalt blue on a white ground with vertical stripes, probably Kashan, early 13thC, 10in (25.5cm) high.
$11,000–12,000 S(NY)

A Persian pottery bowl, decorated in lustre, cobalt blue and splashes of turquoise with cartouches of stylized foliate motifs and palmettes, the interior cobalt blue, Persia, late 12thC, 7in (18cm) diam.
$2,000–2,300 S

An Iznik pottery dish, relief-painted in red, cobalt blue, green and with black outlines, Turkey, c1600, 11¼in (28.5cm) diam.
$5,500–6,500 S

An Iznik pottery dish, decorated in cobalt blue, green, black and red, Turkey, late 16thC, 11¾in (30cm) diam.
$6,500–8,000 Bon

An Iznik pottery dish, decorated in cobalt blue, green, black and raised red with a central leaf flanked by roses and tulips, the exterior with stylized flowerheads, Turkey, early 17thC, 12in (30.5cm) diam.
$2,000–2,300 Bon

An Iznik pottery dish, painted in dark brown, cobalt blue, green and red with stylized flowers and foliage radiating from a central flowerhead, glaze fritting, 17thC, 11¼in (28.5cm) diam.
$1,600–1,800 P

◄ A Chanakkale massive pottery lion, decorated with an ochre glaze with splashes of brown, with applied floral motifs, Turkey, 19thC, 16¼in (41.5cm) high.
$3,000–3,500 Bon

An Istanbul ware porcelain cup and saucer, with moulded relief and gilt decoration of grapes and vine leaves, stamped, Turkey, c1850, saucer 5¾in (14.5cm) diam.
$2,300–2,600 S

Ahmed Fethi Pasha, the minister of the Arsenal, set up a porcelain factory in 1845, in the town of Incirli in Beykoz. The factory functioned for 20 or 30 years, and the earliest wares carried the stamped mark found on this cup and saucer.

◄ A Qajar pottery tile, ith polychrome decoration of a wedding scene, Persia, 19thC, 15½ x 30½in (39.5 x 77.5cm).
$7,500–9,000 S

◄ An Ottoman scribe's table, decorated with mother-of-pearl, bone and ebony, the single drawer with 3 divisions, Turkey, late 16thC, 27in (68.5cm) wide.
$30,000–34,000 S

This impressive box is a rare example of early Ottoman furniture. The works of this period tended to use ebony, with tortoiseshell becoming popular later.

A Damascus parquetry and mother-of-pearl games table, the fold-over top revealing baize, folding again to reveal chess and backgammon boards, with swivel action, late 19thC, 34in (86.5cm) wide.
$1,800–2,000 WBH

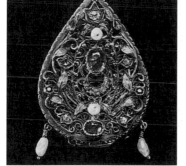

A pair of Qajar enamelled gold earrings, with floral motifs, Persia, 19thC, 2½in (6.5cm) long.
$2,000–2,300 S

A pair of Qajar gold bracelets, each hinged at one side, decorated with a continuous band of raised repoussé conical bosses flanked by raised ropework designs, Persia, 19thC, 2¾in (7cm) diam.
$2,200–2,600 S

A Mughal gold armlet, comprising 9 plaques each set with a stylised floral motif of coral, turquoise, pearl and diamonds, the reverse with a polychrome enamel design of a pair of birds, strung with 5 strands of seed pearls, northern India, late 19thC, 8¼in (21cm) long, in a fitted box.
$2,500–3,000 S

A sapphire and diamond-set filigree amulet, Turkey, 19thC, 2¾in (7cm) high.
$2,100–2,400 S

◄ A Qajar dagger and scabbard, with enamel decoration of figural cartouches and calligraphic bands, Persia, 19thC, 19¼in (49cm) long.
$2,300–2,600 S

A leaf from a manuscript of Persian poetry, gouache with gold on paper, illuminated in colours and gold, Persia, c1560, 11¼ x 7½in (28.5 x 19cm).
$3,000–3,800 S

A leaf from an illuminated Mamluk Qur'an, the heading in ornamental eastern kufic script in white on a ground of lapis and gold arabesque, Syria, late 13thC, 10¼ x 7½in (26 x 19cm).
$2,400–2,800 Bon

Nizami, Laila va Majnun, an illustrated and illuminated Persian manuscript on paper, made for Mirza Aqa Burujirdi, dated for 1813, 6¼ x 3¾in (16 x 9.5cm).
$3,000–3,200 S

◀ A Ghaznavid 'high-tin' bronze bowl, decorated in low relief with a geometric design beneath a band of circular motifs, eastern Persia, 11thC, 9½in (24cm) diam.
$4,000–5,000 S

A Mamluk brass basin, with incised decoration, the interior with a central rosette, Egypt or Syria, early 14thC, 19½in (49.5cm) diam.
$7,500–8,500 S

An Ottoman silver covered cup, the cover and sides with pebbled decoration, engraved with foliage and floral cartouches, and an associated Egyptian saucer, late 19thC/early 20thC, 5in (12.5cm) high.
$650–800 P

A Qajar damascened steel ewer, with incised decoration, the handle terminating in a stylized dragon's head, Persia, 19thC, 17in (43cm) high.
$3,200–3,500 S

A Qajar enamelled-copper dish, decorated in polychrome enamels with a scene of ladies on horseback in a rocky landscape within a border of floral sprays,, the reverse with a riverscape, Persia, 19thC, 6¼in (16cm) diam.
$2,300–2,800 S

▶ A Qajar silver-mounted ostrich egg ghalian, the figural cartouches with calligraphic details, the bowl and shaft with a wood support, Persia, 19thC, 24½in (62cm) high.
$3,800–4,200 S

It is unusual to find a ghalian incorporating an ostrich egg.

An Ottoman silver ewer, the cover with castellated rim and foliate finial, and an associated metalware basin, probably Egyptian, late 19th/early 20thC, ewer 12½in (32cm) high.
$2,800–3,200 P

A silver and copper-inlaid brass inkwell and cover, incised and inlaid with benedictory inscriptions and signs of the zodiac, Khurasan, early 13thC, 4in (10cm) high.
$10,000–11,500 S

A gold scent bottle, with incised foliate motifs, the interior with glass liner, Morocco or Tunisia, c1900, 2¾in (7cm) high.
$7,500–9,000 S

◀ A Safavid brass torchstand, with incised decoration, Persia, c1600, 12¾in (32.5cm) high.
$6,000–7,000 S

▶ An Ottoman silver soap dish and cover, with engraved band and trailing flowers, with liner, late 19thC, 6¼in (16cm) long.
$1,800–2,000 P

An Ottoman salmon pink silk wall hanging, embroidered in raised metal strip and chain stitch, with colours, lined with red cotton, c1720, 82¾ x 59¾in (210 x 152cm).
$2,500–2,800 P

An Ottoman green corded silk wall hanging, of *mihrab* and lamp design, embroidered with plum, yellow and blue silks, lined with pink silk, c1770, 71 x 52in (180 x 132cm).
$3,000–3,300 P

An Ottoman silk panel, the green field embroidered with metal thread, early 19thC, 79 x 66in (200.5 x 167.5cm).
$2,500–3,000 Bon

An Ottoman crimson silk panel, worked with gold and silver thread, 18thC, 27½ x 41¼in (70 x 105cm), mounted, framed and glazed.
$750–900 P

▶ An Ottoman silk tomb cover fragment, with bands of inscription, 18thC, 62½ x 26½in (159 x 67cm).
$3,000–3,200 S

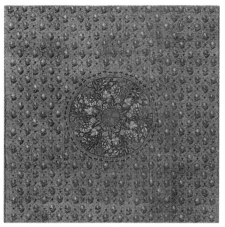

An Ottoman wrapping cloth, the old gold silk satin ground worked in polychrome silk chain stitch, late 18thC, mounted, 39 x 52in (98 x 101cm).
$5,500–6,500 S

A Qajar painted and lacquer frame, enclosing a picture depicting a hunting scene, 19thC, 10¼ x 12¼in (26 x 31.5cm).
$650–750 CGC

A Qajar coco-de-mer begging bowl, worked in relief with depictions of revellers, mounted with a metal chain, Persia, 19thC, 11½in (29cm) wide.
$7,500–8,500 S

An Ottoman tunic of pink silk, with wrapped metal strip embroidery, the back and front panels with birds, branches, flowers and leaves, backed with lime green silk, late 19thC.
$1,600–2,000 P

A Qajar lacquer and papier mâché pen case, 19thC, 10in (25.5cm) long, in an embroidered green velvet bag.
$550–600 SK

Architectural Antiques

BRASS

A Georgian brass and iron boot scraper, cast in the form of 2 griffins, 13in (33cm) wide.
$800–1,000 TMA

A set of 10 Victorian brass curtain rings, 4in (10cm) diam.
$160–200 RUL

A set of 9 Victorian brass curtain rings, 5in (12.5cm) diam.
$300–330 RUL

A pair of French brass door handles, c1900, 6½in (16.5cm) wide.
$100–125 RUL

A Victorian brass coat and hat hook, 9in (23cm) high.
$115–130 RUL

A French brass coat hook, c1900, 11in (28cm) high.
$115–130 RUL

A Victorian brass coat hook, 9in (23cm) high.
$80–100 RUL

BRONZE

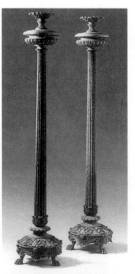

A French bronze fountain, in the form of 3 putti supporting a bowl, c1870, 37in (94cm) high.
$8,000–9,500 S(S)

A French gilt-bronze reeded curtain pole, with fruiting terminals, late 19thC, 66in (168cm) long.
$550–700 P

A bronze fountain figure of a young boy playing the pipes, signed 'A. Rhind Sc, 1926', early 20thC, 35in (89cm) high.
$15,500–18,000 S(S)

LOCATE THE SOURCE
The source of each illustration in Miller's can be found by checking the code letters below each caption with the Key to Illustrations, pages 789–795.

A pair of neo-classical-style patinated-bronze torchères, each with an urn surmounted by a foliate-cast receptacle, on a leaf-cast base, on paw feet, c1900, 80in (203cm) high.
$6,500–8,000 S(NY)

► A pair of neo-classical-style patinated bronze urns, each with a leaf-cast everted rim on a stepped foot, possibly French, late 19thC, 24in (61cm) high.
$3,000–3,300 B&B

IRON

A pair of cast-iron andirons, by Bradley & Hubbard, modelled as owls, signed and dated '1878', 17in (43cm) high.
$650–800 A&A

A Chinese cast-iron bath, with ring handles, the feet with cast animals' masks, 19thC, 43in (109cm) long.
$11,500–13,000 S(S)

A pair of cast-iron boot scrapers, each in the form of a wyvern, with iron scraper and knopped terminals, c1870, 28in (71cm) high.
$1,500–1,700 S(S)

A cast-iron boot scraper, 19thC, 13in (33cm) wide.
$65–80 OCH

◄ A French pierced-iron crucifix, 18thC, 42in (107cm) high.
$300–350 P

A pair of cast-iron boot scrapers, each in the form of a griffin, with cannon barrel bases, 19thC, 24in (61cm) long.
$1,400–1,500 RBB

◄ A pair of Victorian iron shelf or cistern brackets, 9in (23cm) wide.
$30–40 BYG

A Victorian cast-iron rainwater hopper, 16½in (42cm) high.
$50–60 BYG

► A pair of French cast-iron lamp posts, each with stiff-leaf decoration and cast with the shield of the city of Paris, copper tops glazed, late 19thC, 156in (396cm) high.
$16,000–20,000 S(S)

A pair of Coalbrookdale cast-iron three-tier plant stands, stamped and numbered, c1865, 39in (99cm) high.
$3,800–4,400 S(S)

▶ A Victorian cast-iron garden seat, with slatted wooden seat, floral and trellis cast ends, 66in (167.5cm) long.
$350–400 DD

A Regency painted wrought-iron garden seat, with hinged footrest, 49in (124cm) wide.
$1,000–1,200 Oli

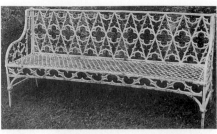

A Victorian Gothic-style cast-iron garden seat, with pierced back and honeycomb seat, 68in (172.5cm) long.
$2,000–2,300 MEA

A pair of Coalbrookdale cast-iron chairs, with Fern and Blackberry pattern, each with a wooden slatted seat, c1870.
$2,300–2,600 S(S)

A set of 6 painted cast-iron garden chairs, each with a shaped back above a circular seat, pierced with foliage and scrolls, on foliate-scrolled legs, late 19thC.
$1,500–1,800 S(NY)

A wrought-iron tree seat, in 2 parts each with segmented back and plain slatted seat, the legs joined by stretchers, on paw feet, 19thC, 57in (145cm) diam.
$3,800–4,200 S(S)

A decorative iron radiator, with warming oven, c1900, 34in (86.5cm) wide.
$1,600–2,000 ACT

A French die-cast solid fuel stove, 1940s, 38in (96.5cm) wide.
$700–800 A&H

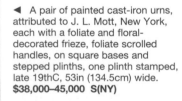

A Continental Selecta solid fuel cooking range, 1950s, 40in (101.5cm) wide.
$1,300–1,500 A&H

◀ A pair of painted cast-iron urns, attributed to J. L. Mott, New York, each with a foliate and floral-decorated frieze, foliate scrolled handles, on square bases and stepped plinths, one plinth stamped, late 19thC, 53in (134.5cm) wide.
$38,000–45,000 S(NY)

▶ A cast-iron corner umbrella stand, c1890, 19in (48.5cm) wide.
$400–500 OCH

MARBLE

A white marble oval cistern, with inverted rim, on an oval base, c1800, 28in (71cm) wide.
$7,000–8,500 S(S)

A pair of Italian white marble lions, each with full mane and roaring, late 19thC, 44in (112cm) long.
$10,000–11,500 S(S)

A carved marble head, weathered, 14thC, 8¼in (21cm) high.
$800–1,000 P

A marble figure of Cupid, one finger slightly damaged, 19thC, 46in (117cm) high.
$60,000–70,000 Doc

It is thought that this figure was made by John Gibson in Italy for the English market. It has never been exposed to the elements, and is in exceptional condition.

A white marble fountain figure of the young Bacchus, reclining on a wine pitcher, drilled for water, on an oval base, 19thC, 28in (71cm) high.
$5,000–6,000 S(S)

A marble figure of Apollo, damaged, 19thC, 41in (104cm) high.
$4,000–4,500 Doc

A *rouge royale* marble columnar fluted pedestal, c1850, 43¾in (111cm) high.
$2,000–2,300 NOA

A pair of Italian marble throne chairs, each back with a medallion carved with a lion holding a shield, the seat flanked by scrolled arm-rests and lion monopodia supports, the sides carved with dolphins, late 19thC.
$14,000–16,000 S(NY)

An Italian Renaissance-style white marble jardinière, late 19thC, 39½in (100.5cm) wide.
$3,200–3,800 B&B

A Venetian marble well-head, carved with an armorial shield, a rosette and a star, 17thC, 32in (81.5cm) wide, with later wrought-iron overthrow.
$23,000–26,000 S(S)

A Regency *verde antico* marble and gilt-brass sarcophagus-shaped jardinière, with reeded canted angles and lion-mask ring handles, on paw feet, 31in (78.5cm) wide.
$20,000–22,500 MCA

◄ An Italian carved marble garden seat, c1890, 65in (165cm) long.
$10,000–11,500 NOA

STONE

Three stone balls, c1900, smallest 6in (15cm) diam.
Pair $300–350
Single $200–250 A&H

A sandstone arch from the entrance of a church, c1897, 88in (223.5cm) wide.
$2,500–3,000 A&H

An Italian carved limestone model of a seated lion holding a shield, 16thC, 15¾in (40cm) high.
$2,000–2,300 P

A carved sandstone figure of a knight, the base inscribed 'Palace of Westminster 1932', early 19thC, 71in (180.5cm) high.
$15,500–17,000 S(S)

A limestone figure of Saint George and the Dragon, 19thC, 66in (167.5cm) high.
$7,500–8,500 Riv

A carved stone figure of Pan, seated on a rock playing pipes, 1920s, 39½in (100.5cm) high.
$2,000–2,500 S(S)

A stone sundial, 18thC, 32in (81.5cm) high.
$725–800 DOR

A pair of reconstituted stone urns, early 20thC, 44in (112cm) wide.
$2,500–3,000 RAW

A stone water trough, c1800, 26in (66cm) wide.
$250–350 A&H

A pair of German limestone urns, by Herman Obrist, Munich, c1901, 8in (20.5cm) high.
$1,000–1,200 ANO

A carved Portland stone sundial, the bronze plate inscribed with hours, foliage, a verse and 'St Peter's, Kew', late 19thC, 55in (139.5cm) high.
$4,000–5,000 S(S)

A pair of sandstone garden urns, on pedestals and square bases, damaged, 19thC, 42in (106.5cm) high.
$600–700 Bea(E)

A pair of carved sandstone urns, carved in relief with stylized fruit and flowers, on a stepped square base, mid-19thC, 38in (96.5cm) high.
$2,800–3,200 S(S)

TERRACOTTA

A pair of Continental glazed terracotta urns, with applied rams' head handles and stiff leaves, early 18thC, 13¾in (35cm) high.
$2,500–3,200 B&B

A terracotta figure of Flora, in classical dress with flowers in her hair, lower arms missing, the base stamped 'M. Blashfield, Stamford', c1850, 63in (160cm) high.
$6,000–7,000 S(S)

A Continental terracotta jardinière and pedestal, the frieze depicting puttis and cherubs, the pedestal with 3 griffins, 19thC, 43in (109cm) high.
$1,800–2,200 SLM

◄ A terracotta oil storage jar, with ribbed decoration, 19thC, 66in (167.5cm) high.
$2,000–2,300 S(S)

WOOD

A pair of Victorian carved wood figures, 30in (76cm) high.
$900–1,000 GAZE

A pair of carved oak parrots, c1880, 23in (58.5cm) high.
$700–800 RUL

A wooden cartwheel, c1860, 44in (112cm) diam.
$160–200 A&H

A pair of carved pine wall brackets, mid-18thC, 17¼in (44cm) high.
$3,250–3,500 P(O)

BRICKS & TILES

Three Dutch terracotta tiles, each
depicting a knight on horseback,
early 17thC, 4in (10cm) square.
$50–65 each BAC

A selection of Georgian
handmade bricks.
$1,100–1,200 per thousand A&H

A Victorian glazed tile, with rope
edging, 7 x 9in (18 x 23cm).
$5–6 BYG

An end tile, 1880–1900,
13in (33cm) high.
$160–200 BYG

An ornamental ridge tile,
1880–1900, 12in (30.5cm) wide.
$10–15 BYG

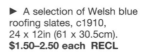

▶ A selection of Welsh blue
roofing slates, c1910,
24 x 12in (61 x 30.5cm).
$1.50–2.50 each RECL

A Victorian blue path edging tile,
c1890, 10in (25.5cm) wide.
$2.50–4 RECL

CHIMNEY POTS

A fired-clay fully-glazed
'king and queen'
design chimney pot,
in brown on a square
base, 1860–80,
22in (56cm) high.
$200–250 BYG

A Gothic-style stone
chimney pot, with
reeded column central
section, 1860–1900,
32in (81.5cm) high.
$200–275 BYG

A Royal Doulton
chimney pot, impressed
'Doulton & Co 98', c1880,
44in (112cm) high.
$400–475 JBe

A salt-glazed 'Long Tom'
chimney pot, c1900,
72in (183cm) high.
$140–160 A&H

BATHROOM FITTINGS

An Empire zinc tub, 19thC,
62¼in (158cm) long.
$1,600–2,000 S(Am)

A French double-ended roll-top bath,
with porcelain-handled lever waste,
early 20thC, 64in (162.5cm) long.
$1,100–1,300 DOR

A cast-iron and enamel roll-top
bath, with high-rise drain overflow,
c1890, 75in (190.5cm) long.
$1,400–1,600 DOR

A ceramic bed pan, by Burgoyne
Burbidges & Co, c1920s,
15½in (39.5cm) long.
$100–115 BYG

◀ A Unitas
relief-decorated
lavatory pan,
slight damage,
c1888, 18in
(45.5cm) high.
$3,000–3,500 ACT

A French double-ended bath,
early 20thC, 64in (162.5cm) long.
$1,300–1,600 POSH

A white porcelain bidet, late
19th/early 20thC, 22in (56cm) wide.
$1,600–1,900 ACT

A low-level copper cistern,
1930–50, 17in (43cm) wide.
$550–600 ACT

An Edwardian porcelain
lavatory pan, by Brown-
Westhead, Cauldon Ltd,
transfer decorated in
blue and white with fruit
and flowers, c1905,
17in (43cm) high.
$800–1,000 M

▶ A French porcelain
double soap dish, 1930s,
10in (25.5cm) wide.
$160–200 AC

A Centaur roll-edge
lavatory pan, 1920s,
15in (38cm) high.
$800–1,000 ACT

A German bronze tap, with stylized bird finial, mounted on turned wooden base, 17thC, 9in (23cm) long.
$320–350 P

A Victorian silvered-brass decorative bath tap, with plug plunger, 7in (18cm) high.
$400–500 RUL

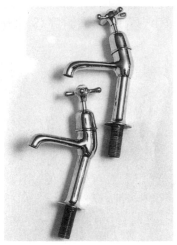

A pair of brass kitchen pillar taps, early 20thC, 8in (20.5cm) high.
$80–130 WRe

A pair of solid nickel 'Globe' bath taps, fully restored, 1920s, 6in (15cm) high.
$150–180 ACT

A brass bath/shower mixer tap, restored, 1930s, 9in (23cm) wide.
$500–600 ACT

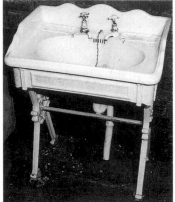

A Victorian washbasin, on original cast-iron base, 27in (68.5cm) wide.
$575–650 A&H

A Victorian corner washbasin, on a cast-iron bracket, 27in (68.5cm) wide.
$400–450 A&H

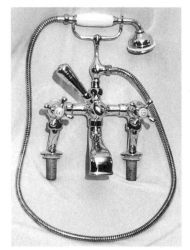

A French roll-edge corner washbasin, original taps and waste, c1920, 30in (76cm) wide.
$1,000–1,200 ACT

A roll-edge washbasin, on cast-iron legs, with taps and waste, c1910, 23½in (60cm) wide.
$1,200–1,400 ACT

A ceramic wash-house sink, on ceramic legs, c1920, 30in (76cm) wide.
$400–500 A&H

A Pyramid roll-edge washbasin, 1920s–30s, 22in (56cm) wide.
$400–450 ACT

► An Art Deco washbasin, 1920s–50s, 22in (56cm) wide.
$125–150 ACT

DOORS & DOOR FURNITURE

A Georgian four-panelled exterior door,
83in (211cm) high.
$150–180 A&H

A pair of Restauration polychromed and grained salon doors, in the style of Jean-Baptiste Huet, damaged, c1810, 100½in (255.5cm) high.
$5,700–6,500 NOA

A Victorian six-panelled pine door, 83in (211cm) high.
$130–160 A&H

A Victorian four-panelled pine door, 78in (198cm) high.
$100–130 A&H

A Victorian brass bell-push, 4in (10cm) high.
$60–70 RUL

A brass bell-push, c1910, 3in (7.5cm) diam.
$40–50 HEM

A Victorian brass door-pull, 5in (12.5cm) diam.
$120–140 RUL

A pair of brass door knobs, c1880, 3in (7.5cm) diam.
$90–100 RUL

A Victorian cast-iron door knocker, 9in (23cm) high.
$35–40 BYG

A rimlock, key and keep, c1910, 7in (18cm) wide.
$65–75 HEM

A pair of Louis XVI-style painted and carved giltwood over-door panels, 19thC, 50in (127cm) wide.
$5,000–5,750 B&B

A Spanish baroque polychrome and parcel-gilt door surround, early 18thC, 104in (264cm) high.
$9,000–10,000 B&B

FIREPLACES

A Georgian pine fire surround, the break-front shelf with dentil and egg-and-dart moulding, the tablet carved in high relief with a festoon of summer flowers, cut down, c1760, 74in (188cm) wide.
$6,000–7,000 S(S)

A Regency marble fire surround, designed by Thomas Hope, possibly carved by John Flaxman, c1810, later shelf, 82¼in (209cm) wide.
$146,000–162,000 S

This fire surround was almost certainly from the Indian Room in Thomas Hope's mansion at Duchess Street, London, and was removed prior to its demolition in 1851.

A George III pine fire surround, the frieze carved with a ribbon bow and pendant floral chains flanked by urns, the pilasters carved with fruit and flowers, c1780, 71½in (181.5cm) wide.
$3,500–4,200 Bon

An Irish Regency white marble fire surround, with free-standing columns, the frieze with geometric pattern in relief, c1820, 72in (183cm) wide.
$3,750–4,500 GKe

An American Federal carved mantelpiece, possibly by Samuel McIntyre, Massachusetts, c1800, 78½in (199.5cm) wide.
$5,000–6,000 SK(B)

A painted pine and carved fire surround, with stepped mantel, the frieze centred by a ram's head within a garland of fruit and flowers, early 19thC, 65in (165cm) wide.
$1,600–2,000 P(Ba)

A carved-oak fire surround, with dentil cornice, decorated with guilloche and flowerhead ornament within fluted columns, 19thC, 120in (305cm) wide.
$2,300–2,600 P(EA)

A Victorian cast-iron breakfront fire surround, the central tablet with an urn and floral swags, 55in (140cm) wide.
$1,200–1,600 A&H

An Irish pine fire surround, c1880, 56in (142cm) wide.
$200–250 TAN

► A brocatelle marble fire surround, the panelled frieze centred with a flowerhead, the fluted jambs surmounted by stop-fluting, late 19thC, 45in (114.5cm) wide.
$1,000–1,150 S(S)

A dark oak fire surround and overmantel, with carved frieze and columns, late 19thC, 84in (213.5cm) wide.
$2,300–2,600 CAG

A Louis XV-style carved white marble fire surround, c1890, 61in (155cm) wide.
$3,500–4,000 NOA

A Regency sarcophagus-shaped cast-iron fire basket, with bronze lions'-mask ring handles and acanthus plates, 46in (117cm) wide.
$12,000–14,000 EH

A neo-classical style cast-iron hob grate, with railed grate, the side panels decorated with medallions, early 19thC, 39¼in (100cm) wide.
$1,400–1,600 P(Ba)

▶ A Victorian oak fire surround, with cast-iron and tiled interior, late 19thC, 62in (157.5cm) wide.
Fire surround $1,300–1,500
Grate $550–730
Tiles $250–325 NOST

A Louis XV-style *rouge* marble fire surround, with serpentine shelf, panelled shaped frieze and jambs, late 19thC, 48in (122cm) wide.
$500–575 S(S)

A pair of fire grates, each pierced frieze centred by an eagle, on scrolling side supports, late 19thC, 20½in (52cm) wide.
$1,600–2,000 P

A Victorian cast-iron combination fire surround, 1930s, 26in (66cm) wide.
$280–350 BYG

A Victorian cast-iron bedroom fireplace, 27in (68.5cm) wide.
$325–400 A&H

A cast-iron fire surround, 1930s, 22in (56cm) wide.
$250–280 BYG

A cast-iron combination fire surround, c1900–10, 30in (76cm) wide.
$350–450 BYG

FIREPLACE ACCESSORIES

A pair of Louis XVI-style gilt and patinated-bronze and jasper ware chenets, c1860, 14in (35.5cm) high.
$3,250–4,000 SK(B)

A pair of brass andirons, with rope-twist guard, 19thC, 28¼in (72cm) high.
$2,000–2,300 P

A pair of ormolu chenets, each in the form of a camel on a shaped rectangular base, late 19thC, 11in (28cm) high.
$16,200–17,800 S(NY)

A brass and iron wire fender, with 3 brass finials, minor imperfections, c1790–1830, 54¾in (139cm) long.
$2,750–3,250 SK(B)

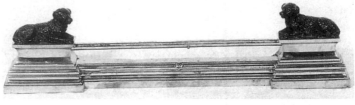

An Empire brass fender, with an adjustable central section, the plinth terminals each with a recumbent hound, 19thC, 50in (127cm) wide.
$800–1,000 HYD

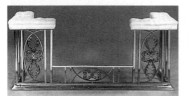

A gilt-brass fender, the corner seats supported on rails inset with foliate cast motifs, 19thC, 54½in (138.5cm) wide.
$800–900 P

A Netherlandish late Gothic cast-iron fire back, probably 16thC, 20¾in (53cm) high.
$3,500–4,000 S(Am)

A cast-iron fire back, with arched top, depicting a classical figure holding an olive branch, inscribed 'PAX 1679', 31in (58.5cm) high.
$500–575 FW&C

A Georgian steel footman, 13in (33cm) high.
$325–400 AnSh

A set of Louis XVI-style brass fire irons, comprising a stand with 4 tools, together with a pair of andirons, c1900, 24in (61cm) high.
$2,750–3,250 SLN

A brass and copper log bin, decorated with swags, leaves and masks, with lion-mask and ring handles, on paw feet, late 19th/early 20thC, 15½in (39.5cm) high.
$5,000–6,000 S

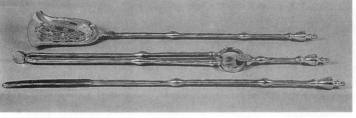

A set of George III steel and brass fire irons, with urn finials, the pan with pierced urn and floral decoration, 30¼in (77cm) long.
$2,300–2,600 P

Sculpture

A Mexican painted and gilt figure of St Ferdinand III of Castile, damaged, 17thC, 37¼in (94.5cm) high.
$8,000–9,500 S(NY)

A Flemish carved lime figure of the Madonna and Child, with traces of gilding and paint, late 17thC, 33½in (85cm) high.
$1,300–1,450 Bon

A Netherlandish boxwood group of the Virgin and Child, damaged, late 17thC, 6¾in (17cm) high.
$6,500–7,500 S

A Spanish polychrome wood figure of the Christ child, damaged, late 17thC, 30in (76cm) high.
$3,700–4,200 S(NY)

A terracotta bust of a young woman, French School, late 18thC, 11in (29cm) high.
$800–900 HOK

A pink and cream mottled terracotta bust of Christoph Willibald von Gluck, from the workshop of Jean Antoine Houdon, with traces of grey-brown pigment, on a marble socle, late 18thC, 20¾in (52.5cm) high.
$9,000–10,500 S(NY)

A pair of Italian carved wood, polychrome and gilt figures of angels, some damage, 18thC, 29in (73.5cm) high.
$9,000–10,500 B&B

A painted plaster figure of Flora, one hand damaged, early 19thC, with later electric light fitting, 69in (175.5cm) high, on a wooden plinth.
$3,000–3,500 S(S)

A terracotta group, by Claude Michel, called Clodion, depicting a faun and a nymph, 1800, 17¼in (44cm) high.
$6,500–7,500 DORO

An Italian neo-classical carved alabaster figure of a maiden, slight damage, c1800, 21in (53cm) high.
$1,100–1,200 SK

A cast-plaster bust of William Pitt, by Humphrey Hopper, after Nollekens, inscribed and dated 'January 3rd, 1814', 29in (73.5cm) high.
$3,300–3,800 S

A bronze figure, entitled 'The Dancing Faun', after Adrien de Vries, 19thC, 22½in (57cm) high.
$2,000–2,300 Bea(E)

A pair of bronze figures of Native Americans, on flared bases with lizard supports, 19thC, 16in (40.5cm) high.
$1,000–1,150 B&W

A Carrara marble figure entitled 'Ruth', or 'The Reaper', by Pietro Barzanti, on a *verde antico* marble support, column and plinth, signed, 19thC, 78½in (199cm) high.
$20,000–23,000 P(Sc)

An alabaster figure of a girl on a fur-covered couch, wearing a serpent bangle on her left arm, one foot missing, 19thC, 25½in (65cm) long.
$750–850 MJB

A carved alabaster model of a stalking tiger, on a naturalistic rocky base, late 19thC, 24¾in (63cm) long.
$2,400–2,700 P(G)

A pair of Egyptian bronze figures of a prince and princess, both on marble and slate plinths carved with scarab wings, late 19thC, 16in (40.5cm) high.
$1,600–2,000 Bon

A bronze heraldic lion, c1870, 9½in (24cm) high.
$1,550–1,800 Cha

▶ A marble figure of a classical maiden, late 19thC, 39¼in (99.5cm) high.
$1,600–2,000 Bon

A bronze bust of a 17thC-style gentleman, wearing a plumed hat, c1870, 7in (18cm) high.
$800–900 ANT

A carved cedarwood bust of William Shakespeare, by W. Perry, dated '1879', on a moulded walnut plinth, 26½in (67.5cm) high.
$4,000–4,500 S

A bronze model of a golden retriever, by Alfred Dubucand, signed, c1880, 6in (15cm) long.
$800–900 WeH

An Italian white marble bust of a young girl, by C. Panati, signed and dated '1886', 25½in (65cm) high.
$2,500–3,000 P(S)

A bronze figure of
Salome, by Dumaige,
signed, c1865,
15in (38cm) high.
$3,000–3,500 ChA

A bronze figure of a
gundog with a snipe,
by Delabrierre, signed,
c1875, 9in (23cm) high.
$3,200–3,600 ChA

An Italian white marble
bust of a girl with a bird
on her shoulder, by Pietro
Barzanti, signed, late 19thC,
20½in (52cm) high.
$4,600–5,200 S(S)

A French bronze figure
of seated girl, late 19thC,
12½in (32cm) wide.
$1,000–1,150 SK

A white marble figure
of a nymph and a winged
putto, by V. A. Bastet,
signed and dated '1894',
52½in (133cm) high.
$30,000–35,000 S

A white marble figure
of a girl, with a string
of pearls around her
neck, late 19thC,
23½in (60cm) high.
$6,000–7,000 P

A gilt-bronze group of
a girl with a tambourine,
a putto at her side, after
Clodion, late 19thC,
12½in (32cm) high.
$1,400–1,600 ChA

◄ A cold-painted-spelter
figure of an Eastern water
seller, on a base with rope-
twist edge, signed 'Mestais'
and 'Guillot', late 19thC,
28½in (72.5cm) high.
$1,000–1,200 Mit

A pair of French terracotta
figures, the man signed
'El Vergnano', the lady
signed 'Calendi', late
19thC, 22in (56cm) high.
$650–800 Mit

An Italian bronze figure
of a soldier, holding
a gun with fixed bayonet,
black patination, on a
marble plinth, c1890,
15in (38cm) long.
$1,300–1,450 WeH

▶ A cold-painted-spelter
figure of a Nubian slave
girl seated on a wall,
by Emmanuel Villanis,
her dress detachable,
signed, c1900,
16in (40.5cm) high.
$1,600–2,000 S(S)

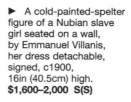

A bronze figure of Diana,
signed 'Houdon', c1880,
23½in (59.5cm) high.
$1,150–1,300 WeH

A bronze figure of a penitent, wearing 17thC dress, signed 'A. Vibert', on a marble plinth, late 19thC, 10in (25.5cm) high.
$2,200–2,400 ChA

A French bronze figure of Joan of Arc, c1880, 17in (43cm) high.
$1,000–1,150 WeH

An Italian veined white marble figure of Bacchus, wearing a fur draped over one shoulder, c1900, 57in (145cm) high, on a wooden pedestal.
$6,000–7,000 S(S)

A marble figure of Saint Francis holding the Christ child and a stem of lilies, c1900, 55½in (141cm) high, on a three-part base.
$4,500–5,000 SK(B)

A terracotta bust, by Goldscheider, entitled 'Les Lys', c1900, 19in (48.5cm) high.
$1,600–2,000 ANO

A terracotta bust, by M. Guiraud Rivière, entitled 'Head of Bacchante', signed, c1900, 22in (56cm) high.
$800–900 JAK

A spelter model of a leaping greyhound, signed 'Carvin', c1910, 11½in (29cm) high.
$750–900 ChA

A bronze group of an Arab mare and stallion, by Pierre-Jules Mêne, entitled 'L'Accolade', incised mark, signed and dated '1865', 25¾in (65.5cm) long.
$10,500–12,000 S(S)

This group, depicting the 2 Arab horses Tachiani and Nedjébé, was first modelled by Mêne in wax and exhibited at the Paris Salon of 1852. The bronze version was exhibited at the Salon the following year.

A painted plaster bust of a young girl, c1920, 14½in (37cm) high.
$160–200 Ber

A bronze figure of a foundry worker, signed 'Winkler', c1910, 23½in (59.5cm) high.
$900–1,000 WeH

Metalware

BRASS

A Continental brass basin on a pedestal, 18thC, 7¾in (19.5cm) diam.
$500–600 SK

A brass counter bell, c1920, 3½in (9cm) high.
$40–50 CHe

A pair of Georgian brass candlesticks, with square bases, 9½in (24cm) high.
$400–450 ANT

A brass candlestick, the triple knopped sconce on a vase-shaped integral stem, the lower section with dished drip-tray, slight damage, late 16thC, 14in (35.5cm) high.
$10,000–11,000 S(S)

A pair of Continental brass pricket candlesticks, with turned stems and mid-drip pans, probably Dutch, c1700, 15in (38cm) high.
$800–900 SK

A pair of brass cassolettes, the reversible covers with pinecone finials, the urn-shaped bodies with scrolled handles, milled socles and square plinths, c1820, 8¾in (22cm) high.
$5,600–6,400 S

A pair of French brass candlesticks, the faceted nozzles raised on mushroom knopped stems and hexagonal bases, late 18thC, 8¾in (22cm) high.
$500–600 P

A pair of Flemish brass pricket candlesticks, each with a knopped stem and on a spreading foot, 19thC, 13in (33cm) high.
$440–520 P(O)

A brass candlesticks, by W. Tonks & Sons, marked, 1866, 6¼in (16cm) high.
$400–500 ChA

Sets/Pairs

Unless otherwise stated, any description which refers to 'a set' or 'a pair' includes a guide price for the entire set or the pair, even though the illustration may show only a single item.

◄ A pair of gilt-brass candlesticks, each in the form of a heron holding 3 leaves in its beak, surmounted by rococo-style sconces, on rockwork bases cast with shells, regilded, stamped 'Abbott', late 19thC, 27in (68.5cm) high.
$3,000–3,500 S

A brass desk set, comprising an inkwell and 2 candlesticks, c1850, candlesticks 7in (18cm) high.
$400–500 STK

A Victorian pierced and moulded-brass casket-shaped inkstand, with lions'-head and cherub decoration, 15¼in (38.5cm) wide.
$525–600 WilP

A gilt-brass inkwell, in the form of a beehive, on an onyx base, c1890, 5in (12.5cm) square.
$400–500 HUM

A Victorian brass inkwell, in the form of a crocodile, the body opening to reveal 2 cut-glass ink bottles, impressed mark to base, 10in (25.5cm) long.
$130–160 HBC

A French brass jardinière, cast and pierced with rococo-style C-scrolls and foliage, with dragon side handles, on foliate scroll feet, with liner, c1880, 21in (53.5cm) wide.
$800–900 S(S)

A French brass table cigarette lighter, c1900, 6in (15cm) high.
$160–200 RUL

A brass paper gauge, with enamel dial, early 19thC, 4in (10cm) long.
$250–300 HUM

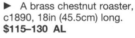

A brass paper clip, by Ratcliff, Birmingham, c1840, 5in (12.5cm) long.
$80–100 HUM

► A brass chestnut roaster, c1890, 18in (45.5cm) long.
$115–130 AL

A gilt-brass letter rack, in the form of a recumbent camel, c1910, 8in (20.5cm) wide.
$180–200 CHe

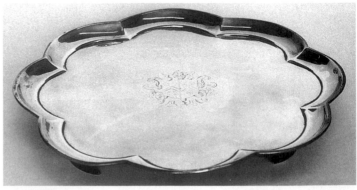

A brass salver, with moulded rim, engraved with a coat-of-arms, on 4 panel feet, 18thC, 14¾in (37.5cm) diam.
$5,700–6,500 CAG

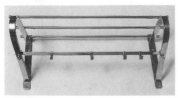

A brass train luggage rack, c1920, 24in (61cm) wide.
$260–300 RUL

◄ A brass tipstaff, commemorating the 150th anniversary of the British Police Force, 1979, 8in (20.5cm) long.
$75–90 WAB

A brass tankard, the domed
cover with scroll thumbpiece and
double scroll handle, repaired,
c1760, 7¾in (19.5cm) high.
$4,000–5,000 S(S)

A brass tobacco jar, c1920,
4in (10cm) high.
$100–115 RUL

A brass vesta, in the form of a bull,
late 19thC, 2½in (6.5cm) long.
$325–375 GH

A Dutch brass hand-warmer, in the
form of a pierced hinged sphere
engraved with birds and flowers,
with a gimballed centre, early 19thC,
6in (15cm) diam.
$500–600 S(S)

A Continental gilt-brass tazza, with
etched geometric design, the edge
with tiger's-eye cabochons, late
19thC, 12in (30.5cm) diam.
$375–425 P

A brass tobacco tin, c1880,
9in (23cm) wide.
$50–60 S

A lacquered-brass vesta case,
in the form of a hip flask, c1870,
2in (5cm) long.
$130–160 HUM

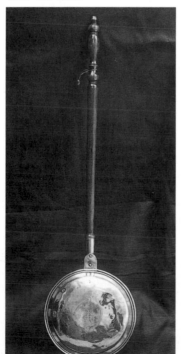

A brass warming pan, with walnut
handle, c1780, 40in (101.5cm) long.
$160–200 KEY

A Dutch brass fireside tobacco box,
with hammered decoration of
farmyard scenes, early 20thC,
6¼in (16cm) wide.
$115–130 CHe

A brass combined vesta and cigar
cutter, in the form of a Veuve Cliquot
champagne bottle, late 19thC,
2½in (6.5cm) long.
$240–280 GH

A brass and tortoiseshell vesta,
in the form of a turtle, late 19thC,
2in (5cm) long.
$120–160 GH

An American brass warming pan,
with painted wooden handle, c1780,
41¾in (106cm) long.
$400–500 A&A

BRONZE

A bronze candlestick, with potpourri container, c1790, 8in (20.5cm) high.
$775–850 ChA

A pair of neo-classical gilt-bronze three-light candelabra, each on a triangular base with conforming white marble plinth, late 18thC, 11in (28cm) high.
$5,000–5,700 B&B

A pair of gilt-bronze candlesticks, cast as a Chinaman and his companion, early 19thC, now mounted as table lamps, 19¾in (50cm) high.
$3,250–4,000 NOA

A pair of French gilt-bronze candlesticks, the sconces supported by figures of cherubic musicians, 19thC, 5in (12.5cm) high.
$725–800 AAV

A pair of French chinoiserie gilt-bronze candlesticks, c1840, 8in (20.5cm) high.
$475–575 ChA

A pair of gilt-bronze and porcelain three-light candelabra, each with scrolling foliate arms applied with flowers surrounding a model of a seated duck, painted in greens, blue and yellow, 19thC, 15¾in (40cm) wide.
$2,750–3,250 P

A pair of Regency bronze candlesticks, each on a triform base of lions' legs with paw feet, and a trefoil yellow marble base, 12¼in (31cm) high.
$725–800 P(S)

A pair of bronze and gilt-brass candlesticks, c1820, 10¼in (26cm) high.
$4,500–5,200 S

A Viennese patinated-bronze candle holder in the form of a frog, late 19thC, 4½in (11.5cm) high.
$1,700–2,100 B&B

A gilt-bronze censer, c1845,
9in (23cm) high.
$2,500–3,000 ChA

A French bronze figure of a child
wearing a helmet, c1865,
3½in (9cm) high.
$250–300 ChA

A Swiss bronze paperweight,
cast with an Alpine scene, c1890,
5in (12.5cm) wide.
$200–230 HUM

A French Egyptian-style bronze
inkwell, c1830, 5in (12.5cm) high.
$325–375 ChA

A gilt-bronze tazza, signed
'Emil Picault, Salon Exhibit 1879',
12½in (32cm) diam.
$6,500–7,000 ChA

**This tazza was part of the collection
of King Leopold II of Belgium.**

An Italian bronze mortar, decorated
with a band of shells and scrolling
foliage, 16thC, 13in (33cm) diam,
with a bronze pestle.
$4,000–5,000 P

A French bronze plaque of a dog,
signed and dated '1925',
4 x 5in (10 x 12.5cm).
$230–260 HUM

An Italian bronze figure of a semi-
naked lady holding a bowl, c1880,
21½in (55cm) high.
$1,600–2,000 WeH

A Danish bronze vase, cast with
winged horsemen, signed
'Lindenberg', 19thC, 16in (40cm) high.
$575–650 P

◄ A matched pair of
bronze Borghese and
Medici vases, early 19thC,
19¾in (50cm) high.
$13,000–14,500 S

► A patinated-bronze
vase, designed by
Gustave-Joseph Chéret,
entitled 'The Water
Babies', c1882,
14½in (37cm) high.
$3,250–4,000 S(Am)

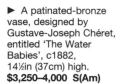

COPPER

An engraved-copper cup, probably French, engraved with a trelliswork pattern filled with flowers, 14thC, 4in (10cm) diam.
$2,000–2,300 S(NY)

An Italian gilt-copper chalice, the bowl and knopped stem applied with angel masks, inscribed, with a plain gilt-copper paten, late 17th/early 18thC, 8in (20.5cm) high.
$2,200–2,600 P

An oak and copper jug, mid-19thC, 8½in (21.5cm) high.
$400–450 ANT

A copper tobacco tin, c1840, 3¼in (8.5cm) wide.
$100–115 S

◀ A copper samovar, with brass spout and tap, early 19thC, 14in (35.5cm) high.
$320–350 WW

A copper kettle and stand, late 19thC, 15in (38cm) high.
$650–730 ASA

IRON

A German iron-bound strong chest, probably Nuremburg, with pierced brass lockplate, the inside of the lid fitted with a steel lock, 16th/17thC, 35½in (90cm) wide.
$2,000–2,300 HOK

A Spanish wrought-iron lectern, the bookrest covered in leather, 16thC, 14¾in (33cm) wide.
$11,500–13,000 S(NY)

An iron figure of a hunter, possibly German, on a red marble base, 17thC, 9¼in (23.5cm) high.
$1,000–1,200 S(NY)

◀ A cast-iron cow doorstop, c1920, 15in (38cm) wide.
$500–575 AWT

▶ A cast-iron model of a cat, standing on a tiled roof, mounted on an alabaster base, slight damage, impressed 'M. Bonnot', early 20thC, 4¾in (12cm) high.
$160–200 P

584 **METALWARE • Copper • Iron**

ORMOLU

A French ormolu three-branch candelabrum, on a figural baluster support, 19thC, 15¼in (39cm) high.
$325–400 P(F)

An Empire ormolu centrepiece, the base cast with masks of Bacchus, with later cut-glass bowl, restored, 13½in (34.5cm) high.
$4,000–5,000 S(NY)

An ormolu five-branch candelabrum, by Elkington, engraved with a coat-of-arms, 19thC, 29in (74cm) high.
$6,500–7,250 HOK

PEWTER

A Dutch pewter wriggle-work beaker, with portraits of William and Mary, maker's mark, c1690, 5½in (14cm) high.
$2,000–2,200 S(S)

A pewter wriggle-work two-handled cup, decorated with flowers, c1680, 6¼in (16cm) high.
$10,500–12,000 S(S)

Touch Marks

Touch marks are makers' marks impressed on pewter items and registered at Pewterers' Hall in London. The earliest marks were small and usually consisted of the pewterer's initials. Later they became more elaborate, often incorporating pictorial designs or symbols. When a date is included, this indicates when the touch was registered and not when the piece was made. Touch marks ceased to be registered in 1824.

A pewter candlestick, late 19thC, 8½in (21.5cm) high.
$65–75 AnSh

A Victorian pewter and leather-bound flask, 5in (12.5cm) high.
$40–50 AnSh

► A pewter wriggle-work bowl, decorated with the arms of the Barbers' and Surgeons' Company, c1657, 9½in (24cm) diam.
$9,000–10,500 S(S)

A pewter saucer or spice plate, decorated with turned lathe rings and hammering, minor damage, c1700, 6in (15cm) diam.
$2,500–3,000 S(S)

A pewter wriggle-work plate, decorated with a coat-of-arms, c1680, 8½in (21.5cm) diam.
$1,100–1,300 S(S)

Two pewter wriggle-work-engraved plates, each decorated with a tulip within a border of foliage, dated '1670', 8½in (21.5cm) diam.
$4,500–5,200 S(S)

A matched pair of pewter plates, by Richard Fletcher, with triple-reeded rims, c1690, 9¼in (23.5cm) diam.
$1,200–1,400 S(S)

A set of 4 pewter wriggle-work plates, by Daniel Barton, London, c1700, 8½in (21.5cm) diam.
$19,000–21,000 S(S)

A sadware pewter plate, maker's touch, 18thC, 9¼in (23.5cm) diam.
$65–80 AnSh

A pewter measure, with curved body, flat cover with reeded edge, stamped, slight damage, late 16thC, 7in (18cm) high.
$7,500–8,000 S(S)

A pewter drinking vessel, by Jacob Nickmüller, Linz, 1790–1830, 5¼in (13.5cm) high.
$65–80 AnSh

A pewter triple-reeded half-pint mug, c1830, 4in (10cm) high.
$65–75 ChA

A pewter 'lighthouse' coffee pot, c1830, 11½in (29cm) high.
$350–400 A&A

A pewter baluster-shaped spice pot, c1800, 4in (10cm) high.
$40–50 AnSh

◄ A pewter wriggle-work flat lid tankard, bearing the touch of John French, initialled 'H.F. 1641', 7½in (18cm) high.
$1,600–1,750 S(S)

Folk Art

Folk Art

Folk Art is a very broad term, encompassing many collecting areas. For other examples refer to the sections on Kitchenware, Marine, Metalware, Treen, Boxes and Textiles.

An American red-painted and carved cherrywood pipe box, with metal-lined interior, Connecticut, late 18th/early 19thC, 8½in (21.5cm) wide.
$5,750–6,500 SK(B)

An American brown-painted wooden sewing box, with thread holes, hinged on top of a larger box with drawer housing a till, an urn and eagle on the top, the smaller box opening to reveal a painted scene of a fox in uniform, possibly Massachusetts, mid-19thC, 11¼in (28.5cm) wide.
$900–1,100 SK(B)

An American Shaker-type wooden box, painted greyish-green, signed 'Currier', Amesbury, Massachusetts, c1860, 6in (15cm) long.
$500–600 A&A

An American fraktur, by Lebanon Co, Pennsylvania, attributed to Abraham Huth, commemorating the birth and baptism of Magdalena Ulrich, born May 31, 1810, in a maple frame, 15½ x 12¾in (39.5 x 32.5cm).
$1,000–1,200 JAA

An American watercolour family register, decorated with blue drapery, hearts, memorial and geometric devices, New Hampshire, dated '1852', 13½ x 9½in (34.5 x 24cm).
$4,500–5,000 SK(B)

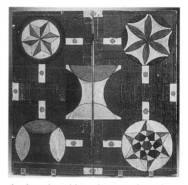

An American hinged games board, painted green with red, yellow, blue and black, late 19th/early 20thC, 19¼in (49cm) square.
$2,800–3,200 SK(B)

A black-painted wrought-iron six-light chandelier, the sides mounted with figures of prancing lambs, mid-19thC, 30in (76cm) diam.
$4,000–4,500 NOA

A wooden lamp, in the form of a boat, *Neonta*, with glass windows, 1930s, 12½in (32cm) long.
$500–600 A&A

▶ An American silk and chenille needlework memorial, on a painted silk ground, depicting a scene commemorating Nath P. Randolph, who died June 23, 1780, with verse 'twice a captive detained by British bands, and four times wounded by their hands', early 19thC, 16½ x 24in (42 x 61cm).
$1,400–1,600 SK(B)

A Map of the United States, Projected by Olive Little Marshfield AD *1830*, a pen and ink and watercolour on paper mounted on canvas, 27 x 38¼in (68.5 x 97cm).
$2,500–2,750 SK(B)

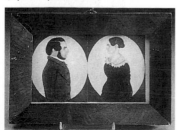

A pair of miniature watercolour portraits of Mr and Mrs E. F. Wade, New York, American School, 1848, 3¼ x 2½in (8.5 x 6.5cm).
$2,200–2,500 SK(B)

An American needlework memorial to George Washington, worked in silk and watercolour on silk fabric, early 19thC, 18¼ x 16¼in (46.5 x 41.5cm).
$2,000–2,200 SK(B)

An American hand-stitched yellow, red and blue quilt, Pennsylvania, 19thC, 70in (178cm) square.
$280–320 OLM

A Waldeboro-style raised hooked rug, wool on canvas, Nova Scotia, mid-20thC, 30 x 54in (76 x 137cm).
$2,500–3,000 A&A

An American painted-zinc trade sign, in the form of a pocket watch, inscribed 'C. W. Hallett', late 19thC, 20½in (52cm) diam.
$500–600 SK(B)

An American sandpaper painting, by E. P. Colby, depicting Lake George, New York, marble dust on coated surface, c1850, 12½ x 16½in (32 x 42cm), in original frame.
$400–500 A&A

An American appliqué quilt, with Rose of Sharon and heart design with scrolling foliate border, worked in green calico and red cotton on a white ground, minor damage, late 19thC, 84 x 82½in (213.5 x 209.5cm).
$800–900 SK(B)

An American needlework sampler, by Sarah Weston, with upper panel of alphabets above family genealogy, the lower panel with trees, bird, flowers and house, 19thC, 16½ x 14¼in (42 x 36cm).
$1,000–1,200 SK(B)

A polychrome and gilt-decorated zinc double-sided optometrist's sign, inscribed 'C. F. Hussey Optometrist', late 19thC, 41in (104cm) long.
$2,650–3,000 SK(B)

A tin plate, with lithograph portrait of George Washington, c1920, 10¼in (26cm) diam.
$130–150 MSB

An American hooked cotton rug, decorated with flowers and birds in red, yellow, browns and cream on a black ground, early 20thC, 32 x 45in (81.5 x 114.5cm).
$850–950 YAG

An American tole figure of a turkey, painted in tones of brown, beige, tan and red, 19thC, 14½in (37cm) high.
$4,500–5,000 B&B

A pair of painted chinoiserie-decorated tea bins, tinned sheet iron with hinged lids, one labelled 'Maracaibo', the other 'Ex. Sup. E. Breakft', maker's mark, mid-19thC, 23½in (59.5cm) high.
$3,750–4,200 SK(B)

Wood & Treen

A Scottish silver-mounted drinking vessel, with feathered staves, c1870, 5in (12.5cm) diam.
$1,000–1,150 AEF

A William IV rosewood portable bookstand, with spindle gallery, mahogany-lined frieze drawer fitted with a pen rest and ink pots with plated lids, 17in (43cm) wide.
$2,500–3,000 WW

An east European wooden bowl, c1890, 20½in (52cm) wide.
$35–40 WEE

A Norwegian burr-maple snuff box, 18thC, 4in (10cm) diam.
$730–830 AEF

An oak miniature post box, the top carved with initials 'H.R.', on a plinth base with a drawer, c1890, 21in (53.5cm) high.
$9,500–10,500 S(S)

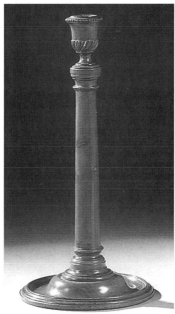

A pair of plum and walnut candlesticks, the urn-shaped sconces carved with beaded and spiral mouldings, c1780, 12¼in (31cm) high.
$3,500–4,000 S

A pair of mahogany candlesticks, c1800, 15½in (39.5cm) high.
$1,300–1,450 GeM

A pair of oak wall brackets, c1880, 17in (43cm) high.
$650–750 MLL

A pair of baroque-style walnut panels, each carved with a grotesque figure surrounded with scrolling foliage, griffins and other animals, 19thC, 29 x 21½in (73.5 x 54.5cm).
$1,400–1,600 B&B

A Continental neo-classical-style marquetry-inlaid panel, framed, c1900, 27½ x 20in (70 x 51cm).
$900–1,000 NOA

A wooden printing block, c1920, 10 x 11in (25.5 x 28cm).
$65–80 RUL

Tunbridge Ware

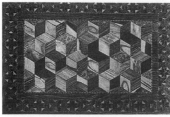

A Tunbridge ware rosewood needlework box, the lid decorated with 'tumbling block' parquetry within a border, on later bun feet, 19thC, 10in (25.5cm) wide.
$550–600 P

A Tunbridge ware rosewood box, c1830, 6½in (16.5cm) wide.
$325–400 MB

A Tunbridge ware box, inlaid with geometric patterns, c1830, 4in (10cm) wide.
$115–130 MB

A Tunbridge ware box, inlaid with a view of Penshurst Place, c1840, 8in (20.5cm) wide.
$1,600–1,800 AMH

A Tunbridge ware glove box, by Edmund Nye, veneered in sycamore, c1855, 9½in (24cm) wide.
$900–1,000 AMH

A Victorian Tunbridge ware walnut work box, the lid inlaid with a picture of the steamship *Dunelm*, the front inlaid with 2 panels depicting recumbent lions, 12¾in (32.5cm) wide.
$600–700 P(L)

A Tunbridge ware ebonized desk stand, by Edmund Nye, ink bottle replaced, 19thC, 10in (25.5cm) wide.
$650–750 BR

A Tunbridge ware rosewood stamp box, c1860, 1½in (4cm) square.
$100–115 MB

A Tunbridge ware travelling inkwell, with glass ink bottle, c1860, 2½in (6.5cm) high.
$400–500 VB

A Tunbridge ware burr-walnut writing box, inlaid with geometric bands, enclosing a fitted interior with velvet writing surface, c1870, 19¾in (50cm) wide.
$525–600 S(S)

A Tunbridge ware box, veneered in coromandel, c1860, 6in (15cm) long.
$400–450 AMH

A Tunbridge ware rosewood writing box, the slope inlaid with a picture of Tonbridge Castle, the border and sides with flowers and foliage, 19thC, 15½in (39.5cm) wide.
$1,200–1,400 E

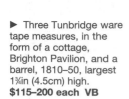

▶ Three Tunbridge ware tape measures, in the form of a cottage, Brighton Pavilion, and a barrel, 1810–50, largest 1¾in (4.5cm) high.
$115–200 each VB

A Tunbridge ware rosewood snuff box, c1840, 2½in (6.5cm) diam.
$115–130 MB

A Victorian Tunbridge ware rosewood box, inlaid with Prince of Wales' feathers and inscribed 'Ich Dien', 7in (18cm) wide.
$325–400 MB

A Tunbridge ware box, inlaid with a picture of a Georgian house, c1850, 3in (7.5cm) wide.
$450–500 AMH

A Tunbridge ware bookstand, inlaid with a view of Muckross Abbey ruins, and the Prince of Wales with a parrot and dog, within a floral border, c1855, 14in (35.5cm) wide.
$1,200–1,400 AMH

A Tunbridge ware pincushion, in the form of a kettle, c1860, 2in (5cm) high.
$400–500 VB

A Tunbridge ware pincushion, c1860, 1½in (4cm) high.
$375–425 AMH

A Tunbridge ware pincushion, in the form of a coffee pot, c1860, 1¼in (3cm) high.
$400–500 VB

A Tunbridge ware rosewood work cabinet, the top inlaid with a picture of Dover Castle, the pair of doors enclosing 4 drawers and with floral and foliate inlay, on a moulded plinth base, 19thC, 8in (20.5cm) high.
$1,000–1,200 WW

► A Tunbridge ware rosewood box, inlaid with a picture of Battle Abbey, c1860, 10in (25.5cm) wide.
$1,000–1,150 MB

A Tunbridge ware needle case, c1870, 2½in (6.5cm) long.
$140–160 AMH

A Tunbridge ware thread winder, c1880, 2in (5cm) wide.
$80–100 VB

◄ A Tunbridge ware rosewood box, the lid inlaid with flowers, c1870, 3in (7.5cm) wide.
$130–150 MB

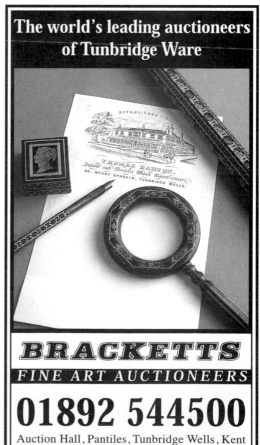
TUNBRIDGE WARE 591

Boxes

An Italian jewellery box, the top inlaid with geometric designs and foliate scroll patterns on the sides and fall-front, damaged, 17thC, 23½in (59.5cm) wide.
$4,000–5,000 S(NY)

A George III fruitwood tea caddy, in the form of an aubergine, 6½in (16.5cm) high.
$8,500–9,500 DN

A Regency tortoiseshell tea caddy, inlaid with mother-of-pearl, the interior with 2 fitted compartments, on ivory ball feet, 8in (20.5cm) wide.
$1,000–1,150 P(NE)

A tortoiseshell tobacco box, inlaid with gold and silver, c1700, 3½in (9cm) wide.
$575–650 HUM

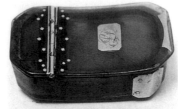

A blonde tortoiseshell and gold-mounted boat-shaped snuff box, c1800, 5in (12.5cm) long.
$200–250 MB

A rosewood box, by Edwards, London, with brass inlay and handle, containing 4 glass bottles, slight damage, c1810, 8½in (21.5cm) wide.
$800–1,000 SPa

A Regency rosewood sarcophagus-shaped tea caddy, with applied mouldings, fitted interior, feet missing, 15in (38cm) wide.
$350–400 Mit

◀ A Regency tortoiseshell pagoda-top tea caddy, inlaid with mother-of-pearl, interior converted to a jewellery box, on ivory ball feet, 12in (30.5cm) wide.
$2,500–3,000 BWe

▶ A rosewood writing slope, inlaid with mother-of-pearl, with secret drawers, c1830, 18in (45.5cm) wide.
$650–750 MB

A Dutch walnut jewellery casket, inlaid with an ivory coat-of-arms, birds and paterae, with secret drawer, on bun feet, c1800, 10in (25.5cm) wide.
$2,500–3,000 S(Am)

A Vizagapatam ivory and horn games box, early 19thC, 18in (45.5cm) wide.
$1,600–2,000 TMi

A George III satinwood, crossbanded and ebony-strung cutlery urn, on a square base with ogee bracket feet, 24¾in (63cm) high.
$4,400–5,200 P(O)

An Italian variegated marble box, the cover mounted with a micro-mosaic of St Peter's, Rome, with chased gold mounts, mid-19thC, 3in (7.5cm) diam.
$3,200–3,700 P(O)

A Victorian rosewood dressing case, by Edwards, London, with silver fittings, silver maker TD, London 1850, 13in (33cm) wide.
$1,450–1,650 P(E)

A coromandel vanity case, with cut-glass silver-mounted fittings in a velvet-lined interior, maker WN, London 1877, 12in (30.5cm) wide.
$1,000–1,150 DD

A Tartan ware box, the lid with a transfer print of Charles Dickens, c1870, 4in (10cm) diam.
$160–200 RdeR

A boulle stationery casket, the domed lid opening to reveal fitted compartments, with inlaid metal rim, 19thC, 7¼in (18.5cm) wide.
$1,200–1,400 Mit

A Welsh slate miniature bureau, with pen holder, 19thC, 6½in (16.5cm) wide.
$130–150 ANV

A coromandel dressing case, by Mechi, with silver-mounted fittings, 1876, 12in (30.5cm) wide.
$1,400–1,550 TMi

A pair of mahogany knife urns, c1900, 25in (63.5cm) high.
$6,000–7,000 GeM

An Edwardian shagreen trinket box, with silver-mounts, by George Fox III, London 1909, 4¾in (12cm) wide.
$2,300–2,600 WW

Music

CYLINDER MUSICAL BOXES

An interchangeable cylinder musical box, by George Baker & Co, playing 6 airs on each cylinder, in a kingwood case with rosewood marquetry panels, c1880, 45in (114.5cm) wide, on a matching cabinet with 4 rows of trays containing 19½in (49.5cm) cylinders.
$22,000–24,500 P(Ba)

A Swiss musical box, by George Bendon, with 13in (33cm) cylinder, in a burr-walnut crossbanded case with gilt scroll side handles, c1870, 24in (61cm) wide.
$2,600–3,000 Bon

A cylinder musical box, by Nicole Frères, with 12¾in (32.5cm) comb and 9 bells playing 8 Scottish airs, contained in a rosewood veneered case, with a floral marquetry panel, boxwood strung and banded, late 19thC, 22¾in (58cm) wide.
$2,600–3,000 DD

A Swiss cylinder musical box, by Paillard Vaucher & Fils, with 13in (33cm) cylinder playing 8 airs, in a walnut and crossbanded case, standing on an ebonized plinth, late 19thC, 22½in (57cm) wide.
$2,200–2,600 Bon

A Swiss musical box, with 13in (33cm) comb playing 12 airs, the rosewood veneered top with musical instrument marquetry decoration, boxwood line inlay and amboyna crossbanding, the front painted with musical motifs, 19thC, 27in (68.5cm) wide.
$1,550–1,650 Mit

A Swiss cylinder musical box, with 14in (35.5cm) cylinder and 6 bells playing 10 airs, contained in an inlaid simulated-rosewood case, 19thC, 24in (61cm) wide.
$680–780 GOR(B)

DISC MUSICAL BOXES

A Capitol disc musical box, the oak case with a watercolour painting inside the lid, c1889, 26in (66cm) wide.
$800–900 JAA

▶ A Stella oak-cased disc musical box, late 19thC, 44in (113cm) high.
$4,000–5,000 WL

A Polyphon 8in (20.5cm) disc musical box, in a mahogany case with print of putti playing musical instruments in lid, Leipzig, c1900, 10in (25.5cm) wide.
$650–800 JAA

MECHANICAL MUSIC

A silver-gilt and enamel singing bird box, the top decorated with figures and sheep in a classical garden setting, the front and back panels with vignettes depicting mountain scenes, early 20thC, 4in (10cm) wide.
$4,000–5,000 DD

◄ A mahogany cabinet barrel organ, by Joseph W. Walker, London, with 2 interchangeable wood cylinders each playing 10 airs, with imitation organ pipes, 19thC, 22½in (57cm) wide.
$2,500–3,000 Bea(E)

A singing bird in a cage, possibly by Bontems, with coin mechanism and drawer, on a giltwood base, c1910, 23in (58.5cm) high.
$3,000–3,500 P(Ba)

PHONOGRAPHS

► An Edison Amberola 50 phonograph, with a diamond Model C reproducer, in fumed-oak cabinet, c1912, 24in (61cm) square.
$480–560 P(Ba)

An Edison Gem Model B phonograph, with spun aluminium horn, playing two-minute cylinders, c1905, 18in (45.5cm) high.
$575–650 HOL

An Edison Fireside phonograph, with Model A reproducer, bentwood oak cover, crank and painted red horn, c1910, 13in (33cm) wide.
$480–560 Bon

A Pathé Democrat phonograph, with spun-aluminium horn, c1903, 13in (33cm) high.
$450–525 HOL

GRAMOPHONES

A Colibri portable gramophone, in black camera-type case, with one Kiddiphone disc, Swiss, c1920, 4¾in (12cm) wide closed.
$160–200 Bon(C)

► A Columbia Type AA gramophone, with reproducer, recorder and spun-aluminium horn, c1915, 11in (28cm) wide.
$525–575 P(Ba)

A Decca Junior portable gramophone, with original crescendo soundbox, c1923, 10in (25.5cm) wide.
$160–180 HOL

A Ginn mahogany gramophone,
with Collaro motor and papier mâché
horn, c1930, 20in (51cm) square.
$1,000–1,150 LAY

An HMV Intermediate Monarch
gramophone, with Exhibition
soundbox, light oak base and
green Morning Glory horn, c1912,
horn 17¾in (45cm) diam.
$680–800 P(Ba)

An HMV Model 460 table grand
gramophone, with Lumière pleated
diaphragm and gilt fittings,
in quarter-veneered walnut case,
parts missing, 1925–30,
20in (51cm) wide.
$730–800 P(Ba)

An HMV 101 portable gramophone,
with original No. 4 soundbox,
needle containers missing,
c1926, 11in (28cm) wide.
$160–200 HOL

A Swiss Mikiphone, c1926,
4½in (11.5cm) wide folded.
$575–650 HOL

**This is the smallest gramophone
that plays a 10in (25.5cm) record.**

A portable gramophone, 1930s,
16in (41cm) wide.
$250–280 OOLA

MUSICAL INSTRUMENTS

A cello, labelled 'Made by
Peter Wamsley at the Harp
and Hautboy in Piccadilly,
London 1735', length of
back 29¼in (74.5cm).
$7,500–9,000 Bon

A cello, by Gerard
J. Deleplanque, Lille,
1720, later scroll, length
of back 28¾in (73cm).
$4,600–5,200 SK

A cello, by Simon
Andrew Forster, London,
c1830, length of back
29in (73.5cm).
$33,000–40,000 Bon

A German cello, by W. H.
Hammig, Leipzig, 1885,
length of back 30in (76cm).
$6,500–8,000 Bon

An American rosewood guitar, by C. F. Martin & Co, Nazareth, Style I-21, with decorative centre strip, inlaid rosewood and pearl finger rest, the cedar neck with pearl inlay and original ivory pegs, inlaid ebony fingerboard, c1865, length of back 19in (48cm), with original wood case.
$1,600–1,800 SK

A Grecian concert harp, by I. & I. Erat, London, with bird's-eye maple soundbox, the capital of the column with elaborate gilded caryatid figures after the Acropolis, the fluted column with anthemion leaf decoration, on a gilded decorated base, c1830, 67in (170cm) high.
$3,500–4,000 P

▶ A Victorian mahogany chamber organ, restored, fitted for electricity, 55in (140cm) wide.
$3,000–3,300 CGC

A Regency giltwood and penwork harp, the fluted upright moulded with winged female figures, griffins and lyres, the ebonized sounding board with leafy scrolls, 67¼in (171cm) high.
$2,200–2,400 HYD

A Neapolitan rosewood mandolin-lyre, by Calace Brothers, with walnut binding, the top with ivory and whalebone inlay, the ebony fingerboard with pearl inlay, signed and dated '1900', 24½in (62cm) long.
$1,000–1,300 SK

A gilt and painted pedal harp, by T. Dodd, the fluted column with classical figures and mythical animals forming the capital, the sounding board painted with scrolling leaves, on a serpentine base with paw feet, early 19thC, 66½in (169cm) high.
$6,500–7,500 MEA

A Regency Grecian double action harp, by I. Erat, London, the sounding board and frame decorated with classical figures and foliage, the fluted pillar applied with gilt-gesso rams' heads, griffins and foliage, minor damage, 66¼in (168cm) high.
$4,500–5,200 Bea

An inlaid mahogany 5-octave square piano, by Martin, London, the fascia board panelled in striped maple, restored, c1780, 60in (152.5cm) wide.
$3,500–4,000 B&B

A Regency mahogany and square piano, by John Broadwood & Sons, crossbanded in rosewood with ebony lines, the top opening to reveal a satinwood and pierced-fret interior, 62in (157.5cm) wide.
$2,800–3,200 P

A Needham walnut pedal organ, with centre bevelled mirror, American, late 19thC, 48in (122cm) wide.
$350–400 WBH

A mahogany square piano, by Robert Fearn Jr, London, with string inlay, minor damage, c1810, 65¼in (165.5cm) wide.
$2,300–2,600 SK(B)

◀ A French upright piano, by Alphonse Blondel, Paris, the ebonized case with brass and tortoiseshell inlay, the under panel inlaid with musical trophies, 19thC, 47in (119.5cm) wide.
$4,500–5,000 MEA

A 5-octave square piano, by John Broadwood & Sons, London, in crossbanded mahogany case, with satinwood fret back to keyboard, early 19thC, 66in (167.5cm) wide.
$1,000–1,200 PCh

▶ A figured-walnut grand piano, by John Broadwood & Sons, late 19thC, 87in (221cm) long.
$1,000–1,150 WBH

◀ A walnut upright piano, with embroidered central panel, c1870, 51in (129.5cm) wide.
$800–900 OOLA

▶ An Art Deco parcel-silvered and ebonized grand piano, in the style of Süe et Mare, early 20thC, the later ebonized walnut case with later silvered stylized fluted cabriole legs, inscribed 'John Strohmenger, London', 54in (137cm) long, with a matching stool.
$5,800–6,800 B&B

A mahogany baby grand piano, by Mason, c1930, 58in (147.5cm) wide.
$1,000–1,100 DuM

An Art Deco maple baby grand piano, by Strohmenger, London, overstrung, the case with sectional veneer, crossbanding and ebonized line inlay, c1938, 57½in (146cm) wide.
$18,500–20,000 RTo

An Art Deco-style mahogany spinet, by Starck, c1950, 58in (147.5cm) wide.
$320–380 DuM

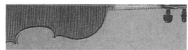

A violin, with a label inscribed 'Anton Zweilinger, Mittwaldi 1734', 23in (58.5cm) long, and a bow, in a fitted case.
$2,750–3,000 HYD

◀ An Italian viola, by Andreas Guarnerius, Cremone, the ribs of bird's-eye maple, c1820, length of back 16¼in (41.5cm).
$10,500–12,000 SK

A viola, by Charles Harris, Addenbury, Oxon, signed and dated '1824', length of back 15¼in (39cm).
$2,500–3,000 Bon

A violin, by Betts, London, c1820, length of back 14in (35.5cm).
$600–700 Bon

◀ A violin, by William Forster, London, 1775, length of back 13¾in (35cm).
$6,500–8,000 Bon

A violin, inscribed 'Charles Harris, Steeple Aston, Oxon, 1835', length of back 14¼in (36cm).
$7,300–8,000 P

An Italian violin, by Eugenio Degani, Venice, labelled and dated '1896', length of back 14¼in (36cm).
$30,000–35,000 Bon

A violin, by Thomas E. Hesketh, Manchester, labelled and dated '1898', length of back 14¼in (36cm).
$6,000–7,000 Bon

A violin, by William Atkinson, Tottenham, 1909, length of back 14in (35.5cm), with case.
$4,000–5,000 P

A violin, by George Pyne, London, 1917, length of back 14in (35.5cm).
$3,250–4,000 Bon

A violin, by G. Wulme-Hudson, London, 1919, length of back 14in (35.5cm).
$8,000–9,500 Bon

A violin, by G. Wulme-Hudson, London, 1924, length of back 14¼in (36cm).
$6,500–8,000 Bon

An American violin, by Ignaz Lutz, San Francisco, 1927, length of back 14in (35.5cm), with 2 bows, one silver-mounted, and case.
$4,600–5,200 SK

A silver-mounted violin bow, school of Tourte, c1780, 50g.
$2,600–3,000 Bon

◄ A violin, by Michael Dötsch after Guarneri del Gesu, labelled and dated '1934', length of back 14in (35.5cm).
$9,000–10,000 Bon

A silver-mounted violin bow, by W. E. Hill & Sons, c1920, 56g.
$2,500–3,000 Bon

A pair of gilt-bronze and Meissen porcelain-mounted wall lights, c1750, 18in (45.5cm) high.
$30,000–35,000 S

A pair of Continental eight-branch chandeliers, converted to electricity, slight damage and repair, early 19thC, 63in (160cm) high.
$52,000–58,000 Bon(C)

An Italian giltwood six-light chandelier, slight damage, c1800, 33½in (85cm) high.
$20,000–23,000 S(Mon)

A bronze hall lantern, with glass smoke deflector and pierced decoration, c1820, 33in (84cm) high.
$37,000–40,000 S

A French ormolu and Chinese rose medallion porcelain seventeen-light chandelier, converted to electricity, late 19thC, 64in (162.5cm) high.
$8,000–9,000 NOA

A Louis XV-style gilt-bronze and blue opaline glass twelve-light chandelier, c1860, 41in (104cm) high.
$5,000–5,500 B&B

A brass gas lantern, with vaseline glass shade, converted to electricity, 1890s, 25in (63.5cm) high.
$1,150–1,300 CHA

A brass six-sided lantern, with 6 green glass panels, c1920, 14in (35.5cm) high.
$220–250 RUL

A patinated and gilt-bronze lamp, attributed to James Smethurst, c1820, 33½in (85cm) high.
$14,000–16,000 S

A set of 4 gilt-metal two-branch wall lights, with flowerhead sconces and tassel supports, 19thC, 21in (53.5cm) high.
$2,000–2,300 RBB

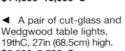

◀ A pair of cut-glass and Wedgwood table lights, 19thC, 27in (68.5cm) high.
$5,000–5,500 S

▶ A Victorian glass oil lamp, the shade etched with flowers, burner stamped 'Hinks's Duples Patent', 29in (74cm) high.
$1,800–2,000 P

A Queen's Burmese Ware lamp, by Thomas Webb & Sons, marked, c1900, 17in (43cm) high.
$11,500–13,000 JAA

An Axminster carpet, by Blackmore Bros, Wilton, reinserted fireplace cut-out, England, c1850, 405 x 274in (1027 x 694cm).
$138,000–154,000 S

A Pontremoli needlepoint carpet, depicting the Tree of Life, in Jacobean style, c1920, England, 223 x 132in (566 x 335cm).
$100,000–110,000 P

A Savonnerie carpet fragment, France, late 17thC, 93 x 59in (236 x 150cm).
$65,000–73,000 S

A 'Savonnerie' carpet, woven in 5 conjoined pieces, rewoven cut-out, probably Cuenca, Spain, c1790, 363 x 216in (945 x 572cm).
$400,000–450,000 S

A Scandinavian kilim, c1930, 45 x 70in (114.5 x 178cm).
$900–1,000 TREA

► A Mashhad pictorial prayer carpet, Khorassan, northeast Persia, c1732, 151 x 115in (383 x 293cm).
$16,500–20,000 S

A Bessarabian kilim, Moldavian/Roumanian border, rewoven areas, late 19thC, 134 x 69in (340 x 175cm).
$2,200–2,400 S(NY)

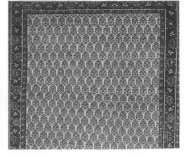

A west Persian carpet, possibly Sultanabad, late 19thC, 238 x 110in (605 x 280cm).
$13,000–16,000 WW

An Afshar rug, southwest Persia, late 19thC, 67 x 51in (170 x 128cm).
$3,500–4,000 SAM

A Ziegler Mahal carpet, west Persia, c1870, 154 x 122in (390 x 310cm).
$10,000–11,500 Bon

◄ A garden carpet fragment, northwest Persia, later border, reduced, c1800, 102 x 85in (257 x 214cm).
$30,000–33,000 P

► A Tabriz silk prayer rug, split to centre, northwest Persia, c1890, 96 x 68in (244 x 172.5cm).
$4,800–5,600 HAM

A sileh 'verneh' horse blanket, damaged and repaired, panels sewn together, Caucasus, c1880, 78in x 89in (198 x 226cm).
$16,000–20,000 S(NY)

A Lesghi rug, east Caucasus, late 19thC, 72 x 46in (183 x 122cm).
$8,000–9,000 SAM

An Amritsar carpet, north India, slight damage, early 20thC, 154 x 121in (391 x 307cm).
$24,000–27,000 S(NY)

A Star Kazak rug, late 19thC, Caucasus, 81 x 60in (206 x 152.5cm).
$16,000–20,000 Bon

A Shirvan rug, east Caucasus, late 19thC, 82 x 53in (208 x 135cm).
$5,600–6,400 WW

A Kazak Karatchop rug, west Caucasus, c1880, 89 x 61in (226 x 155cm).
$13,000–16,000 S

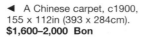

An Indian carpet, with classical Caucasian dragon design, early 20thC, 123 x 116in (389 x 295cm).
$7,000–8,000 S(NY)

◄ A Chinese carpet, c1900, 155 x 112in (393 x 284cm).
$1,600–2,000 Bon

A Kuba runner, northeast Caucasus, c1880, 115 x 47in (291 x 119cm).
$4,000–4,500 P

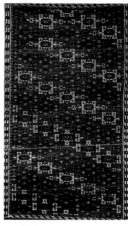

A Yomut Main carpet, northwest Turkestan, ends reduced, c1900, 113 x 69in (287 x 175.5cm).
$2,000–2,500 TREA

An Agra carpet, north India, slight damage, early 20thC, 181 x 134in (460 x 340cm).
$21,000–25,000 S(NY)

A Kaitag silk embroidery,
east Caucasus, small
hole, late 18thC,
39 x 24in (99 x 61cm).
$7,000–8,000 S(NY)

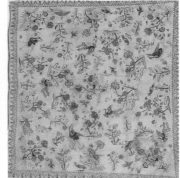

A quilt, embroidered with
floral branch and bird
designs, the whole with
back stitch quilting, signed
and dated 'MW 1695',
66 x 74in (167.5 x 188cm).
$5,000–6,000 RBB

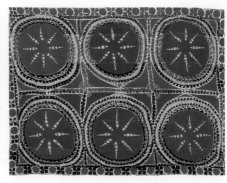

A Tashkent *susani*, Uzbekistan, slight damage,
mid-19thC, 66 x 90in (167.5 x 228.5cm).
$5,000–6,000 S(NY)

► A pictorial needlepoint
wall hanging, woven in
6 panels sewn together,
initialled 'A. P.' and
dated '1740', 83 x 150in
(211 x 381cm).
$57,000–65,000 S(NY)

An American tied comforter
quilt, Pennsylvania,
late 19thC, 77 x 72in
(195.5 x 183cm).
$320–360 OLM

An embroidered silk picture, c1810,
18 x 25in (45.5 x 63.5cm).
$900–1,000 HUM

A petit point picture, slight damage,
late 17thC, 28¼ x 25¼in (72 x 64cm),
in later black frame.
$5,600–6,400 S(NY)

An Irish needlework picture,
depicting Job and his wife, c1860,
30 x 26in (76 x 66cm).
$130–160 EON

A George III sampler, by Charlotte
Ives, the central religious verse
below a red brick house flanked
by vases of flowers, trees, birds,
butterflies and deer, c1818, 15¾ x
12⅛in (40 x 32cm), in a black and
gilded ebonized frame.
$1,600–1,800 CGC

◄ A Victorian crazy patchwork
cushion cover, dated '1887',
7in (18cm) square.
$110–130 L&L

A sampler, worked in silk cross-
stitch and wool satin stitch, with a
panel depicting a country scene with
a barn, trees and a cow standing
in a pond, early 19thC, 17¼ x 12¾in
(44 x 32.5cm), in a giltwood frame.
$3,800–4,200 RTo

A Swiss or German tapestry fragment, woven with The Martyrdom of a Saint, extensively restored, c1470, 22½ x 30½in (57 x 77.5cm).
$20,000–25,000 S(NY)

A Flemish mythological tapestry, by Michael Wauters, after Giovanni Francesco Romanelli, depicting a scene from the story of *Dido and Aeneas*, Antwerp, c1680, 203 x 157in (508 x 400cm).
$24,500–27,000 S(Z)

An Aubusson tapestry, depicting a hunting scene, 18thC, 113 x 129in (287 x 328cm).
$14,500–16,000 B&L

A tapestry fragment, probably Brussels, depicting a musician and a lady, 18thC, 34 x 26¼in (86 x 67cm).
$2,500–3,000 S(Am)

A Brussels mythological tapestry, depicting *The Story of Diana*, restored, late 16thC, 131 x 128in (333 x 324cm).
$32,000–38,000 S

A Continental baroque tapestry, possibly Bruges, made for the Spanish market, late 17thC, 97 x 110in (246.5 x 279.5cm).
$16,000–20,000 B&B

A Brussels tapestry, depicting 2 figures, with a later outer border of stylized flowers, 18thC, 75 x 79in (190 x 200cm).
$4,000–4,500 MEA

A French tapestry, an allegory of Summer, mid-18thC, 110 x 84in (279 x 213cm).
$18,000–20,000 S(NY)

A Brussels tapestry, depicting a hunting scene, 17thC, 117 x 144in (298 x 366cm).
$45,000–52,000 P

This tapestry comes by repute from a Palace in the Andalucian city of Granada, and possibly depicts Queen Juana I of Spain and her husband Felipe el Hermoso.

A post-Mortlake tapestry, depicting *The Story of Diogenes*, probably Hatton Garden or Soho, London, c1700, 94½ x 95½in (240 x 243cm).
$18,000–21,000 S(NY)

An Aubusson tapestry, depicting a hunting scene, repaired, 18thC, 108 x 133in (276 x 340cm).
$12,000–13,500 S(Mon)

A French tapestry, worked in wool and silk, depicting a stag hunt, 19thC, 101 x 83in (256 x 211cm).
$6,800–8,200 WW

A German fan, the paper leaf painted in colours, with tortoiseshell and mother-of-pearl sticks and guards, heightened with two-colour gilding and gilt sequins, c1760, 11¼in (28.5cm) wide.
$1,200–1,400 TEN

An Anglo-Flemish fan, the chicken-skin leaf painted in colours, with ivory sticks and guards, slight damage, c1780, 11⅜in (29cm) wide.
$1,200–1,350 TEN

An ivory fan, printed and hand-coloured on vellum, c1790, 11in (28cm) wide.
$400–500 JPr

A hand-painted silk fan, with carved brisé sticks, c1860, 9in (23cm) wide.
$200–250 JPr

A lace fan, with pierced bone sticks, painted with buttercups, c1870, 14½in (37cm) wide.
$160–200 VB

A fan, with black gauze leaf and spangled motifs, with gilded mother-of-pearl sticks, c1880, 18in (45.5cm) wide.
$325–400 VB

A tortoiseshell fan, the green silk embroidered with sequins, c1880, 15in (38cm) wide.
$250–300 JPr

A bone fan, with painted silk picture, c1890, 11in (28cm) wide.
$80–100 JPr

A Continental hand-painted fan, with bone sticks, decorated with a wedding scene, damaged, c1900, 20in (51cm) wide.
$55–65 AnSh

A Continental hand-painted fan, with wooden sticks, c1920, 16in (40.5cm) wide.
$50–60 AnSh

A white machine lace fan, hand-painted with birds, with ivory sticks, c1920, 13in (33cm) wide.
$100–115 JPr

A French gold and enamel snuff box, maker's mark 'C.L.', c1777, 3¼in (8.5cm) wide.
$18,500–20,000 S(NY)

A gold and enamel combined musical and singing bird box, the movement by Frères Rochat, Geneva, c1825, 3½in (9cm) wide.
$38,000–44,000 S

A silver-gilt and enamel singing bird box, by Charles Bruguier, Geneva, mid-19thC, 3¾in (9.5cm) wide.
$10,000–11,500 S(G)

A gold-mounted ivory patch box, with central cartouche enclosing a woven lock of hair, 19thC, 3½in (9cm) long.
$750–900 RBB

► A gold pedestal seal, mounted with 4 malachite panels, c1835, 2¼in (6cm) long, with original fitted case.
$2,500–3,000 P

A Bilston enamel blue tit bonbonnière, c1775, 2in (5cm) high.
$2,800–3,000 BHa

A Norwegian silver and *plique-à-jour* enamel dish, c1910, 4in (10cm) diam.
$900–1,000 SFL

A south Staffordshire enamel box, late 18thC, 3¼in (8cm) wide.
$1,200–1,400 Bon

A French champlevé enamel and gilt-brass casket, with maroon silk lining, 19thC, 7in (18cm) wide.
$3,000–3,500 JAA

◄ A Bilston enamel combination scent bottle and bonbonnière, c1770, 4in (10cm) high.
$3,000–3,300 BHa

► A Staffordshire enamel étui, the turquoise-green ground with rococo panels painted with figures in rustic landscapes and coloured flowersprays, slight damage, c1780, 3¾in (9.5cm) long.
$900–1,000 P

A Bilston enamel combination bodkin case and thimble, c1775, 3in (7.5cm) long.
$1,800–2,000 BHa

A south Staffordshire enamel combined thimble, scent bottle and bodkin case, with gilt mounts, late 18thC, 5¼in (13.5cm) long.
$2,000–2,200 Bon

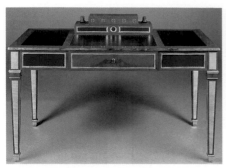

A Russian mahogany and ormolu-mounted *bureau plat*, in the manner of David Roentgen, inset with blue glass panels, restored, late 18thC, 52in (132cm) wide.
$54,000–62,000 P

A Russian neo-classical brass-mounted mahogany and ebonized lady's writing table/jardinière, attributed to Heinrich Gambs, c1800, 44¾in (113.5cm) wide.
$52,000–57,000 S(NY)

A Russian neo-classical inlaid mahogany *secrétaire à abattant*, with white marble and horn mounts, c1820, 40in (101.5cm) wide.
$6,500–7,500 NOA

A pair of Russian karelian birch cabinets, each marble top inlaid with jasper, agate, Siena marble and *verde antico* within a black marble border, c1810, 29½in (75cm) wide.
$78,000–88,000 S

A pair of Russian porcelain figures of a fisherman and his paramour, by the Imperial Porcelain Manufactory, with underglaze blue mark, 1825–55, 15½in (39.5cm) high.
$11,500–13,000 S

A porcelain vase, probably by the Imperial Porcelain Manufactory, decorated on each side with classical motifs and swags, 1825–55, 27½in (70cm) high.
$22,000–25,000 S

A Russian porcelain plate, the centre painted with a lady in a national costume and a washer woman, with green mark of Nicholas II, St Petersburg, 1910, 9½in (24cm) diam.
$2,000–2,500 DORO

A Russian silver bread basket, partly gilded and enamelled to simulate basket-weave and an embroidered napkin, Ovchinnikov, Moscow, c1884, 11¾in (30cm) wide.
$23,000–26,000 S(NY)

A Russian brass samovar, with drip bowl and tray, c1898, 18in (45.5cm) high.
$1,000–1,200 PFK

A Russian icon of The Uncut Stone Mother of God, 18thC, 34 x 27½in (86.5 x 70cm).
$6,800–7,500 JAA

A Russian icon of St Nicholas of Mozhaisk, c1700, 20 x 13in (51 x 33cm).
$6,500–7,500 RKa

A partially gilt silver beaker,
St Petersburg, maker's mark 'MW',
c1735, 4in (10cm) high, 5¼oz.
$2,400–2,700 DORO

A Russian silver and enamel Easter
egg, enclosing an icon, marked,
c1900, 3½in (9cm) high.
$11,500–13,000 S(NY)

An Imperial Russian Siberian
nephrite bell push, c1900,
2½in (6.5cm) long.
$4,000–4,500 SHa

An Imperial Russian gilded silver
and enamel *kovsh*, marked, c1900,
8¼in (21cm) long.
$4,500–5,500 JAA

A Russian silver-gilt and enamel tray,
by Ivan Sazikov, Moscow, 1891,
10½in (27cm) diam.
$1,800–2,000 B&B

A silver-gilt and enamel timepiece,
St Petersburg, 1908–17, 4¼in (11cm)
high, with later fitted case.
$16,000–18,000 S(G)

◄ A Russian
gold bracelet, set
with emeralds and
diamonds, maker's
mark, c1915.
$6,000–7,000 P

An Imperial Russian glass egg,
bearing the Romanoff cipher to
commemorate the coronation of
Nicholas II in 1896, 4in (10cm) high.
$2,000–2,300 SHa

A Fabergé gold, moss agate and
diamond-set brooch, St Petersburg,
marked, 1896–1907, 1½in (4cm) wide.
$11,000–12,500 SHa

A Fabergé enamel cigarette case,
with jewelled gold mounts, mark
of workmaster M. Perchin,
St Petersburg, restored, before
1896, 3¾in (9.5cm) long.
$30,000–33,000 S(G)

A pair of Fabergé silver, translucent
enamel and bowenite table
candlesticks, mark of workmaster
Karl Gustav Hjalmar Armfelt,
St Petersburg, c1900,
4¼in (11cm) high.
$48,000–56,000 S(NY)

► A Fabergé gold, enamel,
carved ivory and linen fan, mark
of workmaster Henrik Wigström,
St Petersburg, c1910, 9in (23cm)
wide, in original fitted box.
$37,000–42,000 S(NY)

A 15ct gold bracelet, c1820,
5in (12.5cm) long.
$1,400–1,550 WIM

A Victorian enamel, diamond
and gold bracelet, with locket
centre, c1865.
$2,600–3,200 P

A gold bracelet, inset with a portrait
miniature depicting the 11th Duke of
Hamilton, c1830.
$1,400–1,700 S

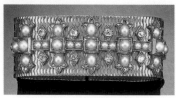

A gold, half-pearl and diamond
bracelet, one diamond missing, c1870.
$6,800–7,500 S

A Scottish gold and agate bracelet,
c1860, 9in (23cm) long.
$1,000–1,200 BWA

A Victorian gold bracelet, the 7 plaques each with a garnet within a gold
corded wire decorated border.
$2,400–2,700 P

A Victorian 15ct gold mesh link bracelet, decorated with
rose diamonds and turquoises, minor repair.
$500–550 FHF

◀ An 18ct
gold bracelet,
the 3 diamond
clusters with
ruby, sapphire
and emerald
centres, c1900,
in a fitted case
by Tiffany & Co.
$10,000–11,000 P

A pink topaz, aquamarine and diamond bracelet,
by Mellerio, signed, c1890, 6½in (16.5cm) long.
$14,500–16,000 S

An 18ct gold bracelet, set with opals, the links set with
a half-pearl, lapis lazuli, turquoise and 2 emeralds,
Birmingham 1900.
$1,600–2,000 DN

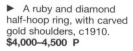

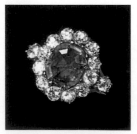

A diamond and emerald
ring, mounted in 18ct gold,
mid- to late 19thC.
$5,500–6,500 S(LA)

A gold ring in the form of a
snake, inset with a ruby
and emeralds, c1800.
$1,000–1,200 WIM

▶ A ruby and diamond
half-hoop ring, with carved
gold shoulders, c1910.
$4,000–4,500 P

A cat's-eye chrysoberyl and
diamond ring, the engraved
gallery, hoop and back of
the bezel decorated with
blue, white and green
enamel, mounted in silver
and gold, some enamel
loss, c1870.
$4,500–5,500 P

▶ An alexandrite and
diamond ring, c1915.
$10,500–12,000 P

A ruby and diamond ring,
mounted in platinum and
gold, c1900.
$2,500–3,000 S(LA)

A topaz and diamond openwork brooch, mounted in silver, silver-gilt and gold, c1720.
$3,700–4,000 P

A Victorian 18ct gold brooch, set with turquoises, diamonds and garnets.
$400–450 AnS

An emerald and diamond brooch, c1910.
$10,000–11,500 S

A diamond, demantoid garnet, peridot and opal necklace, c1900.
$5,500–6,000 P

A 15ct gold necklace, set with amethysts, c1850, 14in (35.5cm) long.
$5,000–5,500 WIM

A Georgian gold brooch, set with 2 rows of 9 garnets.
$400–450 RID

A sapphire and diamond bow brooch, c1890.
$4,500–5,000 P

An onyx cameo and gem-set gold pendant, c1860.
$4,500–5,000 P

A shell cameo brooch, depicting the Three Graces, set in a gold mount, 19thC, 3¼in (8cm) high.
$900–1,000 DN

▶ An opal, enamel and sapphire pendant, with an opal necklace, by C. & A. Giuliano, signed, c1890.
$5,000–5,500 P

A Swiss enamel brooch, c1860, 1¾in (4.5cm) wide.
$1,200–1,400 WIM

An enamelled and diamond-set brooch, in the form of a pansy, c1900, 2¼in (5.5cm) long.
$3,500–4,000 S

A Victorian cameo brooch, with gold wirework surround, 2½in (6.5cm) long.
$900–1,000 FHF

An Iberian gold corsage jewel, set with emeralds, c1750.
$5,000–5,500 P

A Spanish gold brooch, set with diamonds and emeralds, some stones missing, minor repair, late 18thC, 3½in (8.5cm) high.
$9,000–10,000 S(NY)

A turquoise and gold sweetheart pendant/brooch, and a gold rope-twist chain, c1820.
$2,000–2,500 Bon

A Victorian micro-mosaic pendant/brooch, with white glass ground and gold corded wire border.
$730–800 P

A turquoise and diamond brooch/pendant, depicting Medusa, c1880.
$1,800–2,200 S

A turquoise and diamond brooch/pendant, c1880.
$26,000–28,500 P

A pearl, diamond and enamel pendant/brooch, the reverse with glazed compartment, c1900.
$800–1,000 S

An amethyst and diamond brooch, c1900.
$7,300–8,000 P

A pink sapphire and diamond pendant, c1905.
$18,000–20,000 P

An Edwardian peridot, amethyst and half-pearl pendant, on a curb link necklace.
$1,100–1,200 P

◄ A 15ct gold pendant, set with turquoises, natural pearls and diamonds, c1880.
$1,200–1,400 WIM

A filigree silver-gilt, garnet and seed pearl pendant, c1900, 1in (2.5cm) wide.
$300–330 DAC

► A Victorian garnet, diamond and pearl pendant, with gold back, c1880.
$5,500–6,500 P

An enamel and diamond pendant, c1910.
$2,400–2,700 Bon

A pair of Chinese cloisonné enamel models of cranes, 19thC, 28in (71cm) high.
$14,500–18,000 S(NY)

A Japanese cloisonné box and cover, signed 'Kyoto Namikawa zo', late Meiji period, 4¾in (12cm) wide.
$18,000–19,500 S(NY)

A pair of Chinese cloisonné altar candlesticks, 17thC, 13¼in (33.5cm) high.
$4,000–4,500 HYD

A Japanese cloisonné charger, Meiji period, 23¾in (60.5cm) diam.
$2,500–3,000 S(Am)

A Chinese cloisonné charger, the exterior decorated with wire-outlined flowers on a pale blue ground, c1880, 25½in (65cm) diam.
$3,000–3,300 B&B

A Japanese cloisonné enamel jar and cover, by Namikawa Yasuyuki, Meiji period, 4in (10cm) high.
$14,000–15,500 Bon

A pair of Japanese cloisonné enamel vases, late Meiji period, 23½in (60cm) high.
$1,800–2,000 B&L

A pair of Japanese cloisonné vases, Meiji period, 9½in (24cm) high.
$3,300–4,000 MCN

A Japanese cloisonné vase, Meiji period, 9¾in (25cm) high.
$3,300–4,000 MCN

A Chinese Canton enamel lobed box and cover, Qianlong mark and of the period, 4¾in (12cm) wide.
$11,000–12,000 S(NY)

A Chinese silver-gilt and enamelled model of a tree in flower, with a stag and peacocks, slight damage, late 19thC, 13in (33cm) high.
$5,000–5,500 B&B

A Chinese painted enamel yellow-ground censer, minor damage and repair, Yongzheng mark and of the period, 3¾in (9.5cm) diam.
$15,500–17,000 Bon(C)

A Japanese cloisonné vase, late Meiji period, 10in (25.5cm) high.
$1,000–1,300 MBo

A Chinese 'ruby and snowstorm' overlay Peking glass bottle vase, Qianlong seal mark and of the period, 7in (18cm) high.
$57,000–65,000 S

A pair of Chinese yellow glass vases, each carved in high relief with dragons among cloud scrolls, 19thC, 15½in (39.5cm) high.
$21,000–24,500 S(NY)

A Chinese white jade and silver court dress buckle, Ming Dynasty, 3in (7.5cm) wide.
$8,000–10,000 Wai

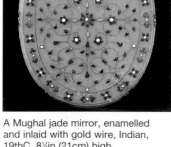

A Mughal jade mirror, enamelled and inlaid with gold wire, Indian, 19thC, 8¼in (21cm) high.
$13,000–14,500 S

A Chinese celadon jade mountain, 18thC, 9¼in (23.5cm) high.
$23,500–27,500 S(NY)

A Chinese jade double gourd-shaped plaque, 19thC, 8in (20.5cm) high.
$4,000–5,000 P

A pair of Chinese lacquer bowls, inlaid with mother-of-pearl, with silver-plated liners, Kangxi period, 7in (18cm) diam.
$2,300–2,600 Wai

A Japanese pieced ivory and polychrome lacquer figure of a Chinese beauty, slight damage, signed 'Kiyonori', Meiji period, 25¼in (64cm) high.
$14,000–15,500 B&B

A Chinese leather-covered box, with gold-painted decoration, 19thC, 23in (58.5cm) long.
$325–375 HGh

► A Japanese boxwood figure of a dancer, signed 'Sansho', Meiji period, 2¾in (7cm) high.
$8,000–9,000 B&B

A Chinese lacquered wood model of a horse, tail missing, some restoration, Western Han Dynasty, 8½in (21.5cm) high.
$18,500–23,500 S

► A Japanese lacquered wood sword stand, decorated with a ho-o bird inlaid in ivory and stained ivory, 19thC, 18¾in (47.5cm) wide.
$3,500–4,000 S(NY)

A Japanese *tosei gusoku*, with a lacquer armour box, signed Mitsutada, Showa period.
$5,000–5,700 B&B

A Chinese lady's silk court dragon robe, inlaid with gold and silver wrapped thread, 19thC.
$1,100–1,300 TEN

A Chinese lady's embroidered silk informal robe, Guangxu period.
$11,500–13,000 B&B

A Japanese silk *haori*, with printed pattern, 1940s.
$65–75 ASG

A Chinese lady's headdress, the silk-wrapped wire mounted with metal plaques set with featherwork and semi-precious stones, minor losses and wear, 19thC, 10½in (26.5cm) wide.
$6,800–7,800 B&B

An Indian diamond, emerald, ruby and pearl-set turban crown, early 20thC, 9½in (24cm) high, with feather plume, in fitted wooden case.
$130,000–136,000 S

A Mughal emerald and diamond-set enamelled gold necklace, Indian, c1900, 6¼in (16cm) long.
$11,500–13,000 S

A Chinese skirt panel, worked in satin stitch and Peking stitch, late 19thC, 12 x 10in (30.5 x 25.5cm).
$250–270 PBr

A Japanese print of the courtesan Kaoyo, by Eisen, published by Koeido, c1830, 15½ x 10in (39.5 x 25.5cm).
$1,800–2,000 JaG

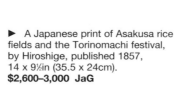

A Chinese poster, 'Watching the Latest Newsreel', 1976, 14½ x 21in (37 x 53cm).
$200–230 Wai

► A Japanese print of Asakusa rice fields and the Torinomachi festival, by Hiroshige, published 1857, 14 x 9½in (35.5 x 24cm).
$2,600–3,000 JaG

A *huanghuali* canopy bed, 17thC,
87in (221cm) wide.
$14,000–15,500 S(NY)

A Chinese four-door cabinet, the 2 side
doors locking to the interior, restored,
19thC, 55in (139.5cm) wide.
$2,000–2,500 B&B

A Chinese gilt and brown lacquer
display cabinet, with carved
ivory detail, slight damage,
early 20thC, 124in (315cm) wide.
$11,000–12,000 B&B

A pair of elm spindle armchairs, with
medallion motif and footrest, c1890.
$1,600–2,000 HGh

A Chinese bamboo double-seated
chair, 19thC.
$900–1,000 SOO

A set of 10 Anglo-Indian rosewood
armchairs, 19thC.
$27,500–32,500 S

A Chinese export carved hardwood
upholstered armchair, late 19thC.
$550–650 AnSh

A Japanese elm clothes chest,
Meiji period, 34in (86.5cm) wide.
$6,000–7,000 KJ

A Mongolian nomadic metal-bound
chest, 19thC, 33in (84cm) wide.
$1,100–1,300 K

A Chinese export mirror painting,
mid-18thC, 19½in (49.5cm) wide.
$29,000–32,500 S(NY)

A Chinese padouk wood table,
with pierced scrolled frieze, 19thC,
46in (117cm) wide.
$1,100–1,300 AH

A Chinese carved wood screen,
with 2 window openings and
hanging brackets, early 19thC,
59in (150cm) high.
$2,500–2,800 HGh

A Chinese jade snuff bottle, decorated with a bird perched on branches, the reverse with a girl collecting flowers, with coral stopper mounted on turquoise, 1780–1850, 2in (5cm) high.
$5,000–5,700 JWA

Early bottles of this type were exported to Japan and decorated by members of the Tsuda family in Kyoto in the early 1900s.

A Chinese pink and blue glass snuff bottle, in the form of a peach, early 19thC, 3in (7.5cm) long.
$1,600–2,000 BOW

A Chinese double overlay glass snuff bottle, the jadeite stopper mounted in a bronze collar, 1780–1880, 2¼in (5.5cm) high.
$11,000–12,000 JWA

A Chinese overlay glass snuff bottle, 1860–1900, 2¼in (5.5cm) high.
$2,500–3,000 S(HK)

◄ A Chinese overlay glass snuff bottle, with jadeite stopper, 19thC, 2¼in (5.5cm) high.
$9,000–10,000 S(NY)

A Chinese inside-painted rock crystal snuff bottle, signed 'Beijing Ye Bengxi', with jadeite stopper, 1930–45, 2½in (6.5cm) high.
$9,500–10,500 JWA

◄ A Chinese green overlay glass snuff bottle, with glass stopper, 19thC, 2¼in (5.5cm) high.
$3,300–3,600 S(NY)

A Chinese glass snuff bottle, decorated with rubies, sapphires, tourmalines, turquoises and emeralds, 18thC, 2⅛in (6.5cm) high.
$2,500–3,300 JWA

A Chinese aquamarine snuff bottle, with a lady carved in high relief, the reverse with flowering plants and rockwork, with tourmaline stopper, 19thC, 2¼in (5.5cm) high.
$9,000–10,000 S(NY)

A Chinese jade snuff bottle, with pink quartz stopper, 19thC, 2¾in (7cm) high.
$2,000–2,200 S(NY)

A Persian or Syrian pottery building maquette, decorated with a turquoise glaze, 11th/12thC, 8in (20.5cm) wide.
$2,300–2,600 Bon

A Persian blue slip-decorated bowl, early 17thC, 15in (38cm) diam.
$65,000–73,000 S

An Ottoman scribe's parquetry table, decorated with mother-of-pearl, tortoiseshell, bone and various woods, Turkey, c1800, 24½in (62cm) wide.
$3,000–3,500 Bon

A Persian bronze model of a bird, c1200, 7¾in (19.5cm) high.
$37,500–42,000 S

◄ An Arab dagger, with rhino horn hilt and silver-decorated scabbard, late 19thC, 11in (28cm) long.
$650–750 GV

A Kashan pottery *albarello*, with stylized foliate motifs, Persia, late 12th/early 13thC, 8in (20.5cm) high.
$7,500–8,000 S

A Safavid Kubachi figural pottery dish, with Chinese-style landscape, Persia, 16thC, 13in (33cm) diam.
$5,000–5,700 Bon

A Qajar pottery panel, Persia, 19¼ x 14½in (49 x 37cm), in a wooden frame.
$4,500–5,000 S

A Khorasan brass inkwell, late 12th/early 13thC, 4¼in (11cm) high.
$14,000–16,000 S(NY)

A Seljuk Minai-ware bowl, Rayy or Kashan, early 13thC, 8in (20.5cm) diam.
$9,000–10,500 S(NY)

A Kütahya polychrome pottery dish, Turkey, mid-18thC, 5¾in (14.5cm) diam.
$2,300–2,800 S

An Ottoman casket, inlaid with mother-of-pearl and tortoiseshell, Turkey, 18th/19thC, 11½in (29cm) wide.
$3,200–3,600 ANT

A Moroccan gem-set gold brooch, 19thC, 5in (12.5cm) high.
$13,000–14,500 S

A Victorian brass ceiling rose and light fitting, 11in (28cm) wide.
$250–300 RUL

Two gilt-brass curtain retainers, c1842, 15in (38cm) wide.
$150–160 AnS

A pair of Italian baroque polychrome and parcel-gilt columns, 18thC, 103in (261.5cm) high.
$13,000–14,500 B&B

A set of Victorian brass mixer taps, 10in (25.5cm) wide.
$260–300 RUL

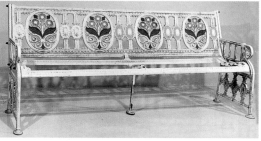

A Coalbrookdale cast-iron garden seat, slatted wood seat damaged, 1883, 75in (190.5cm) wide.
$2,600–3,000 AH

An Edwardian blue and white transfer-decorated lavatory pan, 16in (40.5cm) high.
$1,450–1,550 ACT

A Victorian blue and white transfer-decorated lavatory pan, 16in (40.5cm) high.
$1,000–1,200 ACT

A Coalbrookdale cast-iron plant stand, 1869, 44in (112cm) high.
$18,000–19,500 S(S)

A French cast-stone rustic garden table and 4 chairs, signed 'Lino Lenzi', late 19thC, table 60in (152.5cm) wide.
$5,000–5,700 B&B

A Victorian carved Cotswold stone owl, c1870, 16in (40.5cm) high.
$6,500–7,500 S(S)

◄ A pair of white marble figures of putti, representing Spring and Summer, 19thC, 38½in (98cm) high.
$8,000–9,500 S(S)

A George VI pillar box, 1940s, 60in (152.5cm) high.
$800–1,000 CAB

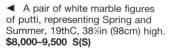

ARCHITECTURAL ANTIQUES • COLOUR REVIEW 619

A George III carved pine fire
surround, 80½in (204cm) wide.
$4,000–4,500 P

A George III-style marble fire surround,
with a recessed Siena marble
border, 19thC, 71in (180.5cm) wide.
$30,000–32,500 S

A French onyx and gilt-bronze fire
surround, c1870, 72in (183cm) wide.
$13,000–16,000 S

A Victorian cast-iron and tiled fire
surround, 34in (86.5cm) wide.
$800–900 A&H

A Victorian cast-iron and tiled fire
surround, on a granite hearth,
52in (132cm) wide.
$1,100–1,200 BYG

A cast-iron and tiled fire surround,
with painted slate panel, 1890s,
48in (122cm) wide.
$1,300–1,600 NOST

An American Empire gilt-bronze fender, early 19thC, 48in (122cm) long.
$3,200–4,000 B&B

An Adam-style cast-iron and brass-
fronted grate, damaged, c1820,
33in (84cm) wide.
$2,600–3,000 CAG

An American Empire ormolu fender, early 19thC, 33in (84cm) long.
$6,800–7,800 S(NY)

A George III carved giltwood lintel
ornament, 45in (114.5cm) wide.
$5,000–5,700 JAd

A pair of chestnut dog-
guard gates, 19thC,
38in (96.5cm) wide.
$570–600 MLL

◄ An American patinated
bronze lintel ornament, in
the form of an eagle, 19thC,
64in (162.5cm) wide.
$4,500–5,000 B&B

A Welsh painted tin purdonium,
early 19thC, 21in (53.5cm) wide.
$4,000–5,000 SPu

A limestone group of the Virgin and Child, possibly French, late 13thC, 29in (73.5cm) high.
$29,000–32,500 S(NY)

A French cast-stone figure of a female saint holding an open book, slight damage, c1470, 20½in (52cm) high.
$13,000–14,500 S(NY)

A Gothic alabaster figure of a female saint, damaged and repaired, 15thC, 33in (84cm) high.
$23,000–26,000 S(NY)

A south German carved wood and polychromed figure of the Virgin Mary, 16thC, 63in (160cm) high.
$5,000–5,500 P

A Neapolitan gilt and polychrome wood figure of an angel, with glass eyes, mid-17thC, 33½in (85cm) high.
$10,000–11,500 S

A Continental carved wood relief panel of the Coronation of The Virgin, damaged and repaired, c1750, 65 x 36in (165 x 91.5cm).
$5,000–5,500 B&B

A carved pine bust of Shakespeare, dated '1754', 10½in (26.5cm) high.
$2,600–3,000 AEF

A French terracotta figure of a nymph, by Joseph-Charles Marin, signed and dated '1784', 11¾in (30cm) high.
$18,000–19,500 S

► An Italian bronze equestrian figure of Gattamelata, after the monument by Donatello, early 19thC, 23in (58.5cm) high, raised on a plinth.
$9,000–10,000 S

A carved marble figure of a young girl, damaged, signed and dated 'Ambrogio Borghi, Milano, 1875', 51in (129.5cm) high.
$9,000–10,000 JNic

◄ A marble bust of a Roman emperor, nose damaged and repaired, 18th/19thC, 34in (86.5cm) high.
$21,000–24,000 S

► A French veined alabaster figure of Minerva, signed 'Angelano', late 18th/early 19thC, 30¾in (78cm) high.
$3,300–3,600 P

A pair of French or Piedmontese terracotta chinoiserie figures, representing the Bird Sellers, in the manner of Pillement, signed, 19thC, 14in (35.5cm) high.
$6,500–8,000 S

A French bronze figure of Milo of Croton, after Edme Dumont, raised on a black marble plinth, mid-19thC, 14½in (37cm) high.
$1,300–1,500 AH

A bronze sculpture entitled 'Albert Durer', by A. E. Carrier-Belleuse, signed, c1855, 24in (61cm) high.
$3,300–3,600 DuM

A gilt-bronze inkstand, surmounted by a model of an Irish wolfhound, mid-19thC, 10½in (26.5cm) wide.
$3,800–4,200 TMA

A gilt-bronze group of a romantic couple, by Joseph Raymond Gayrard, 1850s, 19in (48cm) high.
$5,700–6,500 S(Am)

A pair of Napoleon III gilt-bronze figures of putti, slight damage, mid-19thC, 33in (84cm) high.
$9,000–10,500 B&B

A French terracotta bust of Queen Marie Antoinette, on a white marble socle, late 19thC, 33½in (85cm) high.
$1,300–1,600 NOA

A French bronze figure of Diana, bow missing, late 19thC, 16½in (42cm) high, on a marble plinth.
$730–800 RBB

A French gilt-bronze figure of Juno, late 19thC, 26in (66cm) high.
$2,500–2,700 Bea(E)

A marble figure of a child, late 19thC, 21½in (54.5cm) high.
$800–900 Bon

◄ A bronze figure of a woman, c1900, 18in (45.5cm) high.
$1,100–1,300 DQ

► A French gilt-bronze heroic group, cast after a model by Daniel-Joseph Bacqué, early 20thC, 19½in (49.5cm) high, on a white marble pedestal.
$5,000–5,500 B&B

A French cachepot, decorated with figures within scrolling borders in pewter and brass on a ground of stained green horn, mid-19thC, 6in (15cm) high.
$1,100–1,300 S(NY)

A pair of Regency brass table lustres, with pendant drops and triple bird supports, 11in (28cm) high.
$2,000–2,300 RBB

A French bronze and gilt-brass two-light candelabra, modelled in the form of a putti and figure of Pan, in the style of Clodion, 19thC, 16½in (42cm) high.
$2,000–2,500 CAG

A turquoise and gilt-bronze centrepiece, by Paul Sormani, Paris, signed, c1880, 11in (28cm) high.
$18,000–20,000 S

A pair of French bronze and Siena marble vases-on-stands, c1830, 10¾in (27.5cm) high.
$2,300–2,600 ART

A French gilt-bronze and lapis lazuli inkstand, with hinged lid, the interior with frosted glass inkwell, set overall with semi-precious stones, c1880, 13¾in (35cm) wide.
$9,000–10,500 S(Am)

A marble sweetmeat dish, the applied gilt-metal rim embossed with foliage and studded with gemstones, late 19thC, 4¼in (11cm) diam.
$350–400 AH

A pair of gilt-bronze-mounted *verde antico* marble and Derbyshire spar urns, repaired, 19thC, 5in (12.5cm) high.
$10,500–12,000 S(NY)

◀ A gilt-bronze and *rouge royale* marble urn, supported by 2 sphinxes, late 19thC, 27½in (70cm) high.
$4,000–5,000 Bon

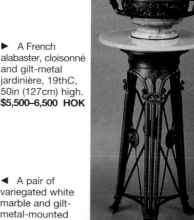

▶ A French alabaster, cloisonné and gilt-metal jardinière, 19thC, 50in (127cm) high.
$5,500–6,500 HOK

A Régence porphyry vase and cover, early 18thC, the ormolu side mounts of later date, 14½in (37cm) high.
$29,000–32,500 S(NY)

◀ A pair of variegated white marble and gilt-metal-mounted vases, late 19thC, 20in (51cm) high.
$3,300–3,600 P(L)

A Tunbridge Ware jewellery box, the interior fitted with red velvet, slight damage, early 19thC, 9¼in (23.5cm) wide.
$500–600 HAM

A Tunbridge Ware bird's-eye maple jewellery cabinet, the top and doors with tessera rose sprays, label for T. Barton to base, late 19thC, 8in (20.5cm) wide.
$1,450–1,600 BR

A rosewood and Tunbridge Ware box, 1870, 4in (10cm) wide.
$130–160 MB

A Tunbridge Ware scent bottle, trinket and sewing stand, c1850, 8½in (21.5cm) high.
$900–1,000 GeM

◄ A Tunbridge Ware writing slope, with a view of Windsor Castle, attributed to George Wise, c1840, 14in (35.5cm) wide.
$3,500–4,000 AMH

A fruitwood and penwork snuff box, in the form of a ship, c1800, 4½in (11.5cm) long.
$500–600 HUM

A carved fruitwood model of a boot, late 19thC, 8in (20.5cm) long.
$1,300–1,500 BLH

A Tunbridge Ware tea caddy, probably by Henry Hollamby, the domed lid inlaid with a view of Eridge Castle, slight damage, c1860, 14in (35.5cm) wide.
$1,200–1,400 CAG

A rosewood and brass-inlaid desk-stand, the tray fitted with 2 cut-glass inkwells, c1815, 13in (33cm) wide.
$1,000–1,200 Bon

◄ A Welsh sycamore love spoon, with chain, early 19thC, 17in (43cm) long.
$1,000–1,100 CoA

A carved wood nutmeg grater, with screw top, c1810, 7in (18cm) high.
$500–600 INC

◄ A Swiss carved wood paper knife, c1820, 9½in (24cm) long.
$730–800 AEF

Icons

A Cretan icon of the Mother of God Glykophilousa, with finely incised halo, in a carved wood frame, 17thC, 13½ x 10½in (34.5 x 26.5cm).
$8,000–9,500 S(NY)

An Italo-Cretan icon of the Galakto-trophousa Mother of God, painted on a gold ground, the haloes with punched decoration, in a giltwood frame, 17thC, 19 x 14½in (48.5 x 37cm).
$3,700–4,400 S

A northern Greek icon of Saint Phillipos, probably from the top of an Iconostasis, late 17thC, 17 x 14¼in (43 x 36cm).
$2,400–2,700 SK

An Italo-Cretan icon of the Madonna and Child, painted on a gold ground, with incised haloes, late 17thC, 11¼ x 9½in (28.5 x 24cm).
$3,800–4,400 JAA

A Melchite icon of the Virgin enthroned, within a raised gesso gilded roundel, the haloes set with coloured pastes, late 18thC, 29 x 19½in (73.5 x 49.5cm).
$5,600–6,400 S(NY)

A Greek two-tier icon, the upper part painted with Christ flanked by the Virgin and Saint John the Baptist, the lower part representing Saint Spiridon and Saint Artemios, c1800, 7 x 6¾in (18 x 17cm).
$575–700 P

A Greek icon of the Hodigitria, the Unfading Rose, the lower part with Saint George and the Dragon and Saint Dimitri, Asia Minor, early 19thC, 14 x 9½in (35 x 24cm).
$1,600–2,000 P

A Greek icon of the Incredulity of Thomas, 19thC, in an 18thC carved gilt frame, 26 x 22½in (66 x 57cm).
$2,000–2,200 S(NY)

Cross Reference

For Russian icons, please see our special Russian Works of Art section on pages 539–545.

A Greek icon of Saint John the Forerunner-Baptist, delivering a blessing and holding a salver containing his head, signed and dated '1925', 16 x 12in (40.5 x 30.5cm).
$575–650 JAA

In this depiction Saint John is called 'Angel of the Wilderness'.

Portrait Miniatures

A portrait miniature of a child with blonde hair, wearing a blue dress trimmed with black lace, by George A. Baker, signed, in a gold mount and leather travelling case, c1815, 22¼in (6cm) diam.
$1,000–1,100 Bon

Baker, born in Strasbourg in 1760, worked chiefly in America, where he died in 1830.

A portrait miniature of Georgiana, Duchess of Devonshire, wearing a cream dress and a blue wrap, by Braddyll, 19thC, 3¾in (9.5cm) high, in a papier mâché frame.
$400–500 S(S)

A portrait miniature of a young woman in a white veil, by Adam Buck, signed and dated '1805', 2in (5cm) high.
$2,700–3,000 BHa

A portrait miniature on ivory of a lady with powdered hair, wearing a white dress, by Frederick Buck of Cork, in a gold and blue enamel frame, c1790, 3in (7.5cm) high.
$2,100–2,300 SIL

A portrait miniature of Violet Bennett as a child, by William J. Carroll, in a flower-decorated gilt-metal frame, signed, c1895, 3in (7.5cm) high.
$730–830 P

A portrait miniature of a young naval lieutenant, wearing a blue coat and black stock, by A. Charles, in a gilt-metal frame, the glazed reverse with plaited hair, signed, c1790, 2¾in (7cm) high.
$1,300–1,450 Bon

A portrait miniature of Mrs Deane, wearing a white dress and cream hat, attributed to Richard Cosway, 19thC, 3in (7.5cm) high, in original leather and velvet-lined cases.
$1,000–1,200 RBB

A portrait miniature of a lady in a blue and white dress, by George Engleheart, c1800, 1¾in (4.5cm) high, mounted as a brooch.
$3,200–3,500 Bon

A portrait miniature of a young boy in a brown suit, by Reginald Eston, in a gilt frame, c1840, 5 x 4in (12.5 x 10cm).
$7,300–8,300 BHa

A portrait miniature of the Hon. Mrs Ronald Lindsay, by Mabel Hankey, signed and dated '1910', 3¼in (8.5cm) high.
$300–330 AG

A portrait miniature of a man wearing a blue coat, by Diana Hill, signed and dated '1790', 2½in (6.5cm) high.
$2,600–3,000 BHa

A portrait miniature on ivory of a gentleman in a blue coat, by Horace Hone, signed and dated '1796', 3in (7.5cm) high.
$2,000–2,300 SIL

A Swiss portrait miniature on ivory of a lady, by Hurter, in a gold frame, c1800, 2¼in (5.5cm) high.
$1,400–1,550 SHa

A portrait miniature of a young officer, wearing a red coat, by W. S. Lethbridge, c1810, 3 x 2in (7.5 x 5cm).
$4,000–5,000 BHa

A portrait miniature of G. Goodwin, attributed to Anne Mee, dated '1798' on reverse, 3¼in (8.5cm) high.
$800–1,000 P

◄ A portrait miniature on ivory, of Lady Pastard wearing a white dress with a pink sash, by Charles Robertson, c1780, 3¼in (8.5cm) high, in a giltwood frame.
$2,500–3,000 SIL

► A portrait miniature of Hyra Elkington's daughter, wearing fancy dress, by Harriet E. Ryder, c1900, 3¼in (8.5cm) high.
$325–400 P

A portrait miniature of a young man, wearing a dark blue coat, by W. Sherlock, c1800, 3in (7.5cm) high.
$3,250–4,000 BHa

A portrait miniature of Samuel Taylor, by Charles Shirref, c1795, 3in (7.5cm) high.
$3,000–3,300 BHa

A portrait miniature of a lady in a blue dress, by John Smart, signed and dated '1783', in a gold frame with silver-mounted paste-set border, the reverse with hair reserve, 1½in (4cm) high.
$6,000–7,500 S

A portrait miniature of Mrs Hamilton, wearing a black cloak and blue ribbon, by Mrs William Walker, c1820, 2¼in (5.5cm) high.
$480–540 Bon

Mrs Walker (née Elizabeth Reynolds) had a distinguished clientele including 5 prime ministers, and was appointed miniature painter to William IV in 1830.

A portrait miniature of a young lady in a red dress, oil on copper, slight damage, Continental School, signed 'CHMP', late 17thC, 2¾in (7cm) high.
$1,300–1,450 WW

A portrait miniature of a young man in a dark jacket, English School, c1800, 3in (7cm) high, in a gold frame with lock of hair and seed pearls on reverse.
$730–830 Bea

A portrait miniature on ivory of a young woman in a blue scarf and white dress, inscribed on reverse 'Mary Gordon, obiit, Sunday 27 Feb 1825, Aged 27', 2½in (6.5cm) high.
$650–750 P(S)

A portrait miniature of a gentleman, with initials 'WPG', the gold frame inscribed 'Died Feb 1814 aged 34', the reverse with blue enamelling and inset with a lock of hair and 3 pearls, English School, 19thC, 2¾in (7cm) high.
$575–650 AG

Cross Reference
See Colour Review

A portrait miniature of a gentleman wearing a brown suit and mauve tie, English School, c1900, 2¼in (5.5cm) high.
$1,300–1,450 BHa

Silhouettes

Collecting silhouettes, or 'black shades' as they were originally known, used to be something of a cult activity. The publication in 1978 of Sue McKechnie's definitive study of the subject, *British Silhouette Artists and their Work 1760–1860*, detailed for the first time the life and work of over 400 artists and added a massive stimulus to the market, which has additionally been boosted in recent years by the sale of several important collections.

Silhouettes come in a variety of media; they can be cut or painted, based on paper, plaster or glass. Their value is dependent upon rarity, condition, and the attractiveness of the sitter. Ideally a silhouette should be in its original frame with an unbroken trade label. The frames, in turned pearwood, stamped-brass or papier mâché, are often works of art in their own right. The elaborately engraved labels often give invaluable information about the artists and how they marketed their wares.

The earliest silhouettes regularly encountered date from the 1770s. The 'hollow-cut' paperwork of Mrs Sarah Harrington dates from this period, and is often surprisingly inexpensive. The 'golden age' of silhouette making was the late Georgian period, and the silhouettes on plaster by John Miers and his partner John Field are among the most technically accomplished. While Miers is undoubtedly the best-known of all silhouettists, his works are not as rare as those painted on glass by Isabella Beetham, or those by William Phelps.

During the Napoleonic period in the early 19th century, John Buncombe and his son Charles specialized in painting military officers in coloured uniforms. Their works are comparatively crudely painted, appeal to a broad spectrum of collectors and are therefore valuable – although beware of fakes! Arthur Lea of Portsmouth, however, was more accomplished and specialized in painting naval officers on the reverse of convex glass.

Full-length silhouettes and 'conversation pieces' featuring groups have become extremely popular in recent years, and particularly appeal to the American market. Late 18th-century groups by Francis Torond fetch good prices, as do the Regency and Victorian works of Auguste Edouart and the Royal Victoria Gallery. After the invention of photography, the quality of silhouettes declined rapidly. The post-1850 products of the 'Pier Head' school of cutters exemplify this trend, which is often reflected in their inexpensive price. **Kevin McSwiggan**

A silhouette of Mr and Mrs Rashleigh, by W. H. Beaumont, cut-out and painted in tones of grey and sepia, heightened with white, wash shadows, mid-19thC, 11½in (29cm) high.
$900–1,000 P

The basket of flowers, and the open book on the knee of the gentleman are features often found in Beaumont's work.

A silhouette of a gentleman, by Mrs Isabella Beetham, painted on card, c1785, 3½in (9cm) high, in a gilded wood frame.
$650–800 Bon

◀ A silhouette of a gentleman, painted and bronzed on ivory, by John Field, signed 'Miers', early 19thC, the reverse with a portrait of a gentleman, by Edward Foster, painted on card 'in red', signed and dated 'Foster 1834', 1½in (4cm) high.
$800–900 P

John Field and Miers worked together, and painted the portrait shown here. Foster, who painted a portrait on the reverse, was known for his 'red' profiles, as he used a reddish pigment in place of the more usual black used by most silhouettists.

A silhouette of an officer of an infantry regiment, his scarlet uniform with blue facings and gold epaulettes, by John Buncombe, painted in colour on card, c1805, 3½in (9cm) high, in an ormolu-mounted papier mâché frame.
$1,400–1,550 P

A silhouette of an interior with 3 ladies and a dog, with pencil and grey wash background, by Auguste Edouart, signed and dated '1826', 13½ x 21½in (34.5 x 54.5cm).
$3,200–3,500 WW

A silhouette of the Rev J. Annesley Burrows, by Augustin Edouart, cut-out on card, signed and dated '1833', 10½in (26.5cm) high.
$500–600 Bon

A silhouette of a gentleman, by William John Jolliffe, painted on glass, backed with silk, mid-18thC, 2½in (6.5cm) high.
$480–560 P

A silhouette of Susan Spencer, by W. Mason, painted on card and bronzed on a sepia background, inscribed and dated '1817', 2¾in (7cm) high, in a papier mâché frame.
$300–350 P

▶ A silhouette of a young girl, by Charles Rosenberg, painted on convex glass, c1810, 3in (7.5cm) high, in a gilt-mounted papier mâché frame.
$650–750 Bon

A silhouette of Mr Pulleine, by Edward Ward Foster, painted in sepia tones on card, signed and dated '1823', 3½in (9cm) high, in a papier mâché frame with *verre eglomisé* border.
$550–600 P

A silhouette of Major Thomas Oldfield, wearing naval uniform, by Arthur Lea, painted on convex glass, inscribed and dated '1799', 3¼in (8.5cm) high, in a pearwood frame.
$5,000–6,000 Bon

A pair of silhouettes of ladies, both wearing elaborate hats, by Benjamin Pearce the Younger, cut-out and bronzed on card, c1890, 5¾in (14.5cm) high, in wood frames.
$200–250 P

A silhouette of Eliza, wearing a bonnet, by Hinton Gibbs, painted on glass, c1800, 3¼in (8.5cm) high, in a papier mâché frame.
$350–400 P

A silhouette of a lady, believed to be Emma Hamilton, by Mrs Mary Lightfoot, on plaster, later inscribed and dated '1855', 3½in (9cm) high, in a hammered-brass frame.
$3,500–4,000 Bon

The headdress and costume suggest that this profile was executed in the 1790s, perhaps to celebrate Emma's marriage to William in 1791.

A pair of silhouettes of Mr Adams and Miss Mary Adams, she wearing a pale green dress, by W. Phelps, painted on plaster, inscribed, signed and dated '1790', 3½in (9cm) high, in hammered-brass frames.
$6,500–7,500 Bon

Examples of Phelps's profiles painted directly on to plaster are rare, and his style is highly individual.

A silhouette of a lady, by Mrs Sarah Harrington, hollow-cut on card, 3½in (9cm) high, in a hammered-brass frame.
$260–300 P

A silhouette of a lady holding a flower, by M. Locke, cut-out on card, lithographic background, signed and dated '1844', 9½in (24cm) high, in a maple frame.
$730–830 P

Silhouettes by M. Locke are rare.

A silhouette of a gentleman wearing a frilled shirt, by John Smith, painted on plaster, c1786, 3½in (9cm) high, in a hammered-brass frame.
$680–750 P

Smith worked in Edinburgh 1786–88. It is possible that he was employed by Miers during his stay in Edinburgh to make hair and pearl fittings for locket silhouettes.

Antiquities

An Egyptian mottled brown and white hardstone vase, Predynastic period, 3500–3100 BC, 3½in (9cm) wide.
$320–350 FW&C

An Egyptian speckled black and white granite bowl, with pouring lip, Predynastic period, 3500–3100 BC, 6¼in (16cm) wide.
$400–450 FW&C

An Egyptian alabaster flask, one handle missing, 18th Dynasty, 1540–1292 BC, 8¼in (21cm) high.
$1,600–2,000 S(NY)

An Egyptian limestone trial piece for a wigged head, damaged, 1000–800 BC, 3in (7.5cm) high.
$1,300–1,600 HEL

An Egyptian white glazed composition ushabti, the details added in dark brown with a single frontal column of hieroglyphs, 19th–20th Dynasty, 1320–1085 BC, 5½in (14cm) high.
$1,250–1,500 Bon

An Egyptian bronze figure of Osiris, holding the crook and flail, 26th–30th Dynasty, 664–342 BC, 12in (30.5cm) high.
$14,500–17,500 S(NY)

An Egyptian bronze figure of Isis seated with Horus on her lap, in a striated tripartite wig, surmounted by horns and sun disc, Late Period, after 500 BC, 13in (33cm) high.
$2,500–3,000 FW&C

> The items in this section have been arranged chronologically in sequence of civilizations, namely Egyptian, Near Eastern, Greek, Roman, Byzantine, Western European, British, Anglo-Saxon and medieval European.

An Egyptian sandstone fragment, carved with the figure of a goddess or queen and the crocodile god Sobek, Ptolemaic Period, 305–30 BC, 23½in (60cm) wide.
$2,000–2,500 B&B

An Egyptian wooden mask from a sarcophagus, circa 500 BC, 12in (30.5cm) wide.
$575–650 BAC

An Egyptian bronze statue of the goddess Mut, wearing a tall crown, Late Period, after 500 BC, 3in (7.5cm) high.
$325–350 RUL

An Anatolian marble schematic figure, circa 2500 BC, 6in (15cm) high.
$320–350 FW&C

A Persian bronze arrowhead, circa 1200 BC, 4in (10cm) long.
$70–80 BAC

A Persian short sword, the hilt flanged to receive now missing inlay, Western Iran, circa 1000 BC, 14½in (37cm) long.
$350–400 ANG

◄ A Syro-Hittite terracotta bird-headed votive goddess, circa 1200 BC, 8in (20.5cm) high.
$160–180 BAC

A limestone figure of a maenad playing the castanets, the back unworked, Cyprus, late 6th century BC, 7in (18cm) high.
$9,000–10,000 S(NY)

A pair of Luristan bronze cheek pieces for the bit of a bridle, north-west Iran, 9–8th century BC, 4in (10cm) wide.
$800–1,000 HEL

A terracotta pottery vessel, from the Holy Land, circa 3200–2600 BC, 9in (23cm) diam.
$250–300 BAC

A red burnished pot, with incised abstract decoration, Cyprus, repaired, mid-3rd millennium BC, 4in (10cm) diam.
$400–500 HEL

A bichrome ware spherical jug, Cyprus, Geometric period, 7th century BC, 12in (30.5cm) high.
$1,000–1,200 BAC

A Bronze Age storage pot, Hungary, 8th century BC, 5in (12.5cm) high.
$90–110 BAC

A Corinthian pottery gamikos, with lid, 6th century BC, 4¼in (11cm) high.
$200–250 HEL

An Attic black figure band cup, each side decorated with an equestrian figure flanked by sprinting athletes and their trainers, circa 6th century BC, 8in (20.5cm) diam.
$2,600–3,000 P

A Celtic bronze sword, the grip decorated with 3 encircling raised bands engraved with chevrons, circa 8th century BC, 23in (59cm) long.
$18,000–21,000 S(NY)

A Hellenistic bronze of a prancing horse, 4th century BC, 3in (7.5cm) high.
$2,000–2,500 P

A Magna Graecia Apulian Red Figure bell krater, circa 350 BC, 7in (18cm) high.
$900–1,000 BAC

A Magna Graecia Black ware jug, 4th century BC, 4in (10cm) high.
$450–500 BAC

Southern Italy was heavily populated by the Greeks in the 4th–3rd centuries BC, and known as Magna Graecia.

A south Italian buff pottery column krater, decorated in crimson, orange and black slip with a frieze of birds, an ivy wreath around the neck, 2 facing birds on each handle, rim repaired, circa 4th century BC, 10in (25.5cm) high.
$900–1,000 Bon

An Apulian column krater, painted on one side with Eros and a robed lady, the reverse with 2 figures, chipped, 4th century BC, 18½in (47cm) high.
$4,000–4,500 Bea (E)

A south Italian Greek black glazed net lekythos, 4th–3rd century BC, 6in (15cm) high.
$450–550 HEL

◀ A Magna Graecia Tarentine terracotta head of Dionysos, surmounted by a stephane decorated with rosettes, early 4th century BC, 5½in (14cm) high.
$3,000–3,500 S(NY)

Ancient Glass

The earliest examples of glass date from the mid-15th century BC in the Near East, where the centres of production remained for over 2,000 years.

Later, when glass production began on a commercial level, Hellenistic and Roman Alexandria was in the forefront of the industry, especially in making multicoloured pieces such as cups and bowls. The basic shape was, however, the amphoriskos, often with two handles. These early vessels were formed by trails of different coloured glass being wound round a sand core and then fired.

Glass blowing was invented in the 1st century BC, probably in Syria, and this allowed different shapes to be produced with ease. Objects of elegant form and of many different colours were soon being exported all over the Roman Empire. By the late 3rd and 4th century AD glass had replaced silver as the usual material for cups, as glassware was cheap and easy to mass produce. Most of the commoner shapes in Roman glass tend to originate from the Syria/Lebanon area from around this time.

A pale green glass bottle, the body divided into 6 panels, the upper parts with 4 birds, alternating with 4 kantharoi and the lower parts with a geometric design, eastern Mediterranean, late 1st–2nd century AD, 3in (7.5cm) high.
$3,500–4,000 Bon

A Roman pale aubergine glass jug, with a rich multicoloured iridescence, the handle and rim in pale green glass, 2nd–3rd century AD, 5in (12.5cm) high.
$1,300–1,500 WW

A Roman blue glass flask, 3rd–4th century AD, 6½in (16.5cm) high.
$600–650 BAC

A Roman greenish-blue glass pilgrim flask, with applied turquoise trailing around the lip exterior, the body decorated with diagonal ribbing, eastern Mediterranean, 4th–5th century AD, 6in (15cm) high.
$2,000–2,500 Bon

A Roman bronze pitcher, 2nd–3rd century AD, 9½in (24cm) high.
$1,000–1,200 B&B

◀ A Roman glass vase, 5th century AD, 6½in (16.5cm) high.
$1,100–1,300 PARS

A Roman hollow gold ring, mounted with a banded-agate intaglio-incised with a lion, 3rd–4th century AD.
$1,400–1,600 HEL

A Late Roman supporting-arm brooch, with moulded decoration on wings and foot, pin and spring missing, Cambridgeshire, 4th century AD.
$100–120 ANG

A Byzantine bronze reliquary cross, in 2 halves, with relief decoration of Christ and various Greek inscriptions, 8th–9th century AD, 5in (12.5cm) high.
$1,300–1,600 HEL

An Anglo-Saxon brooch, 6th century AD, 2¼in (6cm) long.
$80–100 ANG

◀ A Saxon pottery urn, incised with horizontal and vertical lines, 6th century AD, 8½in (21.5cm) diam.
$1,000–1,200 FW&C

An Anglo-Saxon square-headed brooch, pin missing, Norfolk, 6th century AD, 1¼in (3.5cm) long.
$65–80 ANG

Tribal Art

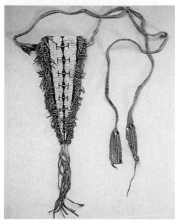

A Central Plains beaded buffalo hide pouch, probably Cheyenne, decorated in black, white and yellow, Native American, c1860, 17in (43cm) long.
$6,500–8,000 SK

A pair of Woodland's lady's quilled and beaded moccasins, Iroquois, the quill colours include yellow, red and blues, the cuffs trimmed in navy silk with white edge beading, Native American, early 19thC, 8¾in (22cm) long.
$9,000–10,000 SK

Native American pieces such as moccasins and hide knife sheaths, decorated with coloured porcupine quills and moosehair, are much rarer (and therefore more valuable) than similar beadwork items. Condition, however, is important as quillwork can easily become frayed, faded and damaged.

A northwest Californian bowl basket, made from willow, pine root, bear grass and maidenhair fern, Native American, c1900, 5¼in (13.5cm) diam.
$750–800 HUR

There is a specialist collectors' market for this type of basketwork, based mainly in the United States, and they consequently command higher prices there.

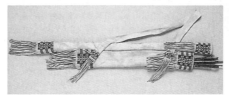

A Cheyenne beaded hide bow case and quiver, with 4 arrows, 2 with iron points, Native American, 34in (86.5cm) long.
$9,000–10,000 B&B

▶ A Southern Plains model of a lattice cradleboard, Comanche, covered in gourd-stitch beadwork with rhomboid devices of red, white and black beads on an opaque light blue ground, the exposed buckskin dyed yellow, a crude doll within, mounted on yellow painted wood lattices, Native American, c1890, 12½in (31cm) long.
$7,000–8,000 SK

A Navajo rug, Native American, c1915, 99 x 81in (251.5 x 205.5cm).
$1,300–1,500 SLN

A pair of Northern Plains beaded hide gauntlets, sewn with numerous shades of glass seed beads, a blue horned elk on the cuff, Native American, 14¾in (37.5cm) long.
$1,600–1,800 B&B

A Woodland's root club, probably Penobscot, with chip-carved and incised handle in the form of a dog or coyote, Native American, late 19thC, 27in (68.5cm) long.
$1,300–1,600 SK

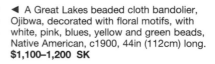

A Sioux beaded, quilled and fringed hide pipe bag, sewn in red, blues and yellow against a white glass bead ground, the red, yellow and purple dyed quillwork with diamond pattern below, Native American, 36in (91.5cm) long.
$800–900 B&B

◀ A Great Lakes beaded cloth bandolier, Ojibwa, decorated with floral motifs, with white, pink, blues, yellow and green beads, Native American, c1900, 44in (112cm) long.
$1,100–1,200 SK

◄ A Native American birch bark and quill scissor case, c1880, 6in (15cm) long.
$600–650 HUM

This type of raised moosehair embroidery was made by the Huron Indians to decorate European-type items such as birch bark calling-card cases, and textile panels used as seat covers. The floral motifs were supposedly inspired by embroideries produced by local orders of French nuns. This scissor case is in particularly good condition and the shape is unusual, which accounts for its higher than average value.

A Dogon wood mask, surmounted by an arc projection, with remains of black and white pigment, Mali, Africa, 26¾in (68cm) high.
$1,000–1,100 P

An Inuit walrus tusk bow drill handle, carved with village, hunting and battle scenes, late 19thC, 19in (48.5cm) long.
$3,700–4,000 SK

A Baule wood mask, carved with slender features and grid scarifications, surmounted by incised lobed coiffure, Ivory Coast, Africa, 11in (28cm) high.
$800–900 P

A Senufo helmet mask, surmounted by stylized hares' ears, flanked by 2 female figures, Ivory Coast, Africa, 21¼in (54cm) high.
$240–260 P

A Yoruba shango staff, carved with a kneeling female figure with incised headpiece, repaired, Nigeria, Africa, 22¾in (58cm) high.
$600–700 Bea

◄ An Eket carved wood figure, on a stand mounted with 4 carved heads, Nigeria, Africa, early 20thC, 35in (89cm) high.
$1,600–2,000 DORO

A Cameroons wood drum, the pierced base carved with 4 figural supports, Africa, 45¾in (116cm) high.
$900–1,000 P

A Pende divination group, the 3 carved wood heads with conjointed body wrapped in fetish material and terminating in a rocker base, Zaire, Africa, 5½in (14cm) high.
$480–540 P

Two Mandinka wood stools, Southern Sudan, Africa, mid-20thC, largest 18in (45.5cm) high.
Large stool $160–200
Small stool $55–70 LHB

A Temba beaded cotton skirt, dyed ochre, South Africa, 50in (127cm) diam.
$800–1,000 Bon

An adze, Western Highlands, Papua New Guinea, 23in (58.5cm) long.
$575–650 BWA

A Zulu meat tray, the under-side scorched and carved with 2 ridged square panels, South Africa, 24in (61cm) long.
$325–400 Bon

A Sumatra Batak magic horn, carved as a head with raised horns and an open muzzle showing an anthropomorphic figure with raised arms flanked by 2 claws, the whole surmounted by various anthropomorphic and zoomorphic figures, Indonesia, 19thC, 21¾in (55.5cm) long.
$30,000–32,500 S(Am)

This piece is desirable because of its size, age and rarity. Moreover, it was sold in Amsterdam where there is a strong market for Indonesian pieces because of Holland's colonial history in the East Indies.

◀ A Central Nias ancestor figure, dressed in a cotton loincloth and a cotton headband, the shoulders and face painted with black dots, Indonesia, 20¼in (51.5cm) high.
$10,500–11,500 S(Am)

A Papua Gulf Ukurawi village ancestor board, carved with an anthropomorphic head between 4 leaf-shaped ornaments carved with zigzag motifs in black and white, Melanesia, 44½in (113cm) long.
$2,750–3,250 S(Am)

◀ A New Ireland Malagan head, the lower face and head with inset fibre bristles, with ochre, black, blue and white pigments forming an ornate motif, Melanesia, 21in (53.5cm) high.
$3,500–4,000 S(NY)

A Lower Sepik gable mask, with red ochre and lime decoration, New Guinea, 22¾in (58cm) long.
$450–525 Bon

An Aborigine wood parrying shield, carved on both sides with panels of ridged linear decoration, Western Australia, 29¼in (74.5cm) long.
$450–525 P

These two illustrations, both of Western Australian parrying shields, demonstrate the importance of condition and how it affects the value of an item. The shield above is smaller and unfortunately heavily chipped around the edges, while the more valuable shield is in almost pristine condition.

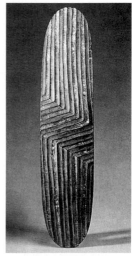

A parrying shield, carved on the front with panelled grooves, the reverse with integral handle and parallel grooves divided by 6 bands painted white, traces of red and white pigment, Western Australia, 31¾in (81cm) high.
$2,000–2,200 Bon

A Iatmul standing figure, with scarification to nipples and navel and traces of lime to the face, Melanesia, 37in (94cm) high.
$350–450 Bon

Books & Book Illustrations

Martin Amis,
The Rachel Papers,
1973, first edition, 8°.
$275–325 HAM

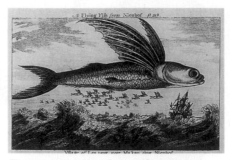

Thomas Astley, *New General Collection of Voyages and Travels*, 1745–47, 4 vols, 4°, including 228 engraved maps, charts and plates by Basire, Parr and others, contemporary mottled calf, gilt, privately printed.
$4,000–4,500 P

John James Audubon, *The Quadrupeds of North America*, with the Reverend John Bachman, published by V. G. Audubon, New York, 1856, 3 vols, hand-coloured lithographs, hand-tooled leather covers and binding, 10½ x 7in (26.5 x 18cm).
$4,000–5,000 NOA

Mrs C. M. Badger,
Wild Flowers Drawn and Coloured from Nature,
New York, 1860, 2°,
22 hand-coloured litho-graphed plates, publisher's gilt pictorial morocco.
$1,800–2,000 SWAN

Aubrey Beardsley,
frontispiece, pictorial title page, 11 illustrations and cover design for *Salome*, by Oscar Wilde, 1894, 4°, limited to 500 copies, original blue cloth gilt.
$1,300–1,600 S

J. M. Barrie, *Peter Pan in Kensington Gardens*, with illustrations by Arthur Rackham, published by Hodder & Stoughton, 1906, 10 x 7in (25.5 x 18cm).
$400–450 DA

John C. Bourne and John Britton, *Drawings of the London and Birmingham Railway*, 1839, 2°, lithographed title, 34 on 29 lithographed plates, 2 maps on one sheet, original roan-backed cloth, gilt.
$1,500–1,800 P

An ink and watercolour illustration by Harmsen van der Beek, 'Mr and Mrs Tubby Read the Song Together', from *Well Done Noddy*, by Enid Blyton, 1952, signed, 6¾ x 4¾ (17 x 12cm).
$1,800–2,000 S

▶ William
Borlase, *The Natural History of Cornwall*, 1758, first edition, 2°, with engraved folding map, 28 engraved plates, contemporary gilt calf.
$575–650 P(B)

A copy of the Holy Bible, 1599, 4°, inscribed 'Imprinted at London by the Deputies of Christopher Barker', woodcut titles and maps, in 18thC gilt calf.
$575–650 DW

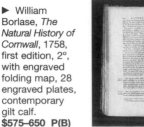

Book Sizes

The size or format of a book is expressed by the number of times a single sheet of paper is folded into the sections which, when gathered and sewn, make up the finished volume.
Shown below are some of the usual descriptions of sizes:

Folio:	1 fold	2 leaves	Fo or 2°
Quarto:	2 folds	4 leaves	4to or 4°
Octavo:	3 folds	8 leaves	8vo or 8°
Duodecimo:	4 folds	12 leaves	12mo or 12°
Sextodecimo:	5 folds	16 leaves	16mo or 16°
Vicesimo-quarto:	6 folds	24 leaves	24mo or 24°
Tricesimo-secundo:	7 folds	32 leaves	32mo or 32°

Edward Browne, *A Brief Account of Some Travels in Europe... Through a Great Part of Germany and the Low Countries...*, 1685, second edition, 2°, 14 engraved plates, contemporary calf, gilt rubbed border.
$450–550 P(B)

Captain James Cook and Captain James King, *A Voyage taken to the Pacific Ocean*, London, 1785, second edition, 3 vols, 4°, near contemporary full calf with gilt tooling, with engraved portrait, 16 maps and charts and 62 plates.
$4,500–5,000 SK

W. R. Burnett, *Iron Man*, Dial Press, New York, 1930, first edition, 8°, author's presentation copy, signed on half-title, original cloth.
$220–260 DW

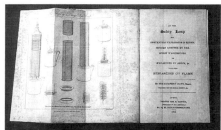

Edward, Earl of Clarendon, *The History of the Rebellion*, 1704, 2°, engraved portrait and title vignettes, contemporary calf.
$725–800 S

Sir Humphrey Davy, *On the Safety Lamp For Preventing Explosions in Mines, Houses Lighted by Gas, Spirit Warehouses, or Magazines in Ships etc... with Some Researches on Flame*, 1825, 8°, contemporary crimson morocco gilt decoration, gilt spine.
$1,800–2,000 P(B)

◄ William Curtis, *Curtis's Botanical Magazine, Or, Flower-Garden Displayed*, 1821–23, vols 48–50, 8°, 252 hand-coloured engraved plates, original half calf.
$1,300–1,500 DW

Hugh Dalziel, *British Dogs*, 1888, third edition, 2 vols, 8°, 16 chromo plates, many black and white wood engraved plates, original decorative cloth gilt.
$500–550 DW

Charles Dickens, *A Christmas Carol in Prose, Being a Ghost Story of Christmas*, Chapman & Hall, London, 1843, 24°, full morocco binding with portrait miniature on ivory of Charles Dickens.
$7,000–8,000 FBG

► Clarence Edward Dutton, *Atlas to Accompany the Monograph on the Tertiary History of the Grand Canyon District*, Washington, 1882, 2°, cloth, stained.
$1,800–2,000 P(B)

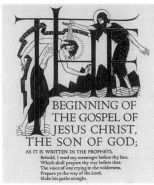

Walt Disney, *Sketch Book*, for *Snow White & the Seven Dwarfs*, 1938, 4°, presentation copy signed by the artist and numbered '4' on the inner flap of dust jacket, 12 tipped-in coloured plates, original cloth.
$7,000–7,800 P

Walt Disney is understood to have signed and numbered 5 copies for presentation at the time of publication, of which the first 2 were presented to Princess Elizabeth and Princess Margaret.

Theodore Henry Fielding and J. Walton, *A Picturesque Tour of the English Lakes*, first edition, R. Ackermann, London, 1821, 4°, hand-coloured engraved title vignette and 48 plates, modern red morocco, spine gilt, gilt edges.
$1,600–2,000 S

The Four Gospels of the Lord Jesus Christ, 1931, 2°, No. 106 of 500 copies, 62 wood-engraved subtitles, pictorial headlines and initials by Eric Gill, original half pigskin.
$8,000–9,000 S

Edward Gibbon, *The History of the Decline and Fall of the Roman Empire*, 1788–89, 6 vols, 4°, 2 folding engraved maps, contemporary full calf, gilt decorated spines with contrasting morocco labels.
$2,000–2,200 DW

Giochimo Greco, *The Royall Game of Chesse-Play*, for Henry Herringman, 1656, first edition, 8°, engraved frontispiece portrait of King Charles.
$2,000–2,500 S

John Franklin, *Narrative of a Second Expedition to the Shores of the Polar Sea*, 1828, first edition, 4°, engraved frontispiece, 30 engraved and aquatint plates, 6 folding maps, later half calf, gilt panelled spine.
$650–800 P

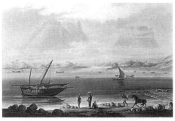

Kate Greenaway, *Mother Goose or the Old Nursery Rhymes*, illustrated by Kate Greenaway, engraved and printed by Edmund Evans, 1881, second issue of first edition, original dust jacket, 5 x 6in (12.5 x 15cm).
$500–575 WW

► Moses Harris, *The Aurelian, or Natural History of English Insects*, 1778, second edition, 2°, inscribed to Mary Coleridge, engraved frontispiece, 44 hand-coloured engraved plates by Harris, contemporary panelled calf, gilt panelled spine.
$7,250–8,000 P

This book is unusually complete. Copies sold at auction in the past 2 decades have rarely contained the full complement of frontispiece, titles, index leaves, diagram and plates.

Captain Robert Melville Grindlay, *Scenery, Costumes and Architecture, chiefly on the Western side of India*, Smith, Elder & Co, London, 1830, 2 vols in one, 2°, engraved title with hand-coloured vignette and 36 hand-coloured aquatint plates, contemporary half morocco, spine gilt.
$8,000–9,500 S

C. Häberlin, *Schreiber's grosses Puppen-Theater*, J. F. Schreiber, Esslingen, c1880, 2°, 9 hand-coloured wood-engraved illustrations, each with moving parts operated by levers, with accompanying verse, original cloth-backed boards.
$2,500–3,000 S

John Harrison, *Medical Receipts*, 1658, 12° manuscript on paper, 506 leaves of text, contemporary blindstamped calf.
$5,500–6,500 Bon

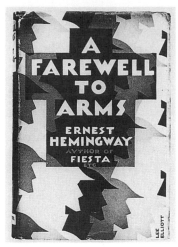

Ernest Hemingway, *A Farewell to Arms*, 1929, first edition, 8°, original cloth gilt.
$260–300 DW

Jean François Galaup de La Perouse, *A Voyage Round the World*, 1798, first edition, 3 vols, 8°, 42 engraved plates & maps, contemporary half calf, gilt spines with morocco labels.
$800–900 P

Thomas Lilford, *Coloured Figures of the Birds of the British Islands*, 1891–97, 2nd edition, 4°, 36 original parts, 421 chromo and hand-coloured lithos, original printed wrappers.
$1,400–1,600 DW

Further Reading
Miller's Collecting Books, Catherine Porter, Miller's Publications, 1995

Nicolaus Joseph Jacquin, *Icones Plantarum Rariorum*, Vienna, 1781–93, 2°, 49 hand-coloured copper engraved plates, contemporary boards.
$1,400–1,600 DW

Ex-libris Wilfrid Blunt, with his signature and note to inside front cover in pencil. The picture of Rhododendron ponticum is possibly the first ever made of this plant.

John Frederick Lewis, *Sketches and Drawings of the Alhambra, Made during a Residence in Granada, in the Years 1833–4*, Hodgson, Boys & Graves, 1835, first edition, 2°, lithographed vignette on title, 25 tinted lithographed plates, dedication leaf to the Duke of Wellington, contemporary quarter purple morocco.
$2,750–3,250 Bon

Jean & Lucien Linden and others, *Lindenia: Iconography of Orchids*, Ghent, 1891–97, vols I–XIII of 17, 2°, titled printed in red and black, 312 plates, 311 chromo-lithographed, contemporary purple half morocco.
$5,000–5,750 RTo

Augustus Koellner, *City Sights for Country Eyes*, Philadelphia, c1850, 4°, with lithograph title and 12 plates, spine missing, original cloth.
$1,000–1,200 SK

John Frederick Lewis, *Lewis's Sketches of Spain and Spanish Character, made During His Tour in that Country, in the Years 1833–4*, 1836, 2°, tinted litho, title and 25 tinted litho plates, original half morocco gilt.
$2,000–2,500 DW

Jane Loudon, *The Ladies' Flower-Garden of Ornamental Bulbous Plants*, 1841, first edition, 4°, 58 hand-coloured engravings, contemporary green half morocco gilt.
$3,500–4,000 DW

John Macculloch, *A Description of the Western Islands of Scotland, including the Isle of Man*, Archibald Constable, 1819, 3 vols, 8° and 4°, 33 engraved plates, 10 engraved maps, 9 hand-coloured, contemporary half morocco, covers detached.
$400–500 Bon

Sir George Steuart Mackenzie, *Travels in the Island of Iceland*, Edinburgh, 1812, 2nd edition, 4°, half title, 8 hand-coloured aquatints, 6 engraved plates, 2 engraved maps, one engraved plate of music, illustrations throughout, later calf-backed boards, gilt panelled spine.
$500–600 P

John Milton, *Early Poems*, 1896, 4°, limited to 310 copies, wood-engraved frontispiece, ornamental border and initials by Charles Ricketts, original buckram, unopened.
$500–600 S

J. & D. Nichol, *Aberdeen Illustrated in Nine Views, with Explanatory Remarks, Plan of the City, and Several Vignettes*, Montrose, 1840, 2°, litho-graphed plan of Aberdeen, 8 tinted lithograph views, loose as issued in publisher's limp cloth portfolio.
$2,000–2,500 Bon

◀ Beatrix Potter, *The Tale of Little Pig Robinson*, 1930, first edition, 4°, 6 colour, 22 black and white plates, cloth boards, gilt titles.
$325–400 HAM

John Milton, *Paradise Lost*, Charles Whittingham, 1846, 4°, large paper copy, 24 mezzotint plates by John Martin, all marked 'proof'.
$3,000–3,500 P

Treadway Russell Nash, *Collections for the History of Worcestershire*, 1799, second edition with additions, 2 vols, tall 2°, folding engraved map, uncoloured copperplate engravings and folding pedigrees, contemporary diced russia, gilt decorated spines.
$500–600 DW

September.

William Nicholson, *An Almanac of Twelve Sports, Words by Rudyard Kipling*, 1898, 4°, 12 coloured wood-block illustrations, original cloth-backed boards, binding detached.
$325–400 P

Philip Rashleigh, *Specimens of British Minerals*, 1797–1802, 2 parts in one volume, 4°, 54 engraved plates, most hand-coloured, calf back cover only, lacks spine and front cover.
$4,000–4,500 P(B)

Thomas McLean, *A Picturesque Description of North Wales*, 1823, 4°, 20 hand-coloured aquatints, contemporary red half morocco.
$1,000–1,200 DW

John Claude Nattes, *Bath, Illustrated by a Series of Views, from the Drawings of John Claude Nattes*, 1806, first edition, 2°, descriptions to each plate, title with hand-coloured vignette, 29 hand-coloured aquatint views, later brown half morocco gilt.
$5,000–6,000 DW

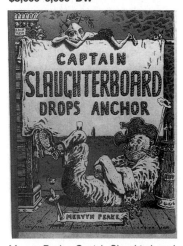

Mervyn Peake, *Captain Slaughterboard Drops Anchor*, Country Life, 1939, first edition, first issue, 4°, black and white illustrations throughout, original pictorial boards.
$4,500–5,000 DW

This was the author's first book, nearly all copies of which are believed to have been destroyed during the London Blitz of WWII.

An illustration by Louis John Rhead, entitled 'The Butterfly', signed, mounted, c1922, 4½ x 9¼in.
$750–900 S

This was reproduced as an illustration in *The Fairy Book*, published in 1922.

Eric Ravilious and others, *The Apocrypha*, Cresset Press, 1929, 2°, 480 copies, one of 30 on hand-made paper, with a separate set of the illustrations in portfolio, 14 full-page wood-engravings, original black vellum, buckram portfolio, in slipcase.
$2,500–3,000 Bon

A complete set of works by William Shakespeare, edited by Charles Knight, 1880, second edition, 8 vols, 10 x 6in (25.5 x 15cm).
$250–300 AnS

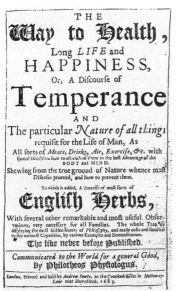

Thomas Tryon, *The Way to Health, Long Life and Happiness*, printed by Andrew Sowle, 1683, first edition, 8°, bound in contemporary calf.
$1,300–1,500 DW

Humphrey Repton and John Adey, *Fragments on the Theory and Practice of Landscape Gardening. Including Some Remarks on Grecian and Gothic Architecture*, J. Taylor, 1816, first edition, 43 plates, 24 hand-coloured aquatints, 18 aquatints, 27 illustrations, contemporary half red morocco gilt.
$5,500–6,500 Bon

Vero Shaw, *The Illustrated Book of the Dog*, London, 1881, 2 vols, 4°, 28 plates, half morocco.
$900–1,000 SK

Reverend W. Wingfield and C. W. Johnson, *The Poultry Book*, 1853, 4°, chromolithographic additional title and 21 plates by Harrison Weir, red stained half calf, spine gilt.
$250–300 L

▶ Virginia Woolf, *The Common Reader*, Hogarth Press, 1932, first edition, second series, 8°, original cloth with original dust jacket designed by Vanessa Bell.
$350–400 DW

An illustration by William Heath Robinson, entitled 'The Ugly Duckling', signed, framed and glazed, c1899, 14¼ x 10in (36 x 25.5cm).
$1,400–1,600 S

This drawing was reproduced in an edition of the stories of Hans Andersen, published in 1899.

James Sowerby, *The Genera of Recent and Fossil Shells for the Use of Students in Conchology and Geology*, edited by G. B. Sowerby, c1820, original printed wraps, 2 boxes, 11 x 8in (28 x 20.5cm).
$2,000–2,500 P(B)

Maps & Atlases

The fascination of collecting old maps lies not only in their appeal as decorative works of art, but also in their ability to take us back in time.

The first atlas is thought to have been printed in 1477, using maps drawn from the calculations of the 1st century AD Greek geographer, Claudius Ptolemy. At this time southern Germany was the centre of engraving and map-making but, by the late 16th century, Gerhard Mercator, with the combination of geographical improvements and superior calligraphy and decoration, had established Dutch supremacy in cartography. Other great map-makers followed, including Abraham Ortelius, the Blaeu and Jansson families, Jocodus Hondius, who was the engraver of many of John Speed's maps, and Christopher Saxton, the first person to publish a National Atlas.

Today, complete atlases are increasingly difficult to find as many have been broken up over the years. One of Saxton's highly decorated county maps published in 1575 would command over $1,600 at auction, depending on the area covered. Smaller scale maps based on Saxton were engraved by Kip and Hole for William Camden's *Britannia* in 1607. These are much less elaborate than Saxton's originals, and are a good starting point for a first-time collector, costing anything from $80 to $250.

For most people an antique atlas is quite simply beyond their financial means, but a single map from one of Speed's atlases can be found at auction for as little as $160. Much depends on colouring and condition, of course, but the county depicted is an important factor too. A collector would expect to pay more for a map of the home counties: for example, maps of Kent and Middlesex, both prosperous and densely populated counties, may realize a figure of over $800 at auction, whereas maps of Glamorgan or Northamptonshire would fetch considerably less.

Recently, with more mobility leading to greater geographical awareness, map collectors are taking a wider view. Maps of America and the World will always be particularly desirable, and maps of places visited on holiday or trips abroad are becoming more popular. This, together with the increasing prosperity of certain counties and countries, is reflected in the higher prices now being seen at auctions. There is no doubt that old maps will continue to appreciate in value and give pleasure to all who behold them.

Amanda Sutcliffe

WORLD

Hartmann Schedel, *Secunda etas mundi*, 1493, 17 x 22¾in (43 x 58cm), a wood-engraved world map from the Latin language edition of the Nuremberg Chronicle.
$8,000–9,000 SWAN

Rumold Mercator, *Orbis Terrae Compendiosa Descriptio*, double-page hand-coloured engraved twin-hemispherical map, set within a strapwork border with an armillary sphere and an elaborate compass rose, French text on verso, old ink inscription in upper margin, 1587, 11¼ x 20½in (28.5 x 52cm).
$5,500–6,500 Bon

Claudius Ptolemaeus, *Geographicae Enarrationis libri octo*, Johannes Grüninger, Strasbourg, 1525, 2°, 27 double-page maps of the ancient world, 22 double-page maps of the modern world and one full-page map of Lotharingia on verso of map 46, contemporary blind-tooled calf.
$27,500–30,000 S

The woodcut borders which enclose the text on the versos of most of the maps are thought to have been the work of Hans Holbein and Albrecht Dürer.

LOCATE THE SOURCE
The source of each illustration in Miller's can be found by checking the code letters below each caption with the Key to Illustrations, pages 789–795.

Abraham Ortelius, *Aevi Veteris Typus Geographicus*, Antwerp, c1590, 2°, Latin text on verso.
$1,200–1,350 NOA

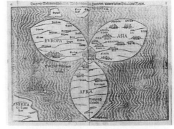

Heinrich Buenting, *Itinerarium sacrae scripturae*, Magdeburg, 1599–1616, 2°, 12 woodcut maps, 3 parts, bound in one volume.
$6,800–7,400 S

The maps include the world in the form of a clover leaf, caricatures of Asia in the form of Pegasus, and Europe in the form of a queen. Buenting rewrote the Bible as a travel book, the last part describing the coinage of biblical times.

Henricus Hondius, *Nova Totius Terrarum Orbis Geographica ac Hydrographica Tabula*, Amsterdam, 1630, 14¾ x 21¼in (37.5 x 54cm), hand-coloured engraved twin hemi-sphere map, depicting the 4 elements, and portraits of Caesar, Ptolemy, Hondius and Mercator, French text on verso, framed and glazed.
$8,000–9,000 P

This map was dated 1630 but is known to have been published later, in 1633.

Philippus Cluverius, *Introduction in Universam Geographiam*, Amsterdam, 1697, 4°, 48 maps, plates and tables.
$2,600–3,000 SWAN

Matthaeus Seutter, *Diversi Globi Terr-Aquei*, Augsburg, c1735, 19¾ x 22¾in (50 x 58cm), an engraved world map with 8 small maps and 4 diagrams in the spandrels, original hand-colouring.
$2,300–2,600 BBA

T. G. Bradford, *A Comprehensive Atlas, Geographical Historical and Commercial*, Boston & New York, 1835, 2°, 68 engraved maps in outline colour and 9 engraved plates, 2 hand-coloured, contemporary blind-stamped morocco, gilt edges.
$8,000–9,000 S

Nicolaes Visscher, *Orbis terrarum nova et accuratissima tabula*, Amsterdam, 1660, 18½ x 22in (47 x 56cm), a twin-hemispherical map engraved by J. de Visscher after N. P. Berchem, with California as an island, inset polar hemi-spheres, contemporary hand-colour.
$6,000–6,500 S

Guillaume Delisle, *Mappemonde*, Paris, 1720, 17¾ x 26½in (45 x 67.5cm), engraved double-hemispheric map, hand-coloured.
$2,000–2,300 SWAN

Composite Atlas, Nürnberg, c1800, 2°, comprising 58 engraved maps, by or after Johann-Baptiste Homann or his heirs, original hand-colouring throughout.
$6,500–8,000 Bon

Robert Montgomery Martin, *Tallis's Illustrated Atlas*, published by John Tallis, 1851, 2°, 81 engraved maps with outline colour, blue quarter calf.
$3,800–4,400 Bon

Carel Allard, *Planisphaerium terrestre sive terrarum orbis*, Amsterdam, 1696, 20½ x 23½in (52 x 60cm), an engraved twin-hemispherical map surrounded by 12 smaller hemispheres and diagrams, contemporary hand-colour.
$4,500–5,000 S

Gerard Mercator, *Universalis Tabula Juxta Ptolemaeum*, c1730, 13½ x 19in (34.5 x 48.5cm), engraved map, hand-coloured, mounted.
$1,450–1,600 SWAN

This map came from a late edition of Mercator's *Tabulae Geographicae*, printed in various places from 1695 to 1730, and used a border illustrated with 4 figures depicting the elements.

Philippe Vander Maelen, *Atlas universel de géographie physique, politique, statistique et minérealogique*, Brussels, 1827, 6 vols, 2°, hand-coloured litho-graphed table of mountains and 382 lithographed map sheets by Henri Ode, contemporary half calf.
$23,000–26,000 S

The maps in the atlas make up the first map of the world on a uniform scale, constructed on a modified conical projection and, if assembled, form a globe with a diameter of 310in (775cm), although only one such was known to have been assembled, by the author himself, and required a specially designed room.

THE AMERICAS

Ferando Bertelli, *Carta da navigare*, 1560, 9½ x 13¾in (24 x 35cm), engraved map of the Atlantic ocean.
$6,800–7,400 S

John Speed, *A Map of Virginia and Maryland*, by Thomas Bassett and Richard Chiswell, 1676, 15 x 20in (38 x 51cm), hand-coloured engraved map.
$1,600–1,800 SLN

Robert de Vaugondy, *Carte du Canada et des Etats Unis de l'Amérique septentrionale*, Jean Baptiste Fortin, Paris, 1778, 19 x 26¼in (48 x 67cm), engraved map, inset of Newfoundland, hand-coloured in outline.
$8,000–9,000 S

This is thought to be the earliest map of the United States.

Cornelis van Wytfliet, *Granata Nova et California*, Douai, 1597 or later, 8¾ x 11¼in (22.5 x 28.5cm), an engraved map showing California as a peninsula and part of Nueva Granada.
$1,000–1,200 Bon

C. van Wytfliet published *A Supplement to Ptolemy's Geography* in 1597, the first atlas devoted to the Americas. It had 19 maps but was enlarged to 23 with the addition of 4 maps of the East Indies in 1605. It is more common than the 1597 issue.

Petrus Bertius and Melchoir Tavernier, *Carte de l'Amérique*, Paris, c1640, 19¾ x 15¼in (50.5 x 38.5cm), engraved map of North and South America, hand-coloured in outline.
$2,000–2,500 SWAN

Lotter, *America Septentrionalis Concinnata Juxta Observationes*, c1770, 17¾ x 22¾in (45 x 58cm), hand-coloured engraved map.
$900–1,000 SLN

◄ F. L. Gussefeld after Homann's heirs, *Charte uber die XIII Vereinigte Staaten von Nord-America ...1784*, 17½ x 22½in (44.5 x 57cm), hand-coloured engraved map.
$1,150–1,300 SLN

California as an Island

Early map-makers such as Mercator in 1531, Ortelius in 1570 and Wytfliet in 1597 correctly showed California as a peninsula. However, by the 17thC many map-makers, particularly the British, including John Speed in 1627, were mistakenly depicting California as an island. There was no copyright at that time, so copying was commonplace. Some Dutch map-makers such as Blaeu in 1635 stuck to the peninsula theory, but it was not until well into the 18thC that new surveys were carried out, and the mistake universally rectified.

ASIA

Abraham Ortelius, *Chinae olim Sinarum regionis, nova descriptio*, Antwerp, c1584, 14¼ x 18½in (36.5 x 47cm), hand-coloured engraved map, French text on verso.
$2,000–2,300 P

Jodocus Hondius, *Iaponia*, Amsterdam, 1628, 13½ x 17½in (34.5 x 44.5cm), a hand-coloured engraved map of Japan, with French text.
$1,300–1,450 S

Thomas Bowen, *A New & Accurate Map of Asia*, London, 1777, 12¾ x 16¾in (32.5 x 42.5cm), engraved map, hand-coloured in outline.
$400–500 SWAN

EUROPE

Giacomo Gastaldi, *Nova descriptione de la Moscovia*, Venice, 1562, 10½ x 14¼in (27 x 36.5cm).
$3,000–3,300 S

G. F. Camocio, *Cyprus insula nobilisima*, engraved map, Venice, 1566, 10¼ x 15¾in (26 x 40cm).
$13,500–15,500 S

John Speed, *The Kingdome of Denmarke*, George Humble, 1626, 15¼ x 19¾in (39 x 50cm), engraved map, side borders with 10 costumed figures, upper border with 6 vignette town views, English text on verso.
$400–500 P

Joannes Janssonius, *Cyprus Insula*, Amsterdam, Johannes Covens and Cornelis Mortier, c1730, 15 x 19¾in (38 x 50cm), engraved general map, Aphrodite lower right and Lusignan arms upper centre.
$680–780 Bon

▶ Imperial Ottoman General Staff, *Map of the Province of the Danube*, Constantinople, c1877, 48 x 71in (122 x 180cm), in Turkish Arabic, a detailed lithographed military-topographical map.
$1,000–1,200 Bon

Cornelis Anthonisz, *Accipe candide lector absolutissimam septentrionalium regionum*, Venice, 1562, 15¼ x 20in (38.5 x 51cm), an engraved map showing Denmark, southern Norway and Sweden, the eastern British Isles and the Baltic shores as far as Helsinki.
$11,500–13,000 S

Vicenzo Maria Coronelli and Girolamo Antonio Parisotti, *Isola di Rodi*, Alla Libraria della Geografia sopra il Ponte Rialto, 1688, 8°, first edition, engraved title, 12 engraved plans, maps or views.
$2,000–2,500 Bon

This map shows other islands and the great fortress at Bodrum.

T. Stackhouse, a steel engraved map of Sweden and Norway, 1795, 15¾ x 14½in (40 x 37cm), with original colour.
$130–150 MAG

Domenico Zenoi, *L'ultimo disegno de l'isola di Malta*, engraved map, Venice, 1565, 13¼ x 16½in (33.5 x 42cm).
$6,000–6,500 S

Printers and map-makers were quick to sense public interest when in 1565 Suleiman the Magnificent sent a large armada to lay siege to the Knights of St John at Malta – just as he had forced them out of Rhodes in 1522. Zenoi produced 5 maps of Malta in 1565. This example shows the withdrawal of the Turkish forces on 8th September following their failure to dislodge the Order, under its Grand Master la Vallette, from Burgu and Senglea.

John Speed, *Europ, and the cheif Cities contayned therin*, George Humble, 1626, 15¼ x 20in (39 x 51cm), hand-coloured, engraved map, framed and glazed.
$750–850 P

DÉP. DU JURA.

V. Levasseur, an engraved map of the Jura region of France, c1860, 16 x 11in (41 x 28cm), with original colour to map section, uncoloured surrounding views.
$40–50 MAG

GREAT BRITAIN & IRELAND

Christopher Saxton, *Anglia*, engraved by Augustinus Ryther, original colouring, 1579, 15¼ x 19¼in (39 x 49cm), modern gilt frame, double-glazed.
$10,500–12,000 DW

Abraham Ortelius, *Angliae, Scotiae et Hiberniae, sive Britannicar: Insularum Descriptio*, 1595, 13½ x 19¾in (34 x 50cm).
$650–750 DW

John Speed, *Dorsetshyre*, 1611 or later, 15 x 20in (38 x 57cm), with an inset plan of Dorchester.
$300–330 KID

William Camden and John Bill, *The Abridgment of Camden's Britannia with the Maps of the Severall Shires of England and Wales*, printed by John Bill, 1626, 4°, 52 engraved maps, all in early hand-colouring, the title panels, distance scales and sea areas fully coloured, borders in outline, old boards.
$13,500–15,500 BBA

This is the only edition of these miniature maps based largely on those of Saxton and notable as the first county maps with markings of latitude and longitude. Coloured copies are rare.

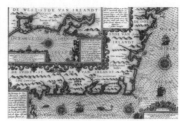

A chart of the east and south coasts of Ireland, by Petrus Kaerius, hand-coloured, 1584, 13¾ x 20in (35 x 51cm).
$3,800–4,200 HOK

This is the first published chart of the Irish coast.

Abraham Ortelius, *Cambriae Typus Auctore Humfredo Lhuydo, Denbigiense Cambrobritanno*, 1607–33, 13¾ x 19¾in (35 x 50cm), an uncoloured map, engraved by Pieter van den Keere, Latin text to verso, mounted.
$420–480 DW

This map is the first printed map of Wales by a Welshman, and in fact the first separate printed map of the Principality to appear (1573–81).

John Speed, *The Countie of Nottingham*, 1611, 15 x 20in (38 x 51cm), a copper engraved map, with later colouring.
$730–830 MAG

John Speed, *The Isle of Man exactly described, and into several parishes divided ...*, a hand-coloured engraved map, 1616, 15 x 20in (38 x 51cm), Latin text to verso.
$480–580 DW

John Speed, *Glamorgan Shyre*, Sudbury & Humble, 1610 or later, 15¼ x 20½in (39 x 52cm), engraved map, later hand-coloured in outline with inset plans of Cardyfe and Llandaffe.
$350–400 P(C)

John Speed, *The Invasions of England and Ireland with al their Civill Wars since the Conquest*, 1611 or later, 15 x 20in (38 x 51cm), engraved, outline colour.
$1,600–1,800 P(NW)

John Speed, *Suffolke*, George Humble, c1627, 15 x 20in (38 x 57cm), described and divided into hundreds, with an inset plan of Ipswiche, framed and double-glazed.
$350–400 KID

Joannes Blaeu, *Somersettensis Comitatus Somersetshire*, 1645 or later, 15½ x 20in (39.5 x 51cm), hand-coloured engraved map.
$250–300 L

Joannes Blaeu, a copper engraved map of the British Isles, 1650, 15 x 20in (38 x 51cm), original colour.
$1,150–1,250 MAG

Joannem Jannsonium, *Hibernia Regnum Vulgo Ireland*, c1670, 15¾ x 16¼in (40 x 41cm), the 4 provinces, hand-coloured.
$2,800–3,200 HOK

Frederick de Wit, *Novissima prae caeteris aliis accuratissima Regnorum Angliae, Scotiae Hiberniae Tabula*, Amsterdam, c1690, 23 x 38½in (58.5 x 98cm), an engraved map with side panels of distances and location tables, original hand-colouring.
$325–400 Bon

William Camden, *Camden's Britannia. Newly Translated ... by Edmund Gibson*, London, 1695, 50 double-page or folding maps, 9 numismatic or antiquarian plates, 2°, first Gibson edition.
$1,100–1,250 SWAN

P. Sanson, a copper engraved map of Scotland, 1705, 16 x 21½in (40.5 x 54.5cm).
$400–500 MAG

C. & J. Greenwood, *County of Worcester*, steel engraved map with original colour, 1834, 23 x 28in (58.5 x 71cm).
$80–100 MAG

Geological Survey of Cornwall, Devon and West Somerset, 1809–39, 2°, edited by E. Bourne, engraved by B. Baker, double-page sheets 20–23 bound in atlas, contemporary half morocco, gilt.
$2,400–2,700 P(B)

Edward Langley and J. Belch, New County Atlas of England and Wales, Joseph Phelps, c1820, 2°, 53 hand-coloured maps, original half red roan.
$2,300–2,600 L

> **Cross Reference**
> See Colour Review

CITY PLANS

Johann Baptist Homann, *Accurater Prospect und Grundris der ... Haupt und Residentz Stadt London*, Nürnberg, 1705, 19 x 22½in (48.5 x 57.5cm), engraved plan of the City with panorama and key below, inset with views of Whitehall and the Royal Exchange, contemporary body colour.
$1,450–1,600 Bon

John Andrews, *A Collection of Plans of the Capital Cities of Europe and ... Asia, Africa and America*, 2 vols in one, by John Andrews, 1792, 4°, 42 engraved plans, contemporary half calf, upper cover detached.
$2,600–2,800 P

A street map of the City of Osaka, Japan, c1860, 38½ x 26in (98 x 66cm), hand-coloured, original wraps.
$1,200–1,300 P(B)

Dolls

SELECTED MAKERS

An Alt, Beck & Gottschalk doll, with parian head and kid body, c1885, 17½in (44.5cm) high.
$400–500 YC

A Carl Bergner bisque-headed two-faced doll, with revolving head, cloth and composition body, c1895, 15in (38cm) high.
$1,200–1,350 YC

A Bähr & Pröschild bisque-headed doll, with jointed wood and composition body, brown eyes, blonde wig, original clothes, impressed 'B&P 320 12', c1910, 21in (53cm) high.
$1,450–1,600 S

A Bru all-bisque doll, c1890, 5½in (14cm) high, with original layette and box.
$2,000–2,250 GrD

This doll is unmarked, but is recognized by collectors and considered to be made by Bru.

◄ A Dressel 'Jutta' bisque-headed doll, with brown mohair wig, weighted blue glass eyes with lashes, on a bent-limb body, teeth and 2 fingers missing, impressed 'Dressel 1920-50 12', c1920, 21½in (54.5cm) high.
$600–650 P(Ba)

► A bisque swivel-headed fashion doll, probably by François Gaultier, with fixed blue glass eyes, dark brown wig, kid arms, original blue silk dress and bonnet, 3 fingers missing, c1865, 11½in (29cm) high.
$750–900 S

A Madame Barrois bisque-headed and shoulder-plate doll, with kid body, dressed in original clothes, incised 'E.B.', c1885, 15¾in (40cm) high.
$2,300–2,600 YC

An E. Denamur bisque-headed *bébé* doll, with jointed composition body, incised 'E.10.D', c1900, 20½in (52cm) high.
$2,100–2,400 YC

A bisque swivel-headed doll, probably by François Gaultier, with fixed blue glass eyes, blonde mohair wig, kid body, individually stitched fingers, original red wool dress with underwear and leather slippers, c1890, 12in (30.5cm) high.
$1,000–1,150 AH

A Heinrich Handwerck bisque-headed doll, with jointed composition body, incised 'Handwerck 99', c1905, 16½in (42cm) high.
$900–1,000 YC

A William Goebel bisque-headed doll, with weighted brown glass eyes, brown mohair wig, on a fully-jointed wood and composition body, wearing a pink dress and cape, white under-clothes, incised 'Bavaria, 120, WG, Bavaria', c1915, 19in (48cm) high.
$450–550 Bon(C)

A Hertel Schwab & Co bisque-headed doll, with grey eyes and delicate colouring, mould No. 151, c1915, 17in (43cm) high.
$1,300–1,450 STK

A Gebrüder Heubach character doll, with sparse hair wig, weighted blue glass eyes, bent-limb composition body, dressed in a whitework dress, impressed '11 Germany' and stamped, c1910, 22½in (56cm) high.
$2,600–3,000 P(Ba)

A Gebrüder Heubach bisque-headed character doll, with solid dome and moulded hair, intaglio eyes, closed mouth, on a bent-limb body, slightly damaged, c1910, 14in (35cm) high.
$650–750 P(Ba)

A Gebrüder Heubach boy doll, with bisque head, shoulder-plate and arms, cloth body, intaglio eyes, c1910, 17in (43cm) high.
$800–900 GrD

A Gebrüder Heubach bisque shoulder-headed boy doll, with cloth body and bisque arms, intaglio eyes, incised with a sunburst, c1910, 15in (38cm) high.
$480–560 YC

A Gebrüder Heubach bisque-headed boy doll, with double-jointed composition body, painted intaglio eyes, incised '6969', c1912, 16½in (42cm) high.
$1,400–1,550 YC

Jumeau (French 1842–99)

The company was founded at Montreuil-sur-Bois by Pierre François Jumeau. Early dolls are marked with a number only but, after 1875, they may feature a red tick mark on the head. The main types of doll produced were:

- **the fashion doll, or Parisienne**, with bisque, swivel head, gusseted kid body and separate fingers and toes. They are renowned for their elegant, fashionable costumes – a doll that comes with an original wardrobe of clothes is particularly desirable.
- **the bébé doll**, invented by Jumeau in 1855 and soon copied by rival firms, was an idealized version of a young girl. Early bébés, usually with closed mouths, fixed wrists and pale bisque heads, are very sought after. Later examples have highly coloured bisque heads, open mouths and articulated wrists.
- **the portrait bébé**, dating from 1870, was allegedly based on real-life models. Most examples have lightly painted eyebrows, blue eyes with long lashes, and jointed composition bodies with eight wooden ball joints and fixed wrists.
- **the Jumeau Triste**, (sad or long-faced doll), dating from c1880.
- **the Tête Jumeau**, dating from 1880–90, has heavy eyebrows, light eyelashes, paperweight eyes, and chubby body with fixed wrists.
- **the two-faced Jumeau**, dating from the turn of the century, operated by a knob on the top of the head that twisted the face around to produce alternately a cheerful and an unhappy doll.

A Jumeau Parisienne doll, with swivel head, fixed brown eyes, brown wig, gusseted white kid body, dressed in original nun's habit with rosary beads, head impressed '5', c1880, 15in (38cm) high, in original box.
$3,200–3,600 S

A Jumeau bisque-headed fashion doll, with shoulder-plate kid body and original clothes, c1880, 15in (38cm) high.
$3,000–3,300 YC

A Jumeau doll, with closed mouth, marked 'Deposé Tête Jumeau' and 'Bte SGDG' in red, 1880–90, clothes later, 24in (61cm) high.
$4,500–3,000 BGC

A Jumeau bisque swivel-headed doll, with fixed brown eyes, blonde wig, gusseted kid body with separately stitched fingers, original Breton-style headdress, impressed '7' with red check mark, c1880, 14¾in (37.5cm) high.
$1,300–1,450 S

A Jumeau bisque-headed bébé doll, with paperweight eyes, fully-jointed body, c1890, 21in (53cm) high.
$4,600–5,200 STK

A Tête Jumeau bisque-headed doll, with blue paperweight eyes, blonde mohair wig, c1890, 18in (45.5cm) high.
$4,000–4,500 STK

A Jumeau bébé doll, with paperweight eyes, slight damage, 1890s, 22in (56cm) high.
$2,500–3,000 STK

A Jumeau porcelain doll, with blue paperweight eyes, dark blonde wig, composition body, damaged and restored, red stamped mark, c1900, 28in (71cm) high.
$3,500–4,000 SK(B)

A Jumeau laughing schoolgirl doll, created for S.F.B.J., jointed body, original clothes, mould No. 236, marked, c1910, 13in (33cm) high.
$975–1,100 GrD

An Emile Jumeau *bébé* doll, c1900, 22in (56cm) high.
$2,500–2,800 GrD

A Kämmer & Reinhardt doll, with jointed body, mould No. 192, c1890, 7in (18cm) long, in original box.
$800–900 GrD

A Jumeau laughing baby doll, created for S.F.B.J., five-part bent limb body, clothes replaced, mould No. 236, small firing crack to forehead, marked, c1910, 13in (33cm) high.
$750–850 GrD

A Kämmer & Reinhardt bisque-headed doll, with jointed composition body, incised 'K☆R', c1900, 28¾in (73cm) high.
$1,200–1,350 YC

A Kämmer & Reinhardt bisque-headed doll, with jointed composition body, incised 'K☆R', c1905, 25½in (65cm) high.
$1,000–1,200 YC

A Kämmer & Reinhardt bisque-headed doll, with sleeping eyes, double-jointed body, incised 'K☆R', c1905, 17in (43cm) high.
$800–950 YC

A Kämmer & Reinhardt bisque-headed doll, with composition body, incised 'K☆R 100', c1908, 19¾in (53cm) high.
$1,150–1,300 YC

This doll was popularly known as the 'Kaiser baby', as it was supposedly modelled on the Emperor's son.

Miller's Compares

A Kämmer & Reinhardt bisque-headed character doll, with painted blue eyes and ball-jointed wood and composition body, slight damage, impressed '114 34', c1909, 13½in (34cm) high.
$575–650 S(S)

I A Kämmer & Reinhardt bisque-headed character doll, with double-jointed toddler body, incised 'K*R 115/A', c1910, 17¾in (45cm) high.
$4,800–5,600 YC

II A Kämmer & Reinhardt bisque-headed character doll, with composition body, incised 'K*R 122', c1912, 15¾in (40cm) high.
$1,400–1,550 YC

In 1908, Kämmer & Reinhardt began producing more realistic dolls, resembling real children, in an attempt to halt falling sales figures. Item I is superbly modelled with closed, pouting mouth and double-jointed toddler body, but this design was not successful as the realistic face did not appeal to children. As it was also more expensive to produce and therefore more costly to buy, fewer examples were made and consequently they are now very rare. Doll collectors consider them exceptionally artistic and desirable, which increases their value. Kämmer & Reinhardt soon began producing dolls with more idealistic faces, of which Item II is a good example. This type of doll was very popular with children in the early 19thC and large quantities were made, with the result that they are less sought after and less expensive today.

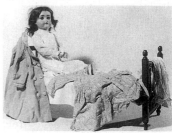

A Kämmer & Reinhardt bisque-headed doll, with closing blue eyes, jointed composition body, c1910, 25in (63.5cm) high, with some clothing and a pine bed.
$1,400–1,550 CAG

A bisque shoulder-headed doll, probably by J. D. Kestner, with solid dome, fixed blue glass paperweight eyes, light brown plaits, gusseted kid body, bisque lower arms, c1890, 25½in (65cm) high.
$750–900 S

A Kämmer & Reinhardt/Simon & Halbig bisque doll, with open mouth, weighted blue eyes and curved limb composition body, impressed '122 42', c1912, 16½in (42cm) high.
$800–900 S(S)

A Kämmer & Reinhardt bisque-headed character doll, with glass eyes, composition double-jointed toddler body, incised 'K*R 116/A', c1912, 16½in (42cm) high.
$2,400–2,750 YC

▶ A J. D. Kestner bisque-headed doll, with sleeping eyes, kid body, bisque lower arms, stamped purple crown on chest, marked 'II/147/Made in Germany', c1892, 20in (51cm) high.
$300–350 DuM

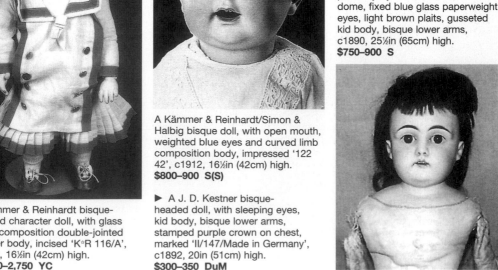

A J. D. Kestner bisque-headed boy doll, with jointed composition body, incised 'J.D.K. 239', c1910, 23in (58cm) high.
$1,000–1,200 YC

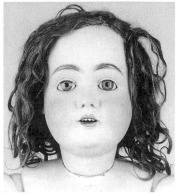

A J. D. Kestner bisque doll, with weighted blue glass eyes, original brown mohair wig, fully jointed wood and composition body, paint slightly flaking, incised '142', c1910, 35in (89cm) high.
$900–1,000 Bon(C)

A J. D. Kestner bisque-headed character doll, with jointed composition body, incised 'J.D.K. 260', c1912, 19¾in (50cm) high.
$1,000–1,200 YC

A Kestner bisque-headed character doll, with blonde mohair wig, weighted blue glass eyes, open/closed mouth with moulded tongue and smiling expression, on a bent limb composition body dressed in a whitework baby's robe, impressed 211 J.D.K., c1910, 11in (28cm) high.
$575–650 P(Ba)

A J. D. Kestner character baby boy doll, incised '226', c1915, 15in (38cm) high.
$1,000–1,200 GrD

A J. D. Kestner character doll, with weighted blue eyes, curved limb body, original clothes, impressed 'Siegfried, Made in Germany 272/9', c1920, 13½in (34.5cm) high.
$3,000–3,300 S

Two Lenci 'art' dolls, both with painted brown eyes, original clothes, trademarks to feet, 1930s, girl 17in (43cm) high.
$3,200–3,600 S

A J. D. Kestner all-bisque Kewpie doll, in original bridegroom's outfit, c1925, 7in (18cm) high.
$800–900 YC

The first bisque Kewpies were made in 1913 at the Kestner factory in Germany, but were soon also being manufactured at other factories in Germany and the United States.

A Käthe Kruse cloth doll, with moulded muslin head, muslin body, jointed knees, separately stitched thumbs, original clothes, Series I, 1910–29, 16in (40.5cm) high.
$5,500–6,500 S(NY)

Two Lenci cloth dolls, with painted features, both with centre fingers stitched together, in original clothes, c1930, largest 22in (56cm) high.
$650–900 each S(S)

A Limoges Cheri bisque-headed *bébé* doll, with paperweight eyes and fully-jointed body, 1900, 14in (35.5cm) high.
$1,200–1,450 STK

A Lenci Dutch boy 300 series felt doll, with blonde hair, painted facial features, wearing a blue embroidered tunic and wooden clogs, cloth and paper label, 1930s, 18in (45.5cm) high.
$1,600–1,750 S(NY)

An Armand Marseille bisque-headed doll, with blonde wig, blue glass eyes, open mouth with 4 teeth, kid body with composition limbs, original clothing and leather shoes stamped 'Natural Form', c1900, 26½in (26cm) high.
$400–500 Bea(E)

An Armand Marseille character doll, mould No. 700, c1910, 15in (38cm) high.
$6,500–8,000 DOL

This doll is very rare, and all original.

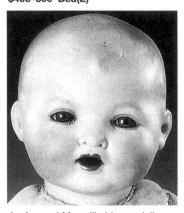

A Limoges bisque doll, with blue eyes and jointed composition body, marked 'France Limoges', 1910, 15in (38cm) high.
$260–300 BGC

An Armand Marseille bisque doll, with weighted blue eyes, cloth body and celluloid hands, repaired, impressed 'Baby Gloria 6', c1910, 17¼in (44cm) high.
$400–500 S(S)

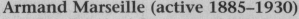

Armand Marseille (active 1885–1930)

Armand Marseille was born in Russia but moved with his family to Thuringia in Germany, where he took over a porcelain factory. By 1890 he was manufacturing bisque-headed dolls with his son, also Armand. Their output was prolific and from 1900 to 1930 they also supplied dolls to other makers.

Marseille's most commonly found doll is the 390 series, made from c1900, but the most popular is the Dream Baby. These were made in vast quantities from life-size to very small, but quality varies. Examples with open mouths are marked '351', and those with closed mouths '341'. Some have a soft stuffed body and composition hands, others have a five-piece, bent-limb composition body. The latter type, with a closed mouth and of small size, are generally more desirable.

An Armand Marseille Dream Baby, c1910, 25in (63.5cm) high.
$525–575 AnS

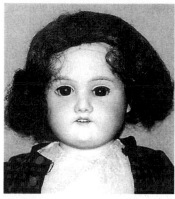

An Armand Marseille bisque-headed doll, with brown sleeping eyes, kid body, original leather shoes, marked 'Floradora/A.4.M/Made in Germany/Armand Marseille', early 20thC, 21in (53.5cm) high.
$200–250 DuM

An Armand Marseille doll, c1915, 24in (61cm) high.
$750–850 AnS

An Armand Marseille sleeping doll, marked '520/6K', early 20thC, 22in (56cm) high.
$260–280 PCh

An Armand Marseille Dream Baby, marked 'A.M.351', c1920, 50in (127cm) high.
$300–350 YC

An Armand Marseille bisque dome-headed life-size doll, with five-piece baby body, mould No. 351, c1920, 25in (63.5cm) high.
$800–900 STK

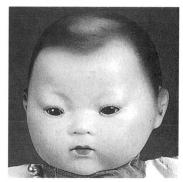

An Armand Marseille bisque Oriental doll, with weighted brown glass eyes, black painted hair, stuffed cloth body with composition hands, original jacket, impressed 'AM Germany 353/2', c1920, 11½in (29cm) high.
$750–900 S

An Armand Marseille Dream Baby, with closed mouth, composition body, mould No. 341, 1920s, 16in (40.5cm) high.
$525–600 GrD

An Armand Marseille bisque Dream Baby, with closed mouth, c1920, 16½in (42cm) high.
$550–600 GrD

An Armand Marseille bisque-headed Dream Baby, with closed mouth, soft body and composition hands, c1920, 22in (56cm) high.
$430–480 GrD

An Armand Marseille bisque-headed Dream Baby, with composition body, 1920s, 10in (25.5cm) high.
$350–400 GrD

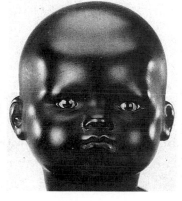

◄ An Armand Marseille Dream Baby, with closed mouth, weighted brown eyes, curved limb composition body, impressed '341/8.K', c1926, 20½in (52cm) high.
$525–575 S(S)

A Pedigree walking doll, c1950, 20in (51cm) high.
$145–160 GAZE

A Bruno Schmidt character doll, with hair wig, jointed toddler body, c1915, 14in (35.5cm) high, with a quantity of clothes and a wicker trunk.
$2,000–2,200 STK

▶ An S.H.P.B. bisque-headed doll, with sleeping blue glass eyes, painted lips, fully-jointed body, 1906, 31in (78.5cm) high.
$550–600 BWe

The initials S.H.P.B. stand for Schoenau & Hoffmeister Porzellanfabric Burggrub.

A Petite Française bisque-headed doll, with jointed wood and composition body, in original underwear, impressed marks, late 19thC, 22in (56cm) long.
$420–480 PCh

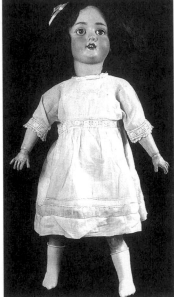

A Pintel & Godchaux bisque-headed *bébé* doll, with paperweight eyes, jointed walking body, mohair wig, wearing Victorian swimming costume, c1880, 16in (40.5cm) high.
$2,200–2,400 STK

A Schoenau & Hoffmeister Mama doll, c1910, 25in (63.5cm) high.
$750–900 AnS

An S.F.B.J. bisque-headed *bébé* doll, with hair wig, jointed body, mould No. 60, c1910, 17in (43cm) high.
$950–1,100 STK

An S.F.B.J. bisque-headed character doll, with side-hip jointed toddler body, mould No. 247, c1915, 21in (53.5cm) high.
$3,000–3,500 STK

An S.F.B.J. bisque-headed doll, with fixed blue glass eyes, blonde wig, jointed wood and composition body, velvet dress and bonnet, impressed 'S.F.B.J. 301 Paris', late 19th/early 20thC, 24in (61cm) high.
$500–575 DA

21 Years Ago ...

A Steiner doll, dressed in original clothes, 1889, 14½in (37cm) high. **L**

Twenty-one years ago this Steiner doll was valued at $1,150–1,300. Although prices for many ordinary dolls have levelled, this is a good all-original example and is sought after by serious doll collectors worldwide. Today it could be expected to realize $3,750–4,250.

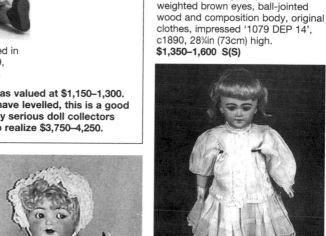

A Simon & Halbig bisque doll, with weighted brown eyes, ball-jointed wood and composition body, original clothes, impressed '1079 DEP 14', c1890, 28¾in (73cm) high.
$1,350–1,600 S(S)

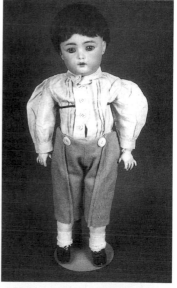

A Simon & Halbig bisque-headed doll, with jointed composition body, incised '1279', c1905, 19in (48cm) high.
$1,300–1,450 YC

This doll was made especially for the Christmas period.

A Simon & Halbig/Kämmer & Reinhardt bisque-headed doll, with sleeping brown eyes, curly fair wig, ball-jointed composition body, mould No. 70, c1900, 28¾in (73cm) high.
$2,000–2,500 Bri

A Simon & Halbig bisque-headed doll, with sleeping eyes, composition body, marked 'K*R, Simon & Halbig', c1900, 22in (56cm) high.
$600–650 DuM

A Steiner pressed bisque doll, with fixed blue glass eyes, blonde wig, jointed wood and composition body, impressed 'A15', stamped 'E. Parisien Ste Sg DG A15', c1890, 22in (56cm) high.
$4,000–5,000 S

A Swaine & Co bisque doll, with flirty brown eyes, ball-jointed wood and composition body, impressed 'S&C 53 3¼', c1910, 21¼in (54cm) high.
$750–900 S(S)

A Simon & Halbig bisque-headed doll, with jointed body, incised '1299', c1910, 19¾in (50cm) high.
$1,450–1,600 YC

UNKNOWN MAKERS

A Grödnertal doll, with gesso head and shoulders, articulated wooden body, original silk dress, c1830, 13¾in (35cm) high.
$850–950 S

A poured-wax shoulder-headed doll, with dark blonde rooted hair, fixed blue glass eyes, cloth-filled body with wax lower limbs, original cotton dress, woollen cape, shoes and socks, slight damage, c1860, 18in (45cm) high.
$650–800 P(Ba)

A Victorian wooden doll, with painted and enamelled face, chamois arms and blonde hair, original bonnet and blue dress, 24in (61cm) high.
$420–480 RID

A bisque swivel-headed Parisienne doll, with fixed dark blue glass paperweight eyes, blonde wig on cork pate, cloth body with bisque lower arms, original silk dress, c1875, 13¼in (33.5cm) high.
$1,450–1,750 S

The term Parisienne was originally used by Jumeau to describe their fashion dolls. These dolls were bought by parents for their daughters as a symbol of their wealth and status. They also helped a young girl develop a fashion sense and improve her sewing skills by adding clothes to the doll's wardrobe.

A Victorian doll, with moulded head, c1880, 13in (33cm) high.
$450–500 AnS

A French swivel-headed fashion doll, with fixed blue glass eyes, remains of sheepskin wig, gusseted kid body with separately stitched fingers, original clothes, c1870, 15in (38cm) high, with a quantity of accessories.
$3,000–3,300 S(S)

◄ A Parisienne swivel-headed doll, with bisque shoulder plate, fixed blue eyes, blonde wig, kid leather body, in a taupe gown and underwear, c1885, and a Motschmann-type doll, with weighted blue eyes, composition body, original clothes, 1860, 13½in (34.5cm) high, box inscribed '2 Dolls given by Queen Victoria to Elo Catherine Leveson Gower'.
$4,000–4,500 S

These dolls were given by Queen Victoria to Elo, who was born at Invercauld Castle, the neighbouring estate to Balmoral. Elo and her sister Louisa were invited to tea by Her Majesty at Balmoral c1876, and each child was presented with one of these dolls.

A pedlar doll, with painted porcelain head, lower arms and legs, late 19thC, 11½in (29cm) high.
$1,300–1,450 DN

A late Victorian Irish papier mâché leprechaun doll, with glass eyes, movable arms, straw hair and beard, wearing velvet clothes, 19in (48cm) high.
$250–275 WA

A German all-bisque doll, with glass eyes, painted shoes and socks, c1910, 11in (28cm) high.
$1,150–1,300 GrD

A German bisque-headed doll, with sleeping eyes, impressed 'Germany 64', c1910, 17in (43cm) high.
$230–260 JBe

A German bisque-headed doll, with weighted blue glass eyes, painted moulded hair, bent limb composition body, wearing a white cotton dress, incised '241-8, Germany', c1915, 23in (58.5cm) high.
$330–380 Bon(C)

A German bisque character doll, with weighted brown eyes, brown wig, curved limb body, impressed 'My Sweet Baby 8', c1920, 23¼in (59cm) high.
$750–900 S

A German all-bisque Oriental doll, with mohair pigtail attached to head, moulded vest and shoes, possibly by Gebrüder Heubach, c1920, 5in (12.5cm) high.
$400–500 STK

A composition character doll, with weighted brown glass eyes, moulded hair, cloth body with composition arms and legs, in original pink dress, probably American, c1930, 24in (61cm) high.
$320–380 Bon(C)

A bisque-headed *poupard* doll, dressed in original clothes, with a musical box, c1900, 16in (40cm) high.
$1,150–1,300 Bea(E)

Dolls' Houses & Furniture

DOLLS' HOUSES

A wooden dolls' house, painted in red, with unglazed windows, opening from the centre to reveal 6 rooms, hall and landing, c1750, 36in (91.5cm) wide.
$3,200–3,600 Bon

Ex-Vivien Greene collection.

A wooden three-storey dolls' house, decorated with flags and bunting to celebrate Queen Victoria's Golden Jubilee of 1887, with 6 rooms, hall and landing, c1880, 45½in (115.5cm) wide.
$6,500–8,000 Bon

Ex-Vivien Greene collection.

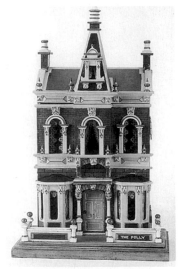

A Moritz Gottschalk dolls' house, the wooden frame with chromo-lithographed paper, the green door flanked by white and gold pillars, the roof painted blue to simulate slate tiles, the front opening to reveal 2 rooms on 2 levels, German, c1885, 19½in (49.5cm) wide, with furniture and fittings.
$10,500–12,000 Bon

Ex-Vivien Greene collection.

A dolls' house, painted yellow with white trim, with 2 rooms on each of 3 floors, c1900, 51in (129.5cm) wide.
$1,600–2,000 SK(B)

An American wooden dolls' house, probably by Bliss, with lithographed paper exterior and a red roof, on a green-painted base with lithographed garden border, front opening to reveal 2 rooms, c1900, 7¾in (20cm) wide.
$480–560 S(S)

An American wooden dolls' house, possibly by Bliss, with 2 floors, the front and sides lithographed with shutters and windows, the porch with turned columns, metal balustrade and front door, balcony above the door, pitched grey roof with central gable, hinged front opening to reveal 2 rooms with original wallpaper and flooring, slight damage, c1900, 10½in (27cm) wide.
$1,000–1,200 S(S)

A dolls' house, in the form of Jedburgh Town Hall, with cream façade and blue roof, opening to reveal 6 rooms, staircase with metal banister and a fireplace, some wiring, c1910, 44in (112cm) high.
$1,100–1,350 Bon(C)

◄ A Lines Brothers wooden dolls' house, lithographed with a brick effect, the façade opening to reveal 4 rooms and a central staircase, c1910, 21in (53.5cm) wide.
$650–800 Bon(C)

DOLLS' HOUSE FURNITURE

A Continental straw-work chiffonier, the top with hinged shelf to a compartment, above a single drawer, the three drawer base enclosed by 2 doors, early 19thC, 8¼in (21cm) high.
$400–500 Bon

An early Victorian 'lacewood' chiffonier, the mirrored shelf above an arched panelled cupboard with dummy doors, 6⅝in (17cm) high.
$550–600 Bon

A gilt-metal five-branch chandelier, with leaf and berry terminal and ruby glass drops, 19thC, 5¼in (13.5cm) high.
$1,150–1,300 Bon

Ex-Vivien Greene collection.

A matched suite of stained mahogany furniture, comprising 14 pieces, one table repaired, one chair missing top splat, c1860, bookcase 6in (15cm) wide.
$2,600–3,000 Bon

A maple grandfather clock, with false door, 19thC, 9in (23cm) high.
$575–650 Bon

Ex-Vivien Greene collection.

> **Cross Reference**
> See Colour Review

A mahogany chest-on-stand, probably American, with swan-neck pediment above a central lunette-carved drawer and 4 long drawers, on a stand with cabriole legs, on claw-and-ball feet, repaired, 19thC, 4in (10cm) high.
$1,000–1,150 Bon

Ex-Vivien Greene collection.

An Art Nouveau bedroom suite, c1900, dressing table 9in (23cm) wide.
$480–560 HOB

A suite of German dolls' house furniture, comprising a sofa and six chairs covered in pink velvet, a table and side table, all with gold paper lining and decoration, late 19thC.
$520–570 Bon

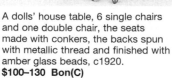

A dolls' house table, 6 single chairs and one double chair, the seats made with conkers, the backs spun with metallic thread and finished with amber glass beads, c1920.
$100–130 Bon(C)

Teddy Bears

A German teddy bear, possibly by Bing, with pale beige mohair plush, an excelsior-filled body with swivel joints and large pads, pads re-covered, c1915, 22in (56cm) high, with his own travel trunk.
$1,300–1,450 P(Ba)

A Chad Valley mohair teddy bear, with glass eyes, replaced paw pads, dress later, c1925–30, 16in (40.5cm) high.
$250–350 TED

A Chad Valley teddy bear, with glass eyes, golden plush fur and squeaker voice, 1930s, 15in (38cm) high.
$320–360 DN

A Chiltern Hugmee mohair teddy bear, with velvet paws and plastic eyes, c1959, 21in (53.5cm) high.
$400–500 TED

A Crämer white mohair teddy bear, the mouth underlined in orange thread, with flat standing feet, c1930, 9in (23cm) high.
$520–570 TED

A Chad Valley mohair teddy bear, with glass eyes and Rexine paws, maker's label in chest seam, c1950, 13in (33cm) high.
$200–250 TED

Facts in Brief

- Condition is very important, particularly in commoner examples. Missing ears or fur cannot be restored, but new paw pads are acceptable.
- Unusual colours add to value.
- Beware of fakes, which are often suspiciously pristine. Check for thickly stitched and uneven seams, unworn noses and old labels on replaced paws.

A Dean's soft-filled teddy bear, with flat face, velvet pads and plastic eyes, c1930, 6¾in (17cm) high.
$120–140 BGC

▶ A Dean's teddy bear, c1950, 14in (35.5cm) high.
$200–220 AnS

A Farnell teddy bear, with clear
glass eyes and felt pads, 1915–20,
19in (48.5cm) high.
$1,450–1,600 BGC

A Hermann straw-filled teddy bear,
with glass eyes, felt pads, 1930s,
16in (40.5cm) high.
$115–130 BGC

A French brown mohair teddy bear,
by J. P. M., Paris, with jointed arms
and legs, pink glass eyes, c1950,
11in (28cm) high.
$325–400 TED

**It is difficult to find French bears
with original makers' labels.**

A Koch shaggy mohair teddy bear,
c1960, 11in (28cm) high.
$275–325 TED

**Hugo Koch, Germany, ceased
business in 1990.**

A Pedigree teddy bear, with felt
pads, orange plastic eyes and label,
c1940, 16in (40.5cm) high.
$115–130 BGC

A Schuco green teddy bear, the
head lifting to reveal lipstick in
neck and powder compact in
body, c1930, 3¼in (8.5cm) high.
$650–800 TED

**This bear is scarcer in green than
the more usual gold mohair.**

A Schuco somersaulting teddy bear,
with original ribbon and key,
c1950, 5in (13cm) high.
$550–650 TED

A Schuco footballer teddy bear,
with mohair head, bendable
wool arms and legs, c1960,
4in (10cm) high, with original box.
$130–160 TED

Beware!
The high prices that Steiff
bears can now command
have resulted in an increasing
number of fakes. Look out for
fake buttons in the ear, or
genuine buttons taken from
less expensive Steiff dolls or
worn-out bears.

A Steiff cinnamon plush teddy bear, with button in ear, black stitched snout, black button eyes, swivel-jointed body with excelsior filling, c1907, 17in (43cm) high.
$3,700–4,000 S(S)

A Steiff black mohair bear, c1912, 20in (51cm) high.
$24,500–26,500 TED

This bear is extremely rare in this size and condition. Steiff made 494 bears for the English market in black mohair, as a mark of respect for those who died on the *Titanic*.

A teddy bear, with black glass eyes, yellow plush fur, felt pads and feet, early 20thC, 15¾in (40cm) high.
$160–200 DN

A straw-filled teddy bear, with snout, c1930, 12in (30.5cm) high.
$250–275 AnS

A teddy bear, with cotton pads and clear glass eyes, 1930–40, 18in (45.5cm) high.
$100–115 BGC

A mohair teddy bear, c1950, 15in (38cm) high.
$100–130 TED

A teddy bear, with mousey face, felt pads repaired, 1920s, 16in (40.5cm) high.
$70–80 BGC

A Continental cream-coloured cotton and silk teddy bear, with a tin nose and glass eyes, 1950s, 13in (33cm) high.
$65–80 CMF

A Polish cotton plush teddy bear, head not jointed, legs jointed with thread, c1960, 6in (15cm) high.
$10–15 TED

Soft Toys

A Merrythought monkey, 1930s, 12in (30.5cm) high.
$65–75 GAZE

A blonde plush bear on wheels, attributed to Steiff, fitted with pull-ring groaner mechanism, c1935, 28in (71cm) long.
$2,400–2,750 S(NY)

A Steiff plush toy giraffe, with growler, 1930s, 10in (25.5cm) high.
$160–200 HUM

A Steiff velvet soft toy, with brown body, striped legs and black mane, 1950s, 6¼in (16cm) high.
$65–75 GrD

A Steiff velvet budgerigar, 1950s, 8in (20.5cm) long.
$55–65 GrD

A Steiff mohair 'Dally' dalmation, with button and tag in left ear, 1957–67, 6½in (16.5cm) high.
$80–100 TED

A Steiff 'Flossy' goldfish, 1965–67, 5¼in (13cm) long.
$50–65 TED

A velvet Mickey Mouse, wearing red shorts, yellow gloves and brown shoes, c1920, 18in (45.5cm) high.
$450–525 Bon(C)

A velvet Mickey and Minnie Mouse, 1920s, 14in (35.5cm) high.
$65–80 GAZE

A mohair straw-filled dog, c1920, 9in (23cm) high.
$40–50 AnS

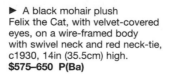

► A black mohair plush Felix the Cat, with velvet-covered eyes, on a wire-framed body with swivel neck and red neck-tie, c1930, 14in (35.5cm) high.
$575–650 P(Ba)

Toys

AEROPLANES

A French tinplate clockwork three-engined aircraft, painted orange, blue and green, the tail with the colours of the French flag, 1930s, 16½in (42cm) long.
$575–650 S

▶ A Japanese chromed-silver twin-engined monoplane, entitled 'The "Castle" Douglas Baby', with 'Silver Streak' in blue across the wings, wingspan 5in (12.5cm) wide, in original cardboard box.
$440–480 P(Ba)

A Dinky Toys Viking plane, c1958, 5½in (14cm) wide.
$40–50 MRW

Further Reading
Miller's Toys & Games Antiques Checklist, Miller's Publications, 1995

SHIPS

A wooden monitor boat, probably by Reed, the sides papered with lithographed scenes of firing cannons and sailors, the rotating gun turrets firing marble shots, c1885, 25½in (65cm) long.
$2,200–2,500 S(NY)

A Bing tinplate clockwork 'Trans-atlantique' three-funnel liner, third series, finished in black, white and red, 2 of 8 lifeboats missing, c1920, 25¼in (64cm) long.
$1,800–2,200 S(S)

▶ A German tinplate clockwork four-funnel liner, repainted in cream, black and red, some parts missing, c1930, 11½in (29cm) long.
$350–400 S(S)

TRAINS

A Bassett-Lowke gauge 0 electric 4-6-2 A3 'Flying Scotsman' locomotive, finished in BR green, 1930s, boxed.
$1,000–1,150 AH

A Bassett-Lowke gauge 0 electric 0-6-0 LMS tank locomotive, finished in black, c1935, boxed.
$400–450 AH

A Bassett-Lowke gauge 0 locomotive with tender, finished in red and brown, 1948, engine 10½in (26.5cm) long, boxed.
$675–750 WaH

A Bowman gauge 0 steam locomotive, fired by methylated spirits, finished in LNER green livery, 1930, 9in (23cm) long.
$200–250 WaH

Hornby Trains

- The first Hornby gauge 0 train sets were launched in 1920 by Frank Hornby, the inventor of Meccano.
- Early, rather crude and clumsy examples were replaced with more realistic designs by 1923, and the first electric train was produced in 1925.
- From the early 1930s the range became increasingly lifelike. Particularly desirable pieces from this period include the bright yellow Colman's Mustard van, and the 4-6-2 LMS Princess Elizabeth train.
- The Hornby-Dublo range was launched in 1938. Inexpensive clockwork versions were also available but only produced until 1940, which has led to their increased value today.
- Trains in the nationalized British Railways liveries were produced from 1953, the range being redesigned and upgraded to a two-rail system in 1957.
- From 1960–64 high-quality plastic was used for a range of freight stock with diecast chassis, and both plastic and tinplate for passenger stock.
- The cost of upgrading resulted in a takeover by Triang in 1964 and, although Triang itself went out of business in 1971, Hornby Railways gauge 00 trains are still in production.

A Bing for Bassett-Lowke gauge II clockwork 4-6-2 tank locomotive, No. 2670, finished in L&NWR black livery, c1920, 17¼in (44cm) long, with 2 coaches and wagons.
$2,700–3,000 S(S)

An Erzgebirge wooden train set, with 'Stephenson' locomotive, with gilt paper lining and printed paper Midland Railway labels, c1870, 35in (89cm) long.
$650–750 S

Two Hornby No. 2 gauge 0 special Pullman coaches, finished in brown and cream with grey roofs, with opening doors, c1930, 13in (33cm) long.
$400–450 WaH

▶ A Hornby gauge 0 'Power Ethyl' tank wagon, finished in green with gold letters and white hand, 1939, 7in (18cm) long.
$200–250 WaH

◀ A Hornby No. 501 gauge 0 clockwork locomotive and tender, 1940s, 11in (28cm) long, boxed.
$160–200 STK

A Carette gauge III live-steam 4-2-0 locomotive, with spirit burner, finished in dark green livery with red and black lining, with a tender and circle of track, c1900, boxed.
$2,600–3,000 AG

A Hornby gauge 0 locomotive and tender, 'Caerphilly Castle', finished in GWR green with gold lining, 1933, 11in (28cm) long.
$650–750 WaH

21 Years Ago ...

A Hornby gauge 0 electric 4-4-0 locomotive, 'Eton', No. 900, 1950s, 15in (38cm) long. **S**

Twenty-one years ago this locomotive was valued at $450–480, a high price to pay for a Hornby steam train. A gauge 0 electric Eton locomotive of this type and condition is very hard to find, and today a good example might cost in excess of $1,200. Hornby gauge 0 items in general have risen in value but not as fast as Hornby-Dublo, which in recent years have increased considerably.

A Hornby-Dublo electric train set, early 1960s, boxed.
$100–120 GAZE

A Hornby-Dublo 'Silver King' locomotive and tender, finished in BR green, 1960s, boxed.
$180–200 AH

An American Ives standard gauge train set, comprising 3243 twin bogie electric locomotive, buffet car, parlour car, observation car, all in orange New York Central & Hudson River livery, the coaches fitted for interior lighting, and a quantity of track, c1920.
$220–260 DN

The American standard gauge is 57mm.

A Hornby Railways gauge 00 'Silver Seal Locomotive' 4-6-0 black 5 class, 1970s, box 14in (35.5cm) long.
$100–115 GAZE

A Lionel diecast and tinplate gauge 0 electric train set, No. 10887E, with 2-4-2 locomotive, 3 goods wagons, track and transformer, 1939, boxed.
$225–275 GAZE

A Lionel 'Pennsylvania' locomotive 681, 12in (30.5cm) long, and twelve-wheel bogie tender, 1960s, boxed.
$220–260 P(Ba)

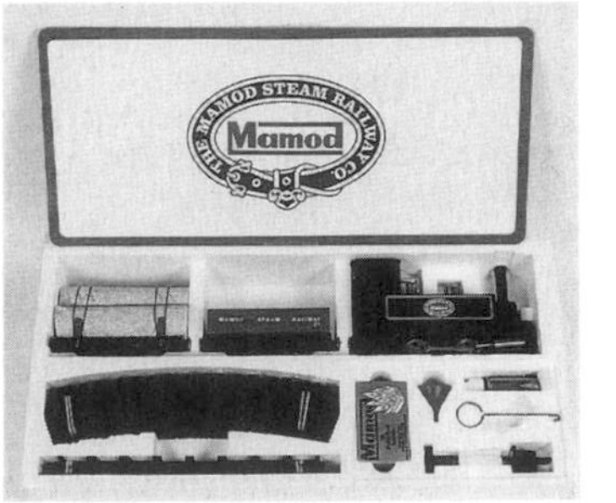

A Mamod live-steam train set, 1960s, box 24in (61cm) wide.
$375–450 GAZE

◄ A Märklin gauge 0 train set, the clockwork engine and tender finished in black, wagons in green, grey and brown, with a quantity of accessories, damaged, some parts missing, c1900.
$8,000–9,000 SK(B)

Toy Train Gauges

The gauge of a train is measured from wheel centre to wheel centre. The table below shows the different measurements of gauges.

All makers	gauge 00/H0	⅝in (16.5mm)
All makers	gauge 0	1⅜in (35mm)
All makers	gauge I	1⅞in (48mm)
All makers	gauge II	2⅛in (54mm)
Bassett-Lowke	gauge III	2⅝in (67mm)
Bing	gauge III	2⅝in (67mm)
Carette	gauge III	2⅝in (67mm)
Märklin	gauge III	3in (75mm)
Schönner	gauge III	3in (75mm)
Bassett-Lowke	gauge IV	3in (75mm)
Bing	gauge IV	3in (75mm)

A Trix Trains gauge 00 'Flying Scotsman' No. 4472 locomotive, finished in LNER green livery, with second tender, c1955, boxed.
$220–260 AH

A Trix Trains gauge 00 'Merlin' A4 4-6-4 locomotive and tender, finished in BR green livery, boxed.
$80–100 AH

VEHICLES

A Britains state coach display, set No. 1476, with figure of King Edward VIII, team of 8 horses, 4 postilions, 6 footmen and 4 yeomen, 1937, boxed.
$1,200–1,400 S(S)

A Britains 59F model Home Farm lorry, finished in yellow with black cab and chassis, metal tyres, c1940, boxed.
$325–375 S(S)

A quantity of Britains garage forecourt items, comprising 101V petrol pumps, 9V Castrol Oil cabinet, 10V Shell Oil cabinet, Castrol XL oil pumps, and No. 787 garage hand, 1956, boxed.
$900–1,000 P(Ba)

A C.I.J. tinplate clockwork Alfa Romeo racing car, finished in blue, with spoked wheels, rubber tyres, repainted, c1927, 21in (53cm) long.
$750–900 Bon(C)

A Dinky Toys No. 49 petrol pumps and oil bin set, pumps in brown, blue, green and red with yellow hoses, c1946, box 5in (12.5cm) wide.
$180–200 DN

A Dinky Toys Gift Set No. 123 'Mayfair', with a Jaguar, Rolls-Royce Silver Wraith, Mercedes-Benz, Bentley, Rolls-Royce Phantom V, Austin Mini Countryman and 3 figures, c1963, boxed.
$750–900 S(S)

A Günthermann tinplate clockwork 'Silver Bullet' record car, with chromium-plated finish and national flags applied to front and tail fins, c1930, 22½in (57cm) long.
$620–680 AH

A Hubley cast-iron coupé, painted red with cream and gold highlights, paint loss, spare tyre and driver missing, 1928, 8¾in (22cm) long.
$1,400–1,550 SK(B)

A German tinplate clockwork racing car, painted grey and maroon, possibly by Max Seidel, Nuremberg, c1920, 11in (28cm) long.
$320–360 MCA

◄ A Schuco Radio 5000 car, finished in red and maroon, c1940, 6in (15cm) long, with damaged box.
$1,000–1,200 P(Ba)

A clockwork racing car, with metallic green painted metal body, 1950s, 13¾in (35cm) long.
$200–250 CGC

A Wyandotte red steel 'La Salle' sedan, with 2 trailers, 1930s, 37in (94cm) long.
$400–500 SLN

SOLDIERS

A Britains set No. 101, The Band of the 1st Lifeguards, the 12 bandsmen wearing blue jackets with gilding, c1908, 2¼in (5.5cm) high, boxed.
$2,600–3,000 S(S)

A Britains set No. 16, The Buffs East Kent Regiment, with 7 soldiers in tan uniforms, 1895–1910, 2¼in (5.5cm) high, boxed.
$1,000–1,150 Bon

A Britains set No. 1641, Mechanical Transport and Air Force Equipment Underslung Lorry with Driver, now fitted with Britains Winch, c1938, 12in (30.5cm) long, boxed.
$400–450 S(S)

A Britains set No. 1870, Historical Series, for F. A. O. Schwartz, New York, with 16 US and foreign troops, c1940, 2¼in (5.5cm) high, boxed.
$5,250–5,750 P(Ba)

▶ A Labayen set of The Marshals of France, with Napoleon in Grenadier uniform and Louis Bonaparte, 1970, 2in (5cm) high.
$575–650 P(Ba)

◀ A Castresana set of 26 Grenadiers of the Walloon Guard, 1960, 2in (2cm) high.
$320–380 P(Ba)

A Britains set No. 29, British Army soldiers and horses, 1950s, soldiers 2¼in (5.5cm) high.
$1,000–1,100 SWO

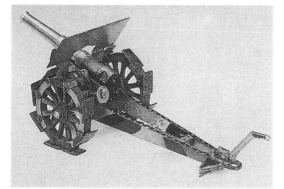

A Märklin heavy field gun, finished in dark and light green camouflage, with brass barrel, 1930s, 5in (13cm) long.
$575–650 S(S)

A set of 17 lead cavalry figures, 1920s, in a fitted box, 13in (33cm) wide.
$115–130 GAZE

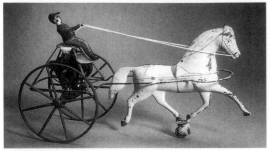

A Stevens & Brown clockwork white horse and gig, the driver in a red jacket and yellow trousers, c1870, 13½in (34.5cm) long.
$4,000–4,500 SK(B)

▶ A French papier mâché nodding minstrel automaton, with brown glass eyes, black flock hair, straw hat, red waistcoat, striped trousers and moulded boots, fingers missing, c1890, 21in (53cm) high.
$1,000–1,150 Bon(C)

An Ives white angora kitten in a black tinplate canister, c1885, 8½in (21.5cm) high.
$8,000–9,000 S(NY)

When wound, the top of the canister rises, revealing the kitten which turns around and sticks out its tongue, then abruptly disappears as the top drops down.

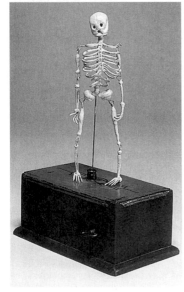

A clockwork skeleton dancer, attributed to Ives, on a tinplate-topped wooden base concealing the mechanism, c1895, 11½in (29cm) high.
$4,000–5,000 S(NY)

This figure is also known as McGinty Dancer.

A monkey trio automaton, with articulated heads and arms, within a floral arch on an ebonized base, the spring drive stamped 'J. Phalibois à Paris', dome and musical movement missing, 19thC, 22in (56cm) high.
$1,000–1,200 P(L)

A French mechanical poodle, c1900, 9½in (24cm) high.
$200–250 GrD

A French clockwork lion, probably by Roullet & Decamps, with skin covering and carved wooden feet, stop/start tail, one eye missing, c1900, 9½in (24cm) long, with lion's cage.
$230–260 Bon(C)

A Schonau & Hoffmeister bisque-headed clown, with wire and wood body, clanging cymbals movement, incised mark, c1900, 12in (30.5cm) high.
$650–750 YC

A German clockwork papier mâché nodding calf, with brown and white hide covering, brown glass eyes, mechanism inoperative, c1900, 20in (51cm) long.
$375–450 S(S)

Cross Reference
See Colour Review

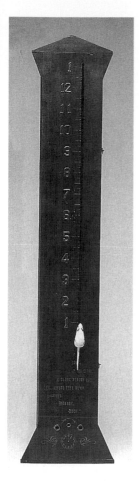

An American celluloid clockwork toy, c1920, 6in (15cm) high.
$1,600–1,800 SMAM

◀ A Dungan & Klump Dickory Dickory Dock clock, the wooden case with brass numerals, original instruction label, Philadelphia, c1900, 42in (106.5cm) high.
$1,450–1,600 S(NY)

▶ A Japanese Popeye the Sailor Man celluloid clockwork toy, c1930, 9in (23cm) high.
$500–600 Bon(C)

A Corgi Magic Roundabout Playground, with hand-operated roundabout and train track, clockwork musical see-saw, c1973, box 16 x 32in (40.5 x 81.5cm).
$575–650 DN

A Mickey Mouse clockwork hurdy-gurdy, with Minnie Mouse dancing on the roof, Minnie and one of Mickey's arms replaced, c1931, 6in (15cm) long.
$4,500–5,500 S(NY)

MONEY BOXES

An American painted cast-iron mechanical money box, c1878, 6in (15cm) high.
$325–400 HUM

A Shephard Hardware Co cast-iron Uncle Sam money bank, patented 1886, 11¼in (28.5cm) high.
$1,100–1,300 Bon(C)

A J. & E. Stevens cast-iron money bank, 'Always did 'spise a mule', with seated jockey on the base, c1890, 10in (25.5cm) wide.
$115–130 EH

An American cast-iron 'Dinah' money bank, late 19thC, 6½in (16.5cm) high.
$115–140 Bon(C)

ROCKING HORSES

A wooden rocking horse, probably by F. H. Ayres, with glass eyes, leather bridle and saddle, original cream finish, on a trestle base, c1880, 44in (111.5cm) high.
$3,000–3,300 S(S)

A carved pine rocking horse, by F. H. Ayres, painted dapple grey, mane replaced, patent stamp for 1880, 60in (152.5cm) long.
$5,200–5,800 MID

An Austrian skin-covered rocking horse, c1880, 42in (106.5cm) long.
$250–300 ESA

A carved-wood rocking horse, with glass eyes, leather saddle, traces of original paint, on pine rockers, 19thC, 36in (91.5cm) high.
$650–800 JAA

A wooden rocking horse, the rockers with 2 seats, repainted grey, base repainted brown, late 19thC, 51½in (131cm) high.
$2,500–3,000 S(S)

A painted pine rocking horse, with horsehair mane and tail, on a stencilled red base, c1900, 37in (94cm) long.
$400–500 DuM

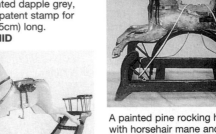

► A wooden rocking horse, painted dapple grey, early 20thC, 32¼in (82cm) high.
$575–650 WL

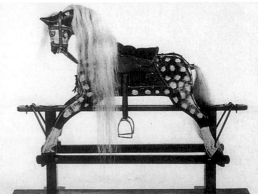

A wooden rocking horse, by Collinson, painted dapple grey, with long white mane and tail, restored, 1950s, 39in (99cm) high.
$1,300–1,450 S(S)

► A stuffed fabric rocking horse, by Pegasus, with leather saddle, 1950s, 36in (91.5cm) high.
$1,150–1,300 OOLA

MISCELLANEOUS TOYS & GAMES

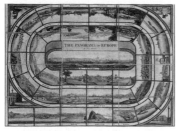

A hand-coloured engraved folding board game, 'The Panorama of Europe, A New Game', by J. & E. Wallis, mounted on linen, depicting 40 European cities with London at the centre, dated 'Nov 1st 1815', 12 x 14in (30.5 x 35.5cm).
$320–380 L

A flip toy, depicting Napoleon III, with 4 double-sided hand-coloured lithographed sections, turned wood handle, in a slip-case, c1850, 7¼in (18.5cm) high.
$680–760 SK(B)

A Victorian walnut, ormolu and agate-mounted box, containing a cribbage board, marker board, 2 ebonized and ivory hand scorers and a pack of cards, gilt engraved plaque for Robinson, Shrewsbury, 7in (18cm) square.
$1,300–1,450 AAV

A Victorian pine games compendium, the hinged lid and front enclosing a chess set, cribbage board and a variety of other games, 12¾in (32.5cm) wide.
$575–650 VOS

A travelling chess set, with bone chessmen, c1890, 10in (25.5cm) square.
$160–200 TMi

An Edwardian mahogany games box, the top with painted ivory dice, domino pieces and counter, the top drawer with wooden chessmen, the lower drawer with poker chips, 17¾in (45cm) wide.
$575–650 SLM

A set of 48 paper-covered wooden blocks, by McLoughlin Bros, with a picture of Santa Claus and 5 other scenes, c1890, 15in (38cm) wide.
$1,800–2,200 S(NY)

A game entitled 'The New Pretty Village School House Set', by McLoughlin Bros, with 4 buildings, figures, trees and hedges, all litho-coloured on card, some wear, c1903, 12 x 15in (30.5 x 38cm).
$140–155 HAM

A 'Taurus' 915-piece jigsaw puzzle, by Parr, predominantly orange with black outlined bull, 1960s, 23¼ x 18½in (59 x 47cm).
$680–760 SK(B)

A French table-top football game, 'Footo-Ballon', by Geogro, with solid-cast lead teams of 11, hooped shirts, red and white against blue and white, leather ball and grid-marked pitch, c1908, pitch 27 x 37in (68.5 x 94cm), in original fitted box.
$1,300–1,450 S(S)

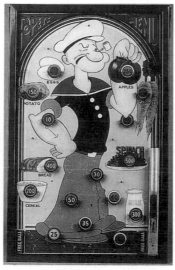

◄ A Popeye bagatelle game, by Durable Toy & Novelty Corp, New York, with brightly-coloured tinplate board and half-circles for catching the balls, c1935, 23 x 14in (58.5 x 35.5cm).
$575–650 Bon(C)

Ephemera

ANNUALS, BOOKS & COMICS

Mickey Mouse Holiday Special, published by Odhams, 1936.
$70–80 CBP

More Adventures of Rupert, Daily Express Annual, 1937, 4°.
$320–350 DW

Kaanga, Jungle King, No. 7, featuring Beast-Men of Mombasa, published by Fiction House, 1951.
$180–200 CBP

◄ *The Dandy Monster Comic*, published by D. C. Thomson, 1952, 2°.
$65–80 DW

► *Dan Dare, Pilot of the Future*, a pop-up book, published by Juvenile Productions Ltd, 1953.
$280–320 CBP

The Beano Comic, No. 1, published by D. C. Thomson, 1938, with free gift whoopee mask.
$11,500–13,000 CBP

There are very few copies in existence, and this whoopee mask is the only example known to have survived.

The Beano Book, No 1, 1940.
$5,000–5,500 CBP

AUTOGRAPHS

George III, a signed letter dated 'June 12th, 1805', to the Commissioners approving the revising of the civil affairs of the Navy, one page, 8°.
$380–420 DW

A Royal Academy admittance card, signed in ink by J. M. W. Turner, 1820, 2¼ x 3½in (6 x 9cm).
$530–600 DW

Walt Whitman, an albumen print portrait photograph, signed in ink and dated '1885', 5¾ x 3½in (14.5 x 9cm).
$680–760 RTo

Edward VII, a signed photograph by Russell & Son, of the King and 4 grandchildren outside Osborne House, dated '1902', 11 x 7in (28 x 18cm).
$1,600–2,000 Bon

Harpo Marx, a signed and annotated photograph, dated '1949', 10 x 8in (25.5 x 20.5cm).
$650–800 Bon

Franklin D. Roosevelt, a signed and inscribed photograph, dated '7 May 1935', 11 x 8¾in (28 x 22cm), framed and glazed.
$1,800–2,200 S(NY)

This is a rare photograph of President Roosevelt in which his leg braces are clearly visible. It was sent to the New England Peabody House for Crippled Children in 1935.

◀ An original painting of Christopher Lee as Dracula, by Elizabeth Roberts, signed by Christopher Lee at his Fan Club Convention, London, 1974, 21 x 15in (53.5 x 38cm).
$180–220 CBP

Charles Chaplin, a signed pencil self-caricature, dated '30th September 1931', 4½ x 3½in (11.5 x 9cm).
$575–650 VS

Harold Wilson, a signed colour photograph dedicated to Sally and James, dated '1984', 11 x 8in (28 x 20.5cm).
$90–110 FRa

CIGARETTE CARDS

Carreras Ltd, Old Staffordshire Figures, set of 24,1926.
$35–40 MAr

W. A. & A. C. Churchman, Well-Known Ties, set of 50, 1934.
$50–60 MAr

W. D. & H. O. Wills, Actresses, set of 52, c1897.
$600–650 VS

Ogdens Ltd, Picturesque Villages, set of 50, 1936.
$50–65 MAr

POSTCARDS

A postcard showing Stockport Fire Brigade turnout, 1900–14.
$35–40 VS

A postcard showing New York City skyline, published by C. G. Frey, New Jersey, c1900.
$55–65 PIn

A postcard showing Waterford Post Office, c1903.
$16–20 WA

A set of 18 postcards showing views of the Saint Louis World's Fair expo exhibit buildings, published in Germany, 1904.
$550–650 PIn

A postcard showing Bray Post Office, Co Wicklow, 1905.
$35–40 WA

A postcard decorated with violets, inscribed 'A Happy Birthday Be Yours', 1908.
$3–5 THA

A postcard showing an accident involving a Whitechapel flat-bed steam lorry, 1906.
$50–55 VS

Two Louis Wain 'Diabolo' postcards, entitled 'The Stick Trick' and 'Quite Professional', Tuck Oilette series 9563, c1908.
$80–100 DN

A postcard showing Southampton Docks Railway Station, 1914–18.
$40–50 VS

"I SHOULD FINK THAT STORK'S ABOUT AGAIN!"

An embroidered Royal Engineers postcard, 1914–18.
$16–20 MAC

◄ A Mabel Lucie Attwell postcard, c1930.
$8–10 CMF

A postcard, by W. R. Ellam, entitled 'Some Story', c1916.
$3–5 JMC

► A postcard of the Cunard ship, *Queen Elizabeth*, 1950–60.
$5–8 COB

POSTERS

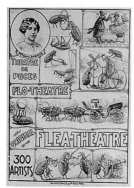

A poster advertising the Théâtre de Puces, with a portrait of the owner Mme Anna Ambros, lithographed in black and mounted on linen, Paris, c1900, 39¼ x 27¼in (99.5 x 69cm).
$600–700 Bon

A poster advertising Peugeot, by Roger Broders, c1923, 63 x 47¼in (160 x 120cm).
$1,400–1,600 ONS

A Red Star Line poster, by L. Rayon, on linen, before 1934, 37½ x 25¾in (95 x 65.5cm).
$525–600 VSP

◄ A poster, inscribed Brioni, with polo player, 1937, 39¼ x 26¾in (99.5 x 68cm).
$650–750 ONS

A poster advertising Jane Eyre, 1943, 36 x 14in (91.5 x 35.5cm).
$525–600 S

An LNER poster, by Septimus Edwin Scott, advertising Dovercourt Bay Holiday Lido, c1935, 40 x 25in (102 x 63.5cm).
$1,300–1,450 Bon(C)

◄ An MGM poster advertising Mutiny On The Bounty, linen-backed, 1935, 81in (205.5cm) square.
$3,250–4,000 S

Further Reading

Miller's Collectables Price Guide, Miller's Publications, 1999–2000.

A poster advertising The Seven Year Itch, 1955, 41 x 27in (104 x 68.5cm).
$1,000–1,250 S

A *Thunderball* poster, 1965, 30 x 40in (76 x 102cm).
$600–700 Bon

Rock & Pop

A manuscript for 'To Know Him Is To Love Him', the words and music in pencil and ink on a sheet of paper, c1958, with Spector's music score and an American copyright document dated '16th July 1958' for the song.
$8,000–9,500 Bon

A signed copy of 'Bob Dylan', Dylan's first LP released in 1962.
$1,300–1,450 Bon(C)

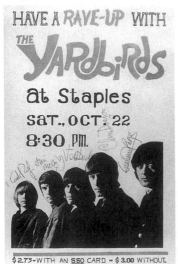

A Yardbirds poster, advertising their concert on October 22nd 1966, Connecticut, signed by each member of the group including Jimmy Page, and 6 previously unpublished black and white photographs of members of the group.
$3,000–3,300 S(NY)

A printed promotional flyer for 'Swinging Lunch Time Rock Sessions', at the Liverpool Jazz Society, starring The Beatles, Gerry and the Pacemakers, and Rory Storm and the Wild Ones, c1961, 7½ x 5½in (19 x 14cm).
$1,000–1,100 Bon

A three-page contract between Andrew Loog Oldham, Eric Easton and Brian Jones, witnessed by Mick Jagger, dated '9th May, 1963' and signed by all parties.
$11,000–12,000 Bon

A typed letter from John Lennon to Mal Evans, addressed from 'Kenwood Mixer Weybridge on Toast', with original envelope postmarked '15 June 1967'.
$4,000–5,000 S(NY)

A black and white photograph of Elvis Presley and Bill Haley, mounted with a signed envelope, c1959, framed and glazed, 23 x 19in (58.5 x 48.5cm).
$650–800 Bon

A handbill for a concert at the Odeon, Leeds, featuring The Beatles, The Brook Brothers, Peter Jay and the Jaywalkers and others, 1963, 12 x 5½in (30.5 x 14cm).
$1,500–1,300 Bon

The Beatles Yellow Submarine, Corgi Toys, in a box, with *The Yellow Submarine Gift Book*, 1968.
$320–360 CBP

Janis Joplin, an autograph on the reverse of part of a piece of International Hotel, Los Angeles, notepaper, 1968.
$900–1,000 S(NY)

A poster advertising The First Jim Morrison Film Festival, 27 March, 1970', 23 x 17½in (58.5 x 44.5cm).
$1,800–2,000 S(NY)

A Jethro Tull black and white concert poster, Detroit, signed in pencil by Gary Grimshaw, 1976, 21 x 14in (53.5 x 35.5cm).
$200–250 Bon(C)

A four-page letter handwritten by Madonna, to Marilyn Fellows, her former history teacher, discussing the influence she had upon her, c1978, and a two-page xerox of a newspaper article, mid-80's, .
$6,500–7,500 S(NY)

◄ John Lennon 'smile' box, walnut veneered and embossed in gold on the lid 'A Box of Smile, Yoko Ono, 1971', 4in (10cms) wide.
$4,000–4,500 S(NY)

According to the vendor, Yoko Ono gave the box to John Lennon as a gift to hold his 'stash'.

A Tristar International Rolling Stones red mouth and tongue telephone, 1984, box 12in (30.5cm) square.
$650–800 Bon

A silver scarf, signed and inscribed by Marc Bolam of T Rex, 1975, 36in (91.5cm) long.
$250–300 VS

A colour cover of *Q Magazine,* signed by Oasis, January 1988, 10 x 8½in (25.5 x 20.5cm).
$80–100 VS

► A photograph of U2, signed by Bono and The Edge, 1997, 11 x 8in (28 x 20.5cm).
$180–200 VS

Scientific Instruments

COMPASSES & DIALS

A Butterfield silver dial, engraved with 4 hour scales, the base engraved with 28 cities and their latitudes, signed, in a fitted velvet-lined fishskin case, French, early 18thC, 2¼in (6cm) wide.
$1,300–1,450 S

A universal equinoctial pocket sundial, probably German, with latitude arc, hinged hour ring and gnomon, base engraved with latitudes for European cities, mid-18thC, 2in (5cm) diam.
$650–800 S

A W. Burucker fruitwood and printed paper cylinder dial, the base unscrews to reveal a floating card compass, single draw, a spyglass in boxwood with marbled paper to the tubes, signed, Nuremberg, c1800, 6½in (16.5cm) high.
$3,250–4,000 S

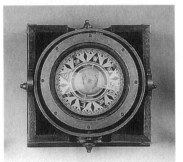

A Husun compass, signed 'H. Hughes & Son', in a brass-bound mahogany case, early 20thC, 7½in (19cm) diam.
$400–450 Bon

An Irish bronze sundial, the plate signed 'James Lynch, Dublin', c1800, 11¾in (30cm) diam.
$1,400–1,600 HOK

A bronze sundial, signed 'D. Voster', Cork, 18thC, 11¾in (30cm) square.
$2,800–3,200 HOK

Daniel Voster was the son of Elias Voster, the first known instrument maker in Cork. Daniel's death is recorded in May 1760.

A brass mining dial, signed 'Troughton & Simms, London', in mahogany case, 19thC, 11½in (29cm) long.
$400–450 Mit

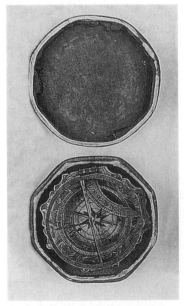

An Andreas Vogler brass universal equinoctial dial, with engraved scroll decoration and inset compass well, with folding hour ring and latitude arc, signed, c1780, 2¼in (5.5cm) wide.
$575–650 Bon

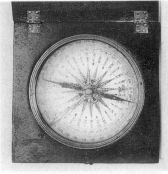

A compass, with blued steel needle, in a mahogany case with hinged cover, mid-19thC, 4¾in (12cm) wide.
$200–250 Bon

◀ An Irish compass, signed 'Yeates & Son, Dublin', in a rosewood case with hinged cover, c1860, 2½in (6.5cm) wide.
$300–330 Bon

GLOBES & SPHERES

A 2¾in (7cm) diam pocket terrestrial globe, retailed by J. Abraham, Bath, in an imitation fishskin-covered case, the inside with printed celestial map, 1843.
$2,000–2,500 BWe

A 15in (38cm) diam collapsible terrestrial globe, by John Betts, London, printed in colour on 8 silk gores mounted on a black enamelled brass umbrella-type frame, c1860.
$575–650 P

This is the first edition of this popular globe, subsequently re-issued by George Philip & Son.

An American floor globe, by A. H. Andrews & Co, Chicago, on a printed papered-wood medial frame with astrological signs and months of the year, raised on a cast-iron stand, late 19thC, 18in (45.5cm) diam.
$1,800–2,200 B&B

A pair of 12in (30.5cm) diam terrestrial and celestial globes, by William Bardin, each with a turned stand, minor losses and damage, c1782.
$13,500–15,500 SK

This model by Bardin was the first to use the term United States of America, only months after the surrender of Cornwallis at Yorktown. William Bardin first began publishing globes in the 1780s in collaboration with Gabriel Wright. William's son Thomas joined the business after Wright's death in 1783.

A 3½in (9cm) diam pocket terrestrial globe, by J. & W. Cary, with 12 hand-coloured paper gores, the oceans recording the 3 voyages of Captain Cook, Tasmania shown joined to Australia, in original fishskin-covered case, the interior with engraved and coloured celestial chart, c1796.
$5,800–6,400 P

A 9in (23cm) diam terrestrial table globe, by J. & W. Cary, showing the various discoveries of Captain Cook and others, c1813.
$14,000–16,000 WW

Globe Stands

The cost of a globe, which in itself was comparatively inexpensive to produce, was determined by the quality of its stand. Examples of globes were usually included in the catalogues of the best cabinet-makers.

Early stands, consisting of four or more turned wood pillars uniting the horizon ring and the circular base, are rarely found. The tripod stand, often in mahogany or walnut, was introduced in the mid-18thC. There were many variations, but elegant examples with a central pillar and cabriole legs were particularly popular.

In the late 18thC globe-makers such as Bardin, Cary and Wright introduced four-pillared table stands with bobbin-turned stretchers. Sometimes a compass was incorporated into the centre, but this was more usual with floor-standing examples.

In the early 19thC smaller globes of less than 18in (45.5cm) diam began to appear. They were often supported on baluster-turned, ebonized, single-pillar stands, and examples in cast-metal are also found.

Towards the end of the 19thC the decorative nature of the globe was taking precedence, and stands often represent both the finest crafts-manship and the prevailing tastes of the day. Examples from this period sometimes incorporated a mechanical device which enabled them to rotate.

A 15in (38cm) diam new terrestrial globe, exhibiting the discoveries in Africa, North Pole, Australia, New Zealand, California, Texas, inscribed 'G. S. Cruchley', on a stand with turned legs, London, 1868.
$2,000–2,500 HYD

A 15in (38cm) diam new terrestrial globe, by Cary, published London, 1844, showing the new discoveries with the tracks of the principal navigators, raised on a mahogany stand with tulip decoration.
$11,500–13,000 B

A French geocentric ptolemaic armillary sphere, by Delamarche, the ecliptic with named zodiac and calendar scales, the horizon ring with zodiac, calendar and wind direction scales supported by 4 quadrants bearing the latitude and longitude of selected places, on an ebonized driftwood stand, late 18thC, 11in (28cm) diam.
$6,500–7,500 P

A 12in (30.5cm) diam terrestrial table globe, by J. Felkl & Son, Rostock & Prague, on an ebonized turned stand, c1870–87.
$650–750 Mit

A Husun star globe, with brass dome framework and circular scale, inscribed 'H. Hughes & Son Ltd, London, 1920, in a stained-wood carrying case, 10½in (27cm) square.
$1,000–1,150 HCC

Husun was the trade name of H. Hughes & Son.

An 18in (45.5cm) diam celestial globe, by Malby, signed and dated for 1855 and 1860, in an engraved brass meridian ring, mid-19thC.
$6,500–7,500 P

Large globes such as this 18in (45.5cm) example are popular today.

A 10in (25.5cm) diam terrestrial table globe, by Thomas Malby & Son, including all the recent geographical discoveries, with brass half circumference, London, 1875, on a turned mahogany stand.
$1,150–1,300 Mit

A 3in (7.5cm) diam pocket celestial globe, by John Newton, with 12 hand-coloured gores, the horizon circle mounted with degrees of celestial longitude and latitude and the hours, the ecliptic circle marked in degrees, in a turned green-painted box, early 19thC.
$2,600–3,200 P

A 12in (30.5cm) diam celestial globe, by John Senex & Benjamin Martin, composed of 12 printed and hand-coloured gores, the constellation figures delicately coloured, with engraved brass hour circle, brass meridian ring engraved on one face, printed and coloured horizon circle, on a stand, late 18thC.
$5,250–6,000 Bon

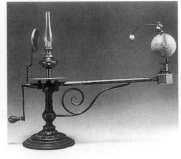

A Continental cast-iron 4in (10cm) diam tellurium globe, within brass bands representing celestial circles and the zodiac, revolving on a hand-cranked turntable-form brass stand with engraved horizon, with an oil lamp, late 19th/early 20thC.
$6,500–7,500 S(NY)

A celestial globe, by Newton & Son, with mahogany stand, mid-19thC, 40½in (103cm) high.
$4,200–4,800 SLN

MEDICAL & DENTAL

A burr-walnut dentist's cabinet, the top doors revealing fitted shelving with 12 graduated drawers below, marblework surface, lower right side door reveals sliding lead-lined specimen drawers with storage space below, mid-19thC, 69in (175.5cm) high.
$2,750–3,250 Bon

An Irish George III brass-bound mahogany apothecary's case, some bottles labelled Francis Scott, Dundalk, a drawer below with secret poison compartment, 8in (20.5cm) wide.
$1,600–2,000 MEA

A mahogany medicine chest, the double doors both revealing 3 shelves of 3 bottles and a shelf containing 5 glass medicine bottles above 4 drawers, the bottom drawer with compartmented test tube holders, early 19thC, 22½in (57cm) high.
$5,200–5,700 S

A similar medicine chest is illustrated in Richard Reece's medical guide from 1814 as a 'Family Dispensary'. In his *Practical Dictionary of Domestic Medicine*, Reece wrote that one person at least in every village or parish where a medical man does not reside, ought to be provided with a medicine chest.

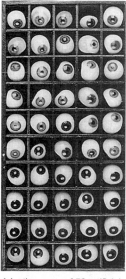

A leather case of 50 artificial eyes, in various shades of blue and brown, late 19thC, 12¾in (32.5cm) wide.
$800–900 Bon

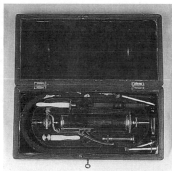

► A lacquered brass enema, with ebony and bone fittings, in a plush-lined mahogany case, c1875, 12¼in (31cm) wide.
$300–330 Bon

An early Victorian rosewood and brass-bound medicine chest, the plush-lined interior with glass bottles, above a drawer with slides and bottles, 12in (30.5cm) wide.
$900–1,000 WW

A mahogany apothecary's chest, with fitted interior, the rear with sliding door containing bottles, early 19thC, 8¾in (22cm) wide.
$1,000–1,150 P(S)

A Victorian glass leech bowl,
13in (33cm) high.
$400–500 RUL

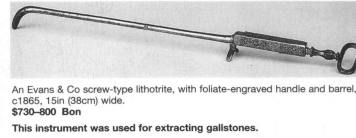

An Evans & Co screw-type lithotrite, with foliate-engraved handle and barrel,
c1865, 15in (38cm) wide.
$730–800 Bon

This instrument was used for extracting gallstones.

Five chemist's ointment jars, c1870, 10in (25.5cm) high.
$600–700 MIL

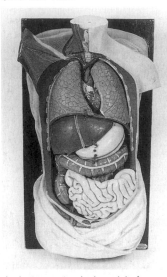

A plaster anatomical model of a
human torso, bearing a label marked
'Prof Dr. W. Benninghoven, Berlin',
early 20thC, 46in (117cm) high.
$575–650 JBe

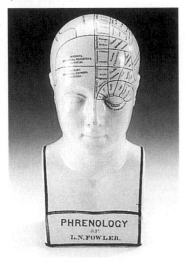

A ceramic phrenology head, by
L. N. Fowler, with dark brown
edge line decoration, mid-19thC,
12in (30.5cm) high.
$2,300–2,600 S

A scarifier, with bleeding cups, in
a mahogany box with brass handle,
early 19thC, box 9½in (24cm) high.
$700–770 DN(H)

A steel tooth key, with ivory handle,
c1840, 6in (15cm) long.
$230–260 HUM

A horn-cased lorgnette, c1840,
4in (10cm) wide.
$160–200 HUM

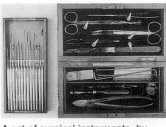

A set of surgical instruments, by
C. Wright & Co, with signed bone-
handled scalpels, suture clips, suture
case forceps, ebony-handled saw
and pliers, c1860, in a mahogany
box 9½in (24cm) wide.
$1,000–1,200 Bon

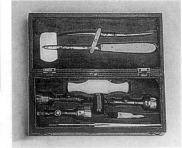

A Millikin trepanning set, signed,
in a red plush-lined mahogany case,
1820–30, 7¾in (20cm) wide.
$1,600–1,800 Bon

◄ A silver medicine spoon, by
Thomas Johnson, London 1874,
4¼in (11cm) long.
£220–240 S(S)

A tortoiseshell table snuff box, inlaid with brass and silver, with articulated tortoiseshell and silver turtle finial, dated '1642', 6in (15cm) wide.
$2,000–2,500 MB

An Italian ebony, rock crystal and glass christening casket, with panels inlaid with agate within chased silver borders, late 17thC, 12½in (32cm) wide.
$68,000–78,000 P

An Italian coral and mother-of-pearl inlaid casket, with red velvet-lined interior, probably Naples, early 18thC, 22¼in (56.5cm) wide.
$113,000–130,000 S(NY)

A mahogany knife box, c1790, 14in (35.5cm) high.
$650–800 AnSh

A French straw-work love token box, c1800, 3in (7.5cm) wide.
$200–250 HUM

▶ A Vizagapatam rosewood and marquetry box, the interior with lidded compartments above a drawer, early 19thC, 12½in (32cm) wide.
$4,200–5,000 DN

A walnut and ebony-veneered collector's cabinet, with side handles, 18thC, 12½in (32cm) wide.
$1,300–1,500 TMA

A kingwood tea caddy, with gilt-metal paw feet, c1810, 8in (20.5cm) wide.
$325–350 Bon

A Regency tortoiseshell, ivory-strung and mother-of-pearl inlaid work box, with silk lined interior, 9¾in (25cm) wide.
$1,600–2,000 P

A rosewood and brass-inlaid dressing case, the fitted interior with silver-mounted jars and bottles, 1821 and later, 13⅛in (34.5cm) wide.
$1,300–1,500 S(S)

A William IV tortoiseshell tea caddy, 8in (20.5cm) wide.
$2,000–2,300 TMi

A straw-work dressing case, the banded lid applied with a print of 2 cherubs, early 19thC, 17in (43cm) wide.
$1,000–1,150 P

◄ A Victorian japanned table desk, the lid forming the slope, 12in (30.5cm) wide.
$500–575 RBB

A rosewood brass-banded and cedar-lined cigar box, c1830, 10in (25.5cm) wide.
$500–575 MB

An agate and marble trinket box, the lid with a star within a gilt-metal engine-turned frame, on ivory ball feet, 19thC, 2¾in (7cm) wide.
$200–250 TMA

A Killarney writing box, the slope with a view of Muckrose Abbey, c1860, 15in (38cm) wide.
$1,200–1,400 STA

A fruitwood box, in the form of a miniature trunk, with brass lock and clasp, late 19thC, 6½in (16.5cm) wide.
$3,800–4,200 S

A fruitwood snuff box, the lid with rolled paper decoration, c1840, 3in (7.5cm) diam.
$300–330 HUM

▶ A carved ivory box, c1900, 10in (25.5cm) wide.
$800–1,000 AnS

A French 'jewelled' turquoise-enamelled and gilt-bronze jewellery box, painted with lovers in 18thC costume, late 19thC, 7¼in (18.5cm) wide.
$2,000–2,300 B&B

A tortoiseshell snuff box, with an enamel plaque of a hound, painted by J. W. Bailey, 19thC, 3in (7.5cm) diam.
$3,000–3,300 BHa

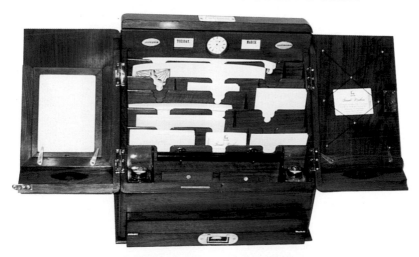

A Victorian rosewood, satinwood-inlaid and walnut-cased brass cylinder music box, playing 10 airs, 20in (51cm) wide.
$2,500–2,700 HAX

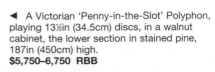

An Edison Red Gem phonograph, playing 2 and 4 minute cylinders, c1910, 25in (63.5cm) high.
$1,300–1,600 HOL

A walnut and marquetry-inlaid Polyphon, c1897, 15in (38cm) wide.
$3,250–4,000 L&E

A 'Penny-in-the-Slot' Polyphon, playing 19¾in (50cm) discs, in a walnut cabinet, damaged, late 19thC, 24½in (62cm) wide.
$5,500–6,000 Bea

A Victorian oak gramophone, with horn, box 18in (45.5cm) wide.
$650–730 RID

An Italian cello, by G. Pedrazzini, Milan, 1922, length of back 29½in (75cm).
$52,000–57,000 Bon

An American Elmer Stromberg arch-top guitar, with maple back and sides, spruce top and ebony fingerboard with pearl block inlay, Boston, c1935, length of back 20¾in (52.5cm).
$18,500–21,000 SK

A Gothic patent concert harp, by Sebastian and Pierre Erard, with bird's-eye maple soundbox and gilt decoration, c1850, 69in (175.5cm) high.
$12,000–14,000 P

A viola, possibly composite, labelled 'Gia Bapt Grancino in contrada, Largha di Milano anno 16', c1770, 16¾in (42.5cm) long.
$14,500–16,000 Bon

A mahogany and satinwood-inlaid piano, by Bland & Weller, London, the 5 octave keyboard fitted with 2 lever stops, c1800, 63in (160cm) wide.
$800–1,000 RBB

A John Broadwood & Sons 'plum pudding' mahogany piano, restored, c1825, 62in (157.5cm) wide.
$10,500–12,000 PPC

A John Broadwood & Sons satinwood and mahogany crossbanded grand piano, with ebony and boxwood inlay, restored, c1810, 90in (228cm) long.
$40,500–48,500 PPC

◄ A Viennese figured-walnut 6 octave piano, by Gyrikowski, Prague, restored, c1825, 92in (233.5cm) long.
$56,500–59,000 PPC

◄ A Erard rosewood 6½ octave grand piano, restored, dated '1840', 94in (299cm) long.
$24,500–27,500 PPC

► A Pleyel 'plum pudding' mahogany 6½ octave grand piano, Paris, restored, c1837, 84in (213.5cm) long.
$35,000–40,000 PPC

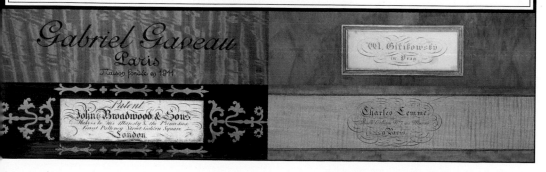

A John Broadwood & Sons
rosewood grand piano, mid-19thC,
54in (137cm) wide.
$1,800–2,000 NOA

A Steinway & Sons ebonized
7 octave grand piano, c1889,
74in (188cm) long.
$8,000–9,000 RBB

A Steinway & Sons mahogany grand
piano, decorated with trophies, floral
sprays and acanthus leaf ornament,
c1907, 83in (211cm) long.
$48,500–53,000 P(Ba)

A Weber Duo Art mahogany
crossbanded and gilt-decorated
grand piano, c1915, 78in (198cm)
wide, with a matching box stool.
$12,000–13,500 P(Ba)

An Erard burr walnut 6½ octave upright
piano, c1854, 55in (140cm) wide.
$11,000–12,000 PPC

A Bechstein mahogany Model B
grand piano, inlaid with ribbons and
swags, c1898, 78in (198cm) long.
$17,000–18,500 P(Ba)

A Gabriel Gaveau satinwood grand
piano, with ormolu mounts, restored,
c1913, 72in (183cm) long.
$24,500–27,500 PPC

An upright piano, by Oskar Dawson
& Son, Haslemere, with overstrung
movement by George Rogers,
London, inscribed with maker's
name and dated '1932', 54in
(137cm) wide, with matching stool.
$1,800–2,000 E

An Erard walnut grand piano, restored,
dated '1861', 102in (259cm) long.
$20,000–22,750 PPC

An Erard carved oak and parquetry-
inlaid straight-strung grand piano,
designed by Bruce Talbot for Gillows,
late 19thC, 105in (266.5cm) long.
$10,500–12,000 P(Ba)

A Louis XV-style bronze-mounted
mahogany and tulipwood parquetry
piano, by Burger and Jacobi,
early 20thC, 70in (178cm) wide.
$38,000–44,000 B&B

A Monington & Weston Art Deco
baby grand piano, black lacquer
trimmed in white, c1930,
56in (142cm) wide.
$21,000–24,500 S(NY)

A portrait miniature of a young man in military costume, by Frederick Buck, c1795, 2½in (6.5cm) high.
$2,400–2,600 BHa

A portrait miniature of a gentleman, by Richard Cosway, signed and dated '1792', 2½in (6.5cm) high.
$2,000–2,500 S

A portrait miniature of Lady Maria Dunglass, by Annie Dixon, signed and dated '1872', 4¼in (11cm) high, in an ormolu frame.
$2,000–2,500 Bon

A silhouette of an officer, probably John Day of the 49th Regiment, by John Buncombe, c1815, 3½in (9cm) high.
$5,000–5,500 Bon

▶ A pair of portrait miniatures of Mr and Mrs Arnold, by J. P. Dunning, in chased gilt-bronze frames, 1821, 5½in (14cm) high.
$1,100–1,300 TMA

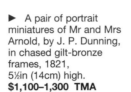

A portrait miniature of a lady, by Samuel Finney, c1770, 5in (12.5cm) high.
$3,250–3,500 BHa

A pair of portrait miniatures of Mr John Steele MP and Mrs Frances Steele, by Andrew Plimer, c1800, 3in (7.5cm) high.
$4,300–5,000 P

◀ A pair of silhouettes of a gentleman and a lady, by the circle of W. Phelps, on paper and stuck to plaster, c1790, 3½in (9cm) high.
$1,200–1,400 Bon

A portrait miniature of a lady, by E. Flavien Chabanne, signed and dated '1832', 5½in (14cm) high.
$2,300–2,600 S(NY)

A portrait miniature of Frances, Countess of Fingall, by Horace Hone, signed with monogram and dated '1786', in a silver-gilt frame, 3in (7.5cm) high.
$5,500–6,000 S

A portrait miniature of Miss Isabel Page, by John Smart, c1776, 1¾in (4.5cm) high.
$19,000–21,000 BHa

An Egyptian alabaster
vase, 2965–2750 BC,
16½in (42cm) high.
$60,000–66,000 S(NY)

An Egyptian sarcophagus lid,
the eyes missing, 1800 BC,
28in (71cm) high, cased.
$21,000–24,500 SK

An Egyptian mummy case
lid, slight damage, face
re-gilded, 1175–945 BC,
75in (190.5cm) high.
$6,500–7,250 B&B

An Egyptian composition
mummiform ushabti, with
single dorsal column of
hieroglyphs, 664–525 BC,
7¼in (18.5cm) high.
$2,600–2,800 Bon

A mummy portrait of a
woman, circa 150–200 AD,
12½in (32cm) high.
$24,500–26,500 S(NY)

A Caucasian bronze finial,
in the form of an ibex, with 2
small balls inside to produce
the effect of a rattle, fitted
into a fragmentary stand,
slight damage, 15th–14th
century BC, 6in (15cm) high.
$12,000–13,000 Bon

An Egyptian linen garment, decorated in white,
grey-black and red-brown pigments, probably
Coptic, 4th–5th century AD.
$1,750–2,000 FW&C

A Cypriot pottery stem cup,
1,000–800 BC, 8½in (21.5cm) diam.
$650–800 HEL

A Greek Black Figure
amphora, repaired,
6th–5th century BC,
9in (23cm) high.
$2,000–2,500 HEL

A Magna Graecia Apulian Red Figure ware kylix,
handle repaired, circa 300 BC, 7in (18cm) diam.
$600–650 BAC

An Anglo Saxon gold ring, misshapen,
late 10th century AD, 1in (2.5cm) wide.
$7,500–9,000 S

◄ A Greek glass amphoriskos, circa
4th century BC, 4¼in (11cm) high.
$9,000–10,500 S(NY)

A mosaic panel of the Triumph of Dionysus,
Roman Imperial, early 3rd century AD,
49½ x 65½in (125.5 x 166.5cm).
$65,000–73,000 S(NY)

An Athabaskan beaded cloth bag, Native American, 18in (46cm) high.
$1,300–1,500 P

A wool rug, Native American, c1920, 45 x 77in (114.5 x 195.5cm).
$730–800 TREA

◄ A Haida polychrome wood model totem pole, Native American, inscribed 'purchased 1939', 28⅕in (72.5cm) high.
$14,500–16,000 S(NY)

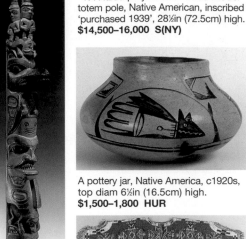

A pottery jar, Native America, c1920s, top diam 6½in (16.5cm) high.
$1,500–1,800 HUR

A Sioux beaded and fringed hide dress, and a beaded and fringed doll, Native American, 14in (35.5cm) high.
Dress $5,800–6,800
Doll $2,500–3,000 B&B

A Navajo pot, Native American, late 19thC, 9in (23cm) high.
$475–650 HEL

An Ekoi skin-covered headdress, Nigeria, 20in (51cm) high.
$1,600–2,000 LHAr

A Fanti drum, Ghana, West Africa, 25⅕in (65cm) high.
$3,000–3,250 S(NY)

A Suku helmet mask, encircled by a raffia headdress, Zaire, Africa, 25in (63.5cm) high.
$13,000–14,500 S(NY)

A Yombe female figure, the eyes inset with glass, Gabon, Congo Region, Africa, probably 19thC, 12¾in (32.5cm) high.
$10,500–11,300 S(NY)

An Admiralty Islands male figure, Melanesia, 12in (30.5cm) high.
$4,500–5,000 S(NY)

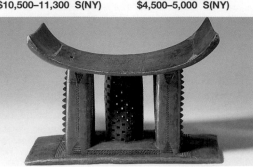

A Papuan Gulf ancestral board, carved in shallow relief with a stylized torso, Melanesia, 41¼in (105cm) long.
$2,500–2,700 P

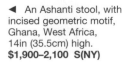

◄ An Ashanti stool, with incised geometric motif, Ghana, West Africa, 14in (35.5cm) high.
$1,900–2,100 S(NY)

A Collection of Caricatures, published by Thomas McLean, London 1829, in contemporary olive half morocco gilt over marbled boards, 20½ x 14¼in (52 x 36cm).
$5,700–6,500 Bon

Rudolph Ackermann, *The Microcosm of London*, 3 vols, first edition, London 1808–10, 10¼ x 13¼in (26 x 33.5cm).
$7,300–8,000 S

Book of Hours, an illuminated manuscript on vellum, in Latin and French, 120 leaves, Paris, c1500, 6¾ x 4¼in (17 x 11cm), rebound in gilt and green morocco.
$21,000–24,500 Bon

Eleazar Albin, *A Natural History of Birds*, and Notes and Observations by W. Derham, 2 vols, 4°, 1738, in contemporary diced calf gilt cover.
$7,300–8,000 DW

William Curtis and others, *The Botanical Magazine or Flower-Garden Displayed*, London 1787–1846, 66 vols, variously bound in 45 vols, 8¾ x 5½in (22 x 14cm).
$18,000–19,500 RTo

John Gould and R. Bowdler Sharpe, *The Birds of New Guinea and the Adjacent Papuan Islands, Including Many New Species Recently Discovered in Australia*, 5 vols, first edition, published by Henry Sotheran, 1875–88, 2°.
$53,000–56,500 Bon

Georges Cuvier, *The Animal Kingdom*, 16 vols, first edition, published by G. B. Whittaker, 1827–35, 9½ x 5¾in (24 x 14.5cm).
$6,500–7,250 S

Jessie M. King, *The High History of the Holy Graal*, translated from the French by Sebastian Evans, No. 25 of 225 copies,1903, 8°.
$17,000–18,500 S

Noel and Bertha Parker, *Jumbo's Jumble Book*, a volume of 14 pages containing nursery rhymes and illustrations of animals, pen and ink and watercolour, 1905–27, 10 x 14in (25.5 x 35.5cm).
$7,250–8,000 P(EA)

An ink and watercolour drawing, entitled *The Badger's Winter Stores*, by Arthur Rackham, c1939, 8¾ x 6½in (22.5 x 16.5cm).
$35,000–40,000 S

This watercolour was commissioned as an illustration for Kenneth Grahame's *The Wind in the Willows*.

► The Hon Lionel Walter Rothschild, *The Avifauna of Laysan and the Neighbouring Islands*, 2 vols, 1893–1900, 4°
$8,000–9,000 DW

◄ Robert Warner and B. S. Williams, *The Orchid Album comprising coloured figures and descriptions of new, rare and beautiful Orchidaceous Plants*, London 1882–97, 11 vols, 527 lithographed colour plates by John Nugent Fitch, original brown cloth cover, 12 x 9½in (30.5 x 24cm).
$18,000–20,000 RTo

A German doll, with Belton bisque head, No. TRX 809, c1880, 17in (43cm) high.
$1,200–1,400 GrD

A Danel et Cie bisque-headed *bébé* doll, c1890, 17¾in (45cm) high.
$5,000–5,750 YC

A Gaultier bisque-headed *bébé* doll, incised 'F.9.G.', c1890, 19¾in (50cm) high.
$4,000–5,000 YC

A Hertel Schwab & Co character doll, c1915, 15½in (39.5cm) high.
$900–1,000 GrD

A Heubach bisque doll, c1905, 25in (63.5cm) high.
$900–1,000 AnS

A Tête Jumeau doll, c1890, 20in (51cm) high.
$4,000–4,500 GrD

A Jumeau *bébé* bisque-headed doll, with fixed blue glass eyes, c1900, 16½in (42cm) high.
$4,500–5,000 AH

A Kämmer & Reinhardt 'Mein Liebling' bisque-headed character doll, with weighted blue glass eyes, c1911, 25in (63.5cm) high.
$5,500–6,000 Bon(C)

A J. D. Kestner bisque-headed doll, with glass eyes, c1900, 15¾in (40cm) high.
$900–1,100 YC

A Limoges bisque-headed doll, c1930, 18½in (47cm) high.
$400–450 GAZE

◄ A Jules Steiner Phénix bisque-headed *bébé* doll, with fixed blue glass paperweight eyes, c1890, 23¼in (59cm) high.
$5,750–6,750 S

An Armand Marseille bisque-headed doll, with weighted blue eyes, c1910, 23½in (60cm) high.
$1,000–1,250 CGC

A Simon & Halbig bisque-headed doll, c1900, 19in (48cm) high.
$800–900 YC

◄ A Simon & Halbig doll, with 'flirty' eyes, c1900, 30in (76cm) high.
$1,250–1,500 AnS

A Steiff golden plush teddy bear, with centre seam, c1908, 18in (45.5cm) high.
$2,500–2,700 Sim

A Steiff teddy bear, with felt pads and glass eyes, c1915, 19in (48.5cm) high.
$1,400–1,600 BGC

A Steiff mohair plush teddy bear, with felt pads and glass eyes, 1940s, 16in (40.5cm) high.
$1,000–1,200 BGC

A teddy bear, with pointed snout, hump and glass eyes, repaired, c1920, 20in (51cm) high.
$525–575 GAZE

An American cotton plush cowboy bear, c1940, 13in (33cm) high.
$300–400 TED

A Merrythought Cheeky silk plush bear, with glass eyes, c1957, 15in (38cm) high.
$275–325 TED

An Austrian white mohair teddy bear, with brown glass eyes, c1950, 19½in (49.5cm) high.
$160–200 Bon(C)

▶ A teddy bear, 1950s, 15in (38cm) high.
$140–160 AnS

A Bowman 0 gauge live-steam tank locomotive, c1935, 9in (23cm) long.
$200–220 DQ

A Hornby Dublo three-rail locomotive and tender, with nickel-plated wheels, c1962, 7in (18cm) long.
$325–375 WaH

A Märklin live-steam locomotive, c1912, 12in (30.5cm) long.
$500–575 DQ

An 0 gauge finescale two-rail motorised LSWR Drummonds 'Bug', c1970, 10in (25.5cm) long.
$1,500–1,750 RAR

A Bing tinplate clockwork 'vis-a-vis' car, slight damage, early 20thC, 10in (25.5cm) long.
$3,250–4,000 Bea

A set of 7 Labayen figures of Napoleon and his Generals, 1970, 2¼in (5.5cm) high.
$850–950 P(Ba)

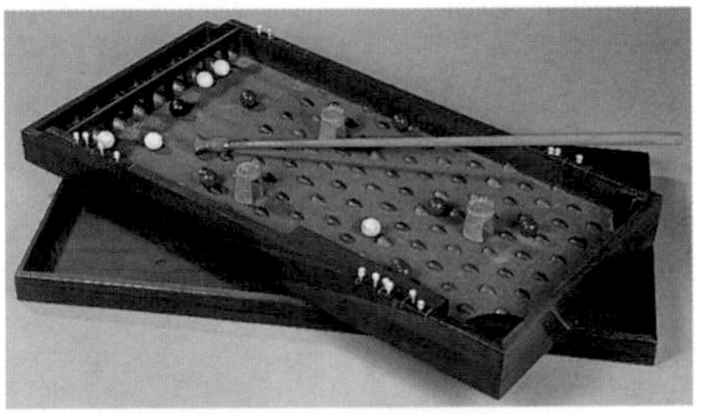

A mahogany travelling cockamaroo, or Russian bagatelle board, 19thC, 24in (61cm) long.
$1,000–1,200 P

A French clockwork figure of a maid, with a pile of plates that scatter when she falls over, c1920, 6in (15cm) high, in original box.
$4,800–5,200 S(NY)

A German bisque-headed clown, with moving head and arms, on a pull-along trolley, c1890, 12in (30cm) high.
$1,000–1,200 YC

A Tudor-style two-storey dolls' house, with battery-operated lighting, partly furnished, 1940s, 29in (73.5cm) wide.
$200–250 GAZE

◄ A carved wooden rocking horse, probably by G. & J. Lines, 1920s, 36in (91.5cm) high.
$625–725 GAZE

► A late Victorian wooden rocking horse, on bow rocker, 29in (74cm) high.
$1,000–1,200 WL

A Victorian 8-day marine chronometer, by D. McGregor & Co, Glasgow and Greenock, signed, c1860, 5¾in (14.5cm) diam, in a mahogany brass-inlaid case.
$8,000–9,000 S(Am)

A French nautical brass clock, aneroid barometer and thermometer, in the form of an anchor, with 8-day movement, c1880, 11in (28cm) wide.
$1,600–1,800 OT

A ship's 8-day desk clock, modelled on HMS *Repulse*'s boiler, c1912, 9½in (24cm) high.
$750–900 K&D

A Napoleonic prisoner-of-war bone model of HM Frigate *Latona*, early 19thC, 22in (56cm) long, resting on a bone base, in a glazed case.
$26,000–30,000 Bon

► A course plotter, by Lilley & Son, London, c1860, 19thC, 5in (12.5cm) wide.
$250–325 HUM

A French prisoner-of-war bone model of a three-masted ship of the line, early 19thC, 19¾in (50.5cm) long, on a parquetry base, in a glazed case.
$14,500–18,000 B&L

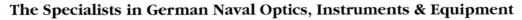

A German brass adding machine, in original chamois-lined fitted leather case with gilt tooled decoration, stylus missing, c1790, 8in (20.5cm) wide.
$10,500–12,000 S

A French ivory multiple dial or compendium, attributable to Pierre Dujardin, dated '1620', 3 x 2in (7.5 x 5cm).
$11,500–13,500 S

A German brass-cased pocket horizontal dial, early 19thC, 1½in (4cm) diam.
$325–400 HUM

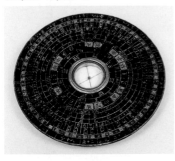

A Chinese geomancer's compass, c1860, 4½in (11.5cm) diam.
$200–250 HUM

A pair of terrestrial and celestial library globes, signed 'Bardin', retailed by W. & S. Jones, London, 1803, 18in (45.5cm) diam.
$40,000–44,000 HYD

◄ A beechwood celestial table globe, by Fortin, Paris, the stand early 18thC, the map c1780, 19in (48.5cm) diam.
$19,000–21,000 S(NY)

A pair of mahogany library globes, the terrestrial by William & Thomas Bardin, 1824, the celestial by Malby & Sons, 1870, 18in (46cm) diam.
$25,000–30,000 Bon

A French 30-minute straw-inlay sand-glass, mid-18thC, 5¾in (14.5cm) high.
$7,250–8,000 S

An Edmund Culpeper compound monocular microscope, in an oak case containing accessories, signed, c1730, 14in (35.5cm) high.
$58,000–65,000 S

Culpeper-type microscopes were made for nearly 150 years. The price of this piece reflects the enormous premium attached to a piece by Culpeper himself.

A brass-mounted 60-minute sand-glass, late 18thC, 7in (18cm) high.
$2,600–2,900 S

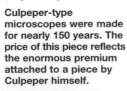

A George III mahogany waywiser, the dial by George Adams, London, 59in (150cm) long.
$3,000–3,300 HAM

A Dutch or German brass sector, mid-17thC, 8¼in (21cm) long.
$7,250–8,000 S

A Negretti & Zambra Jordan's patent sunshine recorder, c1930, 7in (18cm) high.
$400–500 RTW

EARLY TECHNOLOGY

Historic Television Images

Baird Televisor by Plessey 1930

Miniature TVs by Casio, Sony and CMB Corp 1980s

Zarach Sony transparent TV 1972

All types of early electrical and mechanical antiques bought and sold

A page from a catalogue for an exhibition of paintings of Mao Tse-tung, by Andy Warhol, signed in bold blue ink, 1970s, 9 x 8½in (23.5 x 22cm).
$950–1,100 FRa

Gallaher Ltd, Woodland Trees, set of 100 cigarette cards, 1912.
$575–650 MAr

▶ W. A. & A. C. Churchman, Cricketers, set of 50 cigarette cards, 1936.
$200–250 MAr

F. & J. Smith, Football Club Records, set of 50 cigarette cards, 1922.
$800–1,000 MAr

Gallaher Ltd, Aeroplanes, set of 48, 1939.
$50–65 LCC

The Dandy Monster Comic, second *Dandy* annual, 1940.
$1,200–1,400 CBP

The Amazing Spider-Man 3, featuring Dreaded Dr Octopus, 1963.
$850–950 CBP

A poster, by Lem, published by Chaix, on linen, 1899, 62 x 42½in (158 x 108cm).
$575–650 ONS

A poster, advertising Van Nelle's coffee, c1900, 29¼ x 19¾in (74.5 x 50cm).
$380–420 VSP

A travel poster, by R. A. Stone, England, c1905, 40 x 25in (102 x 64cm).
$1,100–1,300 ONS

A poster, Exposition et Mise en Vente, featuring children and toys, c1900, 51 x 38in (129.5 x 96.5cm).
$2,000–2,500 S(NY)

◀ A James Bond poster, advertising the film *You Only Live Twice,* 1967, 30 x 40in (76 x 101.5cm).
$350–400 RBB

▶ An Aer Lingus poster, c1946, 38 x 23in (97 x 59cm).
$2,750–3,000 WA

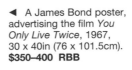

A German etched close helmet, Augsburg, c1550, 15in (38cm) high.
$24,250–26,750 S(S)

► A Victorian officer's dirk of the Cameron Highlanders, by Mortimer & Co, 18¾in (47.5cm) long.
$5,700–6,500 Sp

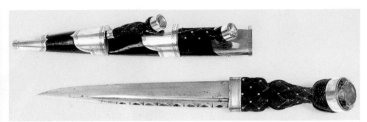

A Scottish silver and leather dirk, decorated with citrines, c1870, 18in (45.5cm) long.
$1,000–1,300 BWA

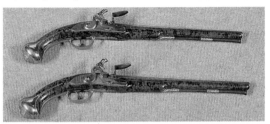

A pair of flintlock holster pistols, by François Formentin, early 18thC, 20in (51cm) long.
$5,000–5,750 B

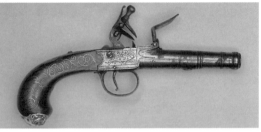

A flintlock boxlock cannon barrelled pocket pistol, by Parkes, London, marked 'HM' for Charles Freeth, Birmingham 1778, 7¾in (19.5cm) long.
$700–800 WAL

A pair of pellet lock duelling pistols, by Charles Moore, London, c1825, 15in (38cm) long.
$10,000–11,250 WSA

► A pair of Bohemian percussion rifled target pistols, by Lebeda, Prague, in a mahogany case, c1835, 14½in (37cm) wide.
$10,500–11,500 S(S)

A pair of French flintlock pistols, by Lepage, Paris, in original lined and fitted case veneered in figured walnut, c1820, 14in (35.5cm) wide.
$18,000–21,000 S(NY)

A percussion sea-service pistol, c1855, 11¼in (28.5cm) long.
$900–1,000 WSA

Ex-Tower of London collection.

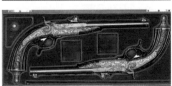

A pair of Liège .380 breech-loading centre-fire target pistols, signed by the retailer 'A. Nouvelle & Cie, Paris', in original fitted velvet-lined wooden case, c1890, 16in (40.5cm) long.
$5,000–5,700 Bon

◄ A 54 bore Beaumont Adams percussion revolver, by E. M. Reilly & Co, London, c1860, in oak case, 12in (30.5cm) wide.
$1,400–1,600 CGC

An Italian swept hilt rapier, signed 'Fedorico Picinino, c1620, 48in (122cm) long.
$19,000–21,000 WSA

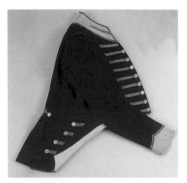

An Argyllshire Volunteers Local Militia officer's coatee, late 18thC.
$2,000–2,500 BOS

A Victorian 12th Lancer's tunic.
$275–325 Q&C

A Royal Irish Fusiliers drummer's scarlet tunic and black trousers with red stripe, c1890.
$650–730 WA

A 1st Volunteer Battalion Royal Lancaster Regiment 'half cheese' drum, c1860.
$1,400–1,600 Q&C

◄ A Victorian model of a 1st Life Guard's bass drum, by Potters, Aldershot, 11in (28cm) high.
$3,250–4,000 Q&C

A group of 7 medals awarded to Flight Lieutenant Copestake, comprising Distinguished Flying Cross, Flying Medal, 1935–45 Star, Air Crew Europe Star with France and Germany bar, Defence Medal, War Medal, Campaign Service Medal with Borneo bar.
$4,000–5,000 Q&C

The Polar Exploration pair of medals, awarded to Herbert 'Ponko' Ponting, official photographer to Scott's last Antarctic Expedition, 1910–13.
$13,500–14,500 Sp

A French grenadier's brass and silver-plated helmet, with feather plume and horse hair, c1880.
$1,300–1,500 Q&C

A copper gun flask, with beaded decoration, c1840, 8in (20.5cm) long.
$140–160 WSA

A 3rd King's Own Hussars officer's sabretache, embroidered with crowned VR cypher, late 19thC.
$1,100–1,300 BOS

A WWII poster, entitled 'Remember Belgium, Enlist Today', slight damage and repairs, 19¼ x 14½in (49 x 37cm).
$160–200 WA

An enamel plaque, depicting General Gordon of Khartoum, c1880–90, 2¾in (7cm) high.
$2,500–3,250 P

A snooker scoreboard, by E. J. Riley, c1930, 27in (68.5cm) wide.
$100–120 WAB

A revolving cue stand, by Burroughes & Watts c1900, 45in (114.5cm) high.
$1,200–1,400 CBC

An Edwardian walnut life pool scoreboard, by Burroughes & Watts, London, on a cupboard with 2 panelled doors, 48in (122cm) wide.
$2,750–3,250 BR

A rosewood, bird's-eye maple, ivory-inlaid and marquetry billiard table, by Brunswick-Balke-Collender Co, c1880, 108 x 59in (276 x 150cm).
$23,500–26,000 B&B

A carved mahogany quarter-size billiard table, c1755, 60¼ x 37½in (153 x 95cm) long.
$73,000–80,000 S

An Arts and Crafts oak steel block billiard table, by Burroughes & Watts, 108 x 59in (276 x 150cm).
$9,500–11,500 WBB

A novelty cricket ball inkwell, c1905, 3½in (9cm) diam.
$325–375 VS

A Topps Gum card, depicting Mickey Mantle, c1953.
$1,400–1,600 HALL

A miniature cricket bat, presented to umpire George Borwick at Adelaide on 19th January 1933, signed by all 11 members of the English team from the 1933 'Bodyline' Tour, England v. Australia, 3rd Test, Adelaide Oval 13–19 January 1933, 17in (43cm) long.
$750–850 FW&C

An MCC touring blazer, by Simpson, London, worn by Geoff Pullar (Lancashire & England) on the tour of the West Indies in 1959–60, slight fading.
$650–730 KNI

'The Northamptonshire Gold Cup', a silver-gilt racing cup and cover, by Benjamin Smith II and Benjamin Smith III, London 1817, 15in (38cm) high.
$10,500–12,000 S

A set of Young's Patent oak and brass-mounted jockey scales, late 19thC, 35in (89cm) wide.
$5,500–6,500 Hal

A red England No. 21 International jersey, worn by Roger Hunt in the World Cup final at Wembley, 30th July, 1966.
$28,500–32,500 S

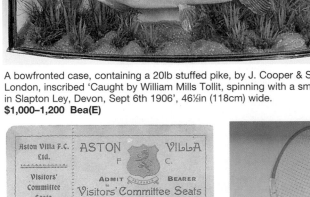

A bowfronted case, containing a 20lb stuffed pike, by J. Cooper & Sons, London, inscribed 'Caught by William Mills Tollit, spinning with a small perch in Slapton Ley, Devon, Sept 6th 1906', 46½in (118cm) wide.
$1,000–1,200 Bea(E)

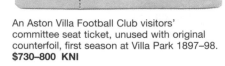

An Aston Villa Football Club visitors' committee seat ticket, unused with original counterfoil, first season at Villa Park 1897–98.
$730–800 KNI

A hand-hammered gutty golf ball, with Forgan patterning, c1855.
$12,000–13,500 S

◄ A Slazenger tennis racket, signed in ink by Fred Perry and impressed with initials 'F.J.P.', c1935.
$500–575 Bea

A Millennium of Craftsmanship

The year 2000 sees both the start of a new millennium and the 21st anniversary issue of *Miller's Antiques Price Guide*. To celebrate the special occasion, Miller's has assembled, on this page and the next, a number of spectacular works of art. Selected from thousands of photographs of beautiful, interesting and rare objects, here is a mere handful of the finest items sold recently which have been produced during the last thousand years – one for each century of the second millennium.

11th Century

A Junyao purple-splashed bubble bowl, Northern Song Dynasty, 3¼in (8.5cm) diam.
$110,000–120,000 S

Jun wares are superb examples of the potter's art. The glazing process was so complicated that each piece fired differently and no one knew how it would look until it came out of the kiln. For each successful piece hundreds were rejected, and perhaps only one in five was a masterpiece, such as this example – as beautiful 900-odd years later as on the day it was made.

13th Century

A Tibetan gilt and polychrome wood manuscript cover, the left side panel carved with a mask emitting 2 foliate sprays, the right side panel painted with lotus petals, 13thC, 10½ x 27½in (26.5 x 70cm).
$6,500–8,000 S(NY)

The manuscript cover was used by Buddhist monks to store scriptures. While the item is not particularly rare, its appeal lies in the intricate carving and vibrant colours.

15th Century

◀ A Venetian enamelled and gilt blue-tinted goblet, c1475–1500, 8in (20.5cm) high.
$235,000–250,000 S

This previously unrecorded goblet was discovered in a Welsh mansion. Although little is known about the piece, it is believed that 15thC Venetian glass was a luxury made to order for Royal families and the aristocracy of Europe, perhaps as engagement or wedding presents, or for use as liturgical vessels. The price paid reflects its superb condition and extreme rarity.

12th Century

A historiated initial cut from a Romanesque Latin Bible manuscript on vellum, depicting the story of Jonah and the Whale, north-eastern France, c1160–75 AD, 4¼in (10.5cm) wide.
$12,000–14,000 S

This miniature is from one of the enormous 12th-century Bibles that were being commissioned by monasteries especially in France and England during the second half of the 12th century. They are thought to have been among the most expensive and complex manuscript projects undertaken up until that date. This example is quite small but it encompasses an entire narrative, illustrating almost all the story of the book of Jonah within a single initial.

14th Century

◀ A French carved white marble figure of the Virgin and Child, damaged and repaired, 14thC, 25in (64cm) high.
$25,000–30,000 P

The facial features, drapery and stance of this figure are typical of northern French sculpture from the second quarter of the 14thC. Although the piece is damaged, its beauty has been unaffected and it is a fine example of the sculptor's craftsmanship.

16th Century

A mazer bowl, with silver-gilt mount, decorated to the centre with an enamel device of a stylized thistle or pomegranate, maker's device of a double-headed arrow, London, 1527, 5¾in (14.5cm) diam.
$325,000–400,000 WW

Mazer bowls, or drinking vessels, were common items in the 16th and 17thC but by 1911 Sir Charles Jackson, writing in *The History of English Plate*, thought that there were no more than 60 still in existence. Unusually, this example – a remarkable survival from the period of Henry VIII – is fully hallmarked.

18th Century

A pair of Sèvres hard-paste porcelain vases, in the form of ewers, painted by Chapuis, gilded by Vincent, dated '1781', 19in (48.5cm) high.
$800,000+ LSK

These vases are similar to a pair in the Royal collection and it has been suggested that they were produced from the same mould. It would appear from the Sèvres factory records that only one pair of vases of this form was decorated in this manner.

20th Century

A porcelain bowl, by Dame Lucie Rie, the rim decorated with fine crisscross sgraffito, c1960, 8½in (21.5cm) wide.
$22,000–26,000 Bon

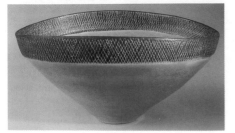

17th Century

An embroidered casket, depicting mythological and religious scenes, containing 2 pewter pots and 2 glass bottles, the top with the date '1660' in seed pearls, 11in (28cm) wide.
$160,000–200,000 DN(H)

Although caskets such as this are not rare, and often found in large country houses, this example is extraordinary because of its pristine condition. It was sold complete with the original leather case which undoubtedly ensured its survival into the late 20thC.

19th Century

A late Victorian D-end writing table, by Jackson & Graham, designed by Owen Jones, inlaid with marquetry of precious woods and ivory, the top and frieze in calamander and rosewood, with a single frieze drawer, the turned legs inlaid with flutes of kingwood and ivory, linked by a similarly-inlaid X-frame stretcher, c1870, 52in (132cm) wide.
$65,000–75,000 MaBh

Jackson & Graham were among the most prestigious cabinet-makers of the 19thC, with extensive premises in London's Tottenham Court Road. They carried out numerous Royal and noble commissions and won prizes in international exhibitions. One of their largest pieces, a side cabinet, is now in the Victoria & Albert Museum. The high quality of their marquetry work necessarily resulted in a low output, which explains the rarity of their furniture and its subsequent collectability. The architect/designer Owen Jones worked closely with the firm in designing their premises and creating some of their most innovative forms.

◄ During her long and distinguished career, Lucie Rie repeatedly explored the sculptural qualities of porcelain. This bowl combines texture, form and a difficult-to-control yellow glaze to create a unique object which sings to the beholder.

METEOROLOGICAL

A sunshine recorder, with glass sphere, anodized copper curved surround to hold recording card, c1910, 7¼in (18.5cm) wide.
$700–800 Bon

A French thermograph, by Maxant, c1910, 14in (35.5cm) wide.
$250–300 RTw

A mahogany thermometer, by Joseph Long, London, with sliding brass scale, signed 'Trotter's Compensation Thermometer No. 632', c1870, 33in (84cm) high.
$1,400–1,650 S

A French thermograph, by Jules Richard, Paris, c1910, 11in (28cm) wide.
$250–350 RTw

An oak-cased weather station, by Negretti & Zambra, London, the 8-day clock with fusee movement, c1890, 18in (46cm) wide.
$4,000–5,000 AW

MICROSCOPES

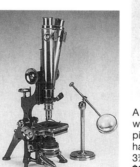

A simple microscope, with sprung brass central pillar and turned bone handles, early 19thC, 3¾in (9.5cm) wide.
$650–750 Bon

A lacquered-brass compound binocular microscope, signed 'C. C. Collins', in a mahogany case with accessories, late 19thC, 18in (46cm) high.
$1,600–1,800 S

A Culpeper-type monocular microscope, by T. Harris & Son, London, with rack-and-pinion focusing, the mahogany base with a drawer containing accessories, in a mahogany pillar case, early 19thC, 16in (40cm) high.
$1,600–2,000 AG

A binocular microscope, signed 'Watson & Sons, London', with rack-and-pinion fine and coarse focusing, with accessories, late 19thC, 16in (40.5cm) high, in a later mahogany carrying case.
$1,600–2,000 S

◄ A lacquered-brass microscope, signed 'Dancer, Manchester', 1850s, 11¾in (30cm) high, with accessories, in a mahogany case.
$1,000–1,200 Bon

John Benjamin Dancer FRAS (1812–87) trained under his father Josiah Dancer, an optician and instrument-maker in London and Liverpool. J. B. Dancer is famous as the inventor of the micro-photograph, but was also a first-class instrument-maker. Dancer was one of the first English provincial opticians to offer achromatic microscopes for sale and developed a series of microscopes somewhat similar to the best examples made by Smith & Beck in London.

A lacquered-brass miniature screw-barrel microscope, probably French, late 19thC, 3in (7.5cm) high, in a fitted wooden case.
$850–950 S

SURVEYING & DRAWING

A lacquered-brass circumferentor, by J. Search, London, signed, late 18thC, in original fitted oak box, 6¼in (16cm) square.
$1,800–2,000 P

A clinometer, signed 'A. J. Thornton, Manchester', the underside of box with provision for mounting, early 20thC, 6¾in (17cm) diam.
$1,600–1,800 S

A silver-mounted folding demi-aune, signed 'Canivet', the ivory rule double-folding through decoratively engraved silver sector-joint hinges, dated '1763', Paris, in a green fishskin case, 6½in (16.5cm) long.
$3,500–4,000 S

**One of the leading instrument-makers of the mid-18thC, Canivet was virtually the only one to undertake large-scale observatory and geodetic instruments. He was also unusual in dating most of his instruments, examples at present known ranging from 1757 to the year of his death, 1774.
A demi-aune is half an aune, a French unit of measure, being 46.79in (119cm).**

A set of Victorian technical drawing instruments, by Dollond, containing pens, compasses, dividers, a brass protractor, an ivory parallel rule, folding rule and other accessories, in a brass-bound walnut-veneered case, box 8in (20.5cm) wide.
$1,000–1,200 Mit

A set of Keuffer & Essel Paragon drawing instruments, with ivory handles, in an oak case lined in green velvet, American, c1895, 15¼in (38.5cm) wide.
$550–650 Bon

A pair of brass proportional dividers, in sharkskin case, c1790, 7in (18cm) long.
$200–250 HUM

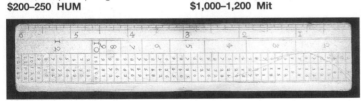

A 6in (15cm) boxwood multiplication rule, stamped and dated '1748', and a fragment of a Gunters scale.
$650–750 P

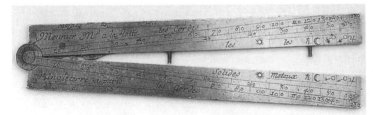

A French brass gunner's sector, engraved with scales on both sides, signed 'Meunier Md. a la flotte d'Angleterre à Paris', 18thC, 6¾in (17cm) long, closed.
$300–350 Bon

A surveyor's compendium, signed 'J. Halden & Co, London', with compass, level and printed tables, in a fitted leather case, early 20thC, 6¼in (16cm) long.
$300–350 Bon

◄ A surveyor's brass level, by Lincoln, London, c1790, 21in (53.5cm) wide.
$650–800 HUM

TELESCOPES

A 6in (15cm) lacquered-brass A-frame theodolite, signed 'Cary', London, early 19thC, in original fitted mahogany box.
$850–950 P

A 2¼in (5.5cm) brass Gregorian reflecting telescope, by B. Martin, London, the 18in (45.5cm) tube with focusing to the secondary reflector by long shank and screw, in mahogany case, 18thC.
$1,800–2,000 Bri

A 2½in (6.5cm) Dudley Adams lacquered-brass telescope-on-stand, with 24in (61cm) body-tube, c1800.
$900–1,000 Bon

A 3in (7.5cm) refracting telescope, by J. H. Steward, London, the body tube with rack-and-pinion focusing, signed, late 19thC, 37in (94cm) long, with a fitted case.
$1,200–1,400 S

A 4½in (11.5cm) brass reflecting telescope, by Watkins & Smith, London, the 24in (61cm) long body tube with screw rod focusing, with associated accessories in the original fitted mahogany box, lid missing, signed, mid-18thC.
$2,100–2,500 P

A silver 13 draw monocular, with a crest stamped 'Warris's Patent', 2in (5cm) lens, early 19thC, 4in (10cm) high, in drum-shaped case with velvet and marbled paper lining.
$1,600–2,000 P

The Warris family were opticians in Sheffield from 1797 to 1822. In 1804 William Warris took out a patent concerning opera glasses.

WEIGHTS & MEASURES

A set of 5 George IV bronze capacity measures, comprising imperial quart, pint, half-pint, gill and half-gill, each signed 'H. Christopherson' and dated for Brighton 1826, largest 5in (13cm) high.
$2,000–2,300 P

A set of 6 brass conical measures, comprising quart, pint, half-pint, gill, half-gill and quarter-gill, each signed for the County Borough of Brighton and by the maker De Grave & Co Ltd, London, early 20thC, largest 5in (12.5cm) high.
$1,400–1,550 P

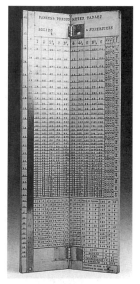

A boxwood Parker's Presto meter tablet, by Isaac Aston, the inner faces with a sliding brass scale, the outer faces stamped with multiplication table, with brass hinges and binding, mid-19thC, 15in (38cm) high.
$500–550 Bon

▶ A set of 14 spherical weights, from 56lb to ½ dram, engraved 'County of Leicester', the larger weight fitted in a painted wooden case, the smaller weights in a mahogany lined case and fitted within the larger case, 10in (25.5cm) high overall.
$1,400–1,600 S

Marine

BAROMETERS

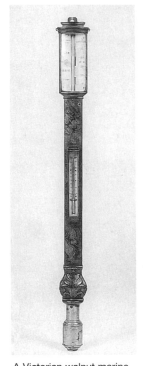

A mahogany sympiesometer, by Duff, Liverpool, with silvered-brass plates, c1870, 22in (56cm) high.
$2,500–3,250 AW

A Victorian walnut marine barometer, by G. & C. Gowland, Sunderland, with an ivorine register scale above a thermometer with a brass reservoir below, 37in (94cm) high.
$3,500–4,000 P(Sc)

A mahogany marine barometer/sympiesometer, by McGregor, Glasgow, on later gimbals, c1880, 36in (91.5cm) high.
$3,700–4,300 AW

A rosewood marine barometer and thermometer, by F. Walker, London, with engraved ivory scale, 19thC, 38in (96.5cm) high.
$2,000–2,300 CAG

CHRONOMETERS & TIMEKEEPERS

A 2-day marine chronometer, the silvered dial signed 'Kelvin Bottomly Baird Ltd, Glasgow', the fusee movement with detent escapement, in a glazed mahogany brass-bound case, c1920, bezel 4¾in (12cm) diam.
$2,200–2,500 S(Am)

A ship's bulkhead clock, by J. Dimmick, Isle of Wight, the 8-day 4-pillar 2-train fusee movement with lever escapement, rack striking with 2 hammers on one bell, late 19thC, dial 9in (23cm) diam, in a brass case.
$1,600–2,000 DN

► A Victorian 2-day marine chronometer, by Victor Kulberg, London, 4¾in (12cm) diam, in a rosewood case with mother-of-pearl plaque.
$5,250–6,250 SK

A Russian mahogany 2-day marine chronometer, the fusee movement with detent escapement in three-tier mahogany case, signed A. Ericsson, St Petersburg, c1900, 4½in (12cm) diam.
$1,550–1,850 S(Am)

MODEL SHIPS

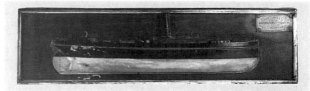

A shipbuilder's model of the SS *Nettleton*, with painted hull, in a glazed mahogany case, c1891, 84in (214cm) long.
$2,000–2,300 TEN

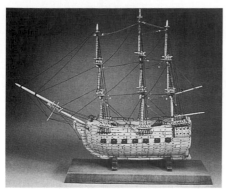

A French prisoner-of-war ivory model three-masted ship, fully rigged and with cannon, on a wooden base, 19thC, 15½in (39.5cm) long.
$3,000–3,300 SK(B)

A half-block model of the SS *The Earl*, by Edward Finch & Co, Chepstow, 1887, 23in (58.5cm) long.
$3,500–4,000 Bon

A model of the opium clipper *Rose*, Swansea, Massachusetts, 1836, in a glazed case, 44in (112cm) wide.
$2,000–2,300 SK(B)

A shipping diorama, depicting a two-masted ship, a paddle steamer and 2 sailing boats, in a glazed case, 19thC, 35in (89cm) wide.
$950–1,150 S

A model of the three-masted schooner, *The Gaxpe Trader*, early 20thC, 42in (106.5cm) long, on a stand.
$350–400 FBG

◀ An Edwardian pond yacht, with teak deck, original sails and transom/rudder mechanism, painted lead-mounted keel, 24in (61cm) long, on a stand.
$240–280 AP

A carved-pine pond yacht, with mahogany deck, oak mast and yardarms, brass fittings, fully rigged with cotton sails, 19thC, 42in (106.5cm) long.
$900–1,000 JAA

▶ A model of the USS *Massachusetts*, built by a crew member, c1910, 43in (109cm) long, in a glazed case.
$1,300–1,600 SLN

◀ A wooden model of a paddle steamer, the hull painted red and black, with paddle wheels each side, early 20thC, 94½in (240cm) long.
$3,250–3,500 Bon(C)

A painted wood pond yacht, *Vitesse*, the weighted keel below a simulated planked deck, with 2 sets of rigging, 1920s, 62½in (159cm) long.
$2,000–2,300 DD

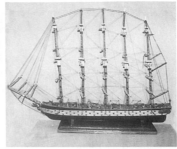

A wooden pond yacht, c1930,
22in (56cm) long.
$90–100 AL

An American wooden model
of a five-masted schooner, c1940,
42in (106.5cm) long, on a pine stand.
$250–300 DuM

A wooden pond yacht, with a green
keel, c1950, 36in (91.5cm) long,
on a wooden base.
$1,300–1,450 DQ

◀ A 1:336in scale model of the *Queen
Mary*, by H. D. Beatty of Cambridge
Engineering, c1950, 35in (89cm) long.
$1,600–2,000 SWO

NAUTICAL HANDICRAFTS

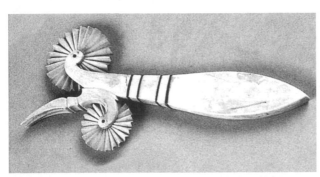

A whalebone and walrus tusk double jagging wheel, 19thC,
7¾in (19.5cm) long.
$1,800–2,200 SK(B)

▶ An engraved whale's
tooth, depicting a three-
masted square rigger
under sail, 19thC,
6in (15cm) long.
$1,000–1,150 SK(B)

A Chinese American school embroidered
picture of HMS *Shannon* and USS
Chesapeake, 19thC, 19 x 26½in (48 x 67cm).
$1,300–1,450 HOK

**The duel between the 38-gun frigates
HMS *Shannon* and USS *Chesapeake* in
1813 is one of the most famous (and
bloodiest) single ship actions. The British
ship captured the American ship in less
than 15 minutes after killing and wounding
146 of the *Chesapeake*'s 300 crew.**

Cross Reference
Textiles

A shellwork picture of flowers in a basket, using limpets,
periwinkles and scallops, the ground decorated with
coral, a seahorse and cowrie shells, damaged, mid-
19thC, 27in (68.5cm) wide.
$750–850 S

A scrimshaw whale's tooth, by James Bute, from
Charles Darwin's voyage aboard HMS *Beagle*, one face
engraved with an image of a whaling boat, the reverse with
a beached vessel, dated 'April 1834', 8in (20.5cm) long.
$12,000–13,500 S

**On 18th April 1834, a party of 25 left the *Beagle*
at the mouth of Santa Cruz for an expedition
of 21 days into the hinterland of Patagonia.**

NAVIGATIONAL INSTRUMENTS

An ebony octant, early 19thC, index arm 10in (25.5cm) radius.
$650–750 Bon

A brass sextant, signed 'Dollond, London', with 2 telescopes, mid-19thC, 9½in (24cm) radius, in mahogany case.
$750–850 S

An anodized brass sextant, signed 'Cox, Devonport', with lattice-shaped frame and mahogany handle, c1800, index arm 7½in (19cm) radius, in a case with accessories.
$480–560 Bon

An iron and brass sextant, signed 'C. Plath, Hamburg', with original certificate No. 5973, dated '14th February, 1930', in a fitted box, 10in (25.5cm) square.
$900–1,000 HOK

◄ A triple circle sextant, signed 'Hayes Brothers, Cardiff & Barry', early 19thC, 8in (20.5cm) radius, in a wooden case with 3 telescope eyepieces.
$700–800 S

MISCELLANEOUS

A pair of iron naval signal cannons, mounted on oak carriages, 19thC, barrels 19¼in (49cm) long.
$2,300–2,600 S

A pair of ivory and brass opera glasses, in a case, a framed letter and a copy of *Nicholls's Seaman-ship Guide*, c1912.
$3,200–3,600 AH

The letter states that the opera glasses were discovered on the body of a passenger found after the sinking of the *Titanic*.

A whalebone diddy box, with wooden top and base, brass tack decoration, 19thC, 8¼in (21cm) wide.
$3,200–3,600 SK(B)

A Royal Navy officer's black beaver-skin cocked hat, a full-dress sword belt and epaulettes, 1930s, in original black tin box.
$575–650 BOS

► A silver vesta case, enamelled with crossed naval flags, inscribed, Birmingham 1912, 2¼in (5.5cm) wide.
$450–525 P

A certificate for a Lloyd's Patriotic Fund award to a Battle of Trafalgar veteran, engraved by E. Scriven after R. K. Porter, recording an award of £10 to William Williams, Seaman, HMS *Neptune*, 1805, 17¼ x 23in (44 x 58cm), in a japanned tube.
$850–1,000 Bon

Cameras

A Canon A1 camera, with 50mm f1.8 FD lens, c1978.
$160–200 VCL

A Contax IIIA Opton Sonnart camera, with 50mm f1.5 lens, c1961.
$300–350 VCL

An Ensign Double-8 folding roll film camera, with f4.5 Ensar lens, c1935.
$55–70 VCL

An Ensign Selfix Autorange 16-20 camera, with Ross 75mm Xpres f3.5 lens, c1950.
$130–160 VCL

A Horne & Thornthwaite wet-plate camera, for 5 x 5in plates, with brass barrel lens No. 1495, c1860.
$900–1,000 Bon

A Kodak Medalist II roll film camera, with coupled rangefinder, Ektar 100mm f3.5 lens, c1950.
$200–250 VCL

An Ensign roll film Reflex camera, with 90mm f4.5 lens, c1920.
$100–130 VCL

A Franke & Heidecke Rolleiflex 4 x 4 Grey Baby TLR camera, No. 2039280, with Xenar 60mm f3.5 lens, case and accessories, c1957.
$225–275 Bon

A Franke & Heidecke Rolleiflex 2.8F camera, c1965.
$400–500 VCL

A W. Kunik vanity outfit, comprising a 16mm Petie camera, 25mm f.11 lens, in a mottled green enamel vanity case, with powder compact, lipstick holder and film holder, c1930.
$575–700 P(Ba)

---

21 Years Ago …

A Rover patent quarter-plate camera, by J. Lancaster & Son, Birmingham, c1891. **P**

Twenty-one years ago this camera was valued at $65–80. In the early days of *Miller's Antiques Price Guide*, one might come across an example of this detective box camera 2 or 3 times a year. Now that the majority have disappeared into collections they are exceedingly rare, with the result that the value has increased dramatically to $650–800. Only very fine and rare items have performed as well as this over the years.

A Leica 1 35mm black camera, No. 11409, with Elmar f3.5 50mm lens, leather case and accessories, c1928.
$400–500 Bon

A Leica 1a camera, No. 27496, with a Leitz Elmar 1:3.5f 50mm lens, c1933.
$600–650 P(Ba)

A Le Coultre Compass 35mm rangefinder camera, with aluminium body, panoramic and stereoscopic heads, c1938.
$850–1,000 S

A Leica M3 camera, No. 1058014, with a Leitz Summilux 1:1, 4/50 lens, No. 1899211, maker's box and accessories, c1951.
$1,300–1,600 P(Ba)

A Leica SL camera, No. 1236025, with a Leitz Summicron-R 1:2/50 lens, No. 2324254, c1960.
$375–400 P(Ba)

A Nikon FM camera body, c1978.
$200–250 VCL

A Pentax MX camera, with 50mm f1.7 SMC lens, c1981.
$160–200 VCL

A Richard Verascope stereo camera, with Saphir Boyer 55mm f4.5 lens, leather case and accessories, c1900.
$400–450 Bon

A Rollei 35 camera, with Tessar 40mm f3.5 lens, c1970.
$200–250 VCL

A Voigtländer Ultramatic camera, with 50mm 2.8 Skopar lens, c1966.
$300–330 VCL

A Yashica 124G TLR camera, with Yashinon 80mm f3.5 lens, c1970.
$200–250 VCL

A Zorki-4K camera, with f2/50mm Jupiter 8 lens, c1975.
$40–50 VCL

◄ A Tropical Una-style quarter-plate camera, with polished teak body, a Carl Zeiss Tessar 1:4.5f=15cm lens, No. 460480, with automatic shutter, canvas case, a quantity of camera bodies and accessories, 1920s.
$1,100–1,250 P(Ba)

Optical Devices & Viewers

A Claude Lorraine glass mirror, c1850, 6 x 7in (15 x 18cm).
$250–325 HUM

A Claude Lorraine glass is a convex mirror used for viewing landscapes. It was named after the 17thC French painter Claude Gelée, known as 'Le Lorrain', who is said to have used such a glass.

A Bing black tinplate magic lantern, with extending lens, c1910, 13in (33cm) wide.
$160–200 Bon(C)

A Rowsell's Patent mahogany graphoscope, 1860s, 15¾in (40cm) wide.
$250–325 Bon

An A. L. Hudson walnut stereopticon, 19thC, 12in (30.5cm) high.
$180–200 DuM

A stereopticon is a double projecting lantern, in which one image dissolves into another.

A German table-top kaleidoscope, mid-19thC, 9in (23cm) wide.
$850–1,000 HUM

A Jules Richard stereo taxiphote, in a mahogany case, c1910, 13in (33cm) high.
$320–350 Bon

A zoetrope, with metal revolving drum and cast-iron foot, on wooden ball feet, with 17 printed and titled strips, late 19thC, 15in (38cm) high.
$650–800 Bon(C)

A table-top stereoscope, in a burr-walnut case inlaid with boxwood and ebony stringing, and a quantity of cards, including scenes of Paris and the Great Exhibition of 1851, mid-19thC, 17½in (44.5cm) high.
$1,100–1,200 S

A table-top stereoscopic viewer, in an oak case, c1910, 18½in (47cm) high.
$575–650 Bon

▶ A German child's zoetrope, the metal body with turned walnut base, with 30 hand-painted picture strips, early 20thC, base 11¾in (30cm) diam.
$480–560 S

Arms & Armour

ARMOUR

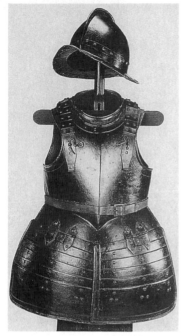

A composite pikeman's armour, later shoulder straps, c1640.
$7,800–9,000 S(S)

A north Italian etched backplate, probably Milanese, decorated with etched trophies, c1580, 14in (35.5cm) high.
$4,800–5,400 S(S)

An Indo-Persian chain mail shirt, of butted links with decorative lines and diamond shapes made from brass links, 19thC.
$400–450 WAL

An English and Dutch composite harquebusier's armour, mid-17thC.
$5,000–6,000 S

A harquebusier's curaiss, with associated backplate, c1650, 15¾in (40cm) high, with later shoulder straps and waist belt.
$2,200–2,400 S(S)

◄ A mail shirt, probably German, formed of alternating rows of flattened riveted iron rings and butted iron rings, early 16thC.
$2,300–2,700 S(NY)

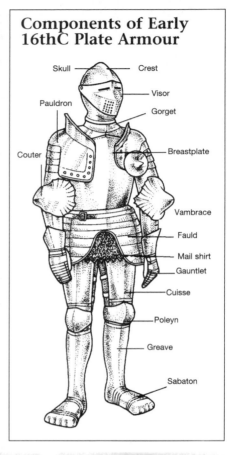

Components of Early 16thC Plate Armour

- Skull
- Crest
- Visor
- Pauldron
- Gorget
- Couter
- Breastplate
- Vambrace
- Fauld
- Mail shirt
- Gauntlet
- Cuisse
- Poleyn
- Greave
- Sabaton

A French carabinier's cuirass, the polished-brass breastplate mounted onto steel, the backplate with brass studs and shoulder straps of steel interlinked rings, the interior with engraved details of the Arsenal and dated '1842'.
$650–750 BOS

A Mahdist pullover style mail shirt, with split links of various size, 19thC.
$300–330 BOS

Two north European cuirassier's tassets, each studded with the letter 'P', for the Earls of Pembroke, c1620.
$4,000–4,500 S(S)

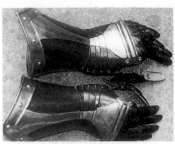

A pair of articulated gauntlets from a black and white armour, mid-16thC, 12in (30.5cm) long.
$1,000–1,100 ASB

A north Italian etched comb morion, decorated on the comb and brim with etched bands of trophies, and on each side of the skull with similar trophies within palm-fronds over a monogram, mid-16thC, 9¼in (23.5cm) high.
$3,700–4,200 S(S)

The etched decoration is of a fashion of about 1570–90, and the helmet was evidently ornamented in that period.

A close helmet, the two-piece skull with overlapping riveted join and incorporating small plume holder to rear, early 17thC.
$4,000–4,500 ASB

Three-quarter suits of armour incorporating helmets such as these were worn during the early years of the English Civil War from 1641 onwards.

A Cromwellian lobster pot helmet, with nasal bar, c1640, 13in (33cm) high.
$2,300–2,600 WSA

A funerary close helmet, pierced at each side with a circle of triangular ventilation holes, late 17thC, 15in (38cm) high.
$1,600–2,000 S(S)

A Civil War cavalry trooper's helmet, the two-piece skull with rolled central ridge, some damage, 1642–49.
$1,600–1,800 ASB

A Zischagge lobster tail cavalry helmet, probably imported from Holland during the Civil War, 1642–49.
$2,400–2,700 ASB

The neck guard of this helmet is of very much broader form than normally encountered, affording a much higher degree of protection.

◄ An Indo-Persian helmet, etched and chiselled with heads and a *koranic* inscription around the head, complete with chain mail neck guard, c1800, 12in (30.5cm) high.
$950–1,100 GV

► An Indo-Persian steel helmet, engraved and damascened with gold, with 3 plume holders, nose guard and chain mail neck guard, 19thC, 8¼in (21cm) high.
$420–520 Bea(E)

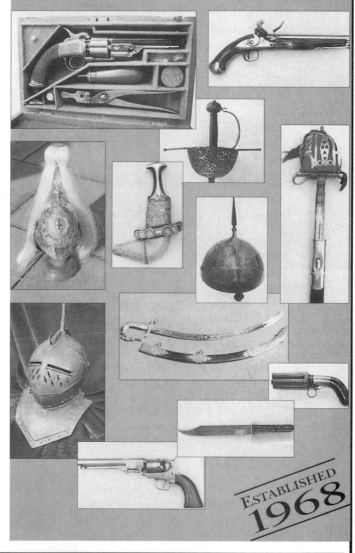

DAGGERS

A Scottish Highlands dirk, c1780, 10in (25.5cm) long.
$570–730 BWA

A Scottish dirk, with silvered pommel and scabbard mounts, mid-19thC, 17in (43cm) long.
$800–900 GV

A dirk, made for the American market by Lingard, Peacroft, Sheffield, the nickel-silver handle decorated with rococo scrolls, in a nickel-silver mounted sheath, mid-19thC, 4¾in (12cm) long.
$200–230 ASB

A Georgian naval midshipman's dirk, the hilt with brass crossguard, the grip of ribbed ivory with gilt pommel and back strap, scabbard missing, 17in (43cm) long.
$350–400 BOS

◄ A twig dagger, 19thC, 8in (20.5cm) long.
$200–250 GV

FIREARMS

A flintlock blunderbuss, the brass barrel inscribed 'Tatham' and 'Mofeleye Mill', crown P and crown V marks, late 18th/early 19thC, barrel 15½in (39.5cm) long.
$2,000–2,300 DuM

A flintlock blunderbuss, the octagonal barrel inscribed 'London' and impressed 'ANNO 1785', 15in (38cm) long.
$1,550–1,800 S(S)

A brass-barrelled flintlock blunderbuss, signed 'Barbar', c1770, 14in (35.5cm) long.
$2,300–2,600 ASB

A flintlock blunderbuss, with figured-walnut stock, signed 'T. Buckley', c1810, 31in (78.5cm) long.
$1,800–2,000 AnSh

James Barbar was a gunmaker in Dover Street, London, from 1739–67. He was appointed Gentleman Armourer to George II in 1741, and Master of the Gunmakers' Company in 1742.

◄ A flintlock blunderbuss, with figured-walnut full stock, foliate-engraved brass mounts, signed 'H. Nock', Birmingham proof marks, early 19thC, 30¼in (77cm) long.
$1,600–1,800 Bon

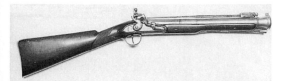

A flintlock blunderbuss, with brass barrel, figured-walnut full stock and engraved brass mounts, signed 'Whaley, Lynn', late 18thC, 31¼in (79.5cm) long.
$2,300–2,600 S(S)

A blunderbuss, with steel barrel, now with percussion action, stamped 'H. Holmes' on the full walnut stock with brass furniture, early 19thC, 14½in (37cm) long.
$1,600–1,800 MEA

An Austrian 12 bore tube lock military percussion saddle carbine, the walnut three-quarter stock with steel mounts, Birmingham proofs, 1847, 30in (76cm) long.
$400–450 WAL

A German 15mm percussion pistol carbine, by V. C. Schilling, Suhl, for use by troops of the Hanseatic League, with walnut stock and iron furniture, c1850, barrel 11in (28cm) long.
$1,600–1,800 ASB

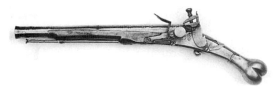

An east Scottish all-steel pistol, with left-hand dog-lock, the four-stage barrel divided by 5 bands of mouldings, c1670, 16in (41cm) long.
$4,200–4,800 Bon

A flintlock service pistol, with banana-shaped border, engraved lock signed 'I. Farmer', full stocked with brass mounts including long-eared butt cap, wood ramrod, mid-18thC, barrel 12in (30.5cm) long.
$1,300–1,450 Gle

A holster pistol, by Heylin, the brass barrel with London proofs, the walnut full stock with engraved brass mounts, c1770, barrel 8in (20.5cm) long.
$2,300–2,600 WSA

A 20 bore flintlock holster pistol, by T. Richards, the walnut full stock with carving around barrel tang, steel mounts, with London proofs, c1760, 15in (38cm) long.
$480–560 WAL

A New Land pattern holster pistol, with ordnance proofs, lockplate with raised pan marked with tower, crown and 'GR', walnut full stock with ordnance marks and brass mounts, swivel ramrod, c1800, barrel 9in (23cm) long.
$1,300–1,450 WSA

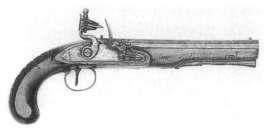

A pair of Irish 18 bore flintlock duelling pistols, by Whitney, Cork, with swamped octagonal sighted barrels struck with Irish census marks, private proof marks, engraved steel trigger-guards decorated with flowers and with engraved pineapple finials, each with horn-tipped wooden ramrod, c1800, 13in (33cm) long.
$2,400–2,600 S(S)

A long sea service flintlock pistol, the barrel with ordnance proofs, with walnut full stock and regulation brass furniture, brass tipped ramrod, c1805, barrel 12in (30.5cm) long.
$2,000–2,300 WSA

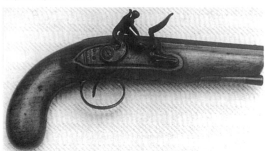

A 15 bore flintlock 'man stopper' overcoat pocket pistol, signed 'Brown, London', with 5in (12.5cm) octagonal barrel and walnut stock, with original horn tipped wooden ramrod, c1820.
$1,000–1,100 ASB

A percussion travelling pistol, signed 'Higham', with twist octagonal sighted barrel, the silver escutcheon engraved with owner's crest and intitials, Birmingham proof marks, mid-19thC, 11½in (29cm) long.
$480–560 Bon

Types of Firearms

The two main types of antique firearms encountered today are as follows:

- **Flintlock:** first appeared mid-17thC, and used a flint to strike sparks from a steel plate in order to ignite the powder charge.
- **Percussion:** invented early 19thC, and used a disposable metal cap containing a minute amount of solid explosive. Although relatively unsophisticated, this method dominated development of firearms until the widespread adoption of the modern metallic cartridge.

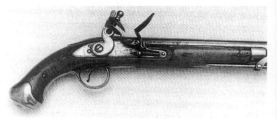

A 16 bore flintlock holster pistol, issued to the 16th Light Dragoons, walnut stock with brass furniture, government proof marks, dated '1805', barrel 9in (23cm) long.
$1,800–2,000 ASB

The 16th Light Dragoons served throughout the Peninsular campaign of 1809–14 and also in the Waterloo campaign. Regimentally marked firearms from the Napoleonic wars are rare.

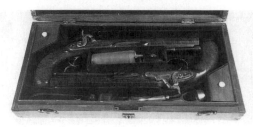

A pair of percussion duelling pistols, by Forsyth, the half stocks with chequered butts and horn fore-ends, c1818, octagonal barrels 10in (25.5cm) long, in velvet-lined mahogany case and most original accessories.
$10,000–11,500 WSA

A brass cannon barrel flintlock travelling pistol, by Perry, London, with carved butt, c1820, 10in (25.5cm) long.
$750–900 GV

A percussion sea service pistol, the walnut full stock with ordnance stamps, c1840, barrel 6in (15cm) long.
$900–1,000 WSA

◀ A Derringer pistol, by Remington, c1860, case 6in (15cm) wide.
$575–650 Q&C

An American .54in model 1842 military percussion holster pistol, the walnut half stock with brass mounts, dated '1850', 14in (35.5cm) long.
$420–480 WAL

A 7mm Woodwards patent over-and-under double-barrelled pinfire pocket pistol, c1855, barrels 1¾in (4.5cm) long.
$550–600 ASB

An Irish 16 bore 'man stopper' percussion pocket pistol, the walnut stock with fishtail butt and brass furniture, signed 'Trulock, Dublin', c1860, 4in (10cm) long.
$650–750 ASB

A Continental back action percussion target pistol, half-stocked in walnut, c1860, 13in (33cm) long.
$570–730 GV

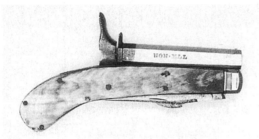

A .25 rimfire knife-pistol, by Unwin & Rodgers, Sheffield, with German octagonal silver barrel, folding trigger and 2 folding knife blades, Birmingham proof marks, stamped, c1862–84, 6½in (16.5cm) long.
$1,300–1,450 S(S)

A Prussian 15mm model 1850 percussion cavalry pistol, marked 'B. G. Schilling, Suhl', repaired, dated '1868', barrel 8½in (21.5cm) long.
$950–1,100 ASB

A pair of Irish target pistols, by M. & B. Anglin, with 8½in (21.5cm) octagonal barrels, 19thC, 14½in (37cm) long, in associated mahogany case.
$2,300–2,600 MEA

A pair of percussion duelling/target pistols, by Joseph Lang, London, gold and platinum lines at the breech and a platinum vent plug, half-stocked in walnut with original ramrods, with 9¾in (25cm) barrels, 19thC, 15in (38cm) long.
$4,500–5,500 GV

A pair of percussion travelling pistols, by Daniel, signed on the locks, with 3½in (9cm) barrels, 19thC, 7½in (19cm) long, in a fitted box.
$1,150–1,300 MEA

A pair of percussion capped pocket pistols, the engraved lockplates with dolphin cocks and trigger guards, 19thC, 7½in (19cm) long.
$320–350 EH

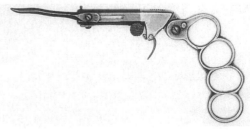

A percussion under-hammer knuckleduster knife-pistol, 'The Sure Defender', No. 517, late 19thC, 8½in (21.5cm) long.
$1,300–1,450 S(S)

A pepperbox revolver, the barrel group with Birmingham proofs, the German silver frame engraved 'Improved Revolving Pistol' and 'Charles Jones' with address, c1845, barrel 4in (10cm) long, in original blue baize-lined mahogany case with most original fittings.
$3,000–3,500 WSA

A .44 Colt 3rd model Dragoon percussion revolver, marked, 1851, 14in (35.5cm) long.
$2,250–2,750 S(NY)

A 54 bore Kerr's Patent revolver, with London proofs, c1860, 10½in (26.5cm) long, in original case with most accessories.
$5,200–5,600 WSA

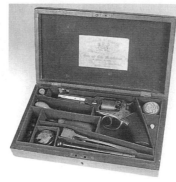

A 80 bore five-shot revolver, by William H. Blanch, Liverpool, c1850, 9in (23cm) long, in a blue baize-lined fitted mahogany case with accessories.
$950–1,150 CGC

A Cooper's patent percussion pepperbox revolver, complete with accessories, c1860, box 10in (25.5cm) wide.
$1,800–2,200 GV

A Massachusetts Arms Company Wesson & Leavitt six-shot belt revolver, with polished-wood grip, mid-19thC, barrel 5in (12.5cm) long.
$950–1,150 BOS

A 39 bore Westley Richards patent five-shot self-cocking percussion revolver, the octagonal barrel engraved at the muzzle, Birmingham proof marks, c1855, 12½in (32cm) long.
$2,400–2,700 Bon

A 54 bore Beaumont Adams revolver, with Kerr's rammer, London proofs, c1855, 11in (28cm) long, in original case with accessories.
$4,500–5,000 WSA

A .32 rim fire Smith and Wesson five-shot single action revolver, model No. 1½, 2nd issue, No. 53468, with mother-of-pearl bird's-head grips, fixed cartridge ejector rod, fluted cylinder and sheath trigger, 1868–75, barrel 3½in (9cm) long.
$480–560 ASB

A Belgian 7mm six-shot double-action pocket revolver, with folding trigger, ivory grips, side ejector rod and loading gate, c1870, barrel 3¼in (8.5cm) long.
$380–420 ASB

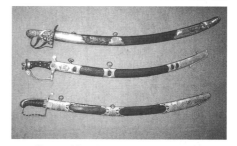

Types of Revolvers

Single action: the weapon is cocked by the firer drawing back the hammer with his thumb.
Double action: when the trigger is pressed the hammer lifts and returns in one movement.
Self-cocking: fitted with double triggers which allow the revolver to be cocked on the first pull of the trigger and fired on the second.

A 12mm Le Faucheux six-shot single action pin fire army revolver, No. 111918, c1870, barrel 6in (15cm) long.
$750–850 ASB

A .38 RF Hopkins and Allen Excel No. 6 five-shot single action revolver, and hardwood bird's-head grips, c1875, barrel 3in (7.5cm) long.
$300–330 ASB

An American .32 rim fire five-shot single action pocket revolver, No. 5199, with sheath trigger and mother-of-pearl grips, c1875, barrel 2¾in (7cm) long.
$520–570 ASB

A Belgian pin fire revolver, with moulded grips, engraved and nickel-plated, c1890, 5in (12.5cm) long.
$275–325 GV

A .44WCF (.44–40) Colt single action revolver, No. 281421, the hard rubber grips with logo, 1907, barrel 7½in (19cm) long.
$2,500–3,000 Bon

A 10mm bore Kentucky rifle, with octagonal barrel, full stocked in tiger-stripe maple with brass mounts and original ivory ramrod, the plate engraved 'C. Bird & Co, Philadelphia Warranted', late 18th/ early 19thC, 47¼in (120cm) long.
$1,800–2,000 GV

Bird & Co were gunsmiths in Philadelphia from 1790 to 1830.

An Ordnance Enfield cavalry rifle, with ordnance proofs and folding leaf rear sight, the lock with engraved crown, VR and 1857 tower, dated '1857', barrel 21in (53.5cm) long.
$1,300–1,450 WSA

A .577 presentation pattern 1853 percussion three-band Enfield rifle, by Isaac Hollis & Sons, dated '1861', barrel 36in (91.5cm) long.
$1,800–2,000 S(S)

A Mk III Snider short rifle, the barrel with ordnance proofs, with iron furniture, the lock marked '1871, Enfield', crown and VR, 48in (122cm) long.
$900–1,000 WSA

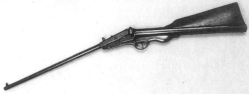

A Britannia air rifle, No. 1058, 177 calibre, c1900, 36in (91.5cm) long.
$1,000–1,100 GV

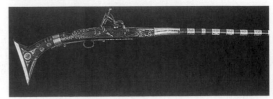

A North African Kabyle Snaphaunce gun, the two-stage barrel with brass inlay on the breech, 19thC, barrel 42in (107cm) long.
$1,000–1,150 Bon

Garth Vincent
Antique Arms and Armour

**I have customers worldwide
and I am interested in purchasing
single items or complete collections,
advice freely given**

**Dealer in antique and reproduction
arms and armour for the collector,
investor and interior decorator
Commission buying at auction**

Access & Visa accepted

Brochure available

**The Old Manor House,
Allington, Nr Grantham,
Lincolnshire NG32 2DH
Telephone: 01400 281358
Fax: 01400 282658
Mobile: 0385 352151**

Email: garthvincent@compuserve.com

Website: http://www.btinternet.com/~garthvincentarmsandarmour/

SWORDS

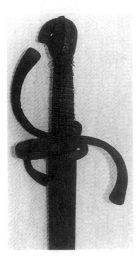

An infantryman's sword, with wire-bound wooden grip, eagle's head shaped pommel and straight single-edged blade, 16thC, blade 25¼in (65cm) long.
$1,100–1,200 ASB

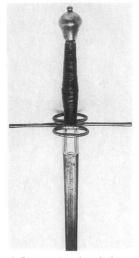

A German two-handed sword, with double-edged blade, inscribed 'In Te Domine' on one face and 'Speravit' on the other, the wooden grip with later tape binding, late 16thC, blade 45¾in (116cm) long.
$4,000–5,000 S(NY)

A military broadsword, inscribed 'Fide Sed CVI Vide', the russet iron hilt with guard formed in one piece, fitted with iron pommel chiselled as a stylized monster head and later wooden grip, English or German, late 16th/early 17thC, blade 28½in (72.5cm) long.
$2,300–2,500 S(S)

A silver-hilted sword, the guard with pierced decoration depicting a hunter, the blade bearing a family crest, c1680, 38in (96.5cm) long.
$2,600–3,000 GV

A silver hilted sword, with a colichemarde blade, the hilt hallmarked 1720, 34in (86.5cm) long.
$1,600–1,800 GV

An American Revolution short sabre, the horn grip bound with a strip of copper, the curved single-edged blade with twin fullers and spear point, c1776, blade 21½in (54.5cm) long.
$750–850 ASB

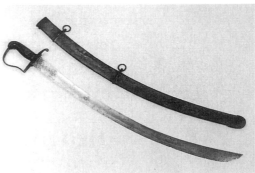

A 1796 pattern cavalry trooper's sword, in steel scabbard, 14th Light Dragoons, blade 30in (76cm) long.
$460–520 RBB

A Continental military rapier, with cup-hilt copper wirework grip, impressed 1797, blade 36½in (92.5cm) long.
$600–700 DD

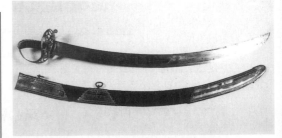

A 1796 pattern cavalry officer's sword, the unusual heavy curved blade engraved with Royal cipher and coat-of-arms, the hilt of gilt ladder-back pattern with horn grip, the leather scabbard with finely engraved gilt-brass mounts, c1800, 40in (101.5cm) long.
$4,000–4,500 WSA

Facts in Brief

- The three main types of military sword are the heavy cavalry (straight blade), light cavalry (curved blade), and infantry.
- Light infantry, bandsmen, pioneer and corps troops also had their own patterns.
- Officers' swords invariably have wire-bound fishskin grips; other ranks' swords have wire-bound leather.
- The amount of decoration on a military sword denotes the owner's status.
- Officers' swords are often found accompanied by symbols of rank, such as epaulettes, gorgets or shoulder belt plates.

A British Military issue sword, with single-edged curved blade, stamped with a crown over 4, the hilt with a brass stirrup guard and ribbed iron grip, scabbard missing, early 19thC, 36in (91.5cm) long.
$450–550 BOS

This example is believed to have been carried by other ranks of the Royal Artillery during the Napoleonic War.

A heavy cavalry pattern trooper's sword, by Woolley Deakin & Co, the polished steel hilt with a pierced design and ribbed leather grip, complete with polished steel scabbard, c1815, 34in (86.5cm) long.
$1,600–1,800 BOS

A Victorian officer's claymore of The Royal Scots Fusiliers, by Thurkle, London, with regulation twin-fullered blade, with etched decoration, the steel basket guard with red liner, fishskin grip, in steel scabbard, blade 33in (84cm) long.
$1,000–1,100 Sp

A Victorian officer's basket-hilted broadsword of the Highland Rifle Militia, with etched bi-fullered Wilkinson blade, No. 19410 for 1874, wire-bound sharkskin grip, blade 32½in (82.5cm) long.
$350–400 WAL

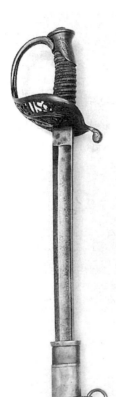

A Knight Templar's dress sword, awarded to John Morro, father of J. B. Morro, c1900, 38in (96.5cm) long.
$1,600–1,800 Q&C

An Edwardian cavalry officer's sword, with slightly curved fullered blade, by Hawkes & Co, London, etched with coat-of-arms and EVIIR cypher, regulation steel guard and fishskin grip, and brown leather scabbard, 35¼in (89.5cm) long.
$300–330 Sp

A British 1900 pattern cutlass, the hilt with sheet iron basket guard and chequered leather grips, the straight single-edged blade with fuller and spear point, in original steel-mounted black leather scabbard with webbing frog, Enfield, 1901, blade 27¾in (69cm) long.
$350–400 ASB

◄ An American naval officer's sword, c1930, 38in (96.5cm) long.
$1,600–2,000 Q&C

This sword belonged to John B. Morro, American Ambassador and father-in-law to the aviator, Charles Augustus Lindbergh.

An American army officer's sword, with slightly curved blade, by Cluberg Solingen, etched with an eagle, motto and military trophies, with brass hilt and wire-bound fishskin-covered grip, in steel scabbard with brass mounts, c1880, blade 26in (66cm) long.
$800–900 WAL

Militaria

COSTUME

A 6th Inniskilling Dragoons officer's tunic, the scarlet melton cloth with white facing to the collar and cuffs and gilt regimental buttons, the plaited shoulder cords with rank stars indicating Lieutenant, 1891.
$900–1,000 BOS

An Edwardian Australian forces tunic, of light khaki fine wool, the collar with white gorget patches, with central scarlet line, the brown leather pouch belt and pouch with a silvered whistle and chain.
$900–1,000 BOS

This tunic is attributed to Col Sir John Michael Fleetwood Miller KCMG, who served as Governor of Victoria and Hon Col of the 19th Australian Light Horse. The rank to the shoulder straps is that of Colonel.

A Hussar's uniform, dated '1904'.
$250–300 Q&C

An Edwardian Indian Army Supply and Transport Corps officer's uniform, comprising a Wolseley pattern foreign service helmet of white doeskin, dark blue melton cloth tunic with white facings to the collar and cuffs, the plaited bullion shoulder cords with rank insignia denoting Colonel, with regimental pattern buttons.
$1,150–1,300 BOS

A German WWII army EM four-pocket M-43 reed-green tunic, factory sewn eagle and collar tabs.
$325–400 JAA

An Edwardian 16th Lancer's tunic.
$250–300 Q&C

A 36th Battery Canadian Field Artillery private's uniform, with grey indication of Division and cuff with 4 blue overseas service chevrons, Royal Artillery buttons, inside label dated '1917', with breeches of the 1918 pattern.
$1,000–1,200 BOS

An American WWII army Major-General's tunic, the left breast with numerous valour and service ribbons, including distinguished service cross with OLC, and purple heart with OLC.
$850–950 DuM

An American WWII leather flying jacket, with fur collar.
$100–115 JAA

HELMETS & HEADDRESSES

A French 2nd Empire bearskin, the brass plate struck with crowned eagle with pierced '2' on sunburst, white plaited lanyard, crimson ostrich feather plume, 1848–70.
$1,450–1,600 S(S)

An officer's bearskin cap of the Scots Fusilier Guards, with brown leather lining throughout, and a cylindrical tin with brass plaque, late 19thC.
$1,600–1,800 Sp

A pair of WWI MkI flying goggles, the tinted tear-shaped lenses with fur mask surround, the reverse fitted with fur and elasticated strap.
$230–260
A WWI British issue soft brown leather cut-down cowl flying helmet, with fur and blanket lining to the interior.
$350–400 BOS

It was common for aircrew to cut down the issue Balaklava style cowl helmet, which was issued during the final stages of the Great War.

A Crimean War period Russian other ranks' black leather helmet, the metal helmet plate in the form of an Imperial crowned eagle, brass flaming grenade spike mount, 1853–56.
$2,200–2,400 WAL

An officer's blue cloth helmet of the Royal Norfolk Regiment, with gilt helmet plate, spike, mounts and chin chain, c1900.
$800–900 AP

A Prussian officer's lance cap of the 13th Uhlans, with white metal fittings and scales, gilt rosettes, Prussian eagle plate in white metal, bearing battle hounours for Waterloo, Peninsula and Garcia Hernandez, issue stamp for 1911.
$2,400–2,600 Sp

▶ A Hampshire regiment blue cloth other ranks' helmet, 1912.
$400–500 Q&C

A Victorian officer's helmet of the 2nd Dragoon Guards (Queen's Bays), the brass skull with traces of gilt, gilt and silver-plated helmet plate with blue and red enamelled centre and black hair plume.
$2,000–2,200 WAL

An Indian policeman's helmet, Madras, c1900.
$220–240 Q&C

▶ A WWI Prussian pickelhaube.
$480–560 AnS

A Victorian Royal Artillery Volunteers other rank's busby, with Lancashire red horse hair plume and sealskin.
$520–560 Q&C

A 17th Lancers officer's lance cap, with black patent-leather skull, the upper portion of white melton cloth ornamented with gold gimp cord, the gold bullion rosette with embroidered Royal cypher of Edward VII, with white swan's-feather plume and Battle Honours including South Africa 1900–02, 1901–10.
$8,000–9,000 BOS

A WWII Japanese naval officer's blue wool cap, with Admiral's rank devices, gold chin strap and bullion service device.
$275–325 JAA

MEDALS

A Sutlej medal 1846
for Sobraon, impressed
'John Winstanley,
1st Dragoon Guards'.
$600–700 WAL

The Punjab Campaign
Medal 1848–49, with
Goojerat and Chilianwala
bars, impressed 'George
Colley, 61st Foot'.
$350–400 Bea(E)

A pair awarded to Ordinary
Seaman J. Davey, Royal
Navy, Crimea Medal,
Sebastopol bar, 1848,
Turkish Crimea Medal, 1855.
$325–375 RMC

A campaign and Colonial Administrator's group of
4 medals awarded to Major-General Sir Archibald Anson,
KCMG, Royal Artillery, Crimea 1854–56, one clasp,
Sebastopol, India General Service 1854–95, one clasp,
Perak, Order of the Medjidie, 5th class breast badge,
silver, gold and enamel, Turkish Crimea 1855, Sardinian
issue, with his ceremonial Tipstaff as Inspector General
of Police in Mauritius 1858–67, with gilt crown finial and
ivory mid-section.
$3,200–3,600 DNW

**Major-General Sir Archibald Anson was Governor of
Penang and administrator of the Straits Settlements
and in charge of the Expedition in Sungei Ujong and
Negri Sambilan during the Perak Campaign 1875–76.**

A Devonshire Regiment group of 6 medals, awarded to
Acting Sergeant Edward Terry, comprising India General
Service Medal, 2 clasps, Queen's South Africa Medal,
5 clasps, King's South Africa, 2 clasps, 1914–15 Star,
British War Medal, Victory Medal.
$750–850 BOS

◄ An India General Service Medal 1895–1902,
3 clasps, Punjab Frontier 1897, Samana 1897,
Tirah 1897–98, awarded to R. J. Chayter,
First Battalion, Northampton Regiment.
$650–750 Q&C

A group of 6 medals, awarded to Private Thomas Allen, Royal
West Kent Regiment, Indian General Service Medal 1895–1902,
with 3 bars, The King's South Africa Medal 1901–02 with 2 bars,
the 1914–18 War Medal, and the 1914–19 Victory Medal.
$575–650 MCA

Facts in Brief

Most 19th & 20thC British medals are inscribed on the edge
with the recipient's name and regiment. Some were issued
unnamed but could be impressed later at the recipient's
request. Continental medals are often uninscribed. Bars
increase a medal's desirability, but it is wise to check the
regimental roll before buying to confirm the recipient was
entitled to the decoration.

A group of 7 medals awarded to
Captain H. P. Gabb MD, comprising
Military Cross awarded 1916 in Mesopotamia
when in the 5th Batallion The Queen's RWS
Regiment, 1914–15 Star and WWI Defence
medals, the Great War for Civilisation Medal
with oak leaves to the ribbon, WWII Defence
Medals and Territorial Army Medal, with
conforming set of dress miniatures.
$900–1,000 HAM

POWDER FLASKS & HORNS

A German cowhorn powder flask, engraved with concentric circles, fruiting scrolling foliage and a medallion flowerhead, early 17thC, 14½in (37cm) long.
$750–850 S(S)

▶ An American Colonial cowhorn powder flask, with traces of original red and green pigment and incised with scrimshaw work depicting the forts and settlements along the Hudson and Mohawk rivers, and views including Lake Ontario, New York and Albany, c1760, 11½in (29cm) long.
$1,300–1,600 Bon

A northern European powder horn, with engraved decoration, dated '1841', 8in (20.5cm) long.
$200–250 HUM

A French copper powder flask, with brass top, decorated with laurel leaves, oak leaves and acorns enclosing crossed pistols and swords and a pike, marked 'B à Paris', c1840, 4½in (11.5cm) long.
$250–300 ASB

MISCELLANEOUS

An English Civil War leather water bottle, bearing the crest of the Percy family of Northumberland, c1640, 10in (25.5cm) high.
$1,200–1,400 GV

An American Civil War snare drum, by A. H. White, Boston, the metal body engraved with a band of five-pointed stars and the Massachusetts State Seal, mid-19thC, 17in (43cm) diam.
$1,000–1,150 SK(B)

Cross Reference
See Colour Review

A George III silver campaign set, comprising a beaker engraved with crest and monogram by Timothy Renou, a combined nutmeg grater and cork-screw, a knife, fork and spoon, a marrow scoop, a pair of mounted glass condiments and a glass smelling salts bottle, c1800.
$12,000–13,500 P

A pair of Georgian tabards, embroidered with Royal Arms, 17¾in (45cm) wide.
$730–830 DNW

A Cambridgeshire Militia drum, c1860, 16in (40.5cm) diam.
$1,200–1,350 Q&C

◀ An original photograph, depicting the Crimean War, inscribed 'Trenches – Crimea', c1855, 8¼ x 10¼in (21 x 26cm).
$200–220 FW&C

Sport

BASEBALL

A baseball bat, used by Mark McGwire, dated '98', 34in (86.5cm) long, with a letter of provenance.
$7,000–8,500 S(NY)

This bat was used in the 1998 historic season whereby McGwire hit 70 home runs breaking Roger Marris's record of 61 home runs in one season.

A baseball, autographed by Babe Ruth on the 'sweet spot', c1942.
$3,500–4,000 HALL

The Sweet Spot

The 'sweet spot' on a baseball is located on the crown of the ball where the stitches come together. It is the narrowest portion of the ball and is considered the most desirable location for an autograph because of its dominant position. Traditionally, the manager of the team would sign on the 'sweet spot', but baseball greats such as Ted Williams, Babe Ruth, and other notable players were also given the honour of signing there. Collectors are always interested in autographs on a baseball, whether or not it has been signed on the 'sweet spot'.

A New York Yankees official baseball, autographed on the 'sweet spot' by the team, including Mickey Mantle, 1953.
$900–1,000 HALL

A baseball, autographed by Joe DiMaggio, c1980.
$250–300 HALL

Joe DiMaggio, born in California in 1914, began his baseball career with the Pacific Coast League in 1932. He was signed by the New York Yankees in 1936 and remained with them until his retirement in 1951.

A Mickey Mantle red, white and blue metal button, c1969, 3in (7.5cm) diam.
$200–250 HALL

Mickey Mantle (1931–95), born in Oklahoma, replaced Joe DiMaggio in centre field when he joined the New York Yankees in 1951. In 1956 Mantle led the league in batting average, home runs and runs batted in, and won baseball's triple crown. He retired in 1969 and was inducted into the Hall of Fame in 1974.

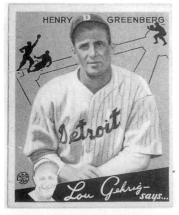

A Goudey Gum baseball card, depicting Henry Greenberg, Lou Gehrig series, 1934.
$350–400 HALL

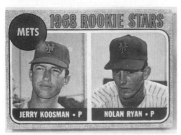

A baseball card, depicting Ted Williams in his rookie year, 1939.
$1,800–2,000 HALL

◀ A Topps Gum rookie card, depicting Nolan Ryan and Jerry Koosman, 1968.
$500–600 HALL

A Hartland statue of Ted Williams, late 1950s, 10in (25.5cm) high.
$200–250 HALL

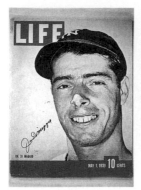

A copy of *Life* magazine, May 1, 1939, autographed by Joe DiMaggio.
$200–250 HALL

A copy of *Baseball Magazine*, August 1951, depicting Mickey Mantle in his rookie year.
$400–500 HALL

A copy of *Daily Record*, September 26, 1960, with headline 'Ted Williams Quits as Player'.
$150–200 HALL

A Brooklyn Dodgers *Year Book*, 1955.
$180–200 HALL

A World Series programme, Yankee Stadium, 1942.
$200–250 HALL

A baseball All Stars game programme, 1946.
$1,000–1,200 HALL

A World Series programme, Yankee Stadium, 1949.
$180–200 HALL

A photographic post-card, signed Jimmy Foxx, c1940.
$400–500 HALL

A World Series ticket stub, Brooklyn Dodgers v. New York Yankees at Brooklyn, New York, 1956.
$180–200 HALL

A wire service photograph of Joe DiMaggio and his son, Joe DiMaggio, Jr, c1946.
$180–200 HALL

A wire service photograph of Joe DiMaggio and Marilyn Monroe at the beach, c1950.
$180–200 HALL

BASKETBALL

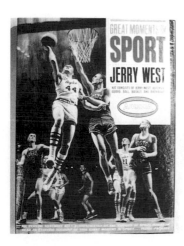

A pair of Nike Air basketball shoes, signed by Derrick Coleman, 1990s.
$50–60 DuM

◀ An Aurora 'Great Moments in Sport' plastic model kit, featuring Jerry West, 1960s, 10 x 8in (25.5 x 20.5cm).
$120–150 HALL

The NBA at Fifty, edited by Mark Vancil, New Jersey, 1996, 4°, with many autographs.
$650–750 FBG

BILLIARDS

A mahogany billiard table, by Burroughes & Watts, late 19thC, 144 x 72in (366 x 183cm), with cues and scoreboard.
$2,500–2,800 MEA

An oak billiard table, by Burroughes & Watts, late 19thC, 144 x 72in (366 x 183cm), with numerous accessories including cues, rests, ivory and compostion balls and cabinet, overhead three-section light shade with five-section slate bed.
$1,600–2,000 HBC

A late Victorian mahogany billiard table, by D. Harris & Son, Dublin, 144 x 72in (366 x 183cm), with a collection of cues and ivory balls.
$5,000–5,000 MEA

A mahogany combined billiard/dining table, by E. F. Riley, Accrington, with slate top, late 19th/early 20thC, 64½ x 34½in (164 x 87.5cm).
$1,000–1,200 FBG

A mahogany billiard table, by George Wright & Co, London, with five-section slate bed, late 19thC, 144 x 72in (366 x 183cm), with numerous cues, accessories and a three-section light.
$4,000–5,000 HBC

A mahogany billiard table, c1900, 144 x 72in (366 x 183cm), with accessories.
$1,000–1,200 SERR

A mahogany billiard table, by Thurston, c1810, 144 x 72in (366 x 183cm).
$35,000–40,000 WBB

An oak combination billiard/dining table, by Cheshire Billiards, 1990s, 84 x 41in (213.5 x 104cm).
$4,000–5,000 CBC

A mahogany scoreboard, by Burroughes & Watts, London, late 19thC, 17in (43cm) wide.
$250–300 GAK

A mahogany scoreboard, by Stevens & Sons, London, with ball box and blackboard, c1890, 42in (106.5cm) wide.
$2,800–3,200 WBB

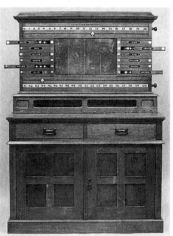

An Edwardian oak scoreboard, by Burroughes & Watts, London, 48in (122cm) wide.
$2,800–3,000 EH

A pair of silver-mounted ash billiard cues, hallmarked London 1896.
$1,100–1,300 S

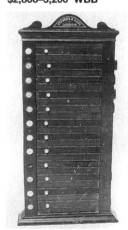

A mahogany scoreboard, by Stevens & Sons, London, 19thC, 11in (28cm) wide.
$550–650 L

A French novelty musical trinket box, in the form of a billiard table, the movement playing 2 airs, the hinged top with ebonized border and green cloth insert, c1840, 12¼in (31cm) long.
$450–500 S(S)

An Italian Renaissance bronze harness mount, late 16thC, 3in (7.5cm) diam.
$300–330 BAC

A presentation hunting tankard, embossed with a hunting scene, the cover with a fox finial, inscribed, maker's mark of the Barnards, London 1843, 11¾in (30cm) high.
$3,200–3,600 Bon

A silver-framed mantel clock, the dial cast with a hunting scene, the numbers in the form of bits and spurs, maker EHS, London 1890, 5in (12.5cm) diam.
$1,150–1,300 RBB

LOCATE THE SOURCE
The source of each illustration in Miller's can be found by checking the code letters below each caption with the Key to Illustrations, pages 789–795.

A Spanish steel spur, with silver inlay, c1750, 5in (13cm) long.
$230–260 HUM

A pair of silver goblets, by Robert Hennell, the sides embossed with a gamekeeper, hounds and pheasants, 1860, 7in (18cm) high, 23¼oz.
$2,750–3,250 P

A brass letter holder, c1900, 10 x 5in (25.5 x 12.5cm).
$480–560 CHe

▶ A sterling silver two-handled trophy cup, by Black, Starr & Frost, engraved to one side '1937 Washington Handicap one mile and a quarter, Laurel, Maryland, Won by War Admiral', 11½in (29cm) high, 50oz.
$675–775 SK

A black and white silk scarf, with a central medallion depicting Blenheim, the Derby winner of 1930, surrounded by small cartouches with previous Derby winners since 1780, within a blue border, framed, 37¾ x 37½in (96 x 95.5cm).
$200–230 SLM

An Irish bronze figure of a polo player, by Walter Roche, signed and dated '1882', 10½in (27cm) high.
$4,500–5,500 P

Roche concentrated mainly on sporting sculpture, working and exhibiting in London.

A leather-cased hunting flask, with silver top, c1920, 10in (25.5cm) high.
$400–450 RTh

FISHING

Angling is one of the world's oldest sports, possibly the most popular, and rich in artefact and invention. It is perhaps surprising, therefore, that collecting angling memorabilia has taken so long to become popular. Tackle collectors are not a new breed, but 20 years ago they were little more than a dedicated few. Today they number in their tens of thousands in the UK, with extensive following overseas. Why this surge in popularity? Several factors have had an impact, not least the advances in technology offered to today's angler. They offer much in strength and convenience, but have stripped the sport of much of its traditional beauty, both visual and tactile, substituting carbon for built cane, plastic for leather wallet, graphite reel for ebonite, walnut or brass. Nostalgia has played its part, together with the appearance in the 1980s of the first dedicated books on the subject. Greater attention by the auction houses and through media coverage has meant that collecting angling memorabilia is here to stay. The first televised auction of fishing tackle was held earlier this year and yet it is only 15 years since tackle first made an appearance in this guide – a remarkable change.

Growth in interest inevitably affects values, but what has risen strongly and what more slowly is complex. Price trends have been affected by public awareness and changes in fashion. Coarse fishing reels like the Allcock Aerials which could have been bought for tens of pounds 20 years ago now fetch hundreds, but the Hardy Silex Major would have cost almost half as much then as today. The prices of rods have also grown more slowly, since most rods are bought for use and therefore collectors are few.

Interest in the hugely diverse area of artificial baits, accessories, paper ephemera etc has risen progressively in recent years. Many early baits, some of which are solid silver, are almost jewel-like and it is hardly surprising they have caught collectors' imaginations. A display which included a few previously unseen examples fetched an amazing $42,000 at Christies recently.

What pointers are there for the future? Fashions continue to change but it is likely that current interest in smaller artefacts will continue apace, while interest in more traditional areas such as reels will see greater selectivity by the collector. The rarest and best items should continue to rise in value, the middle range perhaps less so, although the ever-increasing number of collectors will maintain demand. **Richard Dowson**

Two Allcock Felton Crosswind reels, 1950–60,
l. No. 2 Felton Crosswind with half bale arm,
r. Allcock Felton with full bale arm.
$90–115 each OTB

A 3½in Allcock Aerial centrepin fishing reel, backplate stamped, c1920, in a fitted box.
$800–900 Bon

An Allcock Flick Em Perfection 4in fishing reel, c1940.
$115–130 AnS

▶ A Farlow 2in brass crankwind fishing reel, with curved crank and ivory handle, late 19thC.
$350–400 Bon(C)

A Farlow 4in Patent Lever alloy salmon winch, with wooden handle, in leather reel case, c1910.
$300–350 Bon

A Gowland & Co 4in brass platewind reel, with ivory handle, 1850–90, in unrelated fitted leather reel case.
$230–260 Bon(C)

A Hardy 4in bronzed and half-ebonite Birmingham platewind reel, with horn handle, nickel-silver rims, late 19thC.
$480–560 Bon(C)

A Hardy Uniqua alloy trout fly reel, with caliper spring check, ivorine handle, brass foot, c1912.
$120–145 Bon(C)

A Hardy Silex Major 4in alloy bait casting reel, with twin ebonite handles, c1926.
$320–360 Bon(C)

A Hardy Conquest 4¼in alloy trotting reel, with dark grey enamelled backplate and bright alloy drum, c1960.
$250–325 OTB

A Westley Richards 3in aluminium trout reel, with bronze fittings, c1920.
$65–80 WAB

An Edward vom Hofe Model 722 Commander Ross 12/0 big game multiplier reel, ebonite and nickel-silver construction with turned ebonite handle, in original leather case, 1930s.
$3,200–3,600 AGA

This reel is rare and in fine condition.

◄ A Bakelite salmon reel, with horn handle, German silver fittings and original dry fly line, c1890.
$110–120 WAB

A 4in fishing reel, by W. R. Products, London, c1940–50, boxed.
$145–160 AnS

A 2½in brass crankwind collar winch, with horn handle, mid-19thC.
$575–650 Bon

A brass crankhandle gut twister, with triple iron pick-up hooks, the geared mechanism between 2¼in (5.5cm) brass plates, with bone handle and brass table clamp, 19thC.
$575–650 Bon

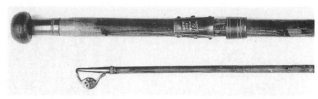

A Hardy two-piece whole cane sea rod, with large snake eyelets and brass roller tip ring, c1893, 100in (254cm) long.
$100–120 Bon(C)

A Farlow's combination rod, incomplete, c1920, longest portion 26in (66cm), in a canvas bag.
$55–65 AL

A 'Scottie VII' special build seven-section cane trout fly rod, by J. S. Sharpe, 1930–32, 108in (274.5cm) long, in maker's bag.
$250–300 Bon

◄ A Gregory nickel-silver bait, c1900, 1½in (4cm) long.
$730–830 Bon(C)

An American Winchester multi-wobbler bait, with box and instruction leaflet, Connecticut, 1921–30, 9½in (24cm) long.
$1,600–2,000 JVM

A black japanned salmon fly reservoir, by J. Bernard & Son, with cream-painted interior of 8 lift-out trays containing 246 fully-dressed gut eyes salmon flies, c1920, 12½in (32cm) wide.
$2,500–3,000 AGA

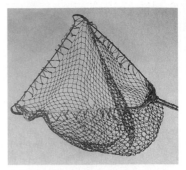

A landing net, with a cane and cork handle, c1920, 47in (119.5cm) long.
$200–250 AL

A black japanned bait can, by Cummins, Bishop Auckland, with belt loops, late 19thC, 7in (18cm) wide.
$230–280 OTB

An American split-willow trapper's basket, Vermont, c1900, 20in (51cm) high.
$200–250 JVM

A bait can, with wooden handle, c1920, 10in (25.5cm) wide.
$35–40 AL

A Gregory glass-eyed Norwich spoon, c1900, 2½in (6.5cm) long.
$525–575 Bon(C)

An Eaton & Deller nickel-silver serrated spoon, c1915, 2½in (6.5cm) long.
$1,000–1,150 Bon(C)

A stuffed and mounted trout in a river-bed setting, inscribed in gilt 'caught by A. H. Ballantyne at Killaloe, County Clare, Ireland 29th May, 1900, Weight 8.5 lbs', in a glazed and ebonized case, 30½in (77.5cm) wide.
$800–950 Oli

A stuffed pike, in a river-bed setting, with inscription, 'Pike. 22½lbs. Caught near Ross-on-Wye, 21st Jan, 1935', in a glazed case, 44in (110cm) wide.
$1,450–1,600 Bea

SOCCER

The Busby Babes, a BEA Manchester–Düsseldorf flight card, 20th November, 1956, autographed by 17 members of the Manchester United party, printed in colour.
$2,300–2,600 S

A Northern Ireland v. Scotland International cap, worn by George Best, 1967–8.
$5,700–7,000 S

A Foster & Co gold velvet peaked cap, with silver wirework decoration and year dates to peak '1888–1891–1895'.
$900–1,000 BWe

This cap was reputedly presented to Billy Bassett, the West Bromwich Albion and England soccer player, 1888–1900.

A Northern Ireland dark green velvet football cap, with gold tassel, awarded to Billy Gillespie, with year dates to peak '1925–26'.
$800–900 VS

▶ A 1923 FA Cup Final 9ct gold Runner's-Up medal, inscribed 'W. G. Moore, West Ham United', 1¼in (3cm) diam.
$3,000–3,250 P(C)

A black and white photograph of Sam Cowan receiving the 1934 FA Cup from King George V, autographed on the mount by the Manchester City team, reserve and trainer, 14½ x 12½in (37 x 32cm).
$850–950 Bon(W)

FOOTBALL

A high-dome leather helmet, 1920s.
$600–700 SMAM

An American football leather helmet, 1930s.
$600–700 SMAM

Two papier mâché candy containers in the form of a football and a baseball, c1930, football 4in (10cm) long.
$35–40 YAG

The official United States Football Association pennant for the USA v. England International match played at Los Angeles, 28th May, 1959, in blue felt with yellow match inscription and fringe, 28¾in (73cm) high.
$600–700 S

◀ A Topps All American football card, depicting Jim Thorpe, 1955.
$350–400 HALL

Jim Thorpe (1887–1953) was born in Oklahoma, of mainly Native American heritage. In 1912 he won the pentathlon and decathlon events in the Olympic Games, and also led his school football team to the national collegiate championship. He played 6 years of major league baseball, but also succeeded in leading the Canton Bulldogs football team to unofficial world championships in 1916, 1917 and 1919. He subsequently played for the Chicago Cardinals until his retirement in 1928.

GOLF

A McEwan golden beech unused long spoon club head, c1875.
$1,600–2,000 S

A David Strath long-nosed long spoon club, with lemon wood shaft and beech head, c1860.
$9,000–11,000 S

A Dot & Dash mesh golf ball box, c1930, 8 x 5in (20.5 x 12.5cm).
$40–50 MURR

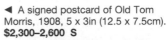

A Chambers patent golf ball marker, c1910.
$800–900 S

◀ A signed postcard of Old Tom Morris, 1908, 5 x 3in (12.5 x 7.5cm).
$2,300–2,600 S

A biscuit tin, inscribed 'The Heath Robinson Golf Course Packed with Peek Frean's Biscuits', with detachable golf course interior and original ball, c1920, 7 x 10½in (18 x 27cm).
$650–800 DW

A pair of bronze and marble bookends, depicting a golfer and his caddy, mid-20thC.
$325–400 MUL

◀ A booklet entitled *Men of America*, cover featuring Bobby Jones, c1920.
$160–200 HALL

RUGBY

A black velvet and silk-lined rugby cap, embroidered 'BRC 1920–22', with silk tassel.
$120–150 MUL

> Miller's is a price GUIDE not a price LIST

A Copeland Spode stoneware jug, decorated with rugby players in relief on a blue ground, with floral decorative border, embossed '1895' to base, 6in (15cm) high.
$800–900 P(C)

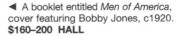

A Tonbridge School cap, worn by G. Hubbard who went on to play for England, embroidered '1919–20–21', 7in (18cm) wide.
$100–125 WaR

A framed menu for England v. Ireland Rugby Union game, played at Lansdowne Road, Dublin, February 6th, 1886.
$500–575 S

SHOOTING

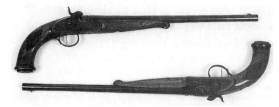

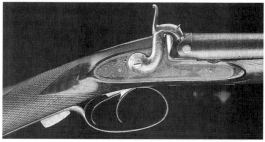

A pair of German hunting pistols, by Johann Andreas Kuchenreuter, the 40cm barrels decorated with geometric scrolling, 1758–1808, 21¼in (54cm) long.
$4,000–4,500 GV

A 5–bore percussion wildfowling gun, by Westley Richards, London, with figured walnut half-stock, Birmingham proof marks, c1840, barrel 42¼in (107.5cm) long.
$1,800–2,000 Bon

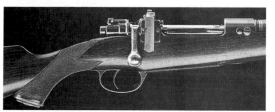

A .375 Magnum bolt-action sporting rifle, by Holland & Holland, the half-length stock with pistol grip and cheekpiece, c1920, barrel 24½in (62cm) long.
$7,500–9,000 S(Sc)

A 13-bore percussion sporting gun, by Thomas Boss & Co, with 30in (76cm) Damascus barrels, half-length figured stock with steel buttplate, c1859.
$2,400–2,800 S(Sc)

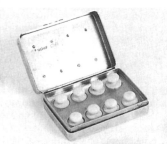

A brass capper, decapper and shot filler for making cartridges, c1880, 11½in (29cm) long.
$40–50 WAB

Six turned ivory egg or tot cups, each engraved and labelled 'Pheasant', 'Red Grouse', 'Black Grouse', 'Chinese Pheasant', 'Ptarmigan' and 'Capercaille', late 19thC, 2½in (6.5cm) high.
$1,300–1,600 Bon

A butt selector, by Sampson Mordan & Co, Chester, the silver box with gilt interior containing 8 numbered ivory pegs, 1912, 1¾in (4.5cm) wide.
$3,000–3,300 P

TENNIS

A lawn tennis racket, c1890, 25in (63.5cm) long.
$300–330 DW

A Birmal aluminium-framed tennis racket, by the Birmingham Aluminium Casting Co Ltd, with metal strings and leather grip, c1920, 27in (68.5cm) long.
$330–380 Bon(W)

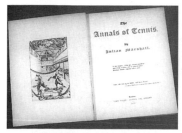

Julian Marshall, *The Annals of Tennis*, illustrated, full embossed cloth with gilt titles, 1878, 4°.
$1,400–1,550 HAM

> **Cross Reference**
> See Colour Review

An earthenware 'lazy Susan', printed and painted overall with tennis nets, balls and rackets within a gilt rim, c1875, 18in (45.5cm) wide.
$900–1,000 S(S)

A mug, with a tennis racket handle, decorated with 1947 Wimbledon winners, 1947, 5½in (14cm) high.
$75–90 WaR

Glossary

We have defined here some of the terms that you will come across in this book. If there are any terms or technicalities you would like explained or you feel should be included in future, please let us know.

acid engraving: Technique of decorating glass by coating it in resin, incising a design and exposing the revealed areas to hydrochloric acid fumes.

acid gilding: 19thC technique for decorating pottery whereby the surface is etched with hydrofluoric acid and the low-relief pattern gilded.

agate ware: 18thC pottery, veined or marbled to resemble the mineral agate.

air-twist: Helical decoration in the stem of wine glasses, developed 1740–70, in which an air bubble in the glass is drawn out and twisted to form complex spirals.

albarello: Pottery vessel used for storing pharmaceutical ingredients.

amboyna: Yellowish-brown burred wood imported from the West Indies and used as a veneer.

anchor escapement: Said to have been invented c1670 by Robert Hooke or William Clement. A type of escape mechanism shaped like an anchor, which engages at precise intervals with the toothed escape wheel. The anchor permits the use of a pendulum (either long or short), and gives greater accuracy than was possible with the verge escapement.

arabesque: Scrolling foliate decoration.

armoire: Large French cupboard or wardrobe, usually of monumental character.

associated: Term used in antiques, in which one part of an item is of the same design but not originally made for it. See **marriage**.

automaton: Any moving toy or decorative object, usually powered by a clockwork mechanism.

barley-twist: Form of turning, popular in the late 17thC, which resembles a spiral of traditional barley sugar.

basalt(es): Black stoneware with a smooth, stone-like finish; perfected by Josiah Wedgwood.

bezel: Ring, usually brass, surrounding the dial of a clock, and securing the glass dial cover.

bisque: French term for biscuit ware, or unglazed porcelain.

bolection moulding: Projecting moulding often used in the late 17thC on furniture to cover the joints between panel and frame. Also found on panelling and fire surrounds.

bombé: Outswelling, curving or bulging. Term used to describe a chest with a bulging front. In fashion from Louis XV period.

bonheur du jour: Small French writing table with a raised back comprising a cabinet or shelves.

boteh: Stylised floral bush found on rugs, similar to a Paisley design.

bracket clock: Originally a 17thC clock which had to be set high up on a bracket because of the length of the weights; now sometimes applied to any mantel or table clock.

bureau de dame: Writing desk of delicate appearance and designed for use by ladies. Usually raised above slender cabriole legs and with one or two external drawers.

bureau plat: French writing table with a flat top and drawers in the frieze.

cabaret set: Tea set on a tray for 3 or more people.

calamander: Hardwood, imported from Sri Lanka (of the same family as ebony), used in the Regency period for making small articles of furniture, as a veneer and for crossbanding.

camaieu: Porcelain decoration using different tones of a single colour.

cameo glass: Two or more layers of coloured glass in which the top layer/s are then cut or etched away to create a multi-coloured design in relief. An ancient technique popular with Art Nouveau glassmakers in the early 20thC.

candle slide: Wooden slide to hold a candlestick.

cartouche: Ornate tablet or shield surrounded by scrollwork and foliage, often bearing an inscription, monogram or coat-of-arms.

caryatid: Strictly a female figure used as a support in place of a column, but frequently used to describe a figure of either sex. See **term**.

cased glass: One layer of glass, often coloured, sandwiched between two plain glass layers or vice versa, the outer layer engraved to create a decorative effect. An ancient technique revived in the 19thC. See **cameo glass** and **overlay**.

celadon: Chinese stonewares with an opaque grey-green glaze, first made in the Song Dynasty and still made today, principally in Korea.

cellaret: Lidded container on legs designed to hold wine. The interior is often divided into sections for individual bottles.

champlevé: Enamelling on copper or bronze, similar to cloisonné, in which a glass paste is applied to the hollowed-out design, fired and ground smooth.

chapter ring: Circular ring on a clock dial on which the hours and minutes are engraved, attached or painted.

character doll: One with a naturalistic face, especially laughing, crying, pouting, etc.

chidori: Japanese for plover. When depicted with waves indicates stormy weather or strife.

chilong: Chinese mythical dragon-type lizard.

Chinese Imari: Chinese imitations of Japanese blue, red and gold painted Imari wares, made from the early 18thC.

chinoiserie: The fashion, prevailing in the late 18thC, for Chinese-style ornamentation on porcelain, wallpapers and fabrics, furniture and garden architecture.

chuval: Turkic word meaning bag.

cistern tube: Mercury tube fitted into stick barometers, the lower end of which is sealed into a boxwood cistern.

cleat: Strip of wood attached to the edge of a flat surface across the grain for neatness and extra strength.

clock garniture: Matching group of clock and vases or candelabra made for the mantel shelf. Often highly ornate.

cloisonné: Enamelling on metal with divisions in the design separated by lines of fine metal wire. A speciality of the Limoges region of France in the Middle Ages, and of Chinese craftsmen to the present day.

coiffeuse: French term for a dressing table.

coromandel: Imported wood from the Coromandel coast of India, of similar blackish appearance to calamander and used from c1780 for banding, and for small pieces of furniture.

countwheel: Wheel with segments cut out of the edge or with pins fitted to one face, which controls the striking of a clock. Also known as a locking plate.

crested china: Porcelain decorated with colourful heraldic crests, first made by Goss but, by 1900, being produced in quantity by manufacturers throughout the UK and in Germany.

cup-and-cover carving: Carved decoration found on the bulbous legs of some Elizabethan furniture.

cut glass: Glass carved with revolving wheels and abrasive to create sharp-edged facets that reflect and refract light so as to sparkle and achieve a prismatic (rainbow) effect. Revived in Bohemia in the 17thC, and common until superseded by pressed glass for utilitarian objects.

Cymric: Trade-name used by Liberty & Co for a mass-produced range of silverware inspired by Celtic art, introduced in 1899 and often incorporating enamelled pictorial plaques.

deadbeat escapement: Type of anchor escapement, possibly invented by George Graham and used in precision pendulum clocks.

Delft: Dutch tin-glazed earthenwares named after the town of Delft, the principal production centre, from the 16thC onwards. Similar pottery made in England from the late 16thC is also termed 'delft' or 'delftware'.

Della Robbia: Florentine Renaissance sculptor who invented technique of applying vitreous glaze to terracotta; English art pottery made at Birkenhead, late 19thC, in imitation of his work.

deng: Chinese ceremonial drinking vessel.

deutsche Blumen: Naturalistically painted flowers, either single or tied into bunches, used as a popular decorative motif on 18thC pottery and porcelain.

diaper: Surface decoration composed of repeated diamonds or squares, often carved in low relief.

diorama: Miniature three-dimensional scene.

écuelle: 17th and 18thC vessel, usually of silver, but also of ceramic, for serving soup. Has a shallow, circular bowl, two handles and a domed cover. It often comes complete with a stand.

enamel: Coloured glass, applied to metal, ceramic or glass in paste form and then fired for decorative effect.

EPNS: Electroplated nickel silver; ie nickel alloy covered with a layer of silver using the electroplate process.

escapement: Means or device which regulates the release of the power of a timepiece to its pendulum or balance.

famille jaune/noire/rose/verte: Chinese porcelain in which yellow, black, pink or green respectively are the predominant ground colours.

fauteuil: French open-armed drawing room chair.

fiddleback: Descriptive of a particular grain of mahogany veneer which resembles the back of a violin.

fielded panel: Panel with bevelled or chamfered edges.

filigree: Lacy openwork of silver or gold thread, produced in large quantities since end 19thC.

flatware (1): Collective name for flat pottery and porcelain, such as plates, dishes and saucers.

flatware (2): Cutlery.

flow blue: Process used principally after 1840, in which powder is added to the dye used in blue and white transferware so that the blue flows beyond the edges of the transfer, making the pattern less sharply defined. Items using this process were made primarily for the American market.

fluted: Border that resembles a scalloped edge, used as a decoration on furniture, glass, silver and porcelain items.

fusee: 18thC clockwork invention; a cone shaped drum, linked to the spring barrel by a length of gut or chain. The shape compensates for the declining strength of the mainspring thus ensuring constant timekeeping.

gadroon: Border or ornament comprising radiating lobes of either curbed or straight form. Used from the late Elizabethan period.

gamikos: Ancient Greek closed vase, often associated with weddings and having appropriate painted scenes.

ghalian: Part of a hookah or hubble-bubble pipe.

gilding: Process of applying thin gold foil to a surface. There are two methods. Oil gilding involves the use of linseed oil and is applied directly onto the woodwork. Water gilding requires the wood to be painted with gesso. The term is also used in ceramics, glass etc.

girandole: Carved and gilt candle sconce incorporating a mirror.

Glasgow School: Term used to describe the style developed in the late 19thC by Charles Rennie Mackintosh and his followers, a simplified linear form of Art Nouveau highly influential on Continental work of the period.

goncalo alves: Brazilian timber sometimes mistaken for rosewood.

grisaille: Monochrome decoration, usually grey, used on ceramics and furniture during the 18th and 19thC.

Grödnertal: Wooden European dolls made during the 18th and 19thC in and around densely forested mountainous regions, such as Grödnertal in Austria.

guéridon: Small circular table designed to carry some form of lighting.

guilloche: Pattern of twisting bands, spirals, double spirals or linked chains.

gul: From the Persian word for flower – usually used to describe a geometric flowerhead on a rug.

halberd: Spear fitted with a double axe.

hard paste: True porcelain made of china stone (petuntse) and kaolin; the formula was long known to, and kept secret by, Chinese potters but only discovered in the 1720s at Meissen, Germany, from where it spread to the rest of Europe and the Americas. Recognised by its hard, glossy feel.

harewood: Sycamore which has been stained a greenish colour. It is used mainly as an inlay and was known as silverwood in the 18thC.

hatchli: Rug used as a tent door by Turkomans.

Hausmaler: German term for an independent painter or workshop specializing in the decoration of faïence, porcelain or glass blanks.

herati: Overall repeating design of a flowerhead within a lozenge issuing small leaves. Used in descriptions of rugs.

hiramakie: Japanese term for sponged gold applied level with the surface.

hirame: Japanese lacquer decorated with gold and silver leaf.

huanghuali: Type of Oriental wood, much admired for its colour.

Imari: Export Japanese porcelain of predominantly red, blue and gold decoration which, although made in Arita, is called Imari after the port from which it was shipped.

indianische Blumen: Indian flowers; painting on porcelain in the Oriental style, especially on mid-18thC Meissen.

inro: Japanese multi-compartmental medicine or seal container, carried suspended from the sash of a kimono.

intaglio: Incised gemstone, often set in a ring, used in antiquity and during the Renaissance as a seal. Any incised decoration; the opposite of carving in relief.

ironstone: Stoneware, patented 1813 by Charles James Mason, containing ground glassy slag, a by-product of iron smelting, for extra strength.

jadeite: Type of jade, normally the best and most desirable.

Jugendstil: German Art Nouveau style.

Kakiemon: Family of 17thC Japanese porcelain decorators who produced wares decorated with flowers and figures on a white ground in distinctive colours: azure, yellow, turquoise and soft red. Widely imitated in Europe.

kantharos: Ancient Greek stemmed deep drinking cup with high flung, ear-like handles.

kiku mon: Japanese stylised chrysanthemum.

kilim: Flat woven rugs lacking a pile.

kirin: Chinese mythical beast with a lion's tail, cloven hooves and the scales of a dragon.

knop: Knob, protuberance or swelling in the stem of a wine glass, of various forms which can be used as an aid to dating and provenance.

koro: Japanese incense burner.

kovsh: Russian vessel used for measuring drink, often highly decorated for ornamental purposes from the late 18thC.

kraak porselein: Dutch term for porcelain raided from Portuguese ships, used to describe the earliest Chinese export porcelain.

krater: Ancient Greek vessel for mixing water and wine in which the mouth is always the widest part.

kufic: Arabic angular script – used in rugs to refer to stylised geometric calligraphy.

lekythos: Ancient Greek flask used for oil or perfume.

linenfold: Carved decoration which resembles folded linen.

loaded: In silverware, a hollow part of a vessel, usually a candlestick, filled with pitch or sand for weight and stability.

lunette: Semi-circular decorative motif popular for carved friezes in the Jacobean and Victorian periods.

made up: Piece of furniture that has been put together from parts of other pieces of furniture. See **marriage**.

maiolica: Tin-glazed earthenware produced in Italy from the 15thC to the present day.

majolica: Heavily-potted, moulded ware covered in transparent glazes in distinctive, often sombre colours, developed by the Minton factory in the mid-19thC.

marriage: Joining together of two unrelated parts to form one piece of furniture. See **associated and made up**.

marvering: Ancient technique where hot threads of softened glass are rolled over a flat surface to smooth and fuse the glass, and to fix trailed decoration.

meiping: Chinese for cherry blossom, used to describe a tall vase, with high shoulders, small neck and narrow mouth, used to display flowering branches.

merese: Flat disc of glass which links the bowl and stem, and sometimes the stem and foot, of a drinking glass.

mihrab: Prayer niche with a pointed arch; the motif which distinguishes a prayer rug from other types.

millefiori: Multi-coloured, or mosaic, glass, made since antiquity by fusing a number of coloured glass rods into a cane, and cutting off thin sections; much used to ornament paperweights.

nashiji: Multitude of gold flakes in Japanese lacquer.

netsuke: Japanese carved toggles made to secure *sagemono* ('hanging things') to the *obi* (waist belt) from a cord; usually of ivory, lacquer, silver or wood, from the 16thC.

niello: Black metal alloy or enamel used for filling in engraved designs on silverware.

nulling (knulling): Decorative carving in the form of irregular fluting which is usually found on early oak furniture.

oinochoe: In ancient times, a small jug with handles.

ojime: Japanese word meaning bead.

okimono: Small, finely carved Japanese ornament.

ormolu: Strictly, gilded bronze but used loosely for any yellow metal. Originally used for furniture handles and mounts but, from the 18thC, for inkstands, candlesticks etc.

overlay: In cased glass, the top layer, usually engraved to reveal a different coloured layer beneath.

overstuffed: Descriptive of upholstered furniture where the covering extends over the frame of the seat.

ovolo (1): Moulding of convex quarter-circle section. Sometimes found around the edges of drawers to form a small overlap onto the carcase.

ovolo (2): Small oval convex moulding chiefly used in repetition.

palmette: In rugs, a cross-section through a stylized flowerhead or fruit.

papier mâché: Moulded paper pulp, suitable for japanning and polishing, used for small articles such as trays, boxes, tea-caddies, and coasters.

pate: Crown of a doll's head onto which the wig or hair is attached, usually of cork in better quality dolls.

pâte-sur-pâte: 19thC Sèvres porcelain technique, much copied, of applying coloured clay decoration to the body before firing.

pier glass: Mirror designed to be fixed to the pier, or wall, between two tall window openings, often partnered by a matching pier table. Made from mid-17thC.

plate: Old fashioned term, still occasionally used, to describe gold and silver vessels; not to be confused with Sheffield plate, or plated vessels generally, in which silver is fused to a base metal alloy.

pole screen: Small adjustable screen mounted on a pole and designed to stand in front of an open fire to shield a lady's face from the heat.

pot: Inexpensive form of bisque used in the manufacture of dolls before the introduction of plastic.

poupard: Doll without legs, often mounted on a stick. Popular in 19thC.

powder flask: Device for measuring out a precise quantity of priming powder, suspended from a musketeer's belt or bandolier and often ornately decorated. Sporting flasks are often made of antler and carved with hunting scenes.

powder horn: Cow horn hollowed out, blocked at the wide end with a wooden plug and fitted with a measuring device at the narrow end, used by musketeers for dispensing a precise quantity of priming powder.

pressed glass: Early 19thC invention, exploited rapidly in America, whereby mechanical pressure was used to form glassware in a mould.

puzzle jug: Type of jug made from the 17thC, especially in delft ware, with a syphon system and several spouts, none of which will pour unless the others are blocked.

quarter-veneered: Four consecutively cut, and therefore identical, pieces of veneer laid at opposite ends to each other to give a mirrored effect.

register plate: Scale of a barometer against which the mercury level is read.

regulator: Clock of great accuracy, thus sometimes used for controlling or checking other time pieces.

rocaille: Shell and rock motifs found in rococo work.

roemer: Originally 16th/17thC German wide bowled wine glass on a thick stem, decorated with prunts, on a base of concentric glass coils, often in green glass (Waldglas). Widely copied throughout Europe in many forms.

rummer: 19thC English low drinking goblet.

seal bottle: Wine bottle with an applied glass medallion or seal personalised with the owner's name, initials, coat-of-arms or a date. Produced from the early 17th to the mid-19thC when bottles were relatively expensive.

SFBJ: Société de Fabrication de Bébés et Jouets; association of doll makers founded 1899 by the merger of Jumeau, Bru and others.

shagreen: Skin of shark or ray fish, often used on sword grips and scabbards.

***shou* symbol:** Formal, artistic version of the Chinese character shou, meaning long-life.

siphon tube: U-shaped tube fitted into wheel barometers where the level of mercury in the short arm is used to record air pressure.

soft paste: Artificial porcelain made with the addition of ground glass, bone-ash or soapstone. Used by most European porcelain manufacturers during the 18thC. Recognised by its soft, soapy feel.

spandrel: Element of design, closing off a corner.

spelter: Zinc treated to look like bronze and much used as an inexpensive substitute in Art Nouveau appliqué ornament and Art Deco figures.

standish: Term for a pre-18thC silver inkstand.

stephane: Curved hair ornament, invariably worn by 'Ladies of Fashion' on south Italian ancient Greek vases.

strapwork: Repeated carved decoration suggesting plaited straps.

stumpwork: Embroidery which incorporates distinctive areas of raised decoration, formed by padding certain areas of the design.

***susani*:** Central Asian hand-embroidered bridal bed-cover.

***suzuribako*:** Japanese writing utensil box.

sympiesometer: Instrument that uses a gas and coloured oil to record air pressure.

table clock: Early type of domestic clock, some say the predecessor of the watch, in which the dial is set horizontally: often of drum shape.

***takamakie*:** Technique used in Japanese lacquerware in which the design is built up and modelled in a mixture of lacquer and charcoal or clay dust, and then often gilded.

tallboy: American term for a chest-on-chest.

tazza: Wide but shallow bowl on a stem with a foot; ceramic and metal tazzas were made in antiquity and the form was revived by Venetian glassmakers in 15thC. Also made in silver from 16thC.

teapoy: Piece of furniture in the form of a tea caddy on legs, with a hinged lid opening to reveal caddies, mixing bowl and other tea drinking accessories.

tear: Tear-drop shaped air bubble in the stem of an early 18thC wine glass, from which the air-twist evolved.

term: Pillar or pedestal terminating in a human head or torso, usually armless. See **caryatid**.

tester: Wooden canopy over a bedstead supported on either two or four posts. It may extend fully over the bed, known as a full tester, or only over the bedhead half, known as a half tester.

tête-à-tête: Tea set for two people.

thuyawood: Reddish-brown wood with distinctive small 'bird's-eye' markings, imported from Africa and used as a veneer.

tin glaze: Glassy opaque white glaze of tin oxide; re-introduced to Europe in 14thC by Moorish potters; the characteristic glaze of delftware, faïence and maiolica.

touch: Maker's mark stamped on much, but not all, early English pewter. Their use was strictly controlled by the Pewterer's Company of London: early examples consist of initials, later ones are more elaborate and pictorial, sometimes including the maker's address.

transfer-printed: Ceramic decoration technique perfected mid-18thC and used widely thereafter for mass produced wares. An engraved design is transferred onto a slab of glue or gelatin (a bat), which was then laid over the body of the vessel, leaving an outline. This was sometimes coloured in by hand.

***tsuba*:** Guard of a Japanese sword, usually consisting of an ornamented plate.

Tudric: Range of Celtic-inspired Art Nouveau pewter of high quality, designed for mass-production by Archibald Knox and others, and retailed through Liberty & Co.

tulipwood: Yellow-brown wood with reddish stripe, imported from Central and South America and used as a veneer and for inlay and crossbanding.

tyg: Mug with three or more handles.

verge escapement: Oldest form of escapement, found on clocks as early as 1300 and still in use in 1900. Consisting of a bar (the verge) with 2 flag-shaped pallets that rock in and out of the teeth of the crown or escape wheel to regulate the movement.

vernier scale: Short scale added to the traditional 3in (7.5cm) scale on stick barometers to give more precise readings than had previously been possible.

***verre églomisé*:** Painting on glass. Often the reverse side of the glass is covered in gold or silver leaf through which a pattern is engraved and then painted black.

vesta case: Ornate flat case of silver or other metal for carrying vestas, an early form of match. Used from mid-19thC.

vitrine: French display cabinet which is often of bombé or serpentine outline and ornately decorated with marquetry and ormolu.

***wan*:** Swastika mark, representing the short writing of the Chinese character *wan*, meaning myriad or ten thousand. Used to represent abundance.

WMF: Short for the German Württembergische Metallwarenfabrik, one of the principal producers of Art Nouveau silver and silver-plated objects, early 20thC.

wrythen: Twisted or plaited.

***wucai*:** Type of five-colour Chinese porcelain decoration.

Directory of Specialists

If you wish to be included in next year's directory, or if you have a change of address or telephone number, please contact Miller's Advertising Department by April 2000. We advise readers to make contact by telephone before visiting a dealer, therefore avoiding a wasted journey.

Antiquities
Dorset
Ancient & Gothic,
PO Box 356,
Christchurch BH23 1XQ
Tel: 01202 478592

Architectural Antiques
Cheshire
Nostalgia,
61 Shaw Heath,
Stockport SK3 8BH
Tel: 0161 477 7706

Devon
Ashburton Marbles,
Grate Hall, North Street,
Ashburton TQ13 7DU
Tel/Fax: 01364 653189

Dorset
Dorset Reclamation,
Cow Drove, Bere Regis,
Wareham BH20 7JZ
Tel: 01929 472200
Fax: 01929 472292

Lincolnshire
Britannia Brass Fittings,
Hemswell Antiques Centre,
Caenby Corner Estate,
Hemswell Cliff,
Gainsborough DN21 5TJ
Tel: 01482 227300

Surrey
Drummonds,
The Kirkpatrick Buildings,
25 London Road (A3),
Hindhead GU26 6AB
Tel: 01428 609444

Yorkshire
Architectural & Historical
Salvage, Spa Street,
Ossett,
Wakefield WF5 0HJ
Tel: 01924 262831
Fax: 01924 281828

Arms & Militaria
Cheshire
Armourer – The Militaria
Magazine,
Published by Beaumont
Publishing Ltd,
25 Westbrook Drive,
Macclesfield,
SK10 3AQ
Tel/Fax: 01625 431583
email: editor@armourer.
u-net.com
Web site: www.armourer.u-net.com
A bi-monthly magazine for military antique collectors and military history enthusiasts offering hundreds of contacts for buying and selling, articles on all aspects of militaria collecting plus the dates of UK militaria fairs and auctions. Available on subscription.

Lincolnshire
Garth Vincent,
Old Manor House,
Allington, Nr Grantham,
NG32 2DH
Tel: 01400 281358

Surrey
West Street Antiques,
63 West Street,
Dorking RH4 1BS
Tel/Fax: 01306 883487

Sussex
Wallis & Wallis,
West Street Auction Galleries,
Lewes BN7 2NJ
Tel: 01273 480208

West Midlands
Weller & Dufty Ltd,
141 Bromsgrove Street,
Birmingham B5 6RQ
Tel: 0121 692 1414

Yorkshire
Andrew Spencer Bottomley,
The Coach House,
Thongs Bridge,
Holmfirth HD7 2TT
Tel: 01484 685234
Fax: 01484 681551

Barographs
Somerset
Richard Twort,
Tel/Fax: 01934 641900

Barometers
Berkshire
Alan Walker,
Halfway Manor, Halfway,
Nr Newbury RG20 8NR
Tel/Fax: 01488 657670

West Yorkshire
Weather House Antiques,
Kym S. Walker,
Foster Clough,
Hebden Bridge HX7 5QZ
Tel: 01422 882808

Beds
Greater Manchester
Victorian Imports,
Prestwich Antiques,
371/373 Bury New Road,
Prestwich M25 1AW
Tel: 0161 798 0911/773 0500

Wales
Seventh Heaven,
Chirk Mill, Chirk,
Wrexham
County Borough LL14 5BU
Tel: 01691 777622/773563

Worcestershire
S. W. Antiques,
Abbey Showrooms,
Newlands,
Pershore WR10 1BP
Tel: 01386 555580

Billiard Tables
Berkshire
William Bentley Billiards,
Standen Manor Farm,
Hungerford RG17 0RB
Tel: 01672 871214
Fax: 01488 685197

Surrey
Academy Billiard Co,
5 Camp Hill Industrial Estate,
Camphill Road,
West Byfleet, KT14 6EW
Tel: 01932 352067

Books
Middlesex
John Ives,
5 Normanhurst Drive,
Twickenham TW1 1NA
Tel: 0181 892 6265
Fax: 0181 744 3944
Reference books.

Surrey
David Aldous-Cook,
PO Box 413, Sutton SM3 8SZ
Tel: 0181 642 4848

Wiltshire
Dominic Winter Book
Auctions, The Old School,
Maxwell St, Swindon SN1 5DR
Tel: 01793 611340

Boxes & Treen
Berkshire
Mostly Boxes,
93 High Street, Eton,
Windsor SL4 6AF
Tel: 01753 858470

London
Coromandel,
PO Box 9772, SW19 3ZG
Tel: 0181 543 9115
Fax: 0181 543 6255

Gerald Mathias,
R5/6 Antiquarius,
135–142 King's Road,
Chelsea SW3 4PW
Tel/Fax: 0207 351 0484

Somerset
Alan Stacey,
Boxwood Antique Restorers,
Appointment only
Tel/Fax: 01963 33988/32555
Cabinet making, polishing, carving and specialists in tortoiseshell, ivory and mother-of-pearl on boxes, caddies and furniture.
See our main advertisement in Boxes (colour section).

British Antique Furniture Restorers' Association
BAFRA Head Office,
The Old Rectory, Warmwell,
Dorchester DT2 8HQ
Tel/Fax: 01305 854822/852104

Bedfordshire
Duncan Michael Everitt,
DME Restorations Ltd,
11 Church Street,
Ampthill MK45 2PL
Tel/Fax: 01525 405819/756177

Berkshire
Graham Childs,
Alpha (Antique) Restorations,
High Street, Compton,
Newbury RG20 6NL
Tel: 01635 578245

Ben R.W. Norris,
Knowl Hill Farm, Knowl Hill,
Kingsclere, Newbury RG20 4NY
Tel: 01635 297950
Fax: 01635 299851
Gilding, carving & architectural woodwork (ie panelling)

Buckinghamshire
David Hordern Restorations
(Thame) Ltd,
8–9 Lea Lane, Thame Road,
Long Crendon,
Aylesbury HP18 9RN
Tel: 01844 202213
Fax: 01844 202214
All aspects of furniture restoration.

Cambridgeshire
Ludovic Potts,
Unit 1 & 1A, Haddenham
Business Park, Station Road,
Ely CB6 3XD
Tel: 01353 741537
Fax: 01353 741822
Traditional repairs, boulle, gilding, walnut, oak, veneering, upholstery, cane, rush

Robert Williams,
Osborn's Farm, 32 Church St,
Willingham CB4 5HT
Tel: 01954 260972

Derbyshire
Anthony Allen,
Antique Restorers &
Conservators,
The Old Wharf Workshop,
Redmoor Lane, New Mills,
High Peak SK22 3JS
Tel: 01663 745274
Boulle, marquetry, walnut, oak, veneering, upholstery. Clocks & clock cases, gold frames & pictures. Comprehensive service.

Devon
Tony Vernon,
15 Follett Road, Topsham,
Exeter EX3 0JP
Tel: 01392 874635
All aspects of conservation and restoration including gilding, carving, upholstery, veneering and polishing. Included on the Conservation Register of the Conservation Unit of the Museums and Galleries Commission.

Dorset
Michael Barrington,
The Old Rectory,
Warmwell, Dorchester DT2 8HQ
Tel/Fax: 01305 852104
Conservation and restoration of antique & fine furniture and clocks. Clock movements and dials, barometers, upholstery, mechanical music, automata and toys, antique metalwork, ferrous and non-ferrous.

Richard Bolton,
Meadow Court,
Athelhampton House,
Dorchester DT2 7LG
Tel: 01305 848346
All aspects of furniture restoration. Courses available.

Philip Hawkins,
Glebe Workshop, Semley,
Shaftesbury SP7 9AP
Tel/Fax: 01747 830830
email:
Hawkinssemley@hotmail.com
Oak and country furniture.

Essex

Clive Beardall,
104B High Street,
Maldon CM9 5ET
Tel: 01621 857890
Furniture.

Gloucestershire

Alan Hessel,
The Old Town Workshop,
St George's Close,
Moreton-in-Marsh GL56 0LP
Tel/Fax: 01608 650026

Stephen Hill,
Brewery Antiques,
2 Cirencester Workshops,
Brewery Court,
Cirencester GL7 1JH
Tel: 01285 658817
Fax: 01285 644060
Mobile: 0976 722028

Andrew Lelliott,
6 Tetbury Hill, Avening,
Tetbury GL8 8LT
Tel: 01453 835783
*Furniture and clock cases.
Included on the Conservation
Unit Register of the Museums
and Galleries Commission.*

Hampshire

Guy Bagshaw,
The Old Dairy, Plain Farm,
East Tisted,
Nr Alton GU34 3RT
Tel: 01420 588362
*Georgian & Regency furniture.
Tutored weekends.*

John Hartley,
Johnson's Barns,
Waterworks Road, Sheet,
Petersfield GU32 2BY
Tel: 01730 233792
Fax: 01730 233922
*Comprehensive furniture
restoration. Large workshop.*

David C. E. Lewry,
Wychelms, 66 Gorran Ave,
Rowner, Gosport PO13 0NF
Tel: 01329 286901
Fax: 01329 289964
Furniture.

Hertfordshire

John B. Carr,
Charles Perry Restorations Ltd,
Praewood Farm,
Hemel Hempstead Road,
St Albans AL3 6AA
Tel: 01727 853487
Fax: 01727 846668
Restoration and conservation.

Kent

Timothy Akers,
The Forge, 39 Chancery Lane,
Beckenham BR3 6NR
Tel: 0181 650 9179
*Longcase, bracket clocks,
cabinetmaking, French polishing.*

Benedict Clegg,
Rear of 20 Camden Road,
Tunbridge Wells TN1 2PT
Tel: 01892 548095

Timothy Long, Restoration,
St John's Church,
London Road,
Dunton Green,
Sevenoaks TN13 2TE
Tel: 01732 743368
Fax: 01732 742206
*Cabinet restoration, polishing,
upholstery, brass and steel
cabinet fittings.*

Bruce Luckhurst,
Little Surrenden Workshops,
Ashford Road, Bethersden,
Ashford TN26 3BG
Tel: 01233 820589
Fax: 01580 243068

e-mail:
restoration@woodwise.
newnet.co.uk
www.bruceluckhurst.co.uk
One-year course available.

Lancashire

Eric Smith,
Antique Restorations,
The Old Church, Park Road,
Darwen BB3 2LD
Tel: 01254 776222
*Furniture, vernacular furniture,
longcase clocks. Registered
with Museums and Galleries
Commission – London and
Lincolnshire.*

Michael Czajkowski,
E. Czajkowski & Son,
96 Tor-o-Moor Road,
Woodhall Spa LN10 6SB
Tel: 01526 352895
*Restoration antique furniture,
clocks and barometers.
UKIC, registered with Museums
and Galleries Commission.*

London

William Cook,
167 Battersea High Street,
SW11 3JS
Tel: 0171 736 5329

Marie Louise Crawley,
39 Wood Vale SE23 3DS
Tel/Fax: 0181 516 0002
*Painted furniture, papier
mâché, tôleware, lacquer
and gilding.*

Robert H. Crawley,
Aberdeen House,
75 St Mary's Road,
Ealing, W5 5RH
Tel: 0181 566 5074

Sebastian Giles,
Sebastian Giles Furniture,
11 Junction Mews W2 1PN
Tel: 0171 402 1535
Comprehensive restoration.

Rodrigo Titian,
Titian Studio,
318 Kensal Road, W10 5BN
Tel: 0181 960 6247
Fax: 0181 969 6126
*Carving, gilding, lacquer,
painted furniture and French
polishing. Caning & rushing.*

Clifford J. Tracy Ltd,
6–40 Durnford Street,
Seven Sisters Rd, N15 5NQ
Tel: 0181 800 4773/4
Fax: 0181 800 4351
*Est. 1961. Restoration of
antique furniture, marquetry,
inlaid ivory, brass and
tortoiseshell, woodturning,
polishing, gilding, cabinetmaking
and complete re-upholstery
service. Worm-infested furniture
guaranteed clear by non-toxic
methods. Free estimates. Our
own transport for collections
and delivery.*

Norfolk

Michael Dolling,
Church Farm Barns,
Glandford, Holt NR25 7JR
Tel: 01263 741115

Roderick Nigel Larwood,
The Oaks, Station Road,
Larling, Norwich NR16 2QS
Tel/Fax: 01953 717937
*Restorers of antique furniture
and traditional finishers.*

Oxfordshire

Alistair Frayling-Cork,
2 Mill Lane,
Wallingford OX10 0DH
Tel: 01491 826221
Antique furniture restoration,

*also stringed instruments,
clock cases and brass fittings
repaired.*

Colin Piper, Conservation,
Highfield House, The Greens,
Leafield, Witney OX8 5NP
Tel: 01993 878593
Fax: 01993 878009
*Conservation and restoration
of fine antique furniture, clocks,
barometers and objets d'art.*
email:
piper.conservation@which.net

Scotland

William Trist,
135 St Leonard's Street,
Edinburgh EH8 9RB
Tel: 0131 667 7775
Fax: 0131 668 4333
*Antique furniture restoration,
cabinet & chairmakers, cane &
rush seating, upholstery.*

Shropshire

Richard A Higgins,
The Old School, Longnor,
Nr Shrewsbury SY5 7PP
Tel: 01743 718162
Fax: 01743 718022
*All fine furniture, clocks,
movements, dials and cases,
casting, plating, boulle,
gilding, lacquerwork, carving,
period upholstery.*

Somerset

Stuart Bradbury,
M & S Bradbury, The Barn,
Hanham Lane, Paulton,
Bristol BS39 7PF
Tel: 01761 418910

Michael Durkee,
Castle House, Units 1 & 3,
Bennetts Field Estate,
Wincanton BA9 9DT
Tel: 01963 33884
Fax: 01963 31278
*Antique furniture conservation
& restoration.*

Robert P. Tandy, Unit 5,
Manor Workshops, West End,
Nailsea, Bristol BS48 4DD
Tel: 01275 856378
*Traditional antique furniture
restoration & repairs.*

Surrey

Booth, David J, 9 High Street,
Ewell, Epsom KT17 1SG
Tel/Fax: 0181 393 5245
*Comprehensive restoration &
large showrooms.*

Michael Hedgecoe,
21 Burrow Hill Grn, Chobham,
Woking GU24 8QS
Tel: 01276 858206
Fax: 01276 857352

Stuart Dudley Hobbs,
Meath Paddock, Meath Green
Lane, Horley RH6 8HZ
Tel: 01293 782349
Furniture & clocks.

Simon Marsh,
The Old Butchers Shop,
High Street,
Bletchingly, RH1 4PA
Tel: 01883 743350
Fax: 01883 744844

Timothy Morris,
Unit 4A, 19 St Peter's Street,
South Croydon CR2 7DG
Tel: 0181 681 2992
Furniture & marquetry.

Timothy Naylor,
The Workshop,
2 Chertsey Road,
Chobham,
Woking GU24 8NB
Tel: 01276 855122

Sussex

William Maxwell Black,
Brookhouse Studios,
Novington Lane,
E. Chiltington, Lewes BN7 3AX
Tel: 01273 890175

Simon Paterson,
Whitelands, West Dean,
Chichester PO18 0RL
Tel: 01243 811900
*Boulle work, marquetry, clock
case & general restoration.*

West Midlands

Phillip Slater,
93 Hewell Road,
Barnt Green,
Birmingham B45 8NL
Tel/Fax: 0121 445 4942
Inlay work, marquetry.

Albert Plumb,
Albert Plumb Furniture,
Briarfield, Itchenor Green,
Chichester PO20 7DA
Tel: 01243 513700
Cabinetmaking, upholstery.

Wiltshire

William Cook,
High Trees House,
Savernake Forest,
Nr Marlborough SN8 4NE
Tel: 01672 513017
Fax: 01672 514455

Yorkshire

Rodney F. Kemble,
16 Crag Vale Terrace,
Glusburn,
Nr Keighley BD20 8QU
Tel: 01535 636954/633702
*Furniture and small decorative
items, carpets.*

Gloucestershire

Samarkand Galleries,
8 Brewery Yard,
Sheep Street,
Stow-on-the-Wold, GL54 1AA
Tel/Fax: 01451 832322
email: mac@samarkand.co.uk
web site:
www.samarkand.co.uk
*Contact: Brian MacDonald
FRGS. Antique rugs from near
east & central Asia. Antique
nomadic weavings.
Decorative carpets.
Tribal artefacts.*

Clocks

Bedfordshire

James B. Chadburn,
Antique Clocks & Restoration,
52 Horton Road, Slapton,
Nr Leighton Buzzard LU7 9DB
Tel: 01525 221325

Cheshire

Coppelia Antiques,
Holford Lodge,
Plumley Moor Road,
Plumley WA16 9RS
Tel: 01565 722197
Fax: 01565 722744

Derbyshire

Dragon Antiques,
1 Tamworth Street, Duffield,
Nr Derby DE56 4ER
Tel: 01332 842332

Devon

Musgrave Bickford Antiques,
15 East Street,
Crediton EX17 3AT
Tel: 01363 775047

Essex

It's About Time,
863 London Road,
Westcliff-on-Sea SS0 9SZ
Tel/Fax: 01702 472574

Village Clocks,
Eastwood House,
32 Eastwood Drive,
Highwood,
Colchester CO4 4EB
Tel: 01787 375896

Gloucestershire

Gerard Campbell,
Maple House, Market Place,
Lechlade-on-Thames,
GL7 3AB
Tel: 01367 252267

Jeffrey Formby,
Orchard Cottage, East Street,
Moreton-in-Marsh GL56 0LQ
Tel: 01608 650558

The Grandfather Clock Shop,
Styles of Stow,
The Little House, Sheep St,
Stow-on-the-Wold,
GL54 1JS
Tel/Fax: 01451 830455

Jillings Antique Clocks,
Croft House,
17 Church Street,
Newent GL18 1PU
Tel: 01531 822100

Hampshire

Bryan Clisby,
Antique Clocks,
at Andwells Antiques,
High Street,
Hartley Wintney RG27 8NY
Tel: 01252 842305

Clock Workshop,
6A Parchment Street,
Winchester SO23 8AT
Tel: 01962 842331

Kent

Gem Antiques,
28 London Road,
Sevenoaks TN13 1AP
Tel: 01732 743540

Gem Antiques,
21 High Street,
Headcorn TN27 9NH
Tel: 01622 890386

Gaby Gunst,
140 High Street,
Tenterden TN30 6HT
Tel: 01580 765818

The Old Clock Shop,
63 High Street,
West Malling ME19 6NA
Tel: 01732 843246

Derek Roberts,
25 Shipbourne Road,
Tonbridge TN10 3DN
Tel: 01732 358986

Leicestershire

Old Timers,
Holmwood,
High Street, Swinford,
Nr Lutterworth LE17 6BL
Tel: 01788 860311

Lincolnshire

Pinfold Wilkinson Antiques,
Open by appointment
Tel: 01476 568791/
01400 251213

London

Chelsea Clocks & Antiques,
Stand H3-4, Antiquarius
135 Kings Road SW3 4PW
Tel: 0171 352 8646
Fax: 0171 376 4591

The Clock Clinic Ltd,
85 Lower Richmond Road,
SW15 1EU
Tel: 0181 788 1407

Newcombe & Son,
89 Maple Road,
Penge SE20 8UL
Tel: 0181 778 0816

Pendulum,
King House,
51 Maddox Street W1R 9LA
Tel: 0171 629 6602

Roderick Antiques Clocks,
23 Vicarage Gate W8 4AA
Tel: 0207 937 8517

W. F. Turk,
355 Kingston Road,
Wimbledon Chase, SW20 8JX
Tel/Fax: 0181 543 3231

Norfolk

Keith Lawson, LBHI,
Scratby Garden Centre,
Beach Road, Scratby,
Great Yarmouth NR29 3AJ
Tel: 01493 730950
antiqueclocks.co.uk

Oxfordshire

Craig Barfoot,
Antique Clocks, Tudor House,
East Hagbourne OX11 9LR
Tel/Fax: 01235 818968
Mobile 0410 858 158

Republic of Ireland

Jonathan Beech,
Killeenacoff House, Cloona,
Westport, Co. Mayo
Tel: 00 353 98 28688

Scotland

John Mann,
Antique Clocks,
The Clock Showroom,
Canonbie, Near Carlisle,
Galloway DG14 0SY
Tel/Fax: 013873 71337
Tel: 013873 71827
Website:
johnmannantiqueclocks.co.uk

Shropshire

The Curiosity Shop,
127 Old St, Ludlow SY8 1NU
Tel: 01584 875927

Somerset

Kembery Antique Clocks,
Bartlett St Antiques Centre,
5 Bartlett St, Bath BA1 2QZ
Tel/Fax: 0117 956 5281

Staffordshire

Essence of Time,
Tudor of Lichfield Antique
Centre, Bore Street,
Lichfield WS13 6LL
Tel: 01543 263951/
01902 764900

Grosvenor Antiques,
71 St Edwards Street,
Leek ST13 5DN
Tel: 01538 385669

Suffolk

Suthburgh Antiques,
Red House, Hall St, Long
Melford, Sudbury CO10 9JQ
Tel: 01787 374818

Wrentham Antiques,
40–44 High Street, Wrentham,
Nr Beccles NR34 7HB
Tel: 01502 675583/675731

Surrey

The Clock House,
75 Pound Street,
Carshalton SM5 3PG
Tel: 0181 773 4844

The Clock Shop,
64 Church Street,
Weybridge KT13 8DL
Tel: 01932 840407/855503

E Hollander,
1 Bennetts Castle,
89 The Street, Capel,
Dorking RH5 5JX
Tel: 01306 713377
Clock restoration.

Horological Workshop,
204 Worplesdon Road,
Guildford GU2 6UY
Tel: 01483 576496

Sussex

Churchill Clocks,
Rumbolds Hill, (Main Street),
Midhurst GU29 9BZ
Tel/Fax: 01730 813891

Samuel Orr Antique Clocks,
34–36 High Street,
Hurstpierpoint BN6 9RG
Tel: 01273 832081

Warwickshire

Summersons,
172 Emscote Road,
Warwick CV34 5QN
Tel /Fax: 01926 400630
*We offer a complete restoration
service for antique clocks &
barometers, and undertake:
dial restoration, cabinetwork &
French polishing, wheel cutting,
one-off parts made, clock
hands cut, fretwork, silvering/
gilding, polishing/lacquering,
parts & materials, insurance
valuations, free estimates &
advice. Wanted: clocks &
barometers in any condition.*

West Midlands

Woodward Antique Clocks,
14 High Street,
Wolverhampton WV6 8QT
Tel: 01902 745608

Wiltshire

P. A. Oxley,
Antique Clocks & Barometers,
The Old Rectory, Cherhill,
Nr Calne SN11 8UX
Tel: 01249 816227

Allan Smith Clocks,
Amity Cottage,
162 Beechcroft Road,
Upper Stratton,
Swindon SN2 6QE
Tel/Fax: 01793 822977

Worcestershire

Brian Loomes,
Calf Haugh Farm,
Pateley Bridge HG3 5HW
Tel: 01423 711163

Time & Motion,
1 Beckside, Beverley HU17 0PB
Tel: 01482 881574

Comics
London

Comic Book Postal Auctions,
40–42 Osnaburgh Street,
NW1 3ND
Tel/Fax: 0171 424 0007/0008
Commemorative ware.

North Yorkshire

Botany Bay Antiques,
8 Grape Lane, Whitby
Tel: 01947 602007
Curios & collectables.

Decorative Arts
Cheshire

Bizarre,
116–118 Manchester Road,
Altrincham WA14 4PY
Tel: 0161 926 8895
Art Deco furniture.

Gloucestershire

Ruskin Decorative Arts,
5 Talbot Court,
Stow-on-the-Wold,
Cheltenham GL54 1DP
Tel: 01451 832254
Fax: 01451 832167
*Decorative Arts 1860–1930.
Arts & Crafts, Art Nouveau &
Art Deco items. Cotswold*

*School Movement incl. Guild
of Handicraft, Gordon Russell,
Gimson, the Barnsleys, etc.*

Greater Manchester

A. S. Antiques,
26 Broad Street,
Pendleton, Salford M6 5BY
Tel: 0161 737 5938
Fax: 0161 737 6626

Kent

20th Century Marks,
12 Market Square,
Westerham TN16 1AW
Tel: 01959 562221
20thC furniture & design.

Delf Stream Gallery,
14 New Street,
Sandwich CT13 9AB
Tel: 01304 617684

London

Nigel Benson,
Art Furniture,
158 Camden Street, NW1 9PA
Tel: 0171 267 4324

20th Century Glass,
Kensington Church Street
Antique Centre, 58–60
Kensington Church St, W8 4DB
Tel: 0171 938 1137/376 0425

Glass

Art Nouveau Originals c1900,
4–5 Pierrepont Row Arcade,
Camden Passage, N1 8EF
Tel: 0171 359 4127
Mobile 0374 718096
Wed & Sat or by appointment.

Artemis Decorative Arts Ltd,
36 Kensington Church Street,
W8 4BX
Tel/Fax: 0171 376 0377/
937 9900

Arts & Crafts Furniture Co Ltd,
49 Sheen Lane, SW14 8AB
Tel: 0181 876 6544

Pieter Oosthuizen,
Unit 4 Bourbon Hanby
Antiques Centre,
151 Sydney Street, SW3 6NT
Tel: 0171 460 3078

Sylvia Powell,
Decorative Arts, 18 The Mall,
Camden Passage, N1 0PD
Tel: 0207 354 2977
Doulton.

Rumours,
10 The Mall, Upper Street,
Camden Passage, N1 0PD
Tel/Fax: 01582 873561
Moorcroft.

Shapiro & Co,
Stand 380, Gray's Antique
Market, 58 Davies St, W1Y 1LB
Tel: 0171 491 2710
Fabergé.

Zoom,
312 Lillie Road SW6 7PS
Tel/Fax: 0171 386 9522
*1950s, 1960s, 1970s furniture
& objects.*

Merseyside

Circa 1900,
11–13 Holts Arcade,
India Buildings, Water Street,
Liverpool L2 0RR
Tel/Fax: 0151 236 1282

Surrey

Gooday Gallery,
20 Richmond Hill,
Richmond TW10 6QX
Tel: 0181 940 8652/
Mobile 0410 124540
*Art Nouveau, Art Deco, Tribal
Art and Post-War Modernism
1890–1980.*

Sussex

Art Deco Etc,
73 Upper Gloucester Road,
Brighton BN1 3LQ
Tel/Fax: 01273 329268
*Decorative Arts ceramics –
Poole Pottery.*

Ephemera
Nottinghamshire

T. Vennett-Smith,
11 Nottingham Road,
Gotham NG11 0HE
Tel: 0115 983 0541

Exhibition & Fair Organisers
Surrey

Cultural Exhibitions Ltd,
8 Meadrow,
Godalming GU7 3HN
Tel: 01483 422562
Fax: 01483 426077

Exporters
Devon

McBains of Exeter,
Exeter Airport Industrial
Estate, Exeter EX5 2BA
Tel: 01392 366261

Pugh's Antiques,
Pugh's Farm, Monkton,
Nr Honiton EX14 9QH
Tel: 01404 42860

Nottinghamshire

Antiques Across the World,
James Alexander Buildings,
London Road/Manvers Street,
Nottingham
NG2 3AE
Tel: 0115 979 9199
Fax: 0115 958 8314

Sussex

International Furniture
Exporters,
The Old Cement Works,
South Heighton,
Newhaven BN9 0HS
Tel: 01273 611251

Lloyd Williams Antiques,
Anglo Am Warehouse,
2A Beach Road,
Eastbourne BN22 7EX
Tel: 01323 648661

The Old Mint House,
High Street,
Pevensey BN24 5LF
Tel/Fax: 01323 762337

Wiltshire

North Wilts Exporters,
Farm Hill House,
Brinkworth SN15 5AJ
Tel: 01666 510876

Fishing
Hampshire

Evans & Partridge,
Agriculture House,
High Street,
Stockbridge SO20 6HF
Tel: 01264 810702

Kent

The Old Tackle Box,
PO Box 55, High Street,
Cranbrook TN17 3ZU
Tel: 01580 713979

London

Angling Auctions,
PO Box 2095, W12 8RU
Tel: 0181 749 4175
Fax: 0181 743 4855

The Reel Thing,
17 Royal Opera Arcade,
Pall Mall SW1Y 4UY
Tel: 0171 976 1840

Monmouthshire

Brindley John Ayers,
River Mill House,
1 Woodside Court,
Llanbadoc,
Usk NP5 1SY
Tel: 01291 672710

Shropshire

Mullock & Madeley,
The Old Shippon,
Wall-under-Heywood,
Nr. Church Stretton,
SY6 7DS
Tel: 01694 771771

Furniture
Bedfordshire

Transatlantic Antiques Ltd,
101 Dunstable Street,
Ampthill MK45 2JT
Tel: 01525 403346

Berkshire

Hill Farm Antiques,
Hill Farm, Shop Lane,
Leckhampstead,
Nr Newbury RG20 8QG
Tel/Fax: 01488 638541

The Old Malthouse,
Hungerford RG17 0EG
Tel/Fax: 01488 682209

Cambridgeshire

Simon & Penny Rumble,
Causeway End Farm House,
Chittering CB5 9PW
Tel: 01223 861831
Oak & country.

Cumbria

Anthemion,
Bridge Street, Cartmel,
Grange-over-Sands
LA11 7SH
Tel: 01539 536295

Derbyshire

Spurrier-Smith Antiques,
28, 30, 39 Church Street,
Ashbourne DE6 1AJ
Tel: 01335 343669/342198/344377

Essex

F. G. Bruschweiler (Antiques)
Ltd, 41–67 Lower Lambricks,
Rayleigh SS6 7EN
Tel: 01268 773761/773932

Gloucestershire

Berry Antiques,
3 High Street,
Moreton in Marsh
GL56 0AH
Tel: 01608 652929

Hertfordshire

Collins Antiques,
Wheathampstead AL4 8AP
Tel: 01582 833111

Kent

Douglas Bryan,
The Old Bakery,
St David's Bridge,
Cranbrook TN17 3HN
Tel: 01580 713103
Fine oak & country furniture.

Flower House Antiques,
90 High Street,
Tenterden TN30 6HT
Tel: 01580 763764

Heirlooms Antiques,
68 High Street,
Tenterden TN30 6AU
Tel: 01580 765535

Pantiles Spa Antiques,
4, 5, 6 Union House,
The Pantiles,
Tunbridge Wells TN4 8HE
Tel: 01892 541377

Gillian Shepherd,
Old Corner House Antiques,
6 Poplar Road, Wittersham,
Tenterden TN30 7PG
Tel: 01797 270236

Sparks Antiques,
4 Manor Row, High Street,
Tenterden TN30 6HP
Tel: 01580 766696

Sutton Valence Antiques,
Unit 4 Haslemere,
Parkwood Estate,
Maidstone ME15 9NL
Tel: 01622 675332

Lincolnshire

Norman Mitchell Simmons Ltd,
The Wong,
Horncastle LN9 6EB
Tel: 01507 523854

Seaview Antiques,
Stanhope Road,
Horncastle LN9 5DG
Tel: 01507 524524

London

Adams Rooms Antiques &
Interiors,
18–20 The Ridgeway,
Wimbledon Village SW19 4QN
Tel: 0181 946 7047

Antique Warehouse,
9–14 Deptford Broadway,
SE8 4PA
Tel: 0181 691 3062

Georg S. Wissinger Antiques,
166 Bermondsey St SE1 3TQ
Tel/Fax: 0171 407 5795

Oola Boola,
166 Tower Bridge Rd, SE1 3LS
Tel: 020 7403 0794/
020 8693 5050

Robert Young Antiques,
68 Battersea Bridge Road,
SW11 3AG
Tel: 0171 228 7847
Country furniture.

Middlesex

Robert Phelps Ltd,
133–135 St Margaret's Road,
East Twickenham TW1 1RG
Tel: 0181 892 1778/7129

Northamptonshire

Paul Hopwell,
30 High Street,
West Haddon NN6 7AP
Tel: 01788 510656
Oak & country furniture.

Oxfordshire

Georg S. Wissinger Antiques,
Georgian House Antiques,
21 & 44 West Street,
Chipping Norton OX7 5EU
Tel/Fax: 01608 641369

Rupert Hitchcox Antiques,
The Garth, Warpsgrove,
Nr Chalgrove,
Oxford OX44 7RW
Tel/Fax: 01865 890241

La Chaise Antiques,
30 London Street,
Faringdon SN7 7AA
Tel: 01367 240427
Upholstered chairs.

Shropshire

Longmynd Antiques,
Crossways,
Church Stretton SY6 6PG
Tel/Fax: 01694 724474
Oak & country furniture.

Somerset

Granary Galleries,
Court House, Ash Priors,
Nr Bishops Lydeard,
Taunton TA4 3NQ
Tel: 01823 432402/432816

Suffolk

Hubbard Antiques,
16 St Margaret's Green,
Ipswich IP4 2BS
Tel: 01473 226033

Oswald Simpson,
Hall Street,
Long Melford CO1O 9JL
Tel: 01787 377523
Oak & country furniture.

Surrey

The Chair Set,
82-84 Hill Rise,
Richmond TW10 6UB
Tel: 0181 332 6454/
Mobile 0411 625477
Chairs.

Dorking Desk Shop,
41 West Street,
Dorking RH4 1BU
Tel: 01306 883327
Desks.

J. Hartley Antiques Ltd,
186 High St, Ripley
GU23 6BB
Tel: 01483 224318

The Refectory,
38 West St, Dorking RH4 1BU
Tel: 01306 742111
*Oak & country – refectory
table specialist.*

Richmond Antiques,
28 Hill Rise,
Richmond TW10 6UA
Tel: 0181 948 4638
*Furniture – chests of drawers.
Weekends only, Sat
10.30–5.30, Sun 2–5.30*

Ripley Antiques,
67 High St, Ripley GU23 6AN
Tel: 01483 224981

Anthony Welling,
Broadway Barn,
High Street, Ripley GU23 6AQ
Tel/Fax: 01483 225384
Oak & country furniture.

Sussex

British Antique Replicas,
School Close,
Queen Elizabeth Avenue,
Burgess Hill RH15 9RX
Tel: 01444 245577

Dycheling Antiques,
34 High Street,
Ditchling BN6 8TA
Tel/Fax: 01273 842929
Chairs.

The Old Mint House,
High Street, Pevensey,
Nr. Eastbourne BN24 5LF
Tel/Fax: 01323 762337

Red Lion Antiques,
New Street,
Petworth GU28 0AS
Tel: 01798 344485
Oak and country furniture.

Stable Antiques,
Adrian Hoyle,
98a High Street,
Lindfield RH16 2HP
Tel/Fax: 01444 483662
Regency furniture.

Wales

Country Antiques (Wales),
Castle Mill, Kidwelly,
Carmarthenshire SA17 4UU
Tel: 01554 890534
Oak.

Russell Worby,
PO Box 43,
Colwyn Bay LL29 8WS
Tel: 01492 512794
*We specialize in Welsh country
furniture and are open at any
time by appointment only.*

Warwickshire

Apollo Antiques Ltd,
The Saltisford,
Birmingham Road,
Warwick CV34 4TD
Tel: 01926 494746
Fax: 01926 401477

Coleshill Antiques & Interiors,
12–14 High Street,
Coleshill B46 1AZ
Tel: 01675 462931
Fax: 01675 467416

Don Spencer Antiques,
36A Market Place,
Warwick CV34 4SH
Tel: 01926 407989/499857
Desks.

West Midlands

L. P. Furniture,
(The Old Brewery),
Short Acre Street,
Walsall WS2 8HW
Tel: 01922 746764
French country furniture.

Martin Taylor Antiques,
140B Tettenhall Road,
Wolverhampton WV6 0BQ
Tel: 01902 751166

Wiltshire

Cross Hayes Antiques,
19 Bristol Street,
Malmesbury SN16 0AY
Tel: 01666 824260/822062
Fax: 01666 823020

Yorkshire

David South,
Kings House, 15 High Street,
Pateley Bridge,
Harrogate HG3 5AP
Tel: 01423 712022
Furniture and upholstery.

Glass
London

Christine Bridge,
Appointment only.
Tel: 07000 445277
Fax: 07000 329452

Andrew Lineham,
Fine Glass, The Mall,
Camden Passage N1 8ED
Tel: 0171 704 0195
Wed & Sat: 01243 576241

Somerset

Somervale Antiques,
6 Radstock Road, Midsomer
Norton, Bath BA3 2AJ
Tel/Fax: 01761 412686

Japanese Prints
London

Japanese Gallery,
66D Kensington Church Street,
W8 4BY
Tel/Fax: 0171 229 2934, and:
23 Camden Passage,
N1 8EA
Tel: 0171 226 3347

Keys
Buckinghamshire

Paul Alan Prescott, MBLI,
20 Cambridge Crescent,
High Wycombe HP13 7ND
Tel: 01494 436307
*Keys made for Bramah and
most other makes of English
patent lock. Postal service only.*

Marine
Gloucestershire

Mark Jarrold,
The Grey House,
Tetbury St,
Minchinhampton GL6 9JH
Tel/Fax: 01453 887074
Marine instruments.

Hampshire

Mariner's Antiques,
Dolphin Quay Antiques
Centre, Queen Street,
Emsworth PO10 7BU
Tel: 0410 330700
Centre tel: 01243 379994
Fax: 01243 379251
*Marine paintings & prints,
Royal Navy & shipping line
memorabilia, nautical books
and antiques, ship models.*

Markets & Centres
Berkshire

Moss End Antique Centre,
Warfield (A3095), RG12 6EJ
Tel: 01344 861942

Stables Antiques Centre,
1a Merchant Place (off Friar
Street), Reading RG1 1DT
Tel: 0118 959 0290
*Open 7 days a week.
Over 40 dealers on 2 floors.
Near station and car parks.*

Buckinghamshire

Marlow Antique Centre,
35 Station Road,
Marlow SL7 1NW
Tel: 01628 473223
*Over 25 dealers. Mon–Sat 10-
5.30. Sun 11–4.30. Furniture,
china, glass, cuff links, pens.
A good secondhand book
department. Trade welcome.*

Derbyshire

Bakewell Antique &
Collectors' Centre,
King St, Bakewell DE45 1DZ
Tel: 01629 812496
Fax: 01629 814531
web site www.chappells-
antiques.co.uk
*30 established dealers (incl.
BADA & LAPADA members)
of quality antiques and
collectables 17th–20thC.
Tea and Coffee House.
Open Mon–Sat 10-5. Sun
11–5. Closed Christmas,
Boxing Day & New Year's Day.*

Belper Antique Centre,
2 Queen St, Belper DE56 1NR
Tel: 01773 823002
Fax: 01332 343575

Duesbury's Antiques Centre,
220 Siddals Road,
Derby DE1 2QE
Tel: 01332 370151

Gloucestershire

Cirencester Arcade &
Ann's Pantry, 25 Market Place,
Cirencester GL7 2PY
Tel: 01285 644214
Fax: 01285 651267
*Antiques, gifts, furnishings
etc. Restaurant/tea rooms,
private room for hire.
Over 60 traders.*

Jubilee Hall Antique Centre,
Oak Street, Lechlade GL7 3AY
Tel: 01367 253777

Hampshire

Dolphin Quay Antiques Centre,
Queen Street,
Emsworth PO10 7BU
Tel: 01243 379994

Herefordshire

Ross-on-Wye Antiques Centre,
Gloucester Road,
Ross-on-Wye HR9 5BU
Tel: 01989 762290

Kent

Copperfields Antiques &
Craft Centre,
3c–4 Copperfields, Spital St,

Dartford DA9 2DE
Tel: 01322 281445
*Open Mon–Sat 10-5.
Antiques, bygones, collectables,
stamps, Wade, Sylvac, Beswick,
Royal Doulton, Victoriana, Art
Deco, 1930s–60s, clocks, crafts,
hand-made toys, dolls' houses
& miniatures, jewellery, glass,
china, furniture, Kevin Francis
character jugs, silk, lace & more.*

Unicorn Antique Centre,
2 Romney Enterprise Centre,
North Street, New Romney
Tel: 01797 361940

Lancashire

GB Antiques Centre,
Lancaster Leisure Park,
(the former Hornsea Pottery),
Wyresdale Road,
Lancaster LA1 3LA
Tel/Fax: 01524 844734/844735
*Over 140 dealers in 40,000 sq
ft of space. Porcelain, pottery,
Art Deco, glass, books and
linen. Large selection of oak
mahogany, and pine furniture.
Open 7 days a week 10.00–5.00.*

Heskin Hall Antiques,
Heskin Hall, Wood Lane,
Eccleston, Chorley PR7 5PA
Tel: 01257 452044

Kingsmill Antique Centre,
Queen Street, Harle Syke,
Burnley BB10 2HX
Tel: 01282 431953
*Open 7 days 10.00–5.00.
8,500 sq ft. Trade welcome.*

Marie English Antiques,
37 New Hall Lane,
Preston PR1 5NX
Tel: 01772 794259

Lincolnshire

Hemswell Antique Centre,
Caenby Corner Estate,
Hemswell Cliff,
Gainsborough DN21 5TJ
Tel: 01427 668389

London

Atlantic Antiques Centres,
Chenil House,
181–183 Kings Road, SW3 5EB
Tel: 0171 351 5353

Bond Street Antiques Centre,
124 New Bond Street, W1
Tel: 0171 351 5353

Bourbon-Hanby Antiques
Centre,
151 Sydney Street,
Chelsea SW3 6NT
Tel: 0171 352 2106
Fax: 0171 565 0003

The Mall Antiques Arcade,
Camden Passage, N1
Tel: 0171 351 5353

Norfolk

Thetford Antiques &
Collectables,
6 Market Place,
Thetford IP24 2AJ
Tel: 01842 755511

Oxfordshire

Antiques on High,
85 High Street,
Oxford OX1 4BG
Tel: 01865 251075
*Open 7 days a week 10–5.
Sun & Bank Holidays 11–5.
35 friendly dealers with a wide
range of quality stock.*

Chipping Norton Antiques
Centre, Ivy House,
Middle Row, Market Place,
Chipping Norton OX7 5NH
Tel: 01608 644212

Didcot Antiques Centre,
220 Broadway,
Didcot OX11 8RS
Tel/Fax: 01235 510819

Lamb Arcade Antiques Centre,
83 High Street,
Wallingford OX10 0BS
Tel: 01491 835166
10–5 daily, Sat till 5.30,
Bank Hols 11–5pm.
*Furniture, silver, porcelain,
glass, books, boxes, crafts,
rugs, jewellery, brass bedsteads
and linens, pictures, antique
stringed instruments, sports
and fishing items, decorative
and ornamental items.
Coffee shop and wine bar.*

Shropshire

Bridgnorth Antique Centre,
High Town, Whitburn Street,
Bridgnorth SY7 9DZ
Tel: 01746 768055
Open 10.00–5.30 7 days a week.

Staffordshire

Tutbury Mill Antiques Centre,
Tutbury Mill Mews,
Tutbury DE13 9LU
Tel: 01283 520074
*Open Mon–Sat 10.30–5.30
Sun 12–5.00.*

Suffolk

Dome Art & Antique Centre,
St Edmunds Business Park,
St Edmunds Road,
Southwold IP18 6BZ
Tel: 01502 722211
Fax: 01520 722734
*6500 sq ft of space.
Open 10–6, 7 days a week.*

Sussex

Churchill Antiques Centre,
6 Station Road,
Lewes BN7 2DA
Tel: 01273 474842

Queens Road Antiques &
Flea Market,
197–198 Queens Road,
Hastings TN34 1RG
Tel: 01424 422955/429754
Open 10.00–5.00 6 days a week.

Wales

Afonwen Antiques & Craft
Centre, Afonwen, Nr. Caerwys,
Mold CH7 5UB
Tel: 01352 720 965
*Open all year Tues–Sun
9.30–5.30, closed Mondays,
open Bank Holidays. The
largest antique & craft centre
in North Wales. 14,000 sq ft
of showrooms, antiques,
collectables, furniture, fine
jewellery. Licensed restaurant.*

Offa's Dyke Antique Centre,
4 High Street, Knighton,
Powys LD7 1AT
Tel: 01547 528635/528940

Romantiques Antique Centre,
Bryn Seion Chapel,
Station Road, Trevor,
Llangollen LL20 7PF
Tel: 01978 752140

Warwickshire

Barn Antiques Centre,
Station Road, Long Marston,
Nr Stratford-upon-Avon,
CV37 8RB
Tel: 01789 721399
*Open 7 days 10–5.
Large selection of antique
furniture, antique pine, linen
and lace, old fireplaces and
surrounds, collectables,
pictures and prints, silver,
china, ceramics and objets*

d'art, antique-style reproduction furniture, clocks including longcase, country kitchens.

Yorkshire

Cavendish Antiques & Collectors Centre,
44 Stonegate,
York YO1 8AS
Tel: 01904 621666
Fax: 01904 644400
Open 9.00–6.00 7 days a week. Over 50 dealers on 3 floors.

Court House Antiques Centre,
Town End Road,
Ecclesfield, Sheffield S35 9YY
Tel: 0114 257 0641

Halifax Antiques Centre,
Queens Road,
Halifax HX1 4LR
Tel: 01422 366657

Sheffield Antiques Emporium & The Chapel,
15–19 Clyde Road,
(off Broadfield Road),
Heeley, Sheffield S8 0YD
Tel: Emporium: 0114 258 4863
Chapel: 0114 258 8288
Over 70 dealers. Collectables, furniture, pictures, books, militaria, linen, kitchenalia, china, Art Deco, clocks, silver and silver plate etc. Excellent coffee shop. Open Mon–Sat 10.00–5.00 Suns and Bank Holidays 11.00–5.00.

Stonegate Antiques Centre,
41 Stonegate,
York YO1 8AW
Tel: 01904 613888
Fax: 01904 644400
Open 9.00–6.00 7 days a week. Over 110 dealers on 2 floors.

Miniatures
Gloucestershire

Judy & Brian Harden,
PO Box 14,
Bourton-on-the-Water,
Cheltenham GL54 2YR
Tel/Fax: 01451 810684
Portrait miniatures.

Money Boxes
Yorkshire

John & Simon Haley,
89 Northgate,
Halifax HX6 4NG
Tel: 01422 822148/360434

Musical Instruments
Gloucestershire

Piano-Export,
Bridge Road, Kingswood,
Bristol BS15 4FW
Tel: 0117 956 8300

Kent

Period Piano Company,
Park Farm Oast,
Hareplain Road,
Biddenden,
Nr Ashford TN27 8LJ
Tel: 01580 291393
Specialist dealer and restorer of period pianos.

Nottinghamshire

Turner Violins,
1–5 Lily Grove, Beeston,
Nottingham NG9 1QL
Tel: 0115 943 0333

Wales

Period Piano Restorers,
878 Carmarthen Road,
Swansea SA5 8HR
Tel: 01792 584584
Piano restorers.

Oriental
London

David Bowden,
12 The Mall,
Upper Street,
Islington N1 0PD
Tel/Fax: 0171 226 3033

Geoffrey Waters Ltd,
F1–F6 Antiquarius Antiques Centre, 135–141 King's Road,
SW3 4PW
Tel/Fax: 0171 376 5467
Chinese ceramics.

Wiltshire

Indigo, Dairy Barn,
Manningford Bruce
SN9 6JW
Tel: 01672 564722
*By appointment only.
18th/19th century furniture & decorative antiques from China, India & the Far East.*

Packers & Shippers
Dorset

Alan Franklin Transport,
26 Blackmoor Road,
Ebblake Industrial Estate,
Verwood BH31 6BB
Tel: 01202 826539

London

Stephen Morris Shipping,
Barpart House,
North London Freight Depot,
York Way,
N1 0UZ
Tel: 020 7713 0080

Somerset

A. J. Williams,
607 Sixth Avenue,
Central Business Park,
Petherton Road,
Hengrove, Bristol BS14 9BZ
Tel: 01275 892166

Paperweights
Cheshire

Sweetbriar Gallery,
Robin Hood Lane,
Helsby WA6 9NH
Tel: 01928 723851

USA

The Dunlop Collection,
PO Box 6269, Statesville,
NC 28687
Tel: 00 1 800 227 1996

Pine
Cheshire

Richmond Galleries,
Watergate Building,
New Crane St,
Chester CH1 4JE
Tel: 01244 317602
Pine, country and Spanish furniture.

Cumbria

Ben Eggleston Antiques,
The Dovecote, Long Marton,
Appleby CA16 6BJ
Tel/Fax: 01768 361849
Trade only.

Derbyshire

Tanglewood Antiques,
Tanglewood Mill,
Coke Street,
Derby DE1 1NE
Tel/Fax: 01332 346005

Essex

English Rose Antiques,
7 Church Street,
Coggeshall CO6 1TU
Tel: 01376 562683
Large selection of English and Continental pine furniture.

Gloucestershire

Parlour Farm Antiques,
Unit 12b, Wilkinson Road,
Love Lane Industrial Estate,
Cirencester GL7
Tel: 01285 885336

Hampshire

Pine Cellars,
39 Jewry Street,
Winchester SO23 8RY
Tel: 01962 867014

Kent

Farningham Pine Antiques,
46 High Street,
Farningham DA4 0DB
Tel/Fax: 01322 863230/863168

Glassenbury Antique Pine,
Glassenbury Timber Yard,
Iden Green, Goudhurst,
Cranbrook TN17 2PA
Tel: 01580 212022

Old English Pine,
100 Sandgate High Street,
Folkestone CT20 3BY
Tel: 01303 248560

The Old Mill,
High St, Lamberhurst TN3 8EQ
Tel: 01892 891196

Up Country,
The Old Corn Stores,
68 St John's Road,
Tunbridge Wells TN4 9PE
Tel: 01892 523341

Lancashire

Enloc Antiques,
96 Keighley Rd, Colne BB8 RPH
Tel: 01282 867101
Fax: 01282 867601

David Roper Antiques
Hill View Farm, Gill Lane,
Longton, Preston PR4 4ST
Tel: 01772 615366/611591
Mobile 0411 069994
Mostly English 18th and 19th century pine & country furniture. Trade suppliers for 30 years. By appointment only.

Netherlands

Jacques Van Der Tol,
Antiek & Curiosa,
Antennestraat 34,
1322 AE Almere-Stad,
Tel: 00 313 653 62050

Oxfordshire

Julie Strachey,
Southfield Farm, North Lane,
Weston-on-the-Green,
OX6 8RG
Tel: 01869 350833
Antique farm & country furniture in pine, oak, etc. Ironwork & interesting pieces for the garden (no repro). By appointment. Junction 9 M40 2 miles. Established 27 years.

Republic of Ireland

Bygones of Ireland Ltd,
Lodge Road, Westport,
County Mayo,
Tel/Fax: 00 353 98 26132/25701

Delvin Farm Antiques,
Gormonston, Co Meath
Tel: 00 353 1 841 2285

Honan's Antiques,
Crowe Street, Gort,
County Galway
Tel/Fax: 00 353 91 631407

Somerville Antiques & Country Furniture Ltd,
Moysdale, Kilkelney,
Ballina, Co Mayo
Tel: 00 353 963 6275
Fax: 00 353 963 6645

Somerset

East Street Antiques,
42 East Street,
Crewkerne TA18 7AG
Tel: 01460 78600

Gilbert & Dale Antiques,
The Old Chapel,
Church Street, Ilchester
Nr Yeovil BA22 8ZA
Tel: 01935 840464
Painted pine & country.

Westville House Antiques,
Westville House,
Littleton,
Nr Somerton TA11 6NP
Tel/Fax: 01458 273376

Staffordshire

Johnson's,
120 Mill Street,
Leek ST13 8HA
Tel/Fax: 01538 386745
Specialists in English & French country furniture. Unique objects & decorative accessories. Most items 18th & 19thC. Open 9–5 Mon–Sat. Export trade welcome.

Surrey

Grayshott Pine,
Crossways Road,
Grayshott,
Hindhead GU26 6HF
Tel: 01428 607478

Sussex

Bob Hoare Antiques,
Unit Q, Phoenix Place,
North St,
Lewes BN7 2DQ
Tel: 01273 480557

Ann Lingard,
Ropewalk Antiques,
Ropewalk,
Rye TN31 7NA
Tel: 01797 223486

Graham Price,
Unit 4, Chaucer Industrial Estate, Dittons Road,
Polegate BN26 6JD
Tel: 01323 487167

Wales

Heritage Restorations,
Llanfair Caereinion,
Welshpool,
Powys SY21 0HD
Tel: 01938 810384

Pot Board,
30 King Street,
Carmarthen SA31 1BS
Tel: 01267 236623

Wiltshire

North Wilts Exporters,
Farm Hill House,
Brinkworth SN15 5AJ
Tel: 01666 510876

Sambourne House Antiques,
Minety,
Malmesbury SN16 9RQ
Tel/Fax: 01666 860288

Porcelain
Bedfordshire

Transatlantic Antiques Ltd,
101 Dunstable Street,
Ampthill MK45 2JT
Tel: 01525 403346

Gloucestershire

Clive & Lynne Jackson,
Tel/Fax: 01242 254375
Parian ware.

David & Sally March,
Oak Wood Lodge,
Stoke Leigh Woods,
Abbots Leigh,
Bristol BS8 3QB
Tel/Fax: 01275 372422

Hampshire

Goss & Crested China Ltd,
62 Murray Road,
Horndean PO8 9JL
Tel: 023 92597440
Goss & Crested china.

London

Marion Langham,
Tel: 0171 730 1002
Belleek.

Northern Ireland

Marion Langham,
Claranagh, Tempo,
Co Fermanagh BT94 3FJ
Tel: 01365 541241
Belleek.

Shropshire

Teme Valley Antiques,
1 The Bull Ring,
Ludlow SY8 1AD
Tel: 01584 874686

Somerset

Andrew Dando,
4 Wood Street, Queen Square,
Bath BA1 2JQ
Tel: 01225 422702
Fax: 01225 310717

Sussex

Jupiter Antiques,
PO Box 609,
Rottingdean BN2 7FW
Tel: 01273 302865
Fax: 01273 889375
*We specialize in English
porcelain from major 18thC
factories and Royal Worcester
and Royal Crown Derby.*

Warwickshire

Coleshill Antiques & Interiors,
12–14 High Street,
Coleshill B46 1AZ
Tel: 01675 462931
Fax: 01675 467416

Yorkshire

The Crested China Co,
The Station House,
Driffield YO25 7PY
Tel: 01377 257042
Goss & Crested china.

Pottery
Berkshire

Special Auction Services,
The Coach House,
Midgham Park,
Reading RG7 5UG
Tel: 0118 971 2949
Fax: 0118 971 2420
*Commemorative ware,
pot lids, Prattware, fairings,
Goss and Crested, Baxter and
Le Blond prints.*

Buckinghamshire

Gillian Neale Antiques,
PO Box 247,
Aylesbury HP20 1JZ
Tel: 01296 423754/
0860 638700
Blue and white.

Hampshire

Millers Antiques Ltd,
Netherbrook House,
86 Christchurch Road,
Ringwood BH24 1DR
Tel: 01425 472062

Kent

Serendipity,
168 High St, Deal CT14 6BQ
Tel: 01304 369165/366536
Staffordshire pottery.

Gillian Shepherd,
Old Corner House Antiques,
6 Poplar Road, Wittersham,
Tenterden TN30 7PG

Tel: 01797 270236
Blue and white transferware.

London

Jonathan Horne,
66b&c Kensington Church St,
W8 4BY
Tel: 0171 221 5658

Valerie Howard,
2 Campden Street, W8 7EP
Tel: 0171 792 9702
Masons Ironstone & Quimper.

Sue Norman, L4 Antiquarius,
135 King's Road, SW3 5ST
Tel: 0207 352 7217
Blue and white transferware.

Jacqueline Oosthuizen,
23 Cale Street,
Chelsea, SW3 3QR
Tel: 0171 352 6071/
376 3852/460 8561
Staffordshire pottery.

Rogers de Rin,
76 Royal Hospital Rd,
SW3 4HN
Tel: 0171 352 9007
Wemyss.

Republic of Ireland

Michelina & George Stacpoole,
Main St, Adare,
Co Limerick
Tel: 00 353 61 396 409

Somerset

Peter Scott,
Bartlett Street Antiques Centre,
Bath BA1 2QZ
Tel: 01225 310457/
0117 986 8468
Blue and white transferware.

Tyne & Wear

Ian Sharp Antiques,
23 Front Street,
Tynemouth NE30 4DX
Tel/Fax: 0191 296 0656

Wales

Islwyn Watkins,
1&4 High Street, Knighton,
Powy LD7 1AT
Tel: 01547 520145

Warwickshire

Paull's of Kenilworth,
16B High Street,
Old Kenilworth CV8 1LZ
Tel: 01926 851311
Masons Ironstone.

Publications
London

Antiques Trade Gazette,
17 Whitcomb St, WC2H 7PL
Tel: 0171 930 9958

Restoration
Essex

Ardley's, 5 East Street,
Coggleshall CO6 1SH
Tel: 01376 563154
Clock restoration.

London

Oliver Clarke,
Heritage Restorations,
96 Webber Street, SE1 0QN
Tel: 0171 928 3624
18th & 19thC furniture.

Leather Conservation Centre,
University College Campus,
Boughton Green Road,
Moulton Park,
Northampton NN2 7AN
Tel: 01604 719766
Fax: 01604 719649
*Conservation and restoration
of leather screens, wall hangings,
car, carriage and furniture
upholstery, saddlery, luggage,
firemens' helmets and much,*

---

*much, more. Included on the
Register maintained by the
Conservation Unit, Museum
and Galleries Commission.*

Rock & Pop
Cheshire

Collector's Corner,
PO Box 8,
Congleton CW12 4GD
Tel: 01260 270429
Fax: 01260 298996

Rocking Horses
Essex

Haddon Rocking Horses Ltd,
5 Telford Road,
Clacton-on-Sea CO15 4LP
Tel: 01255 424745

Scientific Instruments
Cheshire

Charles Tomlinson, Chester.
Tel/Fax 01244 318395
Charles.Tomlinson@lineone.net
Email:Charles.Tomlinson@line
one.net

Scotland

Early Technology,
Monkton House,
Old Craighall, Musselburgh,
Midlothian EH21 8SF
Tel: 0131 665 5753

Services
Hampshire

Securikey Ltd,
PO Box 18,
Aldershot GU12 4SL
Tel: 01252 311888
Underfloor safes.

Kent

Net Publishing Services Ltd,
43 High St, Newington,
ME9 7JR
Tel: 01795 841131

London

Air Improvement Centre Ltd,
23 Denbigh Street,
SW1V 2HF
Tel: 0171 834 2834
*Specialist suppliers of
hygrometers, humidifiers &
dehumidifiers.*

Windsor,
Lyon House,
160–166 Borough High Street,
SE1 1JR
Tel: 0171 407 7144
Antiques & fine art insurance.

West Midlands

Retro Products,
The Yard, Star Street, Lye,
Nr Stourbridge DY9 8TU
Tel: 01384 894042/373332
Tel/Fax: 01384 442065
Fittings and accessories.

Shippers
Shropshire

Big Ben Antiques Shippers Inc,
Rimara, Maesbury Marsh,
Oswestry SY10 8JB
Tel/Fax: 01691 658216

Silver
Bedfordshire

Transatlantic Antiques Ltd,
101 Dunstable Street,
Ampthill MK45 2JT
Tel: 01525 403346

Gloucestershire

Corner House Antiques,
The Corner,
High Street,
Lechlade GL7 3AE
Tel: 01367 252007

London

Daniel Bexfield,
26 Burlington Arcade, W1V 9AD
Tel: 0171 491 1720
Fax: 0171 491 1730

The Silver Fund Ltd,
40 Bury Street, St James's,
SW1Y 6AU
Tel: 0171 839 7664

Republic of Ireland

J. W. Weldon,
55 Clarendon Street, Dublin 2
Tel: 00 353 1 677 1638

Shropshire

Teme Valley Antiques,
1 The Bull Ring,
Ludlow SY8 1AD
Tel: 01584 874686

Sports & Games
Nottinghamshire

T. Vennett-Smith,
11 Nottingham Road,
Gotham NG11 0HE
Tel: 0115 983 0541

Teddy Bears
Oxfordshire

Teddy Bears of Witney,
99 High Street,
Witney OX8 6LY
Tel: 01993 702616/706616

Textiles
Somerset

Joanna Proops,
Antique Textiles,
34 Belvedere, Lansdown Hill,
Bath BA1 5HR
Tel: 01225 310795

Toys
Sussex

Wallis & Wallis,
West Street Auction Galleries,
Lewes BN7 2NJ
Tel: 01273 480208

Yorkshire

Gerard Haley,
Hippins Farm,
Blackshawhead,
Hebden Bridge HX7 7JG
Tel: 01422 842484
Military toys.

John & Simon Haley,
9 Northgate,
Halifax HX6 4NG
Tel: 01422 822148/360434
Money boxes, tinplate toys.

Kent

Bracketts,
Auction Hall, Pantiles,
Tunbridge Wells TN1 1UU
Tel: 01892 544500
Fax: 01892 515191

Watches
London

Pieces of Time,
(1–7 Davies Mews)
26 South Molton Lane,
W1Y 2LP
Tel: 0171 629 2422

Royal Arcade Watch Shop,
4 Royal Arcade,
28 Old Bond St,
W1X 3HD
Tel: 0171 495 4882

Wine Antiques
Buckinghamshire

Christopher Sykes,
The Old Parsonage,
Woburn,
Milton Keynes
MK17 9QM
Tel: 01525 290259

Directory of Auctioneers

Auctioneers who hold frequent sales should contact us by April 2000 for inclusion in the next edition. Unless we are requested otherwise entries will be repeated in subsequent editions.

London

Academy Auctioneers
& Valuers,
Northcote House,
Northcote Avenue,
Ealing W5 3UR
Tel: 020 8579 7466

Angling Auctions,
PO Box 2095,
W12 8RU
Tel: 0181 749 4175

Bloomsbury Book
Auctions,
3–4 Hardwick Street,
Off Rosebery Avenue,
EC1R 4RY
Tel: 0171 833 2636

Bonhams,
Montpelier Street,
Knightsbridge SW7 1HH
Tel: 0171 393 3900

Bonhams,
65–69 Lots Road,
Chelsea SW10 0RN
Tel: 0171 393 3900

Brooks (Auctioneers) Ltd,
81 Westside, SW4 9AY
Tel: 0171 228 8000

Christie, Manson
& Wood,
8 King Street,
St James's,
SW1Y 6QT
Tel: 0171 839 9060

Christie's South
Kensington Ltd,
85 Old Brompton Road,
SW7 3LD
Tel: 0171 581 7611

Comic Book Postal
Auctions Ltd,
40–42 Osnaburgh Street,
NW1 3ND
Tel: 0171 424 0007

Criterion Salerooms,
53 Essex Road,
Islington N1 2BN
Tel: 0171 359 5707

Dix-Noonan-Webb,
1 Old Bond Street,
W1X 3TD
Tel: 0171 499 5022

Stanley Gibbons
Auctions Ltd,
399 Strand,
WC2R 0LX
Tel: 0171 836 8444

Glendinings & Co,
101 New Bond Street,
W1Y 9LG
Tel: 0171 493 2445

Harmers of London,
91 New Bond Street,
W1Y 9LA
Tel: 0171 629 0218

Lloyds International
Auction Galleries,
118 Putney Bridge Road,
SW15 2NQ
Tel: 0181 788 7777

Lots Road Galleries,
71–73 Lots Road,
Chelsea SW10 0RN
Tel: 0171 351 7771

Onslow's, The Depot,
2 Michael Road,
SW6 2AD
Tel: 0171 371 0505

Phillips,
101 New Bond Street,
W1Y 0AS
Tel: 0171 629 6602

Phillips Bayswater,
10 Salem Road,
W2 4DL
Tel: 0171 229 9090

Rosebery's Fine Art Ltd,
Old Railway Booking Hall,
Crystal Palace Station
Road, SE19 2AZ
Tel: 0181 761 2522

Sotheby's,
34–35 New Bond Street,
W1A 2AA
Tel: 0171 293 5000

Spink & Son Ltd,
5 King Street,
St James's,
SW1Y 6QS
Tel: 0171 930 7888

Bedfordshire

Wilson Peacock,
The Auction Centre,
26 Newnham Street,
Bedford MK40 3JR
Tel: 01234 266366

Berkshire

Dreweatt Neate,
Donnington Priory,
Donnington,
Newbury RG13 2JE
Tel: 01635 553553

Padworth Auctions,
30 The Broadway,
Thatcham,
RG19 3HX
Tel: 01734 713772

Special Auction Services,
The Coach House,
Midgham Park,
Reading RG7 5UG
Tel: 0118 971 2949

Buckinghamshire

Amersham Auction
Rooms,
125 Station Road,
Amersham HP7 0AH
Tel: 01494 729292

Bosley's,
42 West Street,
Marlow SL7 2NB
Tel: 01628 488188

Bourne End Auction
Rooms,
Station Approach,
Bourne End SL8 5QH
Tel: 01628 531500

Hamptons,
10 Burkes Parade,
Beaconsfield HP9 1PD
Tel: 01494 672969

Cambridgeshire

Cheffins Grain & Comins,
2 Clifton Road,
Cambridge CB2 4BW
Tel: 01223 58721/213343

Maxey & Son,
1–3 South Brink,
Wisbech PE13 1RD
Tel: 01945 584609

Cheshire

F. W. Allen & Son,
15–15a Station Road,
Cheadle Hulme SK8 5AF
Tel: 0161 485 6069

Dockrees,
Cheadle Hulme
Business Centre,
Clemence House,
Mellor Road,
Cheadle Hulme,
SK8 5AT
Tel: 0161 485 1258

Frank R. Marshall & Co,
Marshall House,
Church Hill,
Knutsford WA16 6DH
Tel: 01565 653284

John Maxwell
of Wilmslow,
133a Woodford Road,
Woodford SK7 1QD
Tel: 0161 439 5182

Phillips North West,
New House,
150 Christleton Road,
Chester CH3 5TD
Tel: 01244 313936

Peter Wilson,
Victoria Gallery,
Market Street,
Nantwich CW5 5DG
Tel: 01270 623878

Wright Manley,
Beeston Castle
Salerooms,
Tarporley CW6 0DR
Tel: 01829 260318

Cornwall

W. H. Lane & Son,
65 Morrab Road,
Penzance TR18 2QT
Tel: 01736 361447

David Lay, ASVA
Auction House, Alverton,
Penzance TR18 4RE
Tel: 01736 361414

Phillips Cornwall,
Cornubia Hall,
Eastcliffe Road,
Par PL24 2AQ
Tel: 0172 681 4047

Martyn Rowe,
Truro Auction Centre,
City Wharf,
Malpas Road,
Truro TR1 1QH
Tel: 01872 260020

Cumbria

Cumbria Auction Rooms,
12 Lowther Street,
Carlisle CA3 8DA
Tel: 01228 25259

Mitchells,
Fairfield House,
Station Road,
Cockermouth CA13 9PY
Tel: 01900 827800

Penrith Farmers'
& Kidd's,
Skirsgill Salerooms,
Penrith CA11 0DN
Tel: 01768 890781

Phillips Carlisle,
48 Cecil Street,
Carlisle CA1 1NT
Tel: 01228 42422

Thomson, Roddick
& Laurie,
24 Lowther Street,
Carlisle CA3 8DA
Tel: 01228 28939/39636

Derbyshire

Neales,
The Derby Saleroom,
Becket Street,
Derby DE1 1HW
Tel: 01332 343286

Noel Wheatcroft,
Matlock Auction Gallery,
The Old Picture Palace,
Dale Road,
Matlock DE4 3LT
Tel: 01629 584591

Devon

Bearnes,
Avenue Road,
Torquay TQ2 5TG
Tel: 01803 296277

Bearnes,
St Edmund's Court,
Okehampton Street,
Exeter EX4 1DU
Tel: 01392 422800

Bonhams West Country,
Devon Fine Art
Auction House,
Dowell Street,
Honiton EX14 8LX
Tel: 01404 41872

Michael J. Bowman,
6 Haccombe House,
Netherton,
Newton Abbot
TQ12 4SJ
Tel: 01626 872890

Eldreds,
13–15 Ridge Park Road,
Plympton,
Plymouth PL7 2BS
Tel: 01752 340066

Robin A. Fenner & Co,
The Stannary Gallery,
Drake Road,
Tavistock
PL19 0AX
Tel: 01822 617799

Phillips,
Alphin Brook Road,
Alphington,
Exeter EX2 8TH
Tel: 01392 439025

Plymouth Auction Rooms,
Edwin House,
St John's Rd,
Cattedown,
Plymouth PL4 0NZ
Tel: 01752 254740

Rendells,
Stonepark,
Ashburton
TQ13 7RH
Tel: 01364 653017

Martin Spencer-Thomas,
Bicton Street,
Exmouth EX8 2SN
Tel: 01395 267403

Taylors,
Honiton Galleries,
205 High Street,
Honiton EX14 8LF
Tel: 01404 42404

Dorset

Chapman, Moore
& Mugford,
9 High Street,
Shaftesbury SP7 8JB
Tel: 01747 852400

Cottees of Wareham,
The Market,
East Street,
Wareham BH20 4NR
Tel: 01929 552826

Hy Duke & Son,
Dorchester Fine Art
Salerooms,
Dorchester DT1 1QS
Tel: 01305 265080

Phillips Sherborne,
Long Street Salerooms,
Sherborne DT9 3BS
Tel: 01935 815271

Riddetts of
Bournemouth,
177 Holden Hurst Road,
Bournemouth BH8 8DQ
Tel: 01202 555686

Semley Auctioneers,
Station Road, Semley,
Shaftesbury SP7 9AN
Tel/Fax: 01747 855122/
855222

Michael Stainer Ltd,
St Andrew's Hall,
Wolverton Rd, Boscombe,
Bournemouth BH7 6HT
Tel: 01202 309999

Essex

BBG Ambrose,
Ambrose House,
Old Station Road,
Loughton IG10 4PE
Tel: 0181 502 3951

Cooper Hirst Auctions,
The Granary Saleroom,
Victoria Road,
Chelmsford CM2 6LH
Tel: 01245 260535

Leigh Auction Rooms,
John Stacey & Sons,
88–90 Pall Mall,
Leigh-on-Sea SS9 1RG
Tel: 01702 77051

Saffron Walden Auctions,
1 Market Street,
Saffron Walden
CB10 1JB
Tel: 01799 513281

G. E. Sworder & Sons,
14 Cambridge Road,
Stansted Mountfitchet
CM24 8BZ
Tel: 01279 817778

Trembath Welch,
The Old Town Hall,
Great Dunmow CM6 1AU
Tel: 01371 873014

Gloucestershire

Bristol Auction Rooms,
St John's Place,
Apsley Road, Clifton,
Bristol BS8 2ST
Tel: 0117 973 7201

Clevedon Salerooms,
Herbert Road, Clevedon,
Bristol BS21 7ND
Tel: 01275 876699

Cotswold Auction Co Ltd,
The Coach House, Swan
Yard, 9–13 Market Place,
Cirencester GL7 2NH
Tel: 01285 642420

Cotswold Auction Co Ltd,
Chapel Walk Saleroom,
Chapel Walk,
Cheltenham GL50 3DS
Tel: 01242 256363

Mallams,
26 Grosvenor Street,
Cheltenham GL52 2SG
Tel: 01242 235712

Moore, Allen & Innocent,
Norcote,
Cirencester GL7 5RH
Tel: 01285 648102

Specialised Postcard
Auctions,
25 Gloucester Street,
Cirencester GL7 2DJ
Tel: 01285 659057

Tayler & Fletcher,
London House, High St,
Bourton-on-the-Water,
Cheltenham GL54 2AP
Tel: 01451 821666

Wotton Auction Rooms,
Tabernacle Road,
Wotton-under-Edge
GL12 7EB
Tel: 01453 844733

Greater Manchester

Bonhams,
St Thomas's Place,
Hillgate,
Stockport SK1 3TZ
Tel: 0161 429 8283

Capes Dunn & Co,
The Auction Galleries,
38 Charles Street,
Off Princess Street,
M1 7DB
Tel: 0161 273 6060/1911

Hampshire

Andover Saleroom,
41a London Street,
Andover SP10 2NY
Tel: 01264 364820

Evans & Partridge,
Agriculture House,
High Street,
Stockbridge SO20 6HF
Tel: 01264 810702

Farnham Auctions Ltd,
169 Fleet Rd,
Fleet GU13 8PD
Tel: 01252 810844

Jacobs & Hunt,
26 Lavant Street,
Petersfield GU32 3EF
Tel: 01730 233933

George Kidner,
The Old School,
The Square, Pennington,
Lymington SO41 8GN
Tel: 01590 670070

May & Son,
18 Bridge Street,
Andover SP10 1BH
Tel: 01264 323417 &
363331

D. M. Nesbit & Co,
7 Clarendon Road,
Southsea PO5 2ED
Tel: 01705 864321

Odiham Auction Sales,
The Eagle Works,
Rear of Hartley Wintney
Garages, High Street,
Hartley Wintney
RG27 8PU
Tel: 01252 844410

Phillips Fine Art
Auctioneers,
54 Southampton Road,
Ringwood BH24 1JD
Tel: 01425 473333

Phillips of Winchester,
The Red House,
Hyde Street,
Winchester SO23 7DX
Tel: 01962 862515

Romsey Auction Rooms,
86 The Hundred,
Romsey SO51 8BX
Tel: 01794 513331

Herefordshire

Morris Bricknell,
Stuart House,
18 Gloucester Road,
Ross-on-Wye
HR9 5BU
Tel: 01989 768320

Russell, Baldwin & Bright,
Ryelands Road,
Leominster HR6 8NZ
Tel: 01568 611122

Nigel Ward & Co,
Border Property Centre,
Pontrilas HR2 0EH
Tel: 01981 240140

Williams & Watkins,
Ross Auction Centre,
Overross,
Ross-on-Wye HR9 7QF
Tel: 01989 762225

Hertfordshire

Brown & Merry
Tring Market Auctions,
Brook Street,
Tring HP23 5EF
Tel: 01442 826446

Andrew Pickford,
The Hertford Saleroom,
42 St Andrew Street,
Hertford SG14 1JA
Tel: 01992 583508/
501421

Humberside

Dickinson Davy
& Markham,
Wrawby Street,
Brigg DN20 8JJ
Tel: 01652 653666

Kent

Bracketts,
Auction Hall, Pantiles,
Tunbridge Wells TN1 1UU
Tel: 01892 544500

Canterbury Auction
Galleries,
40 Station Road West,
Canterbury CT2 8AN
Tel: 01227 763337

Mervyn Carey,
Twysden Cottage,
Benenden,
Cranbrook TN17 4LD
Tel: 01580 240283

Halifax Property
Services,
Fine Art Department,
53 High Street,
Tenterden TN30 6BG
Tel: 01580 763200

Halifax Property Services,
15 Cattle Market,
Sandwich CT13 9AW
Tel: 01304 614369

Hogben Auctioneers,
St John's Street,
Folkestone CT20 1JB
Tel: 01303 240808

Ibbett Mosely,
125 High Street,
Sevenoaks TN13 1UT
Tel: 01732 452246

Lambert & Foster,
77 Commercial Road,
Paddock Wood
TN12 6DR
Tel: 01892 832325

Lambert & Foster,
102 High Street,
Tenterden TN30 6HT
Tel: 01580 762083/
763233

B. J. Norris,
The Quest, West Street,
Harrietsham,
Maidstone ME17 1JD
Tel: 01622 859515

Phillips Fine Art
Auctioneers,
49 London Road,
Sevenoaks TN13 1AR
Tel: 01732 740310

Wealden Auction Galleries
Desmond Judd,
23 Hendly Drive,
Cranbrook TN17 3DY
Tel: 01580 714522

Lancashire

Smythe's,
174 Victoria Road West,
Cleveleys FY5 3NE
Tel: 01253 852184

Leicestershire

Gildings,
64 Roman Way,
Market Harborough
LE16 7PQ
Tel: 01858 410414

Heathcote Ball & Co,
Castle Auction Rooms,
78 St Nicholas Circle,
Leicester LE1 5NW
Tel: 0116 253 6789

Lincolnshire

Escritt & Barrell,
24 St Peter's Hill,
Grantham NG31 6QF
Tel: 01476 65371

Goldings,
The Grantham Auction
Rooms, Old Wharf Road,
Grantham NG31 7AA
Tel: 01476 565118

Thomas Mawer & Son,
The Lincoln Saleroom,
63 Monks Road,
Lincoln LN2 5HP
Tel: 01522 524984

Marilyn Swain Auctions,
The Old Barracks,
Sandon Road,
Grantham NG31 9AS
Tel: 01476 568861

Walter's,
No. 1 Mint Lane,
Lincoln LN1 1UD
Tel: 01522 525454

Merseyside

Cato Crane & Co,
Liverpool Auction Rooms,
6 Stanhope Street,
Liverpool L8 5RF
Tel: 0151 709 5559

Outhwaite & Litherland,
Kingsway Galleries,
Fontenoy Street,
Liverpool L3 2BE
Tel: 0151 236 6561

Worralls,
13–15 Seel Street,
Liverpool L1 4AU
Tel: 0151 709 2950

Norfolk

Garry M. Emms & Co Ltd,
T/A Great Yarmouth
Salerooms, Beevor Road,
Great Yarmouth
NR30 3PS
Tel: 01493 332668/
720179

Ewings,
Market Place,
Reepham,
Norwich NR10 4JJ
Tel: 01603 870473

Thomas Wm Gaze & Son,
Diss Auction Rooms,
Roydon Road,
Diss IP22 3LN
Tel: 01379 650306

G. A. Key,
Aylsham Salerooms,
8 Market Place,
Aylsham
NR11 6EH
Tel: 01263 733195

Knight's,
Cuckoo Cottage,
Town Green,
Alby,
Norwich NR11 7HE
Tel: 01263 768488

Northamptonshire

Merry's Auctioneers,
Northampton Auction
& Sales Centre,
Liliput Rd,
Brackmills,
Northampton
NN4 7BY
Tel: 01604 769990

Northumberland

Louis Johnson,
63 Bridge Street,
Morpeth NE61 1PQ
Tel: 01670 513025

Nottinghamshire

Bonhams,
57 Mansfield Road,
Nottingham
NG1 3PL
Tel: 0115 947 4414

Arthur Johnson & Sons
Nottingham Auction
Centre,
Meadow Lane,
Nottingham NG2 3GY
Tel: 0115 986 9128

Mellors & Kirk,
The Auction House,
Gregory Street,
Lenton Lane,
Nottingham NG7 2NL
Tel: 0115 979 0000

Neales,
192–194 Mansfield Road,
Nottingham
NG1 3HU
Tel: 0115 962 4141

Phillips,
20 The Square,
Retford DN22 6XE
Tel: 01777 708633

T. Vennett-Smith,
11 Nottingham Road,
Gotham NG11 0HE
Tel: 0115 983 0541

Oxfordshire

Dreweatt Neate
Holloways,
49 Parsons Street,
Banbury OX16 8PF
Tel: 01295 253197

Mallams,
24 St Michael's Street,
Oxford OX1 2EB
Tel: 01865 241358

Phillips,
39 Park End Street,
Oxford OX1 1JD
Tel: 01865 723524

Simmons & Sons,
32 Bell Street,
Henley-on-Thames
RG9 2BH
Tel: 01491 571111

Soames County Auctions,
Pinnocks Farm Estates,
Northmoor OX8 1AY
Tel: 01865 300626

Suffolk

Abbotts Auction Rooms,
Campsea Ashe,
Woodbridge IP13 0PS
Tel: 01728 746323

Auction Road Show Co
Unit 23 Maitland Road,
Lion Barn Ind. Estate,
Needham Market IP6 8NS
Tel: 01449 720868

Boardman Fine Art
Auctioneers,
Station Road Corner,
Haverhill CB9 0EY
Tel: 01440 730414

Diamond Mills & Co,
117 Hamilton Road,
Felixstowe IP11 7BL
Tel: 01394 282281

Dyson & Son,
The Auction Room,
Church Street, Clare,
Sudbury CO10 8PD
Tel: 01787 277993

Lacy Scott and Knight,
The Auction Centre,
10 Risbygate Street,
Bury St Edmunds
IP33 3AA
Tel: 01284 763531

Olivers,
Olivers Rooms, Burkitts
Lane, Sudbury CO10 1HB
Tel: 01787 880305

Phillips,
32 Boss Hall Road,
Ipswich IP1 59J
Tel: 01473 740494

Surrey

Chancellors,
74 London Road,
Kingston-upon-Thames
KT2 6PX
Tel: 0181 541 4139

Clarke Gammon,
The Guildford Auction
Rooms, Bedford Road,
Guildford GU1 4SJ
Tel: 01483 566458

Ewbank,
Burnt Common Auction
Room, London Road,
Send, Woking GU23 7LN
Tel: 01483 223101

Hamptons International,
Baverstock House,
93 High Street,
Godalming GU7 1AL
Tel: 01483 423567

Lawrences Auctioneers,
Norfolk House,
80 High Street,
Bletchingley RH1 4PA
Tel: 01883 743323

John Nicholson,
The Auction Rooms,
Longfield, Midhurst Road,
Fernhurst GU27 3HA
Tel: 01428 653727

Phillips Fine Art
Auctioneers, Millmead,
Guildford GU2 5BE
Tel: 01483 504030

Richmond & Surrey
Auctions,
Richmond Station,
Kew Road, Old Railway
Parcels Depot,
Richmond TW9 2NA
Tel: 0181 948 6677

P. F. Windibank,
Dorking Halls, Reigate
Road, Dorking RH4 1SG
Tel: 01306 884556/
876280

Sussex

John Bellman
Auctioneers,
New Pound Business Pk,
Wisborough Green,
Billingshurst
RH14 0AZ
Tel: 01403 700858

Burstow & Hewett,
Abbey Auction Galleries
& Granary Salerooms,
Lower Lake,
Battle TN33 0AT
Tel: 01424 772374

Peter Cheney,
Western Road Auction
Rooms, Western Road,
Littlehampton BN17 5NP
Tel: 01903 722264/
713418

Denham's,
Horsham Auction
Galleries, Warnham,
Horsham RH12 3RZ
Tel: 01403 255699/
253837

Eastbourne Auction
Rooms,
Auction House,
Finmere Road,
Eastbourne
BN22 8QL
Tel: 01323 431444

R. H. Ellis & Sons,
44–46 High Street,
Worthing BN11 1LL
Tel: 01903 238999

Gorringes Auction
Galleries,
Terminus Road,
Bexhill-on-Sea
TN39 3LR
Tel: 01424 212994

Graves, Son & Pilcher,
Hove Auction Rooms,
Hove Street,
Hove BN3 2GL
Tel: 01273 735266

Edgar Horn Fine Art
Auctioneers,
46–50 South Street,
Eastbourne BN21 4XB
Tel: 01323 410419

Raymond P. Inman,
The Auction Galleries,
35 & 40 Temple Street,
Brighton BN1 3BH
Tel: 01273 774777

Lewes Auction Rooms
(Julian Dawson),
56 High Street,
Lewes BN7 1XE
Tel: 01273 478221

Phillips Fine Art
Auctioneers,
Baffins Hall,
Baffins Lane,
Chichester PO19 1UA
Tel: 01243 787548

Rye Auction Galleries,
Rock Channel,
Rye TN31 7HL
Tel: 01797 222124

Sotheby's Sussex,
Summers Place,
Billingshurst RH14 9AD
Tel: 01403 833500

Stride & Son,
Southdown House,
St John's Street,
Chichester PO19 1XQ
Tel: 01243 780207

Rupert Toovey & Co Ltd,
Star Road,
Partridge Green
RH13 8RJ
Tel: 01403 711744

Wallis & Wallis,
West Street Auction
Galleries,
Lewes BN7 2NJ
Tel: 01273 480208

Worthing Auction
Galleries Ltd,
Fleet House,
Teville Gate,
Worthing BN11 1UA
Tel: 01903 205565

Tyne & Wear

Anderson & Garland,
Marlborough House,
Marlborough Crescent,
Newcastle-upon-Tyne
NE1 4EE
Tel: 0191 232 6278

Phillips North East,
St Mary's,
Oakwellgate,
Gateshead
NE8 2AX
Tel: 0191 477 6688

Warwickshire

Bigwood Auctioneers Ltd,
Old School, Tiddington,
Stratford-upon-Avon
CV37 7AW
Tel: 01789 269415

BBG Locke & England,
18 Guy Street,
Leamington Spa,
CV32 4RT
Tel: 01926 889100

West Midlands

Biddle and Webb Ltd,
Ladywood Middleway,
Birmingham
B16 0PP
Tel: 0121 455 8042

Frank H. Fellows & Sons,
Augusta House,
19 Augusta St,
Hockley,
Birmingham B18 6JA
Tel: 0121 212 2131

Phillips,
The Old House,
Station Road,
Knowle,
Solihull B93 0HT
Tel: 01564 776151

Walker, Barnett & Hill,
Waterloo Rd Salerooms,
Clarence Street,
Wolverhampton
WV1 4JE
Tel: 01902 773531

Weller & Dufty Ltd,
141 Bromsgrove Street,
Birmingham
B5 6RQ
Tel: 0121 692 1414

Wiltshire

Henry Aldridge & Son,
Devizes Auction Rooms,
1 Wine Street,
Devizes SN10 1AP
Tel: 01380 729199

Finan, Watkins & Co,
The Square,
Mere BA12 6DJ
Tel: 01747 861411

Swindon Auction Rooms,
The Planks
(off The Square),
Old Town,
Swindon SN3 1QP
Tel: 01793 615915

Dominic Winter
Book Auctions,
The Old School,
Maxwell Street,
Swindon
SN1 5DR
Tel: 01793 611340

Woolley & Wallis,
Salisbury Salerooms,
51–61 Castle Street,
Salisbury SP1 3SU
Tel: 01722 424500

Worcestershire

Philip Laney,
Malvern Auction Centre,
Portland Road,
Off Victoria Road,
Malvern WR14 2TA
Tel: 01684 893933

Philip Serrell,
The Malvern Saleroom,
Barnards Green Road,
Malvern WR14 3LW
Tel: 01684 892314

Yorkshire

BBR,
Elsecar Heritage Centre,
Wath Road,
Elsecar,
Barnsley S74 8HJ
Tel: 01226 745156

Boulton & Cooper,
St Michael's House,
Market Place,
Malton YO17 0LR
Tel: 01653 696151

H. C. Chapman & Son,
The Auction Mart,
North Street,
Scarborough
YO11 1DL
Tel: 01723 372424

Cundalls,
15 Market Place,
Malton YO17 7LP
Tel: 01653 697820

Dee, Atkinson
& Harrison,
The Exchange Saleroom,
Driffield YO25 7LJ
Tel: 01377 253151

David Duggleby,
The Vine St Salerooms,
Scarborough
YO11 1XN
Tel: 01723 507111

Eadon Lockwood
& Riddle,
411 Petre Street,
Sheffield S4 8LJ
Tel: 0114 261 8000

Andrew Hartley,
Victoria Hall Salerooms,
Little Lane,
Ilkley LS29 8EA
Tel: 01943 816363

Lithgow Sons
& Partners,
Antique House,
Station Road, Stokesley,
Middlesbrough
TS9 7AB
Tel: 01642 710158/
710326

Malcolms No. 1
Auctioneers & Valuers,
The Chestnuts,
16 Park Avenue,
Sherburn-in-Elmet,
Nr Leeds LS25 6EF
Tel: 01977 684971

Christopher Matthews,
23 Mount Street,
Harrogate HG2 8DQ
Tel: 01423 871756

Morphets of Harrogate,
6 Albert Street,
Harrogate HG1 1JL
Tel: 01423 530030

Phillips Leeds,
17a East Parade,
Leeds LS1 2BH
Tel: 0113 2448011

Tennants,
The Auction Centre,
Harmby Road,
Leyburn DL8 5SG
Tel: 01969 623780

Tennants,
34 Montpellier Parade,
Harrogate
HG1 2TG
Tel: 01423 531661

Wilkinson & Beighton,
Woodhouse Green,
Thurcroft, Rotherham
SY3 8LA
Tel: 01709 700005

Northern Ireland

Anderson's Auctions,
28 Linenhall Street,
Belfast BT2 8BG
Tel: 01232 321401

Republic of Ireland

James Adam & Sons,
26 St Stephen's Green,
Dublin 2
Tel: 00 353 1 676 0261

Christie's Dublin,
52 Waterloo Road,
Dublin 4
Tel: 00 353 1 6680 585

Drum, Denis Ltd,
New Street,
Malahide,
Co Dublin
Tel: 00 353 1 845 4371

Hamilton Osborne King,
4 Main Street,
Blackrock,
Co Dublin
Tel: 00 353 1 288 5011

Mealy's,
Chatsworth Street,
Castle Comer,
Co Kilkenny
Tel: 00 353 56 41229

O'Regans of Cork,
21 Lavitts Quay,
Cork
Tel: 00 353 21 271550

Whyte's Auctioneers,
30 Marlborough St,
Dublin 1
Tel: 00 353 1 874 6161

Scotland

Christie's Scotland Ltd,
164–166 Bath Street,
Glasgow
G2 4TG
Tel: 0141 332 8134

William Hardie Ltd,
15a Blythswood Square,
Glasgow
G2 4EW
Tel: 0141 221 6780

Macgregor Auctions,
56 Largo Road,
St Andrews,
Fife KY16 8RP
Tel: 01334 472431

Robert McTear & Co,
Clydeway Business
Centre, 8 Elliot Place,
Glasgow G3 8EP
Tel: 0141 221 4456

Phillips Scotland,
65 George Street,
Edinburgh
EH2 2JL
Tel: 0131 225 2266

Phillips Scotland,
207 Bath Street,
Glasgow
G2 4HD
Tel: 0141 221 8377

Sotheby's,
112 George Street,
Edinburgh
EH2 4LH
Tel: 0131 226 7201

Thomson, Roddick
& Laurie,
60 Whitesands,
Dumfries DG1 2RS
Tel: 01387 255366

West Perthshire Auctions,
Dundas Street,
Comrie,
Perthshire PH6 2LN
Tel: 01764 670613

Wales

Peter Francis,
The Curiosity Saleroom,
19 King Street,
Carmarthen SA31 1BH
Tel: 01267 233456

Morgan Evans & Co Ltd,
30 Church Street,
Llangefni, Anglesey,
Gwynedd LL77 7DU
Tel: 01248 723303/
421582

Phillips Cardiff,
9–10 Westgate Street,
Cardiff CF1 1DA
Tel: 01222 396453

Rogers Jones & Co,
33 Abergele Road,
Colwyn Bay LL29 7RU
Tel: 01492 532176

J. Straker, Chadwick
& Sons,
Market Street Chambers,
Abergavenny,
Monmouthshire
NP7 5SD
Tel: 01873 852624

Wingetts,
29 Holt Street,
Wrexham LL13 8DH
Tel: 01978 353553

Channel Islands

Bonhams & Martel
Maides,
Allez St Auction Rooms,
29 High St, St Peter Port,
Guernsey GY1 4NY
Tel: 01481 713463/
722700

Bonhams and Langlois,
Westaway Chambers,
39 Don Street,
St Helier,
Jersey JE2 4TR
Tel: 01534 22441

Austria

Dorotheum,
Palais Dorotheum,
A-1010 Wien,
Dorotheergasse 17
Tel: 00 43 1 515 600

Holland

Van Sabben Poster
Auctions,
Oosteinde 30,
1678 HS Oostwoud
Tel: 00 31 229 20 25 89

Sotheby's Amsterdam,
Rokin 102,
Amsterdam 1012 KZ
Tel: 00 31 20 550 2200

Monaco

Sotheby's Monaco,
Le Sporting d'Hiver,
Place du Casino,
98001 Cedex
Tel: 00 377 93 30 8880

Switzerland

Phillips,
27 Ramistrasse,
8001 Zurich
Tel: 00 41 1 252 6962

Phillips Geneva,
9 rue Ami-Levrier,
CH-1201 Geneva
Tel: 00 41 22 738 0707

Sotheby's,
13 Quai du Mont Blanc,
Geneva CH-1201
Tel: 00 41 22 732 8585

Sotheby's Zurich,
Bleicherweg 20,
Zurich CH-8022
Tel: 00 41 1 202 0011

USA

Butterfield & Butterfield,
220 San Bruno Avenue,
San Francisco
CA 94103
Tel: 00 1 415 861 7500

Du Mouchelles,
409 East Jefferson,
Detroit,
Michigan 48226
Tel: 00 1 313 963 0248

Eldred's,
1475 Route 6A,
East Dennis,
Massachusetts
0796 02641
Tel: 00 1 508 385 3116

Lesley Hindman
Auctioneers,
215 West Ohio Street,
Chicago,
Illinois IL 60610
Tel: 00 1 312 670 0010

Jackson's Auctioneers
& Appraisers,
2229 Lincoln Street,
Cedar Falls IA 50613
Tel: 00 1 319 277 2256

Jones & Horan,
453 Mast Road,
Goffstown,
NH 03045
Tel: 00 1 603 623 5314

New Orleans Auction
Galleries Inc,
801 Magazine Street,
AT 510 Julia,
New Orleans,
Louisiana 70130
Tel: 00 1 504 566 1849

Phillips New York,
406 East 79th Street,
New York
NY10021
Tel: 00 1 212 570 4830

Skinner Inc,
357 Main Street,
Bolton MA 01740
Tel: 00 1 978 779 6241

Skinner Inc,
The Heritage On The
Garden,
63 Park Plaza,
Boston MA 02116
Tel: 00 1 617 350 5400

Sloan's,
4920 Wyaconda Road,
North Bethesda
MD 20852
Tel: 00 1 301 468
4911/669 5066

Sloan's Auctioneers &
Appraisers,
Miami Gallery,
8861 NW 18th Terrace,
Suite 100,
Miami,
Florida 33172
Tel: 00 1 305 592 2575/
800 660 4524

Sotheby's,
1334 York Avenue,
New York NY 10021
Tel: 00 1 212 606 7000

Sotheby's,
9665 Wilshire Boulevard,
Beverly Hills,
California 90212
Tel: 00 1 310 274 0340

Sotheby's,
215 West Ohio Street,
Chicago,
Illinois 60610
Tel: 00 1 312 670 0010

Swann Galleries Inc,
104 East 25th Street,
New York
Tel: 00 1 212 2544710

Treadway Gallery,
2029 Madison Road,
Cincinnati
OH 45208
Tel: 00 1 513 321 6742

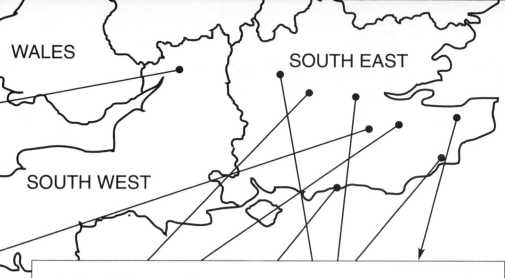

WALES

SOUTH EAST

SOUTH WEST

WALES

SOUTH EAST

SOUTH WEST

EAST
MIDLANDS

EAST
ANGLIA

SOUTH
EAST

SOUTH WEST

Mervyn Carey

Fine Art Auctioneer and Valuer

Regular antiques auctions
held at The Church Hall,
Church Road, Tenterden, Kent

**Enquiries with entries for future
sales welcomed**

Further details and illustrated catalogues
£2 (£2.30 by post) available from
the Auctioneer

**Professionally prepared valuations
carried out in a personal and consid-
erate manner for Insurance, Probate
and Family Division of single items
to complete household contents**

TWYSDEN COTTAGE, BENENDEN,
CRANBROOK, KENT TN17 4LD
TEL: 01580 240283

AYLSHAM SALEROOMS

Norfolk's Leading Fine Art Auctioneers

Conducting:
17 **ANTIQUE SALES** (3 weekly)
6 **PICTURE SALES** (Bi-monthly)
6 **BOOK SALES** (Bi-monthly)
4 **COLLECTOR'S SALES** (Quarterly)
* * *
Free Auction Calendar Available
* * *
Free Advice For Sale by Auction
Freephone Valuation Line 0800 163894
* * *
Professional Valuations for Probate & Insurance
purposes at competitive rates
* * *
Complete House Clearances Undertaken
* * *
Further Details From the Auctioneers

**GA
KEY**

FINE ART AUCTIONEERS

8 MARKET PLACE AYLSHAM NORWICH NR11 6EH
TELEPHONE 01263 733195 FAX 01263 732140

OLIVERS

AUCTIONEERS & VALUERS

REGULAR SALES OF
ANTIQUES & WORKS OF ART

FORTNIGHTLY SALES OF
VICTORIAN & LATER FURNITURE
& HOUSEHOLD EFFECTS

VALUATIONS FOR INSURANCE
PROBATE AND FAMILY DIVISION

OUR OWN COLLECTION SERVICE
AVAILABLE FOR VENDORS

Members of the society of Fine Art Auctioneers

The Saleroom, Burkitts Lane, Sudbury, Suffolk CO10 1HB
Telephone and Fax 01787 880305

THOS. WM. GAZE & SON

DISS AUCTION ROOMS

Weekly Friday Catalogue Sales

comprising

600 Lots of Antique Furniture and Collectables
400 Lots Shipping, Barn Clearance and Pine
800 Lots General Furniture and Effects

also regular

Specialist Fine Art, Architectural Salvage,
Rural and Domestic Bygones,
Decorative Arts, Automobilia,
Toys and Nostalgia Sales

throughout the year

Auction Calendar and Catalogues Available

ROYDON ROAD, DISS, NORFOLK (01379) 650306
Email: auct@twgaze.co.uk

DYSON & SON

AUCTIONEERS & VALUERS

REGULAR THREE WEEKLY SATURDAY AUCTIONS OF
ANTIQUE, OTHER FURNITURE AND EFFECTS.

VIEWING FRIDAY 9 A.M. TO 9 P.M.
SATURDAY FROM 9 A.M. SALE STARTS 11 A.M.
APPROXIMATELY 700 LOTS.
PLEASE PHONE FOR COMPLIMENTARY YEARLY
AUCTION DATE CALENDAR OR VENDORS TERMS.

VISA, DELTA AND DEBIT CARDS ACCEPTED.

The Auction Room, Church Street, Clare, Suffolk. CO10 8PD
Tel: 01787 277 993 Fax: 01787 277996

Heathcote Ball & Co.

INDEPENDENT SPECIALIST
FINE ART AUCTIONEERS
AND VALUERS

Regular Antique & Fine Art Auctions

Country House Sales

Valuations for Sale, Probate,
Insurance, Family Division

House Clearances

**Castle Auction Rooms, 78 St Nicholas Circle,
Leicester, LE1 5NW
Tel: (0116) 253 6789   Fax: (0116) 253 8517**

LT LOUIS TAYLOR
FINE ART AUCTIONEERS & VALUERS
EST 1877

SELL YOUR CERAMICS IN THE HEART OF THE POTTERIES

Due to the large production of fine quality
pottery and porcelain made in the Stoke-on-Trent
area, we naturally specialise in selling ceramics.

Specialist DOULTON and BESWICK Sales

Furniture, Paintings, Silver, Toys
and Objets D'Art

Quarterly Fine Art Sales

Fortnightly Victoriana Sales

For further information please contact the
Auctioneers on (01782) 214111

Britannia House
10 Town Road, Hanley
Stoke-on-Trent ST1 2QG
Tel: 01782 214111
Fax: 01782 287874

Wintertons
fine arts

AUCTIONEERS SINCE 1864

TWO DAY FINE ART SALES
Lichfield Auction Centre - Every two months
VICTORIAN & GENERAL SALES
Lichfield Auction Centre: Every 2-3 weeks
Uttoxeter Saleroom: Monthly
ANTIQUE DISCOVERY DAYS
Regular programme of Valuation Days in
Staffordshire and Derbyshire
SPECIALIST VALUATION SERVICES
Detailed inventories prepared for Probate,
Insurance and Sale Purposes.
FOR DETAILS CONTACT:
Sally Oldham or Sarah Leedham
Lichfield Auction Centre
Fradley Park, Lichfield, Staffs WS13 8NF
Tel: 01543 263256

BBG Locke & England
Auctioneers & Valuers

The Midlands Longest Established Auction House

MONTHLY Fine Art and Antique Auctions

WEEKLY Victoriana Auctions

Full range of PROFESSIONAL VALUATIONS offered

COMPETITIVE commission and removal charges

FREE special request mailing list search service

OFFICES:
**18 Guy Street, Royal Leamington Spa, Warwickshire CV32 4RT
• Enquiries: Tel: 01926 889100 Fax: 01926 470608 •
http://www.auctions-on-line.com/locke**

Auctioneers *Walker Barnett & Hill* Est 1780 Auctioneers **and Valuers**

Hall & Lloyd EST. 1882

**Walker Barnett & Hill
Waterloo Road Salerooms,
Wolverhampton WV1 4JE
Tel No: 01902 773531
Fax No: 01902 712940**

**Hall & Lloyd
South Street Salerooms,
Stafford
Tel No: 01785 258176
Fax No: 01785 228224**

*Weekly Sales of Victorian and General Household Furniture.
Monthly Antique Sales, Country House and Specialist Sales.*
*Valuations and Inventories Compiled for Insurance, Probate, and Family
Division Purposes.*

NORTH
WEST

EAST
MIDLANDS

WEST
MIDLANDS

EAST
ANGLIA

WALES

SOUTH
EAST

SOUTH WEST

SCOTLAND

NORTH

YORKSHIRE & HUMBERSIDE

NORTH WEST

WALES

WEST MIDLANDS

SOUTH WEST

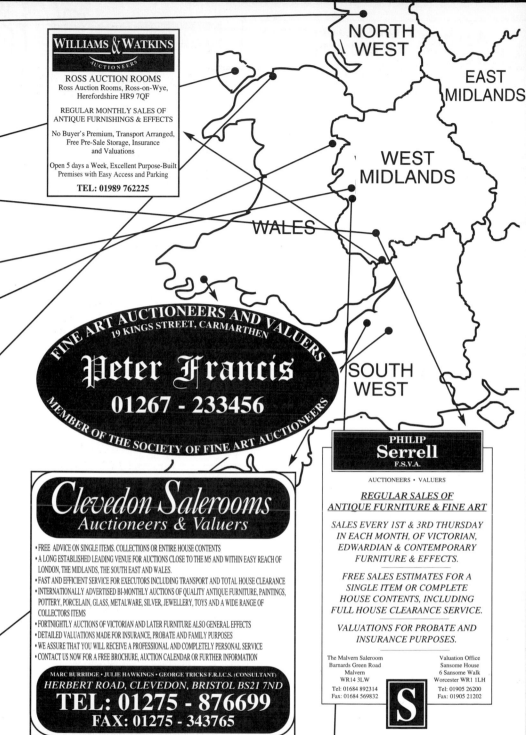

NORTH WEST

EAST MIDLANDS

WEST MIDLANDS

WALES

SOUTH WEST

Index to Advertisers

Key to Illustrations

Each illustration and descriptive caption is accompanied by a letter code. By referring to the following list of Auctioneers (denoted by *) and dealers (•) the source of any item may be immediately determined. Inclusion in this edition no way constitutes or implies a contract or binding offer on the part of any of our contributors to supply or sell the goods illustrated, or similar articles, at the prices stated. Advertisers in this year's directory are denoted by †.

If you require a valuation for an item, it is advisable to check whether the dealer or specialist will carry out this service and if there is a charge. Please mention Miller's when making an enquiry. Having found a specialist who will carry out your valuation it is best to send a photograph and description of the item to the specialist together with a stamped addressed envelope for the reply. A valuation by telephone is not possible.

Most dealers are only too happy to help you with your enquiry, however, they are very busy people and consideration of the above points would be welcomed.

A&A	•	Antiques & Art, 116 State Street, Portsmouth, NH 03802, USA Tel: 00 1 603 431 3931
A&H	•†	Architectural & Historical Salvage, Spa Street, Ossett, Wakefield, Yorks WF5 0HJ Tel: 01924 262831
AAC	•	Arundel Antiques Centre, 51 High Street, Arundel, Sussex BN18 9AJ Tel: 01903 882749
AAN	•	Appledore Antiques Tel: 01233 758272
AAV	*†	Academy Auctioneers & Valuers, Northcote House, Northcote Avenue, Ealing, London W5 3UR Tel: 020 8579 7466
ACT	•	Alscot Bathroom Co, The Stable Yard, Alscot Park, Stratford-upon-Avon, Warks CV37 8BL Tel: 01789 450 861
AEF	•	A & E Foster, Little Heysham, Naphill, Bucks HP14 4SU Tel: 01494 562024
AF	•	Albert Forsythe, The Old Rectory, 24 Carnteel Road, Aughmacloy, Co Tyrone, N. Ireland BT69 2DU Tel: 01662 557522
AG	*	Anderson & Garland (Auctioneers), Marlborough House, Marlborough Crescent, Newcastle-upon-Tyne, Tyne & Wear, NE1 4EE Tel: 0191 232 6278
AGA	*†	Angling Auctions, PO Box 2095, London W12 8RU Tel: 0181 749 4175
AH	*†	Andrew Hartley, Victoria Hall Salerooms, Little Lane, Ilkley, Yorks LS29 8EA Tel: 01943 816363
AHa	•	Adrian Harrington, 64a Kensington Church Street, London W8 4DB Tel: 0171 937 1465
AIL	•	Antique Irish Linen, Dublin Tel: 00 353 1 451 2775
AL	•†	Ann Lingard, Ropewalk Antiques, Ropewalk, Rye, Sussex TN31 7NA Tel: 01797 223486
ALiN	•†	Andrew Lineham Fine Glass, The Mall, Camden Passage, London N1 8ED Tel: 0171 704 0195 Wed & Sat: 01243 576241
ALS	•†	Allan Smith Clocks, Amity Cottage, 162 Beechcroft Road, Upper Stratton, Swindon, Wilts SN2 6QE Tel: 01793 822977 Mobile: 0378 834342
AMH	•	Amherst Antiques, 23 London Road, Riverhead, Sevenoaks, Kent TN13 2BU Tel: 01732 455047
ANG	•†	Ancient & Gothic, PO Box 356, Christchurch, Dorset BH23 1XQ Tel: 01202 478592
ANO	•†	Art Nouveau Originals, Stamford Antiques Centre, The Exchange Hall, Broad Street, Stamford, Lincolnshire PE9 1PX Tel: 01780 762605
AnS	•	Antique Shop, 30 Henley Street, Stratford-Upon-Avon, Warwickshire CV37 6QW Tel: 01789 292485
AnSh	•	Antique Shop, 136A High Street, Tenterden, Kent TN30 6HT Tel: 01580 764323
ANT	•†	Anthemion, Bridge Street, Cartmel, Grange over Sands, Cumbria, LA11 7SH Tel: 015395 36295 Mobile 0468 443757
ANV	•	Anvil Antiques, Cartmel, Grange over Sands, Cumbria LA11 6QA Tel: 015395 36362
AP	*†	Andrew Pickford, The Hertford Saleroom, 42 St Andrew Street, Hertford, Herts SG14 1JA Tel: 01992 583508/501421
ARE	•	Arenski, 185 Westbourne Grove, London W11 2SB Tel: 0171 727 8599
ART	•†	Artemis Decorative Arts Ltd, 36 Kensington Church Street, London W8 4BX Tel: 0171 376 0377/0171 937 9900
ASA	•†	A. S. Antiques, 26 Broad Street, Pendleton, Salford, Greater Manchester M6 5BY Tel: 0161 737 5938
ASB	•†	Andrew Spencer Bottomley, The Coach House, Thongs Bridge, Holmfirth, Yorks HD7 2TT Tel: 01484 685234
ASG	•	Asahi Gallery, 44A Kensington Church Street, London W8 4DB
ASM	•	Art Smith Antiques at Wells Union, Route 1, 1755 Post Road, Wells, ME 04090, USA Tel: 207 646 6996
AW	•†	Alan Walker, Halfway Manor, Halfway, Nr Newbury, Berks RG20 8NR Tel: 01488 657670
AWT	•	Antique Associates at West Townsend, 473 Main Street PO Box 129W, West Townsend, MA 01474 USA Tel: 00 1 508 597 8084
B	*	Boardman Fine Art Auctioneers, Station Road Corner, Haverhill, Suffolk CB9 0EY Tel: 01440 730414
B&B	*	Butterfield & Butterfield, 220 San Bruno Avenue, San Francisco, CA 94103, USA Tel: 00 1 415 861 7500
B&L	*	Bonhams & Langlois, Westaway Chambers, 39 Don Street, St Helier, Jersey JE2 4T Tel: 01534 22441
BAB	•	The Barn at Bilsington, Ashford, Kent TN25 7JR Tel: 01233 720917
BAC	•	Bath Antiquities Centre, 4 Bladud Buildings, Bath, Somerset BA1 5LS Tel: 01225 460408
BaN	•	Barbara Ann Newman, London House Antiques, 4 Market Square, Westerham, Kent TN16 1AW Tel: 01959 564479/Mobile 0850 016729
BBA	*	Bloomsbury Book Auctions, 3–4 Hardwick Street, Off Rosebery Avenue, London, EC1R 4RY Tel: 0171 833 2636
BDA	•	Briar's C20th Decorative Arts, Yorks Tel: 01756 798641
Bea	*	Bearnes, Avenue Road, Torquay, Devon TQ2 5TG Tel: 01803 296277
Bea(E)	*	Bearnes, St Edmund's Court, Okehampton Street, Exeter, Devon EX4 1D Tel: 01392 422800
BEE	•†	Jonathan Beech, Westport, Co Mayo, Republic of Ireland Tel: 00 353 98 28688
BELL	•	Bell Antiques, Glos Tel: 0121 745 9034
Ber	•	Berry Antiques, Berry House, 11–13 Stone Street, Cranbrook, Kent TN17 3HF Tel: 01580 712345
BERA	•†	Berry Antiques, 3 High Street, Moreton in Marsh, Glos GL56 0AH Tel: 01608 652929
BEV	•	Beverley, 30 Church Street, Marylebone, London NW8 8EP Tel: 0171 262 1576
BEX	•†	Daniel Bexfield, 26 Burlington Arcade, London W1V 9AD Tel: 0171 491 1720
BGC	•	Brenda Gerwat-Clark, Granny's Goodies, G2/4 Alfie's Antique Market, 13–25 Church Street, London NW8 8DT Tel: 0171 706 4699

BHa •† Judy & Brian Harden Antiques, PO Box 14, Bourton on the Water, Cheltenham, Glos GL54 2YR Tel: 01451 810684

BIG * Bigwood Auctioneers Ltd, The Old School, Tiddington, Stratford-upon-Avon, Warks CV37 7AW Tel: 01789 269415

BKK • Bona Art Deco Store, The Hart Shopping Centre, Fleet, Hants GU13 8AZ Tel: 01252 616666

BLH *† BBG Ambrose, Ambrose House, Old Station Road, Loughton, Essex IG10 4PE Tel: 0181 502 3951

Bon *† Bonhams, Montpelier Street, Knightsbridge, London, SW7 1HH Tel: 0171 393 3900

Bon(C) * Bonhams, 65–69 Lots Road, Chelsea, London SW10 0RN Tel: 0171 393 3900

Bon(G) * Bonhams & Martel Maides Ltd, Allez St Auction Rooms, 29 High Street, St Peter Port, Guernsey, Channel Islands GY1 4NY Tel: 01481 713463

Bon(M) * Bonhams, St Thomas's Place, Hillgate, Stockport, Gt Manchester SK1 3TZ Tel: 0161 429 8283

Bon(W) * Bonhams West Country, Devon Fine Art Auction House, Dowell Street, Honiton, Devon EX14 8LX Tel: 01404 41872

BOR • Bed of Roses, 12 Prestbury Road, Cheltenham, Glos GL52 2PW Tel: 01242 231918

BOS * Bosley's, 42 West Street, Marlow, Bucks SL7 2NB Tel: 01628 488188

BOW •† David Bowden, 12 The Mall, Upper Street, Islington, London N1 0PD Tel: 0171 226 3033

BR *† Bracketts, Auction Hall, Pantiles, Tunbridge Wells, Kent TN1 1UU Tel: 01892 544500

Bri *† Bristol Auction Rooms, St John's Place, Apsley Road, Clifton, Bristol, Glos BS8 2ST Tel: 0117 973 7201

BRT • Britannia, Grays Antique Market, Stand 101, 58 Davies Street, London W1Y 1AR Tel: 0171 629 6772

BUR • House of Burleigh, The Old Shop Cottage, 2 Braunston Road, Knossington, Oakham, Rutland LE15 8LN Tel: 01664 454570/454114

BUSH • Bushwood Antiques, Stags End Equestrian Centre, Gaddesden Lane, Hemel Hempstead, Herts HP2 6HN Tel: 01582 794700

BWA • Bow-Well Antiques, 103 West Bow, Edinburgh, SEH1 2JP Tel: 0131 225 3335

BWC § British Watch & Clock Collectors Association, Tony Woolven, 5 Cathedral Lane, Truro, Cornwall TR1 2QS Tel: 01872 241953

BWe *† Biddle & Webb Ltd, Ladywood Middleway, Birmingham B16 0PP Tel: 0121 455 8042

BYG • Bygones Reclamation (Canterbury), Nackington Road, Canterbury Kent CT4 Tel: 01227 767453

Byl •† Bygones of Ireland Ltd, Lodge Road, Westport, County Mayo Tel: 00 353 98 26132/25701

C * Christies, 8 King Street, St James's, London SW1Y 6QT Tel: 0171 839 9060

C&C • Cohen & Cohen, 101b Kensington Church Street, London W8 7LN Tel: 0171 727 7677

CAB • Candlestick & Bakelite, PO Box 308, Orpington, Kent BR5 1TB Tel: 0181 467 3743

CaC *† Cato Crane & Co, Liverpool Auction Rooms, 6 Stanhope Street, Liverpool L8 5RF Tel: 0151 709 5559

CAG *† Canterbury Auction Galleries, 40 Station Road West, Canterbury, Kent CT2 8AN Tel: 01227 763337

CARS • C.A.R.S. (Classic Automobilia & Regalia Specialists), 4–4a Chapel Terrace Mews, Kemp Town, Brighton, Sussex BN2 1HU Tel: 01273 601960

CAT • Lennox Cato, 1 The Square, Edenbridge, Kent TN8 5BD Tel: 01732 865988/Mobile 0836 233473

CB •† Christine Bridge, 78 Castelnau, London SW13 9EX Tel: 07000 445277

CBC • Cheshire Billiards Co, Springwood Lodge, Ermine Street, Appleby, Lincs DN15 0DD Tel: 01724 852359

CBP *† Comic Book Postal Auctions Ltd, 40–42 Osnaburgh Street, London NW1 3ND Tel: 0171 424 0007

CCC •† The Crested China Co, The Station House, Driffield, Yorks YO25 7PY Tel: 01377 257042

CCO • Collectable Costume, Fountain Antique Centre, 3 Fountain Buildings, Lansdowne Road, Bath, Somerset BA1 5DU Tel: 01225 428731

CCP • Campden Country Pine, High Street, Chipping Campden, Glos GL55 6HN Tel: 01386 840315

CDC * Capes Dunn & Co, The Auction Galleries, 38 Charles Street, Off Princess Street, Gt Manchester M1 7DB Tel: 0161 273 6060/1911

CEX • Corn Exchange Antiques Centre, 64 The Pantiles, Tunbridge Wells, Kent TN2 5TN Tel: 01892 539652

CF • Country Furniture, 79 St Leonards Road, Windsor, Berks SL4 3BZ Tel: 01753 830154

CGC * Cheffins Grain & Comins, 2 Clifton Road, Cambridge, Cambs CB2 4BW Tel: 01223 358721/213343

CHA • Chislehurst Antiques, 7 Royal Parade, Chislehurst, Kent BR7 6NR Tel: 0181 467 1530

ChA • The Chapel Antiques, The Chapel, Chapel Place, Tunbridge Wells, Kent TN1 1YR Tel: 01892 619921

CHe •† Chelsea Clocks & Antiques, Stand H3-4, Antiquarius Market, 135 Kings Road, London SW3 4PW Tel: 0171 352 8646

ChS •† The Chair Set, 82–84 Hill Rise, Richmond, Surrey TW10 6UB Tel: 0181 332 6454/ Mobile 0411 625477

CHU • Church Street Antiques, 2 Church Street, Wells-Next-the-Sea, Norfolk NR23 1JA Tel: 01328 711698

CMF • Childhood Memories, The Farnham Antique Centre, 27 South Street, Farnham, Surrey GU9 7QU Tel: 01252 724475

CoA •† Country Antiques (Wales), Castle Mill, Kidwelly, Carmarthenshire, Wales SA17 4UU Tel: 01554 890534

CoHA •† Corner House Antiques, High Street, Lechlade, Glos GL7 3AE Tel: 01367 252007

COLL • Collinge Antiques, Old Fyffes Warehouse, Conwy Road, Llandudno Junction, Wales LL31 9LU Tel: 01492 580022 Mobile 0836 506354

CPA • Cottage Pine Antiques, 19 Broad Street, Brinklow, Nr Rugby, Warks CV23 0LS Tel: 01788 832673

CPS • Country Pine Shop, Northampton Road, West Haddon, Northants NN6 7AS Tel: 01788 510430

CS •† Christophe Sykes, The Old Parsonage, Woburn, Milton Keynes, Bucks MK17 9QM Tel: 01525 290259

CSA • Church Street Antiques, 10 Church Street, Godalming, Surrey GU7 1EH Tel: 01483 860894

DA *† Dee, Atkinson & Harrison, The Exchange Saleroom, Driffield, Yorkshire YO25 7LJ Tel: 01377 253151

DAC • Didcot Antiques Centre, 220 Broadway, Didcot, Oxfordshire OX11 8RS Tel: 01235 510819

DaH • Dale House Antiques, High Street, Moreton in Marsh, Glos GL56 0AD Tel: 01608 650763

DAN • Andrew Dando, 4 Wood Street, Queen Square, Bath, Somerset BA1 2JQ Tel: 01225 422702

DBA •† Douglas Bryan Antiques, The Old Bakery, St Davids Bridge, Cranbrook, Kent TN17 3HN Tel: 01580 713103

DD *† David Duggleby, The Vine St Salerooms, Scarborough, Yorks YO11 1XN Tel: 01723 507111

DeA • Delphi Antiques, Powerscourt Townhouse Centre, South William Street, Dublin 2 Tel: 00 353 1 679 0331

DEE • Dee's Antique Pine, 89 Grove Road, Windsor, Berks SL4 1HT Tel: 01753 865627/850926

DFA •† Delvin Farm Antiques, Gormonston, Co Meath, Rep of Ireland Tel: 00 353 1 841 2285

DgC • Dragonlee Collectables, Kent

DHA • Durham House Antiques Centre, Sheep Street, Stow-on-the-Wold, Glos GL54 1AA Tel: 01451 870404

DIC • D & B Dickinson, The Antique Shop, 22 & 22a New Bond St, Bath, Somerset BA1 1BA Tel: 01225 466502

DID • Didier Antiques, 58-60 Kensington Church Street, London W8 4DB Tel: 0171 938 2537/0836 232634

DLP •† The Dunlop Collection, PO Box 6269, Statesville, NC 28687, USA Tel: (704) 871 2626 or Toll Free Telephone (800) 227 1996

DMA • David Masters Antiques, Elm Tree Farm, High Halden, Ashford, Kent TN26 3BP Tel: 01233 850551

DMa •† David March, Abbots Leigh, Bristol, Glos BS8 Tel: 0117 937 2422

DN *† Dreweatt Neate, Donnington Priory, Donnington, Newbury, Berks RG13 2JE Tel: 01635 553553

DN(H) * Dreweatt Neate Holloways, 49 Parsons Street, Banbury, Oxfon OX16 8PF Tel: 01295 253197

DNW * Dix-Noonan-Webb, 1 Old Bond Street, London W1X 3TD Tel: 0171 499 5022

Doc *† Dockrees, Cheadle Hulme Business Centre, Clemence House, Mellor Road, Cheadle Hulme, Cheshire SK8 5AT Tel: 0161 485 1258

DOL • Dollectable, 53 Lower Bridge Street, Chester, Cheshire CH1 1RS Tel: 01244 344888/679195

DOR •† Dorset Reclamation, Cow Drove, Bere Regis, Wareham, Dorset BH20 7JZ Tel: 01929 472200

DORO* Dorotheum, Palais Dorotheum, A-1010 Wien, Dorotheergasse 17, Austria Tel: 0043 1 515 600

DQ •† Dolphin Quay Antique Centre, Queen Street, Emsworth, Hants PO10 7BU Tel: 01243 379994/0800 389142

DRA •† Derek Roberts, 25 Shipbourne Road, Tonbridge, Kent TN10 3DN Tel: 01732 358986

DSG •† Delf Stream Gallery, 14 New Street, Sandwich, Kent CT13 9AB Tel: 01304 617684

DuM • Du Mouchelles, 409 East Jefferson, Detroit, Michigan 48226, USA Tel: 001 313 963 0248

DW * † Winter, Dominic Book Auctions, The Old School, Maxwell Street, Swindon, Wilts SN1 5DR Tel: 01793 611340

E * † Ewbank, Burnt Common Auction Room, London Road, Send, Woking, Surrey GU23 7LN Tel: 01483 223101

EH * † Edgar Horn, Fine Art Auctioneers, 46–50 South Street, Eastbourne, Sussex BN21 4XB Tel: 01323 410419

ELI • Eli Antiques, Stand Q5 Antiquarius, 135 King's Road, London SW3 4PW Tel: 0171 351 7038

EON • O'Neill, Eugene Antique Gallery, Echo Bridge Mall, 381 Elliot Street, Newtown Upper Falls, MA 02164, USA Tel: 00 1 617 965 5965

ESA •† East Street Antiques, 42 East Street, Crewkerne, Somerset TA18 7AG Tel: 01460 78600

FBG * Frank H Boos, Gallery, 420 Enterprise Court, Bloomfield Hills, Michigan 48302, USA Tel: 001 248 332 1500

FD • Frank Dux Antiques, 33 Belvedere, Bath, Somerset BA1 5HR Tel: 01225 312367

FF • Freeforms, Unit 6 The Antique Centre, 58–60 Kensington Church Street, London W8 4DB Tel: 0171 937 9447

FHF * Frank H Fellows & Sons, Augusta House, 19 Augusta Street, Hockley, Birmingham, West Midlands B18 6J Tel: 0121 212 2131

FRa • Frasers, 399 The Strand, London WC2 Tel: 0171 836 9325

FrG • The French Glasshouse, P14/16 Antiquarius, 135 King's Road, Chelsea, London SW3 4PW Tel: 0171 376 5394

FW&C * Finan, Watkins & Co, The Square, Mere, Wilts BA12 6D Tel: 01747 861411

G&CC •† Goss & Crested China Ltd, 62 Murray Road, Horndean, Hants PO8 9JL Tel: (023) 92597440

GAK * † G. A. Key, Aylsham Salerooms, 8 Market Place, Aylsham, Norfolk NR11 6EH Tel: 01263 733195

Gam * Clarke Gammon, The Guildford Auction Rooms, Bedford Road, Guildford, Surrey GU1 4SJ Tel: 01483 566458

GAZE * † Thomas Wm Gaze, & Son, Diss Auction Rooms, Roydon Road, Diss, Norfolk IP22 3LN Tel: 01379 650306

GB • Geoffrey Breeze Antiques, 6 George Street, Bath, Somerset BA1 2EH Tel: 01225 466499

GD •† Gilbert & Dale Antiques, The Old Chapel, Church Street, Ilchester, Nr Yeovil, Somerset BA22 8ZA Tel: 01935 840464

GeC •† Gerard Campbell, Maple House, Market Place, Lechlade-on-Thames, Glos GL7 3AB Tel: 01367 252267

GeM •† Gerald Mathias, Antiquarius, 135 King's Road, Chelsea, London SW3 4PW Tel: 0171 351 0484

GeW •† Geoffrey Waters Ltd, F1-F6 Antiquarius Antiques Centre, 135–141 King's Road, London SW3 4PW Tel: 0171 376 5467

GH * Gardiner Houlgate, The Old Malthouse, Comfortable Place, Upper Bristol Road, Bath, Somerset BA1 3AJ Tel: 01225 447933

GHC • Great Haul of China, PO Box 233, Sevenoaks, Kent TN13 3ZN Tel: 01732 741484

GIN • The Ginnell Gallery Antique Centre, 18–22 Lloyd Street, Gt Manchester M2 5WA Tel: 0161 833 9037

GIO • Giovanna Antiques, Bourbon & Hanby Antiques Centre, Shop16, 151 Sydney Street, London SW3 6NT Tel: 0171 565 0004

GKe • Gerald Kenyon, 6 Great Strand Street, Dublin 1 Tel: 00 3531 873 0625/873 0488

GLD • Glade Antiques, PO Box 939, Marlow, Bucks SL7 1SR Tel: 01628 487255

Gle * Glendinings & Co, 101 New Bond Street, London W1Y 9LG Tel: 0171 493 2445

GN •† Gillian Neale Antiques , PO Box 247, Aylesbury, Bucks HP20 1JZ Tel: 01296 423754/0860 638700

GOR(B) *† Gorringes Auction Galleries, Terminus Road,
GOR Bexhill-on-Sea, Sussex TN39 3LR Tel: 01424 212994

GrD • Grays Dolls, Grays in the Mews, 1–7 Davies Street, London W1Y 2LP Tel: 0181 367 2441/0171 629 7034

GS • Ged Selby Antique Glass, by appointment Yorkshire Tel: 01756 799673

GSP * Graves, Son & Pilcher, Hove Auction Rooms, Hove Street, Hove, Sussex BN3 2GL Tel: 01273 735266

GV •† Garth Vincent, The Old Manor House, Allington, Nr Grantham, Lincs NG32 2DH Tel: 01400 281358

GWA • GB Antiques Centre, Lancaster Leisure Park, (the former Hornsea Pottery), Wyresdale Road, Lancaster, Lancs LA1 3LA Tel: 01524 844734

HA • Haff Antiques

HAC •† French Depot, Halifax Antiques Centre, Queens Road/Gibbet Street, Halifax, Yorks HX1 4LR Tel: 01422 366657

Hal * † Halls Fine Art Auctions, Welsh Bridge, Shrewsbury, Salop SY3 8LA Tel: 01743 231212

HALL * Hall's Nostalgia, 21 Mystic Street, Arlington, MA 02474, USA Tel: 001 781 646 7757

HAM * † Hamptons International, Baverstock House, 93 High Street, Godalming, Surrey GU7 1AL Tel: 01483 423567

Har • Hardy's Collectables/Hardy's Clobber, 862 & 874 Christchurch Road, Boscombe, Bournemouth, Dorset BH7 6DQ Tel: 01202 422407/303030

HAX * Halifax Property Services, Fine Art Department, 53 High Street, Tenterden, Kent TN30 6BG Tel: 01580 763200

HBC * † Heathcote Ball & Co, Castle Auction Rooms, 78 St Nicholas Circle, Leicester, Leicestershire LE1 5NW Tel: 0116 253 6789

HCC * H. C. Chapman & Son, The Auction Mart, North Street, Scarborough, Yorks YO11 1DL Tel: 01723 372424

HEL • Helios Gallery, 292 Westbourne Grove, London W11 2PS Tel: 0411 955 997

HEM •† Hemswell Antique Centre, Caenby Corner Estate, Hemswell Cliff, Gainsborough, Lincs DN21 5TJ Tel: 01427 668389

HEW • Muir Hewitt, Halifax Antiques Centre, Queens Road/Gibbet Street, Halifax, Yorks HX1 4LR Tel: 01422 347377

HGh • Hungry Ghost, 1 Brewery Yard, Sheep Street, Stow on the Wold, Glos GL54 1A Tel: 01451 870101

HIG • Highcroft Antiques, Red Lion, 165 Portobello Road, London W11 2DY

HOA •† Bob Hoare Antiques, Unit Q, Phoenix Place, North Street, Lewes, Sussex BN7 2DQ Tel: 01273 480557

HOB • Hobday Toys, Middlesex Tel: 01895 636737

HofB • Howards of Broadway, 27A High Street, Broadway, Worcs WR12 7DP Tel: 01386 858924

HOK * Hamilton Osborne King, 4 Main Street, Blackrock, Co Dublin Tel: 00 353 1 288 5011

HOL • Holmfirth Antiques (Ken Priestley), Yorks Tel/Fax: 01484 686854 Mobile 0973 533478

HON •† Honan's Antiques, Crowe Street, Gort, County Galway, Rep of Ireland Tel: 00 353 91 631407

HRQ • Harlequin Antiques, 79–81 Mansfield Road, Daybrook, Nottingham, Notts NG5 6BH Tel: 0115 967 4590

HUB •† Hubbard Antiques, 16 St Margaret's Green, Ipswich, Suffolk IP4 2BS Tel: 01473 226033

HUM • Humbleyard Fine Art, Unit 32 Admiral Vernon Arcade, Portobello Road, London W11 2DY Tel: 01787 379287

HUR • Hurst Gallery, 53 Mt. Auburn Street, Cambridge, MA 02138, USA Tel: 617 491 6888 Internet: www.hurstgallery.com

HVH • Horta, Hotel de Ventes, 16 Avenue Ducpetiaux, 1060 Bruxelles Tel: 02 533 11 11

HYD * HY Duke & Son, Dorchester Fine Art Salerooms, Dorchester, Dorset DT1 1QS Tel: 01305 265080

INC • The Incurable Collector, Surrey Tel: 01932 860800

IS •† Ian Sharp Antiques, 23 Front Street, Tynemouth, Tyne & Wear NE30 4DX Tel: 0191 296 0656

JAA * Jackson's Auctioneers & Appraisers, 2229 Lincoln Street, Cedar Falls, IA 50613, USA Tel: 00 1 319 277 2256

JAd * James Adam & Sons, 26 St Stephen's Green, Dublin 2 Tel: 00 3531 676 0261

JaG •† Japanese Gallery, 23 Camden Passage, London N1 8EA Tel: 0171 226 3347

JAK •† Clive & Lynne Jackson, Glos Tel: 01242 254375 Mobile 0589 715275

JAS • Jasmin Cameron, Antiquarius J6, 131–141 King's Road, London SW3 5ST Tel: 0171 351 4154

JBB • Jessie's Button Box, Fountain Antique Centre, 3 Lansdown Road, Bath, Somerset BA1 5DY Tel: 0117 929 9065

JBe • John Bellman, Auctioneers, New Pound Business Park, Wisborough Green, Billingshurst, Sussex RH14 0AZ Tel: 01403 700858

JD *† Lewes Auction Rooms (Julian Dawson), 56 High Street, Lewes, Sussex BN7 1XE Tel: 01273 478221

JH *† Jacobs & Hunt, 26 Lavant Street, Petersfield, Hants GU32 3EF Tel: 01730 233933

JHa • Jeanette Hayhurst Fine Glass, 32a Kensington Church Street, London W8 4HA Tel: 0171 938 1539

JHo •† Jonathan Horne, 66b&c Kensington Church Street, London W8 4BY Tel: 0171 221 5658

JIL •† Jillings Antique Clocks, Croft House, 17 Church Street, Newent, Glos GL18 1PU Tel: 01531 822100 Mobile 0973 830110

JM *† John Maxwell of Wilmslow, 133A Woodford Road, Woodford, Cheshire SK7 1QD Tel: 0161 439 5182

JMC • J & M Collectables, Kent Tel: 01580 891657

JNic * John Nicholson, The Auction Rooms, Longfield, Midhurst Road, Fernhurst, Surrey GU27 3HA Tel: 01428 653727

JO •† Jacqueline Oosthuizen, 23 Cale Street, Chelsea, London SW3 3QR Tel: 0171 352 6071

JP •† Paull's of Kenilworth, 16B High Street, Old Kenilworth, Warwickshire CV8 1LZ Tel: 01926 851311/0831 691254

JPr •† Joanna Proops Antique Textiles, 34 Belvedere, Lansdown Hill, Bath, Somerset BA1 5HR Tel: 01225 310795

JSC * J. Straker, Chadwick & Sons, Market Street Chambers, Abergavenny, Mon, Wales NP7 5SD Tel: 01873 852624

JUP • Jupiter Antiques, PO Box 609, Rottingdean, Sussex BN2 7FW Tel: 01273 302865

JVa • Jenny Vander, 20–22 Market Arcade, George Street, Dublin 2 Tel: 00 353 1 677 0406

JVM • Malchione Antiques & Sporting Collectibles, 110 Bancroft Road, Kennett Square, PA 19348, USA Tel: 00 1 610 444 3509

JWA • J.W.A. (UK) Limited, PO Box 6, Peterborough, Cambs PE1 5AH Tel: 01733 348344

K • Kite, 15 Langton Street, Chelsea, London SW10 0JL Tel: 0171 351 2108 Mobile 0411 887120

K&D •† Kembery Antique Clocks, Bartlett Street Antiques Centre, 5 Bartlett Street, Bath, Som BA1 2QZ Tel: 0117 956 5281/0850 623237

KEY • Key Antiques, 11 Horsefair, Chipping Norton, Oxon OX7 5AL Tel: 01608 643777

KID *† George Kidner, The Old School, The Square, Pennington, Lymington, Hants SO41 8GN Tel: 01590 670070

KJ • Katie Jones, 195 Westbourne Grove, London W11 2SB Tel: 0171 243 5600

KNI * Knight's, Cuckoo Cottage, Town Green, Alby, Norwich, Norfolk NR11 7HE Tel: 01263 768488

L * Lawrence Fine Art Auctioneers, South Street, Crewkerne, Somerset TA18 8AB Tel: 01460 73041

L&E *† BBG Locke & England, 18 Guy Street, Leamington Spa, Warks CV32 4RT Tel: 01926 889100

L&L • Linen & Lace, Shirley Tomlinson, Halifax Antiques Centre, Queens Road/Gibbet Street, Halifax, Yorks HX1 4LR Tel: 01422 366657

LaM • La Maison, 410 St John Street, London EC1V 4NJ Tel: 0171 837 6522

LAY * David Lay, ASVA, Auction House, Alverton, Penzance, Cornwall TR18 4RE Tel: 01736 361414

LBr • Lynda Brine, Assembly Antique Centre, 5–8 Saville Row, Bath, Somerset BA1 2QP Tel: 01225 448488

LCA •† La Chaise Antiques, 30 London Street, Faringdon, Oxon SN7 7AA Tel: 01367 240427

LCC • The London Cigarette Card Co Ltd, Sutton Road, Somerton, Somerset TA11 6QP Tel: 01458 273452

LF *† Lambert & Foster, 77 Commercial Road, Paddock Wood, Kent TN12 6DR Tel: 01892 832325

LHAr • Artifacts, USA Tel:/Fax: 00 1 415 381 2084

LHB • 'Les Hommes Bleus' Gallery, Bartlett Street Antique Centre, 5–10 Bartlett Street, Bath, Somerset BA1 2QZ Tel: 01225 316606

LPA •† L.P. Furniture, (The Old Brewery), Short Acre Street, Walsall, West Midlands WS2 8HW Tel: 01922 746764

LRG * Lots Road Galleries, 71–73 Lots Road Chelsea, London SW10 0RN Tel: 0171 351 7771

LSK * Lacy Scott & Knight, Fine Art Department, The Auction Centre, 10 Risbygate Street, Bury St Edmunds, Suffolk IP33 3AA Tel: 01284 763531

M * Morphets of Harrogate, 6 Albert Street, Harrogate, Yorks HG1 1JL Tel: 01423 530030

MaBh • Mallet at Bourdon House Ltd, 2 Davies Street, Berkeley Square, London W1Y 1LJ Tel: 0171 629 2444

MAC • The Mall Antique Centre, 400 Wincolmlee, Hull, Humberside HU2 0QL Tel: 01482 327858

MAG • Magna Gallery, 41 High Street, Oxford, Oxfordshire OX1 4AP Tel: 01865 245805

MANS• Mansell William, 24 Connaught Street, Marble Arch, London W2 2AF Tel: 0171 723 4154

MAr • Mint Arcade, 71 The Mint, Rye, Sussex TN31 7EW Tel: 01797 225952

MARK•† 20th Century Marks, 12 Market Square, Westerham, Kent TN16 1AW Tel: 01959 562221

MAT * Christopher Matthews, 23 Mount Street, Harrogate, Yorks HG2 8DQ Tel: 01423 871756

MB •† Mostly Boxes, 93 High Street, Eton, Windsor, Berks SL4 6AF Tel: 01753 858470

MBo • Michael E. Bound, Portobello, London

MCA *† Mervyn Carey, Twysden Cottage, Benenden, Cranbrook, Kent TN17 4LD Tel: 01580 240283

MCN • MCN Antiques, 183 Westbourne Grove, London W11 2SB Tel: 0171 727 3796

MEA *† Mealy's, Chatsworth Street, Castle Comer, Co Kilkenny, Rep of Ireland Tel: 00 353 56 41229

MEG • Megarry's & Forever Summer, Jericho Cottage, The Duckpond Green, Blackmore, Essex CM4 0RR Tel: 01277 821031/822170

MER • Mere Antiques, 13 Fore Street, Topsham, Exeter, Devon EX3 0HF Tel: 01392 874224

MGC • Midlands Goss & Commemoratives, The Old Cornmarket Antique Centre, 70 Market Place, Warwick, Warks CV34 4SO Tel: 01926 419119

MiA • Old Mill Antiques Centre, Mill Street, Low Down, Bridgnorth, Shropshire WV15 5A Tel: 01746 768778

MID • Richard Midwinter, 31 Bridge Street, Newcastle-under-Lyne, Staffs ST5 2RY Tel: 01782 712483/01630 672289

MIL • Milverton Antiques, Fore Street, Milverton, Taunton, Somerset TA4 1JU Tel: 01823 400592

Mit * Mitchells, Fairfield House, Station Road, Cockermouth, Cumbria CA13 9PY Tel: 01900 827800

MJB * Michael J. Bowman, 6 Haccombe House, Netherton, Newton Abbot, Devon TQ12 4SJ Tel: 01626 872890

MLa •† Marion Langham, London Tel: 0171 730 1002

MLL •† Millers Antiques Ltd, Netherbrook House, 86 Christchurch Road, Ringwood, Hants BH24 1DR Tel: 01425 472062

MoS • Morgan Stobbs, by appointment Tel: Mobile 0402 206817

MRW • Malcolm Russ-Welch, PO Box 1122, Rugby, Warks CV23 9YD Tel: 01788 810 616

MSB • Marilynn and Sheila Brass, PO Box 380503, Cambridge, MA 02238-0503, USA Tel: 00 1 617 491 6064

MSW *† Marilyn Swain Auctions, The Old Barracks, Sandon Road, Grantham, Lincs NG31 9AS Tel: 01476 568861

MTa • Maggie Tallentire, Cousy 82160 Caylus, Tarn et Garonne, France Tel: 0033(0)5 63 24 05 27

MTay •† Martin Taylor Antiques, 140B Tettenhall Road, Wolverhampton, W Midlands WV6 0BQ Tel: 01902 751166

MUL •† Mullock & Madeley, The Old Shippon, Wall-under-Heywood, Church Stretton, Shropshire SY6 7DS Tel: 01694 771771

MURR• Murrays' Collectables Tel: 01202 309094

NCA • New Century, 69 Kensington Church Street, London W8 4BG Tel: 0171 376 2810

No7 • No 7 Antiques, 7 Nantwich Road, Woore, Shropshire CW3 9SA Tel: 01630 647118

NOA * New Orleans Auction Galleries Inc, 801 Magazine Street, AT 510 Julia, New Orleans, Louisiana 70130, USA Tel: 00 1 504 566 1849

Nor •† Sue Norman, L4 Antiquarius, 135 King's Road, London SW3 5ST Tel: 0171 352 7217

NOST •† Nostalgia, 61 Shaw Heath, Stockport, Cheshire SK3 8BH Tel: 0161 477 7706

NP • Neville Pundole, 8A & 9 The Friars, Canterbury, Kent CT1 2AS Tel: 01227 453471

OCH • Gillian Shepherd, Old Corner House Antiques, 6 Poplar Road, Wittersham, Tenterden, Kent TN30 7PG Tel: 01797 270236

OL * Outhwaite & Litherland, Kingsway Galleries, Fontenoy Street, Liverpool, Merseyside L3 2BE Tel: 0151 236 6561

Oli *† Olivers, Olivers Rooms, Burkitts Lane, Sudbury, Suffolk CO10 1HB Tel: 01787 880305

OLM •† The Old Mill, High Street, Lamberhurst, Kent TN3 8EQ Tel: 01892 891196

ONS * Onslow's, The Depot, 2 Michael Road, London SW6 2AD Tel: 0171 371 0505 Mobile 0831 473 400

OO •† Pieter Oosthuizen, Unit 4 Bourbon Hanby Antiques Centre, 151 Sydney Street, London SW3 6NT Tel: 0171 460 3078

OOLA •† Oola Boola, 166 Tower Bridge Road, London SE1 3LS Tel: 0171 403 0794/0181 693 5050

ORI • Oriental Gallery, Glos Tel: 01451 830944

OT • Old Timers, Box 392, Camp Hill, PA 17001-0392, USA Tel: 00 1 717 761 1908

OTB •† Old Tackle Box, PO Box 55, Cranbrook, Kent TN17 3ZU Tel/Fax: 01580 713979

OTT • Otter Antiques, 20 High Street, Wallingford, Oxon OX10 0BP Tel: 01491 825544

P *† Phillips, 101 New Bond Street, London W1Y 0AS Tel: 0171 629 6602

P(B) * Phillips, 1 Old King Street, Bath, Somerset BA1 2JT Tel: 01225 310609

P(Ba) * Phillips Bayswater, 10 Salem Road, London W2 4D Tel: 0171 229 9090

P(C) * Phillips Cardiff, 9–10 Westgate Street, Cardiff, Wales CF1 1DA Tel: 01222 396453

P(D) * Phillips Sherborne, Long Street Salerooms, Sherborne, Dorset DT9 3BS Tel: 01935 815271

P(E) * Phillips, Alphin Brook Road, Alphington, Exeter, Devon EX2 8TH Tel: 01392 439025

P(EA) * Phillips, 32 Boss Hall Road, Ipswich, Suffolk IP1 59J Tel: 01473 740494

P(Ed) * Phillips Scotland, 65 George Street, Edinburgh, Scotland EH2 2JL Tel: 0131 225 2266

P(F) * Enquiries Phillips Sevenoaks, Kent

P(G) * Phillips Fine Art Auctioneers, Millmead, Guildford, Surrey GU2 5BE Tel: 01483 504030

P(Gen) * Phillips Geneva, 9 rue Ami-Levrier, CH-1201 Geneva, Switzerland Tel: 00 41 22 738 0707

P(HSS) * Phillips, 20 The Square, Retford, Notts DN22 6XE Tel: 01777 708633

P(L) * Phillips Leeds, 17a East Parade, Leeds, Yorks LS1 2BH Tel: 0113 2448011

P(NE) * Phillips North East, St Mary's, Oakwellgate, Gateshead, Tyne & Wear NE8 2AX Tel: 0191 477 6688

P(NW)* Phillips North West, New House, 150 Christleton Road, Chester, Cheshire CH3 5TD Tel: 01244 313936

P(O) * Phillips, 39 Park End Street, Oxford, OX1 1JD Tel: 01865 723524

P(R) * Phillips Fine Art Auctioneers, 54 Southampton Road, Ringwood, Hants BH24 1JD Tel: 01425 473333

P(S) * Phillips Fine Art Auctioneers, 49 London Road, Sevenoaks, Kent TN13 1AR Tel: 01732 740310

P(Sc) * Phillips Scotland, 207 Bath Street, Glasgow, Scotland G2 4HD Tel: 0141 221 8377

P(W) * Phillips of Winchester, The Red House, Hyde Street, Winchester, Hants SO23 7DX Tel: 01962 862515

P(WM)* Phillips, The Old House, Station Road, Knowle, Solihull, W Midlands B93 0HT Tel: 01564 776151

P(Z) * Phillips, 27 Ramistrasse, 8001 Zurich, Switzerland Tel: 00 41 1 252 6962

PAC • The Potteries Antique Centre, 271 Waterloo Road, Cobridge, Stoke-on-Trent, Staffs ST6 3HR Tel: 01782 201455

PAO •† P. A. Oxley, The Old Rectory, Cherhill, Nr Calne, Wilts SN11 8UX Tel: 01249 816227

PARS • Pars Antiques, Stand A14–15, Grays in the Mews, 1–7 Davies Street, London W1Y 1AR Tel: 0171 491 9889

PBr • Pamela Brooks, Leics Tel: 0116 230 2625

PC Private Collection

PCh *† Peter Cheney, Western Road Auction Rooms, Western Road, Littlehampton, Sussex BN17 5NP Tel: 01903 722264/713418

PF *† Peter Francis, The Curiosity Saleroom, 19 King Street, Carmarthen, South Wales SA31 1BH Tel: 01267 233456

PFK *† Penrith Farmers' & Kidd's plc, Skirsgill Salerooms, Penrith, Cumbria CA11 0DN Tel: 01768 890781

PGA • Paul Gibbs Antiques, 25 Castle Street, Conwy, Gwynedd, Wales LL32 8AY Tel: 01492 593429

PHA •† Paul Hopwell, 30 High Street, West Haddon, Northants NN6 7AP Tel: 01788 510636

PIn • Postcards International, Vintage Picture Postcards, PO Box 2930, New Haven, CT 06515-0030, USA Tel: 00 1 203 865 0814

POSH• Posh Tubs, Moriati's Workshop, High Halden, Ashford, Kent TN26 3LZ Tel: 01233 850155

POW • † Sylvia Powell Decorative Arts, 28 The Mall, Camden Passage, London N1 0PD Tel: 0171 354 2977

PPC • † Period Piano Company, Park Farm Oast, Hareplain Road, Biddenden, Nr Ashford, Kent TN27 8LJ Tel: 01580 291393

PrB • Pretty Bizarre, 170 High Street, Deal, Kent CT14 6BQ Tel: 0973 794537

PSA • † Pantiles Spa Antiques, 4, 5, 6 Union House, The Pantiles, Tunbridge Wells, Kent TN4 8HE Tel: 01892 541377

PSG • Patrick & Susan Gould, Stand L17 Gray's Mews Antique Market, Davies Mews, Davies Street, London W1Y 1AR Tel/Fax: 0181 993 5879

PT • † Pieces of Time, 1–7 Davies Mews, 26 South Molton Lane, London W1Y 2LP Tel: 0171 629 2422

Q&C • Q&C Militaria, 22 Suffolk Road, Cheltenham, Glos GL50 2AQ Tel: 01242 519815/Mobile 0378 613977

RAG * † Rye Auction Galleries, Rock Channel, Rye, Sussex TN31 7HL Tel: 01797 222124

RAR * † Romsey Auction Rooms, 86 The Hundred, Romsey, Hants SO51 8BX Tel: 01794 513331

RAW • The Original Reclamation Trading Co, 22 Elliot Road, Love Lane Estate, Cirencester, Glos GL7 1YS Tel: 01285 653532

RBA • Roger Bradbury Antiques, Church Street, Coltishall, Norfolk NR12 7DJ Tel: 01603 737444

RBB * † Russell, Baldwin & Bright, Ryelands Road, Leominster, Herts HR6 8NZ Tel: 01568 611122

RD • Davidson, Richard Antiques

RdeR • † Rogers de Rin, 76 Royal Hospital Road, London SW3 4HN Tel: 0171 352 9007

RECL • Reclamation Services Ltd, Catbrain Quarry, Painswick Beacon, Above Paradise, Painswick, Glos GL6 6SU Tel: 01452 814064

RED • † Red Lion Antiques, New Street, Petworth, Sussex GU28 0AS Tel: 01798 344485

REF • † The Refectory, 38 West Street, Dorking, Surrey RH4 1BU Tel: 01306 742111

RHE * R. H. Ellis & Sons, 44–46 High Street, Worthing, Sussex BN11 1LL Tel: 01903 238999

RID * † Riddetts of Bournemouth, 177 Holden Hurst Road, Bournemouth, Dorset BH8 8DQ Tel: 01202 555686

Riv • Riverbank Antiques, Wells Union, Route 1, PO Box 3009, Wells ME 04090 USA Tel: 207 646 6314

RKa • Richardson & Kailas, London Tel: 0171 371 0491 By appointment

RMC • Romsey Medals, 5 Bell Street, Romsey, Hampshire SO51 8GY Tel: 01794 512069

ROS * Rosebery's Fine Art Ltd, Old Railway Booking Hall, Crystal Palace Station Road, London SE19 2AZ Tel: 0181 761 2522

RPh • † Robert Phelps Ltd, 133–135 St Margaret's Road, East Twickenham, Middlesex TW1 1RG Tel: 0181 892 1778/7129

RTh • † The Reel Thing, 17 Royal Opera Arcade, Pall Mall, London SW1Y 4UY Tel: 0171 976 1840

RTo * † Rupert Toovey & Co Ltd, Star Road, Partridge Green, Sussex RH13 8RJ Tel: 01403 711744

RTw • † Richard Twort, Somerset Tel: 01934 641900

RUL • Rules Antiques, 62 St Leonards Road, Windsor, Berkshire SL4 3BY Tel: 01753 833210/01491 642062

RUM • † Rumours, 10 The Mall, Upper Street, Camden Passage, Islington, London N1 0PD Tel: 01582 873561/0836 277274/0831 103748

RUSK • Ruskin Decorative Arts, 5 Talbot Court, Stow-on-the-Wold, Cheltenham, Glos GL54 1DP Tel: 01451 832254

RWB • Roy W Bunn Antiques, 34/36 Church Street, Barnoldswick, Colne, Lancs BB8 5UT Tel: 01282 813703

RYA • † Robert Young Antiques, 68 Battersea Bridge Road, London SW11 3AG Tel: 0171 228 7847

S * Sotheby's, 34–35 New Bond Street, London W1A 2AA Tel: 0171 293 5000

S(Am) * Sotheby's Amsterdam, Rokin 102, Amsterdam, Netherlands 1012 KZ Tel: 31 (20) 550 2200

S(G) * Sotheby's, 13 Quai du Mont Blanc, Geneva, Switzerland CH-1201 Tel: 00 41 22 732 8585

S(HK) * Sotheby's, Li Po Chun Chambers, 18th Floor, 189 Des Vouex Road, Hong Kong, China Tel: 852 524 8121

S(LA) * Sotheby's, 9665 Wilshire Boulevard, Beverly Hills, California 90212 Tel: (310) 274 0340

S(Mon) * Sotheby's Monaco, Le Sporting D'Hiver, Place du Casino, 98001 Cedex, Monaco Tel: 00 377 93 30 8880

S(NY) * Sotheby's, 1334 York Avenue, New York, USA NY 10021 Tel: 00 1 212 606 7000

S(S) * Sotheby's Sussex, Summers Place, Billingshurst, Sussex RH14 9AD Tel: 01403 833500

S(Sc) * Sotheby's, 112 George Street, Edinburgh, Scotland EH2 4LH Tel: 0131 226 7201

S(SI) * Sotheby's (Singapore) Pte Ltd, 1 Cuscaden Road, 01-01 The Regent, Singapore Tel: (65) 732 8239

S(Z) * Sotheby's Zurich, Bleicherweg 20, Zurich, Switzerland CH-8022 Tel: 41 (1) 202 0011

SA • Somerville Antiques & Country Furniture Ltd, Moysdale, Killanley, Ballina, Co Mayo, Rep of Ireland Tel: 00 353 963 6275

Sam • † Sambourne House Antiques, Minety, Malmesbury, Wilts SN16 9RQ Tel: 01666 860288

SAM • Samarkand Galleries, 8 Brewery Yard, Sheep Street, Stow-on-the-Wold, Glos GL54 1AA Tel: 01451 832322

SAS * † Special Auction Services, The Coach House, Midgham Park, Reading, Berks RG7 5UG Tel: 0118 971 2949

SCO • † Peter Scott, Stand 39, Bartlett Street Antiques Centre, Bath, Somerset BA1 2Q Tel: 01225 310457 or 0117 986 8468 Mobile 0850 639770

SeH • † Seventh Heaven, Chirk Mill, Chirk, Wrexham, County Borough, Wales LL14 5BU Tel: 01691 777622

SER • † Serendipity, 168 High Street, Deal, Kent CT14 6BQ Tel: 01304 369165/366536

SERR * † Philip Serrell, The Malvern Saleroom, Barnards Green Road, Malvern, Worcs WR14 3LW Tel: 01684 892314

SFL • † The Silver Fund Ltd, 40 Bury Street, St James's, London SW1Y 6AU Tel: 0171 839 7664

SHa • † Shapiro & Co, Stand 380, Gray's Antique Market, 58 Davies Street, London W1Y 1LB Tel: 0171 491 2710

SIL • The Silver Shop, Powerscourt Townhouse Centre, St Williams Street, Dublin 2 Tel: 00 3531 6794147

Sim * † Simmons & Sons, 32 Bell Street, Henley-on-Thames, Oxon RG9 2BH Tel: 01491 571111

SK * Skinner Inc, The Heritage On The Garden, 63 Park Plaza, Boston, MA 02116, USA Tel: 001 617 350 5400

SK(B) * Skinner Inc, 357 Main Street, Bolton, MA 01740, USA Tel: 00 1 978 779 6241

SLM * Sloan's Auctioneers & Appraisers, Miami Gallery, 8861 NW 18th Terrace, Suite 100, Miami, Florida 33172, USA Tel: 00 1 305 592 2575/800 660 4524

SLN * Sloan's, C G Sloan & Company Inc, 4920 Wyaconda Road, North Bethesda, MD 20852, USA Tel: 00 1 301 468 4911/669 5066

SMAM • Santa Monica Antique Market, 1607 Lincoln Boulevard, Santa Monica, California 90404, USA Tel: 310 314 4899

SMI •	Janie Smithson, Lincolnshire Tel/Fax: 01754 810265 Mobile 0831 399180	
SO •†	Sam Orr Antique Clocks, 36 High Street, Hurstpierpoint, Nr Brighton, Sussex BN6 9RG Tel: 01273 832081	
Som •†	Somervale Antiques, 6 Radstock Road, Midsomer Norton, Bath, Somerset BA3 2AJ Tel: 01761 412686	
SOO •	Soo San, 239a Fulham Road, London SW3 6HY Tel: 0171 352 8980	
SoS/ SOS •	Styles of Stow, The Little House, Sheep Street, Stow-on-the-Wold, Glos GL54 1JS Tel: 01451 830455	
Sp *	Spink & Son Ltd, 5 King Street, St James's, London SW1Y 6QS Tel: 0171 930 7888	
SPa •†	Sparks Antiques, 4 Manor Row, High Street, Tenterden, Kent TN30 6HP Tel: 01580 766696	
SPU /SPR •†	Spurrier-Smith Antiques, 28, 30, 39 Church Street, Ashbourne, Derbyshire DE6 1AJ Tel: 01335 343669/342198	
SSP	Stanley Stripped Pine	
STA •†	Michelina & George Stacpoole, Main St, Adare, Co Limerick, Rep of Ireland Tel: 00 353 61 396 409	
STG •	Stone Gallery, 93 The High Street, Burford, Oxfordshire OX18 4QA Tel/Fax: 01993 823302	
STK •	Stockbridge Antiques, 8 Deanhaugh Street, Edinburgh EH4 1LY Tel: 0131 332 1366	
SWA •†	S.W. Antiques, Abbey Showrooms, Newlands, Pershore, Worcs WR10 1BP Tel: 01386 555580	
SWAN *	Swann Galleries Inc, 104 East 25th Street, New York, USA 10010 Tel: 00 1 212 2544710	
SWB •†	Sweetbriar Gallery, Robin Hood Lane, Helsby, Cheshire WA6 9NH Tel: 01928 723851	
SWN •	Swan Antiques, Stone Street, Cranbrook, Kent TN17 3HF Tel: 01580 712720	
SWO *†	G. E. Sworder & Sons, 14 Cambridge Road, Stansted Mountfitchet, Essex CM24 8BZ Tel: 01279 817778	
TAC •	Tenterden Antiques Centre, 66–66A High Street, Tenterden, Kent TN30 6AU Tel: 01580 765655/765885	
TAN •†	Tanglewood Antiques, Tanglewood Mill, Coke Street, Derby, Derbyshire DE1 1NE Tel: 01332 346005	
TB •	Millicent Safro Tender Buttons, 143 E.62nd Street, New York NY10021, USA Tel: (212) 758 7004 Fax: (212) 319 8474	
TC •	Timothy Coward, Devon Tel: 01271 890466	
TCG •	20th Century Glass, Kensington Church Street Antique Centre, 58–60 Kensington Church Street, London W8 4DB Tel: 0171 938 1137/376 0425	
TED •†	Teddy Bears of Witney, 99 High Street, Witney, Oxon OX8 6LY Tel: 01993 702616/706616	
TEN *†	Tennants, The Auction Centre, Harmby Road, Leyburn, Yorks DL8 5SG Tel: 01969 623780	
TEN *	Tennants, 34 Montpellier Parade, Harrogate, Yorkshire HG1 2TG Tel: 01423 531661	
TH •	Tony Horsley, Sussex Tel: 01273 550770	
THA •	Town Hall Antiques, Market Place, Woburn, Bedfordshire MK17 9PZ Tel: 01525 290950	
TIM •	Timepiece Antiques, 58 Patrick Street, Dublin 8 Tel: 00 353 1 454 0774	
TMA *	Brown & Merry Tring Market Auctions, Brook Street, Tring, Herts HP23 5EF Tel: 01442 826446	
TMi •	T. J. Millard, Antiques, Assembly Antiques, 5–8 Saville Row, Bath, Somerset BA1 2QP Tel: 01225 448488	
TPC •†	Pine Cellars, 39 Jewry Street, Winchester, Hants SO23 8RY Tel: 01962 777546/867014	
TREA *	Treadway Gallery, 2029 Madison Road, Cincinnati, OH 45208, USA Tel: 00 1 513 321 6742	
TRL *	Thomson, Roddick & Laurie, 60 Whitesands, Dumfries DG1 2RS Tel: 01387 255366	
TRL *	Thomson, Roddick & Laurie, 24 Lowther Street, Carlisle, Cumbria CA3 8DA Tel: 01228 28939/39636	
TRU •	The Trumpet, West End, Minchinhampton, Glos GL6 9JA Tel: 01453 883027	
TT •	Treasures in Textiles, 53 Russian Drive, Liverpool, Merseyside L13 7BS Tel: 0151 281 6025	
TVM •	Teresa Vanneck-Murray, Vanneck House, 22 Richmond Hill, Richmond-upon-Thames, Surrey TW10 6QX Tel: 0181 940 2035	
TWa •	Time Warp, c/o Curiouser & Curiouser, Sydney Street, Brighton, Sussex BN1 Tel: 01273 821243	
VB •	Variety Box, 16 Chapel Place, Tunbridge Wells, Kent TN1 1YQ Tel: 01892 531868	
VCL •	Vintage Cameras Ltd, 254 & 256 Kirkdale, Sydenham, London SE26 4NL Tel: 0181 778 5416/5841	
VH •	Valerie Howard, 2 Campden Street, London W8 7EP Tel: 0171 792 9702	
VI •†	Victorian Imports, Prestwich Antiques, 371/373 Bury New Road, Prestwich, Gt Manchester M25 1AW Tel: 0161 798 0911/0161 773 0500	
VOS *	Vost's, Newmarket, Suffolk CB8 9AU Tel: 01638 561313	
VS *†	T. Vennett-Smith, 11 Nottingham Road, Gotham, Notts NG11 0HE Tel: 0115 983 0541	
VSP *	Van Sabben Poster Auctions, Oosteinde 30, 1678 HS Oostwoud, Holland Tel: 00 31 229 20 25 89	
W&S •	Pat Woodward and Alma Shaw, Unit G43, Ground Floor, Gloucester Antiques Centre, In The Historic Docks, Severn Road, Gloucester, Glos GL1 2LE	
WA *†	Whyte's Auctioneers, 30 Marlborough St, Dublin 1 Tel: 00 353 1 874 6161	
WAB •	Warboys Antiques, Old Church School, High Street, Warboys, Cambridge, Cambs PE17 2S Tel: 01487 823686	
WaH •	The Warehouse, 29-30 Queens Gardens, Worthington Street, Dover, Kent CT17 9AH Tel: 01304 242006	
Wai •	Peter Wain, Glynde Cottage, Longford, Market Drayton, Salop TF9 3PW Tel: 01630 639613	
WAL *†	Wallis & Wallis, West Street Auction Galleries, Lewes, Sussex BN7 2NJ Tel: 01273 480208	
WaR •	Wot a Racket, 250 Shepherds Lane, Dartford, Kent DA1 2PN Tel: 01322 220619	
WBB •†	William Bentley Billiards, Standen Manor Farm, Hungerford, Berkshire RG17 0RB Tel: 01672 871214	
WBH *†	Walker, Barnett & Hill, Waterloo Road Salerooms, Clarence Street, Wolverhampton, W Midlands WV1 4JE Tel: 01902 773531	
WDG *	William Doyle Galleries, 175 East 87th Street, New York, NY 10128, USA Tel: 212 427 2730	
WEE •	Weedon Bec Antiques, 66 High Street, Weedon, Northants NN7 4QD Tel: 01327 349910	
WeH •	Westerham House Antiques, The Green, Westerham, Kent TN16 1AY Tel: 01959 561622/562200	
WELD •†	J. W. Weldon, 55 Clarendon Street, Dublin 2 Tel: 00 353 1 677 1638	
WELL •†	Anthony Welling, Broadway Barn, High Street, Ripley, Woking, Surrey GU23 6AQ Tel: 01483 225384	
WilP *	Wilson Peacock, The Auction Centre, 26 Newnham Street, Bedford, Beds MK40 3JR Tel: 01234 266366	
WIM •	Wimpole Antiques, Stand 349, Grays Antique Market, South Molton Lane, London, W1Y 2LP Tel: 0171 499 2889	
WL *†	Wintertons Ltd, Lichfield Auction Centre, Wood End Lane, Fradley, Lichfield, Staffs WS13 8NF Tel: 01543 263256	
WRe •	Walcot Reclamations, 108 Walcot Street, Bath, Somerset BA1 5BG Tel: 01225 444404	
WSA •†	West Street Antiques, 63 West Street, Dorking, Surrey RH4 1BS Tel: 01306 883487	
WW *	Woolley & Wallis, Salisbury Salerooms, 51–61 Castle Street, Salisbury, Wilts SP1 3SU Tel: 01722 424500	
YAG •	The York Antiques Gallery, Route 1, PO Box 303, York, ME 03909, USA Tel: 207 363 5002	
YAN •	Yanni's Antiques, 538 San Anselmo Avenue, San Anselmo, CA 94960, USA Tel: 00 1 415 459 2996	
YC •	Yesterday Child, Angel Arcade, 118 Islington High Street, London N1 8EG Tel: 0171 354 1601	
ZOOM •†	Zoom, 312 Lillie Road, Fulham, London SW6 7PS Tel: 0171 386 9522	

Index

Italic page numbers denote colour pages; **bold** numbers refer to information and pointer boxes.